Hellenic Studies 53

FROM LISTENERS TO VIEWERS

Recent Titles in the Hellenic Studies Series

http://chs.harvard.edu/chs/publications

FROM LISTENERS TO VIEWERS

SPACE IN THE *ILIAD*

CHRISTOS TSAGALIS

CENTER FOR HELLENIC STUDIES
Trustees for Harvard University
Washington, D.C.
Distributed by Harvard University Press
Cambridge, Massachusetts, and London, England
2012

From Listeners to Viewers: Space in the Iliad
   by Christos Tsagalis
Copyright © 2012 Center for Hellenic Studies, Trustees for Harvard University
All Rights Reserved.
Published by Center for Hellenic Studies, Trustees for Harvard University, Washington,
   D.C.
Distributed by Harvard University Press, Cambridge, Massachusetts, and London,
   England
Production: Ivy Livingston
Cover design and illustration: Joni Godlove
Printed by Edwards Brothers, Inc., Ann Arbor, MI

LIBRARY OF CONGRESS CATALOGING-IN-PUBLICATION DATA

Tsagalis, Christos
From listeners to viewers : space in the Iliad / by Christos Tsagalis.
p. cm. — (Hellenic studies ; 53)
ISBN 978-0-674-06711-0 (alk. paper)
1. Homer. Iliad. 2. Space and time in literature. I. Title. II. Series: Hellenic studies ; 53.
PA4037.T7893 2012
883'.01--dc23

                                                                            2012024442

Contents

Preface

IN TRANSCRIBING GREEK NAMES FROM HOMER, I have generally followed modern principles of strict transliteration, for example rendering υ as *u*, ου as *ou*, and χ as *kh*: thus *Antilokhos, Ekhemmon, Othruoneus, Thumbraios,* and *Lukourgos.* In the case of some well-known names, however, I have opted to retain more familiar traditional spellings such as *Achilles, Cilicia, Circe, Lycia, Myrmidons, Typhoeus,* and *Pylos.*

In researching this book, I have consulted works published to the end of 2011. The recently published volume from E. J. Brill, *Space in Ancient Greek Literature,* edited by I. J. F. de Jong, unfortunately appeared too late to be included.

Acknowledgments

AS WITH MANY THINGS IN LIFE, so with books, ends and beginnings come strangely close. The completion of what started as a research project four years ago makes me think of all those who have helped me bring this book to its present form. Different people have offered different kinds of assistance, but they are all to be dearly thanked for having graciously given so much of their time, effort, and patience. It is, therefore, my pleasure to acknowledge my debt to them.

Elizabeth Minchin, Alex Purves, Antonios Rengakos, Michael Squire, the anonymous referee, and the entire CHS team have read parts or the whole of my manuscript at various stages. They have all made instructive comments, helped clarify my thinking on a number of issues, and suggested further secondary literature on certain topics treated in my book. Patrick Finglass was so kind so as to polish my English; he read the entire manuscript from beginning to end with his usual precision and keen eye for detail. David Weeks also helped me get rid of various mistakes and made my English more idiomatic. Thanks are also due to Jenny Strauss Clay, who made available to me a penultimate draft of her book *Homer's Trojan Theater: Space, Vision, and Memory in the* Iliad (Cambridge, 2011), when I was still working on my manuscript.

I would also like to express my gratitude to Pietro Pucci and Greg Nagy, both for the ongoing influence that their scholarship continues to exercise on my view of many things Homeric and for being always there for me in so many different ways.

On a personal note, space has made me reconsider the human absence and presence that so influence one's life. My twin brother's emigration to France and the coming birth of my second daughter are constant reminders of spaces left void and then filled, of memories and love mixed so painfully and healingly in our brief and, perhaps, trivial life stories.

Introduction

THE AIM OF THIS BOOK is to offer a comprehensive study of space in the *Iliad*. Space constitutes a wide-ranging area of research, well beyond the limited concepts of landscape or setting.[1] Space in narrative is of prime importance for understanding the inner mechanics of the plot, and covers a wide spectrum of roles that have not been adequately studied in the *Iliad*. I will argue that both the development of its plot and its delineation of character are heavily conditioned by the function of space in its various manifestations, extending from the most elementary features of scenery to perspective and mental mapping.

Lessing's dictum that literature is a temporal art,[2] and the obvious but misleading imbalance of time and space in narrative, have been partly responsible for the abundance of studies dealing with time and the dearth of those examining space. It was not until the late twentieth century that this disparity began to disappear, as scholars realized that space is a far more complicated concept, and that both background settings and more profound aspects of narrative space are of pivotal importance for understanding literature as a whole.[3] Foucault, for example, almost prophesied that in contrast to the nineteenth-century obsession with history, "the present epoch will perhaps be above all the epoch of space."[4] Although literary critics were not ready to endorse concepts like Bakhtin's groundbreaking "chronotopes" (i.e. timespaces), which echoed Einstein's theory of relativity and were deemed rather eccentric for literary use, recognizing the paramount role of space, now on an almost equal footing with time, opened a new window into the world of narrative art. Nowadays, spatial metaphors are part of the language of narrative theory, and constitute an essential underpinning of contemporary approaches to literature.[5] Despite a slow

---

[1] On landscape in Homer, see Hellwig 1964; Elliger 1975:29–102 (*Iliad*) and 103–156 (*Odyssey*); Andersson 1976; Hölscher 1989; Purves 2002:136–167; Purves 2010a:24–64; Clay 2011.

[2] Lessing 1893 (1766).

[3] Soja 1989.

[4] Foucault 1986:22.

[5] On modern narrative theory and space, see Frank 1963; de Certeau 1974; Frank 1978; O'Toole 1980; Mickelsen 1981; Van Baak 1983; Zoran 1984; Ronen 1986; Friedman 1993; Bachelard 1957;

start, classical scholars are becoming more and more interested in the study of space in ancient literary texts, as the books by Purves, Chaston, and Clay show.[6] In this respect, I would like to present some of the important recent steps in the study of space in literature.

> Raum ist in literarischen Texten nicht nur Ort der Handlung, sondern auch kultureller Bedeutungsträger. Die Raumdarstellung bildet eine der grundlegenden Komponenten der (fiktionalen) Wirklichkeitserschließung. Kulturelle Normen und Wertehierarchien finden im literarischen Raum eine konkret anschauliche Form; umgekehrt haben literarischen Räume maßgeblichen Anteil an der Aushandlung kultureller Raumordnungen.[7]

> Space in literary texts is not only the location of the plot, but also a vehicle of cultural meaning. Spatial representation forms one of the most basic components of illustrating fictional worlds. Cultural norms and hierarchies of values find in literary space a concrete and vivid form; conversely, literary spaces have a huge share in the treatment of cultural organizations of space.

The study of space and spatial representation in literature originated in research on the semantic field of *topos* ("place" and "landscape")[8] in the form of lays and motifs. In recent times, the studies of Alexander Ritter (*Gestaltung von Landschaft und Raum in der Erzählkunst*)[9] and Thomas Kullmann (*Vermenschlichte Natur: Zur Bedeutung von Landschaft und Wetter im englischen Roman von Ann Radcliffe bis Thomas Hardy*)[10] showed that certain literary texts display a close relationship between their descriptions of landscape and their delineation of character. One of the key contributions of Kullmann's research was that it laid the foundation for a poetics of spatial representation in literature.

Of paramount importance for the construction of a poetics of space were the pioneering work of Jurij Lotman on space and semiotics[11] and of Manfred Pfister on theater semiotics.[12] Lotman argued that the spatial structure of a

---

Duchan, Bruder, and Hewitt 1995; Friedman 1996; Pier 1999; Herman 2001, 2002; Ryan 2003; Buchholz and Jahn 2005; Bridgeman 2007; Ryan 2009.

[6] Purves 2010a; Chaston 2010; Clay 2011. There is also a forthcoming volume on space in ancient Greek literature, to be edited by de Jong as part of the series *Studies in Ancient Narrative*.

[7] Extract from the back cover of Hallet and Neumann 2009.

[8] On defining place, see Tuan 1977, 1978; Merrifield 1993; Hirsch 1995:9.

[9] Ritter 1975.

[10] T. Kullmann 1995.

[11] Lotman 1972.

[12] M. Pfister 1977:338–359.

text can be used as a model for that of the entire world.[13] For Lotman, reality is shaped by spatial representations; they constitute the material for forming and structuring cultural models, which are then mapped by humans onto the ideological schemata they use to organize and interpret the world. Pfister suggested that in drama, where the difference between the real space of the theater and the fictive space where the plot of the play unfolds is stark, space is represented by both language and stage techniques (theatrical scenery, costumes, lighting, etc.) that create a complex but effective nexus between on- and offstage action, within onstage events, or among multiple stages. Semiotics and structuralism, therefore, brought to the fore the need for an interdisciplinary approach to space that would incorporate the findings and insights of different fields of study. The foundations were thus laid for constructing a poetics of space that would combine comprehensiveness, interdisciplinarity, and flexibility, allowing for enough variation and divergence to cater to both the rules and constraints of diverse literary genres[14] and the tastes of different eras.[15]

Although a definition of space that would cover an extremely large array of approaches seems difficult, it is fair to say that space is "the boundless, three-dimensional extent in which objects and events occur and have relative position and direction."[16] Since "objects and events" form part of this definition, it is to be understood that human agency and its products constitute an integral part of the way this three-dimensional extent, in all its multiple manifestations, interacts with the way we perceive and define reality. Thus when discussing space in literature we need to consider the convergence and interaction of two factors: the first pertains to the uses of space by human civilization, and the second is the wide variety of active spatial representations.

Space: An Interdisciplinary Approach

Modern companions and handbooks classify space under various categories. For example, Stephan Günzel's handbook on *Raum*[17] classifies space in no fewer than fourteen distinct areas of research:

1. *Historical space:* archive and place of remembrance

2. *Political space:* public and state of emergency

---

[13] Lotman 1972:312.
[14] For an instructive presentation of studies on the semiotics of space, see Nünning 2009:35–38.
[15] Goetsch (1977) has shown how different types of drama (realistic, expressionistic, epic, and absurd) employ diverse forms of spatial representation.
[16] See Britannica Online Encyclopedia, s.v. "Space."
[17] Günzel 2010.

3. *Economic space:* megacities and globalization

4. *Corporeal space:* gender and performativity

5. *Postcolonial space:* thinking about borders and thirdspace

6. *Social space:* spatialization

7. *Technological space: Enträumlichung*

8. *Media space:* images—signs—cyberspace

9. *Cognitive space:* orientation—mental maps—organizing and processing data

10. *Topographical space:* nature and heterotopy

11. *Urban space:* square—city—agglomeration

12. *Tourist space:* mobility and imagination

13. *Poetic space:* chronotopos and geopolitics

14. *Epistemological space:* labor and the geography of knowledge

Such a systematic and detailed classification of space may seem overwhelming to any modern reader of Homer, but a closer look shows that some of the insights of this type of spatial study are also applicable to the *Iliad*. Leaving aside cognitive space, which I will treat later on, I will now summarize the findings of recent research on space that are relevant to my topic. Of the fourteen categories of space studied by modern research, the six that are applicable to the *Iliad* are historical, political-social, corporeal, cognitive, topographical, and poetic space.

Historical space:[18] Pierre Nora's *Realms of Memory* (*Lieux de mémoire*) reflects the shift of interest from a chronological interpretation of history to a spatial one. His famous formulation "memory fastens upon sites, whereas history fastens upon events"[19] is virtually a prelude to his writing of a history of places of memory. According to his argument, collective consciousness, especially in the case of nations, tends to be shaped and crystallized around places, which acquire a secondary, symbolic meaning that is then mapped onto the nation's self-definition to such an extent that it reshapes it.[20] One other key notion that research on historical space has brought to the fore, mainly in the German-speaking world, is that of *spacing history*, as advocated by Karl Schlögel[21] and

[18] For an overview of research on historical space, see Ebeling 2010.
[19] Nora 1996:18.
[20] See Anderson 1991:187–206.
[21] Schlögel 2003:11.

enriched by Reinhart Koselleck.[22] Both of these scholars emphasized a return to the study of space as a factor in shaping historical reality, and tried to reconcile time and space as the two crucial factors that help us understand not simply events but also *why* events unfolded the way they did.

These powerful insights into the function of historical space are also applicable to the *Iliad*. Heroes tend to construct highly thematized notions of their past by recourse to their places of origin. For example, Achilles' memory of his past life makes Phthia a symbolic reality that contrasts with his present situation at Troy. By projecting this highly personalized, positively presented picture of his past, Achilles shapes and justifies his actions in the present. His abstention from the war is filtered through his use of his place of origin as a *site of memory* against which his rejection of Agamemnon's leadership and the importance of the expedition are constantly measured (*Iliad* I 152–157; XIX 315–330).

Political-social space:[23] Although sociologists clearly distinguish between political and social space, there is no reason to apply such rigid categorizations in the case of the *Iliad*. As an introduction, it will suffice to mention Giorgio Agambens, whose work has convincingly shown that in the modern world place has been identified with political space, and Anthony Giddens,[24] whose theory of *structuration* focuses on the question of priority between individuals and social forces with respect to their role in the formation and shaping of social reality. What is also important to our discussion is the fact that owing to technological advances and the globalization process, traditionally conceived political and social organization and power reside not so much in territories determined by concrete borders or clearly delineated social classes as in complex systems of parallel worlds that have reconceptualized the way political and social space works. In this light, various aspects of modern life whose spatial representation has shaped people's identity, like sports, work, and entertainment, constitute sophisticated forms of political and social space, since they function as the ideological arenas of a constant struggle for authority, power, and control. But what also matters for understanding the way political and social space functions is that reality is constructed by a complex interaction between agency and structure, that is, between the actions of individuals and the constraints implied by a given system. Systems contain the situated activities of human agents and the patterning of social relations across a space-time axis, but structuration means that what has been formed within a structure can also exist outside it,

---

[22] Koselleck 2000.

[23] On political space, see Geulen 2010; on social space and the sociology of space, see Schroer 2006; Kajetzke and Schroer 2010; for an anthology of important texts on political space, see Dünne and Günzel 2006:371–446.

[24] Giddens 1984 and 1995.

the typical example being the relation between teacher and student, which is preserved irrespective of spatial constraints (both in class and in the street) and temporal ones (even after many years, when both agents have lost their previous status as teacher and student).

This last observation is of crucial importance for exploring the way political-social space works in the *Iliad*. The poem's structure includes a series of thematic rules and constraints that determine the horizon of events that can take place and the kind of relations that can be developed between individuals. Certain combinations are by definition excluded. For example, Achilles and Agamemnon must disagree, since they cannot solve their differences in a manner that will not end in dissension and strife.[25] The structure also provides rules that enable the narrator to create novel and dramatically effective "courses of action." In this respect, space does play an important role, as tensions between individuals are also mapped onto several spatial features of the inner organization of the Achaean camp. For example, the placement of Achilles' hut at the far end of the camp—as far as possible from the headquarters of Agamemnon—symbolically underlines their different political viewpoints. The Panhellenic character of the expedition, an idea that belongs to the deep structure of the Trojan War tradition, is shaped in the *Iliad* into what we might call an early form of globalization, since the individual interests of the various leaders tend to be absorbed by a powerful mechanism of assimilation, with its own rhetoric. Achilles' stubborn resistance to this assimilation is spatially marked by both his withdrawal from the war and his remaining in his own "territory," in a parallel world that keeps him, for most of the poem, apart from the rest of the army.

Corporeal space:[26] As the subtitle "gender and performativity" in the above list shows, feminist critics have devoted much ink (and also some bile) to their protest against androcentric dichotomies and symbolisms according to which the female was basically corporeal, the male predominantly spiritual. Such biased, scientifically unsupported views had often been used as arguments for the construction of hierarchies that reinforced the inferior position of women. Julia Kristeva and Luce Irigaray use Plato's *Timaeus* as the basis for further developing the concept of *khōra* (χώρα) that they attribute to the female body: a receptive, open, and formless space, yet a "womb" and an unexpressed totality,

---

[25] See Aristotle Poetics 1453a 35–39: ἔστιν δὲ οὐχ αὕτη ἀπὸ τραγῳδίας ἡδονὴ ἀλλὰ μᾶλλον τῆς κωμῳδίας οἰκεία· ἐκεῖ γὰρ οἳ ἂν ἔχθιστοι ὦσιν ἐν τῷ μύθῳ, οἷον Ὀρέστης καὶ Αἴγισθος, φίλοι γενόμενοι ἐπὶ τελευτῆς ἐξέρχονται, καὶ ἀποθνῄσκει οὐδεὶς ὑπ' οὐδενός ("Yet this is not the pleasure to expect from tragedy, but is more appropriate to comedy, where those who are deadliest enemies in the plot, such as Orestes and Aegisthus, exit at the end as new friends, and no one dies at anyone's hands"; trans. S. Halliwell).

[26] For a concise presentation of corporeal space, see Postl 2010; for a collection of important texts, see Dünne and Günzel 2006:195–285.

whose urges and impulses on the one hand and comfort and healing on the other result in a combination of antithetical features.[27]

Corporeal space, though, is not linked only to women. The "body" as a site of social and ideological concerns has been systematically employed throughout human history. In the *Iliad*, the bodies of both men and women are at times treated as sites of aesthetic and ideological, but also poetic considerations, intricately entwined with the medium of oral epic. Helen's body is the epitome of corporeal space, since it symbolizes a creature that provokes male awe and sensation (as in the Trojan elders in *Iliad* III 156–158) and effectively "plays" with notions of hierarchy, which it tellingly challenges. The male body, armed or naked,[28] lies at the center of attention, as it constantly becomes the symbol of military excellence, heroic prowess, and κλέος. More specifically, the body of the fallen hero constitutes one of the major themes of the entire *Iliad*, one whose special weight has been emphasized from the very proem (*Iliad* I 4–5).

Topographical space:[29] By the term *topographical space* I denote landscape and the way it is linked to the people who inhabit it. I will briefly give some examples that are typical of the *Iliad*. Although there are no landscape descriptions in the poem, the narrator constantly uses certain topographical markers such as the oak and fig trees, the rivers Simoeis and Skamandros, Mount Ida, the Hellespont, the islands (Tenedos, Lesbos etc.) off the coast of Asia Minor near Troy, and so on. He also makes use of other geographical entities like Lycia (denoted by a feature of its landscape, the river Xanthos), Phthia (connected to Mount Peleion), and other localities in both Greece and Asia Minor. The epic presents a blurred picture, since it fuses imagined features (the oak and fig trees) with real landscape elements (Ida; the rivers in the Troad), which it employs to further its own poetic ends. In this light, some of the ideas developed by the human geographer Carl O. Sauer are also applicable to the *Iliad*. In a pioneering study with the suggestive title "The Morphology of Landscape,"[30] Sauer argued in favor of a phenomenology of landscape, in the sense that human culture shapes physical and natural elements of a given landscape into a cultural one. The term "cultural landscape," of course, has undergone various changes down the years, but Sauer's basic idea that nature with its topographical features is the medium that humans mold according to their own culture (as a set of rules for understanding their condition in the world) is valid for our interpretation of the *Iliad*. For Briseis, Phthia, a place far away from her native land, acquires meaning through certain cultural premises. Since her husband and family have

---

[27] Kristeva 1974; see also Irigaray 1974 and 1977.
[28] Analyzed in an exemplary manner by Vernant 1996:91–101.
[29] See Christians 2010.
[30] Sauer 1925.

been killed and her city sacked by the Achaeans (*Iliad* XIX 291–297), she faces the danger of becoming a slave in the service of some king. Patroklos' promise to make her Achilles' wife when they return to Phthia turns a mere place-name into a cultural landscape: topography is thus replaced by culture, since Phthia is for Briseis not a sum of topographical features, but the site where lies the promise of and hope for the life of a wedded and honorable wife. One more example is characteristic of the process I am describing: when in *Iliad* XXII Achilles is chasing Hektor around the walls of Troy, they pass from the washing-places "where the wives of the Trojans and their lovely / daughters washed the clothes to shining, in the old days / when there was peace, before the coming of the sons of the Achaians" (XXII 154–156).[31] A topographical detail, the washing-places situated somewhere near Troy, is a solid natural feature that the epic tradition uses only as a medium, subsequently shaping it according to its own set of epic rules. The washing-places are turned into cultural space, standing for the peaceful years Troy enjoyed before the outbreak of the war.

Poetic space:[32] Bakhtin's theory about the constitutive and interactive function of space and time[33] has recently become the focus of renewed scholarly interest, since some critics favor a reversal of Bakhtin's famous *chronotopoi* into *topochronoi*, thus emphasizing the need of "a *topochronic* narrative poetics, one that foregrounds *topos* in an effort to restore an interactive analysis of time with space in narrative discourse."[34] Specific *chronotopes* are spatiotemporal concepts corresponding to particular viewpoints or sets of ideological tenets. That said, the whole of the *Iliad* may be seen as a huge chronotope, where the pair "Troy–present time" means war and suffering, whereas "Greece–past time" stands for peace and happiness. This does not mean there are no smaller chronotopic building blocks within the Iliadic narrative, but this large dichotomy is of profound significance for the poetics of the *Iliad*, since it is against this background that the entire horizon of false expectations, credible and impossible scenarios, hopes and promises, disappointments and grief—that is, what Iliadic tragedy is all about—emerges.

I have deliberately excluded *cognitive space* from this presentation, since it constitutes the prime methodological tool that I would now like to discuss in some detail. In this way, the reader will be better equipped to follow the arguments to be developed later, which combine the insights of various branches of

---

[31] Unless otherwise indicated, I have used Lattimore's 1951 translation of the *Iliad*.
[32] For a brief overview, see Sasse 2010.
[33] Bakhtin 1981.
[34] Friedman 2005:194.

learning, from classical philology to cognitive science and from narratology to the social sciences.[35]

Cognitive Space

According to cognitive theory, which studies the perception and active representation of space,[36] the position of a person or an object is mapped onto various modalities such as location, distance, color, size, sound, and imagery. Let us consider the following examples:

(a) John's house is in London.

(b) John's house is near the lake.

(c) John's house is painted white.

(d) John's house is two acres in size.

(e) John's house is very noisy.

(f) John's house is like one of those old farm houses built in the middle of a prairie.

(g) John's house is of traditional style, large, with a garden filled with dozens of trees, two kitchens (one for the maids and the butler in the basement), two halls on the first and second floors, a spacious living room in the second floor leading to a separate room with a large pool table, three bathrooms (all upstairs with the exception of one in the basement), seven bedrooms (including a cozy attic), and what you would consider the best view from the third floor balcony.

In all these cases, space is represented by means of different spatial modalities. In (a), the placement of John's house is described in terms of its location. Location in itself is only relative, for when the speaker wishes to locate a person or an object, he also needs to identify the place where the person or object is. In other words, he needs to determine a "there" by using further spatial details. Here, the use of the place name "London" allows the speaker to avoid spatial subdivisions, since it supplies the reader with all the necessary information, given that he is expected to know where London is. Turning to the *Iliad*, we can see that this form of spatial representation, which is only used with place names, may be divided into two smaller but distinct groups: one that pertains to real topographies, that is, locations where part of the plot takes place, and

---

[35] For one of the fullest presentations of the current state of research with respect to space, see Günzel 2010.

[36] See the useful summary offered by C. Wagner 2010.

another referring to imaginary ones—absent locations that (mainly but not solely) feature in the speeches of certain characters. Mount Ida, for example, or Samothrace belong to the first category, as they are used as vantage points where the gods stand to watch the fighting in the plain of Troy. Phthia, Pylos, or Lycia need no further geographical determination, but also constitute locations *in absentia* that are regularly summoned to the *hic et nunc* of the plot by means of analeptic or proleptic references endorsed respectively (but not solely) by Achilles, Nestor, Sarpedon, and Glaukos. Having said this, I will try to explore how the tradition of the *Iliad* has devised a system of spatial representation that fully exploits the traditional referentiality of these place names, which in the process of growth and shaping of the epic tradition have acquired a secondary function that has gradually absorbed their first meaning. Because these locations have shaped their epic identity by being tied to figures that are emblematic of the heroic tradition, it is fair to say that they have been transformed into metonymic pathways, leading to a whole nexus of associations with each hero and the tradition that has developed around his persona.

In (b), the placement of John's house is determined by its distance from a spot (the lake) whose position is either known to the reader or functions as an orientation point at the time the utterance is made. In this case, contextual constraints are essential, since the lake is used as a signpost that has played, or will play, some role in the unfolding narrative. In this example, the signpost "lake" is fixed, since its location cannot change. If instead of "lake" the signpost were, for example, "Peter," then the fact that "Peter" is not bound to any given location, but would presumably change places while the narrative unfolds, would create a dynamic form of spatial representation, since the reader would need to create different visualizations of "Peter" and then anchor to one of them the visualization of "John's house." This form of dynamic spatial representation is typical of the *Iliad*, which contains a system of *immobile* signposts on the battlefield (the oak and fig trees, the hill of Kallikolone, the rivers Simoeis and Skamandros, the rise in the plain, and the Wall of Herakles, as well as the large landmarks of the walls of Troy and the Achaean camp), but also uses "mobile shifters," such as other warriors or the troops, as signposts to determine the place where a hero stands on the battlefield, to follow his movement in the plain, and often to visualize the place where he falls.

In (c), the placement of John's house is determined not externally (as in the former two examples, where its location depends on its relative position with respect to another place—"London" or "the lake") but internally, since it arises from a characteristic of the house itself. Such a formulation creates in the reader's or listener's mind a picture of John's house that is marked by its whiteness. Cognitive research has shown that color "is one feature of visual stimuli that has a known separate neuroanatomical basis, and people who lose their color perception due to brain damage often lose their ability to image in color."[37] Imaging in color allows for visual clarity, which as a form of spatial representation enables both speaker and listener or reader (depending on the medium) to produce a mental picture of John's house in space by determining its position against a darker background, one that would contrast with the brightness of the imagined object. Brightness, in particular, is an effective spatial mechanism, and therefore a mnemonic cue, since it functions as an "internal lamp" that sheds light on different areas of memory, turning what is blurred into a clear mental picture.[38]

Before I turn my attention to the *Iliad*, there is one more point to make with respect to color as a form of spatial representation: given that transformational thinking—that is, shifting rapidly from one situation to another—is very much at work in certain oral traditions, the need to visualize and mentally locate moving agents of the plot makes it an extremely dynamic and efficient device for spatial representation. In this respect the *Iliad* is of paramount importance, since the continual movement of the various heroes, Trojans and Achaeans alike, on the vast, uncharted area of the battlefield is visualized better by means of frequent references to the shining effect of their armor. Helmets, breastplates, shields, greaves, spears, and swords all produce a gleaming effect so constantly repeated that it has become almost an integral feature of the tradition. I will show that this emphatic reiteration and emphasis on the shining armor is a spatial cue for recall and organization of material, since it allows the narrator to "see" with his mind's eye where the warriors whose actions he is going to describe are positioned on the battlefield. This mechanism is all the more crucial in light of the narrator's frequent use of transformational thinking that necessitates a continual shifting of situations and locations alike.[39]

In example (d), John's house is visualized in terms of the large area it covers. As in the previous case, the house's position is determined by means of implicit coding that stems from a feature of the house itself. This feature has to be specific and concrete, not general and abstract. Concepts and ideas are hard to visualize, and in the framework of oral storytelling they have to be linked to or absorbed by the actions of actors and agents who perform specific deeds, presented in imageable forms.[40] At this point it is helpful, as we are about to turn

---

[37] Rubin 1995:57.
[38] The expression "internal lamp" was coined after the case of the Russian mnemonist Shereshevsky, who used to insert a street lamp into his memorized scene for the purpose of illumination, or added a contrasting background in order to avoid confusion and achieve mental clarity. See Whitehead 2009:28 and my own remarks in chapter 5, below.
[39] On transformational thinking, see Paivio 1971:28–33; Rubin 1995:48–49.
[40] See Rubin 1995:60.

our attention to the *Iliad*, to repeat some of Havelock's observations with respect to oral epic tradition:

> Actions and their agents are in fact always easy to visualise. What you cannot visualise is a cause, a principle, a category, a relationship or the like ... To be effectively part of the record they [concepts] have to be represented as agents or as doings particular to their context and sharply visualised. [41]

From this perspective, the qualitative difference between the formulation "John's house is magnificent" and "John's house is two acres in size" is that while the former employs the abstract idea of beauty and magnificence, the latter promotes a specific feature of the house, namely its huge size. The advantage from the point of view of visualization and memory recall becomes obvious: whereas "beauty" as an abstract concept is hard to visualize, size determined by specific numerical data helps the speaker and listener alike create a concrete mental image of John's house, as "a house two acres in size." Analogous arguments can be applied to the *Iliad*. The size of the heroes and gods who inspire awe, and the emphasis on their armament and stature and their glorious deeds, are to a great extent substitutes for causal chains of events and ideas that have been fused into the particular sets of actions and behavioral systems that these agents embody. The tradition of oral epic storytelling has internalized the entire world into its own system of associations, developed around specific, concrete actions that are readily imagined and evoked during the performance of oral song. Moreover, apart from their usefulness for memorability, specificity and concreteness are particularly effective for a kind of elliptical thinking typical of oral song-making. As the reader or listener is expected to infer that John is probably a very wealthy man, since he owns such a big house, so the Homeric audience is expected to figure out that a warrior's twelve-cubit spear indicates his exceptional heroic prowess and status, a point that the narrator can also use to create unexpected but dramatically powerful tropes in his narrative.

In case (e), the position of John's house is identified through sound, which is employed as a spatial marker that allows the reader or listener to mentally place himself with respect to the object in question. Sound is an implicit form of deixis that emphasizes perspective, and is based on the location of an observer with respect to the person or thing mentioned. A loud noise, such as that associated with John's house, indicates proximity, since the listener is situated close enough to the house to perceive the sound as loud. Conversely, a quiet sound suggests that the observer is not near the house. In the *Iliad*, sound is regularly

---

[41] Havelock 1963:188.

employed as a spatial mechanism that allows the audience to be immersed in the plot: the clang of weapons, the noise of the troops marching on the plain, Zeus' thundering, and the sound of the sea are among the wide array of manifestations of a kind of spatial representation that transforms the telling of the epic story and remembering an event of the past into "seeing it, and describing it as if it were happening before one's eyes."[42] The mental transportation of the audience from the present to the past and the bringing of a distant past to the present of the performance have been often discussed by Homerists, but mainly in temporal terms. Sound testifies to a hitherto unexplored facet of the bard's imaginative way of plunging his audience into the midst of his narrative, since it breaks down the distinction between the "here" of the performance and the "there" of the events narrated. Moreover it creates a synesthetic effect, since proximity to the hubbub of battle is achieved almost at the same time through the audience's "hearing" the loud sound produced by the clash of the troops and its "seeing" this clash taking place from a (mentally) short distance.

Example (f), "John's house is like one of those old farmhouses built in the middle of a prairie," belongs to the realm of mental imagery, perhaps the strongest cue to recall. Imagery[43] is a dynamic form of spatial representation and an important feature of memory,[44] enabling narrator and audience alike to associate attributes or stimuli by pairing them with locations in a consistent way.[45] Imagery is also a way of organizing isolated units by mapping them onto a solid and specific spatial background. In our example, John's house is mentally visualized by means of a simile, which we can treat as an illustrative analogy between an unknown or new item and a familiar and easily recognizable one. The speaker attempts to picture the object in question, John's house, in his mind's eye by reference to a well-known and common mental image of one of "those old farmhouses built in the middle of a prairie." The generalizing tone of this last expression indicates that both speaker and audience are expected to bring the image readily to their mind's eye, for there are many old farmhouses and so everybody is expected to know what they look like. The illustrative simile has the advantage that it evokes a whole nexus of links, some explicitly stated (old, farmhouse, middle of the prairie) and others, much greater in number, implicitly alluded to. For example, the image of an "old house built in the middle of a prairie" may trigger in the listeners' minds various verbally unexpressed features: bad state of the house, abandonment, isolation, a rural environment, a large family

---

[42] Bakker 2005:146.
[43] On imagery, see Rubin 1995:39–64.
[44] Underwood 1969.
[45] See Rescorla and Cunningham 1979; Geiselman and Crawley 1983; Winograd and Church 1988; see Rubin 1995:51 for further bibliography.

with many children living there, a lot of land around it, horses and animals in a nearby stable, and so on. In other words, imagery is about ellipsis, and elliptical thinking is very much counterbalanced in oral traditional song-making by the inherent pictureability of the mental imagery. In this light, it is fair to say that the spatial representation activated by the illustrative analogy that the simile so aptly creates equals a whole universe of signifiers, and is like a tide of memory that brings to the surface a deep-rooted and complex set of interconnections. Imagery enables the listener to picture much more than what it explicitly tells him to visualize. The extremely rich system of extended similes for which the *Iliad* is so famous testifies to the importance of imagery within the medium of oral song. The fact that similes are replete with imagery allows the storyteller to organize his narrative and visualize the placement of his actors and agents against the backdrop of a strong and dynamic set of easily recognizable spatial representations. Moreover, the kind of interactive imagery that the similes so powerfully embody increases distinctiveness and specificity, two of the most useful requirements for mental recall. Seen from this angle, the extended simile is a trademark of the Homeric tradition of oral song-making, since its nature, shape, and function constitute an inseparable whole, in contrast to the brief simile devoid of any spatial mappings.

Case (g) is a typical form of description that displays a high proportion of spatial features. John's house is described by means of various modifiers, whose juxtaposition in asyndeton elevates them to equal descriptive status without any hint as to possible subdivisions. As the reader or listener hears the gradually unfolding array of features that characterize John's house, he begins to follow a mental path that guides him to the various aspects of the described house. He visualizes first a house in traditional style, whatever "traditional" means within the context of this particular communicative situation; he then glances at its enormous size, which is further specified (but not subdivided) by the enumeration of various spatial accoutrements like a garden, in which dozens of trees create concrete mental pictures and indicate its size. The second list within the larger descriptive list of characteristics of John's house offers the reader or listener various clues that facilitate his mental tour:[46] as he moves visually from the garden to the kitchens, and mentally visits the basement where the servants' kitchen is situated, he realizes that John is a very rich person, whose house is in fact an estate where there are various servants (including a butler, whose presence suggests that John is a member of the aristocracy). Our mental tour of the house continues as further information is marshaled through spatial organization: we go from the basement to the first and then the second floor

---

[46] See de Certeau 1974:118–122.

where the two halls are situated, and see there a spacious living room, through which we arrive at a separate room with a large pool table. In the time it takes for the listener to cross it, the scale of the living room becomes almost real. Ascending further to the upper (third) floor, we see the three bathrooms, the seven bedrooms, and above them the cozy attic. This vivid visual journey concludes with the addition of one more detail, tellingly placed at the very end of the description: the view from the third-floor balcony is a revealing piece of spatial information, for not only does it lead us from the enclosed area of the rooms to the open area of the balcony, but it is also accompanied by a guiding reference, the only one that fuses the actual description with the rather separate register of the discourse. The speaker aims at involving his listeners even more effectively in the process of visualizing John's house. Since he has, after all, guided them all around this enormous estate, it is now time, assuming that they have followed him in his mental pathway, to stand by them as they gaze together out of the common window of their imagination.

Similarly, the Iliadic storyteller engages in descriptions of prized objects, the most notable example being, of course, the long ecphrasis on the shield of Achilles in *Iliad* XVIII.[47] He lays great emphasis on the position of the beholder, who determines the particular way the description will unfold. Like the speaker in the example of John's house, the Homeric bard regularly, but not solely, employs the method of the *visual tour*, taken by a notional "mobile" beholder who moves his mind's eye in a certain direction or along a visual path. Taking a cue from this observation, I intend to explore the full range of descriptive techniques the storyteller employs, which go far beyond the *tour strategy*. In the *Iliad*, objects whose static nature is regularly taken as given often move in space, as they are transferred from one owner to another. By cataloguing the various owners of an object, the storyteller translates time (the remote and vast period of the past) into space. Apart from this dynamic form of spatial representation, the *Iliad* is also fond of static spatial description, either through the use of spatial pairs (near-far, foreground-background, dark-shining, center-periphery) or by highlighting one or two noteworthy features of a prized object.

---

[47] Describing the shield of Achilles, the storyteller-observer, though invisible, follows a visual tour by moving not only from one boss of the shield to the next but also from one section of each boss to another section of the same boss. The sequentiality of his description (he never omits a section or a boss to return to it later) and its comprehensiveness (he moves to the next section only when he has finished with the previous one) is analogous to the linearity and comprehensiveness of the visual tour of John's house in the example discussed above.

Space in the *Iliad*

The study of space in the *Iliad* is related to two sets of rules and constraints, the former reflecting what one considers to be a working model of analysis, the latter imposed by the particular poetic grammar of Iliadic epic. Before I go through the organization of material to be adopted in this book, let me briefly dwell on these two sets of rules and constraints.

Following recent approaches to the study of space, I devote separate sections (parts 1–4) to the three principal forms of spatial representation attested in literature (setting, imagery, and description), and further divide one of these forms (setting) into two subgroups, on the basis of narrative perspective. In particular, what is generally (and in the case of the *Iliad* rather misleadingly) called *setting* will be the subject of two chapters, one dedicated to *simple story space* and one to the *"offstage" story space embedded in character speech*. Parts 1 and 2 of this book correspond to the real and imaginary topographies as mapped out by the actants of the plot. As will become obvious from the presentation of the relevant material, this distinction is of paramount importance for the poetics of the *Iliad* as a whole. Parts 3 and 4 are devoted to the study of imagery and description, where space looms large and which in the case of the *Iliad* mainly pertain to the extended similes and the description of prized objects.

This "vertical" classification of space in the *Iliad* will be combined with a "horizontal" one, comprising all the relevant types of analysis of space that I discussed briefly above. This interdisciplinary approach is, in my view, much needed for the study of such a complex semantic field as the one represented by space.

In part 1, I will study *simple story space*,[48] which constitutes one of the two principal forms of narrative space, and can be defined as the primary spatial form with its various framed and framing spaces. Story space encompasses a broader spectrum than both *landscape* and *scenery*, as it includes *perspective*, that is, the way the narrator helps his audience "view" the content of his narrative. The cartography of mortal space and the division between the mortal and immortal spheres of activity follow a carefully constructed narrative blueprint, which facilitates the unraveling of the plot and accentuates basic beliefs about the heroic world. More specifically, the threefold organization of human space, with the plain at the center and the city of Troy and the Achaean camp on the edges of a notional map, aims at keeping the audience's attention on the action and the actors. Iliadic theatricality, one of the key factors enhancing

---

[48]   See Chatman 1978:96–107.

dramatization, results from this visually frugal but highly effective spatial mapping.[49] The tradition's unflagging reluctance to promote impressionistic descriptions and spectacular scenery and its concentration on a visually limited space give special weight to the narrated events and make the delineation of character all the more significant. Moreover, the story space shifts as the plot unfolds: from the plain of Troy and the fighting at the beginning of the epic, the narrator briefly moves to the city of Troy, preparing Hektor's great return to the battlefield;[50] the fulfillment of Zeus' plan transfers the audience in front of and inside the Achaean camp, until Patroklos' intervention and his subsequent death; with Achilles' return to war, the emphasis shifts again to the whole range of the battlefield until the final encounter with Hektor; and as the epic ends, the Achaean camp and the city of Troy (where Patroklos and Hektor are lamented respectively) are overwhelmed by grief and lamentation.

In part 2, my focus will be on *embedded* story space, a secondary form of space which is evoked by characters and stands beyond the boundaries of the *primary* story space where the action takes place. By allowing characters to refer regularly to absent places from their past or future lives, the *Iliad* turns geographical locations into *thematized spaces* against which a character's role and personality are sketched. More or less in the manner of a theatrical play, where the action is spatially concentrated in a given, clearly delineated area that is immensely expanded by the characters' mythical armature, the limited story space of the simple narrative is absorbed or expanded by the much wider embedded story space alluded to in character speech. Such dynamic interaction creates a complex form of space, which redefines the setting and allows characters to function not only within the narrow frame of the Trojan plain, city, and Achaean camp, but also in light of their coming from other areas, which symbolically stand for their "other" lives that have been lost during the perils of war and to which they long, often ironically, to return. Given that time and again this extended story space is based on the extratextual role of certain characters in other epic traditions, the *Iliad* invites its audience to reconsider the presentation of a character and evaluate the poem's dramatic outlook on the world of heroes.

Part 3 will focus on such topics as *pictureability*, *foregrounding*, and *mental imaging*, which all pertain to the special register represented by the extended Homeric simile.[51] Seen from the perspective of space, Homeric epic contains—

---

[49] Compare the apt title of Clay's recent book *Homer's Trojan Theater: Space, Vision, and Memory in the Iliad* (Clay 2011).

[50] On war in the *Iliad*, see W.-H. Friedrich 1956; Fenik 1968; Latacz 1977; van Wees 1997; Hellmann 2000.

[51] I am not suggesting that these three features pertain only to the Homeric simile. For the relation between body language, pictureability, and memorability in the *Iliad*, see Minchin 2008b.

and uses as almost a kind of stylistic trademark—an extended form of simile that, unlike the spatial thriftiness of its narrative, is remarkably rich in active spatial representations. My main argument, which stems from the observation that the pictorial abundance of the similes is mainly and predominantly spatial, is that the Iliadic storyteller employed *homologous image-mappings for the space of narrative scenes and corresponding similes.*[52] As long as the visual setting of a given narrative unit remains the same, the space delineated in an extended simile also remains the same, or at least of the same sort as that of the previous simile. In addition, I will suggest that this technique, which is clearly a result of the process of mnemonic association enhanced by spatial unity, and has been recognized in cognitive psychology as a powerful cue to recall, has far-reaching consequences for the bard's mode of performance, or composition in performance.

Extending the Parry-Lord hypothesis with respect to the dictional and formulaic economy imposed by the system of oral song-making, I will argue that an equivalent form of economy is at work in the similes, that is, that special register which displays a rather low degree of formulaic repetition: it seems that the bards who shaped the system of traditional oral epic during centuries of performance followed what is known in cognitive theory as the "dual coding" system,[53] according to which the human brain uses two different areas for mapping stimuli, one for words and another for images.[54] This theory effectively explains the fact that narrative and simile seem to be in complementary distribution: whereas the former is rich in formulas and poor in spatial representation due to lack of imagery, the latter displays a remarkable wealth of imagery-oriented spatial mappings, but a low-level formulaic system. This dissonance between the view promoted by the narrator and the multiple image-mappings employed by listeners *relativizes perspective*: the simile, though an attempt to assimilate story space to a *paratopic space*, through its innate pictureability ends by creating multiple mental spaces. Such active engagement of the audience members gives them the opportunity to experience the tragedy of the plot not only through the narrator's suggested visual imaging in simple narrative, but also by their own mental means while visualizing similes.

Another spatial feature of the Homeric simile to be explored is its ontological boundaries: the narrator uses spatial imagery so abundantly in the similes

---

[52] Although based on externally perceived objects that are then mapped mentally, the idea of spatial analogy between two different levels of perception lies in the core of the so-called *index projection hypothesis* developed by Pylyshyn (2007:178–179).

[53] See Paivio 1971, 1975, 1986.

[54] See the apt formulation by Bruford and Todd 1996:8: "Although the insights of Parry and Lord into the use of formulae and themes have opened our eyes to several aspects of how epic narratives are produced, they are of little help in explaining the *mnemonic processes* which come into play when the singer is singing his tale."

in order to effect for his audience a "mental leap" from the world of the plot to different visual spheres. To this end, he promotes a boundary-crossing experience, and breaks down the illusion created by the distance between the world of the narrative and the real world of the performance.[55] It is in this cognitive perspective that I will discuss various aspects of the extended simile, such as its *bilaterality* (the split of the simile marker into two domains, the target domain and the base domain), its ability to expand in complex ways (stemming from the simile's openness and traditional referentiality), mapping inconsistency between the target and base domains, and the *multiplied simile*, an interpretive crux stemming from the imperfect combination of dictional ellipsis and the interlacing of two visually superimposed structures.

Last, I will study how the shift of spatial register from simple narrative to simile, which exploits at length the audience's familiarity with the natural world, immerses the listeners in a starkly different mental cartography, where the narrator's suggested vision does not necessarily coincide with the visualization of space evoked in each member of the audience, in accord with individual mnemonic storage. In tandem with their visual familiarity with the simile's content, listeners tend to tread their own mental paths in the process of visual imaging. From the narrator's standpoint, the simile embodies his attempt to limit the audience's variety of possible image-mappings by directing them toward his own visualization of the simile's content.[56]

In part 4, the emphasis will be on description formats, mnemonic strategies, and narrative role. Taking my cue from the work of Elizabeth Minchin on descriptive segments,[57] I will investigate the function of perspective in object-description. I contend that the way the narrator views an object or presents a work of art is based on the activation of specific mental formats that are readily available to his audience. Some of these formats, like those dealing with the size, color, and shape of the object or its history (often expressed through the object's *journey* and passage from one person to another), constitute forms of spatial organization. In the light of the role of perspective, ecphrastic space may be considered a means of *marking and prolonging events* that appear in the same context with the described objects. Extended space often results in the interruption of temporal sequence, since object description is a kind of piling up of spatially oriented data. Such explicit indications of space are often linked to

---

[55] Critics have noted the tendency of the Homeric simile to bring the audience back from the story-world to the realm of the performance. See S. Richardson 1990:66; Minchin 2001:43; Bakker 2005:114–135; Clay 2011:21.

[56] See Lakoff and Turner 1989:91; Minchin 2001:145; Teng and Sun 2002; Tsagalis 2008b:272–285.

[57] Minchin 2001:100–131.

the narrator or a character.[58] As in the simile, where listeners can evaluate its content on the basis of their own individual image-mappings, so in ecphrastic and descriptive segments the narrator takes it for granted that his listeners will employ their visual memory to supplement and complete his description. Along these lines, it may be argued that the narrator expands and maximizes an object's limited importance in ecphrastic space by interrupting story time and creating a pause. When no-fabula time matches text time, he can introduce his audience, temporarily, to a world of pure wonder, like that of Achilles' shield which makes them realize the contrast between the grimness of war and the beauty of human craftsmanship. By *spacing time*, the tradition of the *Iliad* almost creates for its audience an alternative world, whose mental reconstruction is interrupted by the shockingly horrible reality of the narrative. Scattered throughout the epic, descriptions (more or less like similes) fail to form a coherent totality, since they delineate spaces that the listeners view only in passing: the whole will remain endlessly suspended.

Space in the *Iliad* is built upon the epic's specific poetic grammar. It will be the main aim of this book to offer a comprehensive treatment of all these types of spatial representation, and to explore how they contribute to and reflect the logic and flow of a deeply tragic narrative.

---

[58] See Bal 1997:141.

PART ONE

VIEWING SIMPLE STORY SPACE
IN THE *ILIAD*

I N THIS PART, I will explore how the narrator organizes and "views" simple story space in the *Iliad*.[1] The tripartite mapping of mortal space (the plain, the Achaean camp, the city of Troy) and the twofold division between the areas of mortal and immortal activity intersect with a bipartite distinction between the base-level setting—the battlefield—and other framing spaces such as the Achaean camp, the city of Troy, and places of solely divine access. More specifically, the plain of Troy is presented as both a dynamic martial space, where most of the fighting takes place, and as a static space containing either certain microsettings where martial activity is replaced by other activities (like oath-taking or assemblies) or specific locus-images (such as the oak tree of Zeus and the fig tree, the river and ford of Skamandros, etc).

The Achaean camp, the city of Troy, and the divine world represent background and closed spaces that communicate only temporarily with the base-level space of the battlefield. The threefold organization of human space with the plain at the center and the city of Troy and the Achaean camp on the edges of a notional map aims at keeping the audience's attention on the action and the actors. By refusing to describe the landscape or any setting at length, the Iliadic tradition was able to focus on character interaction as dictated by the unraveling of the plot. Unfailing reluctance to promote impressionistic descriptions and spectacular scenery was a conscious choice, true to the perception of the heroic code that this epic tradition fostered.[2] The scenic frugality of the locale and the concentration on a visually limited space gives special weight to the narrated events and makes character delineation all the more significant. Moreover, the story space shifts as the plot unfolds: from the plain of Troy and the massive fighting between the two sides in the beginning of the epic, the narrator's lens briefly zooms in on the city of Troy, preparing Hektor's impressive return to the battlefield; the audience is then transferred in front of and inside the Achaean camp, up until Patroklos' intervention and his subsequent death; when Achilles returns to the war to avenge the death of his friend, the focus is again on the battlefield until the fated duel with Hektor; and the epic

---

[1]   For a penetrating introduction to space from a narratological point of view, see Chatman 1978:9–107; Bal 1997²:132–142.

[2]   Contrast the "attitude" of other epics with respect to one aspect of story space, i.e. the setting or landscape. The *Cypria*, the *Nostoi*, the *Odyssey,* and even epics such as Eumelus' *Titanomachy, Corinthiaca,* and *Europia* include multiple settings. For this aspect of the *Odyssey*, see Parry 1957; Nestle 1968; Treu 1968:82, 87–101; Elliger 1975:103–156; Andersson 1976:37–45. On the sociology of space in the *Odyssey*, see Finley 2002; Thalmann 1998; Purves 2006a; Vidal-Naquet 1996; Haller 2007. On taxonomic approaches to landscape, see E. Bucholz 1871; Bonnafé 1984:119–175. On Eumelus and a Corinthian epic tradition, see West 2002a; see also Bethe 1907; Bowra 1938; Dunbabin 1948; Will 1955; Capovilla 1957; Bowra 1963; Huxley 1969:63–64, 67–68; Untersteiner 1971; Drews 1976; Lecomte 1998; Debiasi 2004:19–69.

comes to an end with a touching view of the Achaean camp and the city of Troy filled with grief and lamentation for Patroklos and Hektor respectively. Mapping the plot in terms of spatial shifts reveals that the narrator aims at signaling to his audience the most grim realization of this, and any war: namely that the only spaces shared by enemies are those of death and grief.

The distinction between the worlds of mortals and immortals highlights the disparity between human sorrow and divine imperviousness.[3] By laying special emphasis on the spatial coordinates of divine intervention in the world of mortals, the *Iliad* invites its audience to reinterpret distance as a form of irony, for gods enter and exit the mortal world with great ease, whereas mortals are trapped in it: in fact, one of the principal dilemmas of the two major Iliadic heroes, Hektor and Achilles, is based on the very idea of their literal and figurative entrapment, the former between city and battlefield, the latter between battlefield and Phthia. In this light, space becomes a means for a profound ironic twist between gods and men.

The triple division of the world of mortals between the plain, the city of Troy, and the Achaean camp is so characteristic of the *Iliad* that it is almost taken for granted.[4] Scholars have rarely questioned this division or asked how it came into being. This might seem like trivial quibbling, given that it is virtually impossible to discuss such thorny topics without a considerable degree of speculation. Yet this tripartite structure of the Iliadic story space conforms with what one could call the default mode of all military confrontations: two camps, one for each adversary, and the plain between as a "disputed area" for combat. This basic visual imaging is at odds with that of a city under siege, where the set of icons in the audience's minds would no doubt normally be those of the defending army *inside* the city and only the attacking army *outside* the city walls. The awkward thing about Iliadic story space, which is of course directly connected to the city of Troy, is that there is no real siege, but a clear confrontation in the vast, open area of the plain separating the city of Troy and the Achaean camp by the sea. This choice, however, must have been a conscious and deliberate one on the part of the tradition crystallized in our *Iliad*, since it has two important advantages for the plot. First, it invites the audience to concentrate on a contested space, and therefore to appreciate the denser action that

---

[3]   On the Homeric gods, see Willcock 1970; Tsagarakis 1977; Griffin 1980:144–204; Thalmann 1984; Erbse 1986; W. Kullmann 1992; Emlyn-Jones 1992; Yamagata 1994; Kearns 2004.

[4]   The tripartite division of the world of mortals in the *Iliad* corresponds to three zones, two peripheral and one central, of fluctuating sharpness and resolution: the city of Troy and the Achaean camp are less "sharp" and more liminal with respect to the dramatic tension of the plot. Such a cognitive map allows for a balanced construction of narrative space that is based on the symmetry between mental topographies and narrative action. For the use of an equivalent, four-zone model, see Ryan 2003, who studies Marquez's *Chronicle of a Death Foretold*.

takes place in this space; and second, it allows the principal heroes of the two armies to engage in close combat. The effect of this second choice is noteworthy, since the high pitch and deep pathos of Iliadic fighting presuppose personal contact between the opposing warriors, something unlikely if the Trojans fought the Achaeans from the city walls. In fact, the *Iliad* constantly capitalizes on such themes, as when Priam and Hekabe beg Hektor to return to the safety of the city and avoid fighting Achilles on the battlefield (*Iliad* XXII 38–40, 84–85). Moreover, this tripartite organization of mortal space accords with the Aristotelian notion of the "*eusynoptic* landscape or object being of a size that cannot exceed the capacity of the human eye, and also, by extension, the limits of human memory."[5] The tripartite division of story space is thus closely linked both to the aim of visual comprehensiveness that would be effectively grasped by the audience and to the dramatic tension of the epic, almost a prerequisite for actively engaging the listeners in a dense plot, devoid of variant settings and attention-catching scenery but replete with pathos, tragedy, and grief.

---

[5] Purves 2010a:63. On Aristotle, see *Poetics* 1450b34–1451a6 and 1459a30–34; see also Purves 2010a:24–64.

1

The Base-Level Setting
The Battlefield

R EFLECTING THE TRIPARTITE STRUCTURE of Iliadic story space, the plain of Troy represents an extended area lying between the Achaean camp and the city of Troy.[1] Despite the lack of description, it can be further divided into the following subsettings: (1) the battlefield, (2) microsettings (oath-taking, friendly meetings, assemblies), and (3) locus-images (the oak and fig trees, the tombstone of Ilos, the tomb of Myrine, the ford of Skamandros, the "rise in the plain").

The Dynamics of Martial Space

The ἐς μέσον character of combat undoubtedly represents its most salient feature, and is of paramount importance for the staging of the Iliadic war.[2] In order to appreciate how the Iliadic tradition makes the battlefield an inter-mediate space, and the consequences of this narrative strategy, it is essential to recall that crucial phases in the evolution of the plot take place away from the battlefield, in the Achaean camp and, to a lesser extent, in the city of Troy. Hellwig has argued that only in the beginning of the epic is the battlefield the center of the fighting between the two armies.[3] Although her argument is based on a rather idiosyncratic definition of what she calls "die Stadt" (the city of Troy), which includes a number of places situated outside the city walls,[4] it is still on the right track, since it brings to the fore a crucial aspect of the battle-field's function as a channel leading the action either to the Achaean camp or to the city of Troy.

---

[1]   On the Trojan plain, see Thornton 1984:150–163; Clay 2007.
[2]   See also its use in tragedy: Sophocles *Women of Trachis* 513–514; Euripides *Suppliant Women* 699; *Phoenician Women* 1361. I owe these references to Diggle 1973:265.
[3]   1964:24–25.
[4]   Such as the monument of Ilos (*Iliad* XI 166).

To say that the battlefield is a space purely devoted to military activities seems so banal that it risks stating the obvious. In this light, it may come as a surprise when we suggest that it is this military space that shapes the various forms of Iliadic war (ἀνδροκτασίαι, smaller-group combat, formal duels, ἀριστεῖαι), and that its rather vague topography is part of a sophisticated staging of the fighting, pointing to important themes that permeate the entire epic. In fact, as I am about to suggest, the presentation and the function of military space entail important consequences for the work's perception of and outlook on the heroic world.

The study of military space will be organized on the basis of the main forms of fighting: the ἀνδροκτασίαι, the smaller-group combat, the formal duels, and the ἀριστεῖαι.

Androktasiai

These catalogues of second-tier warriors typically consist of the names of the slayer and the slain, a verb meaning "to kill," and quite often brief biographical information concerning the victim (patronymic or father's name, place of origin, short aretalogy).[5] With respect to space, the ἀνδροκτασίαι stand somewhere between the formal duels and the ἀριστεῖαι: each item of the catalogue[6] has to do with basically two warriors, but seen as a whole they occupy a rather dynamic, ever-expanding space. The narrator's camera moves from one group of warriors to the next, and—what is even more interesting—switches perspectives. In contrast to the ἀριστεία, where the expanding space is presented by following the trail of the protagonist, in the ἀνδροκτασία there is not a single trail,[7] but a zigzag technique.[8] From the narrator's global, panoramic visual scanning of the battlefield when the armies approach each other for massive fighting, we turn back and forth between close-ups of lesser heroes.[9] Fully

---

[5]   See Strasburger 1954:15–18; Ciani 1963–1964; Latacz 1977:82–89; Hellmann 2000. According to C. Armstrong 1969:30, the father's name is recorded ninety-eight times in the casualty lists of the *Iliad*.

[6]   See Beye 1964.

[7]   The *trail* is the continuous action space created by a character who moves from one spot or area to another and is uninterruptedly "visible" to the audience; see Konstan 2002:2.

[8]   I am hereby giving the term "zigzag" a "spatial turn." I am therefore not using it in its temporal aspect, for which see Barthes 1989:129.

[9]   See de Jong and Nünlist 2004a. The core of this observation was anticipated by Aristotle (*Poetics* 1459a30–34), Goethe (in his letter to Schiller in 1798), and Wood (in his treatise *On the Original Genius of Homer*, published in 1775). The most eloquent formulation is that of Jebb 1883:520 ("... and it is in taking a bird's-eye view from a height, not in looking around one on the level, that the comprehensive truth of Homeric topography is most vividly grasped. Homer is as his own Zeus or his own Poseidon, not as one of the mortals warring on the lower ground"). I owe all these citations to Purves 2010a:2–3, who in turn owes them to James Porter.

exploiting the deictic potential of the Greek language, the narrator traces his path by shifting the focus, as he sees the field through spatial snapshots, leaving his listeners to complete the larger tableau for themselves.[10]

One of the most noteworthy examples of this technique can be seen in the first large-scale battle (*Iliad* IV 446–544), which is divided into five parts: an introduction and four ἀνδροκτασίαι.

οἳ δ' ὅτε δή ῥ' ἐς χῶρον ἕνα ξυνιόντες ἵκοντο,
σύν ῥ' ἔβαλον ῥινούς, σὺν δ' ἔγχεα καὶ μένε' ἀνδρῶν
χαλκεοθωρήκων· ἀτὰρ ἀσπίδες ὀμφαλόεσσαι
ἔπληντ' ἀλλήληισι, πολὺς δ' ὀρυμαγδὸς ὀρώρει.
ἔνθα δ' ἅμ' οἰμωγή τε καὶ εὐχωλὴ πέλεν ἀνδρῶν
ὀλλύντων τε καὶ ὀλλυμένων, ῥέε δ' αἵματι γαῖα.[11]

Now as these advancing came to one place and encountered,
they dashed their shields together and their spears, and the strength
of armoured men in bronze, and the shields massive in the middle
clashed against each other, and the sound grew huge of the fighting.
There the screaming and the shouts of triumph rose up together
of men killing and men killed, and the ground ran blood.[12]

The introduction to this extended battle scene is a global view of the two armies standing in front of each other. Having previously referred to the movement of Achaeans and Trojans (*Iliad* IV 332, IV 427 κίνυντο φάλαγγες),[13] the narrator orients his listeners by offering a panoramic scan[14] of the opposing contingents and framing a common ground (*Iliad* IV 446 ἐς χῶρον ἕνα) for the actual combat. *Orientation* and *framing* have time and again been pointed out as typical tendencies, if not techniques, used by the Homeric narrator, who aims at guiding his audience by presenting the general framework of a scene, and only then proceeds to its constituent members.[15]

---

[10] On the use of deixis in Homer to shift the audience's attention to different paths, see Bakker 1997:54–122.

[11] The text of the *Iliad* is that of West 1998–2000 in BT, with some changes.

[12] All translations are from Lattimore 1951.

[13] Hellmann 2000:138 points out the discrepancy between the moving of the two armies in phalanx formation and the actual fighting being conducted by πρόμαχοι. This paradox can be resolved by viewing the battle space as described earlier: the narrator does not reenact phalanx fighting because this would eliminate, or at least downplay, personal excellence, the *raison d'être* of Homeric heroes. Instead, he is interested in *close-ups* between individual warriors; see van Wees 1997:673.

[14] See P. Wilson 1951–1952:269, who notes that the poet aims at making his audience see everything very clearly.

[15] Krischer 1971:132 observes this technique in Homeric catalogues; see also Bakker 1997:86.

With the expression ὅτε δή, the narrator invites the audience to follow his path and join him in the act of viewing space.[16] This mutual seeing, with an emphasis on the *hic et nunc* of the narration, has a direct bearing on the presentation of space. The stress laid on the *mutual approach* and *balanced opposition* of the two armies, as indicated by various markers (ἐς χῶρον ἕνα, ξυνιόντες, σύν ῥ' ἔβαλον, σὺν δ', ἀλλήλῃσι, ἅμ', ὀλλύντων τε καὶ ὀλλυμένων), suggests to the listener a comprehensive view of the battlefield, like that of a bird that swoops down and then lands in a single area.[17] This studied symmetry, based on the shared mental tendency to see in frames, facilitates viewing for the audience and results in a vivid picture of the actual scene.[18]

Space is also denoted by the adverb ἔνθα, which in general can indicate either time or place. In contrast to the standard use of ἔνθα (or ἐν), which is regularly employed in descriptions of scenery[19] containing items strung together by refrain composition, its function here is quite different. After referring to the clashing of the shields and swords and emphasizing the sound of the fighting, the narrator aims at making his listeners realize that this space where the combat has just begun will be not merely an area of impending warfare but also, and perhaps more significantly, a place of suffering and death. In this light, ἔνθα designates an internal deictic shift, not to another place but to a different function of the same space. We may ask why this dramatization is highlighted for the listeners by a deictic marker denoting space: the answer is, in my view, typical of the very process of the performance of oral song. Deictic markers both help mental icons take shape, by opening a path for them to follow, and allow the bard to find his way "on the fly," while performing his song. ἔνθα sustains and renews the listeners' interest in visualizing this space, marks and prolongs the description, and by turning their mind's eye from the impressive meeting of the two armies to the appalling spectacle of slaughter, it previews the tragic unfolding of the war from the very first day of battle.

This introductory passage is followed by an extended simile that gives the impression of having been intercalated between the panoramic view of the two clashing armies and the subsequent close-ups on the individual warriors.

> ὡς δ' ὅτε χείμαρροι ποταμοὶ κατ' ὄρεσφι ῥέοντες
> ἐς μισγάγκειαν συμβάλλετον ὄβριμον ὕδωρ

---

[16] Bakker 1997:79.

[17] On bird's-eye view, see de Jong and Nünlist 2004a:69–70.

[18] On the importance of spatial symmetry and the technique of midpoints with respect to mnemonic recall, see Aristotle *On Memory and Reminiscence* 452a17–24 and the analysis by Sorabji 1972:31–34.

[19] See Hellwig 1964:32–35; Müller 1968:89–153; Elliger 1975:103–165; Andersson 1976:37–52; Hölscher 1989:186–209; S. Richardson 1990:50–61; de Jong 2001:xvii n47.

κρουνῶν ἐκ μεγάλων κοίλης ἔντοσθε χαράδρης,
τῶν δέ τε τηλόσε δοῦπον ἐν οὔρεσιν ἔκλυε ποιμήν,
ὣς τῶν μισγομένων γένετο ἰαχή τε φόβος τε.

As when rivers in winter spate running down from the mountains
throw together at the meeting of streams the weight of their water
out of the great springs behind in the hollow stream-bed,
and far away in the mountains the shepherd hears their thunder;
such, from the coming together of men, was the shock and the
     shouting.

Iliad IV 452–456

Although the simile refers to the preceding narrative, the narrator is well aware that he is now inviting his listeners to adopt a significantly different view of the fighting armies. Not simply adding material to the previous description, he is rather "mapping" the combat action onto a different mental grid, by temporarily stepping outside of story space and "leaping" into what I shall call paratopic space (παρά + τόπος 'place'), the extratextual and atextual space of the Homeric simile.

In terms of view, the common denominator with the preceding narrative is the symmetrical display of space: the "hollow stream-bed" (κοίλης ἔντοσθε χαράδρης) where the two rivers coalesce on the one hand, and the "one place" (ἐς χῶρον ἕνα) where the armies clash on the other. Researchers who have studied two distinctive types of pictorial display, the metaphor and the simile, have argued that in terms of pictureability, metaphor and simile differ with respect to image grouping:[20] symmetrical image alignment of pictorial components depicting things of the same kind is apt for expressing pictorial metaphor, whereas describing things of different kinds is suitable for expressing pictorial simile.[21] In this light, both story space and paratopic space employ the mental imaging process of symmetry, making personal immersion and individual engagement on the part of the listeners coincide with the narrator's suggested drawing of space. Image groupings of different things such as armies and rivers display symmetrical image alignment and are placed on the same mental grid,[22] promoting a balanced organization of space and enhancing pictureability.[23]

---

[20] Teng and Sun 2002.
[21] On the role of psychological or cognitive factors with respect to metaphors and similes, see Paivio 1979; Ortony 1979a; Miller 1979.
[22] Cf. Herman 2001:535, who argues that narrative entails "a process of cognitive mapping that assigns referents not merely a temporal but a spatiotemporal position in the storyworld."
[23] On pictureability in Homeric similes, see Minchin 2001:133–137.

The actual fighting is presented in four distinct phases, each one containing a short catalogue of individual conflicts. In order to make this division clear for his audience, the narrator views the battle in terms of four spatial snapshots. The first snapshot (*Iliad* IV 457–472) is carried out in three movements, which create smaller spatial units: (1) Antilokhos kills the Trojan Ekhepolos; (2) Elephenor drags the corpse of Ekhepolos to seize his armor; (3) Agenor kills Elephenor and the battle flares up around his body.

The narrator informs his audience that he is turning his camera on Antilokhos by using the term πρῶτος (*Iliad* IV 457), which is here employed as a *chronotopic* term,[24] since it denotes both time and space: the action starts not only *when* Antilokhos strikes but also at the spot *where* he stands. This spatiotemporal function of πρῶτος is corroborated by the fact that the narrator hastens to indicate to his listeners where Antilokhos is located. The expression ἐνὶ προμάχοισι (458), designating the first ranks of the phalanx, selects for narrative elaboration a given group of warriors standing in the front line. By determining the place where these heroes are located, without any landscape reference, the narrator flags them as important for the ensuing action. Additionally, he is able to deal with the problem of presenting contemporaneous actions. Having offered a summary overview of the armies approaching each other, he is now ready to focus his attention on the individual warriors, by splitting the time of the battle's introductory phase into temporal anachronies.[25] What has escaped attention is that this technique is equally applied to the organization of space: the global view of the Greek and Trojan armies is followed by a zooming in on snapshots occurring in the space already delineated. To this extent, we can speak of *spatial anatopies*, for the same space is visualized again, not as a compact whole but as smaller areas of dense action. These individual scenes, which have been called "highlights of action,"[26] do not represent the end product of spatial splitting, but in their turn constitute areas where the narrative lens zooms in even further, thus shaping the audience's perspective. In fact, there are three distinct camera shots in the description of Antilokhos' killing of Ekhepolos: first we get a side view of Antilokhos striking the horn of Ekhepolos' helmet (459); second, we follow the course of his spear and visualize a single spot, Ekhepolos' forehead, where it strikes (460), and then we track the spear's path until we see it reaching the bone (460–461); finally, we get a side view of Ekhepolos falling down like a "tower (462)". This meticulous depiction of the fighting between two individual heroes represents a succinct organization of space down to its

---

[24] On the term *chronotope*, see Bakhtin 1981:84.
[25] See Latacz 1977:77–81; Rengakos 1995:32–33; Hellmann 2000:94–95.
[26] Van Wees 1997:673.

most minute elements. It is based on a ring-form principle,[27] whose beginning and end consist of side shots, while its middle is based on the technique of *tracking in* on the path of the spear.[28] Focused shots of this kind direct the listeners' attention to ever smaller areas of space. The death of a warrior signals the completion of this zooming technique, making the audience realize through their own visualization that the appalling grimness of death lies in the gradual experience of its most shocking details.

Next, the narrator moves his camera to the corpse of Ekhepolos being dragged away from under the arrows by Elephenor, who wants to take his armor (*Iliad* IV 463–466): we "see" him from a side angle dragging the dead Trojan by his feet, while missiles are flying over his head. This could have been the end of the scene, if the poet had wanted to allow Elephenor to despoil Ekhepolos. Instead, it is only the prelude to the camera's ensuing move to a third warrior, the Trojan Agenor, who upon seeing what is going on strikes Elephenor in the ribs. The narrator makes sure to describe this event by inverting the regular order of aggressor-victim: we first follow Agenor's spotting of the unprotected side of Elephenor, who bends over the corpse of Ekhepolos (468), and only then see the spear stabbing his ribs (469). This technique of *backward zooming*, which is also employed just before the death of Hektor at the hands of Achilles (*Iliad* XXII 321–327), constitutes a "visual allusion" to an ensuing action; the narrator capitalizes on the visualization of a specific spot of a very limited space—the ribs of the enemy—and only then mentally follows the course of the future victor's deadly weapon. By entwining temporal and spatial elements, he throws into sharp relief the climactic tension of this first section of ἀνδροκτασίαι. As the scene shifts to massive fighting over the body of Elephenor, the audience realizes that during these ἀνδροκτασίαι it has been visualizing nothing else than a single string of interrelated killings. The poet's covert comment has by now become overt: the catalogue has been turned into drama.

The second snapshot (*Iliad* IV 473–504) consists of three parts: (1) the killing of Simoeisios by Telamonian Ajax, (2) the killing of Leukos by Antiphos, and (3) the killing of Antiphos by Odysseus. The beginning of the snapshot is again indicated by ἔνθα, the function of which remains undetermined in terms of setting, since it is not clear whether it refers to the space around the corpse of Elephenor, where the battle has flared up, or marks a deictic shift and designates a new space. But this ambiguity is only part of the whole picture, since ἔνθα may be indicating that the narrator notionally places himself "on the battlefield."[29]

---

[27] On ring-composition in fighting scenes in the *Iliad*, see Hainsworth 1966.

[28] On the use of this term in film theory, see Crisp 1993:1–15.

[29] Cf. the similar use of ἐνθάδε in the *Homeric Hymn to Apollo* 168; on this metaleptic effect, see de Jong 2009:111 and n58. Sometimes, a metaleptic function based on spatial deictic markers is

This temporary collapse of the distinction between the spatiotemporal levels pertaining to the narrator and the narrated world is known by the term *metalepsis*. In oral song, where spatial memory plays a key role, such imaging hesitation and narrative merging is closely connected with the reality of performance. The bard momentarily hesitates, since in self-contained narratives like the catalogues of ἀνδροκτασίαι he is uncertain about the direction he should move; expansion of and focus on details constitute choices he has to make in real time, while performing his song. At the same time, such a blurring of narrative levels has no "antiillusionistic"[30] effect, but is "aimed at increasing the authority of the narrator and the realism of his narrative (rather than breaking the illusion)."[31] This oscillation, which resembles what film directors call an *out-of-focus* shot,[32] where a scene or figure or object appears blurred for a very limited period of time, is especially apt for expressing confusion: the audience is able to view the havoc wreaked on the battlefield by being deprived of any spatial designation.[33]

This outcome is only temporarily effective, for the narrator soon embarks on a description of the killing of the Trojan Simoeisios by Telamonian Ajax. In contrast to the previous catalogue, where warriors are presented either by their bare name (*Iliad* IV 457 Ἀντίλοχος, 467 Ἀγήνωρ) or accompanied by their patronymics (IV 458 Θαλυσιάδην Ἐχέπωλον, 463–464 Ἐλεφήνωρ / Χαλκωδοντιάδης), he now expands on the victim's genealogy. Simoeisios' pedigree is expressed mainly by means of spatial imagery: after his double designation by his periphrastic patronymic (473 Ἀνθεμίωνος υἱόν) and his name and age (474 ἠΐθεον θαλερὸν Σιμοείσιον),[34] the narrator uses the reference to his mother not to talk about her lineage but to describe the place of his birth at the banks of the river Simoeis for which he was named. By expressing this analeptic reference in terms

---

closely connected to the visual quality of Homeric discourse, on which see Bakker 1997:77 and n58.

[30] See Fludernik 2003a:392.

[31] De Jong 2009:115.

[32] Sharff 1982; Mamer 2000:3–26. On the filmic features of Homeric battle scenes, see van Wees 1997:673–674; and of Homeric similes and the scenes on Achilles' shield, see Winkler 2007:52–57 and 57–63 respectively.

[33] Epic hesitation, such as rhetorical questions that a character addresses to his own θυμός (e.g. *Iliad* XI 407, XVII 97, XXII 122) and second-person apostrophes (e.g. to Menelaos and to Patroklos) often have a metaleptic effect; see Culler 1981:135. From a comparative point of view, it may be observed that Homeric epic differs from other oral traditions (like South Slavic epic) with respect to such "performative" devices: whereas South Slavic epic constantly employs expletives as extrametrical features, Homeric epic has incorporated them into the metrical structure of the dactylic hexameter. On θυμός-speeches, see Pelliccia 1995; on various forms of epic metalepsis, see de Jong 2009. On metalepsis in general, see Genette 1980:234–237, 1988:58–59; McHale 1987; Herman 1997; F. Wagner 2002; Fludernik 2003a; Genette 2004; Pier–Schaeffer 2005.

[34] See Tsagalis 2004:179–188.

of the calm and serene environment of the river's banks, the narrator is able to translate the antithesis between past and present into a purely spatial code.

The emphasis on spacing the past is an effective prelude to the actual description of the killing of Simoeisios. Having visualized his birth on the banks of a river, the audience is invited, after a brief tracking in on the spearhead driving through the victim's shoulder, to view a vivid simile: Simoeisios is compared to a falling poplar "which in the land low-lying about a great marsh grows" (*Iliad* IV 483 ἥ ῥά τ' ἐν εἰαμενῆι ἕλεος μεγάλοιο πεφύκηι). The spatial coding of the previous analepsis is followed by the simile's paratopic space. The difference between river banks and the marsh is only superficial, for both spatial visualizations are linked by a downward motion: Simoeisios' mother is pictured descending from Mount Ida to the river (475 Ἴδηθεν κατιοῦσα), and Simoeisios himself falls like a tree. Next, the camera takes a worm's-eye view (484 ἀτάρ τέ οἱ ὄζοι ἐπ' ἀκροτάτηι πεφύασιν ["yet with branches growing at the uttermost tree-top"]) by pointing directly upward, looking straight up from the ground to the branches, reaching the upper part of the poplar, and then again downward from a bird's-eye view (487 ἥ μέν τ' ἀζομένη κεῖται ποταμοῖο παρ' ὄχθας ["and the tree lies hardening by the banks of a river"]). At the end of the simile the two spatial views merge to such an extent that the banks of the river, representing deeper-level mnemonic images, take the place of the marsh (487) which stands for surface-level spatial organization. The first part of this snapshot is completed through a vivid visualization of the banks of a river, as *the space where Simoeisios' life began and ended.*[35]

The transfer from the world of the simile that describes Simoeisios' death to the ἀνδροκτασίαι is initiated by the deictic shift τοῦ δ' (*Iliad* IV 489), turning the mind's camera to a new person: the Trojan Antiphos, aiming his spear against Ajax, the slayer of Simoeisios. This time, though, the narrator varies his material by moving his camera further on, not to Ajax but to Leukos, Odysseus' comrade who is hit by Antiphos' spear. The audience tracks the course of the spear: the initial side view of it narrowly missing Ajax is followed by an extremely brief close-up of the spear striking the victim's groin and a medium close shot of Leukos dragging a corpse away from the battle (492);[36] then comes a high-angle view of Leukos falling down upon the corpse, which falls from his hands (493). The killing of Leukos is only an excuse for the narrator to turn the focus on Odysseus. By carefully introducing Leukos as Odysseus' comrade, he paves the way for a further move of his camera to Odysseus, who will now become

---

[35]   Therefore, both the space delineated by the simile of the two clashing armies as rivers and that of Simoeisios' dying at the river's bank draw on related river-oriented imagery.

[36]   According to Kawin 1992, a medium close shot brings the camera nearer than a medium shot, but not so near as a close-up.

the center of attention until the completion of this brief new episode. In film theory, this technique of presenting space is called a *long take*, where all the action is recorded in one uninterrupted movement, during which the camera runs continuously. In this way, the conventional segmentation of cuts and, in our case, smaller images, is avoided by downplaying their transitory function until the key figure Odysseus is located and visualized. The only trace of the individual cuts, to stick to terms of film theory, are the deictic markers τοῦ δ'/ τοῦ μέν/τοῦ δ' (489, 491, 494) which signal the passage from Ajax to Leukos and finally to Odysseus, with whom the fast-track move will be over: a dramatic close-up will now be developed in the form of a brief narrative.

Having shifted the listeners' attention to Odysseus, the narrator lays special emphasis on placing him in space. Once more, it is by means of a long take that the camera follows Odysseus as he moves through the front ranks (*Iliad* IV 495 διὰ προμάχων):[37] in his helm of shining bronze (495 κεκορυθμένος αἴθοπι χαλκῶι), he stands close to the Trojans (496 στῆ δὲ μάλ' ἐγγὺς ἰών), and strikes (496 καὶ ἀκόντισε δουρὶ φαεινῶι) after looking around him (497 ἀμφὶ ἓ παπτήνας). In contrast to what was described before, Odysseus does not miss (498 ὃ δ' οὐχ ἅλιον βέλος ἧκεν) and kills not Antiphos, as expected, but Demokoön, a bastard son of Priam. Viewing space by means of a long-take camera shot prevents the audience from perceiving the effect of this technique before it is over, at the moment when Odysseus' spear hits Demokoön: it is only then that listeners understand that the ambiguity of the obscure ἀμφὶ ἓ παπτήνας (497) and the unexpected death of Demokoön (instead of Antiphos) entail a hidden irony, since it is not clear whether Odysseus was looking for Antiphos, or protecting himself (unlike Elephenor in the previous scene).[38] Odysseus is not like Elephenor, as he knows how to protect himself, but he is like Antiphos in the sense that he kills the "wrong" person. The designation of Demokoön as a (bastard) son of Priam who came from Abydos (499–500), and the reiteration of the fact that he was killed by Odysseus on account of the latter's anger at the death of Leukos (501), draw attention to the deep irony of this passage. As the episode closes, by balancing the description of Antiphos striking Leukos' groin with a zoom in on Demokoön's temple pierced by Odysseus' sharp bronze, we realize that space has been visualized as a foil for a comment on the quirks of fate: the long-take shots make the listeners a specific category of spectators, invited to linger and explore through continuous visualization the havoc of war, where spaces

---

[37] On theoretical aspects of the long-take moving camera, see Read 1932; Sontag 1966:242–245; Durgnat 1968; Fry 1970; Harpole 1978; Bordwell 1977; Bacher 1978; Burch 1979:217–230; Henderson 1980:16–81; Sontag 1982:95–104; Deleuze 1986; Henderson 1986; Deleuze 1989; Johnson and Graham 1994; Le Fanu 1997; Mitry 1997:183–190; B. Kennedy 2000; Schwab 2000.

[38] See scholia on *Iliad* XVIII 497.

are constantly violated, and where even revenge (a necessary concomitant to heroic fighting) may ironically underline the tragic nature of the human world as presented by the *Iliad*.

The third snapshot (*Iliad* IV 505–516) marks a change from individual fighting to the description of the armies at large. In a panoramic view, the narrator presents both Trojans and Greeks collectively, the former retreating, the latter shouting in triumph, carrying their dead off the battlefield and moving forward. The use of the bird's-eye view technique[39] immediately keys the audience to the global perspective employed in the beginning of this entire scene. The intercalated catalogues of ἀνδροκτασίαι are pushed aside, so to speak, and the camera lens opens wide to overlook the whole battlefield.[40] This temporal halt before the battle-action resumes amounts to a short break, as if the bard is trying to see where he stands in the midst of the countless details he has presented while depicting the various *Einzelkämpfe*. At the same time, his view indicates to the audience what is happening on a larger scale: the broadening of space leads to an enlargement of the action, a summary of the progress made thus far. The initially symmetrical space occupied by Greeks and Trojans has now given way to an expanded Greek and a compressed Trojan space. The action resumes with the intervention of Apollo and Athena, who stir the Trojans and the Greeks to fight. The fourth snapshot (*Iliad* IV 517–538) begins with the typical deictic marker ἔνθ' (517).

These three catalogues of ἀνδροκτασίαι offer a sequence of two interrelated killings: after the divine intervention, the focus is first on a Trojan killing a Greek, and then on a Greek avenging the death of his comrade-in-arms. The twofold division of this fourth snapshot highlights its greater balance as compared to the first and second.[41] The symmetrical description of its two episodes is anticipated by a preview of the outcome of the first encounter: using the technique of backward zooming, the narrator designates first the victim (*Iliad* IV 517 Ἀμαρυγκείδην Διώρεα), then the deadly weapon (518 χερμαδίωι) and the part of his body where the wound is inflicted (518–519 παρὰ σφυρὸν ὀκριόεντι / κνήμην δεξιτερήν), and only then reveals the slayer (519–520 βάλε δὲ Θρηικῶν ἀγὸς ἀνδρῶν, / Πείρως Ἰμβρασίδης). Once he has indicated who the killer is, the narrator allows the description to follow its regular course of *forward zooming*, presenting no fewer than seven separate images: the tendons are smashed (521–522 ἀμφοτέρω δὲ τένοντε καὶ ὀστέα λᾶας ἀναιδής / ἄχρις ἀπηλοίησεν), the victim falls backwards into the dust (522–523 ὁ δ' ὕπτιος ἐν κονίηισιν /

---

[39] See S. Richardson 1990:119–123; de Jong and Nünlist 2004a:69.

[40] On ἀνδροκτασίαι, see Strasburger 1954; Fenik 1968; Latacz 1977; van Wees 1997; Hellmann 2000.

[41] In each case there are three victors: Greek-Greek-Trojan in the first snapshot, Greek-Trojan-Greek in the second.

κάππεσεν) and stretches his hands to his comrades for help (523 ἄμφω χεῖρε φίλοις ἑτάροισι πετάσσας), the enemy approaches (524 ὃ δ' ἐπέδραμεν) and strikes the victim with his spear next to the navel (525 οὖτα δὲ δουρὶ παρ' ὀμφαλόν), his guts are poured on the ground (525–526 ἐκ δ' ἄρα πᾶσαι / χύντο χαμαὶ χολάδες), and finally darkness covers the victim's eyes (526 τὸν δὲ σκότος ὄσσ' ἐκάλυψεν). The reversal of the typical order of spatial organization is here very effective: first, it facilitates the transition from the previous snapshot to the new one by reminding the audience of the unbridgeable gap that separates the worlds of gods and men. The snapshot begins with ἔνθα (517), indicating that it was there, that is, at the very place where the gods stirred mortal men to fight, that fate ensnared Diores, son of Amarunkeus. Second, by designating the part of his body where the stone hit, the narrator previews the action to follow, and then meticulously describes his death. Third, it draws a line between the second snapshot, where both Antiphos and Odysseus failed to kill the warriors they wanted, and the fourth, where the revenge factor is paramount.

The "syntax of movement," to use Bakker's apt phrase,[42] is carried out by the deictic τὸν δὲ (*Iliad* IV 527), designating the victor of the previous episode, who is now a victim: "[It was] him [whom] Thoas the Aetolian attacked and hit with the spear on his chest above the nipple," strengthening the link between the two episodes. Spatial organization then follows its typical order: the audience sees from a side view Thoas running and striking Peiros in the chest with his spear (527–528); a momentary zoom on the bronze spear lodged in the lung (528) is followed by another side view of Thoas approaching Peiros (529). At the climax of this scene, there is a masterful double zooming, out from the spear being pulled out of the dead man's chest (529–530) and in on Thoas' sharp sword piercing the victim in the middle of the belly (530–531). The episode is completed by a panoramic view of the Thracians protecting the corpse of their leader and the two dead bodies of Diores and Peiros lying on the ground in the midst of much killing and fighting (532–538).

In this third snapshot, space is viewed through the detailed descriptions of the wounding of the two heroes. The symmetrical presentation of material includes a balanced emphasis on shocking minutiae: the appalling picture of Diores' guts being spilled on the ground, vividly described with the triple alliteration χύντο χαμαὶ χολάδες, and the double zooming in on the fatal wounding of Peiros throw into sharp relief the cruelest aspect of war. From the first snapshot, where the catalogues of ἀνδροκτασίαι were turned into dramatic encounters, and the second where accidental death signaled the ironic twist of human fate, the narrator offers a view of story space in its most gruesome and appalling details.

---

[42] See Bakker 1997:54–58.

The whole scene is completed by a global, synoptic view of the battlefield. The initial symmetrical approach of the two armies, followed by catalogues of ἀνδροκτασίαι organized in three snapshots,[43] has now come full circle, as space is once again symmetrically mapped (*Iliad* IV 541). We are situated in exactly the same place as when the clash began; this time, though, there is no orientation,[44] no landmarks, no escape for the audience through similes, only suspended action and human bodies of both Greeks and Trojans lying next to each other in the open space (543–544), dismembered, cut wide open, united in death.

Fighting in small groups

Apart from the catalogues of ἀνδροκτασίαι, the *Iliad* views the space of the battlefield in terms of fighting in small groups, whether in reference to a pair of victors and victims or a group of θεράποντες and ἑταῖροι.[45] In tandem with the technique of *close-ups*, which we explored with respect to the ἀνδροκτασίαι, the narrator further miniaturizes the space by means of *spotlighting*: attention is drawn to a person who is placed on the battlefield indirectly, through the positions of ancillary groups of people. In the wake of the special spatial existence of the characters, who are physical bodies in space[46] and function as plot coordinators, the narrator's encyclopedic vision is implicitly transmitted to the audience, who are invited to realize that spatial proximity expressed via deictic markers such as "next to," "together," or "behind" thematizes space. Seeing by spotlighting emphasizes a synoptic point of view, which makes narrative presentation equivalent to the very process of mental imaging. Scale and measurement are appropriately exhibited when space is relativized and listeners are able to place characters with reference to others.[47]

Pairs of warriors

Pairs of warriors fighting together, victors or victims alike, often include brothers (Hektor and Paris, Telamonian Ajax and Teukros) or simply characters who are mythically related in the epic tradition (Idomeneus and Meriones, Odysseus and Diomedes).[48] In *Iliad* XI 401–488, when Trojan supremacy is turning the tide against the Achaeans and their leaders retreat as a result of

---

[43] With the addition of an intervening snapshot (*Iliad* IV 505–516).

[44] Notice the use of the expression κατὰ μέσσον 'in the middle'.

[45] On fighting in small groups, see Strasburger 1954; Trypanis 1963; Fenik 1968; Singor 1995; Hellmann 2000:112–121.

[46] See Zoran 1984:317.

[47] On associative mnemonic mechanisms with special reference to oral storytelling, see Rubin 1995:31–35.

[48] On fighting pairs, see Fenik 1968:22, 23, 60–66, 82, 91, 92, 191, 196, 226.

their wounds, the narrator focuses on Odysseus, who suddenly finds himself alone amid a throng of Trojans.[49] At first his isolation is emphasized (401 οἰώθη δ' Ὀδυσεύς; 406 μοῦνος), but then the hard-pressed hero is able to kill a number of enemies (420–425). Even though he presents these victims in catalogue form, the narrator unexpectedly informs the audience that Odysseus "left them lying" (426 τοὺς μὲν ἔασ'), and pierced with his spear Kharops, the son of Hippasos, whose brother Sokos came to help him. Then the narrator embarks on a whole scene with the two warriors fighting each other and exchanging speeches; Sokos retreats and Odysseus, who has been wounded by his enemy's blow, manages to stab him in the back and kill him. Severely wounded and bleeding, Odysseus is attacked by more Trojans, but Telamonian Ajax and Menelaos hear him calling for help and save him from certain death. The summary of this brief episode is instructive for the way the narrator employs the motif of a "pair of warriors" both to thematize space with respect to the brothers Kharops and Sokos and to emphasize the spatial existence of Odysseus, who in two successive scenes of the same episode is both victor and victim.

> τοὺς μὲν ἔασ', ὃ δ' ἄρ' Ἱππασίδην Χάροπ' οὔτασε δουρί,
> αὐτοκασίγνητον εὐηγενέος Σώκοιο.
> τῶι δ' ἐπαλεξήσων Σῶκος κίεν, ἰσόθεος φώς,
> στῆ δὲ μάλ' ἐγγὺς ἰὼν καί μιν πρὸς μῦθον ἔειπεν·

> These he left lying, and stabbed with the spear the son of Hippasos,
> Charops, full brother of Sokos, a man rich in substance. And Sokos
> moved in, a man like a god, to stand over the fallen brother
> and came and stood close by Odysseus and spoke a word to him ...

> *Iliad* XI 426–429

The privileged treatment of Sokos has already been signaled by the narrator's refusal to deal with Odysseus' other victims and his subsequent focus on Sokos' brother Kharops. In order to create a special space for the encounter with Sokos, the narrator describes Kharops by giving both his father's and his brother's names. Since the latter reference does not form part of a hero's typical epic presentation, listeners realize that such a compressed foregrounding of a soldier's brother is narratively significant. As soon as Sokos is designated as the brother of the victim, the audience is presented with a vista of his coming to save his brother Kharops. In contrast both to Odysseus' previous victims, who are bare items in a list, and to Kharops' father Hippasos, who is a mere name in the victim's pedigree, Sokos is "here to stay," as he will be given a whole scene.

---

[49] On this episode, see Fenik 1968:98–99.

The space is designated in terms of deictic proximity to the place where Kharops has fallen: Sokos comes close and stands (στῆ δὲ μάλ' ἐγγὺς ἰών) to protect his brother. By combining movement and standing, the narrator hints at fraternal solidarity, which is here expressed by means of typical epic diction. The vagueness of the place where the ensuing encounter will occur is replaced by a heavily thematized space, delineated not in terms of description but of cooperation and camaraderie. In this light, space becomes not a container of action but action itself: *where* is effectively replaced by *what* and *who*.

After the death of Sokos, Odysseus, who finds himself bleeding and once more outnumbered by the Trojans, calls three times for help. He is three times heard by Menelaos, who together with Telamonian Ajax standing next to him comes to his aid. This time, the narrator enriches the palette of presenting narrative space by effectively bringing to the fore new aspects of spatial organization.

> Τρῶες δὲ μεγάθυμοι ὅπως ἴδον αἷμ' Ὀδυσῆος,
> κεκλόμενοι καθ' ὅμιλον ἐπ' αὐτῶι πάντες ἔβησαν·
> αὐτὰρ ὅ γ' ἐξοπίσω ἀνεχάζετο, αὖε δ' ἑταίρους.
> τρὶς μὲν ἔπειτ' ἤϋσεν, ὅσον κεφαλὴ χάδε φωτός,
> τρὶς δ' ἄϊεν ἰάχοντος ἀρηΐφιλος Μενέλαος,
> αἶψα δ' ἄρ' Αἴαντα προσεφώνεεν ἐγγὺς ἐόντα·
> "Αἶαν διογενὲς Τελαμώνιε, κοίρανε λαῶν,
> ἀμφί μ' Ὀδυσσῆος ταλασίφρονος ἵκετο φωνή,
> τῶι ἰκέλη, ὡς εἴ ἑ βιώιατο μοῦνον ἐόντα
> Τρῶες ἀποτμήξαντες ἐνὶ κρατερῆι ὑσμίνηι.
> ἀλλ' ἴομεν καθ' ὅμιλον· ἀλεξέμεναι γὰρ ἄμεινον."

But the great-hearted Trojans, when they saw the blood of Odysseus,
cried aloud through the close battle and all made a charge against
    him.
He gave back a little way and called out for his companions.
Three times he called, as much voice as a man's head could hold,
and three times Menelaos the warlike heard him shouting
and immediately spoke to Aias, who was near by him.
"Son of Telamon, seed of Zeus, Aias, lord of the people,
the war cry of patient Odysseus is ringing about me
with a sound as if he had been cut off by himself, and the Trojans
were handling him violently in the strong encounter. Therefore
let us go to him through the battle. It is better to defend him against
    them."

Iliad XI 459–469

Αἴας δ' ἐγγύθεν ἦλθε φέρων σάκος ἠΰτε πύργον,
στῆ δὲ πάρεξ· Τρῶες δὲ διέτρεσαν ἄλλυδις ἄλλος.
ἤτοι τὸν μὲν Μενέλαος ἀρήϊος ἔξαγ' ὁμίλου
χειρὸς ἔχων, εἵως θεράπων σχεδὸν ἤλασε ἵππους·

Now Aias came near him, carrying like a wall his shield,
and stood forth beside him, and the Trojans fled one way and
    another.
Then taking Odysseus by the hand warlike Menelaos
led him from the battle, while his henchman drove the horses close
    up.

Iliad XI 485–489

Sound is also an aspect of space.[50] Since Menelaos and Ajax can hear Odysseus' shout, the audience visualizes them at some distance but not far away from him. Their movement through the ranks of the army (*Iliad* XI 469 καθ' ὅμιλον) and their realization that Odysseus is left alone among the Trojans (470 μονωθείς, picking up line 467 μοῦνον ἐόντα) are combined,[51] as in the previous case of Sokos, with coming close (485 ἐγγύθεν ἦλθε) and standing next to (486 στῆ δὲ πάρεξ), but also with carrying the wounded Odysseus away from the enemy lines (487 ἔξαγ' ὁμίλου). The use of similar diction, further accentuated by its use in two successive scenes of the same episode, shows that the thematized space of brotherhood and comradeship, of solidarity and cooperation, applies to victims and victors alike, irrespective of their nationality. In this light, listeners are invited to ponder such minutiae from these episodes and realize that they form part of a coherent organization of space, with far-reaching consequences for both character delineation and the development of the plot as a whole. The *Iliad* establishes and exploits intrinsic visual norms that require listeners to learn the epic's unique storytelling strategies. By learning the *Iliad*'s grammar of space, the audience is constantly expected to expand these superficially miniaturized battle scenes and piece them together within a larger and complex story-world. Viewed from this perspective, the repeated lessons on warrior solidarity and comradeship, expressed in the motif of fighting pairs and the diction of spatial deixis (coming to the aid of and standing next to), create highly engaged listeners, able to decode and appreciate the epic's technique of building macronarrative dramatic tension. The thematized space explored above, and systematically reiterated in equivalent scenes throughout the poem,

---

[50] See Bal 1997:133–134.
[51] Notice the contrast with the Trojans fleeing one way and another (*Iliad* XI 486 Τρῶες δὲ διέτρεσαν ἄλλυδις ἄλλος).

reaches its sublime climax in the fatal encounter between Achilles and Hektor in *Iliad* XXII. When Hektor decides to stop running, deceived by Athena who is standing next to him disguised as his brother Deiphobos (*Iliad* XXII 226–247), the audience is expected to comprehend the deep irony based on the illusion of heroic solidarity. The Iliadic grammar of space allows the listeners to recall numerous scenes of warrior and fraternal solidarity, and realize that the shocking overturning of Hektor's expectations amounts to a violation of the thematized space of solidarity, which now becomes a space of betrayal and death.

Groups of θεράποντες and ἑταῖροι

Apart from pairs of warriors, the narrator systematically exploits the function of larger masses of the army, who are described as they fight behind the πρόμαχοι. What is of special interest is that the narrator almost always treats these groups of θεράποντες and ἑταῖροι within the framework of a binary opposition, consisting of the elite warriors fighting in front and the ordinary and anony-mous groups of soldiers standing behind them. As in the case of ἀνδροκτασίαι and pairs of fighters, so with larger numbers of troops, the battle descriptions use warriors as space-organizers.[52] Such thematizing of space becomes particu-larly effective given that in the *Iliad*, characters move in what seems to be an empty space. In this light, the interplay between the front line and the rear ranks creates a visual contour that is intricately entwined with the unraveling of the epic plot.

A standard connection between a front-line warrior and the contingent behind him concerns the moment he retreats to the rear ranks of the army. This rearward movement of a πρόμαχος is typically expressed by the formula ἑτάρων εἰς ἔθνος ἐχάζετο ("he shrank into the host of his own companions," attested nine times in the *Iliad*.[53] The movement of a leading figure through space consti-tutes a mechanism of spatial organization. By laying emphasis on the abstract delineation of space, where the setting exists only in relation to the placement and movement of characters, the narrator is able to focus on the action itself, and even more importantly to tailor deictic manifestations of space to unrav-eling and building the climax of the Iliadic plot.

> τὸν δ' ὡς οὖν ἐνόησεν Ἀλέξανδρος θεοειδής
> ἐν προμάχοισι φανέντα, κατεπλήγη φίλον ἦτορ,
> ἂψ δ' ἑτάρων εἰς ἔθνος ἐχάζετο κῆρ' ἀλεείνων.

---

[52] The narrative lens follows the movement of a hero among the mass of the army and virtually turns the place or area of his activity into a space of either protection or danger.

[53] See *Iliad* III 32; XI 585; XIII 165; XIII 533; XIII 566; XIII 596; XIII 648; XIV 408; XVI 817.

But Alexandros the godlike when he saw Menelaos
showing among the champions, the heart was shaken within him;
to avoid death he shrank into the host of his own companions.

Iliad III 30–32

Here (as in *Iliad* XI 585 and XIII 596), the πρόμαχος retreats among his companions standing behind him and saves his life (κῆρ' ἀλεείνων), whereas in two other cases Meriones continues his withdrawal and returns temporarily to the ships and his hut in search of a new spear (*Iliad* XIII 165–168), with which he wounds Deiphobos and then retreats among his fellow warriors (XIII 533). This particular thematization of "space behind" signals protection and safety, and demarcates notional zones that are presented in terms of bipolar antitheses between isolation and contiguity, separation and solidarity. The *Iliad* thus introduces a notion of space that capitalizes on Greek views of the alien and unknown as something standing beyond an enclosed area,[54] where knowledge and therefore safety are guaranteed. In the military cosmos of the *Iliad*, uncharted space is the area where there are no comrades-in-arms, who represent a hero's only familiar topos.[55]

In this type of retreat scene (as in *Iliad* XIII 566, XIII 648, XIV 408, and XVI 817), the narrator offers a telling variation of a hero's withdrawal among his companions to save his life: in XIII 566–570 and 648–655, Meriones manages to kill an opponent by striking him in the back, at the very moment he is withdrawing into the mass of his companions; in XIV 408 Ajax wounds Hektor by hurling a stone at him, also just as the Trojan hero is retreating into the host of his own companions. This sophisticated variation is a disguised allusion to the death of Patroklos in *Iliad* XVI, where the hero finds himself away from the protection of the army: after being hit from behind (in the back) by Apollo (791–792 στῆ δ' ὄπιθεν, πλῆξεν δὲ μετάφρενον εὐρέε τ' ὤμω / χειρὶ καταπρηνεῖ) and Euphorbos (806–808 ὄπιθεν δὲ μετάφρενον ὀξέϊ δουρί / ὤμων μεσσηγὺς σχεδόθεν βάλε Δάρδανος ἀνήρ), he retreats and tries to find refuge among the

---

[54] This process is equivalent to what cognitive scientists have called *image schemata*. An image schema is "a recurring, dynamic pattern of our perceptual interaction and motor programs that gives coherence and structure to our experience" (M. Johnson 1987:xiv) or an "extremely skeletal [image] which we use in cognitive operations" (Turner 1992:728). One of these schemata is what has been labeled "containment-boundedness (in-out)"; see M. Johnson 1987:30; Dannenberg 2008:75.

[55] In scenes of this type, if examined as *Kettenkämpfe*, i.e. as short military vignettes, we can see one of the more typical manifestations of the spatial form of narrative. Within the focalized microcosm of these fighting snapshots, sequences are of minor importance; what really matters is juxtaposition, placement—in cognitive language horizontality: *nacheinander* 'one after the other' becomes *nebeneinander* 'one next to the other'; see Mickelsen 1981:64–65.

multitude of his ἑταῖροι. It is exactly at this moment, when Patroklos aims at leaving the perilous space of isolation and plunging himself into the protective space of companionship, that Hektor strikes the fatal blow:

Πάτροκλος δὲ θεοῦ πληγῆι καὶ δουρὶ δαμασθείς
ἂψ ἑτάρων εἰς ἔθνος ἐχάζετο κῆρ' ἀλεείνων.
Ἕκτωρ δ' ὡς εἶδεν Πατροκλῆα μεγάθυμον
ἂψ ἀναχαζόμενον, βεβλημένον ὀξέϊ χαλκῶι,
ἀγχίμολόν ῥά οἱ ἦλθε κατὰ στίχας, οὖτα δὲ δουρί
νείατον ἐς κενεῶνα, διάπρο δὲ χαλκὸν ἔλασσεν·

Now Patroklos, broken by the spear and the god's blow, tried
to shun death and shrink back into the swarm of his own
   companions.
But Hektor, when he saw high-hearted Patroklos trying
to get away, saw how he was wounded with the sharp javelin,
came close against him across the ranks, and with the spear stabbed
   him
in the depth of his belly and drove the bronze clean through.

                                         Iliad XVI 816–821

In this way, the *Iliad* makes a telling gesture to its audience, who are invited to realize the profound paradox of heroism: to acquire κλέος within warrior society by isolating oneself from it, that is, by fighting as a πρόμαχος away from the protection of the army.

Iliadic heroes experience space in terms of *edges* and *boundaries* that they must not cross.[56] These unseen boundaries correspond to a thematized topography, geographically uncharted but narratively mapped out by the epic's consistent recycling of spatial snapshots of juxtaposed warriors or heroes trying to reenter the mass of the army standing behind them.

Formal duels

The formal duels between Patroklos and Sarpedon, Patroklos and Hektor, and Achilles and Hektor are instructive for exploring how space functions in individual fighting between members of the heroic elite. Given that these three encounters are connected and constitute integral parts of the process that culminates in the death of Hektor, they allow for a comparative analysis in terms

---

[56] On the interplay in the *Odyssey* between the πείρατα 'edges' of the earth and Odysseus' uncharted topography of an alien space located *inland* (in the story of the oar), see Purves 2002:136–167.

of spatial organization. As I will show, they comprise a three-step climactic process.

(1) In contrast with individual fighting between second-tier warriors who are not among the πρόμαχοι, the duels of Sarpedon and Patroklos are first presented as successive separate images of each one attacking the other (*Iliad* XVI 419–426 Σαρπηδὼν δ' ὡς οὖν ἴδ' ἀμιτροχίτωνας ἑταίρους / χέρσ' ὕπο Πατρόκλοιο Μενοιτιάδαο δαμέντας, … ἐξ ὀχέων σὺν τεύχεσιν ἆλτο χαμᾶζε;[57] XVI 427 Πάτροκλος δ' ἑτέρωθεν, ἐπεὶ ἴδεν, ἔκθορε δίφρου.[58] In the duel between Patroklos and Sarpedon, the victim strikes first and misses, before the victor strikes second and fatally wounds him.

The situation is strikingly different in the case of the duel between Patroklos and Hektor, since the Trojan hero spots Patroklos trying to retreat into the host of his companions (*Iliad* XVI 818–819) only after he has been wounded by Apollo and Euphorbos.[59] The symmetrical delineation of the fighting space in the encounter between Sarpedon and Patroklos is here intentionally undermined by a shifting emphasis on different preliminary opponents, until the final and fatal stroke by Hektor. Seen from this angle, the very concept of the duel is put in doubt: Patroklos is initially hit by Apollo, who comes from behind, then receives a wound in the back from Euphorbos (who appears out of the blue), and is finally given the death blow by Hektor, who strikes Patroklos as he is retreating to the safety of the Achaean army. The almost complete overturning of the most elementary rules governing a duel emphatically results in an unparalleled disturbance of balanced space within the *Iliad,* and underscores the tragic doom of Patroklos, who is deprived of his most elementary right according to the heroic code, that is, to fight face to face. In this way, the audience follows Patroklos in his vain effort to escape, and painfully realizes, through the successive attacks on him by different (mortal and immortal) enemies, that his fate is sealed, as if the whole universe is conspiring against him.

In the duel between Hektor and Achilles, the typical dueling space is violated in a radically different way, since the audience is invited to assume that Hektor will stand and fight Achilles. The poet has carefully built this expectation since the beginning of *Iliad* XXII, thanks to two factors: the Trojan army's retreat into the city while Hektor stays deliberately on the battlefield, and the hero's refusal to return to Troy despite the successive entreaties by Priam and

[57] "But Sarpedon, when he saw his free-girt companions going down underneath the hands of Menoitios' son Patroklos, … sprang to the ground in all his arms from the chariot."
[58] "… and on the other side Patroklos when he saw him leapt down from his chariot."
[59] On this episode, see the remarks of Clay (2011:86–90), who shows how Patroklos' ἀριστεία "can be plotted onto the plain of Troy as a zig-zagging path" (90).

Hekabe. Even the Trojan hero's monologue, a speech addressed to his own θυμός (*Iliad* XXII 99–130), indicates his resolve to confront the son of Thetis once and for all. This systematic misdirection[60] of the audience is only temporary, since Hektor will ultimately fight against Achilles, but its function is paramount for comprehending and evaluating the temporary metamorphosis of the balanced and symmetrical dueling space into the unequal and lopsided space of a hunt: as warriors lose all sense of honor and bravery, they do not stand against each other and fight but run like predators and prey. This encroachment on the standard expectations of the warrior code evokes the wild backdrop of combat, where men can turn into animals. The abundant use of animal similes supports the audience's misdirection and postpones the real duel, which will take place only when its special space is restored, that is, only when Hektor stands face to face with Achilles and decides to fight. In a remarkable display of careful planning, the poet has even decided to violate once more the expectations created by the formal repetition of motifs, and thus maximize the impact of this duel on his audience. In order to understand his technique, we must first consider another point.

(2) In the Sarpedon-Patroklos[61] and Hektor-Patroklos episodes, the description of the actual fight is interrupted by a change of focus from the one of the two combatants to his ἑταῖρος, θεράπων, or ἡνίοχος (Thrasudemos[62] in the case of Sarpedon, Kebriones for Hektor). This shift of focus gives the narrator the opportunity to introduce an internal preview, a preliminary minor episode that prepares the audience for forthcoming information.[63] Only after presenting Patroklos killing his enemy's acolyte does the narrator allow the fighting

---

[60] On misdirection in the *Iliad*, see Morrison 1992a:30, who argues that "at each stage of the narrative, the narrator introduces explicit alternatives to the actual outcome." After the presentation of the potential paths the plot could take, the second or last alternative is realized, exactly as with decision-making (cf. Agenor in *Iliad* XXI 531–570); see Arend 1933:106–115; Fenik 1968:68; Lohmann 1970:37–40; Morrison 1992a:130n8.

[61] See W.-H. Friedrich 1956:103–112; Aceti 2008:1–269.

[62] On the variant Thrasumelus, cf. West's BT edition *ad loc.*

[63] In the case of Kebriones, this preview uses previous references to Hektor's charioteer (*Iliad* VIII 318–319; XI 521–532; XII 91–92; XIII 790) as a backdrop for violating the audience's expectations: the accidental killing of Arkheptolemos, who was Hektor's charioteer, by Teukros in *Iliad* VIII transforms Kebriones, Hektor's half-brother, into Hektor's new charioteer, who in *Iliad* XI is presented as urging Hektor to drive their chariot with him through the tumult of battle and fight Telamonian Ajax. In *Iliad* XVI, the situation is dramatically reversed: this time it is Hektor who orders Kebriones to lead the chariot into the battle, thus—unwittingly—causing his death. Unlike Teukros in *Iliad* VIII, Patroklos does not miss (XVI 737 οὐδ' ἁλίωσε βέλος) but kills Kebriones, the only charioteer left to Hektor. Thus, Kebriones begins and ends his life in the poem by becoming Hektor's charioteer (VIII 318–319 Κεβριόνην δ' ἐκέλευσεν ἀδελφεὸν ἐγγὺς ἐόντα / ἵππων ἡνί' ἑλεῖν) and dying as such (XVI 738–739 Κεβριόνην, νόθον υἱὸν ἀγακλῆος Πριάμοιο, / ἵππων ἡνί' ἔχοντα). On Kebriones, see Bassett 1920; M. Reichel 1994:286. On the motif of the "death of the charioteer," see Bannert 1988:30–39.

between the two main opponents to resume. In his effort to designate space with greater precision and given that setting is virtually absent, or at least significantly downplayed in the *Iliad*, the bard encourages his audience to realize that this minor incident occurs in the same area where the main confrontation will take place. In this way, when it comes to narrating the actual duel he can count on a space they have already visualized. This technique, which has not yet been analyzed in terms of spatial organization, is particularly effective, since it functions as an introduction to and a justification of the ensuing duel. The bard is thus able to guide the listeners through the successive killings committed by Patroklos during his ἀριστεία to his main targets, the confrontations with Sarpedon and Hektor. The deaths of Thrasudemos and Kebriones introduce the audience to a special space, delineated in terms not of setting but of thematic importance. Suddenly, all peripheral fighting disappears from sight, and Patroklos is found in the very center of the highly thematized space of a formal duel.[64] Having been familiarized with this notional space through the deaths of Thrasudemos and Kebriones, the audience can now easily focus on the reactions of Sarpedon and Hektor to the killing of their θεράπων and ἡνίοχος respectively.[65] By previewing the ensuing duel, the narrator makes sure that listeners have mastered his special grammar of space and are now in a position to take full advantage of its merits: mentally situated in the familiar space of the killings of the heroes' acolytes, the audience are expected to immerse themselves in the dramatic description to follow, and compare Patroklos' victorious first duel against Sarpedon with his fatal second one against Hektor.[66]

In contrast to the Sarpedon-Patroklos and Hektor-Patroklos duels, the duel between Achilles and Hektor contains no minor incident, because the staging of the entire encounter is based on Hektor's complete isolation. In other words, the *Iliad* makes the most of his marginalization within the Trojan army. As Achilles finds himself excluded from the Achaean warrior society for a large part of the plot because of his idiosyncratic interpretation of the heroic code, so Hektor too is now imprisoned in his own heroic logic. Isolation and separation are the painful nuggets the poet digs up to describe the ultimate remoteness of all great heroes. With flashes of ingenious handling, his prolonged view of

---

[64] On the pair "center-periphery (inner-outer)" as one of the principal image schemata that humans regularly employ in perceptual interactions, see M. Johnson 1987:124 and Dannenberg 2008:76.

[65] The subversive association between the two duels is enhanced, on a secondary level, by the fact that in both cases, the eventual victim (Sarpedon, Patroklos) kills the victor's horse or charioteer (Pedasos, Kebriones).

[66] On the poetics of immersion, see Ryan 2001. Preview is one of the strategies used by oral traditional epic to create immersion and, by offering alternative spatial versions of parts of the battlefield, generate *tellability*; see Labov 1972; Ryan 1991.

the duel evolves into a theatrical display: two internal audiences, the Trojans from the walls and the Achaeans from the plain, watch the two heroes, tragically alone[67] and ready to face each other.

In the duel between Achilles and Hektor the first violation of expectations ends with a second, even more sinister: Hektor is led to believe in the illusion of an actual heroic duel, since he thinks that his brother Deiphobos is standing next to him and that they will face Achilles together. Given that "standing next to" indicates solidarity and comradeship, the audience realizes that by manipulating the typology of dueling space, the *Iliad* knocks down conventional heroic themes one by one, like skittles. This climactic encounter of the epic's greatest heroes is thus a crisp synopsis of the poet's attitude to thematizing space and using it as a covert criticism of the fallout of the warrior code.

(3) Finally, the victor stands above his victim (in the case of Patroklos the victor is Hektor, not Apollo or Euphorbos) and pulls out his spear by pushing against the body of his dead opponent with his feet. The three aforementioned duels present an ascending climax of dramatic intensification: Sarpedon asks Glaukos to help him (*Iliad* XVI 492–501) and the latter prays to Apollo (XVI 514–526). Patroklos puts his foot on Sarpedon's chest and pulls out his spear, while the Myrmidons stand close holding his horses (XVI 503–507). Things become more tragic after the duel between Patroklos and Hektor: the Trojan hero reminds Patroklos of his arrogance, Patroklos foretells that Hektor will die at the hands of Achilles, and Hektor angrily replies that he may kill Achilles first (XVI 830–861), standing on the chest of Patroklos and withdrawing his spear (XVI 862–863). Finally, in the duel between Achilles and Hektor, the rapid exchange of speeches (three by Achilles, two by Hektor) quickens the dramatic pulse: Achilles reminds Hektor of his own arrogance when he killed Patroklos, Hektor begs him to return his body to his parents in exchange for an enormous ransom, Achilles in an uncontrollable outburst of anger reveals his almost bestialized self, Hektor prophesies Achilles' death at the hands of Paris and Apollo, and finally Achilles replies that he will accept his fate when the gods decide his death (*Iliad* XXII 331–366). When the speeches are over, every Achaean soldier who comes close pierces the dead body of Hektor with his spear (*Iliad* XXII 370–371).

The built-in aesthetic of the body[68] serves as the focus of the listeners' gaze, for the space around the prostrate corpse illuminates the body and exposes its fine details, thus casting individual heroes in sharp relief and making them the center of attention. The telling repetition of *Iliad* XVI 855–857 = XXII 361–363

---

[67] Hektor's gradual isolation, physical and psychological, in *Iliad* XXII is effectively indicated by the fact that οἶος 'alone' is used only for him (XXII 39; XXII 507).

[68] Cf. *Iliad* XXII 370–371 οἳ καὶ θηήσαντο φυὴν καὶ εἶδος ἀγητόν / Ἕκτορος ("and gazed upon the stature and on the imposing beauty / of Hektor").

(ὣς ἄρα μιν εἰπόντα τέλος θανάτοιο κάλυψεν, / ψυχὴ δ' ἐκ ῥεθέων πταμένη Ἄϊδόσδε βεβήκει / ὃν πότμον γοόωσα, λιποῦσ' ἀνδροτῆτα καὶ ἥβην)[69] for the corpses of both Patroklos and Hektor constitutes an implicit eulogy of the young hero's body,[70] by means of a powerful metaphor and an effective manipulation and reversal of typical funerary language: the soul, like a human being, laments leaving the manhood and youth of the body, though in funerary epigrams of both the archaic and the classical period the standard formulas employ the same diction to describe the pain of those left behind when a dear one departs for the underworld.[71]

In this constellation, those standing nearby and (especially in the case of Hektor) piercing the deceased's body with their spears identify with the previous duel, collectivizing the experience of the one-on-one heroic performance of first-rank warriors. A victorious battle constitutes a powerful experience for the great heroes and the armies standing behind them, and the body of the fallen enemy becomes a vehicle for personal and collective empowerment. In the event of a heroic performance, then, it is not only the main warriors who embrace the glory, but anyone who claims a stake in the fight is entitled to his own share of heroism. The inherent spatial boundedness of the warrior's fallen body at the end of a heroic duel becomes apparent in its topological oscillation: the body is neither here nor there, as both armies claim it with ferocious tenacity.

The nonidentification of the duel's physical space not only calls attention to the actual combat, but also offers a dramatic forum for presenting the desire for self-characterization in the fighting tradition of the heroic community. When victorious warriors take control of the immediate topology of the battlefield, they construct a public image of their heroic selves. This offers a unique opportunity to other preeminent heroes on the victim's side to move forward through the army's ranks and rise to the center stage of communal attention, by defending the body of their fallen comrade. In the purely agonistic hierarchy of warrior society, the limelight of the space around the body provides the perfect forum in which to visibly establish one's eminence: the closer one stands to the place where the duel happened, the stronger his claim to heroic status. Heroic duels best epitomize the spatial reorganization of social relations. The center stage where the duel

---

[69] "He spoke, and as he spoke the end of death closed upon him, / and the soul fluttering free of the limbs went down into Death's house / mourning her destiny, leaving youth and manhood behind her."

[70] Cf. Priam's speech of supplication to Hektor in *Iliad* XXII 71–73 νέῳ δέ τε πάντ' ἐπέοικεν/ ἄρηϊ κταμένῳ, δεδαϊγμένῳ ὀξέϊ χαλκῷ / κεῖσθαι· πάντα δὲ καλὰ θανόντι περ, ὅττι φανήῃ ("For a young man all is decorous, when he is cut down in battle and torn with the sharp bronze, and lies there / dead, and though dead still all that shows about him is beautiful.") On this topic, see Vernant 1996:91–101.

[71] See Tsagalis 2008a:200–204.

takes place becomes a spectacular space for the overpowering of an opponent. The implication is that by coming close to Hektor's corpse and repeating what Achilles first achieved on his own (piercing Hektor's body with the spear), ordinary, anonymous soldiers appropriate the space that Hektor occupied so proudly on the battlefield, disregard differences in status, and call for their own victory.

The body of the deceased warrior constitutes a framed space that marks the completion of the duel. The interconnection and gradual intensification of the Iliadic tragedy is imposing and taxing, for it requires that the audience realize that the body of the deceased designates both the boundary of the framed space of the duel and the opening of a new space, since the armies will plunge themselves into renewed carnage in their effort to claim the corpse. The double function of the space around the body capitalizes on the difference between ending and stopping, and regards such open endings in which nothing is concluded as closure, and not finality. Postponing or even canceling a conclusive ending, it appears, adds an extra twist to the plot, creating the expectation of a more conclusive ending, which is in itself postponed and finally deferred to another epic poem (narrating the death of Achilles). Such a belated ending plays on more complex or contrapuntal relationships and marks the space of the dead body not only as the terminal point of a duel but also as a notional path, a narrative corridor leading to other related duels and dead bodies, prolonging death endlessly. Moreover, the deceased's body has a stark chronotopic aspect, since it evokes the past and places it next to the present. In the case of Hektor's body, spatiotemporal features are deftly employed as the Achaeans approach and pierce his corpse with their spears. The body of "great Hektor" makes them recall the past (when Hektor "set the ships ablaze with the burning firebrand") and contrast it with the present ("See now, Hektor is much softer to handle than he was").[72] The body may thus be "an accumulation of relative perspectives and the passages between them, an additive space of utter receptivity retaining and combining past movements, in intensity, extracted from their actual terms. It is less a space in the empirical sense than a gap in space that is also a suspension of the normal unfolding of time. Still, it can be understood as having a spatiotemporal order of its own."[73]

These three successive camera shots invalidate all claims of a static aspect of space in duels. Contrary to previous beliefs that space is suddenly frozen when it comes to a duel, the narrator's eye creates a dynamic scene, with first a sidelong but close-up view of the two warriors, and second a face-to-face view, which in

---

[72] *Iliad* XXII 373–374 "ὢ πόποι, ἦ μάλα δὴ μαλακώτερος ἀμφαφάασθαι / Ἕκτωρ ἢ' ὅτε νῆας ἐνέπρηθεν πυρὶ κηλέωι."
[73] Massumi 2002:57.

the case of the death of Patroklos is profoundly—and significantly—undone. The narrator leads his camera behind each warrior who takes part in the duel, and changes his position to track the direction of the weapons thrown against the opponent. This zooming technique "spaces" duel-time into distinct parts, which are visualized as space-blocks, more or less in the manner of camera frames shot by the main narrator. The death of Patroklos offers much to explore, especially since the Achaean hero virtually loses his orientation, cannot properly retreat, and is fatally wounded by Hektor. In this light, the audience is invited to evaluate the importance of space for any warrior: whereas in the case of Sarpedon Patroklos emerges victorious by controlling the space where the fighting will take place, in the ensuing episode his disorientation leads to his death. This is also the case with Achilles' pursuit of Hektor around the walls of Troy, the more so since this climactic encounter is intricately entwined with spatial constraints. Hektor, knowing that there is no space favorable to him for fighting Achilles, refuses to stand and fight and runs around the walls. In other words, he tries to nullify the very notion of a framed space, the basic prerequisite for the duel. This is done the same number of times that Patroklos was disoriented before being killed by Hektor. Seen from this angle, these three interrelated duels are a poetic exercise on space, which thus becomes the crucial test for viewing a duel.

With respect to the spatiality of the fighting space, warriors do not fight in a physically confined setting. Their isolation and remoteness from the rest of the surrounding armies is not geographical but emotional. The dueling space is open and exposed on all sides, but at the same time impenetrable by other warriors as long as the duel lasts—a topography that is ideal on the one hand for promoting the theatricality[74] of the fighting, and on the other for representing the heroes' symbolic entrapment.

The urge to switch from the plurality of massive fighting to the singularity of one-to-one heroic encounters jolts the poet into a manipulation of space that evolves in a remarkably dynamic manner and is, after all, the lasting hallmark of great poetry.[75]

Aristeiai

An ἀριστεία presents a single character, moving around the battlefield and killing one enemy after the other. Since this form of fighting combines features of both the ἀνδροκτασίαι (successive killings) and the duel (emphasis on an individual

---

[74] On the theatricality of the Trojan plain, see Clay 2007 and 2011.

[75] On the interplay between plurality and singularity with respect to multiple fronts versus a single front, or spot, in the long stretch of the central fighting books of the *Iliad* (XII–XVII), see the analysis in Clay 2011:38–95.

warrior), we expect the organization and the narrative function of space to be especially complex. In fact, we may even speak of a dynamic space, which expands by following a *trail*,[76] a character's course through space. Although the protagonist moves across the battlefield as he kills one enemy after the other, and despite the fact that the narrator interrupts the ἀριστεία by turning his lens on other episodes of fighting, the audience is invited to view the protagonist's action as having a single trajectory. This *continuous action space*[77] is the result of the visual imaging of the scene offered to the listeners by the narrator. The main agent or hero moves on the battlefield while the narrator's spotlight tracks his movement.

Whether seen as a strategic device for promoting individual κλέος and accentuating heroic ideology, or a heuristic tool in the topological planning of fighting and the unfolding of the plot, Iliadic ἀριστεῖαι comprise a dense network of narrative snapshots of various competing heroic agendas that consistently create false expectations—credible scenarios that remain permanently suspended. Major warriors get involved in a series of heroic exploits where space constitutes a critical connection between individual power, recognition within the warrior community, and implicit claims to preeminence among the army. Moreover, in an epic where excellence on the battlefield represents a figurative locus for confirming one's status, the ἀριστεία as a form of heroic distinction is always tied to the ebb and flow of the plot's currents.

The narrative strategy of creating this continuous action space is fundamental to the Iliadic staging of war. It allows the audience to "see and follow" the rise and fall of warriors in terms of their illusion of ultimate success. Great heroes excel, and entertain for a moment the thought that they will reach each other's space (the city of Troy or the Achaean ships) victorious and bring the war to an end, but they are all made to realize, in a very painful way, that the epic's *Kriegsanschauung* is one of suspension, lack of resolution, and tormenting oscillation.

On the Trojan side, Hektor is left to believe that he will burn the ships of the Achaeans, and as it appears, he comes dangerously close to accomplishing his goal:

> Ἕκτωρ δὲ πρύμνηθεν ἐπεὶ λάβεν, οὔ τι μεθίει,
> ἄφλαστον μετὰ χερσὶν ἔχων, Τρωσὶν δ' ἐκέλευεν·
> "οἴσετε πῦρ, ἅμα δ' αὐτοὶ ἀολλέες ὄρνυτ' ἀϋτήν.
> νῦν ἥμιν πάντων Ζεὺς ἄξιον ἦμαρ ἔδωκεν,
> <u>νῆας ἑλεῖν</u> ..."

---

[76] Konstan 2002:2.
[77] The term was coined by Konstan (2002:2).

> Hektor would not let go of the stern of a ship where he had caught
>   hold of it
> but gripped the sternpost in his hands and called to the Trojans:
> "Bring fire, and give single voice to the clamour of battle.
> Now Zeus has given us a day worth all the rest of them:
> *the ships' capture ...*"

> *Iliad* XV 716–720

By penetrating deep into enemy space after breaking the Achaean wall with a stone (*Iliad* XII 445–462), Hektor makes his claim to foreign territory an almost tangible reality. Contrary to what is expected to happen in a poetic tradition culminating in the sack of Troy, it is not the city walls that are invaded but the enemy's mirror city, the secluded space of the Achaean camp. In this light, the audience interprets the symbolic function of the play between insiders and outsiders, and evaluates the violation of spatial frames against the backdrop of the Iliadic plot.[78] Hektor's attempt to burn the ships not only risks the safety of the Achaeans, who would be unable to return to Greece, but also contrasts with the audience's expectations based on the Iliadic tradition's subject matter. By entertaining such a scenario through Hektor's ἀριστεία, the *Iliad* flirts with the transgression of spatial boundaries that its plot has, until this moment, carefully delineated, and creates such strong puzzlement and agony[79] in the audience that it almost needs an equally powerful mechanism to restore the shattered balance. This mechanism will be nothing else than a new violation of spatial boundaries, this time by Patroklos, who in his arrogance will first push back the Trojans and then entertain the thought that he may sack Troy:[80]

> ἔνθά κεν ὑψίπυλον Τροίην ἕλον υἷες Ἀχαιῶν
> Πατρόκλου ὑπὸ χερσί, περίπρο γὰρ ἔγχεϊ θῦεν,
> εἰ μὴ Ἀπόλλων Φοῖβος ἐϋδμήτου ἐπὶ πύργου
> ἔστη, τῶι ὀλοὰ φρονέων, Τρώεσσι δ' ἀρήγων.
> τρὶς μὲν ἐπ' ἀγκῶνος βῆ τείχεος ὑψηλοῖο
> Πάτροκλος, τρὶς δ' αὐτὸν ἀπεστυφέλιξεν Ἀπόλλων,
> χείρεσσ' ἀθανάτηισι φαεινὴν ἀσπίδα νύσσων.
> ἀλλ' ὅτε δὴ τὸ τέταρτον ἐπέσσυτο δαίμονι ἶσος,

---

[78] This strategy is based on the activation of the inbuilt image schema of containment-boundedness (in-out), which is "one of the most pervasive features of our bodily experience ... [as] [w]e move in and out of rooms, clothes, vehicles, and numerous kinds of bounded spaces," as M. Johnson has eloquently put it (1987:21).

[79] On suspension and agony in Homer, see Rengakos 1999.

[80] The gist of this scene is reported to Hephaistos by Thetis in *Iliad* XVIII 454–456.

δεινὰ δ' ὁμοκλήσας ἔπεα πτερόεντα προσηύδα·
"χάζεο, διογενὲς Πατρόκλεις· οὔ νύ τοι αἶσα
σῶι ὑπὸ δουρὶ πόλιν πέρθαι Τρώων ἀγερώχων
οὐδ' ὑπ' Ἀχιλλῆος, ὅς περ σέο πολλὸν ἀμείνων."
ὣς φάτο· Πάτροκλος δ' ἀνεχάζετο πολλὸν ὀπίσσω,
μῆνιν ἀλευάμενος ἑκατηβόλου Ἀπόλλωνος.

There the sons of the Achaians might have taken gate-towering Ilion
under the hands of Patroklos, who *raged* with the spear *far before*
    them,
had not Phoibos Apollo taken his stand on the strong-built
tower,[81] with thoughts of death for him, but help for the Trojans.
Three times Patroklos tried to mount the angle of the towering
wall, and *three times* Phoibos Apollo battered him backward
with the immortal hands beating back the bright shield. As Patroklos
for the fourth time,[82] like something more than a man, came at him
he called aloud, and spoke winged words in the voice of danger:
"Give way, illustrious Patroklos: it is not destined
that the city of the proud Trojans shall fall before your spear
nor even at the hands of Achilleus, who is far better than you are."
He spoke, and Patroklos gave ground before him a great way,
avoiding the anger of him who strikes from afar, Apollo.

Iliad XVI 698–711

Like Hektor before him, Patroklos extends the limits of the area within which he is supposed to act (and has actually been advised by Achilles to do so)[83] and thus violates all the rules of its symbolic function. Such a transgression of one's heroic space furnishes an unmistakable clue to decoding his concomitant arrogance. Space saturates Iliadic narrative to such an extent that it undergirds heroic action and behavior:[84] craving ultimate victory, Patroklos tries to overcome the very boundaries of the plot within which he functions as a heroic figure. Apollo's

---

[81] On the so-called *suspense of anticipation*, see Reinhardt 1961:107–117; Schadewaldt 1966:150–161; de Jong 1987a:68–81; M. Lang 1989; Morrison 1992b; Nesselrath 1992; Louden 1993, 1999:124–129; Schmitz 1994; Rengakos 1999:315–320.

[82] On the pattern "x times + 1," see Fenik 1968:46–48; Janko 1992:400; Kelly 2007:194–197.

[83] Cf. *Iliad* XVI 87–96, where Achilles advises Patroklos not to lead the Myrmidons away from the ships and think that he may sack Troy.

[84] Muellner (1996:15) shows that in fear of Apollo's threat, Patroklos "retreats an ironically great distance in order to avoid his *mênis*," and argues (15n22) by comparing the relevant cases of Diomedes and Achilles that "the distance that the hero retreats is in inverse proportion to the distance between god and mortal to which he admits."

intervention, which makes effective use of typically Iliadic spatial protocols (*Iliad* XVI 707–709), reminds the audience that the son of Menoitios is just the surrogate of Achilles. There is no *esprit de corps* here, for Patroklos has already pushed the Trojans back from the ships. His action does not even abide by heroic etiquette, in the sense that his overconfidence stems from his military disguise. In light of the fact that the most elementary tenet of heroic behavior is eponymity, that is, being recognizable by the enemy as a noble and mighty warrior of status and prestige, from the very beginning of his ἀριστεία Patroklos has also violated a figurative notion of Achilles' personal space. By wearing Achilles' divine armor,[85] a remarkable piece of weaponry testifying to his special connection to the divine world,[86] Patroklos even transgresses the notional boundaries of his own self: he enters an unknown and dangerous space, that of being thought of as and acting like Achilles, a space that Hektor will also enter (after killing Patroklos and putting on Achilles' armor), and will never be able to leave until his own demise. Seen from this angle, Achilles' premonition is telling:

"πείθεο δ', ὥς τοι ἐγὼ μύθου τέλος ἐν φρεσὶ θείω,
ὡς ἄν μοι τιμὴν μεγάλην καὶ κῦδος ἄρηαι
πρὸς πάντων Δαναῶν, ἀτὰρ οἳ περικαλλέα κούρην
ἂψ ἀπονάσσωσιν, ποτὶ δ' ἀγλαὰ δῶρα πόρωσιν.
ἐκ νηῶν ἐλάσας ἰέναι πάλιν· εἰ δέ κεν αὖ τοι
δώηι κῦδος ἀρέσθαι ἐρίγδουπος πόσις Ἥρης,
μή σύ γ' ἄνευθεν ἐμεῖο λιλαίεσθαι πολεμίζειν
Τρωσὶ φιλοπτολέμοισιν· ἀτιμότερον δέ με θήσεις·
μηδ' ἐπαγαλλόμενος πολέμωι καὶ δηϊοτῆτι
Τρῶας ἐναιρόμενος προτὶ Ἴλιον ἡγεμονεύειν,
μή τις ἀπ' Οὐλύμποιο θεῶν αἰειγενετάων
ἐμβήηι—μάλα τούς γε φιλεῖ ἑκάεργος Ἀπόλλων—
<u>ἀλλὰ πάλιν τρωπᾶσθαι</u>, ἐπὴν φάος ἐν νήεσσιν

---

[85] The armor is a marked form of clothing, which constitutes a form of spatial relation through the perceptual involvement of sight (and sometimes sound). The armor of Achilles figuratively brings Patroklos, who is now wearing it, outside the boundaries of his own self. The same, tragically, will happen to Hektor when he puts on Achilles' (Patroklos') armor. On the various senses involved in the perceptual representation of space, see Bal 1997:133–135.

[86] The *Iliad* carefully indicates to the audience that neither Patroklos nor Hektor is "worthy" of wearing this divine armor. This is effected by a three-step process: Patroklos' wearing of the first armor of Achilles (*Iliad* XVI 130–144) ends with an overt reference to his inability to bear his friend's Pelian spear, which only Achilles could wield (XVI 140–144), while Hektor's wearing of Achilles' first armor that he took from the dead Patroklos is mentioned in a highly compressed form, not more than two lines (XVII 194–195). The detailed description of Achilles wearing the new armor (XIX 369–391) concludes with a reminder to the audience that Achilles is now brandishing his superb Pelian spear, which nobody else (Patroklos or Hektor) could bear.

θήῃς, τοὺς δέ τ' ἐᾶν πεδίον κάτα δηριάασθαι.
αἲ γάρ, Ζεῦ τε πάτερ καὶ Ἀθηναίη καὶ Ἄπολλον,
μήτέ τις οὖν Τρώων θάνατον φύγοι, ὅσσοι ἔασιν,
μήτέ τις Ἀργείων, νῶϊν δ' ἐκδυῖμεν ὄλεθρον,
ὄφρ' οἶοι Τροίης ἱερὰ κρήδεμνα λύωμεν."

"But obey to the end this word I put upon your attention
so that you can win, for me, great honour and glory
in the sight of all the Danaans, so they will bring back to me
the lovely girl, and give me shining gifts in addition.
When you have driven them from the ships, come back; although
     later
the thunderous lord of Hera might grant you the winning of glory,
you must not set your mind on fighting the Trojans, whose delight
is in battle, without me. So you will diminish my honour.
You must not, in the pride and fury of fighting, go on
slaughtering the Trojans, and lead the way against Ilion,
for fear some one of the everlasting gods on Olympos
might crush you. Apollo who works from afar loves these people
dearly. *You must turn back* once you bring the light of salvation
to the ships, and let the others go on fighting in the flat land.
Father Zeus, Athene and Apollo, if only
not one of all the Trojans could escape destruction, not one
of the Argives, but you and I could emerge from the slaughter
so that we two alone could break Troy's hallowed coronal."

Iliad XVI 83–100

Achilles' forewarning is accompanied by his shocking hunch about the doom of Patroklos. He not only advises his friend about what to do but also implicitly reveals, through a moving tragic irony, what will happen to him if he does not follow his advice. What is of particular interest to my investigation concerns the *proxemics* upon which Achilles' advice is based:[87] he explicitly tells Patroklos that only together will they be able, if the gods grant them victory, to sack the city of Troy (XVI 89, 97–100).[88] By translating their standing next to each other in combat into spatial terms, Achilles makes a personal comment on the heroic code. Lack of honor (XVI 90 ἀτιμότερον δέ με θήσεις) is tied to Patroklos'

---

[87] On proxemics as a spatial term with particular reference to the *Odyssey*, see Lateiner 1995:136.

[88] The phrasing of *Iliad* XVI 89 μὴ σύ γ' ἄνευθεν ἐμεῖο λιλαίεσθαι πολεμίζειν will be ironically echoed in XXIII 83-84 μὴ ἐμὰ σῶν ἀπάνευθε τιθήμεναι ὀστέ' Ἀχιλλεῦ, / ἀλλ' ὁμοῦ; the two friends will finally be reunited, albeit in death.

potential refusal to fight together with Achilles, a statement that injects space into the rhetoric of pride, distinction, and reputation. Likewise, Hektor's taunting speech to Patroklos after inflicting a fatal wound on him (XVI 830–842) begins by offering another aspect of a heroic rhetoric of space:

> "Πάτροκλ', ἦ που ἔφησθα πόλιν κεραϊξέμεν ἀμήν,
> Τρωϊάδας δὲ γυναῖκας ἐλεύθερον ἦμαρ ἀπούρας
> ἄξειν ἐν νήεσσι φίλην ἐς πατρίδα γαῖαν,
> νήπιε·"

> "Patroklos, you thought perhaps of devastating our city,
> of stripping from the Trojan women the day of their liberty
> and dragging them off in ships to the beloved land of your fathers.
> Fool!"

Iliad XVI 830–833

Hektor adopts the stance of the protector of Troy, whose women would have been taken to Greece as slaves by the Achaean ships. He thus confirms his own status as savior of his city, and even verbalizes ironically distorted imaginary advice from Achilles to Patroklos. Whereas Achilles has actually warned Patroklos not to follow the panic-stricken Trojans into the plain, away from the Achaean ships,[89] Hektor imagines Achilles putting a heavy burden on his friend's shoulders by asking him to return to the ships only after killing Hektor (XVI 839–842). This rhetoric of space is based on the way individual heroes highlight different aspects of the heroic code. Achilles emphasizes to Patroklos the honor and glory (XVI 84 ὡς ἄν μοι τιμὴν μεγάλην καὶ κῦδος ἄρηαι) he himself (i.e. Achilles) is going to win if Patroklos pushes the Trojans back, but warns him of the danger of winning glory for himself without him (XVI 87–88 εἰ δέ κεν αὖ τοι / δώηι κῦδος ἀρέσθαι ἐρίγδουπος πόσις Ἥρης). Hektor, on the other hand, painfully reminds Patroklos that by violating his personal heroic space he has lost both his life and his honor, as his body will be devoured by vultures *in this place* (XVI 836 σὲ δέ τ' ἐνθάδε γῦπες ἔδονται), that is, in an area located *outside* Patroklos' proper space. In a remarkable dramatic reversal of the previous situation, Hektor distorts Achilles' advice[90] and creates a shocking image of Patroklos,

---

[89] Cf. *Iliad* XVI 83–96.

[90] The use of similar language by Achilles (*Iliad* XVI 87 ἐκ νηῶν ἐλάσας ἰέναι πάλιν) and by Hektor (XVI 839–840 μή μοι πρὶν ἰέναι ... / νῆας ἔπι γλαφυράς), in his imaginary reconstruction of Achilles' speech to Patroklos, is an ironic twist applied to the technique of *transference* (μετακένωσις): whereas a character of the plot is sometimes presented as possessing knowledge that he could not possibly have had but which is accessible to the external narratees, here Hektor employs language recalling Achilles' earlier speech to Patroklos (the content of which

who—if victorious—would have returned to the Achaean ships with Hektor's blood-stained chiton (XVI 839–841).

Although the death of Achilles lies outside the thematic scope of the *Iliad*, it is systematically foreshadowed throughout the entire epic. In the light of the foregoing analysis of the violation of heroic space and the poem's creation of false expectations, Achilles' own violation of Achaean space and his flirtation with the idea of conquering Troy are dramatically foreshadowed during his ἀριστεία:

> "ἦ δή που μάλ' ἔολπας ἐνὶ φρεσί, φαίδιμ' Ἀχιλλεῦ,
> ἤματι τῶιδε πόλιν πέρσειν Τρώων ἀγερώχων,
> νηπύτι'· ...
>   σὺ δ' ἐνθάδε πότμον ἐφέψεις ..."

> "You must have hoped within your heart, o shining Achilleus,
> on this day to storm the city of the proud Trojans.
> You fool! ...
>   but in this place you will find your destiny ...”

> *Iliad* XXI 583–588

Agenor's vague foreshadowing of Achilles' death will become more explicit when the dying Hektor, using language that recalls Agenor's prophetic words, even mentions the names of his opponent's future killers:

> "ἤματι τῶι, ὅτε κέν σε Πάρις καὶ Φοῖβος Ἀπόλλων
> ἐσθλὸν ἐόντ' ὀλέσωσιν ἐνὶ Σκαιῆισι πύληισιν."

> "... on that day when Paris and Phoibos Apollo
> destroy you in the Skaian gates, for all your valour.”

> *Iliad* XXII 359–360

The reference to the Skaian Gates implicitly points to Achilles' violation of heroic space. Taken together with Agenor's telling ἐνθάδε (XXI 588), they indicate that the tradition of the *Iliad* sees Achilles' extra-Iliadic death in terms of his violation of his personal heroic space, which amounts to his arrogant claim that he can sack Troy. Space thus becomes such a profoundly linked feature of the way the poem deals with the world of heroes that it even postulates a similarly defined heroic attitude for Achilles in another epic tradition.[91]

Hektor could not have known), but distorts its content. On transference, see Bassett 1938:130–140; J. Kakridis 1982.

[91] See Proclus' summary of the *Aethiopis* on the death of Achilles: τρεψάμενος δ' Ἀχιλλεὺς τοὺς Τρῶας καὶ εἰς τὴν πόλιν συνεισπεσὼν ὑπὸ Πάριδος ἀναιρεῖται καὶ Ἀπόλλωνος (§ 62 Kullmann =

When placed against the backdrop of a whole range of military activity, the politics of space reveal the interdependence of individual and communal identity formation. Agamemnon's superb performance on the battlefield in *Iliad* XI, as highlighted by the expanded area in which he triumphantly moves, magnifies and exemplifies his heroic prowess, against the strongly negative background of his initial verbal haughtiness during his conflict with Achilles. Furthermore, the extended area where his ἀριστεία takes place aims at doing justice to the figurative place he occupies owing to his high status among the Achaean army. Given that Agamemnon's movement is expressed not through place markers but by means of individuals or pairs of opponents, space acquires a strongly personalized dimension.

The audience is encouraged to reconceptualize Agamemnon's identity by realizing that his status is dynamically invigorated and affirmed on the battlefield. The invocation of the Muses (*Iliad* XI 218), before the beginning of a catalogue of warriors to be killed by the son of Atreus, is reminiscent of an epic proem. The result of such a marked opening up of his ἀριστεία is noteworthy, for it lets listeners reevaluate Agamemnon's role. The power dynamics inherent in such expressions are considerable, since the bard's recourse to divine authority reflects the sheer scope of the subject matter to be sung: by invoking the Muses, the poet implies that Agamemnon's heroic exploits surpass human measure.

The immense authority inscribed in an ἀριστεία is closely connected to the spatial aspects of such a heroic performance: by offering a unique combination of fighting ahead of the whole army and protecting those behind by pushing the enemy back, the hero who performs an ἀριστεία activates a whole set of power dynamics consisting in the symbiotic relationship between center and periphery.[92]

Diomedes, whom the narrator places "in the middle" (*Iliad* V 8 κατὰ μέσσον) of the fighting at the beginning of his ἀριστεία,[93] soon displays a remarkable mobility as he rushes across the battlefield (V 87 θῦνε γὰρ ἂμ πεδίον; 96 θύνοντ' ἂμ πεδίον; 250 θῦνε διὰ προμάχων). Faced with a wealth of enemies but a

---

191–192 Severyns = Allen 106.7–9). In this light, the expression σὺ δ' ἐνθάδε πότμον ἐφέψεις used by Agenor (*Iliad* XXI 588) amounts to an intertextual allusion. See Burgess 2009:44–45, who gives a full list of such passages (*Iliad* XIX 416–417, though no reference to place is included; *Iliad* XXIII 80–81), and discusses (44–55) the various elements comprising *Iliad*ic allusions to his death.

[92] On the mental pattern or image schema "center-periphery," see M. Johnson 1987:124 and Dannenberg 2008:76.

[93] The frequent position of some character "in the middle" may be seen within the larger framework of immersion techniques employed by the Homeric storyteller, who aims to "place" his audience, at least at times, right in the middle of the events taking place on the battlefield or in the Achaean camp. See Detienne 1965 on the use of τὸ μέσον as public space; Clay (2011:43) states with respect to the Achaean camp that "the center constitutes both the religious and the public space where the community assembles."

shortage of comrades (85–86 Τυδείδην δ' οὐκ ἂν γνοίης ποτέροισι μετείη, / ἠὲ μετὰ Τρώεσσιν ὁμιλέοι ἦ μετ' Ἀχαιοῖς),[94] Diomedes indirectly reaffirms the core-periphery dynamics of Iliadic warfare. Sometimes, a hero's military prowess is exemplified through his engagement in combat in a marginal space even beyond the other πρόμαχοι. In particular, the poet redefines Hektor's heroism by stressing that he is fighting ahead of his own army, which stands some distance behind him (XXII 459 ἀλλὰ πολὺ προθέεσκε, τὸ ὃν μένος οὐδενὶ εἴκων). Given that second- and third-tier warriors are always placed at the core of the army and never in its peripheral front lines, they can hardly claim a stake in a community where hierarchies are clearly reflected in the spatial arrangement of the troops. These lesser warriors, representing the "mainstream" segments of heroic society, often serve as victims of the first-rank heroes during their heroic exploits. In the world of Iliadic fighting, where penetrating the enemy lines is virtually reserved for preeminent heroes, power relations reside in space, and become the arena for individual empowerment by means of the interplay between center and periphery.

Consequently, through individual corporeal activity and by appropriating space as their own, heroes use the various abstract spaces of the Iliadic battle-field to match class hierarchies. The ἀριστεία provides claims to inclusion and exclusion, and by mirroring dichotomies between insiders and outsiders leads to the evaluation of power relations, enables identity formation, and last, but certainly not least, creates a single, unified action space.

Static Space

The battlefield is used mainly, but not solely, for the presentation of martial activity. It is also transformed so as to include friendly encounters between enemies, oath-swearing, and assemblies. Moreover, it contains certain locus-images (the oak tree of Zeus and the fig tree, the river and ford of Skamandros, the tombstone of Ilos and the tomb of Myrine, the rise in the plain), which mark simple story space and are employed as mental tags that cue both bard and audience to specific associations.

---

[94] "… you could not have told on which side Tydeus' son was fighting, / whether he were one with the Trojans or with the Achaians …" The use of ἂν γνοίης indicates that we are dealing here with a "descending" metalepsis (i.e. from embedding to embedded story level), where the "intrametaleptic" transgression results in the collaboration between storyteller and audience. In fact, the storyteller invites his listeners to experience the havoc of war on their own, since they cannot possibly distinguish whether Diomedes is among the ranks of the Trojans or the Achaeans. On the various forms of metalepsis, see Genette 1980:234–237, 1988:58–59; McHale 1987; Herman 1997; F. Wagner 2002; Fludernik 2003a; Genette 2004; Pier & Schaeffer 2005; de Jong 2009.

Microsettings

The martial space of the battlefield is occasionally transformed into a nonmilitary space, when an oath is sworn or an impending duel is turned into a friendly exchange of arms. Both these deviations from the formal function of the battlefield space are worth considering, the more so since they take place in a purely martial space that is basically devoted to combat.

With respect to the swearing of oaths, I will examine only two cases: the oaths before the duel of Menelaos and Paris in *Iliad* III and before the duel of Ajax and Hektor in *Iliad* VII, which have to do with a temporary cease-fire and the creation of a special space for the performance of sacrifices and the swearing of the oaths.

In *Iliad* III 67–70, Paris tells Hektor that he is ready to fight Menelaos in a duel, after swearing a promissory oath that the winner will take Helen and all her possessions and the Achaeans will return to Greece: [95]

> "νῦν αὖτ' εἴ μ' ἐθέλεις πολεμίζειν ἠδὲ μάχεσθαι,
> ἄλλους μὲν <u>κάθεσον</u> Τρῶας καὶ πάντας Ἀχαιούς,
> αὐτὰρ ἔμ' <u>ἐν μέσσωι</u> καὶ ἀρηΐφιλον Μενέλαον
> συμβάλετ' ἀμφ' Ἑλένηι καὶ κτήμασι πᾶσι μάχεσθαι·"

> "Now though, if you wish me to fight it out and do battle,
> make the rest of the Trojans *sit down*, and all the Achaians,
> and set me *in the middle* with Menelaos the warlike
> to fight together for the sake of Helen and all her possessions."

Iliad III 67–70

Both the verb κάθεσον (line 68) and the expression ἐν μέσσωι (69) are essential for understanding how the *Iliad* transforms the battlefield, the space of martial violence par excellence, into a space of sanctified violence. By calling the armies to "sit down" or by "seating" them, the narrator aims to curtail the visual fluidity[96] of the battlefield and delineate a space where the ensuing episode will occur. In the light of Paris' determination to fight Menelaos ἐν μέσσωι 'in the middle', it becomes clear that the *Iliad* aims at highlighting the theatricality of the scene to follow, as the armies are transformed into seated spectators and the protagonists of the duel into stage actors. This "internal" transformation

---

[95] On oaths, see Hirzel 1902; Plescia 1970; Sommerstein and Fletscher 2007. On Homeric oaths, see Callaway 1993.

[96] On the elusiveness of Iliadic landscape, see Andersson 1976:16–17.

mirrors an "external" one that converts auditors into spectators.[97] Consider the remarks of Clay:

> Cognitive studies have demonstrated the importance of visual imagery in remembering and, more particularly, the role of visual memory in oral traditions of storytelling. Traditional storytellers frequently speak of seeing the story unfold before their eyes "like a silent movie, a set of slides, or even a dramatic play ..." (Labrie 1981:91).... "In an oral tradition, imagery involves the transformation of a sequential verbal input into a spatial image and back to a sequential verbal output" (Rubin 1995:62). This phenomenon is encapsulated in the old term, *enargeia*, that characteristic vividness so much admired by the ancient critics of the Homeric epics, a vividness that transforms auditors into spectators.[98]

This almost cinematic character is not limited to battle scenes, but pervades Homeric epic as a whole. It allows the traditional storyteller to present the tale to his audience as a series of slides, which they are able to watch in their minds' eye.[99] In order to underpin visual and spatial imagery, he lays special emphasis on placing himself in a privileged position, in this case at the very center where Paris and Menelaos will fight each other.[100] The narrator, though, will exploit this central space by turning it, temporarily, into the space where the oath will be sworn.

This dramatization and manipulation of martial space acquires an even more profound meaning when we consider the swearing of oaths. Hektor goes between the two armies (*Iliad* III 77 καί ῥ' ἐς μέσσον ἰών) and repeats his brother's words almost verbatim. This detail—that Hektor stands in the middle—has not attracted the attention it deserves. Hektor could very well have shouted to the Achaeans to stop the fighting, or could have addressed one of the leaders who command the two armies. Why then does he go between them and put

---

97 See Goldhill 1996:17.

98 2007:238 and 2011:29n42 with further bibliography. On other devices employed by the Homeric bard in his attempt to turn his auditors into spectators (like the potential optative in the second or third person), see Clay 2011:23–26 and n25; see also Pseudo-Longinus (*On the Sublime* 26.1), who states that in *Iliad* XV 697–698 the "shift of addressees" (ἡ τῶν προσώπων ἀντιμετάθεσις) is "vehement/active/vivid" (ἐναγώνιος) and "often makes the listener seem to find himself in the middle of perils" (πολλάκις ἐν μέσοις τοῖς κινδύνοις ποιοῦσα τὸν ἀκροατὴν δοκεῖν στρέφεσθαι).

99 See Winkler 2007:50, who argues that "to an astonishing degree, the *Iliad*, the very first work of Western literature, reveals features of the art of cinematic storytelling long before modern technology made this art a reality."

100 On the duel between Paris and Menelaos, see Bergold 1977.

his life at risk?[101] The answer to this question is essential for comprehending the critical intersection and contrast between the scene of oath-sacrifice and the scene of the ensuing duel.[102] Swearing an oath requires the creation of an agreement, a pact between two or more individuals, which is ritually configured through a series of symbolic acts (words, gestures, exchange of artifacts, sacrifice). Moreover, the oath delineates a notional space within which the two sides operate, an area—real or imaginary—where special rules are in effect. This special space is implicit in the ancient testimonies concerning the taking of an oath. According to Pausanias,[103] Tundareos had asked all the suitors of Helen to stand on the τόμια ('parts of a sacrifice') of a horse and swear an oath that they would help Helen and her husband in case they were in trouble in the future. The sacrificial parts of the horse stand for the special space within which the oath is sworn.[104] Since this space becomes sacred for those swearing the oath, it may be that the very expression ὅρκια τέμνειν, which is used in Homer time and again for swearing an oath, has kept something of its older function, indicating the process of cutting up sacrificial victims and stepping on them. Moreover, the term ὅρκος, like its cognate ἕρκος, is a figurative *fence* "which confines or constrains," and thus keeps out or fences off violators and intruders.[105] In the purely martial space of the battlefield, the narrator makes Hektor stand, as the emissary of a proposed duel, in the middle between the two armies in order to flag the space as sacred for taking a promissory oath. This interpretation is supported by the language used by Menelaos on the importance of bringing sacrificial victims to this sacred place (III 103–104 οἴσετε ἄρν', ἕτερον λευκόν, ἑτέρην δὲ μέλαιναν, / Γῆι τε καὶ Ἠελίωι· Διὶ δ' ἡμεῖς οἴσομεν ἄλλον ["Bring two lambs: let one be white and the other black for / Earth and the Sun God, and for Zeus we will bring yet another"]) and fetching Priam as a trustworthy representative of the Trojans (III 105 ἄξετε δὲ Πριάμοιο βίην ["Bring ... the strength of Priam"]; III 107 μή τις ὑπερβασίηι Διὸς ὅρκια δηλήσηται ["lest some man overstep Zeus' oaths"]). The special place where the oath will be taken must include all prerequisites, animal and human alike, since it needs to keep out possible violators. It is from this angle that we must interpret the description of the Trojans and Achaeans while they dismount their horses (III 113 καί ῥ' ἵππους μὲν ἔρυξαν ἐπὶ στίχας, ἐκ δ' ἔβαν αὐτοί) and take off their weapons and place them nearby on the ground (III 114–115 τεύχεά τ' ἐξεδύοντο· τὰ μὲν κατέθεντ' ἐπὶ γαίηι / πλησίον ἀλλήλων). Their coming together around this sanctified area is implied

---

[101] Cf. *Iliad* III 79–83.
[102] As well as other scenes of killings on the battlefield. On this topic, see Kitts 2005:124–125.
[103] 3.20.9; see also Stesichorus fr. 190 (PMGF) and Σ on Sophocles' *Ajax* 1113 (Christodoulou).
[104] See Karavites 1992:62–63.
[105] See Plescia 1970:1.

by the narratorial comment "so there was little ground left between them" (III 115 ὀλίγη δ' ἦν ἀμφὶς ἄρουρα). The emphasis on the disarming and mutual approach of the two armies underpins the theatricality of the whole episode. The ritually sanctified space of the oath exercises its force on the warriors of both sides, as the *Iliad* plays with the visual representation of a nonmartial scene within a martial context par excellence. What is of particular importance is that this pause does not bring the narrative to a standstill, but "corresponds to a contemplative pause by the hero himself."[106] By making Hektor transform Paris' desire to create a special martial space for the duel into a sanctified space for oath-exchange, the storyteller encourages the audience to see this as a potential terminal space, a symbolic *where* for the war to end.

After the interlude of the τειχοσκοπία episode, when Priam and Antenor arrive at the battlefield, the narrator carefully accentuates the fact that they stood between the two armies and that it was there that they "led up the victims for the gods' oaths" (*Iliad* III 269 ὅρκια πιστὰ θεῶν σύναγον). Once all the necessary preparations for the ensuing oath-swearing have been completed, Agamemnon raises his hands towards the sky (275) and utters the oath (276–291), an important aspect of which is that its unwavering fulfillment will result in a radical change of space for both armies. In other words, should both Trojans and Achaeans abide by the oath, the battlefield where this whole scene takes place will cease to exist, since the Achaean army will return to Greece, the Trojan allies to their respective countries, and the Trojan army to the city of Ilion. The power of the oath is so great that it can bring the war to an end, and thus deprive the battlefield of its martial aspect and transform it into the peaceful plain of Troy. This last observation, which is prominently spelled out in the utterance of the oath, allows the narrator to make full use of the sanctified space where the oath is sworn, in order first to create a highly thematized juncture of ritual and martial space, and then to elicit comparison with the wider bipolar space bordered by Greece and Troy that the *Iliad* takes for granted.

Just before the duel, Hektor and Odysseus, representing the Trojan and Achaean sides respectively, "measured out the distance first" (*Iliad* III 315 χῶρον μὲν πρῶτον διεμέτρεον); then "when these two [Paris and Menelaos] were armed on either side of the battle, / they strode into the space between the Achaians and Trojans" (340–341 οἳ δ' ἐπεὶ οὖν ἑκάτερθεν ὁμίλου θωρήχθησαν, / ἐς μέσσον Τρώων καὶ Ἀχαιῶν ἐστιχόωντο), and "they took their stand in the measured space not far from each other" (344 καί ῥ' ἐγγὺς στήτην διαμετρητῶι ἐνὶ χώρωι). Notwithstanding the elusiveness of Iliadic landscape, especially of Iliadic martial space, the narrator emphatically stresses the careful delineation

---

[106] Genette 1980:100.

of the space of this duel because it is identical with the ritual space where the oath has been sworn.[107] By presenting his listeners with a sanctified, closed space that stands in sharp contrast to the vastness and vagueness of the battle-field, and by attempting to miniaturize space and imbue it with the ominous tone of a solemn ritual, the *Iliad* offers a highly ritualized fusion of sacrifice and war, and presents one more credible scenario of its coming to an end.[108] This attempt to decide the universal (Trojan War) by means of the particular (a single duel) aims at a complete reversal of space, since the Achaeans will return home and the Trojans will continue to live in their city. This effort to return to the very origin of the war—the abduction of Helen—and "correct" the initial wrongdoing is effectively carried out in spatial terms that allow for a "meta-phorical switch," which remains suspended as the Trojans violate the oath, and their perjury becomes a powerful leitmotif persisting for four more books.

Another case worth exploring in this respect is the swearing of oaths before the duel between Hektor and Ajax in *Iliad* VII. Here the situation is rather different from the oath-exchange and duel in *Iliad* III, for Apollo and Athena, who set this plan in action, aim at stopping all military activity only for this day (VII 29–30 νῦν μὲν παύσωμεν πόλεμον καὶ δηϊοτῆτα / σήμερον). Even when Apollo talks Hektor into this duel, he refrains from explaining the aim of this one-on-one fight, despite the fact that he employs the same diction (49 ἄλλους μὲν κάθεσον Τρῶας καὶ πάντας Ἀχαιούς) we have observed in the episode between Menelaos and Paris in *Iliad* III 68. The same is true of the expression ἐς μέσσον ἰών (VII 55) used of Hektor and the "sitting down" of the Achaean army, as well as of the two gods—in the guise of vultures—on Zeus' lofty oak tree (60 φηγῷ ἔφ' ὑψηλῇι) and the mutual approach of the ranks of the two armies (61 τῶν δὲ στίχες εἴατο πυκναί). The privilege of determining the wording of the oath is left to Hektor, who—after the Trojan perjury in *Iliad* III—proposes that the winner shall take the arms of his defeated opponent but return his body to his comrades. In this light, this oath entails no radical change of space, like that in *Iliad* III, but rather advocates respecting and preserving the current spatial symmetry between Troy and the Achaean camp. Along the same lines, there is no clear demarcation of the oath or the martial space where the duel will take place. On the other hand, there is a notable effort to view the two heroes as they approach each other: Ajax "takes huge strides forward" (VII 213 ἤϊε μακρὰ βιβάς), whereas Hektor "can no longer find means to take flight and shrink back into / the throng of his men" (*Iliad* VII 217–218 ἀλλ' οὔ πως ἔτι εἶχεν ὑποτρέσαι

---

[107] On the careful delineation of this space and the ordered preparation of the troops, see Kitts 2005:123–125.

[108] On credible impossibilities or scenarios in the *Iliad*, see Scodel 1999:33–42, 49–57, 59–60, 63–65, 66–69, 70–74, 80–82.

οὐδ' ἀναδῦναι / ἂψ λαῶν ἐς ὅμιλον). Moreover, the duel comes to a halt when the rather elusive space where it occurs is violated by Talthubios and Idaios, the Achaean and Trojan heralds, who stand in the middle holding their scepters (277 μέσσωι δ' ἀμφοτέρων σκῆπτρα σχέθον), while Idaios suggests that the duel end in a draw, now that Zeus has shown his love for both heroes (279–282).

The marked differences from the oath-exchange in *Iliad* III are instructive with respect to the function of space. The elusiveness of the area where this episode takes place, the absence of any radical spatial shift if the oath is observed, and the violation of the space of the duel by the heralds indicate the complete collapse of the oath. This time it comes about not as the result of perjury (as in *Iliad* III), but in the form of a deviation from or transgression of various topological factors that chart a ritual space for fulfilling this sacred agreement.

Apart from oath-exchanges, the organization of space entails inherent difficulties for the Iliadic tradition, since it lacks another form of setting where a friendly meeting, like that between Diomedes and Glaukos, can take place.[109] In order to overcome such problems of staging,[110] the *Iliad* creates an internal space within the battlefield, a space that is not delineated by specific landscape markers, and as a result is not narratively autonomous. It is denoted, in semiotic terms, by the following series of signs,[111] which represent the inversion of a corresponding chain of features of a formal duel: instead of moving aggressively one against the other, the two adversaries stop and stand close together; they do not resort to the typical exchange of taunting speeches but speak in a friendly manner; they do not throw their spears or arrows but exchange weapons;[112] they dismount their chariots and shake hands.[113] This *deroutinization* process, by which features from a given type-scene are transferred to another, in this case its direct opposite, is enhanced even more through a *zooming* technique that is equally employed in formal duels: the main narrator turns the attention of his audience to a specific pair of warriors who are narratively "isolated" within

---

[109] On this episode, see Tsagalis 2010b:87–113.

[110] I use the term "staging" here deliberately with its theater-oriented overtones; cf. Hellwig's (1964:28) use of *Schauplatz* to denote the Trojan plain.

[111] On signs and the role of memory in Homer, see Scodel 2002; on the indexicality of signs, see Sourvinou-Inwood 1995:136–139; on signs within the context of *traditional referentiality* that reach outside the poem, see Foley 1997; 1999a:25–34; 1999b. Although the word σῆμα is not used in the particular passage I am discussing, nevertheless, for the external audience of an epic song, typologically established steps forming part of a type scene or a traditional structural pattern are signs, in the sense that their presence or absence keys listeners to specific interpretive notes. On the importance of "recognition" and "interpretation" of the σῆμα by plot agents and the extension of signs, typical and metonymical alike, by the audience, see Nagy 1990a:202–222.

[112] See Karavites 1992:54; Lateiner 1995:49–56; Kitts 2005:84.

[113] See Maronitis 2004:37.

the battlefield. Such a technique results in the creation of an internal stage, a smaller story space where the ensuing episode will take place. Given that no spatial indicators are employed to mark the setting, the *Iliad* sets up an empty space for the listeners in the form of camera position.[114] The main narrator's lens is suddenly focused on a single spot on the battlefield, an almost indescribable or ineffable stationary point. The spectators are guided to a place that is both already present (since it forms part of the battlefield) and absent (in the sense that it is devoid of topography), and subsequently encouraged to visualize the specific scene on their own. Following Ryan's model of reconstructing maps of fictional worlds, we can see that the literary cartography of the place where the encounter between the two heroes takes place is what discourse analysts have felicitously called a *map* strategy, where "space is represented panoramically from a perspective ranging from the disembodied god's-eye point of view of pure vertical projection to the oblique view of an observer situated on an elevated point."[115] In light of the complete absence of typical spatial indicators, it is worth investigating the process of tacit instruction to the listeners to re-create space, by capitalizing on certain mental strategies employed in visual imaging. Examined against this background, certain deictic terms referring to distance may in fact be cues offered to the audience for a suggested mapping of the given scene, the more so since such hints encompass built-in, so to speak, mental models of narrative structure.[116]

After the introduction of the two heroes in typical epic manner (*Iliad* VI 119 Γλαῦκος δ' Ἱππολόχοιο πάϊς καὶ Τυδέος υἱός), space is roughly indicated by the line ἐς μέσον ἀμφοτέρων συνίτην μεμαῶτε μάχεσθαι (120), which allows the narrator to differentiate Glaukos and Diomedes from the rest of the two armies and zoom his narrative lens in on them.[117] This very same line is also attested two more times in the *Iliad* (XX 159, XXIII 814), always anticipating an impending duel that is going to take place between foot-soldiers;[118] let us therefore compare all three passages:

> Γλαῦκος δ' Ἱππολόχοιο πάϊς καὶ Τυδέος υἱός
> ἐς μέσον ἀμφοτέρων συνίτην μεμαῶτε μάχεσθαι.

---

[114] On empty space, see Fludernik 1996:192–201, with further bibliography. On applying filmic terminology to the Iliadic plot, see Winkler 2007.

[115] Ryan 2003:218.

[116] Along these lines, N. Richardson 2006:51, following Esrock 1994, has convincingly argued that the *Iliad* exploits at length the human eye's "natural attraction to bright patches in the visual field [termed "radiant ignition"], as when Homer helps us image a field of armed warriors by describing the light reflecting off their bronze helmets."

[117] See scholia on *Iliad* VI 120 (Erbse) ὡς διεστώτων καὶ ἀναπαυομένων ("as if they were standing apart and resting").

[118] πεζῇι. On this important point, cf. *Iliad* VI 232–236.

οἳ δ’ ὅτε δὴ σχεδὸν ἦσαν ἐπ’ ἀλλήλοισι ἰόντες,
τὸν πρότερος προσέειπε βοὴν ἀγαθὸς Διομήδης·

Now Glaukos, sprung of Hippolochos, and the son of Tydeus
came together in the space between the two armies, battle-bent.
Now as these advancing came to one place and encountered,
first to speak was Diomedes of the great war cry:

Iliad VI 119–122

δύο δ’ ἀνέρες ἔξοχ’ ἄριστοι
ἐς μέσον ἀμφοτέρων συνίτην μεμαῶτε μάχεσθαι,
Αἰνείας τ’ Ἀγχισιάδης καὶ δῖος Ἀχιλλεύς.
. . . .
οἱ δ’ ὅτε δὴ σχεδὸν ἦσαν ἐπ’ ἀλλήλοισιν ἰόντες,
τὸν πρότερος προσέειπε ποδάρκης δῖος Ἀχιλλεύς·

Two men far greater than all the others
were coming to encounter, furious to fight with each other,
Aineias, the son of Anchises, and brilliant Achilleus.
. . . .
Now as these in their advance had come close to each other
first of the two to speak was swift-footed brilliant Achilleus ...

Iliad XX 158–160, 176–177

ὣς ἔφατ’· ὦρτο δ’ ἔπειτα μέγας Τελαμώνιος Αἴας,
ἂν δ’ ἄρα Τυδείδης ὦρτο κρατερὸς Διομήδης.
οἳ δ’ ἐπεὶ οὖν ἑκάτερθεν ὁμίλου θωρήχθησαν,
ἐς μέσον ἀμφοτέρων[119] συνίτην μεμαῶτε μάχεσθαι

So he spoke, and there rose up huge Telamonian Aias,
and next the son of Tydeus rose up, strong Diomedes.
When these were in their armour on either side of the assembly,
they came together in the middle space, furious for the combat ...

Iliad XXIII 811–814

The formulaic material employed in all these instances includes a two-step process: (1) the introduction of the two warriors in stark epic manner by means of patronymics and typical epithets accompanying their names; (2) a

---

[119] West opts for the reading ἀμφοτέρω, despite the fact that he prints ἀμφοτέρων for the same formulaic line in both *Iliad* VI 120 and XX 159.

designation of space in two phases, including their coming close together or separating themselves from other bystanders and standing between the two armies.[120]

With respect to the first step, although patronymics constitute a general characteristic of epic diction, their use before such scenes may also, on a secondary level, entail claims to authority and prestige. The warriors approach each other in majestic grandeur, figuratively carrying with them legitimization[121] and status stemming from their genealogical pedigrees, which are here fossilized in formulaically appropriate patronymics.[122] Patronymics may thus testify to the heroes' esteem and stature,[123] projecting their past into the present of the epic performance.[124]

For the second step, the Homeric narrator has a twofold goal: first, he tries to create a symmetrical space for the two heroes, by making them stand between the two armies surrounding them, and then he attempts to isolate them from the rest of their armies by bringing them close. The formulaic line ἐς μέσον ἀμφοτέρων συνίτην μεμαῶτε μάχεσθαι, verbalizing the narrator's first aim, subordinates the first phase to the second, which is also expressed formulaically (οἳ δ' ὅτε δὴ σχεδὸν ἦσαν ἐπ' ἀλλήλοισι ἰόντες).

In tandem with this, and given that the formula οἳ δ' ὅτε δὴ σχεδὸν ἦσαν ἐπ' ἀλλήλοισι ἰόντες is attested twelve times in the *Iliad*[125]—always before the formula τὸν πρότερος προσέειπε + epithet + nominative proper name of one of the two heroes—it is clear that both the shaping and the content of this formula fit a military context, as the two protagonists are narratively isolated from the rest of the two armies and approach each other ready for combat.

When we apply these findings to the meeting between Diomedes and Glaukos, it becomes clear that: (1) the Iliadic tradition designates the story space for the friendly encounter between the two heroes through the typical means of epic diction, namely by employing formulas pertaining to a formal duel; (2) the emphasis on creating symmetrical space by making the two heroes stand in the middle accords with the cognitive aesthetics of reception, that is,

---

[120] The order of these two phases can vary slightly: in *Iliad* VI 119–122 and XX 158–160, 176–177, the two warriors are first presented standing in the middle of the two armies and then approach each other, whereas in XXIII 811–814 they first take their place on either side of the assembly, then come together in the middle space, and finally approach each other (816).

[121] See Grethlein 2006:63–84.

[122] The use of what Kirk 1962:164–166 has called *abbreviated* style epitomizes the heroes' grandeur and stature in pure epic terms.

[123] See Scodel 1992:76.

[124] See Higbie 1995:69–109, who argues for the existence, in modern oralist terms, of a "naming type-scene" in Homer.

[125] *Iliad* III 15; V 14, 630, 850; VI 121; XI 232; XIII 604; XVI 462; XX 176; XXI 148; XXII 248; XXIII 816.

the interrelation between literary imagery and audience imagination, and in particular with the human mind's tendency to create visual fields on the basis of analogy and symmetry.[126] In particular, by adopting a panoramic perspective, the external narrator encourages the audience to create on their own the space where the first part of the episode takes place. The phrase "now as these advancing came to one place and met" invites the audience to visualize the mutual approach from the side, as if standing outside and above. This map strategy (in Ryan's terminology) uses certain modes of perspective-taking (like the adverbial and verbal expressions denoting motion[127] and mutual approach[128]), and turns the initial zooming in of the narrator's lens on a particular spot on the battlefield to an *angling* of his narrative camera.

After the exchange of speeches by the two warriors, Diomedes—having realized that he is related to Glaukos—"drove his spear deep into the prospering earth" (*Iliad* VI 213 ἔγχος μὲν κατέπηξεν ἐπὶ χθονὶ πουλυβοτείρηι). The formula ἐπὶ χθονὶ πουλυβοτείρηι, which is attested (together with its allomorphs) fourteen times in the *Iliad*, evokes the brief postponement of military activity through traditional referentiality:[129] in *Iliad* III 89–91, Hektor repeats the gist of Paris' previous speech (68–70) and urges both Greeks and Trojans to "lay aside on the bountiful earth their splendid armour / while he himself in the middle and warlike Menelaos / fight alone for the sake of Helen and all her possessions"; in III 195 Priam asks Helen, who is standing next to him on the walls of Troy, to identify the Achaean hero (Odysseus) whose armor "lies piled on the prospering earth…." In this light,[130] it may be plausibly argued that—this time—the narrator appropriates the formulaic diction attested in character speech, aiming at extending its functional use. He does not employ, as he did before, the technique of *contextual deroutinization* of formulaic material, but that of *intensification*: in the meeting between Diomedes and Glaukos, placing the weapons on the ground is a prelude to the heroes' ensuing disarmament (VI 235–236). The postponement of warfare has here become cancellation and annulment, as

---

[126] See Kosslyn and Koenig 1992.

[127] συνίτην and ἐπ' ἀλλήλοισι ἰόντες.

[128] ἐς μέσον and σχεδὸν ἦσαν.

[129] On traditional referentiality, see Foley 1991:24; Danek 2002; Tsagalis 2008b:188, 205.

[130] The use of the expression ἐν μέσωι by both Paris and Hektor shows that all three contexts (temporary postponement of military activity for the preparation of a very important duel, formal duels, and friendly encounters such as that between Diomedes and Glaukos) share the same formulaic diction, and more importantly that the first and the third have been shaped on the basis of the second. Since the formal duel is the default mode of close encounters in a military epic like the *Iliad*, it is possible that it has bestowed its diction on other scenes, which were shaped, in pure Parrian terms, according to the principle of *formulaic economy*.

the traditional referentiality of a formula has been pushed to its most extreme limits.

The mutual exchange of weapons builds on the standard Iliadic representation of the actual combat between warriors. When weapons (spears and arrows) are thrown by one warrior at another, what actually falls on the ground is the body of the defeated hero who thus meets his doom.[131] By driving his spear into the ground, Diomedes inverts the typical use of a weapon and reveals his friendly feelings towards Glaukos: when weapons are placed on the ground, then words become gentle and soothing (μειλιχίοισι), and the potential conflict turns into an amicable meeting. Seen from this angle, Diomedes' thrusting his spear into the ground may also look forward to Hektor's placing of his helmet, the symbol of his military might that terrifies baby Astuanax, on the ground in his meeting with Andromakhe on the walls (*Iliad* VI 473). The expression καὶ τὴν μὲν κατέθηκεν ἐπὶ χθονὶ παμφανόωσαν ("and laid it in all its shining upon the ground") reproduces the syntax of line 213: ἔγχος μὲν κατέπηξεν ἐπὶ χθονὶ πουλυβοτείρηι ("he drove his spear deep into the prospering earth"). The narrator's reference to the "prospering" earth (χθονὶ πουλυβοτείρηι) exploits the scene's formulaic military substratum, paving the way for the emotionally loaded meeting between Andromakhe and Hektor.

Given the rather fixed framework of such scenes, it is worth investigating how space is important for exploring the gradual shift of focus within the limited setting of this encounter. In the beginning of the episode, when the narrator described the two heroes moving forward and standing between the two armies, he adopted a lateral view,[132] that is, he viewed the two heroes from the side or an elevated point; conversely, when the heroes start speaking and are looking at each other, the position of the narrator (and of course the visual imagination of the listeners) becomes a face-to-face view, as if space shifted according to the focalization presented in each case.[133] This spatial reorganization of the scene according to continuous shifts of the narrator's eye is also reflected in some seemingly unimportant topographical hints, like Diomedes' stabbing his spear into the earth. Seen from the vantage point of the shift of space, the technique of *formulaic intensification* builds upon another mental strategy called the *tour*,[134] which "represents space dynamically from a perspective internal to the

---

[131] See the following remarks on the falling of the leaves on the ground (ἔραζε) as a compressed metonym for death.

[132] On laterality as one of many possible relationships between located and reference objects (or *figure* versus *ground* in theoretical terminology), see Herman 2002:274–277.

[133] This face-to-face visual imaging and mental organization of space is also at work in the meeting between Hektor and Andromakhe, especially when the Trojan hero places his shining helmet on the ground.

[134] On the distinction between *map* and *tour*, see de Certeau 1974:118–122.

territory to be surveyed."[135] This time, members of the audience would have placed themselves right behind the two heroes; they would have created visual images of them looking at each other face-to-face, and would have mentally seen through the eyes of Glaukos Diomedes driving his spear on the ground. This ever-changing presentation of story space indexes modes of perspective-taking that make full use both of the mental charts regularly employed by audiences and of traditional diction, the path to evoking and activating such charts within the medium of epic song.

Toward the end of the episode, the designation of simple story space acquires an unexpected trope: the two heroes dismount their horses, shake hands, and exchange oaths of friendship:

> ὣς ἄρα φωνήσαντε, καθ' ἵππων ἀΐξαντε
> χεῖράς τ' ἀλλήλων λαβέτην καὶ πιστώσαντο.
>
> So they spoke, and both springing down from behind their horses
> gripped each other's hands and exchanged the promise of friendship.
>
> *Iliad* VI 232–233

The use of the expression καθ' ἵππων ἀΐξαντε, which always refers to chariots,[136] has caused much trouble for Homeric scholars, since it is contrasted with the beginning of the entire scene, where Diomedes and Glaukos stand as foot-soldiers one against the other. One can speculate that the *Iliad* has shaped the end of this episode by conflating a typical scene of gift-exchange[137] and reconcil-

---

[135] Ryan 2003:218.

[136] "ἵππων: chariot horses and hence chariot" (Graziosi and Haubold 2010:143 on *Iliad* VI 232). Cf. *Iliad* XI 423; XVII 460; XX 401. Kirk 1990:190, on *Iliad* VI 232 notes: "That they were in chariots is not suggested by the introduction to their encounter in 119–121."

[137] The unequal exchange of gifts has generated considerable discussion among scholars: the scholia offer a variety of explanations, ranging from the removal of Glaukos' wits by Zeus to the suggestion that this outrageous imbalance was aimed at pleasing a Greek or pro-Greek audience; Aristotle (*Nicomachean Ethics* 1136b:9–14) thought that Diomedes is not unjust, while other ancient scholars (sch. A, μετατιθέασί τινες ἄλλοσε ταύτην τὴν σύστασιν) moved this scene elsewhere. Craig (1967:243–245) and Walcot (1969:12–13) suggest that Glaukos accepts the unequal exchange as the price for his life; Calder (1978:34–35) argues that the unequal exchange of gifts is a by-product of the poet's effort to interpret the episode of Diomedes and Glaukos with its many arcane points; Donlan (1989) suggests that Glaukos is expected to receive fewer gifts because he is a lesser warrior; Martin (1989:286–289), following Maftei (1976:52), believes that Diomedes has invented the ξενία element in this episode in order to win the "flyting" contest and manipulate the exchange of armor; Traill (1989:301–305) has suggested that Zeus tries to compensate Diomedes for his failure to win a great duel and kill a preeminent figure during his ἀριστεία in *Iliad* V; Kirk (1990:171) maintains that the odd end of the episode may have been the poet's intention, if he wanted to mark in a stark manner the transition to the Hektor episode that occupies the rest of *Iliad* VI; Parks (1990:77–79) argues that verbal duels often turn into guest-friendships,

iation between two warriors with one of fighting, in which the two adversaries would have dismounted their chariots to engage in close combat, as is highly likely given the military context of *Iliad* XI 423, XVII 460, and XX 401, where the same expression is used. After all, it is often the case that the borrowing of diction from one scene and its transfer to another is only partial and imperfect, resulting in thematic gaps.

One last type of transformed martial space pertains to the summoning of an assembly within the area of the battlefield, after martial activity has been temporarily suspended. The double meaning of the word ἀγορή 'assembly', which can be translated as both "gathering" and "place of gathering,"[138] testifies to the role of spatial features in the various denotations of this term. Space here operates on both the literal and the figurative level, as "assemblies" view social space as a metaphor for the temporary postponement of built-in antitheses between various individuals or groups of people within a given community.

The Trojans hold an assembly during a temporary halt before their great assault on the Achaean wall. This stationary location is designated by an extremely brief description:

> Τρώων αὖτ' ἀγορὴν ποιήσατο φαίδιμος Ἕκτωρ,
> νόσφι νεῶν ἀγαγών, ποταμῶι ἔπι δινήεντι,
> <u>ἐν καθαρῶι, ὅθι δὴ νεκύων διεφαίνετο χῶρος.</u>

> Now glorious Hektor held an assembly of all the Trojans,
> taking them aside from the ships, by a swirling river
> *on clean ground, where there showed a space not cumbered with corpses.*

> *Iliad* VIII 489–491

Homeric epic systematically employs discourse markers indicating visual shifts that help the audience mentally locate themselves with respect to the characters of the plot. By using αὖτ(ε), the narrator suggests to his listeners that they will now "see" with their minds' eye the Trojans whom they visualized before the action was briefly transferred to Olympos. This spatial orientation of the audience is based on the metanarrative aspect of the particle αὖτ(ε), since it amounts to a covert way of enhancing the role of the omnipotent narrator who has total control over the different parts of his song.[139] Once the shift from

---

as is the case in *Beowulf*, when the hero meets with the Danish coast guard; Scodel (1992:76) accentuates the strangeness of the whole episode and argues that "Zeus here acts, without clear motive, on the mind of a character who has, exceptionally and perhaps uniquely, no previous inclination at all to act as Zeus causes him to act."

[138] Cf. LSJ s.v. ἀγορά I and II.

[139] See Bonifazi 2008:50.

Olympos to the plain of Troy is complete, the narrator informs his audience about the new "setting" of the Trojans, whom Hektor has led away from the ships, next to "a swirling river." The spatial coordinates of this place are problematic, for if the river is identified with Skamandros,[140] then the Trojan army must be visualized as being at a considerable distance from the ships (*Iliad* VIII 490 νόσφι νεῶν), and not close to them (IX 76 ἐγγύθι νηῶν, IX 232 ἐγγὺς γὰρ νηῶν καὶ τείχεος). Although topographical discrepancies of this sort can be easily explained away by resorting to general features of oral performance, such as a certain degree of inconsistency with respect to geographical details, this kind of explanation would do little justice to the complexity of visualizing epic space. Apart from the fact that IX 76 and IX 232 echo the focalization of the Achaeans (Nestor and Odysseus respectively), who have every reason to stress the danger posed by the Trojans' approach to the Greek camp, and should not be interpreted at face value, the narrator takes pains to anchor in his listeners' minds the mental image of an area of the battlefield devoid of dead bodies. The adverb ὅθι, accompanied by δή, is called a "marker of evidentiality." In the words of Bakker,

> The *dé* clause, being directed to an addressee, signals that the speaker assumes that the hearer is capable of witnessing the same evidence, and in uttering the *dé* clause the speaker wants to convey that the addressee shares the same evident environment. [141]

By creating the conditions for a "shared vision" between himself and his audience,[142] the narrator offers his listeners a vivid image of a place without slain warriors. The rare use of χῶρος, which testifies to the importance given to the spatial aspect of the assembly scene that is about to begin, as well as the emphatic ἐν καθαρῶι, help the audience view the area where the assembly is held not so much in terms of a geographical location but rather of a nonmartial space. It is as if the performer of the song encourages his listeners to clear their minds of the larger space of the battlefield covered by corpses of warriors, and visualize it again as a new thematized space, where there is a place for an exchange of opinions, and room for an assembly.

In *Iliad* X 194–203, it is time for the Achaeans to hold an assembly. Oddly enough, the assembly takes place "in the open" and not in the Achaean camp:

ὣς εἰπὼν τάφροιο διέσσυτο· τοὶ δ' ἅμ' ἕποντο
Ἀργείων βασιλῆες, ὅσοι κεκλήατο βουλήν.

---

[140] Narratively identified, not historically.
[141] Bakker 1997:75.
[142] See Bakker 1997:76.

τοῖς δ' ἅμα Μηριόνης καὶ Νέστορος ἀγλαὸς υἱός
ἤϊσαν· αὐτοὶ γὰρ κάλεον συμμητιάασθαι.
τάφρον δ' ἐκδιαβάντες ὀρυκτὴν ἑδριόωντο
ἐν καθαρῷ, ὅθι δὴ νεκύων διεφαίνετο χῶρος
πιπτόντων, ὅθεν αὖτις ἀπετράπετ' ὄβριμος Ἕκτωρ
ὀλλὺς Ἀργείους, ὅτε δὴ περὶ νὺξ ἐκάλυψεν.
ἔνθα καθεζόμενοι ἔπε' ἀλλήλοισι πίφαυσκον.
τοῖσι δὲ μύθων ἦρχε Γερήνιος ἱππότα Νέστωρ·

So he spoke, and strode on through the ditch, and there followed
    with him
the kings of the Argives, all who had been called into conclave,
and with them went Meriones and Nestor's glorious
son, since the kings themselves called these to take counsel with
    them.
After they had crossed the deep-dug ditch they settled
on clean ground, where there showed a space not cumbered with corpses
of the fallen, *a place whence Hektor the huge had turned back*
from destroying the Argives, after the night had darkened about him.
There they seated themselves, and opened words to each other,
and the Gerenian horseman Nestor began speaking among them ...

Iliad X 194–203

The place where the assembly takes place has troubled scholars. Why should the Achaeans hold a meeting outside the ditch? The storyteller aims to create a bridge between this assembly, the equivalent Trojan one in VIII 489–491, and Hektor's overwhelming presence on the battlefield. This plan is effectively carried out (1) by the reiteration of similar language that visually designates the assembly area as the one from which Hektor withdrew after killing many Achaeans,[143] and (2) by the pragmatic function of αὖτις, which is not only propositional but also a discourse adverb cueing the audience both to a locus already mentioned by the poet, and also to the *hic et nunc* of the performance. It is as if the performer, in his aim to mark a "performative peak in the narration,"[144] evokes a parallel action or event in the memory of his audience, as if he were telling them: "The Achaeans are holding their assembly out of the ditch, in a place clear of dead bodies, from which Hektor withdrew, as *I told you before*."

---

[143] The deliberation that takes place in the ὅθεν clause in *Iliad* X 200 is a kind of explanation on the narrator's part of the Achaeans' apparently paradoxical decision to summon a meeting of their leaders outside the ditch. See also *Iliad* XXIII 60–61.

[144] Bonifazi 2008:57.

Drawing on Ryan's[145] route-like as opposed to map-like spatial models, Bonifazi has summarized the visual aspect and the procedural meaning of *au*-words, such as αὖ, αὖτε, αὖτις, αὖθις, and αὐτοῦ in the following way:

> The procedural meaning of the ancient Greek words considered here rests primarily on the visual discontinuities existing between different sections of the epic narration. In particular, they work as "road-signs" of the discourse, prompting specific cognitive activities related to visual imagery: shifting between different kinds of shots (long shots, mid shots, and close-ups), shifting between less and more detailed depictions (zooming in), and shifting between ordinary moments and special instants of the narration (flashes). By means of these markers the mind's eye of the performer and of the audience, who both re-see the mythical events, is helped in visualizing the next focus of the visual field.[146]

As these astute remarks suggest, the audience visualizes the area where the Achaean assembly takes place by reactivating in their minds' eye the image they created when they visualized Hektor's slaughter of the Achaeans before the nightfall.[147] Given that the pragmatic function of αὖτις reenacts not only a previous event but also a recent moment of the performance,[148] the listeners, transformed into spectators, "see" the Achaeans reclaiming the space held by Hektor and the Trojans. In other words, the storyteller uses space to create a thematic link between two distinct scenes, and at the same time bridges two separate performance instances. The twofold meaning of the word "assembly" is fully exploited: the gathering of the Achaean leaders and the place where this gathering takes place, which constitutes an intermediate space claimed by both sides, are parallel to the metaphorical coming together of storyteller and audience at the very point where the earlier and the more recent visualizations are mentally evoked. Seen from this angle, most of the diction employed in *Iliad* X 194–203 works also on the level of the discourse. Like Nestor, the heroic archetype of the wise hero of a distant past, the storyteller rushes (διέσσυτο)[149] to an

---

[145] Ryan 2003.

[146] Bonifazi 2008:59–60.

[147] The repetition of the phrase ἐν καθαρῷ, ὅθι δὴ νεκύων διεφαίνετο χῶρος (*Iliad* VIII 491 = X 199), which is attested *only* in these two passages, and the explicit reference to Hektor's turning back to this place after "destroying the Argives, after the night had darkened about him" (X 200–201) are clear indications of this internal cross-reference.

[148] On reenactment, see Martin 1989:12–37 and 231–239; Nagy 2004:27.

[149] The use of διέσσυτο (τάφρου) is important, since as in the case of Andromache in *Iliad* XXII 460 (μεγάροιο διέσσυτο), it indicates a transition from familiar to unknown space, or to somebody else's space.

uncharted area (τάφροιο, τάφρον ἐκδιαβάντες), outside the limits of the well-described Achaean camp; he is mentally followed by his audience (τοὶ δ' ἕποντο) with whom he will share his thoughts (συμμητιάασθαι); they will mentally move into an unfamiliar, clear space (ἐν καθαρῶι), away from the previous narration of the battlefield killings, and there they will communicate while refraining from other action (ἔνθα καθεζόμενοι ἔπε' ἀλλήλοισι πίφαυσκον). This reading conceives the flow of Homeric narration as "cinema in the mind," a process where story and discourse do not represent separate registers of action but share a symbiotic relationship. In the dynamic universe of oral performance, the delineation of space for the agents of the plot is inseparable from the designation of mental space for the audience. The storyteller invites his listeners to visualize the space where the assembly takes place in performative terms, by allowing the image of a previous visualization to re-emerge in their minds. Following the pragmatic "stop sign" of αὖθις, the world of the story and that of the discourse come closer, as the listeners become spectators who mentally transfer themselves over the ditch into an uncharted area, and, suspending their previous visualization of the action, are ready to listen to the storyteller, just as the Achaean leaders refrain from fighting and listen to wise Nestor.

Locus-images

The Iliadic battlefield contains a series of locus-images, which help the narrator "construct a narrative on the run ... [and] pin the narrative content down locally on the Homeric plain of Troy."[150] Locus-images not only allow the bard to find his way while performing his song,[151] but he can also link them to specific narrative situations. They are a form of mental tag,[152] creating and then systematically evoking associations that the performer does not need to spell out again. These locus-images perform a double task: first, they mark narrative space in

---

[150] See Thornton 1984:368. I have not included in the following discussion the "tomb of Aisuetes" (*Iliad* II 793), for it is not thematically exploited by the storyteller. According to Brügger et al. (2003:258), it is uncertain whether this Aisuetes is the same as the father of Alkathoös, who is killed by Idomeneus in XIII 427–444. Further interpretive considerations can only be grounded on an identification of the two. On the other hand, it is interesting that Polites, whom the Trojans station on Aisuetes' tomb to watch the Greek army (II 791–794), features again in the episode of Idomeneus fighting Aineias in *Iliad* XIII, which immediately follows the killing of Alkathoös, Aisuetes' son. When Aineias' spear misses his target and hits Askalaphos, Deiphobos and Meriones engage in close fighting over his body. Meriones then wounds Deiphobos, who is saved by Polites (XIII 518–539). On the conflation of material belonging to different mythical cycles with respect to Alkathoös, see Janko 1992:100–101 on *Iliad* XIII 427–433.

[151] See Massumi 2002:180: "The way we orient is more like a tropism (tendency plus habit) than a cognition (visual forms plus configuration)."

[152] See Ferguson and Hegarty 1994, who speak about "anchors," i.e. landmarks serving as points of reference for the location of other items; see also Ryan 2003:223.

specific ways and are closely intertwined with the unfolding of the Iliadic plot; second, they constitute lasting markers that function as memory cues[153] to a reality standing beyond the limits of the poem and having a strong metonymic power.[154]

Protection and danger: The oak tree of Zeus and the fig tree

In the large, blank landscape of the *Iliad*'s background setting, listeners come across several landmarks, scattered at random here and there. Audiences are encouraged to visualize the Trojan plain as a flat area, devoid of almost any form of elevation, where background markers appear only when useful to the plot.[155]

One such spot is the oak tree (φηγός), which is attested seven times in the *Iliad*.[156] In V 693–695, after the wounded Sarpedon has begged Hektor not to let him die on the plain, the Trojan hero pushes back the Achaeans and thus allows Sarpedon's comrades to carry him under the oak tree and remove the spear from his thigh. In VII 22, Apollo and Athena meet next to the oak tree (ἀλλήλοισι δὲ τώ γε συναντέσθην παρὰ φηγῶι), where he convinces her that a duel should be organized between Hektor and one of the Achaean leaders. In VII 59–60, the two gods, having taken the form of vultures (59 ἑζέσθην, ὄρνισιν ἐοικότες αἰγυπιοῖσιν), sit on the tall oak tree of father Zeus who bears the aegis (60 φηγῶι ἔφ' ὑψηλῆι πατρὸς Διὸς αἰγιόχοιο) and watch with pleasure the preparations for the duel (ἀνδράσι τερπόμενοι). In IX 354, Achilles tells Odysseus, Phoinix, and Ajax that as long as he was fighting, Hektor would not dare step beyond the Skaian Gates and the oak tree. In XI 170, the Trojans find safety when they reach the oak tree, which Agamemnon will never reach, as he is wounded and forced to retreat (XI 251–274).[157] In XXI 549, Apollo prevents Achilles from sacking Troy by placing Agenor in his way, while he himself "leaned there on an oak tree with close mist huddled about him" (φηγῶι κεκλιμένος· κεκάλυπτο δ' ἄρ' ἠέρι πολλῆι). This crucial delay gives the Trojans time to retreat inside the city.

Hence the oak tree "stands ... by the Scaean Gate, that is close to the Trojan walls, and is associated with safety for the Trojan troops, but also with a

---

[153] See Scodel 2002; and cf. Massumi 2002:179: "Landmarks I remembered. Sporadically. Rising to the light from rhythms of movement, as from an unseen ground of orientation, in flux."

[154] On the traditional referentiality of signs, see Foley 1997; 1999a:25–34; 1999b:11–13. On the semiotics of σῆμα in Homeric and Hesiodic poetry, see Nagy 1990a:202–222.

[155] See Andersson 1976:23–24.

[156] As West 1998:190 on *Iliad* VI 237 (Ἕκτωρ δ' ὡς Σκαιάς τε πύλας καὶ πύργον ἵκανεν) has suggested, πύργον (not φηγός) is the correct reading, since the oak tree is outside the gates, whereas the women are inside. φηγόν has replaced the correct reading πύργον under the influence of the formula Σκαιάς τε πύλας καὶ φηγὸν ἵκανεν/-οντο (*Iliad* IX 354 and XI 170 respectively).

[157] *Iliad* XVI 767 is of no importance to this study, since that simile mentions not the oak tree of the Trojan plain but any oak tree.

foreboding of death for Hector."[158] This is all certainly true, but there is more to it. We need to look into its metonymic force as a sign, and then decode its function not only within the plot, from a literary point of view, but also as emanating from and associated with a reality that transcends the borders of the Iliadic epic. Such an approach can be better understood if we ask, for example: Why is the oak tree specifically connected with the Trojans, why does it symbolize protection, and why does it have a special foreboding for Hektor?

In Indo-European myth, the oak is closely connected with the god of thunder. *Perkúnas* in the Lithuanian tradition, *Pērkons* in Latvian, *Perún* in Slavonic (Old Russian *Perunŭ*, Belorussian *Piarun*, Slovak *Parom*), all strike with their fire oak trees, which are sacred to them and are called "Perun's oak."[159] In Greek tradition, where the Indo-European thunder-god appeared as the supreme sky-god Zeus, the oak tree acquired a close association with him as well. In West's words,

> Perkunas' and Perun's special relationship with the oak tree is not foreign to Zeus. His holy oak at Dodona was famous from Homer on (*Od.* 14.327 f. = 19.296 f.), and he had another at Troy (*Il.* 5.695, 7.60). His partiality for oaks is implied by a joke in Aristophanes (*Av.* 480, cf. schol.; Eust. in Hom. 594.35). His habit of striking them with lightning is noted (*Il.* 14.414, Ar. *Nub.* 402, Luc. *Dial.* 20.16).[160]

After Aiakos, Apollo, and Poseidon had completed the walls of Troy, three series of stones started falling down. Two of them fell from the part of the wall built by Apollo and Poseidon, while the third collapsed from the side built by Aiakos and rolled inside the city. This was interpreted as a sign that this particular part of the walls of Troy would be vulnerable to an attack from the first and fourth descendants of Aiakos.[161] Troy was indeed attacked by the descendants of Aiakos, the Aiakidai (Achilles being Aiakos' grandson).[162] Aiakos is closely connected both with the oak tree, for he repopulated desolate Aegina by asking Zeus to turn the ants on the sacred oak tree into men (thus creating Achilles' famous warriors the Myrmidons),[163] and with stones, which were used to build the walls of Troy. Stones or rocks and oak may seem an odd combination, but in fact they are both related to the god of the thunderbolt, to whom they are

---

[158] Thornton 1984:358–359. Minchin (2008a:25) argues that both the fig tree and the oak tree become emblems of Troy and promise safety within its walls.

[159] See West 2007:238–242.

[160] West 2007:248.

[161] On this myth, see Pindar *Olympian* 8.30–46.

[162] Ajax's father Telamon is not known to Homer as one of the sons of Aiakos and the brother of Peleus. See Toepffer s.v. "Aiakos," RE 1.1:923–926.

[163] See Ovid *Metamorphoses* 7.520–567.

sacred.[164] Nagy has shown that Hittite *peruna-* 'rock' is cognate with Slavic *perunŭ* '[god of] the thunderbolt', in the same way that Latin *quercus* 'oak' is connected with Baltic (Lithuanian) *perkū́nas*.[165] Given this mythological context on the one hand, and on the other the strong Indo-European link between the oak, rocks, and the god of the thunderbolt,[166] who in Greek tradition was assimilated to the sky-god Zeus, we can form the following tentative hypothesis: the function of the oak tree, which in its most traditional (formulaic) attestation is connected to the Skaian Gates (Σκαιάς τε πύλας καὶ φηγὸν ἵκανεν/-οντο), represents a Hellenized version of the power inherent in the sacred tree of Zeus. The oak tree offers safety to the Trojans because it stands for an inviolable place protected by Zeus.[167] On the other hand it symbolizes danger for Hektor, by being associated through Aiakos, who took part in the building of the city's famous walls and from whose side of the walls the stones collapsed, with his descendant Achilles, who is destined to kill the preeminent Trojan hero Hektor. In other words, the oak and the stones offer protection to the Trojans, but also allude to the future death of Hektor, just as Aiakos' mythological contexts link him with both building the walls of Troy and being a future menace to it, through the Myrmidons and especially his grandson Achilles. The antithetical, twofold function of the oak and the stones reflects the equally antithetical double association of Aiakos with Troy.

In this light, the oak tree standing close to the Skaian Gates has preserved in the Homeric tradition something that we can see more clearly through the cognate Indo-European tradition of the Celts. In Celtic mythology the oak tree is *the tree of doors*, believed to be a gateway between worlds, or a place where portals could be erected. The oak is a figurative threshold, a symbolic gateway on whose two sides Zeus' power becomes alternately protective and destructive. Seen from this angle, it is tempting to suggest that its formulaic symbiosis in the Skaian Gates reflects a latent feature of its mythological background, which bespeaks its function as *transitory space*.

The fig tree (ἐρινεός) is mentioned three times in the *Iliad*: In VI 433–439, Andromakhe's unexpected military advice to Hektor concerns a weak spot on the walls next to the fig tree.[168] In XI 166–168, the retreating Trojans hasten

---

[164] Nagy 1990a:190.

[165] 1990a:185–190. He also discusses the meaning and function of the Greek proverbial phrase "from the oak and the rock," which he connects with the relation between thunder and the creation of humankind.

[166] See Chadwick 1900.

[167] See Chadwick 1900:41.

[168] λαὸν δὲ στῆσον παρ' ἐρινεόν, ἔνθα μάλιστα / ἀμβατός ἐστι πόλις καὶ ἐπίδρομον ἔπλετο τεῖχος. / τρὶς γὰρ τῇ γ' ἐλθόντες ἐπειρήσανθ' οἱ ἄριστοι / ἀμφ' Αἴαντε δύω καὶ ἀγακλυτὸν Ἰδομενῆα / ἠδ' ἀμφ' Ἀτρείδας καὶ Τυδέος ἄλκιμον υἱόν· / ἤ πού τίς σφιν ἔνισπε θεοπροπίων εὖ εἰδώς, / ἤ νυ καὶ

by the fig tree after passing the σῆμα of Ilos, son of Dardanos;[169] and in XXII 145–148, during Achilles' pursuit of Hektor, the two heroes go past the lookout places and the "windy fig tree."[170] In all these passages, the fig tree is presented not on its own as a single spot but in association with an imminent danger for the Trojans (VI 433–434; XI 166–168; XXII 145 [σκοπιήν]). [171]

In coming to grips with the function of locus-images, we must realize that space becomes epitomized in (in cinematic terms "is zipped into") a landmark feature of the setting through association with and evocation of collectively shared cultural experience. Within the medium of traditional oral song, myth is by definition a strong means of transforming landscape markers, such as the oak and fig trees, into signs. Spatial contiguity is of vital importance for comprehending this transformation process: when the oak and the wild fig tree are mentioned, they trigger in the bard's mind an association with another mental image (of the Trojan walls, the grave of Ilos, etc.), and form a mental pair or visual chain. These pairs include a marked and an unmarked element, the former being pulled to its new function by the latter. The unmarked element that is closely associated with the past of Troy "absorbs" the marked one and anchors it to a new meaning. Thus the Skaian Gates are the unmarked element, "pulling" the oak tree into their own interpretive and functional orbit. The oak and fig trees are signs of the past, which on the surface structure of the Iliadic epic appear as setting markers. They are not described or glossed by the narrator, but are tagged to other landscape pointers. This associative topography, where something is not described per se but is linked to something else, testifies to a process of mnemonic encoding based on nodes of mental vistas, which the oral tradition has shaped into culturally charged signs or pairs of signs.

Associations have long been known as a typical means of memory organization. In oral traditions, pairings of ideas or words are commonplace, the

---

αὐτῶν θυμὸς ἐποτρύνει καὶ ἀνώγει ("'... but draw your people up by the fig tree, there where the city / is openest to attack, and where the wall may be mounted. / Three times their bravest came that way, and fought there to storm it /about the two Aiantes and renowned Idomeneus, / about the two Atreidai and the fighting son of Tydeus. / Either some man well skilled in prophetic arts had spoken, / or the very spirit within themselves had stirred them to the onslaught'").

[169] οἳ δὲ παρ' Ἴλου σῆμα παλαιοῦ Δαρδανίδαο / μέσσον κὰπ πεδίον παρ' ἐρινεὸν ἐσσεύοντο / ἱέμενοι πόλιος ("The Trojans swept in their flight past the barrow of ancient Ilos / Dardanos' son, to the centre of the level ground and the fig tree, / as they made for the city").

[170] οἳ δὲ παρὰ σκοπιὴν καὶ ἐρινεὸν ἠνεμόεντα / τείχεος αἰὲν ὕπεκ κατ' ἀμαξιτὸν ἐσσεύοντο. / κρουνὼ δ' ἵκανον καλλιρρόω· ἔνθα δὲ πηγαί / δοιαὶ ἀναΐσσουσι Σκαμάνδρου δινήεντος ("They raced along by the watching point and the windy fig tree / always away from under the wall and along the wagon-way / and came to the two sweet-running well springs. There there are double / springs of water that jet up, the springs of whirling Skamandros").

[171] Iliad XXI 37 is a different case altogether, since it refers to another fig tree from which Lukaon was cutting boughs when abducted by Achilles.

more so since they constitute mechanisms used to generate traditional mean-ings.[172] This item-to-item cueing has been discussed either as operating serially or, recently, as working in large networks of associations. In South Slavic epic, which offers the greatest amount of comparable data, nodes are activated on three different scales: (1) the positive or excitatory one, in which both members of the associative pair are either present or absent in the majority of perfor-mances; (2) the neutral level, where both members of the associative pair are either present or absent in half the number of tellings of a song; and (3) the negative or inhibitory level, where both nodes are present or absent in less than half of performances.[173] With this schema in mind, it is possible to argue that the associative pairings including the oak or fig tree on the one hand and another landscape spot on the other display the following fluctuation in scale: (1) they appear most often in association with the walls; (2) they are also connected, though less often, with the fate of an individual, mainly Trojan, hero; (3) they are associated with the meeting place of two gods (Apollo and Athena). In this light, it becomes plausible that the pair "trees-Trojan walls" represents the deep structure or nucleus of an associative link, and that the replacement of the walls by individual heroes results from the thematic contiguity of Trojan walls and Trojan heroes. What we see at work here is an effective mnemonic mechanism based on association, operating within the constraints imposed upon it by the strict rules of oral song. In such a traditional medium, space is organized in order to ensure, enhance, and ease memorability, and in doing so it generates meaning by effectively anchoring the secondary item of the associative pair within the semantic realm of the primary item.

The river and the ford of Skamandros

Cognitive psychology has time and again emphasized the importance of visual imagery as one of the strongest and most widely employed factors enhancing memory. Paivio has argued that the effectiveness of imagery in memory recall is felt mainly in three domains: (1) the preference for concrete versus abstract, (2) the predilection for parallel and spatial versus sequential, and (3) fondness for dynamic versus static processing.[174] Oral traditions constitute complex sets of multiple constraints that limit the infinite possibilities for presenting their material. These constraints are partly, and primarily, systemic, that is, they are imposed by the very system of oral composition and are almost built in. Constraints are of various sorts and have their own sets of rules, which

---

[172] F. Andersen 1985; Foley 1991, 1992; Rubin 1995:31.
[173] See Rubin 1995:33.
[174] Paivio 1971, 1986. See also Yates 1966; Rubin 1995:11.

are conditioned by different neurophysical factors of the human brain. They operate with such force and precision and are so intricately interwoven into the very system of oral storytelling that they are able to create levels of stability and fixation that would otherwise have been unthinkable.[175]

The preference for concreteness instead of abstract concepts is seen in the case of the ford of Skamandros, which constitutes a "tangible" and "solid" location that triggers narrative development and eases mnemonic recall. Moreover, the formulaic fixity of the way the ford is mentioned (*Iliad* XIV 433–434 = XXI 1–2 ἀλλ' ὅτε δὴ πόρον ἷξον ἐϋρρεῖος ποταμοῖο / Ξάνθου δινήεντος, ὃν ἀθάνατος τέκετο Ζεύς)[176] indicates the importance of dynamic versus static processing of mnemonic data. In particular, the pair "location-movement" (πόρον ἷξον) lies at the heart of spatial imagery: it sets a boundary, which is expressed by the cluster ἀλλ' ὅτε δή, and introduces an antithesis with what happened before. The narrative *incipit* of the episode is thus "prefaced by the movement of the characters into position. Only when he has carefully positioned everyone does the poet commence his narration of the episode."[177] In fact, the cluster ἀλλ' ὅτε δή functions as a mental stop, indicating that the narrator has reached a point where he wants to change narrative direction. The individual concrete location he mentions immediately allows him to pass on to a new scene, once he has placed all characters on his mind's visual map. The ford of Skamandros is a concrete location that evokes new cues, a spatial image that shapes a sequential verbal and thematic output.[178]

On another level, locations pin down specific associations developed around abstract concepts, which are tied to images subsequently organized "in coherent, easy-to-recall sequences of narrative."[179] Let us briefly survey all the relevant passages.

---

[175] See Oesterreicher 1997.

[176] "But when they came to the crossing place of the fair-running river, / of whirling Xanthos, whose father was Zeus the immortal ..." The phrase ἀλλ' ὅτε δή, which is employed with respect to the ford of Skamandros, signals the completion of a particular action and the subsequent shift in the content of the narrative. The adversative force of ἀλλ'(ά) is here felt on the level of the discourse, since the storyteller *sees* the events he describes as a process that has to be segmented in his mind so that it can be readily recalled. The use of an adversative particle tied to a temporal conjunction (ὅτε) and followed by a marker of evidentiality, suggesting a "joint seeing" by narrator and audience (δή), shows that the need to remember by pointing to specific spatial locations (the ford of Skamandros) configures the need to tell, and telling requires, unavoidably, a temporal sequence (change of action). See Bakker 1997:74–80; on space-time and memory, see also Calame 2006:40–42.

[177] Minchin 2008a:18–19.

[178] See Rubin 1995:63.

[179] Rubin 1995:61.

In *Iliad* XIV 433–439, Hektor, who has been wounded and carried out of battle in a chariot, reaches the ford of Skamandros, where his companions help him recover.[180] In *Iliad* XXI 26–33, Achilles captures twelve young Trojans at the ford, whom he carries to the Achaean camp and later decapitates before Patroklos' funeral. Achilles also kills the Trojan Lukaon in the same place, and throws his corpse into the water (XXI 34–135). In XXIV 349–351, Priam and Idaios meet Hermes by this ford on their way to Achilles' hut. And in XXIV 692–694, Hermes departs for Olympos and leaves Priam and Idaios alone to bring Hektor's corpse back to Troy.

In the light of these passages, it becomes clear that the ford of Skamandros has acquired an almost metonymic function within the Iliadic narrative. Its easy-to-recall concrete location allows the narrator to anchor to it different manifestations of the same abstract idea, namely that of danger for the Trojans. According to this argument, the mnemonic function of visual imagery that enhanced spatial memory through specific locations on the Trojan plain was followed, during the period of shaping of the Homeric tradition, by metonymic referentiality: abstract ideas, which were shaped into concrete action, were tied to concrete locations.[181] Through the system of oral song-making, therefore, associative recall acquired a metonymic aspect[182] that allowed the bards to turn

---

[180] Rivers were considered the source of regenerative powers; see Onians 1951:230; Thornton 1984:152–153. Hektor named his son Skamandrios (*Iliad* VI 402), while the rest of the Trojans called him Astuanax. In later tradition about the fate of Troy after the Trojan War (Hellanicus of Lesbos FGH 4 F31, according to Dionysius of Halicarnassus *Roman Antiquities* 1.47.5–6), it was under this name, and not that of Astuanax, that he and the other descendants of Hektor approached Askanios after being released by Neoptolemos, who had taken them captive to Greece, and were subsequently restored to their old Trojan kingdom. For a full treatment of the various traditions concerning the foundation and refoundation of certain cities in the Troad by the descendants of Hektor and Aineias, see Aloni 1986:22–23; Erskine 2001:102–108; Nagy 2009c: part II, §§168–180.

[181] See also Hellwig 1964:35–36, who draws attention to the fact that the poet refers in passing to certain factual appearances ("faktische Aussehen"), like the banks of the river (*Iliad* XXI 10 ὄχθαι), tamarisks (XXI 18 μυρίκῃσιν), eels and fish (XXI 203 ἐγχέλυές τε καὶ ἰχθύες), and an elm (XXI 242 πτελέην), in his attempt to present his listeners with an indirect description of the ford of Skamandros. In fact, this is a typical mnemonic strategy of building up fixed visual imagery, by adding various details in the process of the performance.

[182] On how concrete σήματα or signals allude to a metonymic reality within the system of oral song-making, see Nagy 1990a:202–222; consider also the remarks of Foley: "Those phenomena and objects named as *sēmata* of course have a special force: in these cases traditional referentiality is not simply realized but explicitly stipulated with what I take as a term in the native Homeric poetics. But we should also remember that metonymic projection, the part standing for the whole, is a quality of the idiom or register at large, and that far the greater number of its occurrences are unmarked by the term *sēma*. Thus the noun-epithet formulas and myriad other aspects of phraseology, the typical scenes, and the story-patterns all participate in the driving reception: in addition to their nominal surfaces, they are responsible for providing access to an extrasituational, extratextual, and finally untextualizable context" (1997:81).

the river and the ford of Skamandros from a static spot into a dynamic, evolving area, cueing the content of the episode at whose beginning it stands.[183]

Timemarks: The tombstone of Ilos and the tomb of Myrine

The narrator and the characters of the plot in the *Iliad* often use tombs as points of orientation.[184] These landmarks help the poet space the past and translate it into his authoritative spatial idiolect, that is, into concrete and hero-oriented signposts pinned down on the Trojan plain. Chapman has used the term *time-marks* to describe the transformation of place into space by recourse to socially and emotionally charged experience.[185] In his groundbreaking study of the creation of collective memory and the process of social shaping of the past,[186] Zerubavel has used the term *time maps*, which like Chapman's concept is based on the combination of temporal and spatial vocabulary. In the case of the tombstone of Ilos, an ancestor of Priam who evokes the Trojan past, time and space are fused into a specific location on the battlefield, a landmark that maps out the mythical prehistory of Troy. Zerubavel has also emphasized the importance of what we may call "the same place" process, or cultural bridging.[187] Constancy of place facilitates sameness and continuity, since it allows both individuals and communities to construct chronological continua, establishing connections between noncontiguous points in history. Unconnected aspects of history, or in our case of myth, are thus presented first as sharing some sort of link and later as forming part of a continuous, diachronic sequence, almost travelling in time. By cultivating the idea of permanence, individuals and communities alike (not to mention modern states) have thus been able to enhance whole sets of ideological tenets with respect to continuity, permanence, and—almost unavoidably—a feeling of nostalgia. Longing for the past is often interpreted within the premises of a historical or mythical continuum that has been interrupted by some violent change.[188] This last observation is fundamental to the function of timemarks in the *Iliad*.

The tombstone of Ilos, the grandfather of Priam,[189] is understandably associated with the Trojans. In *Iliad* X 415–416, Hektor holds a council next to it, away from the din of the battle (θείου παρὰ σήματι Ἴλου, / νόσφιν ἀπὸ

---

[183] See also Minchin 2008a:26–28.

[184] See Grethlein 2008.

[185] Chapman 1997:43.

[186] Zerubavel 2003.

[187] Zerubavel 2003:40–43.

[188] The same is true of the washing-places (*Iliad* XXII 153–156), which constitute a timemark in the sense that they evoke a feeling of nostalgia for the past, "before the coming of the sons of the Achaians" (XXII 156 τὸ πρὶν ἐπ' εἰρήνης, πρὶν ἐλθεῖν υἶας Ἀχαιῶν).

[189] See *Iliad* XX 236–237.

φλοίσβου).[190] In XI 166–168, the retreating Trojan troops rush past the monument (οἳ δὲ παρ' Ἴλου σῆμα παλαιοῦ Δαρδανίδαο, / μέσσον κὰπ πεδίον παρ' ἐρινεὸν ἐσσεύοντο / ἱέμενοι πόλιος), whereas in XI 371–372, Paris shoots an arrow and wounds Diomedes as he leans against a column on the gravestone of Ilos (στήλῃ κεκλιμένος ἀνδροκμήτῳ ἐπὶ τύμβῳ / Ἴλου Δαρδανίδαο παλαιοῦ δημογέροντος). Last, in XXIV 349–351, Priam and Idaios drive past the tombstone of Ilos and water their mules and horses in the river Skamandros (οἳ δ' ἐπεὶ οὖν μέγα σῆμα πάρεξ Ἴλοιο ἔλασσαν, / στῆσαν ἄρ' ἡμιόνους τε καὶ ἵππους, / ὄφρα πίοιεν, / ἐν ποταμῷ) before the appearance of Hermes, who is going to lead them safely past the Achaean guards to the hut of Achilles.[191] The narrative function of the tombstone of Ilos is not apparent, and scholars have expressed divergent points of view.[192] It seems clear, though, that what really matters in this case is that "the narrator uses the tomb to set the present action against the backdrop of the past."[193]

In all these passages, either Ilos or his tombstone is modified by an epithet (θείου 'divine', παλαιοῦ 'ancient', μέγα 'great'), while Ilos is twice accompanied by his patronymic (Δαρδανίδαο) and once by a reference to his identity (δημογέροντος). These features belong to a coherent and systematic buildup of authority. Ilos and his σῆμα are presented as a source of power stemming from the past; they are the visible signs of Troy as past, reminding the audience of the antiquity and power of this city and, by inference, of its tragic present situation.[194] Ilos' patronymic traces the city's history back to Dardanos, the founder of Troy, and reminds listeners that the name "Dardanians" (Δάρδανοι) constantly employed for them in the *Iliad* points to permanence and continuity: this is the great city of Dardanos and Ilos, which is now under attack by the Achaeans. By making the very landscape of the battlefield testify to the antiquity and fame of Troy, the *Iliad* turns ancestors into a source of status and legitimacy, a "sacred thread linking past and present."[195]

---

[190] The fact that assemblies are held near tombs implicitly indicates the latter's authority and social status; on this point, see Grethlein 2008:28–29. On tombs in Homer, see F. Pfister 1909:541–543; Mannsperger and Mannsperger 2002.

[191] See Thornton 1984:152–153.

[192] Griffin (1980:23) maintains that there is a contrast between the grave and the battle, whereas Thornton (1984:154) regards the grave of Ilos as a symbol of power for the Trojans. It is difficult to decide between these two alternatives, the more so since, as Grethlein notes, "while the transmitted text of scholion T ad *Il.* 11.372 prefigures Thornton's interpretation, Erbse's conjecture of ἀν‹τ›άξιον for ἀντάξιον suggests Griffin's reading: ἐπὶ δὲ τῷ μνήματι τοῦ παλαιοῦ προγόνου ἐστι, μηδὲν ἀν‹τ›άξιον ποιῶν" (2008:29n24).

[193] Grethlein 2008:29.

[194] On the double function of σῆμα as 'sign' and 'tomb', see Niemeyer 1996:12–18. Cf. also Nagy 1990a:202–203. On the *Odyssey*, see especially Purves 2006a.

[195] Hale 1998:124.

Seen from this perspective, Ilos' tombstone also implies a social punctuation of Troy's past that is worth considering. In *Iliad* XX 199–241, Aineias presents Achilles with his entire pedigree, which goes back to the founding of Troy:

τὸν δ' αὖτ' Αἰνείας ἀπαμείβετο φώνησέν τε·
"Πηλείδη, μὴ δή μ' ἐπέεσσί γε νηπύτιον ὥς
ἔλπεο δειδίξεσθαι, ἐπεὶ σάφα οἶδα καὶ αὐτός
ἠμὲν κερτομίας ἠδ' αἴσυλα μυθήσασθαι.
ἴδμεν δ' ἀλλήλων γενεήν, ἴδμεν δὲ τοκῆας,
πρόκλυτ' ἀκούοντες ἔπεα θνητῶν ἀνθρώπων·
ὄψει δ' οὔτ' ἄρ πω σὺ ἐμοὺς ἴδες οὔτ' ἄρ' ἐγὼ σούς.
φασὶ σὲ μὲν Πηλῆος ἀμύμονος ἔκγονον εἶναι
μητρὸς τ' ἐκ Θέτιδος καλλιπλοκάμου ἁλοσύδνης·
αὐτὰρ ἐγὼν υἱὸς μεγαλήτορος Ἀγχίσαο
εὔχομαι ἐκγεγάμεν, μήτηρ δέ μοί ἐστ' Ἀφροδίτη.
τῶν δὴ νῦν ἕτεροί γε φίλον παῖδα κλαύσονται
σήμερον· οὐ γάρ φημ' ἐπέεσσί γε νηπυτίοισιν
ὧδε διακρινθέντε μάχης ἒξ ἀπονέεσθαι.
εἰ δ' ἐθέλεις καὶ ταῦτα δαήμεναι, ὄφρ' εὖ εἴδῃς
ἡμετέρην γενεήν, πολλοὶ δέ μιν ἄνδρες ἴσασιν.
Δάρδανον ἄρ πρῶτον τέκετο νεφεληγερέτα Ζεύς·
κτίσσε δὲ Δαρδανίην, ἐπεὶ οὔ πω Ἴλιος ἱρή
ἐν πεδίῳ πεπόλιστο, πόλις μερόπων ἀνθρώπων,
ἀλλ' ἔθ' ὑπωρείας οἴκεον πολυπίδακος Ἴδης.
Δάρδανος αὖ τέκεθ' υἱὸν Ἐριχθόνιον βασιλῆα,
ὃς δὴ ἀφνειότατος γένετο θνητῶν ἀνθρώπων·
τοῦ τρισχείλιαι ἵπποι ἕλος κάτα βουκολέοντο
. . . .
230   Τρῶα δ' Ἐριχθόνιος τέκετο Τρώεσσιν ἄνακτα·
Τρωὸς δ' αὖ τρεῖς παῖδες ἀμύμονες ἐξεγένοντο,
Ἶλός τ' Ἀσσάρακός τε καὶ ἀντίθεος Γανυμήδης,
ὃς δὴ κάλλιστος γένετο θνητῶν ἀνθρώπων·
τὸν καὶ ἀνηρείψαντο θεοὶ Διὶ οἰνοχοεύειν
κάλλεος εἵνεκα οἷο, ἵν' ἀθανάτοισι μετείη.
Ἶλος δ' αὖ τέκεθ' υἱὸν ἀμύμονα Λαομέδοντα·
Λαομέδων δ' ἄρα Τιθωνὸν τέκετο Πρίαμόν τε
Λάμπόν τε Κλυτίον θ' Ἱκετάονά τ' ὄζον Ἄρηος.
Ἀσσάρακος δὲ Κάπυν, ὃ δ' ἄρ' Ἀγχίσην τέκε παῖδα·
αὐτὰρ ἔμ' Ἀγχίσης, Πρίαμος δ' ἔτεχ' Ἕκτορα δῖον.
ταύτης τοι γενεῆς τε καὶ αἵματος εὔχομαι εἶναι."

Then in turn Aineias spoke to him and made his answer:
"Son of Peleus, never hope by words to frighten me
as if I were a baby. I myself understand well enough
how to speak in vituperation and how to make insults.
You and I know each other's birth, we both know our parents
since we have heard the lines of their fame from mortal men; only
I have never with my eyes seen your parents, nor have you seen
    mine.
For you, they say you are the son of blameless Peleus
and that your mother was Thetis of the lovely hair, the sea's lady;
I in turn claim I am the son of great-hearted Anchises
but that my mother was Aphrodite; and that of these parents
one group or the other will have a dear son to mourn for
this day. Since I believe we will not in mere words, like children,
meet, and separate and go home again out of the fighting.
Even so, if you wish to learn all this and be certain
of my genealogy: there are plenty of men who know it.
First of all Zeus who gathers the clouds had a son, Dardanos
who founded Dardania, since there was yet no sacred Ilion
made a city in the plain to be a centre of peoples,
but they lived yet in the underhills of Ida with all her waters.
Dardanos in turn had a son, the king, Erichthonios,
who became the richest of all mortal men, and in his possession
were three thousand horses who pastured along the low grasslands,

. . . .

230 Erichthonios had a son, Tros, who was lord of the Trojans,
and to Tros in turn there were born three sons unfaulted,
Ilos and Assarakos and godlike Ganymedes
who was the loveliest born of the race of mortals, and therefore
the gods caught him away to themselves, to be Zeus' wine-pourer,
for the sake of his beauty, so he might be among the immortals.
Ilos in turn was given a son, the blameless Laomedon,
and Laomedon had sons in turn, Tithonos and Priam,
Lampos, Klytios and Hiketaon, scion of Ares;
but Assarakos had Kapys, and Kapys' son was Anchises,
and I am Anchises' son, and Priam's is Hektor the brilliant.
Such is the generation and blood I claim to be born from."

Iliad XX 199–241

89

According to this genealogy, Ilos was the son of Tros, grandson of Erikhthonios, great-grandson of Dardanos, and great-great-grandson of Zeus. In other words, there are three generations of Trojan ancestors before Ilos, not counting Zeus. Likewise, Hektor and Aineias (who offers this genealogy) belong to the third generation after Ilos (> Laomedon > Priam > Hektor) or his brother Assarakos (> Kapus > Ankhises > Aineias). So Ilos stands in the very middle of the entire pedigree of Trojan kings, separated by three generations from Dardanos and Hektor respectively. Ilos' importance is based not only on his occupying the center of the entire line of Trojan kings, but also on the fact that the city of Ilion bears his name and that it was in the time of his ancestor Dardanos that the first city, called "Dardania," was built "to be a centre of peoples" who at the time lived in the foothills of Mount Ida (*Iliad* XX 216–218). What we see at work here is the sociomnemonic process of *periodization*, according to which communities articulate their past by emphasizing certain "historical" events, which they consider watersheds in their life and their future. By employing such processes, communities often engage in selective obliteration: they tend to select events that fit their desired self-image and erase disturbing events or darker periods of their history that negatively affect the construction of their fictive self. Seen from this angle, the emphasis on Ilos among Troy's ancestors is conditioned by the desire to create a point of historical departure, of "resetting a mnemonic community's 'historical chronometer' at zero."[196]

Other landscape markers, such as the σῆμα of Myrine and the peak of old Aisuetes' tomb (*Iliad* II 793), where Polites stood to see when the Achaean army would start marching from the ships, constitute visual markers that enhance memorability. The narrator creates both for himself and his audience specific "hooks" on which he can visually "hang" certain mental pictures he is going to describe in detail, such as the Trojan and allied contingents (tomb of Myrine) and the "imagined" march of the Achaean army (tomb of Aisuetes).[197]

The tomb of Myrine bears two different names: men call it Βατίεια 'the Hill of the Thicket', and gods σῆμα πολυσκάρθμοιο Μυρίνης 'the tomb of dancing or bounding Myrine':

> ἔστι δέ τις προπάροιθε πόλιος αἰπεῖα κολώνη,
> ἐν πεδίῳ ἀπάνευθε, περίδρομος ἔνθα καὶ ἔνθα,
> τὴν ἤτοι ἄνδρες Βατίειαν κικλήσκουσιν,
> ἀθάνατοι δέ τε σῆμα πολυσκάρθμοιο Μυρίνης·
> ἔνθα τότε Τρῶές τε διέκριθεν ἠδ' ἐπίκουροι.

---

[196] Zerubavel 2003:91.
[197] See Grethlein 2006:146.

Near the city but apart from it there is a steep hill
in the plain by itself, so you pass on one side or the other.
This men call the Hill of the Thicket, but the immortal
gods have named it the burial mound of dancing Myrina.
There the Trojans and their companions were marshalled in order.

Iliad II 811–815

Alternative human and divine names for the same locations are attested three times in the *Iliad* (II 813–814; XIV 290–291; XX 74).[198] No satisfying general explanation of this phenomenon has been advanced. Scholars tend to interpret it as an indication of divine supremacy, or of renaming by mortals who have lost track of its earlier identity. According to Grethlein,

This not only underscores the gap between humans and gods, but it also shows that tombs can slip into oblivion. For men, the marker of Myrine has turned into merely landscape; artefact has become nature. Only the gods, who are endowed with a better memory, are aware of its original significance. The underlying semiotic process is implied in the Greek word σῆμα, which can signify both "sign" and "tomb." For humans, the "sign" of Myrine's "tomb" has lost its original significance and has gained a new one. [199]

This is true, but I think that there is more to it. Given that the tomb of Myrine points to the past, its double naming not only reflects the divergence between divine and human knowledge of the past, but also different or conflicting points of view about the past. Naming is a powerful means of culturally appropriating or even reclaiming the past. According to the ancient scholia,[200] Myrine was the name of an Amazon, and some scholars[201] have argued that this scant reference may be a hint at the existence of a local myth concerning a war between the locals and the Amazons. In fact, the *Iliad* (III 184–189) may refer to such a war between the Phrygians (with Priam as their ally) and the Amazons, though Kullmann regards it as an anachronism, since the Amazons about whom Priam

---

[198] In the *Odyssey*, no specific human name is given in the case of μῶλυ (x 305) or the Πλαγκταί (xii 61).

[199] Grethlein 2008:30–31. On divine supremacy, see also Clay 1972:128.

[200] A and D; see also Strabo 12.8.6.6–12.8.6.13 ἐν δὲ τῷ Ἰλιακῷ πεδίῳ κολώνη τις ἔστιν "ἣν ἤτοι ἄνδρες Βατίειαν κικλήσκουσιν, ἀθάνατοι δέ τε σῆμα πολυσκάρθμοιο Μυρίνης," ἣν ἱστοροῦσι μίαν εἶναι τῶν Ἀμαζόνων ἐκ τοῦ ἐπιθέτου τεκμαιρόμενοι· εὐσκάρθμους γὰρ ἵππους λέγεσθαι διὰ τὸ τάχος· κἀκείνην οὖν πολύσκαρθμον διὰ τὸ ἀπὸ τῆς ἡνιοχείας τάχος· καὶ ἡ Μύρινα οὖν ἐπώνυμος ταύτης λέγεται.

[201] See Heubeck 1949/1950:202–206 (= 1984:99–103).

speaks attacked not Troy but Phrygia.[202] I would not press this point. The double naming may be indicative of two different focalizations of the same landmark, based on the propensity of humans to reappropriate painful memories of the past. Perhaps the narrator's formulation silently implies the erasing of the name "tomb of the Amazon Myrine" (who had fought against the alliance of Trojans and Phrygians) and its replacement by a neutral term devoid of emotional involvement. The idea of the supreme knowledge of the gods with respect to an older name may be right, but it has to be combined with that of "reclaiming the past," which, though the myth surrounding Myrine has faded in the course of time, is a strong tendency as far as the working of collective memory is concerned.

The rise in the plain

The "rise in the plain" (θρωσμὸς πεδίοιο) appears three times in the *Iliad*: in X 160, Nestor urges Diomedes to wake up because the Trojans are sitting close to the Achaean ships, at the rise of the flat land; in XI 56, when the Trojan army has marched to the other side of the rise of the flat land (Τρῶες δ' αὖθ' ἑτέρωθεν ἐπὶ θρωσμῷ πεδίοιο), the situation becomes even more grave for the Achaeans; and in XX 3, when Achilles and the Achaeans are preparing for battle next to the ships, the Trojans are again standing on the other side of the rise in the flat land (Τρῶες δ' αὖθ' ἑτέρωθεν ἐπὶ θρωσμῷ πεδίοιο). Thornton, who was working on a purely literary register, has argued that "the image of the 'rise in the plain' is used by the poet to mark both physically and emotionally the turn of events from Achaean defeat while Achilles is absent, to their victory when he returns to battle."[203] This interpretation is on the right track, but fails to explain *why* the storyteller has used the visual imagery of a "rise in the plain" to indicate such a turning point in the plot.

By focusing our attention on the deictic strategies employed by the storyteller in order to suggest specific mental visualizations to his audience, it becomes clear that he places himself centrally, offering a viewing of the Achaeans on one side and the Trojans on the other (ἑτέρωθεν), as they prepare for battle. Such verbal signposts show that references to Iliadic landscape do not follow a map with cartographic and isotropic principles,[204] but exploit landmarks,

---

[202] See W. Kullmann 1960:303. Moreover, the traditional way of interpreting the phrase σῆμα πολυσκάρθμοιο Μυρίνης as "burial mound of dancing Myrina" is incompatible with an Amazon; it is much more probable that the epithet "dancing" or "leaping" refers to some ritual and not to a female warrior. See also Kirk 1985:247.

[203] 1984:362.

[204] Gehrke 1998:164. On *hodological space* ("*spazio odologico*"), see Janni 1984:85.

paths, edges, and nodes.[205] This matches the typical strategies employed by people when they create a mental map. The imaginary landscape of Homer is constructed more or less in the same way, because the performance of oral song requires mental viewing by means of visual imagery, in the manner of a person describing his house to an interviewer *in absentia*. When presented with the inherent difficulties of offering somebody a mental tour, we invent signposts to navigate the vistas that appear in our mind one after the other. These signposts create order in the flow of mental images, giving us time to organize them and use them effectively. That is why a visual image of a "rise in the plain" or "a break in the flat land" constitutes a mnemonic device of visual taxonomy. In Lynch's terminology, it is an *edge*, since it is different from the default imagery of the flat Trojan plain. While navigating his mind across this fictional flat plain of Troy, the narrator is able to stop where he finds an edge, a point of departure for a shift to another visual zone before the outbreak of generalized action.[206]

---

[205] See Lynch (1960:89), who calls it *hodological*. On this issue, see Lynch 1960:46–90; Downs and Stea 1977; on Homer, see Clay 2007:247.

[206] This argument is corroborated by the use of imperfect tenses; see Clay 2007:246, who shows that imperfect, or rather *imperfective,* tenses indicate "generalized actions that often form transitions between different zones of combat." Clay (2011:65) makes the same argument for transitional similes in *Iliad* XII.

2

Framing Spaces
The Achaean Camp, Troy, and the World of the Immortals

A S WE SAW IN CHAPTER 1, the base-level space of the battlefield is part of a set of *framing spaces* that are deployed around and above it. The Achaean camp and the city of Troy encircle the Trojan plain on a horizontal level, while the various places where the immortals live and travel enclose the battlefield from above. These framing spaces are deftly employed to create multiple polarities between intense and peaceful activity, open and closed areas, and dynamic and static spaces.

The Achaean Camp

Brigitte Hellwig has convincingly argued that the Achaean camp is used as a place for: (1) councils, (2) observation of the enemy, (3) prayer, and (4) lament.[1] These four functions represent the wide variety of activities that take place in the camp, and are linked with certain locations within it. My main aim in this section is twofold: first, I will try to show that each location of the Achaean camp is paired with specific functions, and second, I will examine the mnemonic strategies underlying this internal topography.[2]

The main areas included in the Achaean camp are: (1) the headquarters of Agamemnon and Achilles; (2) the seashore; (3) the Achaean Wall; and (4) the ships.

---

[1]   See Hellwig 1964:26.
[2]   On the positioning of the various Achaean kings within the camp, see Willcock 1984:225; Clay 2011:48–51. On left and right with respect to Iliadic topography and the placement of various heroes, see Cuillandre 1944; Mannsberger 2001; Trachsel 2007; Clay 2011:48n13.

The headquarters of Agamemnon and Achilles

When the action is located within the hut or in the headquarters of an Achaean leader, be it Agamemnon in *Iliad* I or Achilles in *Iliad* IX and XXIV, the role of space becomes all the more important, since the particular location is used not as a place where an event occurs, but as the framework within which the narrator unfolds the story of a particular event. In other words, the place delineated by the hut or headquarters of a given Achaean hero constitutes a special *social space*, which shapes the particular events occurring there and, more significantly, functions as a code for "reading" the episode at hand.

It is no coincidence that the Achaean presence in the *Iliad* begins and ends with two episodes situated in the headquarters of Agamemnon and Achilles, in *Iliad* I and XXIV respectively. The quarrel between Agamemnon and Achilles takes place in the ἀγορή 'assembly', while the meeting between Priam and Achilles happens at the latter's hut. Moreover, a serious attempt to annul the dire consequences of the wrath of Achilles resulting from his quarrel with Agamemnon is made, almost halfway through the poem (*Iliad* IX), in Achilles' hut. My argument is that the huts or headquarters of these two important Achaean heroes constitute a thematized space that embeds crucial social concerns and attitudes toward questions concerning the heroic code, authority and status, honor, and exclusion and inclusion in the heroic community.[3]

Although the exact location of the Achaean assembly in *Iliad* I is not explicitly stated, we can assume that it takes place close to the ships of Agamemnon. This is overtly indicated by the fact that when the assembly is over, Achilles goes back to his shelter and the ships with Patroklos and his companions,[4] whereas Agamemnon, after preparing a ship that carried a hecatomb and Khruseis,[5] orders Talthubios and Eurubates to go to Achilles' hut and take Briseis. When this is accomplished, the two heralds return with Briseis "beside the ships of the Achaeans," that is, to Agamemnon's headquarters.[6] In fact, the very withdrawal

---

[3] On the interdependence between space and social theory, see Soja 1989.

[4] *Iliad* I 306–307 Πηλείδης μὲν ἐπὶ κλισίας καὶ νῆας ἐΐσας / ἤϊε σύν τε Μενοιτιάδῃ καὶ οἷς ἑτάροισιν ("Peleus' son went back to his balanced ships and his shelter / with Patroklos, Menoitios' son, and his own companions").

[5] *Iliad* I 308–311 Ἀτρείδης δ' ἄρα νῆα θοὴν ἅλαδε προέρυσσεν, / ἐν δ' ἐρέτας ἔκρινεν ἐείκοσιν, ἐς δ' ἑκατόμβην / βῆσε θεῷ, ἀνὰ δὲ Χρυσηΐδα καλλιπάρῃον / εἶσεν ἄγων· ἐν δ' ἀρχὸς ἔβη πολύμητις Ὀδυσσεύς ("But the son of Atreus drew a fast ship down to the water / and allotted into it twenty rowers and put on board it / the hecatomb for the god and Chryseis of the fair cheeks / leading her by the hand. And in charge went crafty Odysseus").

[6] *Iliad* I 320–326 ἀλλ' ὅ γε Ταλθύβιόν τε καὶ Εὐρυβάτην προσέειπεν, / τώ οἱ ἔσαν κήρυκε καὶ ὀτρηρὼ θεράποντε· "ἔρχεσθον κλισίην Πηληϊάδεω Ἀχιλῆος· χειρὸς ἑλόντ' ἀγέμεν Βρισηΐδα καλλιπάρῃον. / εἰ δέ κε μὴ δώῃσιν, ἐγὼ δέ κεν αὐτὸς ἕλωμαι / ἐλθὼν σὺν πλεόνεσσι, τό οἱ καὶ ῥίγιον ἔσται." / ὣς εἰπὼν προΐει, κρατερὸν δ' ἐπὶ μῦθον ἔτελλεν ("... but to Talthybios he gave his

of Achilles, his "moving away" from the place where the assembly takes place, that is, where the heroic community is summoned to decide on a crucial matter as a cohesive and coherent entity, contrasts with Agamemnon's constancy (he goes only from the assembly to the nearby seashore). The *Iliad* invites the audience to realize that the assembly is held at a place dominated by Agamemnon, and that Achilles' departure for his shelter and the ships epitomizes his withdrawal from the set of common tenets shared by the other Achaean kings. Marginalization and withdrawal are spatial metaphors, and the same holds for steadiness of space. In the world of the *Iliad* strife derives meaning through space, while space reflects boundaries of power and authority.[7]

In *Iliad* IX, Agamemnon sends his heralds Talthubios and Eurubates, the very same people who had fetched Briseis to his hut in *Iliad* I,[8] together with Odysseus, Phoinix, and Ajax, to Achilles' shelter to ask him to accept the gifts that Agamemnon is offering him and return to the war. The epic carefully uses the distance between the locations of Agamemnon's hut, where the Achaean elders are summoned, and Achilles' hut, to where the ambassadors are dispatched, in order both to suggest the distance separating the two heroes and to make clear that the place where Achilles lives is a space of his own, a world untouched by the politics of Agamemnon. With the underlying premise that identity formations derive meaning through spatial organization, I would argue that the locations of the headquarters of these two emblematic heroes and the distance that the ambassadors have to cover evoke Achilles' withdrawal in *Iliad* I and accentuate the interaction between an individual's sense of space and his place in society. These particular heroes understand their role as shaped by the realities attached to their surrounding heroic communities; both of them consider their headquarters as their proper space, an area where they tend to construct and recreate their status-based worldview (Agamemnon) or their personal lives, ideals, and identities.[9]

---

orders and Eurybates / who were heralds and hard-working henchmen to him: 'Go now / to the shelter of Peleus' son Achilleus, to bring back / Briseis of the fair cheeks leading her by the hand. And if he / will not give her, I must come in person to take her / with many men behind me, and it will be the worse for him.' / He spoke and sent them forth with this strong order upon them.") and I 347 ... τὼ δ' αὖτις ἴτην παρὰ νῆας Ἀχαιῶν ("and they walked back beside the ships of the Achaians").

[7] On the elusive spatiality of power relations, see Soja 1989, who builds upon the work of Lefebvre 1974, Poulantzas 1978, Giddens 1981, and others.

[8] Given that Briseis is a kind of "second Helen" within the plot of the *Iliad*, the embassy to Achilles in Book IX may, to some extent, have been patterned on an "archetypal" embassy to Troy by Odysseus and Menelaos to reclaim Helen; see *Iliad* III 205–224. On Briseis as a "second Helen," see Suzuki 1989:21–29; Dué 2002:39–42.

[9] One can even speak of a "spatiality of being" with respect to the way Agamemnon and Achilles, these two emblematic Iliadic heroes, construct and deconstruct their heroic identities. Achilles,

The Achaean camp seems to be a socially constructed map, not merely an agglomeration of huts and shelters of the Achaean kings but a chart of different centers of control and domination, authority and self-esteem. Achilles' self-enclosure and confinement to his own part of the camp is about the heroic dynamics of partition reflected in distance, segmentation, and spatial "parceling out." The idea of Achilles as the solitary hero builds on what Foucault called "the little tactics of the habitat," a social topography of tension. The "politicized spatiality of heroic life"[10] is based on carefully delineated policies and politics of inclusion and exclusion from the Achaean camp. In the epic universe of the heroic community, where inclusion and participation, recognition and honor are the very essence of a hero's existence, spatial demarcations of the sort observed in the ongoing strife between Agamemnon and Achilles point to a thematization of space already present in the epic's famous proem: *Iliad* I 6-7 ἐξ οὗ δὴ τὰ πρῶτα διαστήτην ἐρίσαντε / Ἀτρείδης τε ἄναξ ἀνδρῶν καὶ δῖος Ἀχιλλεύς ("since that time when first there stood in division of conflict / Atreus' son the lord of men and brilliant Achilleus").[11] The very use of a "spatial" verb (διαστήτην 'stood apart') prefigures the role of space in presenting the conflict between Agamemnon and Achilles, whose names are, almost symbolically, pushed to the two edges of the next line. Along the same lines, the placement of Odysseus' ship at the center of the Achaean camp reflects his occupying the political center point in the quarrel between Achilles and Agamemnon. Being in the middle (VIII 223 ἐν μεσσάτῳ), the storyteller uses it as a platform for Agamemnon to address the whole army (VIII 220-226), and for and Eris (XI 6), who is unleashed by Zeus (XI 3-4).[12]

In the case of Priam's visit to Achilles' hut in *Iliad* XXIV, spatial considerations are strongly spelled out to the audience: first by narratively highlighting the Trojan king's journey, and second by presenting the audience with a dramatic change in the spatial politics used for Achilles' headquarters in his strife with Agamemnon.

Priam's departure (*Iliad* XXIV 322-328) is highly emotional, since all the Trojans think he is going to be killed by Achilles (XXIV 328 πόλλ' ὀλοφυρόμενοι, ὡς εἰ θανατόνδε κιόντα). In the collective conscience of the Trojan people the Achaean camp, and more significantly the hut of Achilles, epitomize suffering and death. What is remarkable in this episode is that these grim expectations

---

for example, follows the typical process of "objectification," objectifying the heroic community and setting himself apart from it. He does so "by creating a gap, a distance, a space," as Soja 1989:132 has aptly described the tendency of humans to stand apart from the whole, after seeing the whole as something potentially "other" than themselves.

[10] Soja 1989:2.

[11] See also Stesichorus *Iliou Persis* fr. S88. 11 (PMGF), where the form διάσταν is used.

[12] See Nagy 2009c II 7.73-74; Clay 2011:43.

constitute a timely expression of internal misdirection, as the change of place will indeed signify a change of condition, primarily for Achilles, and only secondarily for Priam. The brief stop at the tombstone of Ilos and the ford of Skamandros (XXIV 349–351), where the meeting with Hermes takes place, constitutes a hint that Priam's journey may take an unexpected turn by means of divine help. Hermes puts the guards in the ditch to sleep and easily brings the chariot of Priam and Idaios to Achilles' hut. Then, for the first time in the *Iliad*, the bard takes the time to describe the area outside the hut of Achilles (XXIV 448–456):

> ἀλλ' ὅτε δὴ κλισίην Πηληϊάδεω ἀφίκοντο
> ὑψηλήν—τὴν Μυρμιδόνες ποίησαν ἄνακτι
> δοῦρ' ἐλάτης κέρσαντες, ἀτὰρ καθύπερθεν ἔρεψαν
> λαχνήεντ' ὄροφον λειμωνόθεν ἀμήσαντες·
> ἀμφὶ δέ οἱ μεγάλην αὐλὴν ποίησαν ἄνακτι
> σταυροῖσιν πυκινοῖσι· θύρην δ' ἔχε μοῦνος ἐπιβλής
> εἰλάτινος, τὸν τρεῖς μὲν ἐπιρρήσσεσκον Ἀχαιοί,
> τρεῖς δ' ἀναοίγεσκον μεγάλην κληῖδα θυράων,
> τῶν ἄλλων, Ἀχιλεὺς δ' ἄρ' ἐπιρρήσσεσκε καὶ οἶος—

> But when they had got to the shelter of Peleus' son: a towering
> shelter the Myrmidons had built for their king, hewing
> the timbers of pine, and they made a roof of thatch above it
> shaggy with grass that they had gathered out of the meadows;
> and around it made a great courtyard for their king, with hedgepoles
> set close together; the gate was secured by a single door-piece
> of pine, and three Achaians could ram it home in its socket
> and three could pull back and open the huge door-bar; three other
> Achaians, that is, but Achilleus all by himself could close it.

> *Iliad* XXIV 448–456

The emphasis on detail and the almost idyllic atmosphere created by this elaborate description preface the meeting between Priam and Achilles and set the tone for a profound shift in the function of space. Only within this locus-image can the two heroes use narratives that build on the politics of pity. By reminding Achilles of his father Peleus in distant Phthia, Priam plays a powerful game with his interlocutor's emotions, as their lives are revealed to be remarkably complementary: Priam is at home and knows the fate of his son, who lies dead, while Achilles is alive but not at home and does not know the fate of his father. Seen from this angle, space becomes an integral part of Priam's emotional politics.

Proximity and distance, far and near, Troy and Phthia are bipolar antitheses transformed into symmetrical analogies of pain and suffering. The larger space of the two heroes' fates encroaches upon the smaller space of Achilles' headquarters and turns it from the marginalized, unfriendly, and deadly habitat of Hektor's killer into a locus of pity and sharing. At the end of the epic, Achilles' hut becomes a place of reconciliation, not only between the old Trojan king and the young Achaean hero but also between Achilles and the heroic community to which he finally returns.

Seen from this perspective, the headquarters of Agamemnon and Achilles are mainly used as loci where important deliberations are made about the cohesion of the heroic community. They are both centers of authority and self-esteem, and constitute a form of social space that allows the *Iliad* to explore the inner tensions, concerns, and ideological preoccupations of the world of heroes.

The seashore

The seashore comprises a highly thematized area, a place of isolation and sadness, of prayer and lament.[13] It is closely associated with Achilles, who meets his mother Thetis there in *Iliad* I and XVIII,[14] but as the episode with Khruses shows (he prays to Apollo while walking along the shore), it is also a "break-off" space where mortals and immortals meet.

The seashore constitutes a place of unhappiness and loneliness: Khruses "went silently away beside the murmuring sea beach" (*Iliad* I 34 βῆ δ᾽ ἀκέων παρὰ θῖνα πολυφλοίσβοιο θαλάσσης) and "walked in solitude" (I 35 ἀπάνευθε κιών), and Achilles "weeping went and sat in sorrow apart from his companions / beside the beach of the grey sea looking out on the infinite water" (I 348–350 ... αὐτὰρ Ἀχιλλεύς / δακρύσας ἑτάρων ἄφαρ ἕζετο νόσφι λιασθείς / θῖν᾽ ἔφ᾽ ἁλὸς πολιῆς, ὁρόων ἐπ᾽ ἀπείρονα πόντον).[15] Here, location and action are intricately entwined, though with shifting degrees of emphasis. In contrast with Khruses, who walks along the seashore, Achilles sits in sorrow on the beach and looks at the endless high sea. Although in both situations the murmuring of the sea contrasts with the silence of the two figures,[16] silence takes two different forms based on two distinct aspects of the same location: the priest is walking

---

[13] See Minchin 2008a:20.

[14] In *Iliad* XXIV, Thetis and Achilles meet at the latter's hut (see 122–123).

[15] See also *Iliad* XXIII 144 (Achilles addressing the river Sperkheios in Greece while looking at the sea in the Troad); *Odyssey* ii 260–266 (Telemakhos prays to Athena at the seashore before departing in search of his father). For ἐπ᾽ ἀπείρονα intead of ἐπὶ οἴνοπα (*Iliad* I 350), I am following Aristarchus; see the critical apparatus ad loc. in West's edition.

[16] On the interplay of silence and speech in *Iliad* I, with reference to the Agamemnon episode, see Montiglio 2000:56–59. On this topic, see also Kirk 1985:56–57.

away from the Achaean camp, whereas Achilles stays within its limits. Space is used here as a litmus test for the dramatically different outcomes of the problems Khruses and Achilles are facing. By leaving the Achaean camp, Khruses figuratively breaks loose from Agamemnon's threats and insolent behavior, although he obeys his order temporarily. Apollo will listen to Khruses' prayer and fulfill his wish. Conversely, Achilles is "trapped" within the Achaean camp, which is not so much a location but a space of social and heroic self-awareness and recognition. He gazes at the "endless sea" as if gazing at the endless troubles and pain he is and will be facing.[17] His wish too will be fulfilled, but only after he pays the high price of losing his dear friend Patroklos.

Landscape features are paired with emotional stimuli, and even with sets of ideological tenets (Achilles, despite his threats, cannot leave the camp that epitomizes his heroic identity), and enhance mnemonic recall, in the sense that abstract ideas are expressed or deployed through mental and visual association with concrete features of the setting. This is part of why there is generally no landscape description in the *Iliad*. The setting exists in its particulars, not as a whole, because it is these particular features that serve to draw the characters.[18]

In the last books of the *Iliad*, the seashore is often used as the locus of lamentation at the death of Patroklos:[19] Achilles (*Iliad* XVIII),[20] Achilles together with the Myrmidons (*Iliad* XXIII),[21] and again on his own (*Iliad* XXIV).[22] This does not mean that lamentation for Patroklos takes place only at the seashore,[23] but that the gradual change of the seashore's associative role from a place of prayer at the beginning of the epic to a place of lamentation towards its end is parallel to the gradual shift of the associative role of the walls of Troy, which in *Iliad* VI are a location of prayer (to Athena and Zeus), but at the end of the poem (*Iliad* XXII

---

[17] Lesky 1947:185; Elliger 1975:67.

[18] Elliger 1975:69.

[19] See Elliger 1975:67–68.

[20] The only place away from the ships that Achilles can be is the seashore, cf. *Iliad* XVIII 3 τὸν δ' ηὖρε προπάροιθε νεῶν ὀρθοκραιράων.

[21] *Iliad* XXIII 59–61 Πηλεΐδης δ' ἐπὶ θινὶ πολυφλοίσβοιο θαλάσσης / κεῖτο βαρὺ στενάχων πολέσιν μετὰ Μυρμιδόνεσσιν / ἐν καθαρῷ, ὅθι κύματ' ἐπ' ἠϊόνος κλύζεσκον ("... but along the beach of the thunderous sea the son of Peleus / lay down, groaning heavily, among the Myrmidon numbers / in a clear place where the waves washed over the beach"); XXIII 143 ὀχθήσας δ' ἄρα εἶπεν ἰδὼν ἐπὶ οἴνοπα πόντον ("and gazing / in deep distress out over the wine-blue water, he spoke forth.")

[22] *Iliad* XXIV 3–4 αὐτὰρ Ἀχιλλεύς / κλαῖε φίλου ἑταίρου μεμνημένος ("only Achilleus / wept still as he remembered his beloved companion"); XXIV 12 δινεύεσκ' ἀλύων παρὰ θῖν' ἁλός ("and [would] pace turning / in distraction along the beach of the sea").

[23] The antiphonal laments for Patroklos by Briseis (*Iliad* XIX 287–300) and Achilles (XIX 315–337) are uttered in Achilles' hut, cf. XIX 280 καὶ τὰ μὲν ἐν κλισίῃσι θέσαν, κάθεσαν δὲ γυναῖκας ("and stowed the gifts in the shelters, and let the women be settled"). On these laments, see Pucci 1998:97–112; Tsagalis 2004:139–143, 148–151.

and XXIV) are a place of grief and mourning for Hektor. The walls of Troy and the seashore are therefore employed as a form of interactive imagery, which, as cognitive psychologists have shown, reinforces distinctiveness, accentuates specificity, and enhances memorability by linking abstract ideas or feelings to particular locations.[24] At a later phase in the evolution of the Iliadic tradition, mnemonic recall through interactive imagery was further improved through a process of *visual pairing*, through which interactive imagery created nets of parallel, not sequential, imagery. Hektor and Achilles/Patroklos are the two sets of great heroes whose actions and inaction dramatically punctuate the epic. Prayer and lamentation, representing the two edges of their bifurcated life stories, were gradually associated with particular locations, the walls of Troy and the seashore respectively. These locations were gradually reconfigured as the *Iliad* reserved terminal space (the walls of the city and the sea) for the expression of terminal conditions—praying for the preservation of life and mourning the loss of it.

The seashore also constitutes a place that one cannot get beyond, either as an extra-Iliadic space of departure (memory of arrival) or as a limit for short journeys by ship (*Iliad* I). It is a spatiotemporal marker, since it marks beginnings and ends for the Achaeans, signposts by which they can orient themselves in time. This function accords with the *Iliad*'s limited time frame. By concentrating on the wrath of Achilles, an event occurring in the tenth year of the war, the epic systematically engages with both the past and the future. Within this universe of associations the seashore, though a spatial element, acquires a chronotopic dimension: it recalls the Achaean arrival at Troy and facilitates the play of irony with the evasive illusion of sailing back to Greece, only to limit itself to a notional frontier that is briefly crossed (as when Khruseis is returned to her father).

The Achaean wall

The Achaean wall and ditch[25] are first mentioned in *Iliad* VII 336–343, when Nestor advises the Achaeans to "gather and pile one single mound on the corpse-pyre / ... and build fast upon it / towered ramparts, to be a defence ..." and to "dig a deep ditch / circling it, so as to keep off their people and horses ..."[26] Once the wall is built and the ditch dug, Poseidon complains to Zeus that the fame of

---

[24] See Buggie 1974; Marschark and Hunt 1989; Hintzman 1993; Rubin 1995:54–56.

[25] On the Achaean Wall, see Mannsperger 1998.

[26] "τύμβον τ' ἀμφὶ πυρὴν ἕνα χεύομεν ἐξαγαγόντες / ἄκριτον ἐκ πεδίου· ποτὶ δ' αὐτὸν δείμομεν ὦκα / πύργους ὑψηλούς, εἶλαρ νηῶν τε καὶ αὐτῶν. / ἐν δ' αὐτοῖσι πύλας ποιήσομεν εὖ ἀραρυίας, / ὄφρα δι' αὐτάων ἱππηλασίη ὁδὸς εἴη. / ἔκτοσθεν δὲ βαθεῖαν ὀρύξομεν ἐγγύθι τάφρον, / ἥ χ' ἵππον καὶ λαὸν ἐρυκάκοι ἀμφὶς ἐοῦσα, / μή ποτ' ἐπιβρίσῃ πόλεμος Τρώων ἀγερώχων."

this wall will surpass that of the walls of Troy that he and Apollo built together (VII 446–453), and Zeus assures him that the wall will be destroyed as soon as the Achaeans return home (VII 455–463). In *Iliad* VIII 175–183, Hektor tells the Trojans that Zeus stands on his side and that the Achaean wall will not stop him from burning the enemy's ships. In IX 232–233, Odysseus warns Achilles that the Trojans have encamped just outside the wall, and Achilles ironically refers to the vain effort of Agamemnon to stop the Trojans by building a wall (IX 349–352). Achilles' words make it clear that the wall is connected with the activity of one man, Agamemnon, although it was Nestor who proposed its construction. Through the focalization of Achilles, the space of the wall is anchored to the theme of his wrath, his own strife with Agamemnon. The wall is the last recourse the arrogant son of Atreus has at his disposal. Once he is deprived of it, the need for Achilles will become even more prominent. In X 126–127, Agamemnon advises Nestor to go with him beyond the "boundary" of the ditch, to the spot on the plain where the leaders of the Achaeans will hold a council. In *Iliad* XII, the wall and ditch are the focus of action: after imagining their future destruction by the gods, the narrator turns to the imminent attack by Hektor and the Trojans. The space delineated by the wall and the ditch has now been tied to the action of one preeminent Trojan hero, Hektor, whose martial activity is highlighted by his ability to do intratextually what Zeus promises to do, *mutatis mutandis*, extratextually. In *Iliad* XII 257–264 and XII 290–291, specific parts of the wall are brought to the foreground by focusing on the activity of both Achaeans and Trojans. In XIV 55–82 Nestor informs Agamemnon that the Trojans have invaded the Achaean camp, and Agamemnon acknowledges what has been expressed time and again since the wall was built: that it will be of no use to the Achaeans. In *Iliad* XV, the ditch becomes the center of opposing movements by the two armies: first the Achaeans push the Trojans back across it (XV 1–4), and then the Trojans press the Achaeans, who retreat behind the wall (XV 344–345). In XVI 368–371, the Trojans cross the ditch in panic as Patroklos has broken their lines, while in XVII 760–761 the Achaeans take shelter behind the wall as they try to save the body of Patroklos. In XVIII 215–217 and 228, Achilles appears in the ditch and wreaks havoc among the Trojans by shouting three times. The divine battle (θεομαχία) begins when Athena raises a war cry while standing beside the ditch in front of the wall (XX 48–50). Finally, Hermes puts the Achaean guards to sleep and opens the gates of the wall with ease (XXIV 443–447), letting Priam inside so that he can go to the hut of Achilles.[27]

The Achaean wall and ditch fulfill three functions: (1) they help the narrator pin down the various phases of both the Achaean retreat and the Trojan attack,

---

[27] See Thornton 1984:362–365.

as Zeus starts fulfilling the promise he made to Thetis in *Iliad* I; (2) they function as a means of intratextual misdirection, creating the illusion of safety for the Achaeans; and (3) they delay the return of Achilles to the war.

With respect to the first function, the wall and ditch constitute a point of reference for the narrator as he gradually moves his visual center from the battle-field to an uncharted area, close to, but not within, the camp of the Achaeans. The various landscape markers he has used while referring to the battle on the Trojan plain are of no help now; he needs another signpost, a new mental guide to lead him and his audience to another phase of his narrative. The wall and ditch are a concrete point of reference that allows him to anchor various activi-ties of both armies until Hektor and the Trojans invade the Achaean camp. This effective strategy of "mental touring" shows that the wall and ditch, in terms of mnemonic recall, are the visual stepping stones that facilitate the transition to a new focus in the narrator's field of vision. The unfolding of the narration is like a "path" (οἴμη),[28] a mental journey in which the bard resembles a traveler in constant need of points of orientation, in order to find his way and activate the vast, uncharted areas of his memory.[29]

As far as the plot is concerned, the wall and the ditch constitute an effec-tive intratextual misdirection. The narrator lets the Achaeans believe that with these they will be able to stop the Trojan advance. This illusion is not only short-lived and dramatically contradicted, but also linked to certain heroes whose role in the Iliadic plot is of paramount importance. In *Iliad* XIV 55–81, Nestor tells Agamemnon that the wall will not protect them from the Trojans, and Agamemnon acknowledges that all this effort has been in vain. His words echo Achilles' ironic twist in *Iliad* IX 349–352, when he presents Agamemnon as responsible for building the wall. Achilles even engages in a telling wordplay based on the double reference of the word τεῖχος 'wall', designating both the Achaean wall and the walls of Troy. "And yet," he says, "when I was fighting

---

[28] See Bakker 1997:60–61: "The epic story is like a hike, longer or shorter, along a trail that may be more readily visible or less at various places ... Path and space are realities in terms of which the presentation of the epic tale is viewed by the performers and their audiences; the epic story involves not only a continuously shifting present moment, but also a given location, not only a *now* but also a *here*" (the emphasis is my own). See also Clay 2011:115–119, who shows how the semantics of οἴμη and οἶμος on the one hand and typical epic terminology for "telling the story" (ἐννέπω, *insece*) on the other reveal the spatial aspect of the very act of the performance. This does not mean that οἴμη and οἶμος should be derived simply from εἶμι. See Nagy 2009b 2.92–93; 2009c I 4.209, who argues on the basis of Attic φροίμιον and Old Icelandic *seimr* 'thread' that "the primary meaning of *oimos* and *oimē* can be reconstructed as 'thread, threading', and the mean-ings 'song' or 'way, pathway' can be explained as secondary: that is, 'song' and 'way, pathway' are metaphorical generalizations derived from the meaning 'thread, threading'."

[29] See Bakker 1997:70: "The main concern of the Homeric narrator is movement, an activity that requires a continuous channeling and monitoring of the speech flow through time."

among the Achaians / Hektor would not drive his attack beyond the wall's shelter / but would come forth only so far as the Skaian gates and the oak tree. / There once he endured me alone, and barely escaped my onslaught" (IX 352–355). Intratextual misdirection concerns only the Achaeans, for the audience has been told since *Iliad* VII that the wall is weak and will offer no shelter to the Achaeans. The function of this false illusion is to dramatize the situation the Achaeans are facing, as they gradually run out of means to turn the tide of events to their benefit: the embassy in *Iliad* IX fails, the main Achaean leaders are wounded one after the other, and the wall and ditch cannot save them. The wall and the ditch are therefore the ultimate step in the process of gradually preparing for the return of Achilles. Patroklos' crossing of the ditch and his advance in the plain, contrary to Achilles' advice, is the remaining piece in the dramatic puzzle the epic has so meticulously completed.

Finally, the Achaean wall and ditch are a means of delaying the return of Achilles. The ditch is associated with the dramatic tension gradually built up since Achilles' withdrawal from battle. Whatever measures the Achaeans take to prevent a Trojan victory, they are unable to stop Hektor. The wall is the very last protection, not only because it virtually speaks for their having retreated to their ships, but also because it turns the basic staging of Iliadic war upside down. Instead of pushing the Trojans back to their city, the Achaeans are besieged in their own pseudo-city, whose protective wall, unlike the Trojan ones, is very weak. By using the space of the wall and the ditch as a mechanism that temporarily casts doubt on the most essential condition of the Iliadic war (that the Achaeans are the aggressors and the Trojans the defenders), the tradition of the *Iliad* highlights the fact that the plan of Zeus will be fulfilled and that the wall and the ditch are one more mechanism for delaying the return of Achilles to the battlefield.

The ships

The area of the ships is sometimes used as a lookout, from which the Achaeans observe what is going on in another part of the camp.[30] In *Iliad* XI 599–601 Achilles, while "standing on the stern of his huge-hollowed vessel / looking out over the sheer war work and the sorrowful onrush," sees Nestor's horses carrying the wounded Makhaon. In XIV 3–8 Nestor hears the outcry of war and tells Makhaon that he will search for a vantage point to see what is happening. But as soon as he steps outside his hut, he is able to see the confusion of the battle (line 13). Winfried Elliger has suggested, following Schadewaldt,[31] that the

---

[30] Hellwig 1964:25–26.
[31] Elliger 1975:62; Schadewaldt 1966:120n5.

area of the Achaean camp and the vaguely charted space of the ships undergo an internal expansion and, we may add, provide the necessary background for placing specific narrative events. In the two aforementioned examples, separated by three books but linked through their subject matter (the second "continues" the first), two different spots in the area near the ships are used as observation posts. As the action has been transferred inside the Achaean camp, the story-teller has to narrate various events, which he has to pin down to specific locations so that he can recall them with ease. To make this possible, he makes these events perceptible to certain figures of the plot, situated in specific locations in the Achaean camp. Achilles is presented doing what he often does in the *Iliad*, that is, looking or watching, but this time not at the sea; when he realizes that the horses of Nestor are carrying the wounded Makhaon, he decides at once to dispatch Patroklos and learn whether what he sees is true. What is at work here is a process of mnemonic recall, by which the bard notionally puts himself at the stern of Achilles' ship, and then makes Achilles see from this location what is going on in another area of the camp.[32] What the narrator can remember easily is the concrete location, typified by the Iliadic tradition, of Achilles on the shore looking at the vast sea, which he now alters by placing him on the stern of his ship. He then ties to this image another one, which he has already mentioned, namely that of Nestor's chariot carrying the wounded Makhaon. While bringing to his mind's eye the formulaic image of Achilles abstaining from the battle, he adds to it a new visual image, as seen through Achilles' own eyes. Since common images are easily retrieved and visualized by the human mind, they facilitate the recall of added material. The fact that the narrator first tells his audience what is going on and then presents Achilles seeing what is going on amounts to an almost innate tendency of oral storytelling, in which the narrator first offers a preview of the event to be described and then orients his listeners to the direction he is going to follow in his narrative. He first frames the event (Makhaon carried by the horses of Nestor) and then offers a *close-up*,[33] a more careful look at what happens. While visualizing Achilles looking at what the storyteller has narratively prefaced, the audience has the sense of being mentally involved, of being there on Achilles' ship, looking together with him at Nestor's horses carrying the wounded Makhaon off the battlefield.

In *Iliad* XIV 13, the area near the ships, this time just outside Nestor's tent, is used as an observation post. Here, space is delineated first in terms of sound and

---

[32] See de Jong and Nünlist 2004a:70–71, who call this "a scenic standpoint, fixed on one character, actorial." Nagy (2009c II 7.69–78), commenting on Achilles' watching the fighting in *Iliad* XI 600, argues that "the narrative point of reference in the *Iliad* consistently follows the north-to-south perspective of the Achaeans." See also Cuillandre 1944:41, 69, 96–100, who makes the same point.

[33] On close-ups, see de Jong and Nünlist 2004a:72–73.

then of location. Nestor hears the battle cry (XIV 1 Νέστορα δ' οὐκ ἔλαθεν ἰαχή) and informs the wounded Makhaon that he will look for a "watchpoint" (XIV 8 αὐτὰ ἐγὼ ἐλθὼν τάχα εἴσομαι ἐς περιωπήν),[34] which "happens" to be outside his tent. The clamor of the fighting indicates that the Trojans have now come very close, which is corroborated by the fact that Nestor expects to find soon what is going on (XIV 8) and that this happens "even sooner than he wishes" (which means that the battle is happening almost next door).[35] In this case, the perceptual representation of space is effected first through *sound*,[36] and then through *sight*. This is a different strategy, but as successful as the previous one, of involving the audience in the tale. The outcry of war is not just a verbal input employed by the narrator: it almost acquires "flesh and bones"; it becomes a "tangible" reality, so to speak, as Nestor sees what he has just heard. In like manner, the storyteller almost carries his listeners into his narrative: once they hear about the hubbub of war, they are invited to visualize it, by placing their minds' eye on a mental watchpoint, that is, by connecting, Nestor-like, sound and sight.

The literary topography of space: The funeral games for Patroklos

Visualizing the funeral games for Patroklos must have been one of the most demanding tasks that the Iliadic storyteller had to carry out for his audience. From the area where the games would be held to the complexity of the eight different contests, the narrator faced the challenge of creating a clear mental vista for his listeners. In addition, the contextualization of these athletic contests according to the rules and tenets of heroic society, with its inner tensions and almost systemic rivalries, would have made presenting them even more difficult.[37]

---

[34] Janko 1992:152 on *Iliad* XIV 8 suggests that περιωπή may even be the stern of a ship, which is all the more significant since Achilles has seen Nestor's chariot carrying the wounded Makhaon from his ship's stern (*Iliad* XI 599–601).

[35] Janko 1992:152 on XIV 8.

[36] On space and sound, see Bal 1997:133–134.

[37] Rivalry is a deep-seated feature of the heroic world, but within the highly competitive framework of the funeral games for Patroklos it becomes overt; verbal abuse is here tied, or rather subordinated, to the notion of *spatial ordering*. When heroes turn themselves into *athletes*, their military skills as well as the very means by which they conduct fighting are turned into means of social and political rivalry. The chariot race, boxing, wrestling, running, armed combat, weight-throwing, archery, and spear-throwing contests span the range of Iliadic fighting. Heroes in the *Iliad* often fight while driving their chariots; they throw rocks at each other (like Ajax and Hektor in their duel in *Iliad* VII), run after one other (Achilles chasing Hektor in *Iliad* XXII), and of course constantly engage in spear-throwing as well as in regular armed combat. Although warriors do not engage in boxing or wrestling, most of the athletic contests in the funeral games for

The contest area

His first task was to picture for his audience the place where the games would be held. To this end, he had to transform an area inside the camp into an ἀγών, a "contest space." To effect such a transformation, he opted for a gradual pinpointing of an area that would be suitable for the first and most demanding of the various contests, the chariot race. Visualizing such an area was carried out by two different means: (1) by emphasizing where Achilles stands, who was going to organize the actual events, and (2) by picturing an area that would be inside the Achaean camp but also at some distance from the huts of the army.

As soon as *Iliad* XXIII begins, the storyteller helps his listeners visualize Achilles lying among the Myrmidons on the sea shore and lamenting Patroklos. He is situated "in a clear place where the waves washed over the beach" (61 ἐν καθαρῷ, ὅθι κύματ' ἐπ' ἠϊόνος κλύζεσκον). After the appearance of Patroklos' ghost and the collection of wood needed for his pyre, the πομπή of chariots led by the Myrmidons and Achilles himself, with Patroklos' body in the middle (134), arrives at a place indicated by Achilles (138–139),[38] where the final stage of the funeral will take place. When the burning of Patroklos' body, the gathering and preserving of his bones in a golden jar, the heaping of the earth, and the piling of the tomb are completed, the storyteller emphatically states that it was Achilles who "held the people there, and made them sit down in a wide assembly, / and brought prizes for games out of his ships ..." (258–259).[39] The lack of any specific place marker, which is consistent with the oral storyteller's process of mental visualization, makes this area hard to picture in the mind's eye. This "disadvantage," though, is counterbalanced by the stress laid on Achilles: the narrator's mental camera has been following him, with a few short breaks, since the very beginning of *Iliad* XXIII. As it monitors Achilles, the audience is invited to realize

---

Patroklos represent a metaphorical field of combat, which concerns only the Achaeans, but is marked by its profound analogy to the world of the battlefield. Of the various winners of the funeral games, four are first-rank Iliadic heroes (Diomedes in the chariot race, Odysseus in the foot race, Meriones in the archery, and Agamemnon in the spear-throwing, though he gets the first prize without a contest); two are lesser figures (Epeios in boxing and Eurualos in weight-throwing); finally two contests featuring first-line Achaean heroes (Ajax and Odysseus in wrestling, and Diomedes versus Ajax in armed combat) end in a draw. Notwithstanding the intertextual associations of the actual winners and protagonists of the various contests, the games repeat, enrich, and reconfigure certain overt and covert tensions between Iliadic heroes. See Lohmann 1992.

[38] This must have been along the beach, where the woodcutters had placed their logs after returning from Ida. This was the spot Achilles had chosen for making a huge grave mound for Patroklos (*Iliad* XXIII 125–126). According to West, the ambiguity of αὐτοῦ (258) "may result from using a verse originally composed for Ach.'s funeral, where Ag. might have 'kept the army there' for the games" (2011:400).

[39] αὐτοῦ λαὸν ἔρυκε καὶ ἵζανεν εὐρὺν ἀγῶνα. / νηῶν δ' ἔκφερε ἄεθλα ...

that the games will take place *where Achilles has moved to, that is, in the very same area where the tomb of Patroklos has been piled.*[40] In this way the topography of the contest area is thematized, since it is inextricably linked to the place where Patroklos' σῆμα is situated. Thus the dead comrade is notionally present in the games held in his honor, thanks to Achilles who has organized them next to his friend's tomb.[41]

The contests

Having paved the way to visualizing the area where the games would take place, the storyteller had to do the same thing with the individual contests to be presented. In this case, two factors may have determined his choice: (1) the importance he had decided to give to the chariot race, and (2) the difference between individual contests, which he has treated visually by dividing them into two groups: (2a) contests involving physical contact between the participants, and (2b) throwing events (weight, archery, javelin). As I will show, even running, which belongs to neither (2a) or (2b), is presented as part of (2a) by virtue of the particular type of visualization employed by the narrator. In view of these two factors, the bard has used two techniques of visual representation, the zoom-in and high-angle long or medium camera shot, both of which he has applied to the chariot race, employing the former for contests belonging to category (2a) and the latter to events in category (2b).

The chariot race

For the actual chariot race (*Iliad* XXIII 287–538), the storyteller has employed the techniques of both zooming in and the high-angle long or medium camera

---

[40] Given that space in the *Iliad* is as free with its accuracy as it is with its visualization, it is not surprising that the games take place in a rather uncharted area. The use of the word χῶρος, deprived of any sort of modification but the orders of Achilles, is telling in itself, for it shows that we will be dealing not so much with a location but with space, i.e. *a place with which people do something* (to rephrase de Certeau's famous expression "l'espace est un lieu pratiqué" [1980:208]). The place where the games are held is subordinated to the function of the games. This area becomes so closely associated with athletic events that it actually fades away. We are dealing here not with a system of specific points and locations but with a network of movable and moving features that are deployed in it. The games are a place in flux, an interactive universe of movement, shift, tensions, and conflicts.

[41] See Whitman 1958:215, who emphasizes the return of Achilles to the world of heroes from which he has abstained for a large part of the epic. The person who refused to accept the gifts offered to him by Agamemnon in *Iliad* IX is now presented as a dispenser of prizes in enormous quantities. His epic life, as well as that of Agamemnon, who will receive the first award in spear-throwing from Achilles, though the contest never really takes place, is replayed. On the ritual form of the narrative of the funeral games for Patroklos in the *Iliad* and the fact that "even the Great Panhellenic Games were originally conceived as funeral games for heroes," see Nagy 1979:117.

shot. The special weight of the chariot race must have exerted significant pressure on how it was presented. The strong intertextual background of this event may also have played a role, since the storyteller was aware of other important chariot races that had taken place in funeral games, such as those held in honor of Achilles and Amarunkeus in earlier oral traditions, which we may call for practical reasons *Memnonis*[42] and *Nestoris*[43] respectively. The most significant factor, though, was in all probability the storyteller's decision to present the chariot race on two separate, yet complementary levels: that of the actual event and that of the internal spectators watching this event. To this end, he has employed the technique of zooming in for the actual race, while reserving the high-angle long and medium shots for the watching of the event.

The presentation of the five contestants is interrupted by the dialogue between Antilokhos, the fourth contestant, and his father Nestor, who tells his son about the tactics he should use to defeat his opponents, since his horses are slow.[44] Nestor offers a detailed mental tour of the impending event, which the narrator presents by means of a high-angle long shot, since the king of Pylos "watches" with his mind's eye a potential race that he describes to his son. The implications of this detailed mental tour are important for interpreting the spatial representation of the contest area. It may well be that Nestor's emphasis on the turning post, which is not a spatial preview of the contest, since it plays no role in the race in honor of Patroklos, may be due to an oral tradition concerning Nestor's participation in the funeral games for Amarunkeus, in which he had triumphed in four events but lost to the Aktorione-Molione twins in the chariot race, *as his chariot crashed while trying to pass the turning-post.*[45] Although Nestor

---

[42] With respect to the *Memnonis*, see Pestalozzi 1945:40; Schadewaldt 1965:155–202; W. Kullmann 1960:333–335, 350, 356; N. Richardson 1993:201–203. This is a neoanalytical argument based on the funeral games held in honor of Achilles in the post-Homeric *Aethiopis* by Arctinus of Miletus.

[43] On the so-called *Nestoris*, see Bölte 1934; Frame 2009:105–172.

[44] Nagy (1990b:207–214) stresses the parallelism between Antilokhos and Patroklos by means of their overt connection in the chariot race of the funeral games (*Iliad* XXIII). The double meaning of σῆμα as 'sign' and 'tomb', which is employed in the context of Nestor's advice to Antilokhos before the actual race and is presented as a set of two alternatives (either the tomb of a man who died long ago [line 331] or the turning point in a race of men who lived in the past [332]), has now become a τέρμα 'turning point' for Achilles in the present (333). Drawing on the analogy of the Panhellenic games, "where the turning points of chariot racecourses were conventionally identified with the tombs of heroes," Nagy (1990b:210) shows that the σῆμα Nestor gives to Antilokhos concerning the σῆμα (i.e. the τέρμα of the chariot race) is a reminder of the κλέος of Patroklos in particular, whose very name means "he who has the κλέα of his ancestors" (Πάτροκλος).

[45] Frame 2009:131–172. Frame argues that Nestor and Patroklos share certain mythical features with respect to the process of their becoming *horsemen*. Patroklos begins to be called Πατρόκλεες ἱππεῦ and Πατρόκλεες ἱπποκέλευθε 'horseman Patroklos' in *Iliad* XVI, when he takes the place of Achilles (a substitution reinforced by the fact that Patroklos wears Achilles' armor). It is telling that in doing so he is carrying out Nestor's advice, who in book XI advised him to seek

seems to be intentionally concealing some elements of how he lost to the twins in Bouprasion, he stresses that their greater number was the crucial reason for his defeat (XXIII 638–642). In the words of Frame,

> Nestor says that the twins drove past him because of their "number" (*plḗthei*). He then expands on this by saying that each twin had a different function in the race, for while one of them steadily held the reins, the other urged the horses on with the whip. The fact that the twins have different functions clearly suggests the Indo-European twin myth, and the reason for their victory seems rooted in an opposition between their very natures. But if the twins won by their greater number, we may turn this around and say that Nestor lost by the fact that he was only one against two, and this brings us straight to his variant use of the twin myth. [46]

Nestor offers the audience a potential, but never realized, visual preview of the actual race, which will be used as a backdrop against which the audience is invited to evaluate the real race that takes place in the funeral games for Patroklos. This process is complete when Achilles gives out the prizes at the end of the race. Instead of Eumelos, who finishes last, Nestor is awarded this prize, as an implicit recognition of his participation in another chariot race that took place in another time and place, and in which Nestor was defeated. By offering this prize to Nestor, Achilles makes a gesture to another oral tradition, the recollection of which by Nestor himself is an acknowledgment of "his role in Patroclus' fate."[47] Nestor's visual preview, like his double function with respect to both his role in another tradition and his involvement in the events that lead to Patroklos' death in the *Iliad*, operates both intertextually and intratextually: it feeds on his crashing the chariot while trying to pass a turning-post in the chariot race against the Aktorione-Molione twins, but also paves the way for the

---

Achilles' help. Frame shows that just as Nestor becomes ἱππότα Νέστωρ when he replaces his twin brother Periklumenos, the foremost Pylian hero after whose death Pylos' enemies have the upper hand, so Patroklos becomes a *horseman* when he is turned into a surrogate of Achilles, after failing to rouse him to battle (2009:125). But in contrast to Nestor, who survived the war against the Epeians and reached old age, Patroklos dies. Nestor's presence in the funeral games for Patroklos, and moreover his being awarded a prize *honoris causa* though he does not take part in the chariot race, reflects not only the similarities he shares with Patroklos, but also the fact that he had been defeated in the funeral games in honor of Amarunkeus *before becoming a horseman* (Frame 2009:131).

[46] Frame 2009:133.

[47] Frame 2009:135.

listeners to picture more clearly what is going on when the real race takes place and the technique of zooming in is employed.[48]

The storyteller applies the technique of zooming in for the actual race by focusing his attention on the various contestants. To this end, he employs a device he has also used in his visualization of fighting scenes throughout the epic: he "sees" in pairs, dividing the various contestants into groups of two and mentally following them as they drive their chariots during the race. By "seeing" through associative pairs he facilitates visualization and data recall, since the mnemonic links created are much stronger, and therefore more easily activated. Associative visualization through pairing is a key factor in the process of spatially mapping the chariot race, as can be seen by comparing the three lists of contestants offered by the storyteller. In order to make this point clear, let us first look at the order in which the five participants are presented at different points in the entire episode (Table 1):

Table 1: Order of participants in the chariot race (*Iliad* XXIII 287–538)

1. First Introduction	2. Start	3. Finish
Eumelos	Antilokhos	Diomedes
Diomedes	Eumelos	Antilokhos
Menelaos	Menelaos	Menelaos
Antilokhos	Meriones	Meriones
Meriones	Diomedes	Eumelos

What becomes obvious even after a cursory look is that the first and last list are the important ones for the storyteller, since Eumelos-Diomedes and Menelaos-Antilokhos constitute the two pairs of contestants on whose action the visualization of the area of the chariot race is founded. This visual pairing is based on the first list of participants, which the narrator keeps in his mind and activates when he zooms in on the race. In particular, we can even discern the pattern he has followed in his "treatment" of these pairs: he has selected the second contestant of each pair, whom he has turned into a "winner" of one of the

---

[48] Nestor *tours* the turning-post by mentally "leading" his son through the race, by visualizing Antilokhos driving his chariot past the turning-post. In this way, he creates a strong sense of "being there" and gives the turning-post a *spatial turn*, since it embodies *his own* concern for the victory and acquiring fame for his son. From the very beginning of this episode, then, the audience is invited to read the games as the space of a dynamic social and heroic topography.

smaller, internal races into which he has divided the overall event. Diomedes (second in his initial pairing with Eumelos) defeats Eumelos, just as Antilokhos (second in his initial pairing with Menelaos) defeats Menelaos.[49] This process shows that the associative pairing of the contestants is so strong that it virtually encroaches on the mental picturing of the entire event, which is "divided" into two smaller chariot races between the two pairs of participants, Eumelos-Diomedes and Menelaos-Antilokhos.

Taking my cue from this line of argument, I will now deal with two related questions: first, what is the role of Meriones, and second, why does the storyteller forget or put aside the second list, referring to the placement of the contestants at the start?

According to the scholia,[50] Meriones is added to the list of contestants because of the ensuing quarrel between his commander Idomeneus and Locrian Ajax. This explanation is based on the storyteller's aim of including in the games as many as possible of the first-rank Achaean heroes. Nestor and Idomeneus, who cannot take part in the games because of their age,[51] are given prominent roles as speakers.[52] But while the former is understandably presented as the wise advisor of his son Antilokhos, the latter does not express his concern for his comrade Meriones.[53] Instead, he gets into an argument with Locrian Ajax. Why, then, is Meriones completely left out of the picture when Idomeneus is introduced as a spectator? Associative pairing is once more the answer, though this time it is shaped by both immediate and traditional referentiality: the storyteller had planned to introduce Idomeneus as a spectator, but the antagonistic and verbally competitive presentation of the previous pair of heroes (Menelaos-Antilokhos) was so strong that it easily spilled over to the Cretan king, who was also presented quarrelling with Locrian Ajax. In addition, and given the typical tendency of Iliadic heroes to rivalry and their almost innate propensity to strife,[54] the narrator thought it fit to introduce Idomeneus as expressing no concern for his comrade Meriones.

---

[49] Eumelos finishes the race dead last because his chariot crashes.

[50] bT on *Iliad* XXIII 351; see N. Richardson 1993:213; West 2011:403 on *Iliad* XXIII 448.

[51] On Nestor's inability to take part in the games, see *Iliad* XXIII 621–623; on Idomeneus' age, see XIII 361 (μεσαιπόλιος 'greying', cf. XIII 512–515), XXIII 476 (οὔτε νεώτατός ἐσσι ["you are not by so much the youngest"]). The same applies, though for reasons of overlordship, to Agamemnon, who wins the final event *honoris causa*; see West 2011:400 on *Iliad* XXIII 257–897.

[52] See *Iliad* XXIII 305–350 (Nestor-Antilokhos) and XXIII 456–489 (Idomeneus-Locrian Ajax).

[53] Ameis and Hentze (1906:68 on *Iliad* XXIII 450) explain the storyteller's interest in Idomeneus as due to Meriones' participation in the chariot race. Idomeneus, however, says nothing about his comrade.

[54] The funeral games for Patroklos constitute a complex space where certain concerns endemic to the prize-fighting and agonistic nature of the heroic community converge with metaliterary considerations pertaining to archaic epic at large. The athletic contests for Patroklos represent

As to why the storyteller changes the order of the contestants at the start of the race, and then completely ignores it, one should bear in mind that the first introduction, like the order of presentation of the various competitors in all the events included in the games, is based on the heroes' notional quality.[55] In other words, the storyteller has decided to create a second, short-lived list that is based neither on the contestants' notional quality nor on their final placement at the finish line. A careful look at the table above, where all three lists are presented, shows that the narrator has moved only two heroes from his first list: namely Diomedes and Antilokhos, whom he has placed last and first in the second list. Since order is a form of spatial organization, it becomes plausible that the list of contestants is restructured so as to help the narrator "keep apart" those heroes whom he is going to favor in the ensuing chariot race. Diomedes and Antilokhos will be the two contestants who rise victorious against Eumelos and Menelaos respectively, in the two smaller chariot races into which the storyteller has divided the presentation and mental visualization of the chariot race at large. Since the narrator organizes space in this entire event by exploiting associative pairing, Diomedes and Antilokhos constitute another pair that signifies victory. They are therefore singled out in the second list, and moved so as to frame it.

The actual race is visually split into two smaller races, preceded by a brief depiction of the contestants at the starting line. After the drawing of lots, all the competitors are visualized as standing in line (*Iliad* XXIII 358 στὰν δὲ μεταστοιχεί), while Achilles shows them the turning-post far away on the level plain,[56] where he has stationed Phoinix as judge "to mark and remember the running and bring back a true story" (XXIII 361). The storyteller basically follows the same process of mental picturing he has employed in battle descriptions: a

---

in miniature form the entire range of heroic dynamics that permeate the *Iliad*. The power and tension revealed in the games is so intense that the Iliadic tradition takes pains to delineate a spatial framework within which these prized contests will take place. Notwithstanding the hefty rewards for those winning or excelling in each of the eight athletic contests, the funeral games are beleaguered by various unexpected practices and outcomes, resulting in glaring conflicts and verbal abuse, cut short by the intervention of a "cooperative" instead of a "competitive" Achilles, whose new persona contrasts with his attitude throughout the rest of the poem. The multiple grievances of the games are largely a result of the competitive spirit of most of the participants, who opt for self-assertion, not self-control. See Grethlein 2007.

[55] West 2011:401 on *Iliad* XXIII 288–351.

[56] Achilles is beyond competition; he is clearly the best, as he has immortal horses that were given to Peleus by Poseidon, and would easily have won the chariot race if he had wanted to (*Iliad* XXIII 274–286). Achilles' exclusion from contests with multiple participants is almost endemic in epic tradition; see his exclusion from the catalogue of Helen's suitors in Hesiod's *Catalogue of Women*, fr. 204.87–92 (Merkelbach-West). His exclusion is accompanied by the motif of "he would have won easily, if he had been a contestant," which is also employed in XXIII 274–278.

brief general view followed by zooming his mind's lens in on pairs of contestants.[57] Phoinix, who was last heard from in XIX 311, is turned into a judge, who in the manner of a bard will remember what happened in the race and report it accurately. As far as the representation of space is concerned, Phoinix is one of the three poles on which the notion of an internal audience is based. As Nestor advised Antilokhos by mentally picturing a proposed race, Phoinix will do the same with the actual race, and finally Idomeneus and Locrian Ajax will also bring forward their own versions of what happened in the race as they watched it from a distance. By insisting on various Iliadic heroes' watching the chariot race, the narrator facilitates the external audience's own visualization of the same event. All internal spectators pave the way so that the external audience may not just see the narrated event, but also picture others watching this event, and consequently place themselves in the position of those heroes watching the race. The result is ἐνάργεια, a vivid representation that turns listeners into viewers.

The description of the actual race continues with a medium-angle camera shot of the chariots being driven at great speed through the plain. When the chariots approach the end of the road and come to the sea, then the storyteller zooms his lens in on the participants, whom he visualizes in groups of two. The narrator offers a visualization of the pair Eumelos-Diomedes in a single shot. As soon as he pictures Eumelos and his chariot in the lead, he makes it clear that Diomedes' chariot is very close behind him (*Iliad* XXIII 378–381).[58] Once he has zoomed in on this group of contestants, the storyteller begins to use a visual zigzag, zooming in further on one or the other hero (382–400): first on Diomedes' chariot, by presenting Apollo snatching the whip away from the son of Tudeus and Athena giving it back; then to Eumelos' chariot, the yoke of which is smashed by Athena; and finally to Diomedes' chariot, which passes Eumelos and leaves the others far behind. The narrator gradually decreases the width of his mental camera as he aims at offering a close look at the actual race. Zooming in is therefore combined with a zigzag visualization of the two heroes.

When the winner from the first pair of contestants has been decided, and given that he is going to be the winner of the entire race, as this was the leading

---

[57] See West 2011:401 on *Iliad* XXIII 362–372.

[58] ... οὐδέ τι πολλὸν ἄνευθ' ἔσαν, ἀλλὰ μάλ' ἐγγύς. / αἰεὶ γὰρ δίφρου ἐπιβησομένοισιν ἐΐκτην, / πνοιῇ δ' Εὐμήλοιο μετάφρενον εὐρέε τ' ὤμω / θέρμετ· ἐπ' αὐτῷ γὰρ κεφαλὰς καταθέντε πετέσθην ("... not far behind at all, but close on him, / for they seemed forever on the point of climbing his chariot / and the wind of them was hot on the back and on the broad shoulders / of Eumelos. They lowered their heads and flew close after him.") Notice that the rhetorical figure of κατ' ἄρσιν καὶ θέσιν 'parallelism of negative and positive', which expresses the same idea twice, negatively by rejecting its opposite and positively by stating what happens, intensifies the clarity of the visualization, since it creates a stronger mental picture.

group, the bard switches to the Antilokhos-Menelaos pair. He begins with Antilokhos, who is seen urging his horses to run faster. This incitement is in fact a prelude to the double zooming-in that lies at the heart of this scene: first, the bard focuses his attention on the narrowing of the hollow way, and then further zooms in with his mind's eye on a break in the ground because of winter water (419–421). This intensified zooming amounts to the technique of *internal preview* that is also used in certain battle scenes:[59] the narrator first visually familiarizes his audience with a specific spot within a smaller frame (the break in the ground within the narrowing of the hollow way), and then places there the thematic core of his scene. The agonistic tone and rivalry between Antilokhos and Menelaos, highlighted by their exchange of angry words, contrasts with the preceding presentation of the Eumelos-Diomedes pair where there is no direct speech.[60] Variation has played its role here, although in both cases the result has been decided by some unexpected event: divine interventions in the former, human poor sportsmanship in the latter.

Once Antilokhos has emerged victorious in the second-pair chariot race, the bard turns his attention to a group of spectators watching the event. He first adopts a high-angle medium shot that allows him to visualize the internal audience from some distance.[61] Then, with a low-angle shot, he pictures Idomeneus sitting apart from the others, on high ground so as to see in all directions (*Iliad* XXIII 451 ἧστο γὰρ ἐκτὸς ἀγῶνος ὑπέρτατος ἐν περιωπῇ). On hearing Diomedes calling, he is able to see at a distance his chariot taking the lead, and as if being informed by the narrator, he suggests that Eumelos' mares have had an accident at the turning-post. His speech is followed by an angry reply from Locrian

---

[59] See chapter 1 above.

[60] Critics have emphasized how the Iliadic storyteller uses these potential conflicts to present an alternative picture of Achilles, who is transformed from the hero of μῆνις into a hero of arbitration and wisdom. Achilles restrains the inbuilt tendency of heroes toward strife, as with Antilokhos in the chariot race. It has been recently argued that the famous "smile" of Achilles in *Iliad* XXIII 555–557, at the very moment that Antilokhos behaves like a second Achilles, having been deprived of the second prize because of the action of a god (Athena being responsible for Diomedes' victory), reflects a metaliterary, poetological gesture by the "poet of the *Iliad*," who smiles at his own work of art (Rengakos 2006a:18 = 2007:101). The role of space in the process of Achilles' transformation, as well as in the presentation of the rest of the Achaean leaders who participate in the games, is noteworthy. The various contests that make up the games, as is the case with modern prize-fighting, are overt or covert "nom de guerre aliases" (Heiskanen 2004:242). Space here takes the form of classification and order: ordinal numerals make κλέος, with respect not so much to the actual result, but more importantly to the awarding of prizes that symbolize the heroes' recognition among their peers. Space becomes the means by which collective awareness and credit are measured and evaluated. In the end, they are subsumed under a narrative that bridges the power dynamics of the battlefield and the prizewinning ideology of the games, which both belong to the same chain of heroic ideological concerns and epitomize symmetrical underlying assumptions concerning the world of heroes.

[61] On this technique, see Winkler 2007:53.

Ajax, who thinks that the leading chariot is still that of Eumelos. Idomeneus answers back, and Achilles intervenes before the matter gets out of control (XXIII 448–498). Having discussed above the importance and function of this mirror scene for the visualization of the actual race, I will explore here only its spatial features. Although the inherent tensions between members of the heroic community may sufficiently explain the disagreement between Idomeneus and Locrian Ajax, the two figures constitute one more pair that translates the picturing of the place of the assembly into character action. As with the actual chariot race, in which the greatest and most important component of mental visualization was based on the actions of two pairs of contestants and not on a description of the contest area, so with the assembly place, the initial low-angle camera shot that singled out Idomeneus soon takes the form of a flyting between two first-rank heroes. Once more, dynamic space delineated by the concrete action of characters on whom the storyteller zooms his mind's lens is the central means of achieving a clear mental picture.

The finish of the race is visualized in three camera shots, each zooming in on a pair of heroes. The first shot is continuous, since it follows Diomedes arriving in his chariot, stopping at the middle of the assembly area, and leaping down from his chariot in a symbolic gesture at the end of the race. The majestic presentation of Diomedes is coupled with the insertion of Sthenelos into the storyteller's mind's camera frame, since it is he who awards him the first victory prize. Traditional referentiality on the one hand (the two Theban heroes Diomedes and Sthenelos often appear together in the epic), and associative pairing as a spatial cue for data recall on the other, have both played their role in the visualization of this scene. Likewise in the second camera shot, in which the narrator sees with his mind's eye Antilokhos and Menelaos as a pair of contestants arriving at the finish line one after the other: the emphasis on their closeness (*Iliad* XXIII 516–527) is consistent with the earlier presentation of the actual race, but also reflects the bard's technique of "seeing" jointly, that is, including the pair of contestants in a single mental vista. The third and last camera shot contains Meriones and Eumelos, the great outsider and the favorite in the chariot race respectively. Once more, visualization is realized by means of associative pairing based on the spatial aspect of order, which is here deftly employed to allude to the contrast between expected (Meriones) and unexpected (Eumelos) failure.

Boxing

Boxing is the first in a group of four events (boxing, wrestling, running, duel in armor) involving mainly (with the exception of running) physical contact between contestants and presented by means of the zooming-in technique.

The space where the event takes place is visualized by a close camera shot on the pair of boxers, Epeios and Eurualos. The narrator employs multiple means to make this possible: he places them in the spotlight by having them move, "girt up," to the middle of the circle (*Iliad* XXIII 685 τὼ δὲ ζωσαμένω βήτην ἐς μέσσον ἀγῶνα); zooms in on them facing each other (686 ἄντα); capitalizes on their closeness and subsequent mutual attack by exploiting the spatial aspect of sound (686–688 ... ἀνασχομένω χερσὶ στιβαρῇσιν ἅμ' ἄμφω / σύν ῥ' ἔπεσον, σὺν δέ σφι βαρεῖαι χεῖρες ἔμιχθεν. / δεινὸς δὲ χρόμαδος γενύων γένετ' ...); concentrates on details of the bodies of the two boxers, like the sweat running all over their limbs or the cheek of Mekisteus receiving a blow from Epeios (688–690 ... ἔρρεε δ' ἱδρώς / πάντοθεν ἐκ μελέων ... / κόψε δὲ παπτήναντα παρήϊον);[62] locates Mekisteus' collapse at the very same spot where he was standing, that is, at the middle of the circle (690–691 ... οὐδ' ἄρ' ἔτι δήν / ἑστήκειν, αὐτοῦ γὰρ ὑπήριπε φαίδιμα γυῖα); pictures Epeios helping him stand up (694–695 αὐτάρ μεγάθυμος Ἐπειός / χερσὶ λαβὼν ὤρθωσε); and finally visualizes his comrades, who are standing nearby, carrying him out of the circle (695–698 φίλοι δ' ἀμφέσταν ἑταῖροι, / οἵ μιν ἄγον δι' ἀγῶνος ἐφελκομένοισι πόδεσσιν, / αἷμα παχὺ πτύοντα, κάρη βάλλονθ' ἑτέρωσε· / κὰδ δ' ἀλλοφρονέοντα μετὰ σφίσιν εἷσαν ἄγοντες).

In this way, the narrator has been able to offer his audience a vivid vista of the actual encounter, which they (like the internal audience of other heroes) can see happening in front of their eyes. By highlighting proximity, the zooming-in technique immerses listeners into the narrated scene and results in a feeling of presence, as if they can hear the loud noise produced by the fighting and almost "see" the sweat running off the bodies of Epeios and Eurualos.[63]

Wrestling

The wrestling contest between Ajax and Odysseus is visualized in two phases, the former bringing to the spotlight the initial engagement, the latter zooming in on their failed efforts to lift each other and their subsequent mutual fall on the ground. Like the boxing contest, the first phase of this event is visualized

---

[62] The visualization of these details creates the illusion of "being close" to the event taking place. The sweat running off the bodies of the two boxers can only be seen by someone standing next to the two contestants. Likewise for the determination of the particular part of the face (cheek) that receives Epeios' punch.

[63] Epeios and Eurualos are not first-rank Iliadic heroes. The former features only in the funeral games, and the latter, apart from the Catalogue of Ships (*Iliad* II 565–566), is mentioned in passing in VI 20. It is undoubtedly their rich intertextual background that must have influenced the narrator's choice to use them in the boxing contest. Epeios, as the builder of the wooden horse (*Odyssey* viii 493; xi 523), was a key figure in the *Little Iliad* and probably the *Iliou Persis*, and Eurualos, son of the boxer Mekisteus who triumphed in the funeral games of Oedipus and one of the Epigonoi, featured in the Theban epic tradition.

by almost the same means, since both games are based on the physical contact of the two participants: the bard pictures the pair of contestants girding up and moving to the middle of the circle (*Iliad* XXIII 710 ζωσαμένω δ' ἄρα τώ γε βάτην ἐς μέσσον ἀγῶνα),[64] zooms in on them grappling each other (711 ἀγκὰς δ' ἀλλήλων λαβέτην χερσὶ στιβαρῇσιν), takes full advantage of the spatial aspect of sound to create the feeling of presence for his audience (714 τετρίγει), and focuses on particular features of the bodies of the two wrestlers, like their sweat and the bruises on their ribs and shoulders (716 πυκναὶ δὲ σμώδιγγες ἀνὰ πλευράς τε καὶ ὤμους).

The second phase, comprising no fewer than twelve camera shots, is further divided into three parts. The first two, focusing on the failed attempts of Ajax and Odysseus to lift each other and their falling on the ground, are symmetrically balanced, since each of them contains five camera shots. By offering an even closer zoom in on this pair of contestants, they capitalize on the notion of proximity and presence, while the third one brings Achilles into the picture, who stops the contest:

Phase A:

(1) Ajax tries to lift Odysseus (725 ὣς εἰπὼν ἀνάειρε)

(2) Odysseus strikes him at the hollow of his knee (725–726 Ὀδυσσεύς· / κόψ' ὄπιθεν κώληπα τυχών)

(3) Odysseus throws Ajax over backward (727 κὰδ δ' ἔβαλ' ἐξοπίσω)

(4) Odysseus falls on his chest (727–728 ἐπὶ δὲ στήθεσσιν Ὀδυσσεύς / κάππεσε)

(5) The internal audience looks on in wonder (728 λαοὶ δ' αὖ θηέοντό τε θάμβησάν τε)

Phase B:

(6) Odysseus attempts to lift Ajax (729 δεύτερος αὖτ' ἀνάειρε πολύτλας δῖος Ὀδυσσεύς)

(7) Odysseus is able to move him just a little from the ground (730 κίνησεν δ' ἄρα τυτθὸν ἀπὸ χθονός, οὐδ' ἔτ' ἄειρεν)

(8) His knee is hooked behind (731 ἐν δὲ γόνυ γνάμψεν)

(9) They both fall on the ground next to each other (731–732 ἐπὶ δὲ χθονὶ κάππεσον ἄμφω / πλησίοι ἀλλήλοισι)

(10) They are "soiled in the dust" (732 μιάνθησαν δὲ κονίῃ)

---

[64] See *Iliad* XXIII 685 τὼ δὲ ζωσαμένω βήτην ἐς μέσσον ἀγῶνα.

Phase C:

(11) Achilles intervenes (734–737 εἰ μὴ Ἀχιλλεὺς αὐτὸς ἀνίστατο καὶ κατέρυκεν· / "μηκέτ' ἐρείδεσθον, μὴ δὲ τρίβεσθε κακοῖσιν. / νίκη δ' ἀμφοτέροισιν· ἀέθλια δ' ἶσ' ἀνελόντες / ἔρχεσθ', ὄφρα καὶ ἄλλοι ἀεθλεύωσιν Ἀχαιοί")

(12) The two contestants wipe the dust from their bodies and put on their tunics (738–739 ὣς ἔφαθ', οἳ δ' ἄρα τοῦ μάλα μὲν κλύον ἠδ' ἐπίθοντο, / καί ῥ' ἀπομορξαμένω κονίην δύσαντο χιτῶνας)

The five camera shots that make up each of the first two phases make use of the sequential technique employed in the case of fighting duels, in which the bard presents one warrior aiming first and only then turns to his opponent aiming second. In that case, the first throw of a spear is presented in full until that shot is completed; only then does the narrator turn his lens to the second attempt. Here, though, there is a notable difference: the storyteller's camera moves vertically, not horizontally as it does for an armed duel. By using the same number of "cuts" (in cinematographic terminology) for the attempt of each contestant, the bard is able to make clear for his audience the similarity of both failed efforts, leading to the same result. This subtle technique further builds on the fact that the final draw is effectively connected to the final placement of the bodies of Ajax and Odysseus in horizontal position on the earth.[65] Thus, the event that started with the participants' "standing up" (707–709 "ὄρνυσθ', οἳ καὶ τούτου ἀέθλου πειρήσεσθον". / ὣς ἔφατ'· ὦρτο δ' ἔπειτα μέγας Τελαμώνιος Αἴας, / ἂν δ' Ὀδυσεὺς πολύμητις ἀνίστατο, κέρδεα εἰδώς) ends with their lying on the ground. This interplay between verticality and horizontality that is shared by the two heroes is a further spatial association that involves the audience in producing vivid mental images.[66]

The event is completed with two camera shots (phase C), in the first of which Achilles intervenes. The "cuts" on Achilles standing up, and on the two heroes cleaning the dust from their bodies and wearing their tunics, are a visual repetition of the initial shots with which the actual event started: after Achilles stood up and called for a wrestling event, Ajax and Odysseus rose too and put on their gear ready to wrestle.

---

[65] In contrast to the boxing event, which ended with the collapse of only the defeated contestant, Eurualos, in the wrestling event there is no winner. On the neoanalytical arguments about echoes of the contest of arms featuring in the *Aethiopis*, see Pestalozzi 1945:51; W. Kullmann 1960:81, 335. Differently West (2011:407 on *Iliad* XXIII 708–709), who finds no indication of such a link.

[66] See Garcia 2007:181.

Running

The foot race is characterized by a clear analogy with part of the chariot race:[67] the three competitors are lined up while Achilles determines the finish line (757 ~ 358), the presentation is based on the technique of associative pairing (Locrian Ajax and Odysseus: 758–766), as it was with the first group of competitors in the chariot race (Eumelos and Diomedes: 375–381). The third competitor (Antilokhos) is completely left out of the actual race—exactly as with Meriones, the nonpaired fifth contestant in the chariot race—and there is a divine intervention by Athena, who harms the leader (Locrian Ajax in the foot race, Eumelos in the chariot race) and helps her favored contestant (Odysseus and Diomedes) by listening to Odysseus' prayer (770–771) and making Eumelus' chariot collapse (391–396).

On the level of mental visualization, the use of the zoom technique for an event that does not involve physical contact (unlike boxing, wrestling, or dueling) is surprising. What has really determined the emphasis on the proximity of the two contestants, the focus on their contest, and the complete ignorance of the third competitor who is virtually left out of the picture? Associative pairing is both a powerful cue to recall and an effective means of spatial organization. The bard pictures the actual area where the contest takes place in terms of the progressive action of a pair of contestants, whose course he mentally follows. The visual link between them is significantly strengthened when they are presented as a pair, that is, by means of single "cut." The nondiegetic insertion of an extended simile picturing the proximity between a woman's chest and the shuttle she holds in her hands while weaving (760–763) brings to mind the filmic technique of *montage*,[68] in which one shot merges with another that is superimposed on it. Thus the two competitors are seen as a single visual unit as far as the narrative is concerned. Next to them is placed a nonnarrative "cut" that spills over to the associative pairing of the two competitors and becomes mentally tied to it. The single shot of the main narrative is based on the Homeric narrator's tendency to "depict all bodies and single objects only through their contribution towards this [progressive] action, and commonly by a single trait."[69] This dynamic process of creating mental images is based on the activation (comprising selection and juxtaposition) of small amounts of information in the

---

[67] See West 2011:408 on *Iliad* XXIII 757–797.

[68] See Garcia 2007:177. See also Bakker 1993, who refers to the segmentation of Homeric speech into discrete units that are subsequently joined together into chains or sequences.

[69] The full quotation in German is as follows: "Ich finde, Homer mallet nichts als fortschreitende Handlungen, und alle Körper, all einzelne Dinge mallet er nur durch ihren Antheil an diesen Handlungen, gemeiniglich nur mit einem Zuge" (Lessing 1893:117). The translation is my own.

form of visual elements and on their sequential arrangement or interweaving. In the words of Garcia, "Homer is no painter; he is a cinematographer."[70]

Duel in Armor

This is the last of the first category of events involving physical contact. Once more, the storyteller employs the technique of associative pairing by presenting the armed duel of Telamonian Ajax and Diomedes. As expected from the nature of this contest, the duel is visualized in terms of the same spatial features used for duels on the battlefield. First, the two competitors are mentally pictured in opposition to the crowd of spectators (*Iliad* XXIII 813–814 οἳ δ' ἐπεὶ οὖν ἑκάτερθεν ὁμίλου θωρήχθησαν, / ἐς μέσον ἀμφοτέρω συνίτην μεμαῶτε μάχεσθαι ["When these were in their armour on either side of the assembly, / they came together in the middle space, furious for the combat"]). This spatial partition, applied time and again in formal duels, helps the audience visualize the two contestants by using the multitude of internal viewers as a backdrop against which attention can be focused on the pair of antagonists, who are thus brought to the spotlight. Then, the bard visualizes the two competitors approaching and attacking each other three times at close range (816–817 ἀλλ' ὅτε δὴ σχεδὸν ἦσαν ἐπ' ἀλλήλοισιν ἰόντες, / τρὶς μὲν ἐπήϊξαν, τρὶς δὲ σχεδὸν ὡρμήθησαν ["Then as, moving forward, the two were closing in on each other, / there were three charges, three times they swept in close"]). Both their mutual approach and the repeated attacks invite the audience to picture Ajax and Diomedes up close, to see the actual contest with their minds' eye *again and again*.

It is exactly at this moment that the narrator zooms his camera in on the actual fight. He is in a position to do this because he has gradually narrowed his field of vision: leaving aside the crowd of spectators, he now focuses on the competitors, who are brought to the middle; are then presented by means of dynamic space, that is, by moving close together; and are subsequently pictured as attacking each other. In this light, the further details of the duel can be easily visualized. Each hero's attempt is given by three close "cuts":[71]

A. ἔνθ' Αἴας μὲν ἔπειτα κατ' ἀσπίδα πάντοσ' ἐΐσην νύξ',	A. Then Aias on the shield [of Diomedes], the circular one on all sides [he] stabbed

---

[70] 2007:179.

[71] *Iliad* XXIII 818–821; the translation is adapted from Lattimore 1951, so as to show the way visual "cuts" are arranged.

B. οὐδὲ χρό᾽ ἵκανεν   B. but did not reach the skin,

C. ἔρυτο γὰρ ἔνδοθι θώρηξ   C. for the corselet inside it guarded him.

A. Τυδείδης δ᾽ ἄρ᾽ ἔπειτα ὑπὲρ σάκεος μεγάλοιο   A. Then the son of Tudeus, over the top of the huge shield,

B. αἰὲν ἐπ᾽ αὐχένι κῦρε   B. was always menacing the neck [of Ajax]

C. φαεινοῦ δουρὸς ἀκωκῇ   C. with the point of the shining spear

Each visual "cut" is based on a different spatial aspect of the duel, which becomes a cue for visualizing the last phase of this event. In terms of speech organization, these mental "shots" are verbalized by means of three *intonation units*:[72] in the case of Diomedes, the first translates the spatial feature of the round shield, the second that of the skin, and the last that of the hero's corselet.[73] In the case of Ajax, the first is based on Ajax's famous eight-layered shield, the second zooms in on his neck, and the third on the point of the shining spear, each one visualizing a different phase of the actual duel. This is an important detail, since it shows that the storyteller is either picturing with his mind's eye the moment when the spear hits the opponent's shield (in the case of Ajax's attempt) or is visualizing the potential flight of the spear (in the case of Diomedes' throw). In the latter case, the audience is invited to adopt first the focalization of Diomedes, who sees the unprotected neck of Ajax, and then that of the internal audience of Achaean spectators, who see the point of the shining spear in Diomedes' hand, ready to be thrown at Ajax's neck. The symmetrical arrangement of "cuts" allows the bard to create a balance between the outcome of the event and the way it is visualized.[74] Selection and highlighting of spatial aspects is his own, but it will also be shared by his audience, if they see what he sees, and most importantly the way he sees it.

---

[72] On intonation units and frames, see Bakker 1997:100–111.

[73] This tiny regression is introduced by the γάρ-clause, which is "no more than additional visual detail pertaining to the picture verbalized in a preceding unit" (Bakker 1997:112). From the point of view of cognitive science, the regression is carried out by a spatial feature, the corselet (θώρηξ), which is of course placed above the skin (χρόα). This small anachrony is thus effected by means of space.

[74] Symmetrical arrangement facilitates data organization and eases recall.

Weight-throwing

The event of weight-throwing is the first in the list of three contests that do not involve physical contact. The very nature of these events determines to a considerable extent the kind of visualization the storyteller will adopt. In this particular case, though, the narrator will first offer his list of the four competitors, who—perhaps unexpectedly—are not presented in order of merit. To explore the cognitive process of picturing the various heroes when they rise to take part in the event and when the results are presented, let us compare the three relevant lists given by the bard (Table 2):

Table 2: Order of participants in the weight-throwing contest
(*Iliad* XXIII 826–849)

1. First Introduction	2. Order of Throwing	3. Results
Polupoites	Epeios	Polupoites
Leonteus	Leonteus	Telamonian Ajax
Telamonian Ajax	Telamonian Ajax	Leonteus
Epeios	Polupoites	Epeios

Although the bard does not make clear at all whether Epeios threw the weight further than Leonteus or vice versa, the audience is expected to assume that Leonteus surpassed Epeios, since the latter's throw causes laughter, whereas the former's does not. What is beyond doubt, of course, is that Polupoites is the winner and that Ajax's throw outdistanced those of both Epeios and Leonteus (843 ὑπέρβαλε σήματα πάντων).

The comparison of these three lists shows that the second and the third have been verbally conflated in a single list, presenting the four competitors in the order they threw the weight, but also containing, in reverse form, the results of their attempts. In other words, the second and third lists exist as separate categories only cognitively or visually, although they have been subsumed into one list by the narrator. I stress this point because I regard it as of key importance for exploring the process of spatial organization of this event. With the first list, the storyteller has decided to introduce an associative pair of contestants, the Lapithai Polupoites and Leonteus, who have appeared earlier in the plot (*Iliad* II 740–746; XII 129–130), and then two other competitors who readily came to his mind as typical examples of exceptionally strong heroes who have systematically been presented as first participants in previous contests (Epeios in boxing,

Telamonian Ajax in both wrestling and armed duels). As to their order, given that Ajax has been mentioned more often and more recently than Epeios, he comes before him in the storyteller's mind. With respect to the order of throwing, the bard has exchanged the positions of the first and last participants, placing the first (Polupoites) last, and the last (Epeios) first.[75] This choice is very much at odds both with the technique of associative pairing, since the two Lapithai are now separated as they occupy the second and fourth positions in the second list (that of the order of throwing), and with ring composition, a traditional epic technique that one would expect to be employed in cases like this.[76] Why, then, has the storyteller opted to switch the positions of the first and last participants? The answer is based on the cognitive process at hand, which pertains to the spatial visualization of this entire event. When a contest does not include physical contact, the bard does not "see" it performed by pairs of competitors. On the contrary, he sees by long "cuts" that allow him to capture in his mind's eye the whole distance that the various heroes will cover with their throws. In particular, he visualizes the event by gradually widening the angle of his mental lens: first he sees the hero whose throw will cover the smallest distance, Epeios; then, using him as a visual basis, he will go a bit further and picture Leonteus' throw, who will surpass Epeios; next, he will see Telamonian Ajax's throw, which surpasses the marks of the previous two contestants; last, he will picture Polupoites' throw, which goes so far beyond all others that the narrator will avail himself of a simile as a mental aid to intensify and clarify the distance it covers (XXIII 845–847). Such progressive visualization based on linear mental movement along a spatial chain, each link of which allows the storyteller to transfer himself to the next, is analogous to the well-known mnemonic technique of *increment recall*, employed in list-learning. Although not the same, both techniques capitalize on serial progression and additive, linear expansion, that is, on mental spatialization.[77]

The verbal convergence of the second and third lists is thus the product of two cognitive schemata activated in the narrator's mind: the order of throwing is determined by the mental picturing of the space covered by each competitor's throw. This is a remarkable example of the transformation of a temporal process (who threw first, second, third, and fourth) into a spatial arrangement (whose throw went further). The visual tracking of an entire event has therefore been shaped by means of the gradual mental "imaging" of the dynamic and expanding space of the distance covered by the weight throwing.

---

[75] The same point is also made by West 2011:409 on *Iliad* XXIII 836–838.
[76] If ring composition had been used, then we would expect the order of throwing to be Epeios, Telamonian Ajax, Leonteus, Polupoites.
[77] See Baddeley 1990:40–42, 156–158. On the use of this technique in epic catalogues, see Tsagalis 2009:165.

Archery

The archery contest between Teukros and Meriones involves hitting a pigeon tied by a string to a ship's mast-pole at a considerable distance.[78] Achilles makes it clear that the competitor who succeeds in hitting the pigeon will be awarded the first prize, while the one who only hits the string will be given the second.

The event is presented in three phases, each visualized by means of a long-distance camera frame. The first frame is pictured by following the narrator's lens, which first tours the area where the target is placed and only then sees the target (*Iliad* XXIII 852–854):

A. ἱστὸν δ' ἔστησεν νηὸς κυανοπρώροιο	and planted the mast pole of a dark-prowed ship
B. τηλοῦ ἐπὶ ψαμάθοις,	far away on the sands
C. ἐκ δὲ τρήρωνα πέλειαν	and a tremulous wild pigeon to it
D. λεπτῇ μηρίνθῳ δῆσεν ποδός	he tethered by a thin string attached to her foot

This four-shot process is typical for viewing this event, and will also be employed (in a slightly expanded form) in presenting the two subsequent phases, the actual attempts of Teukros and Meriones. When viewing the place where the target will be, the storyteller first sees the particular spot he will be focusing on, the ship's mast, and then moves with a second "cut" further down to the sand far away. Only when he has toured the entire contest area does he view the "tremulous pigeon" on the mast and, again by a vertically moving "cut," pictures the tiny string attached to its foot. The way he has visualized the contest area is telling for his subsequent picturing of the entire event: the audience realizes not only that the target is far away but that it is also placed high up. By combining distance with verticality, the bard provides a clear mental vista of the forthcoming event. His audience has been now familiarized with the scene he is going to offer them, and the shooting can begin.

Both Teukros' and Meriones' attempts are visualized by not only the same number but also the same kind of "cuts." Let us first see how these camera shots are presented by separate intonation units (*Iliad* XXIII 865–869 and 874–883; Lattimore's translation, modified), and then examine them through a comparative presentation (Table 3, below):

[78] Teukros and Meriones are the only notable archers among the Achaeans (apart from Philoktetes, who is a member of the army but not present in Troy). On the connotational function of archery as a way of fighting, see H. Mackie 1996:49–55.

A. ὄρνιθος μὲν ἅμαρτε·...

He missed the bird ...

B. αὐτὰρ ὃ μήρινθον βάλε πὰρ πόδα, τῇ δέδετ' ὄρνις,

but ... hit the string beside the foot where the bird was tied

C. ἀντικρὺ δ' ἀπὸ μήρινθον τάμε πικρὸς ὀϊστός.

and straight through cut the string the bitter arrow

D. ἣ μὲν ἔπειτ' ἤϊξε πρὸς οὐρανόν,

and she leapt towards the sky

E. ἣ δὲ παρείθη / μήρινθος ποτὶ γαῖαν·

while the string dropped and dangled / toward the ground

A. ὕψι δ' ὑπὸ νεφέων εἶδε τρήρωνα πέλειαν·

Way up under the clouds he saw the tremulous pigeon

B. τῇ ῥ' ὅ γε δινεύουσαν ὑπὸ πτέρυγος βάλε μέσσην.

and as she circled struck her under the wing in the body

C. ἀντικρὺ δὲ διῆλθε βέλος·

and the shaft passed clean through and out of her,

D. τὸ μὲν ἂψ ἐπὶ γαίῃ / πρόσθεν Μηριόναο πάγη ποδός·

and dropped back on the ground and stuck before Meriones' foot,

E. αὐτὰρ ἣ ὄρνις /... τῆλε δ' ἀπ' αὐτοῦ / κάππεσε·

but the bird ... fell far away from there

Table 3: Teukros' and Meriones' attempts in the archery contest

Teukros	Meriones
1. Misses pigeon	1. Sees pigeon
2. Hits the string attached to the pigeon's foot	2. Hits pigeon under the wing
3. Arrow pierces the string	3. Arrow pierces pigeon
4. Missed target (pigeon) flies to the sky	4. Arrow falls on the ground
5. Hit target (string) falls on the ground	5. Pigeon flies back to the mast pole but then falls down

Meriones' attempt, organized in five "cuts" (sees, hits, pierces, arrow falls, pigeon falls) mirrors Teukros' previous attempt, also visualized in five "cuts," with slight changes (misses, hits, pierces, pigeon flies to the sky, string falls). The symmetrical depiction of long-distance space makes its visualization clearer, since narrator and audience alike are mentally viewing the same space over and over again. It is exactly within this framework that the use of the same weapon (just as in the weight-throwing and javelin contests) enhances visual connections and analogies.[79] By seeing Meriones taking the bow Teukros has just used in his hand, the audience can clearly evaluate the link between the two attempts: all elements that need to be mentally pictured are the same (mast, pigeon, string, ground), with the exception of the two arrows and the two competitors. The impact of visual space on the articulation of this event is such that some details seem to have been invented as a visual reflex to what was depicted in Teukros' first attempt. After piercing the pigeon, Meriones' arrow falls down in front of his foot *because* the pigeon was pictured in the previous phase as tied to the mast by its foot. There is no causal connection here, only a visual one. The image of the foot has been mentally carried over from the pigeon to Meriones. Associative links of this sort testify to the spatial substratum of visual memory.

The javelin

The javelin contest never really takes place, since Agamemnon is awarded the first prize and Meriones the second without ever throwing the spear. The award reflects the recognition of Agamemnon's preeminence on the basis of his strength and throwing ability (XXIII 890–891 ... ἴδμεν γὰρ ὅσσον προβέβηκας ἁπάντων / ἠδ᾽ ὅσσον δυνάμι τε καὶ ἥμασιν ἔπλε᾽ ἄριστος).[80] Meriones is simply a "filler," visually available from the previous contest (860 = 888).[81]

Here, though, visual memory may have played a crucial role that has gone unobserved. Critics have discussed the "problem" of the unexpected order of the two prizes (the prize mentioned first is the second awarded, while the one mentioned second is the first to be given), as well as the triviality of the spear as a prize. It has been suggested that the spear "was not initially intended as a prize at all, only as the spear to be used in the contest, and then Ach. made it a complimentary prize for Meriones."[82] This cannot be true, since the μέν in 884 should be followed by a δέ referring to the two prizes. There is no alternative, for

---

[79] Such considerations have not attracted scholarly interest with respect to the abrupt syntax of *Iliad* XXIII 870–871; see both Leaf 1900–1902:533 and N. Richardson 1993:268 on this passage.

[80] "... for we know how much you surpass all others, / by how much you are greatest for strength among the spear-throwers."

[81] See West 2011:410 on *Iliad* XXIII 884–897.

[82] This is W. Jordan's suggestion, taken from West 2011:419 on *Iliad* XXIII 884.

only one "means" can be used for each contest. This point is further supported by *Iliad* XXIII 798–799 (αὐτὰρ Πηλεΐδης κατὰ μὲν δολιχόσκιον ἔγχος / θῆκ' ἐς ἀγῶνα φέρων, κατὰ δ' ἀσπίδα καὶ τρυφάλειαν ["Then the son of Peleus carried into the circle and set down / a far-shadowing spear, and set down beside it a shield and a helmet"]), where the two prizes are designated.[83] There, Achilles' speech followed, in which the nature of the actual contest was explained and Asteropaeus' sword was also put down as a prize. Such a speech, in which Achilles would define the nature of the spear contest, is lacking here for two reasons: first because it is inherent in the expression (886 καί ῥ' ἥμονες ἄνδρες ἀνέσταν ["and the spear-throwers rose up"]), and second because the participation of Agamemnon decides the result without the need for an actual event. The storyteller needs to seal the reconciliation between the two heroes with a telling gesture of acknowledgement of status. The bard makes Achilles speak with *Iliad* I in mind:[84] the prize is given to Talthubios to be carried to the ships.[85] Long- and short-term memory are therefore "responsible" for the presentation of this last event. The standing up of the two would-be competitors, this time, is visualized in such a stark manner that it determines not only the nature of the contest and the end result, obviating the actual event, but also the "absorption" of the contest by the end result: by picturing Agamemnon, the storyteller immediately skips the actual contest before the mnemonic "tide" created by the all-powerful image of his carrying Achilles' female prize, Briseis, to the ships in *Iliad* I. It is because of this process that Talthubios surfaces in his mind.

Troy

The city of Troy includes the following subsettings: (1) the walls, (2) the palace, and (3) the entrance to the city. In this section, I will explore the evocative concept of the locale "Troy," and discuss how it is presented and the necessary implications stemming from such a presentation within the narrative of the *Iliad*. As with the Achaean camp, the city of Troy fufills four distinct functions, as a place of: (1) councils, (2) observation of the enemy, (3) prayer, and (4) lament.[86]

---

[83] I take the shield and the helmet as one prize, since they are clearly presented together / (799).
[84] Achilles awards the prize for the spear-throwing contest to Agamemnon without even allowing the contest to take place. This gesture of acknowledgement of Agamemnon's status stands in contrast to the ἔρις of the two Achaean heroes at the beginning of the poem. The games, therefore, begin and end by highlighting a profound transformation of Achilles, who averts strife in the case of Antilokhos and "corrects" his improper behavior towards Agamemnon in *Iliad* I.
[85] See *Iliad* I 320–347.
[86] See Hellwig 1964:25.

The walls

The basic threefold setting promoted in the *Iliad* (Troy, plain, Achaean camp) offers a general mnemonic blueprint that the narrator can easily recall and follow during the performance of his song. The city of Troy, as a single locale, constitutes the other end of the visual spectrum activated in the bard's and the audience's minds, and represents the global or, if I may use this term, the "macromnemonic" aspect of mental recall. In other words, this ABA´ visual pattern, with Troy (A) and the Achaean camp (A´) standing for the two symmetrical edges of the narrator's mnemonic chart and the plain of Troy in the middle (B), is a simple and especially effective visual plan that bard and listeners can readily follow during the performance of an oral song. In addition, there is also a "micromnemonic" aspect related to the specific presentation of Troy in the *Iliad*. The macrostructure aside, the dichotomy between the walls of the city and the palace, or in postmodern geographical terminology between center and periphery, is also visually effective, for it is an essential feature of interactive imagery, based on the pairing of mental icons through either association or contrast. The narrator, having no clear picture in his mind of the city of Troy, uses the standard pair "center-periphery" in order to cue the actions of his heroes to specific spatial locations.

This mnemonic strategy does not exhaust the function of the spatial dichotomy between center and periphery with respect to the city of Troy. On the contrary, it allows the tradition of the *Iliad* to explore a territorially demarcated area in terms of heroic topography. The locale of a city (like Troy, of which the walls are a subsetting) is linked, in the words of the geographer Edward Soja, to "another social specificity of social being which ... may be described as the nodality of social life, the socio-spatial clustering or agglomeration of activities around identifiable geographical centres or nodes."[87]

This clustering of activities around the walls of Troy[88] is not only exploited in the narrative, but also allows the audience to glimpse a "hidden" world with its own social dynamics. The three key scenes that take place on the walls of Troy are essential both to the dramatic input of the plot and to notions of control, heroism, family, and jurisdiction. In this light, the idea of *nodality*, which entwines together different activities around the fixed setting of the walls, becomes the centerpiece of a narrative geography of enclosure and confinement that brings to the fore the conflict between the family and the heroic world, the two poles

---

[87] Soja 1989:149.

[88] Of the two sets of gates, the Skaian and the Dardanian, only the former are exploited as a thematized space *forming part of the walls*. The Dardanian Gates seem to be a sally port; see Scully 1990:41–68; Trachsel 2007:12–32; Clay 2011:38.

around which Helen's and Hektor's tragic life stories unfold. The walls are the meeting place of the Trojan elders and the spot from where Helen will watch the duel between Menelaos and Paris (*Iliad* III), the meeting area for Hektor's family (*Iliad* VI), and the spot for Hektor's supplication by his parents and their subsequent observation of his duel with Achilles, as well as the dragging of Hektor's body by Achilles across the plain and the lament by his relatives (*Iliad* XXII).

The distinction between the world of the battlefield and the walls of a besieged city is one of the hallmarks of the Iliadic presentation of warfare. As I have suggested above, the apparent paradox of the Trojan army's leaving the city and fighting the enemy on open ground has important interpretive consequences for the plot of the *Iliad* and the dramatic outlook that the epic fosters.[89] The picture becomes more complicated when one considers the function of the walls of a city, which have been narratively deprived of their most elementary reason for existing, that is, to protect the city's inhabitants from threat or attack. In the world of the *Iliad*, the plain of Troy and the walls of the city constitute the main nodal locations of two distinct forms of heroic interaction, the war and the family. The epic systematically employs their locational separation and territorial demarcation to present the inner dynamics of the conflict between the family and the battlefield which generate much tension and drama for the main figures of the plot.

The meeting of the elders on the walls of Troy is, of course, conditioned by narrative requirements, since Priam will ask Helen to tell him the names of certain Achaean leaders standing on the plain. At the same time, the council of elders represents the voice of the Trojan people, epitomized in their uttering a single, collective speech without any indication of individual speaker:[90]

[89]   This aspect of Iliadic warfare may be a relatively "recent" development. According to Sale (1987:21–50), the fact that "there are few or no pre-Homeric formulae for 'in Troy-city' and none for 'from Troy'" indicates that pre-Homeric poetry did not involve—at least not frequently—scenes taking place inside Troy. Sale carefully adds that this does not mean that scenes taking place inside Troy are overall less formulaic, but that they may have developed only in a "late" phase in the evolution and shaping of the *Iliad*, since there was no pressure to create such formulas due to the lack of relevant scenes. Though it is hard to decide about this issue, Sale's observation accords well with the fact that the Trojan army does not fight from inside the city, i.e. from the walls, but in the plain. If the Theban tradition was the only well-known example of fighting from the walls of a besieged city, then the Iliadic tradition may have been the one that introduced the innovation of having the defender's army exit the city and fight in the battlefield. This decision, as argued in part 1, has crucial dramatic implications for the epic's plot.

[90]   The collective voice of the Trojan elders must be examined together with the silence of the two maidens, Aithre and Klumene, who accompany Helen. This is one of the very rare occasions when collective speech is voiced in Homeric epic, which usually employs τις-speech to express either common feelings (in narrative parts) or imaginary fears and anxieties of a figure of the plot (embedded in speeches). On τις-speeches, see J. Wilson 1979; de Jong 1987b. These figures not only form the internal audience of the conversation between Priam and Helen, but

"οὐ νέμεσις Τρῶας καὶ ἐϋκνήμιδας Ἀχαιοὺς
τοιῇδ' ἀμφὶ γυναικὶ πολὺν χρόνον ἄλγεα πάσχειν·
αἰνῶς ἀθανάτῃσι θεῇς εἰς ὦπα ἔοικεν.
ἀλλὰ καὶ ὣς, τοίη περ ἐοῦσ', ἐν νηυσὶ νεέσθω,
μηδ' ἡμῖν τεκέεσσί τ' ὀπίσσω πῆμα λίποιτο."

"Surely there is no blame[91] on Trojans and strong-greaved Achaians
if for long time they suffer hardship for a woman like this one.
Terrible is the likeness of her face to immortal goddesses.
Still, though she be such, let her go away in the ships, lest
she be left behind, a grief to us and our children."

Iliad III 156–160

The sheer wonder at the divine beauty of Helen walking towards the tower (*Iliad* III 154 Ἑλένην ἐπὶ πύργον ἰοῦσαν) indicates a specific attitude toward what the French sociologist Pierre Bourdieu has called the *socializing of the body*.[92] The very appearance of Helen on the walls and the display of her body constitute a real social event, marking the walls as social space.[93] What is of particular importance to this scene is that although there is no single expression in the text describing Helen's bodily deportment, sight becomes the key factor in the perceptual representation of space.[94] This time, though, sight acquires a specific social dimension, as it reveals the inner tensions within the Trojan community concerning Helen as the cause of the war, and consequently of Troy's present suffering.[95] The divine movement of her body (154 ἰοῦσαν), contrasted with the

---

also represent the social dynamics of this scene: Priam is the head of the council and Helen is a member of the royal house (as the wife of Paris). At the same time, the presence of Aithre points to the older phase of the myth, when she was brought to Sparta as a slave by the Dioscuri in retaliation for the earlier abduction of Helen by Theseus (Aithre was Theseus' mother). At a later stage, Aithre followed her lady, Helen, to Troy. On this topic, see Jenkyns 1999; on the absence of the Dioscuri from the *Iliad*, see Clader 1976:48–53; Austin 1994:48n35; and cf. *Cypria* (§§14–16 Kullmann = Severyns 106–109 = Allen 103.13–17). With respect to the authenticity of *Iliad* III 144, I side with W. Kullmann (2002:164–165). Differently West 1999:186–187 and Krieter-Spiro 2009:62, who argue that this verse is an Athenian interpolation.

91 On the "voice of νέμεσις" with respect to Helen's varied language styles in Homer (with special reference to the τειχοσκοπία), see Ebbott 1999; Worman 2001; Tsagalis 2008b:112–134.

92 Bourdieu 1991:81–89.

93 On the concept and function of the "body" in Homer, see Vernant 1996:7–79.

94 See Bal 1997:133.

95 With respect to Helen's body—as she is moving and being watched by the Trojan elders—the words of Massumi (2002:57) are especially appropriate: "an accumulation of relative perspectives and the passage between them, an additive space of utter receptivity retaining and combining past movements ... [I]t is less a space in the empirical sense than a gap in space that is also a suspension of the normal unfolding of time." The body of Helen thus has "a spatiotemporal order of its own," as it epitomizes and thematizes past, present, and future.

immobility of the seated elders (149 εἴατο), turns her temporarily into a viewed object, whose eyes and face recall those of a goddess (158 αἰνῶς ἀθανάτῃσι θεῇς εἰς ὦπα ἔοικεν). Helen's body constitutes a site,[96] not only in narrative terms,[97] but also with respect to its political underpinnings and implications for Trojan society at large. In an attempt to reappropriate and embed Helen, who inspires awe and fear at the same time, into the hierarchy and framework of Trojan society, Priam asks her to approach and sit next to him (162 "δεῦρο πάροιθ' ἐλθοῦσα, φίλον τέκος, ἵζε' ἐμεῖο"). In other words, he tries to turn Helen from a viewed object into a viewing audience.[98] In this light, the walls—in the τειχοσκοπία scene—are the locus for social performance, the site where the embedding of another site—Helen herself—is made possible, at least briefly, until it is subsumed by the social framework represented by the seated Trojan elders.

The socializing of Helen's body in the scene on the walls is founded on the storyteller's use of *kinesics*, one of the three broad categories of nonverbal communication. Kinesics includes body movements and positions ranging from gestures and body postures to facial expressions, eye movements, and automatic psychological reactions.[99] Since nonverbal communication in a given society involves deep-rooted cultural knowledge that is shared by all members of a community, the narrator can use it to facilitate "pictureability," that is, to make a moment memorable by creating a clear mental image.[100] By making full use of the audience's familiarity with the mental picture of a beautiful woman making an impressive entrance and attracting male attention, the bard is able

---

[96] Given that the viewers, Helen and Priam (and the elders), are figures of both the Iliadic plot and an epic tradition, their watching the Achaean leaders on the plain is transformed into a gaze at the epic tradition itself. The view soon becomes a recollection of the epic past, a temporal turn that is based on an equivalent spatial subversion: as the walls constitute a locus of memory (for Antenor of Troy, for Helen of her past in Greece), so Helen's body introduces a jarring reconfiguration of the entire landscape. In Helen's world, the elements of the setting (the walls, the plain of Troy, her palace in Sparta which she recalls) are not external entities in which she lives or has lived, but a nexus of interrelated concepts such as body, memory, and desire. By "rejecting" the selective memory of Trojan or Achaean interests developed around the key question of responsibility for the Trojan War, Helen sees Troy and Sparta not as lands but as spaces tied to her body's personal history, the former being her body in the present, the latter her body in the past. In this way, she fosters a spatiotemporal malleability that makes her, in de Certeau's terminology (I owe this reference to Rofel 1997:170), "poach" on the walls' function as the epitome of division, bordering, limitation, and separation. See Brady 2002:152.

[97] Worman 2002:102.

[98] On Helen's oscillation between viewed object and viewing audience, see Worman 2002:102.

[99] See Minchin 2008b:20. The other two categories of nonverbal communication include *haptics* (touching) and *proxemics* (behavior in space). See Korte 1997:37–82; Mayo and Henley 1987:6–7; on body language, see also Argyle 1988.

[100] On the use of nonverbal communication as a method for information recall, clear visualization, and vividness in various Homeric scenes, see Minchin 2008b.

to capitalize on the visual dimension and use speech[101] (the brief comments of awe uttered by the elders) to mirror his audience's unspoken impression.[102] The vivid mental image of a beautiful woman is expected to create the same powerful impression of wonder that the elders express when they see Helen on the walls. In turn, this process helps capture the tension lurking in the background of this scene: the cause and prize of the war, Helen herself, appears on the walls of Troy and identifies for Priam the great heroes she has made—by her decision to follow Paris—cross the sea to destroy his city.

The walls also feature in another major episode of the Iliadic plot, the meeting between Andromakhe and Hektor in *Iliad* VI. Both protagonists have moved away from their "proper" space, the chamber and the battlefield respectively; moreover, each of them is looking for the other in his or her own space, that is, Hektor is searching for Andromakhe in the palace, while Andromakhe is going to the walls to see what happened to Hektor in the plain of Troy. The placement of the actual meeting between husband and wife at the *transitory space* of the Skaian Gates (*Iliad* VI 392–394) accentuates the polarity of two different worlds: the world of the city and the family, symbolized in the figure of Andromakhe, and the world of the heroes and the battlefield represented by Hektor.[103]

The walls are an intermediate space in terms of the polarity between city and battlefield. This is spatially denoted by the interplay between the initial movement of the two characters towards the Skaian Gates and their subsequent stop once they arrive at their meeting place.[104] In this way, Andromakhe and Hektor are able to look at the deeply divided world of the *Iliad,* and by suggesting the *centrality of the body to the making of space,* to reconfigure the walls as a "border" that makes the temporal and the spatial converge. In fact, the placement of the meeting between husband and wife at the Skaian Gates, which are treated as a transitory space forming part of the walls, turns the two protagonists into commentators on the very polar antitheses they themselves stand for.

Andromakhe aims at convincing Hektor to fight the Achaeans from the walls, and even advises him to place part of his army next to the fig tree, where there is a weak spot in the walls (*Iliad* VI 433–434). In fact, the Achaeans have already tried three times to invade the city from there (435–439). Andromakhe's words,

---

[101] Minchin (2008b:30, 38) argues that information offered by nonverbal communication can turn out to be richer than that given by speech. This is the kind of expressive economy that Homeric poetry is famous for.

[102] See Lateiner 1995:281, who observes that "nonverbal messages override verbal messages in importance."

[103] See Schadewaldt 1965:214–217; Tsagalis 2008b:10–11.

[104] See Schadewaldt 1965:214–217. On polarity as an epic "law" manifested by means of contrast and contraposition, see Schadewaldt 1965:369, 1966:133–134.

with their paradoxically military tone, constitute a brief but sharp commentary on the spatial polarities of the Iliadic war. They verbalize an attempt to annul all kinds of crossings, both the one that the Trojan army regularly makes, as it crosses the walls and fights the Achaeans in the open space of the plain, and the Achaeans' attempts to cross the walls and enter the city. In this respect, her words constitute not simply a piece of military advice to Hektor, but also a form of criticism of the nature of Iliadic fighting.

Hektor's answer implicitly points to his notion of heroic κλέος. Since both his father's fame and his own require that he fight in the front rank, that is to say in the open space, the walls constitute an obstacle to his κλέος. Having learned to be an ἐσθλός (*Iliad* VI 444–445 … ἐπεὶ μάθον ἔμμεναι ἐσθλός / αἰεὶ καὶ πρώτοισι μετὰ Τρώεσσι μάχεσθαι), he refuses to fight from the walls because he regards this attitude as a kind of escape. He even expresses his concern about the accusation of "escaping war" that might be raised against him (441–443 … ἀλλὰ μάλ᾽ αἰνῶς / αἰδέομαι Τρῶας καὶ Τρῳάδας ἑλκεσιπέπλους, / αἴ κε κακὸς ὣς νόσφιν ἀλυσκάζω πολέμοιο ["yet I would feel deep shame / before the Trojans, and the Trojan women with trailing garments, / if like a coward I were to shrink aside from the fighting"]). Hektor effectively reminds both Andromakhe and the external audience that walls "may keep people in as well as keep people out";[105] that what constitutes protection and safety for Andromakhe represents the loss of heroic κλέος for him. The space of the walls means his rejection of his very identity as well as of his family's fame (VI 446 ἀρνύμενος πατρός τε μέγα κλέος ἠδ᾽ ἐμὸν αὐτοῦ ["winning for my own self great glory, and for my father"), and in this light he refuses to comment on Andromakhe's reference to the Achaean leaders' previous attacks at the weak spot of the walls.

The walls allow the two protagonists of this scene to endorse two different "archaeologies" of space: whereas Andromakhe focuses on the walls as a means of keeping the enemy out and her husband in, Hektor sees the walls as a potential threat to his heroic fame, an imprisonment of his own military skills and heroic status. In this way the *Iliad*'s attempt to hint at the history of the walls, so closely linked to the foundation of Troy and the protective role of Apollo and Poseidon, remains suspended, since Hektor replaces Andromakhe's allusion to the spatial archaeology of the walls with his own spatial archaeology of the battlefield: like his father before him,[106] he will cross the walls, the metaphorical

---

[105] I owe this phrase to Brady 2002:70.

[106] See *Iliad* III 184–189 "ἤδη καὶ Φρυγίην εἰσήλυθον ἀμπελόεσσαν, / ἔνθα ἴδον πλείστους Φρύγας ἀνέρας αἰολοπώλους, / λαοὺς Ὀτρῆος καὶ Μυγδόνος ἀντιθέοιο, / οἵ ῥα τότ᾽ ἐστρατόωντο παρ᾽ ὄχθας Σαγγαρίοιο· / καὶ γὰρ ἐγὼν ἐπίκουρος ἐὼν μετὰ τοῖσιν ἐλέγμην / ἤματι τῷ, ὅτε τ᾽ ἦλθον Ἀμαζόνες ἀντιάνειραι" ("Once before this time I visited Phrygia of the vineyards. / There I looked on the Phrygian men with their swarming horses, / so many of them, the people of Otreus / and godlike Mygdon, / whose camp was spread at that time along the banks of Sangarios: / and

border separating men from heroes, and stand in the front rank, even at the cost of his own life.

The walls become the center of the narrative yet again in the beginning, middle, and end of *Iliad* XXII. At the outset of the book, Priam and Hekabe, standing on the walls, virtually beg Hektor to return to the city and not stay on the plain to fight Achilles. As the plot unfolds, action takes place around the walls, as Achilles chases Hektor, and at the end Hektor's parents together with Andromakhe lament from the walls Hektor's death at the hands of the best of the Achaeans. The walls' inherent theatricality allows for their effective dramatic exploitation. In the course of the action, Hektor's decision to stand outside the Skaian Gates (XXII 6), his subsequent pursuit by Achilles around the walls, and his vain attempts to get near the Dardanian Gates (XXII 194–198) picture in spatial terms his dramatic oscillation between the worlds of the family and the battlefield. The symmetrical, almost ring-like use of the walls at the beginning and end of *Iliad* XXII frames the action and imbues it with a certain autonomy that rings a familiar bell when compared to the larger narrative pattern of the epic. In *Iliad* XXII the walls are turned from a location into a space of supplication (beginning), dramatic oscillation (middle), and lament (end), just as supplication, oscillation, and lament feature in the beginning, middle, and end of the entire *Iliad*: Khruses' failed supplication of Agamemnon causes Apollo's punishment and brings death to the Achaean camp in *Iliad* I; the shifting tide of war makes victory change sides during the course of the plot; and Priam's supplication of Achilles in *Iliad* XXIV results in the return of Hektor's body and the proper lamentation for him. Seen in this light, *Iliad* XXII is framed in the same way that the whole epic begins and ends.

The walls thus become not only a highly thematized space, but also a space where the larger trends that permeate the *Iliad* are reasserted. It seems, therefore, that they are used as a *spatial epitome* of the whole flow of the action. At the same time, the walls reconfigure one of the pervasive thematic tenets of the entire epic, namely the dilemma between life and heroic death. In the case of Achilles, an equivalent choice is made on the basis of the polarity between Phthia and Troy, which in his diction are constantly turned from geographical locations into signposts of unheroic and heroic space respectively. In the case of Hektor, where geography does not really help in emblematizing such crucial polarities, the walls become the symbolic means whereby the drama of his life is played out. As a result of Hektor's choice not to listen to the entreaties of his loved ones, who are watching—as if from their theater seats[107]—the final

---

I myself, a helper in war, was marshalled among them / on that day when the Amazon women came, men's equals").

[107] On the theatricality of the *Iliad*, see now Clay 2011.

act of his life, the walls revert from a place of protection into a viewing space: the hero's denying any *fiat* to his loved ones translates the walls into a heroic ecology, which for Hektor represents a waning identity, facing the peril of entrapment within the fenced-off world of the city and the family. By walking away from the walls, Hektor moves into the vast space of heroism, where he will face the other great lonely hero, Achilles.

The city

The city of Troy figures mainly in the activities of Helen and Paris in *Iliad* III, Hektor's visit in *Iliad* VI, and brief references to Andromakhe in *Iliad* XXII and Priam in *Iliad* XXIV. The perceptual representation of the city by the Homeric narrator combines short descriptions of the settings of the houses or chambers of these figures and also, perhaps tellingly, a focus on visible stature, which unfolds by referring to the antithesis between brightness and dirtiness on the one hand and marriage and death on the other.

The spatial representation of the city of Troy, which is limited to the houses of Priam, Paris, and Hektor and the temple of Athena, includes two types of relations: the frame, that is, the space where these characters are situated, and the way this space is filled.[108] This is achieved in the case of the palace by means of brief descriptions and the use of three kinds of spatial features, namely shapes, sizes, and colors, which "are perceived visually, always from a particular perspective."[109] In the case of the Trojan palace, spatial representation follows a twofold pattern, starting with a brief description of the particular location and followed by ample use of color-based images, developed around the social space of themes such as clothing and cleanliness.

The meetings between Helen and Paris in *Iliad* III 421–423 and Hektor and Hekabe in *Iliad* VI 242–250 begin with short descriptions of the setting. This is the frame within which the ensuing episodes will take place. What is of particular importance is that the frame is described in terms of shape, material, and size, which are purely spatial factors. In III 423, the chamber of Paris is called ὑψόροφος θάλαμος 'high-vaulted bedchamber', and in VI 242–250, shape and material (243 ξεστῆς αἰθούσῃσι τετυγμένον, 244, 248 ξεστοῖο λίθοιο, 248 τέγεοι) and size (244 πεντήκοντ' ἔνεσαν θάλαμοι, 248 δώδεκ' ἔσαν ... θάλαμοι) are emphatically stressed. The use of spatial aspects such as shape, material, and size, next to the traditional means of symmetrical spatial representation based on the analogy between the families of Priam's sons and daughters (cf. VI 244–246 and 248–250), bestows on the brief description of the houses of Paris

---

[108] Bal 1997:134.
[109] Bal 1997:133.

and Priam a sense of magnitude and royal status. The city of Troy, epitomized in the description of the houses of the epic's protagonists, is thus depicted in all its splendor and glory. The antithesis between the huge and beautiful houses (III 421 and VI 242 δόμον περικαλλέ'[α]) and the future destruction of the city turns the royal palaces into a spatial foreshadowing of Troy's unfolding tragedy. The Iliadic storyteller can count on his audience's ability to interpret the underlying reality of such vivid visualizations: his listeners have no clear mental picture of Paris' or Priam's house, but they surely know what a palace looks like. By evoking a familiar picture, the narrator can ease the visualization of these two scenes and make a moment memorable.[110]

Apart from these descriptions pertaining to the spatial frame of the relevant episodes, the Iliad emphasizes the use of the senses, through color, touch, and smell. In Iliad III 382, Aphrodite places Paris in "his own perfumed bedchamber" (ἐν θαλάμῳ εὐώδεϊ κηώεντι); in III 385 she "laid her hand upon Helen's fragrant robe and shook it" (χειρὶ δὲ νεκταρέου ἑανοῦ ἐτίναξε λαβοῦσα),[111] and in III 419, Helen walks away in silence "shrouding herself about in the luminous spun robe" (κατασχομένη ἑανῷ ἀργῆτι φαεινῷ). As these references make clear, the space of the bedchamber of Helen and Paris is represented in terms of color, touch, and smell. Touch indicates proximity, and the shining color of the robe and its perfume, together with the fragrance of the bedchamber, create strong mental icons and a feeling of "being there" on the part of the audience. While the meager description of the house and chamber in III 421–423, where the working activity of the maids is placed next to the beauty of the outer and inner buildings (421 δόμον περικαλλέ'[α], 423 ὑψόροφον θάλαμον), delineates the spatial frame of the scene, the use of senses indicates the specific way this frame is to be filled. The audience is thus transferred to the very location where the protagonists of this scene are placed, and is invited to "experience" what is going on by adopting their perspective: the seductive power of Aphrodite, the pleasant scent and shining dress of Helen—that is, a glimpse of a world of fragrant smells and shining colors, like the one the two lovers first experienced when they met in Sparta. In this way, the antithesis between past and present, the momentary and the enduring, once more keys the audience to the dramatic tone of the Iliad.

Likewise, during Hektor's visit to Troy in Iliad VI, the spatial representation of the palace and the temple of Athena, where his mother Hekabe is heading, is accomplished both through a brief reference to its location (297 ἐν πόλει

---

[110] On the use of pictureability as a vehicle evaluating hidden tensions or future dramatic developments, see Minchin 2008b.

[111] The translation is mine. Lattimore translates νεκταρέου as "immortal."

ἄκρῃ) and by means of the shining effect[112] of the great πέπλος 'robe'[113] that is to be dedicated to Athena. Whereas the former sets the general spatial frame, the latter indicates *how* this space is to be interpreted: namely in terms of the wealth and awe of the Trojan people, in one of the rare collective representations in the entire poem. The same strategy is employed in the brief description of Paris' house, which like Athena's temple is situated on the peak of the citadel (317 ἐν πόλει ἄκρῃ). This is done mainly by reference to Paris' shining armor (321 περικαλλέα τεύχε'[α]) and Helen's "directing the magnificent work done by her handmaidens" (324 ... καὶ ἀμφιπόλοισι περικλυτὰ ἔργα κέλευεν). Hektor, despite Helen's offer, refuses to sit down and share the world of Helen and Paris, even for a while. His house is empty, since Andromakhe and Astuanax have gone to the walls. In this light, space points to the contrasting fates of Hektor and of the other preeminent Trojans. The ever-growing distance is strengthened even more since Andromakhe and Astuanax are placed outside the limits of their proper space, in fact at the very site where Astuanax will meet his death in the non-Iliadic epic tradition.[114]

The spatial frame of a given scene often has a highly symbolic role,[115] since it plays on sets of antitheses such as inside-outside, regular-irregular, and positive-negative. Spatial subversion requires an easily recognizable spatial frame, whose regular and positive function will be overturned. In *Iliad* XXII 440–448, Andromakhe is presented weaving at her loom, while the maids are preparing a bath for Hektor. The spatial frame of this scene is, as usual, described in a laconic manner (XXII 440 μυχῷ δόμου ὑψηλοῖο "in the inner room of the high house"; 442 κατὰ δῶμα "through the house"), but the narrator carefully hints at the possibility that this peaceful space where the regular activities of everyday life take place will be subverted. The frame is described not only as the place where Andromakhe is, but also as the place where Hektor is not (439 πόσις ἔκτοθι μίμνε πυλάων "her husband had held his ground there outside the gates"; 445 μάλα τῆλε λοετρῶν "far from waters for bathing"), silently indicating that in the light of Hektor's impending death, the audience must interpret the peaceful space of the chamber, where Hektor's bath is being prepared and Andromakhe performs a housewife's primary duty, that of weaving, as a form of tragic irony.[116] The

---

[112] *Iliad* VI 294–295 ὃς κάλλιστος ἔην ποικίλμασιν ἠδὲ μέγιστος, / ἀστὴρ δ' ὡς ἀπέλαμπεν ("that which was the loveliest in design and the largest, / and shone like a star").

[113] See *Iliad* VI 271–273, 289–295.

[114] See *Iliad* XXIV 734–735 ἤ τις Ἀχαιῶν / ῥίψει χειρὸς ἑλὼν ἀπὸ πύργου, λυγρὸν ὄλεθρον ("or else some Achaian / will take you by hand and hurl you from the tower into horrible / death"); *Iliou Persis* (§97 Kullmann = 268 Severyns = Allen 108.8) Ὀδυσσέως Ἀστυάνακτα ἀνελόντος.

[115] See Bal 1997:134.

[116] On the function of the house as a special space where traditionally conceived female activity is placed and interpreted, see Wigley 1992.

secluded space of the chamber contrasts with the vast space of the battlefield, and is therefore to be taken as a symbolic opposition between life and death.

In *Iliad* XXIV 160–165, Priam is presented in his yard amidst his sons, who cover his body with a cloak and pour dung on his head and neck. Moreover, in XXIV 719–720, the κλυτὰ δώματα 'renowned house' virtually signifies Hektor's deathbed, as it is there that the ritual lamentation for him will take place. The spatial frame of these two scenes comprises the yard of Priam's house and the palace respectively, but what really matters is how this space is filled. By juxtaposing the spare description of the frame with a rich harvest of topological references to what this space contains, the *Iliad* moves from description to interpretation. Helen's shining and fragrant clothing in *Iliad* III and the beautiful bright robe dedicated to Athena in *Iliad* VI are strongly contrasted with the futile preparation of Hektor's bath by Andromakhe and her maids in *Iliad* XXII, Priam's being covered by a simple cloak and rolling in the dung in *Iliad* XXIV, and the mourning for Hektor in the palace. The world of the city of Troy, which is radically changed into a place of grief and mourning at the end of the poem, constitutes an evolving space, whose dynamic nature follows the unraveling of the plot and is based not on the way it is framed but on the way it is filled.

The World of the Immortals

The fact that the world of the immortals is separate from that of mortals, and inaccessible to them, underlines the unbridgeable gap between gods and men. Particular spatial features of the purely divine world are deftly employed to underscore its profound difference from the plain of Troy and the mortal world at large. The stress on the spatial aspect of divine intervention in the mortal realm aims at "flagging" distance as a form of irony, since gods enter and exit the mortal world with such ease that the disparity between human sorrow and divine imperviousness to suffering is further emphasized.[117] That said, one should not undervalue the fact that by moving freely back and forth, Homeric gods offer unity to the realms of sky, earth, and sea.[118]

Spatial theography: Height and depth

Any discussion of divine space in the *Iliad* has to distinguish between form and function, for Olympos and the depths of the sea constitute the two poles of a

---

[117] Gods and goddesses who engage in fighting *never* kill anyone themselves (C. Armstrong 1969:30). This feature may be due to epic convention, but it abides quite effectively by the Iliadic *Weltanschauung*: divine involvement constitutes the backdrop against which human suffering and grief are measured.

[118] Other than XXIII 71–74, there are hardly any descriptions of the underworld in the *Iliad*.

coherent spatial theography, whose language of localization and orientation is of prime importance for understanding the role of the gods.

Olympos is regularly characterized by its various spatial aspects, such as color (*Iliad* I 532 αἰγλήεντος; XVIII 186 ἀγάννιφον), size (I 402 μακρόν; I 530 μέγαν; XX 5 πολυπτύχου), shape (V 367 αἰπύν; XXI 505 χαλκοβατὲς δῶ), and elevation (VIII 25 περὶ ῥίον; XIV 154 ἀπὸ ῥίου). As is often the case with Iliadic locations, the gods' abode is devoid of topography. The narrator has no clear picture of Olympos, and his brief presentation is a composite mental image of Greek landscape characterized by spatial manifestations of the idea of extremity: Olympos is high, vast, distant, and radiantly shining. Before we consider *why* Olympos is presented in this way, we should bear in mind that we are dealing not with static but with dynamic space: almost every single time the narrative lens turns to Olympos, it is following the trail or path of a particular god or group of gods returning from the plain of Troy, the depths of the sea, or the land of the Ethiopians. The spatial presentation of Olympos is closely linked to its dynamic nature: height, size, distance, and optical salience constitute useful mnemonic tools for referring to it. Given that the narrator does not possess any clear picture in his mind's eye of the divine abode per se, he employs a variety of spatial mechanisms that facilitate his mental mapping of all the relevant material.

Apart from the use of spatial memory for visualizing Olympos, dynamic space creates associations of cognitive and hierarchical factors which take the form of social and axiological coding.[119]

> ἠερίη δ' ἀνέβη μέγαν οὐρανὸν Οὔλυμπόν τε.
> ηὗρεν δ' εὐρύοπα Κρονίδην ἄτερ ἥμενον ἄλλων
> ἀκροτάτῃ κορυφῇ πολυδειράδος Οὐλύμποιο·

> in the morning and went up to the tall sky and Olympos.
> She found Kronos' broad-browed son apart from the others
> *sitting upon the highest peak of rugged Olympos.*

> *Iliad* I 497–499

> ηὗρον δὲ Κρονίωνα θεῶν ἄτερ ἥμενον ἄλλων
> ἀκροτάτῃ κορυφῇ πολυδειράδος Οὐλύμποιο.

> They found the son of Kronos sitting apart form the other
> gods, *upon the highest peak of rugged Olympos.*

> *Iliad* V 753–754

---

[119] Olympos, like Helikon in Hesiod's *Theogony*, points to a markedly different topography of time, but unlike the Hesiodic Helikon it has no metaliterary connotations. On topographies of time in the *Theogony*, see Purves 2002:16–71.

Ζεὺς δὲ Θέμιστα κέλευσε θεοὺς ἀγορήνδε καλέσσαι
κρατὸς ἀπ᾽ Οὐλύμποιο πολυπτύχου· ἢ δ᾽ ἄρα πάντῃ
φοιτήσασα κέλευσε Διὸς πρὸς δῶμα νέεσθαι

But Zeus, *from the many-folded peak of Olympos*,
told Themis to summon all the gods into assembly. She went
everywhere, and told them to make their way to Zeus' house.

Iliad XX 4–6

The contrast between higher and lower loci within the realm of Olympos points to the higher divine status of Zeus, who is first among all the Olympian gods. Along the same lines, the emphasis on both the (often) lonely figure of Zeus, whom divine travelers visit at Olympos, and the fact that Zeus never travels in order to meet with another god, connects the cognitive schema that highlights the importance of "one" versus "many" with the primacy of Zeus, who domi-nates Olympos. In other words, figures and place references within the realm of Olympos are mentioned according to axiological, not topological order.[120]

With respect to the function of Olympos, we have to distinguish between its thematic and symbolic roles, the former pertaining to the evolution of the plot, and the latter referring to the fact that space may be semantically charged with its own meaning.[121] As thematic space, Olympos is mainly associated with the gods' travelling to the world of mortals and back again, which allows the action to proceed. This vertical aspect has important implications for the plot, not only because the gods regularly interfere in human affairs and attempt to determine the action, but also because the speed and ease of divine move-ment to and from Olympos nullifies (for the immortals) typical divisions of space. Thus the gods can be far away from the human world of suffering, but can also visit it in a second. Although they can cover distances quickly when they move, the Olympians cannot be in different places at the same time. The far-off, unchanging world of Olympos is thus integral to the notion and func-tion of the divine body, which "Homer places ... at the intersection of the mortal and immortal worlds."[122] Seen from this angle, Olympos acquires an impor-tant thematic function for the Iliadic plot, not merely as a backdrop against which events are developed, but as a parallel notion of space, one that high-lights vertical versus horizontal movement. This inherent spatial verticality of Olympos is also noticed when the divine abode par excellence is employed as an

---

[120] At the same time, one has to acknowledge that gods achieve Panhellenic status by ascending to Olympos; see Nagy 2009a:278.

[121] On the symbolic function of space, see Bachelard 1957, Meyer 1975 [=1963], and Hoffmann 1978.

[122] Purves 2006b:206.

observation point. The *Iliad* exploits the dramatic contrast between the verticality of Olympos and the walls of Troy, the divine and human points of observation respectively. Whereas the divine vantage point makes gods intervene in human affairs, mortals standing on the walls watch what is happening in the plain of Troy but cannot change its course.[123]

As far as the symbolic function of Olympos is concerned, we can speak, as the subtitle of this section suggests, of a *spatial theography*,[124] which translates the thematic aspect of divine travel into a symbolic one based on standardized antitheses of status, such as high (gods) versus low (men), or even higher (the Olympians) versus lesser gods (Thetis, Iris). Travel of the lower to the abode of the higher, from which the lesser divinities (and of course humans) are excluded, spatially underscores social categorizations that originate in the human world. The *Iliad* turns Olympos from a mere place into one end of a whole set of bipolar oppositions between the divine and the human worlds, systematically employing the principal oppositions of far-near, mountain-plain, infinite-finite, safe-unsafe, and accessible-inaccessible.[125] At the same time, Olympos stands as a symbol of divine unity, since the *Iliad* systematically capitalizes on the contrast between the assemblies of gods held there and the human assemblies taking place on earth: whereas the former are often used as a benchmark for divine unity, and there are no direct consequences for the divine world even when they are characterized by dissension that leads to opposing initiatives by individual gods, the latter reveal the inner conflict of the heroic community, and result in suffering and death. Seen in this light, the divine assembly at the end of *Iliad* I becomes an ironic rereading of the human assembly at the beginning of the same book: conflict occurs in both of them, but where in the former it is followed by laughter and enjoyment, in the latter it becomes the beginning of unfathomable suffering and death.

The depths of the sea are also employed as a divine abode in the *Iliad*, though not so often as Olympos. Their use is based not so much on random references to Poseidon's realm as to Thetis' underwater abode. The latter reference shows that the sea-depths are a highly thematized space within the plot of the *Iliad*, since they are employed as the locus where narrative shifts really begin: the three cardinal changes in the behavior of Achilles are anchored to the action of his mother Thetis, who listens to her son or the other gods (as in *Iliad* XXIV) from her home at the bottom of the sea, and subsequently gets involved in the Iliadic plot.

---

[123] See Purves 2006b:196. There are, though, a few exceptions: in *Iliad* XVI 431–461 and XXII 167–187 respectively, Zeus sees Sarpedon's and Hektor's imminent deaths from Olympos, but is unable to intervene and save them.

[124] I owe this term to van Noppen 1996.

[125] On the spatial aspect of these bipolar oppositions, see Bal 1997:216.

In *Iliad* XIII 20–38, the narrator offers a majestic description of Poseidon's palace:

τρὶς μὲν ὀρέξατ' ἰών, τὸ δὲ τέτρατον ἵκετο τέκμωρ,
Αἰγάς· ἔνθα δέ οἱ <u>κλυτὰ δώματα</u> βένθεσι λίμνης
χρύσεα μαρμαίροντα τετεύχαται, ἄφθιτα αἰεί.
ἔνθ' ἐλθὼν ὑπ' ὄχεσφι τιτύσκετο χαλκόποδ' ἵππω
ὠκυπέτα, <u>χρυσέῃσιν</u> ἐθείρῃσιν κομόωντε,
<u>χρυσὸν</u> δ' αὐτὸς ἔδυνε περὶ χροΐ, γέντο δ' ἱμάσθλην
<u>χρυσείην</u> εὔτυκτον, ἑοῦ δ' ἐπεβήσετο δίφρου.
βῆ δ' ἐλάαν ἐπὶ κύματ'· ἄταλλε δὲ κήτε' ὑπ' αὐτοῦ
πάντοθεν ἐκ κευθμῶν, οὐδ' ἠγνοίησεν ἄνακτα,
γηθοσύνῃ δὲ θάλασσα διίστατο· τοὶ δ' ἐπέτοντο
ῥίμφα μάλ', οὐδ' ὑπένερθε διαίνετο χάλκεος ἄξων·
τὸν δ' ἐς Ἀχαιῶν νῆας ἐΰσκαρθμοι φέρον ἵπποι.
ἔστι δέ τι σπέος εὐρὺ βαθείης βένθεσι λίμνης,
μεσσηγὺς Τενέδοιο καὶ Ἴμβρου παιπαλοέσσης·
ἔνθ' ἵππους ἔστησε Ποσειδάων ἐνοσίχθων
λύσας ἐξ ὀχέων, παρὰ δ' ἀμβρόσιον βάλεν εἶδαρ
ἔδμεναι· ἀμφὶ δὲ ποσσὶ πέδας ἔβαλε <u>χρυσείας</u>
ἀρρήκτους ἀλύτους, ὄφρ' ἔμπεδον αὖθι μένοιεν
νοστήσαντα ἄνακτα· ὃ δ' ἐς στρατὸν ᾤχετ' Ἀχαιῶν.

He took three long strides forward, and in the fourth he came to his
     goal,
Aigai, where his *glorious house* was built in the waters'
depth, glittering with gold, imperishable forever.
Going there he harnessed under his chariot his bronze-shod horses,
flying-footed, with long manes streaming of *gold*; and he put on
clothing of gold about his own body, and took up the *golden*
lash, carefully compacted, and climbed up into his chariot
and drove it across the waves. And about him the sea beasts came up
from their deep places and played in his path, and acknowledged
     their master,
and the sea stood apart before him, rejoicing. The horses winged on
delicately, and the bronze axle beneath was not wetted.
The fast-running horses carried him to the ships of the Achaians.
     There is a cave, broad and deep down in the gloom of the water,
lying midway between Tenedos and Imbros of the high cliffs.
There Poseidon the shaker of the earth reined in his horses,

and slipped them from the yoke, and threw fodder immortal before
them
so they could eat, and threw around their feet *golden* hobbles
not to be broken or slipped from, so they would wait there steadfast
for their lord gone. And Poseidon went to the ships of the Achaians.

Iliad XIII 20–38

The shining palace (κλυτὰ δώματα ... μαρμαίροντα) of Poseidon and the repeated references to gold (δώματα ... χρύσεα, χρυσέῃσιν ἐθείρῃσιν, χρυσόν, ἱμάσθλην χρυσείην, πέδας ... χρυσείας) are not only "the simplest and most popular way of giving emphasis,"[126] but when combined with the presentation of nature as the partner of the god, it becomes clear that they constitute an *espace vécu*, a "lived space" "whose elements, loci, dimensions, and directions are fraught with affective charges."[127] Emphasis on movement is here combined with a massive, almost complete participation of nature in divine activity.[128] That said, it is no surprise that divine immortality is transferred to elements of Poseidon's world (his palace and the fodder for his horses). This brief view of the underwater palace of the supreme sea god is, as usual, associated with his involvement in the plot, but it also suggests a particular form of spatial theography: depth is seen as simply a mirror of height,[129] the other side of a vertical path or continuum straddled by the gods, who can easily move from one end to the other.

Unlike the *Odyssey*, the sea and its depths in the *Iliad* have hardly any negative connotations, mainly because they are presented in connection only with divine activity. In the *Iliad*, virtually no action takes place at sea, with the (perhaps telling) exception of Odysseus' brief sea journey to Khruse to return Khruseis to her father.[130] At the same time, the sea depths are associated with the only type of divine journey that becomes dramatically charged within the plot of the epic, since it involves Thetis, the "bridge" between the principal Iliadic hero (Achilles) and the immortal world.

Thetis' underwater abode is presented in terms of her constant journeys to both Olympos and the shore next to the Achaean ships, and of a brief description of her cave in *Iliad* XVIII. Her journey from the depths of the sea either to

---

[126] J. Kakridis 1949:121.
[127] Van Noppen 1996:681.
[128] See Vivante 1970:115–116; Elliger 1975:69–71.
[129] Cf. *Iliad* XV 189–195, where the division of the world among Zeus, Poseidon, and Hades is presented.
[130] This is the most complete πλοῦς type-scene in both Homeric epics, since Odysseus, the hero of the *Odyssey* and the sea journey par excellence, is imbued with the fullest list of maritime features even in the *Iliad*.

Olympos or the shore of the Achaean camp[131] is always expressed in two phases: the opening of the waves (I 496 ἀνεδύσετο κῦμα θαλάσσης; XVIII 66–67 περὶ δέ σφισι κῦμα θαλάσσης / ῥήγνυτο; XXIV 96 λιάζετο κῦμα θαλάσσης) and her upward movement (I 497 ἀνέβη μέγαν οὐρανὸν Οὔλυμπόν τε; XVIII 68 ἀκτὴν εἰσανέβαινον; XXIV 97 ἀκτὴν δ' εἰσαναβᾶσαι). The common denominator in all these is the emphasis on her ascending movement. This may seem trivial, but Thetis' vertical itinerary has a symbolic as well as a thematic function. The representation of the world as a vertically organized hierarchy is, of course, an almost global feature of various religions and cultures, and as anthropologists have argued, it derives from the "fundamental human experience of the body's erect position, from the difficulty experienced in elevating the body from the earth's horizontal surface."[132] This is certainly true, but next to the widespread diffusion of this belief stands its specific poetic acculturation, its distinct epic function. The ascending movement of Thetis, expressed by the verbs ἀναδύεσθαι and (εἰσ)αναβαίνειν, points to her main function in the poem. Thetis is preeminently a goddess who supplicates: she begs both Achilles not to make certain decisions that will lead to his death, and Zeus to give victory to the Trojans so that her son will be satisfied. In fact, by situating Thetis in a world that is neither Olympos nor the human world, the *Iliad* "can have the cake and eat it too": her underwater realm keeps her apart both from the divine abode of the gods par excellence (Olympos) and from the world of mortal men to which her son belongs. Her upward movement symbolically points to the act of a suppliant, who kneels and begs a god to grant her wish. This time, depth is not, as with Poseidon, a mirror of the divine world above. It is a reconfigured sphere of divine activity, a highly thematized and symbolic area with a specifically female bent, the space of a "fallen" mother and an "upright" goddess. Sitting in a cave (XVIII 65 σπέος) next to her aged father in the depths of the sea (XVIII 36 ἡμένη ἐν βένθεσσιν ἁλὸς παρὰ πατρὶ γέροντι), surrounded by her sisters, she is ironically reminiscent of the standard picture of a woman still living in her father's house. Thetis' special status reconfigures the space of the sea and allows it to be symbolically decoded as a locus situated in the "geography of marginality." The deliberate blurring of the boundaries between motherhood and abandonment of the family's abode in Phthia suggests a reappraisal of Thetis' underwater habitat, which is now seen as a gender-specific space, a place where her contrasting roles and functions as both goddess and the mother of a mortal son are fused. In addition, by exploring the depths of the sea as a

---

[131] In *Iliad* I, XVIII, and XXIV.
[132] Van Noppen 1996:682.

special feminine space where the divine and human elements coalesce, the *Iliad* throws male claims to authority and territoriality into sharp relief.

The division of the divine world into three realms (*Iliad* XV 189–195), distributed among Zeus, Poseidon, and Hades and reflecting the strong male instinct for appropriating territory, can now be seen against the backdrop of the feminine space of the sea, where fame, recognition, and authority (as emblems of male arrogance for possession and power) are replaced by understanding, caring, and eagerness to help. Apart from scenes in which Thetis' sea abode is presented in relation to Achilles, in both *Iliad* VI 135–137 and XVIII 395–409 Thetis is presented as living at the bottom of the sea, where she rescues and cares for persecuted gods, Dionysus and Hephaistos (together with Eurunome) respectively.[133]

Minor spaces

The *Iliad* avails itself of a number of locations used by the gods as observation posts. From these, immortals watch what is going on either on the plain of Troy or in the Achaean camp and decide to intervene and influence the action. The only exception to this pattern is the land of the Ethiopians (*Iliad* I 423), which falls outside this framework. The spatial function of this location, where the gods enjoy a marvelous feast (*Iliad* I 423) and the locals offer sacrifices to them, has both a thematic and a symbolic aspect. The Iliadic narrator uses the land of the Ethiopians, situated at the borders of the world as the early Greeks imagined it, for quite different effects. In I 423–427, it creates a pause and allows for the unraveling of another narrative thread, since the return of Khruseis to her father Khruses happens within the twelve-day period during which the gods stay with the Ethiopians. Moreover, it prolongs Achilles' anger and makes Thetis' visit to Olympos more dramatic.[134] Conversely, in XXIII 205–211, it is used to speed up the intervention of the Winds in favor of Achilles. Iris states that she cannot stay at the banquet held at Zephuros' house, and that she will go to the other gods in the land of the Ethiopians, so that the Winds can act at once and make Patroklos' funeral pyre finally burn. In its symbolic function, the land of the Ethiopians epitomizes the notion of a perfect community of gods and men, a place where both parties act in flawless harmony: men offer sacrifices to the gods and the immortals rejoice in them. Within this framework, the spatial aspect of distance (this land is situated at the borders of the world, and in any case far from the Trojan theater of action) intensifies even more the ironic contrast with Troy. It seems that the *Iliad* allows for a brief glimpse of an alternative world, one of serenity and harmony, where gods and men are presented in purely positive

---

[133] See Hellwig 1964:26. On gender and space, see Higgonet and Templeton 1994.
[134] See Tsagalis 2008b:216–219.

terms. Seen from this angle, the land of the Ethiopians constitutes a symbolic space that stands in contrast to the grimness of the Iliadic world.

Mount Ida and the highest peaks of a mountain in Samothrace form a visual pair that offers views of the human theater of operations from two different angles. Both mountains constitute thematic and symbolic spaces: their locations determine which gods use them as observation posts.[135] Zeus, who is a pro-Trojan god for most of the plot, goes to Ida to observe the city of Troy and the ships of the Achaeans.[136] Given that the location of Ida in the interior of the Troad, somewhere beyond Troy, turns it into a "friendly" space for the Trojans, the narrator is not coy about positioning Zeus in such a pro-Trojan space. Likewise Poseidon, who acts as a pro-Achaean god, is placed on the highest peaks of a mountain on the island of Samothrace (*Iliad* XIII 10–16), which lies rather close to the Achaean camp.[137] In the light of these passages, it becomes evident that distance is thematically spatialized: proximity means support. A second aspect of these landmarks concerns the way space is presented, namely the particular viewpoint adopted by the narrator. That said, and taking into account that the phraseology employed for these mountains does not differ from that used for Olympos, the viewpoint adopted in this spatial presentation becomes all the more crucial.

> οὐδ' ἀλαοσκοπιὴν εἶχε κρείων Ἐνοσίχθων·
> καὶ γὰρ ὃ θαυμάζων ἧστο πτόλεμόν τε μάχην τε,
> ὑψοῦ ἐπ' ἀκροτάτης κορυφῆς Σάμου ὑληέσσης
> Θρηϊκίης· ἔνθεν γὰρ ἐφαίνετο πᾶσα μὲν Ἴδη,
> φαίνετο δὲ Πριάμοιο πόλις καὶ νῆες Ἀχαιῶν.
> ἔνθ' ἄρ' ὅ γ' ἐξ ἁλὸς ἕζετ' ἰών, ἐλέαιρε δ' Ἀχαιοὺς
> Τρωσὶν δαμναμένους, Διὶ δὲ κρατερῶς ἐνεμέσσα.

> Neither did the powerful shaker of the earth keep blind watch;
> for he sat and admired the fighting and the run of the battle,
> aloft on top of the highest summit of timbered Samos,
> the Thracian place; and from there all Ida appeared before him,
> and the city of Priam was plain to see, and the ships of the Achaians.
> There he came up out of the water, and sat, and pitied the Achaians
> who were beaten by the Trojans, and blamed Zeus for it in bitterness.

> *Iliad* XIII 10–16

---

[135] See Trachsel 2007:104–105.

[136] See *Iliad* VIII 47, XI 183, XIV 157, XIV 293, XV 5.

[137] On the analogy between Zeus' journey in *Iliad* VIII 41–46 and Poseidon's in *Iliad* XIII 23–28, see Schadewaldt 1966:115n1; Reinhardt 1961:279; Kakridis 1980:81–88.

ἔγρετο δὲ Ζεύς
Ἴδης ἐν κορυφῇσι παρὰ χρυσοθρόνου Ἥρης.
στῆ δ' ἄρ' ἀναΐξας, ἴδε δὲ Τρῶας καὶ Ἀχαιούς,
τοὺς μὲν ὀρινομένους, τοὺς δὲ κλονέοντας ὄπισθεν
Ἀργείους, μετὰ δέ σφι Ποσειδάωνα ἄνακτα·
Ἕκτορα δ' ἐν πεδίῳ ἴδε κείμενον, ἀμφὶ δ' ἑταῖροι
εἵαθ'· ὃ δ' ἀργαλέῳ ἔχετ' ἄσθματι, κῆρ ἀπινύσσων,
αἷμ' ἐμέων, ἐπεὶ οὔ μιν ἀφαυρότατος βάλ' Ἀχαιῶν.

But now Zeus wakened
by Hera of the gold throne on the high places of Ida,
and stood suddenly upright, and saw the Achaians and Trojans,
these driven to flight, the others harrying them in confusion,
these last Argives, and saw among them the lord Poseidon.
He saw Hektor lying in the plain, his companions sitting
around him, he dazed at the heart and breathing painfully,
vomiting blood, since not the weakest Achaian had hit him.

Iliad XV 4–11

In both passages, the gods adopt a panoramic,[138] actorial, and fixed stand-point. They assume a "bird's-eye view," as they are located in a fixed place and look upon the human world from above. The narratological terminology reveals that this is not the usual way a panoramic standpoint is presented in Homeric epic. The narrator normally adopts a nonactorial, panoramic view, that is, he does not identify himself with a particular figure, when he wants to offer descriptions of large groups of characters.[139] This departure from the usual practice has a special effect: by offering such a view of the human world at Troy, the narrator temporarily assumes the position of one of his characters who is endowed with special abilities, as he can raise himself high and take a global view of the world. By adopting a divine viewpoint, the omniscient and omnipresent narrator is able to mirror his ability to take a bird's-eye view of a figure of the plot. In this way, the fighting and slaughter on the battlefield are not seen panoramically, by the narrator standing outside the plot, but from the point of view of the gods, that is, from within the plot. The gain from this shift is considerable: the gods, who become spectators of the human suffering,[140] react in various ways, yet their panoramic view is a metaliterary comment on the

---

[138] Panoramic standpoints are regularly used with temporal devices like a summary, or as a marker of a starting or end point; see de Jong and Nünlist 2004a:69.

[139] de Jong and Nünlist 2004a:70.

[140] See Griffin 1978:1–22; de Jong and Nünlist 2004a:70.

traditional dichotomy of viewer and viewed object. By turning plot characters (the gods) into external spectators and then again into characters, the Homeric narrator mirrors his own double stance toward his work: he can both see it from a distance and be immersed in it.[141]

The Wall of Herakles (*Iliad* XX 145) and the Hill of Kallikolone (XX 151) represent two symmetrical[142] landmarks used by the gods as observation points within the plain of Troy. They are both highly thematized spaces, since their location determines the gods who will be placed there: the Wall of Herakles is occupied by the pro-Achaean gods because it is beyond the ramparts and ditch of the Achaean camp, next to the sea, while the Hill of Kallikolone is used by the pro-Trojan gods since it is located between the city of Troy and Ida.[143] Both observation points are situated at the limits of human space, thus underlining their function as a bridge between direct observation and direct intervention.[144] It is no coincidence that both of them are mentioned mainly in the episode of the θεομαχία, where the gods will get involved in the fighting in the most blatant way.

At the same time, the Wall of Herakles and the Hill of Kallikolone both refer to the past.[145] The former was built by the Trojans and Athena in order to help Herakles escape from a sea beast "when the charging monster drove him away to the plain from the sea-shore" (*Iliad* XX 148),[146] and the latter was the hill where the Judgment of Paris took place. This archaeology of space evokes by means of specific locations two different phases of the Trojan past. Herakles had led an expedition to Troy in the distant past (V 638–642; XIV 250–262; XV 25–30; XX 144–148),[147] while the episode between Paris and the three goddesses stands at the very beginning of the Trojan War mythic saga. By using these signposts as time markers, the *Iliad* entwines space with time and creates two effective chronotopes.[148] What is important with respect to these two signposts is that

---

[141] In this respect, the analogy with the shield of Achilles becomes all the more telling. On such metaliterary comments, see W. Kullmann 1956:84; de Jong 2009, 2011.

[142] *Iliad* XX 151 ἑτέρωσε 'to the other side'; 153 ἑκάτερθε 'on either side'.

[143] According to the scholia (bT on *Iliad* XX 53c), Demetrius of Scepsis (fr. 23.b1–7), and the *Mythographus Homericus* (*P. Berol.* inv. 13930 [*P. Schub.* 21], in van Rossum-Steenbeek 1998:299–300 [n. 54, lines 17–23]).

[144] Trachsel 2007:105–108.

[145] See Trachsel 2007:99–108.

[146] According to Pseudo-Apollodorus *Library* 2.103–104, 134–136 and Diodorus Siculus *Library* 4.42, 49 (see Gunning 1924:750–754), Laomedon did not reward Poseidon for building (with Apollo) the walls of Troy, and the angry sea-god sent a monster against the city. Laomedon promised the gift of his divine horses to anyone who would help, but refused to give them to Herakles, who went to Troy to offer his support. As a result, Herakles sacked the city of Troy.

[147] See Boardman 2002:36; Grethlein 2008:33n42.

[148] See Bakhtin 1981; Riffaterre 1996.

their older use or significance "remains in the world but in a new form of being in time and space," since it becomes the "other side" of the new form that has replaced it.[149] The Wall of Herakles and the Hill of Kallikolone bring the past of the Trojan landscape to the present of the Iliadic narrative. They are still visible, but their function has changed. The memory of the past invades specific locations, which the new mythical tradition of the *Iliad* reappropriates within the confines of its own plot. In this way, time colors space and imbues it with connotations that comment on the present state of things. Unlike Herakles, who tried to escape from a danger (a beast) coming from the sea by means of Trojan help (the wall), the Achaeans are trying to protect themselves from a threat (the Trojans) coming from the land.[150] As far as the hill of Kallikolone is concerned,[151] it symbolizes the beginning of the Trojan War myth, the Judgment of Paris which led to the abduction of Helen and the expedition of the Achaeans against Troy. By using the Wall of Herakles and the Hill of Kallikolone as symmetrically located observation points for the pro-Achaean and pro-Trojan gods respectively, the *Iliad* employs "the present only as a foil for the privileging of the permanent and absolute heroic past."[152]

---

[149] See Bakhtin 1984:410.

[150] Grethlein (2008:34n44) sees the reference to the fight between Herakles and the Sea Beast as an allusion to the subsequent fight between Achilles and the river Skamandros.

[151] See Eustathius *Commentary on Homer's Iliad* (1195, 43–44 = vol. 4, p. 365, l. 17 van der Valk), who calls Kallikolone βραχύτατός τις Ὄλυμπος "a kind of very small Olympos."

[152] Nagy 2001:78–79. See also Haubold 2005:95, who argues that "the Homeric bard sees in Herakles a potential challenge to the heroes."

PART TWO

HOME IS THE HERO
EMBEDDED STORY SPACE

THE TRADITIONAL NARRATOLOGICAL DIVISION between narrator and character text entered the field of classics via a monograph on Homer.[1] I. J. F. de Jong's systematic analysis of Iliadic narrative has shown, once and for all, the importance of adopting the basic distinction between διήγησις (narrator text) and μίμησις (character text), which is as old as Plato.[2] But narratology was far from alone in studying these two registers of Homeric poetry. Oralists, for example, had also explored the similarities and differences between διήγησις and μίμησις with respect to such dictional features as noun-epithet formulas, evaluative language, and abstract terms, as well as specific stylistic features and syntax.[3] Not surprisingly, narrator and character text, or simple narrative and speeches, show crucial differences that highlight their functioning on different, yet complementary levels.

Space has barely featured in this respect. This may be because it forms a general category, comprising several smaller sections that operate on multiple levels, such as language, topography, myth, and cognitive representation, and create a complex nexus of associations hard to pinpoint and pigeonhole. Part of the explanation, at least, is also the fact that literary interest in space virtually began in the Romantic period, during which description was considered to be the basic, if not the only, spatial aspect of any worth.

M. Fludernik's theory of *natural narratology*,[4] and in particular the notion of *experientiality*, can be accommodated, *mutatis mutandis*, to the narrative framework of archaic Greek epic. More significantly, it can help us see focalizers[5] as "cognizers," that is, as thinking agents whose stored experiences shape their perception of what is going on in the story-world. In other words, despite the fictionality of Iliadic heroes, such as Achilles or Nestor, it is clear that they are treated as independent mental entities, sharing human consciousness but also having personal traits based on their epic biographies. In this light, they exert a certain pressure on the narrator, limiting his ability to define their roles in the epic. *Traditional referentiality*,[6] a term that aptly describes each hero's epic input, points to the fact that "each act of perception is carried out by a mind which has previous knowledge, memories, and expectations, all of which play a

---

I have borrowed the first part of the title from Martin's influential article "Home is the Hero: Deixis and Semantics in Pindar's *Pythian* 8," published in *Arethusa* 2004:343–363.

[1]   De Jong 1987a.

[2]   Plato *Republic* 3.392c–394b. Plato distinguishes between three types of narration (διήγησις): "single" (ἁπλῆ), "effected through impersonation" (διὰ μιμήσεως γιγνομένη), and "effected through both" (δι᾽ ἀμφοτέρων). See de Jong 1987a:2–5.

[3]   See Griffin 1986:36–57.

[4]   1996; 2000; 2003b; 2008.

[5]   I.e. characters whose own point of view is presented.

[6]   See Foley 1991:24; Danek 2002; Tsagalis 2008b:123, 154, 187–188.

decisive role in shaping the inner representation of the input data."[7] Within the universe of oral song, this stock of knowledge, memories, and expectations of individual characters has more or less crystallized in their epic cognizance, that is, in the traditional medium's awareness and typified expression of their epic personas. At the same time, we would expect the oral tradition represented by our *Iliad* to have emphasized, highlighted, downplayed, and (re)shaped some of the typical features of any hero's experiential inventory, in order to make him abide by its particular presentation of the story-world. Odysseus, for example, has a general epic persona, with certain fixed characteristics that can be seen in the entire epic tradition. On the other hand, each song tradition, say the Iliadic, the Odyssean, or the Thesprotian-Telegonian, treats him in a way that suits its plotline and narrative aims. Odysseus' aspect of "husband," for example, is positively highlighted only in the Odyssean tradition, whereas it is absent from the Iliadic, and is rather distorted or ironically twisted in the Thesprotian-Telegonian (in which he marries Kallidike, queen of the Thesprotians, and is killed by Telegonos, his son by Circe[8]).

In the *Iliad*, the experiential content of individual heroes may belong to their crystallized epic personas, but their particular representation reflects their role in a specific epic tradition. Given that their representation is twofold, in narratological terms, since it comes from both the main narrator and other focalizers—either other characters of the plot or the heroes themselves—the notion of cognizance becomes all the more important.

I will therefore explore the possibility that focalizers in the Iliadic tradition are cognizers, whose accumulated experience allows them to function systematically and coherently as *chronotopic agents*, that is, as thinking minds that constantly use time not as a separate entity, but always in unison with space.[9] External analeptic and proleptic references[10] by characters are very often—and certainly more frequently than in the epic's narrative segments—*explicitly* spatial references, but whereas the external analepses refer to events taking place outside the Iliadic story space, external prolepses are almost equally divided between Trojan War (sack of Troy) and post–Trojan War story space (return to Greece). The embedded story space of the *Iliad* is marked by the constant mention of absent space, which is of a *chronotopic* nature.

Given that space encompasses all aspects of time and memory, I will investigate how embedded story space veers in a new direction, looking in particular

[7]   Margolin 2003:282.
[8]   On this episode, see Tsagalis 2008b:63–90 with all the relevant bibliography.
[9]   See Bakhtin 1981; Riffaterre 1996:244–266.
[10] On the narratological terms *prolepsis* and *analepsis*, see Genette 1980:35–36; Reichel 1994:47–98; Bal 1997:84; de Jong 2001:xi, xvi; de Jong et al. 2004b:xv, xvii–xviii.

at the way "terms of geography and spatial perception are dramatically recast to expose spaces that had previously been lost or hidden within the topography of a particular genre or tradition."[11] By inviting audiences to place the plot of the *Iliad* within the wider framework of the Trojan War, the storyteller was able to create an all-encompassing vision of the wider space within which it had originated and would end, a space that epic characters would constantly make use of in accessing and citing the entire Trojan War epic tradition.

Spacing Time

Characters of the plot often map the past, present, and future along the spatial axis *Greece-Troy*. In particular, whereas in the speeches past and future are often translated into the spatial term "Greece," the present is mainly spatialized through "Troy," a term I shall soon return to. Additionally, the spatial pair *here-there* is basically marked by nationality, since the Trojans refer principally to the spatial location of Troy ("here"),[12] whereas the Achaeans think of the past and the future in terms of their past life in or returning to Greece ("there").

Before I embark on a detailed examination of the various ramifications and interconnections of this polar space with time and the plot of the *Iliad*, I would like to linger briefly on the meaning of such broad and rather vague terms as "Greece" and "Troy." In other words, what do we define as "Greece" and "Troy" within the realm of Iliadic epic? With respect to Greece, the *Iliad* contains a useful guide: the Catalogue of Ships in *Iliad* II attempts to put in order the epic memory concerning the various participants in the Trojan War, with special emphasis on their places of origin and their strengths.[13] Leaving aside questions of historical accuracy, the Catalogue of Ships provides a rather thorough overview of the Mycenaean world, with some "later" additions, part of which modern scholars have tried to explain by means of the history and transmission of the Iliadic text.

Despite the fact that a catalogue of the Trojans and their allies is "appended" to the Catalogue of Ships, things are quite different for what we would call "Troy." The term "Troy" is generally used for the city of Troy (Ilion), the Troad (the broad area around Troy including a number of smaller cities taking part in the war on the Trojan side), and even the Trojan War as a whole. This is of course the modern use of the term, but since it is rather widespread, it is crucial to emphasize the differences between these three uses. Scully, who has meticulously

---

[11] Purves 2002:134–135.

[12] πρὶν ἐλθεῖν υἶας Ἀχαιῶν is uttered either by the narrator (*Iliad* XIII 172, XXII 156) or by Achilles (IX 403), never by the Trojans.

[13] On the Catalogue of Ships, see Visser 1997 and Brügger et al. 2003.

studied the ways Troy is presented in both Homeric epics, believes that its walls, its sacredness, and its populace living within this closed area create the Homeric vision of a city closer to the new polis of Ionian times than to the fortified citadels of the Mycenaean period.[14] Although my focus is different from Scully's, his three aspects comprising the Homeric vision of Troy will be at the center of my discussion. As I will show, for the characters of the plot, Troy constitutes a space that extends well beyond the physical locality of the city: it embodies a whole set of beliefs concerning social cohesion and survival through time, a common bond keeping a populace together. Space in Troy acquires an almost metaphorical meaning, which in the course of time evolves from the citadel of Ilion to the wider Troad, and eventually to the entire Trojan War. This progressive expansion of the meaning of the word "Troy" shows how time becomes spatialized: first the inner area of the citadel is identified with the wider term "Troy," then the term absorbs a broader geographical area where Trojan control is exercised, and finally it subsumes the entire poetic tradition developed around this city. The Iliad, therefore, uses "Troy" as what I would call a "flexi-space," one that shrinks and expands according to contextual factors, to accommodate shifting perspectives on the city, its people, and the war.[15]

Before examining in detail the various places Iliadic characters constantly refer to, I shall offer some statistical data on the spatial differences between narrator and character text, in an attempt to combine the methodological tools of narratological analysis with the emphasis of oral theory on the dictional differences between narrative and speeches. This approach offers a "panoramic" view of what I would call a deep spatial divide between narrator and character speech in its representation of space (see Table 4).[16]

Table 4: Spatial distribution of narrator vs. character text

Greece	Narrator Text (NT)	Character Text (CT)
Phthia	[1]	13
Argos (Agamemnonis urbs)	1	7

---

[14] See Scully 1990:81–99.

[15] I have coined the term "flexi-space" on the model of "flexi-narrative," for which see Jones 2005:585–589.

[16] In the case of narrator text (NT), bracketed numbers indicate that the given place-name is attested in the Catalogue of Ships, whereas unbracketed numbers designate the rest of NT in the *Iliad*.

Greece	Narrator Text (NT)	Character Text (CT)
Argos (Diomedis urbs)	[1]	6
Argos Pelasgicum	[1]	0
Argos (Peloponnese/Greece)	0	13
Sparta	[1]	1
Ithaka	[1]	1
Pylos	2 [1]	10
Mycenae	2 [1]	4
Skyros	1	2
Lemnos	6 [1]	5
Lesbos	1	3
Boeotian Thebes	1	8
Crete	[1]	3
Total	22 (22.4%)	76 (77.6%)

Asia Minor	Narrator Text (NT)	Character Text (CT)
Lycia	2 [1]	19
Hypoplakian Thebes	2	2
Khruse	1	4
Killa	0	2
Arisbe	5 [2]	0
Zeleia	2 [1]	1
Pedasos	1	4
Pedaios/-on	1	0

Asia Minor	Narrator Text (NT)	Character Text (CT)
Thymbre	0	1
Dardania	0	1
Tenedos	2	2
Imbros	3	1
Total	19 (33.9%)	37 (66.1%)

These statistics amply show that characters refer to Greece and Asia Minor much more often than the narrator does (77.6 and 66.1% vs. 22.4 and 33.9%). If we take into account that some of the narrator-text attestations of these places come from the Catalogue of Ships in *Iliad* II, which belongs to narrator text but constitutes a rather separate subcategory, the difference between narrative and speeches with respect to place-names increases even more, as the percentage of references in narrator text drops to 13.3 percent for Greece and 26.8 percent for Asia Minor. On the other hand, the divergence between narrator and character text with respect to space in the case of Asia Minor place-names may be illusory, since it is mainly due to the inclusion of Lycia. I have decided to include Lycia in the same catalogue with the "wider Troad" both because of the Catalogue of Ships, where Trojans and allies are grouped together, and because Lycia, where Sarpedon and Glaukos come from, is so important for the development of the Iliadic plot.[17] That said, we should bear in mind that Lycia is the only distant place among all the Asia Minor locations. In that sense, it resembles more the "absent" places of mainland Greece and the Aegean that are constantly mentioned by the Achaean heroes. When one takes Lycia out of the picture, and given that the notion of "wider Troy" (the Troad with a few islands) could accommodate with some flexibility all the other places in Asia Minor, the numbers can change drastically, giving a total of seventeen references in narrator text[18] and eighteen in character text—almost perfect equality. In this light it becomes clear that differences between narrator and character text with respect to place-names are significant only when distant locations are involved. In order to explore this important observation further, I will first turn my attention to the limited number of references to place-names in narrator text, including the Catalogue of Ships.

[17] See chapter 4, below.
[18] After omitting the references to Lycia in the Catalogue of Ships.

Narrator Text and the Catalogue of Ships

Of the twenty-two attestations in narrator text of significant place-names pertaining to Greece, nine come from the Catalogue of Ships (CS) (41%). The relevant figures for the Trojan world are nineteen and four respectively (21%). If we compare these figures, it becomes clear that the much more extended Greek part of the Catalogue of Ships represents almost half of important Greek place-names in the *Iliad*, while the smaller section devoted to the Trojans and their allies (CT&A) contains only one fifth of the total number of place-names in Asia Minor attested in the *Iliad*. In other words, the narrator (the CS and CT&A excluded) tends to use place-names from the general theater of war (the Troad) much more often than he does Greek place-names. It seems, then, that such a choice may have been conditioned by the subject matter of his epic, which takes place in the Troad. The narrator places himself within the larger setting of the theater of war and adopts the north-to-south perspective of the Achaeans. His manner is more restrained, since he is more focused on the *hic* (as opposed to the *nunc*) of his story.[19] The only notable exception on the Greek side is Lemnos, which appears six times in narrator text (once in the CS) and five times in character text.[20] Taking into account that small numerical differences are statistically unimportant, we can see that there is almost perfect equality in the attestation of a place-name in narrator and character text when we are dealing with a non-distant place. Significant numerical differences are observed only for certain distant places (Phthia, Argos, Pylos, Boeotian Thebes, Lycia). In this light, Lemnos is not unique: it forms part of the narrator's treatment of localities close to the Troad, which he considers part of his greater theater of war. It can be no coincidence that of the five attestations of Lemnos in character text (the CS excluded),[21] three are associated with the good relations between the Achaeans and the local king (*Iliad* VII 467; XXI 40, 46) and two with Hera's plan to seduce Zeus (XIV 230, 281). In other words, the narrator treats Lemnos as an integral part of his plot, not as a background space particularly linked with a single hero or a group of heroes, as with Phthia, Argos, Boeotian Thebes, or Lycia. This observation has far-reaching consequences for the role of the

---

[19] This observation accords with Griffin's point that narrator language is more apt to let words or terms from the storyteller's own time slip into the text (1986:37–38).

[20] On the Trojan side, Arisbe, Zeleia, and Imbros are more often attested in narrator than in character text, but since the numerical difference is small, I will not examine them in detail.

[21] The *Iliad* refers to Lemnos in the Catalogue of Ships (II 722) as the place where Philoktetes was bitten by a snake and subsequently abandoned, whereas in the *Cypria* (§33 Kullmann = 144–146 Severyns = Allen 104.21–23) the incident with the snake takes place in Tenedos, and only then is Philoktetes left in Lemnos. The version offered by the *Cypria* presupposes that the Achaean fleet went back from Tenedos to Lemnos.

narrator. It becomes clear now that he is much more restrained than his characters not only in the use of moral or evaluative terms, as Griffin has shown,[22] but also in his focus on the action itself. In this respect he is much different from his greatest hero, Achilles, who constantly raises himself "beyond the immediate confines of the action"[23] and thinks of distant places, or from Nestor, who regularly contemplates the past by referring to remote areas in mainland Greece.

The CS and CT&A, which depend heavily on spatial memory, are marked by the longest and most detailed concentration of place-names in the *Iliad*. Thus we see that the presentation of place-names in the poem is strongly polarized: whereas references to various localities are much more common in character speech, the narrator has reserved for himself an almost programmatic and globalizing panorama of geographical locations in the form of an extended catalogue in the beginning of his epic.

Despite the vast bibliography on the CS and CT&A, there has been no systematic attempt to determine how the storyteller uses spatial memory to organize and recall this extended material. The arrangement of the data offered by the CS and CT&A has been treated mainly in terms of the origins of the two catalogues and the question of whether they are a late insertion in the main body of the *Iliad*. Recently, important studies by Marks and Sammons have shed new light on the way the CS in particular participates progressively in the Iliadic plot: Marks has argued that certain clusters of heroes appear jointly or close to one another in the following narrative on the basis of either their geographical contiguity or their placement in the CS. Sammons has forcefully suggested that some key Iliadic themes, like that of Agamemnon's preeminence for most of the Iliadic plot and Achilles' role as the "absent leader,"[24] are programmatically mirrored in the CS.[25] These insights have far-reaching consequences for the interpretation of the role of space within the CS and the CT&A, since they not only indicate that these two catalogues in *Iliad* II "cross over" to the poem's narrative, but also point to the use of specific cognitive mechanisms that keep together the programmatic panorama offered by the narrator and the individual embedded spaces thematized by plot agents in character speech. Seen from this perspective, the catalogues suggest that the narrator has used their subject matter not as an "index" but as a "table of contents," on the one hand (a) turning the sequential arrangement of names into a device that determines the role of some characters in the narrative, and on the other (b) mirroring

---

[22] 1986:37–40.
[23] Griffin 1986:56.
[24] Stanley 1993:19; Sammons 2010:188–193.
[25] 2010:181.

the external patterning of geographical areas through the function of certain thematized spaces in character speech.

With respect to (a), keeping track of a large number of characters, especially second-rank figures, must have been a pressing need for the narrator, who to meet this demanding challenge resorted to character clustering on the basis of geographical contiguity. Thus, for example, Meges of Elis, who is placed immediately before Odysseus and his Kephallenians (*Iliad* II 625–630) is consistently associated in battle with Idomeneus and Meriones (V 43–69) and Thoas (together with Idomeneus and Meriones: XV 300–302), as well as with Odysseus (together with Meriones and Thoas: XIX 239). In other words, Meges' function in the narrative reflects his position in the CS, since the heroes he is associated with are placed either before him (Odysseus) or after him (Thoas, Idomeneus, and Meriones) in the CS.[26]

As far as (b) is concerned, the larger framework of the two catalogues programmatically points to the use of thematized space in character speech: thus the placement of the contingent of Achilles and the Lycians in the most distant geographical zones (northern Greece and southern Asia Minor respectively) is mirrored in their use of the "coming from afar" motif in the plot of the epic, since both of them complain to those who brought them to Troy (the Atreidai and Hektor respectively) that they have come from afar to fight a war that is not their own. The two catalogues, therefore, inform and feed the plot of the *Iliad*. It is under this theoretical premise that I propose to explore the following topic: since both the CS and the CT&A refer to a number of geographical "zones," can we trace and study the particular techniques employed by the storyteller both externally, within the larger scale of each catalogue, and internally, within each zone?

Let us start, then, from the beginning of the CS. Seen from the point of view of cognitive science,[27] catalogues form a special register, heavily based on spatial memory, the fundamental mechanism for activating mental images during the performance of oral song.[28] Catalogues can be of different sorts (genealogical, thematic, of objects), and they can serve various functions (paradigmatic, descriptive, emphatic, etc). According to Pucci's formulation:

> The catalogue, as a speech act, manifests a prowess of memory, and points to poetry as its privileged means. Cataloguing constitutes the

---

[26] See Marks 2012:107; the author carefully reminds us of the caveats of this approach: "proximity in the Catalogue is only one of several tendencies that underlie the relationships among Iliadic characters."

[27] See Ryan 2003:214–242.

[28] See Bal 19972:147; Minchin 2001:73–99.

supreme distillation of poetry's capabilities for truth, rigor, order, history, sequentiality: mere names, mere numbers, and no *mêtis*; or as we would say no connotations, no rhetoric, no fiction. Almost no poem.[29]

Pucci emphasizes the catalogue's lack of narrative and its almost complete erasure of time and action, the most elementary prerequisites for poetry of any sort. Yet catalogues such as the CS and the CT&A are not mere lists of items added one after the other,[30] but are marked by their succinct organization of information that brings together time and space into one indivisible unit, which is regarded as of such paramount importance that the narrator invokes the Muses and asks for their help in order to perform a task of truly gigantic proportions:[31]

> ἔσπετε νῦν μοι, Μοῦσαι Ὀλύμπια δώματ' ἔχουσαι—
> ὑμεῖς γὰρ θεαί ἐστε, πάρεστέ τε, ἴστέ τε πάντα,
> ἡμεῖς δὲ κλέος οἶον ἀκούομεν, οὐδέ τι ἴδμεν—
> οἵ τινες ἡγεμόνες Δαναῶν καὶ κοίρανοι ἦσαν.
> . . . .
> ἀρχοὺς αὖ νηῶν ἐρέω, νῆάς τε προπάσας.
> Βοιωτῶν μὲν Πηνέλεως καὶ Λήϊτος ἦρχον
> Ἀρκεσίλαός τε Προθοήνωρ τε Κλονίος τε,
> οἵ θ' Ὑρίην ἐνέμοντο καὶ Αὐλίδα πετρήεσσαν,
> . . . .
> τῶν μὲν πεντήκοντα νέες κίον, ἐν δὲ ἑκάστῃ
> κοῦροι Βοιωτῶν ἑκατὸν καὶ εἴκοσι βαῖνον.

> Tell me now, you Muses who have your homes on Olympos.
> For you, who are goddesses, are there, and you know all things,
> and we have heard only the rumour of it and know nothing.
> Who then of those were the chief men and the lords of the Danaans?
> . . . .
> I will tell the lords of the ships, and the ships numbers.
> Leïtos and Peneleos were leaders of the Boiotians,
> with Arkesilaos and Prothoenor and Klonios;
> they who lived in Hyria and rocky Aulis

[29] Pucci 1996:21.
[30] See Sammons 2010:9. On catalogues in Homeric poetry, see Beye 1964:345–373; Powell 1978:255–264; Edwards 1980:81–105; Barney 1982:191–192; Thalmann 1984:25–26; Minchin 1996:4–5, 2001:74–76.
[31] See also Tsagalis 2010a:323–347.

....
Of these there were fifty ships in all, and on board
each of these a hundred and twenty sons of the Boiotians.

Iliad II 484–510

The CS is a complex and concise catalogue, for although its rubric is straightfor-
ward, it is basically subdivided into two (occasionally three) items in each entry.
As early as *Iliad* II 493, the poet defines his rubric as "lords of the ships and all the
ships numbers" (ἀρχοὺς αὖ νηῶν ἐρέω, νῆάς τε προπάσας);[32] he then proceeds
to describe the individual items, which are developed into two-level entries,
one for each leader and one for the number of ships. By making constant reference to geographical location, the CS clearly follows a geographical blueprint,[33]
although "no entry begins with a relative marker such as 'to the north, south
of there.'"[34] This last observation is accurate, but I think it overstates the notion
of "geographical orientation" to require the narrator to use distinct and clear
directional markers. But what if the storyteller sees the topography of Greece
and of Asia Minor in his mind's eye as a spatial diptych, that is, as both a *tour*
and a *map*, in which geographical contiguity applies to the internal "sections"
he creates, whereas the external arrangement of the sections is based on his
attempt to create a structural bridge between the CS and the CT&A? To explore
this possibility, let us take into account the following remarks:

    1.   The storyteller's overarching principle (1) is to begin from core regions,
determined by the nature of each catalogue. Since the CS reflects the movement
of the ships and troops from the various regions of mainland Greece and the
islands to Aulis, the core region is Aulis. Likewise in the CT&A: the gathering of
all the allies at Troy means that the core region is Troy.

    2.   The storyteller has decided first to divide each catalogue into smaller
sections, and then to follow the principle (2) of geographical contiguity both
internally, within each section, and externally, in the transition from the CS to
the CT&A. If principle 1 and principle 2 are combined, then he has to end the CS
with northern Greece, since it is closest to the core area (Troy) of the CT&A that
will come first in the second catalogue.

    3.   According to principle 1, he begins the CS with Aulis in Boeotia and
follows a clockwise movement, based on geographical contiguity, towards

---

[32] See Marks 2011:101–112.

[33] Various theories have been put forward concerning the way the Catalogue of Ships proceeds
with respect to the geographical placement of the Greek troops. See Brügger et al. 2003:153–154,
with a summary of previous bibliography.

[34] Sammons 2010:14n31.

Orkhomenos, Phokis, Lokris, Euboea, Athens, and Salamis (*Iliad* II 494–558). That this is the end of a smaller zone within his first section is indicated by the fact that though he still operates on the principle of geographical proximity, he changes the way he tours this specific area. He first moves to the south (southern Argolid), then to the north (northern Argolid), then to the southeast (Laconia), southwest (Pylos), central (Arcadia), and northwest Peloponnese (Elis) (*Iliad* II 559–624). He now moves on to a third zone within this same section by following a counterclockwise movement: Doulikhion, Kephallenia, and Aetolia (*Iliad* II 625–644). At this point, the narrator's mental tour of section 1 is complete.

4.   The storyteller now makes a huge leap from Aetolia to Crete, in the southern Aegean, and then moves counterclockwise toward the eastern islands of Rhodes, Syme, Karpathos, and Kos (*Iliad* II 645–680). This discontinuity has been called unavoidable,[35] but for the wrong reason. In my view, it is a by-product of the ensuing discontinuity with northern Greece. As I have just argued, the latter is a discontinuity only if the CS is seen independently of the CT&A. When examined as a spatial diptych, the placement of Thessaly at the very end of the CS makes perfect sense. The narrator is employing the principle of *economy*, according to which geographical contiguity will enhance spatial memory only if used at the lowest cognitive cost.

5.   In northern Greece, the storyteller moves first to Pelasgian Argos and then goes northeast (Phthiotis, Pelasgiotis, Magnetis); he now changes direction and turns toward the northwest (Hestiaiotis), then southeast (Thessaliotis) and northeast (Perrhaibia); a surprising turn off course towards the west (Aenienis) is explained by the fact that in this and the following location the narrator is mainly touring the courses of the rivers Titaressos (on the west) and Peneios (on the east). The entire section ends with Peleion in the northeast, the closest point for the mental leap to the beginning of the CT&A that will soon follow (*Iliad* II 681–759). Having paved the way so as to decrease the cognitive cost of passing from one mental map to another, the storyteller is now ready to move on to the CT&A.

6.   The CT&A is divided into four zones, which belong to two larger sections. The first section covers a vast area in the north, stretching from Europe to the Pontos region, while the second stretches toward the south. The first section includes three geographical zones. The storyteller begins, as he did in the CS, with the core region of Troy, following a counterclockwise course from Ilion to Zeleia, the Propontis, the southwestern Hellespont, and Pelasgian Larisa (*Iliad* II 816–843). He then moves northwest to Europe, touring areas on the basis of geographical contiguity: the Thracians, the Kikones, and the Paiones (II

---

[35]   Jachmann 1958:184–185.

844–850). The third and last zone of this northern section contains a leap toward the northeast, to Asia, again according to geographical contiguity. The narrator seems to be touring areas as they appear on a map: first the Paphlagonians, then the Halizones (II 851–857). One can see that it is the combination of geographical contiguity and beginning with the core region that determines the mental blue-print adopted by the storyteller in the CT&A; that is, just as in the CS.

7.   Having toured a vast area in the north, the storyteller now moves toward the south. He first follows a course toward the Musoi in the southwest, then to the Phrygians in the southeast, and the Maiones further south (*Iliad* II 858–866). His mental journey continues further south with the Carians and southeast to the Lycians (867–877). In this case section and zone coincide, since the storyteller uses a single technique of mental "navigation": in contrast to the previous section on the north, in which he used two different techniques (coun-terclockwise and linear progression), he now follows a single path as he moves almost vertically toward the south.

8.   The CS and CT&A form a spatial diptych, based not only on their sharing the same organizing principles (beginning from the core region, geographical contiguity, and low cognitive cost) but also on their symmetrical arrangement: both emphasize their beginning and end, to which they devote the largest amount of textual space: CS core region (sixty-four verses)—CS last section (seventy-eight verses), and CT&A core region (twenty-seven verses)—CT&A last section (twenty-two verses); both use water in the form of a gulf, sea, or river as the outer limit of each section: in the CS, these are Khalkis in Aetolia, Karpathos/Kos in the eastern Aegean, and Peneios in northern Greece; the CT&A has the river Halys in the land of the Halizones (implicit in their name as well as in the place-name Alybe)[36] and the river Xanthos in Lycia at the very end. Symmetry and analogical arrangement, together with the organizing principles discussed above, strongly indicate that space plays a major role in the structure of both catalogues, which must be examined not separately but as belonging to a spatial diptych. Juxtaposition, concatenation, and seriality[37] have all played their roles in the internal organization of the two catalogues.

The CS contains 29 entries referring to 43 leaders, 1186 ships, and 152 place-names. The sheer size of this material, however, obscures the different levels on which these data operate: the entries refer to textual size and classification,

---

[36]   See Brügger et al. 2003:281 on *Iliad* II 857.

[37]   Contrast, for example, Aratus' *Phaenomena,* which belongs to written literature, in which the poet constantly employs directional markers to describe the constellations of the zodiac. In this case and very much unlike the Homeric storyteller, Aratus is following a map of the sky based on two works of Eudoxus of Cnidus in prose, the *Phaenomena* and *Enoptron.*

the leaders (at least some of them) to the characters of the plot, the ships and the place-names to the movement of the various smaller flotillas from the individual homelands to Aulis,[38] where the gathering of the army took place. This cluster of information reflects the dual nature of the CS, pointing to both the past and the present. In the words of Sammons,[39]

> The mention of ships and many hometowns in the catalogue transforms what would be a static list into a dynamic image of movement; not only the movement of the army before Troy, but the movement of the army *from* Greece.

The much smaller CT&A, which contains sixteen entries referring to the twenty-seven leaders and nineteen place names, is devoid of any reference to ships, since the Trojans are fighting in their own country and their allies have all come to Troy by inland routes, though for some of them, such as the Carians and the Lycians, a sea journey would not have been unthinkable. In this way, the lack of a previous gathering of the Trojans and their allies contrasts with the mustering of the Achaean army at Aulis. On the other hand, place-names, which are also used in this smaller catalogue, indicate that they form the main linking mechanism between the two catalogues on the level of structure. Statistics may also be of help here: the ratio between individual homelands and number of leaders is for the CS 28.3 percent (152:43) and for the CT&A 142.1 percent (19:27).[40] These numbers show that while in the CS multiple place-names are associated with the area controlled by a given leader, in the CT&A multiple leaders are often associated with a given place-name. The Boeotian and Phrygian entries of the CS and the CT&A respectively show this feature clearly: whereas in the Boeotian entry (*Iliad* II 494–510), twenty-nine place-names are linked to five leaders (493–494), in the Phrygian entry (862–863) the relevant numbers are one place-name and two leaders. Before considering the significance of this disparity, we should also keep in mind another divergence between the two catalogues, in the ratios between specific geographical features of the

---

[38] Giovannini (1969:23–50) argues that the arrangement of locations in the CS reflects the political reality of the archaic period and not the Mycenaean past. See also Kullmann 1993:132–138. For criticism of Giovannini's other thesis that the CS reflects the itineraries of Delphic θεωροί (1969:53–71), see Kirk 1985:183–186.

[39] 2010:154.

[40] For the relevant numbers, see the tables in Brügger et al. 2003:146, 264. My only difference with them concerns the Lycian contingent, whose *Ortsname* is given (*Iliad* II 877 τηλόθεν ἐκ Λυκίης) in the manner of the Halizones (*Iliad* II 857 τηλόθεν ἐξ Ἀλύβης), and in which there is only one (not two, as indicated in the list offered by the commentary) geographical feature (*Iliad* II 877 Ξάνθου ἄπο δινήεντος). As a result, the total number for place-names and geographical features or references in the CT&A should be corrected to nineteen and twelve respectively.

various homelands, like rivers or mountains, and regions (= entries).[41] The CT&A displays a higher proportion of geographical features or references per entry than the CS, the relevant figures being for the former 12:16 (133.3%), and 35:29 (82.9%) for the latter.

These data should be interpreted with caution, the more so since they are based on two different groups (leaders and regions). Since the CT&A is marked by higher percentages of place-names per leader and geographical features per region than the CS, it is clear that place-names and geographical features tend to cluster more in the CS than in the CT&A. In other words, place-names and geographical features are presented in groups more often in the CS than in the CT&A. Given that both place-names and geographical features are spatial markers,[42] it seems that the narrator has employed them in clusters so that he can exploit them more effectively as cues to recall of material. The fact that the CS is much more extended in comparison to the CT&A (CS: 266 verses, 29 entries referring to 43 leaders, 1186 ships, 152 place-names, and 35 geographical features or references; CT&A: 61 verses, 16 entries referring to 27 leaders, 19 place-names, and 12 geographical features or references) is reflected, in my view, in the more dense clustering of spatial features that ease the mnemonic process for the storyteller. Low cognitive cost and readiness for data recall, especially in a catalogue context that represents a storehouse of names and numbers, have determined a number of structural and organizing choices by the storyteller in the arrangement and presentation of their material.

The CS and the CT&A are good examples of the transformation of time into space. Their lack of subordination,[43] which is best seen in the complete absence

---

[41] Geographical features should be examined in reference to regions (= entries) and not with respect to place-names, since there are cases where a geographical feature is given but not the relevant place-name.

[42] The fact that place-names are used as mnemonic "tags" can be seen in their increased numbers in the core regions placed at the beginning of the two catalogues. The greater the number of spatial tags, the stronger the mental links created (fifty-five and nine place-names for the core areas of the CS and the CT&A respectively). Seen from this angle, the increased number of place-names (twenty-nine) from Boeotia, which is placed first in the entire CS, shows both how strong the initial mental tag must be for such an extended and demanding mnemonic undertaking as the CS and how ignorant of the reality of performance are arguments of interpolation; see Visser 1997:359.

[43] The emphasis on the ordering of the troops reflects the arrangement of data in the narrator's mind. The two catalogues with their extremely limited narrative element (e.g. the Thamyris digression), their linear progression, and their almost algebraic tone mirror the narrator's organization of material on a cognitive level. Place-names distributed on a notional map of Greece and Asia Minor are deftly employed as the mnemonic GPS guiding him in the arrangement of his material. As the leaders κοσμοῦσι "organize" their troops, so the narrator κοσμεῖ "organizes/ arranges" his catalogues by using spatial features as mnemonic hooks, on which he hangs an impressive accumulation of names and numbers.

of any temporal markers, the most elementary prerequisite of all narrative, is coupled with multiple spatial pointers, making possible a "double view" of past and present, which are translated into "there" and "here." By touring the various locations and regions from which the Achaean and Trojan armies come, the two catalogues programmatically participate in the unfolding of the Iliadic plot. In placing the kingdoms of Achilles and the Lycians at the end of both catalogues, the Iliadic tradition epitomizes in the register of space an important part of the plot's dramatization.

Finally, one of the catalogue's striking features is its comprehensiveness, its bold aim to achieve a totality that the Iliadic song excludes by its very nature and thematic scope.[44] One is entitled, of course, to interpret this feature of the two catalogues within the wider framework of other devices by which the narrator is able to offer his audience a panoramic view of the entire Trojan War. In fact, it may be seen as forming an integral part of a whole nexus of mechanisms, such as anachronies (analepses and prolepses), intertextual associations with other song traditions, references to the history of prized objects, and even, through the extended ecphrasis on the shield of Achilles, mental vistas of imagined (but not fantastic) worlds. At the same time, the alleged "totality" of the CS and the CT&A stands at odds with the viewpoint of the Iliadic song tradition, which artfully entertains the possibility of an alternative tradition of "pure information," of completeness, only to undercut it. The CS and the CT&A embody in a truly emblematic way an epic otherness, and at the same time an idealization of epic song,[45] in which the tradition would abide by the rules of a comprehensive presentation of the past. By undermining such a tradition, the *Iliad* promotes its own poetic credo: a song highlighting selectivity instead of comprehensiveness, dramatic cohesion instead of episodic sequence, a single underlying narrative thread instead of multiple plot lines, a tragic thrust moving steadily towards its painful resolution instead of impressionistic scenes and warrior exploits, and finally a thought-provoking, self-conscious look at its own subject matter, the heroes and the heroic world, instead of a pompous glorification of heroic deeds.

---

[44] See Sammons 2010:79, who observes that a purely catalogic poem like the *Catalogue of Women* must have aimed (very much unlike the *Iliad*) at "something like a comprehensive vision of mythological history."

[45] See Pucci 1996:5–24; Sammons 2010:20.

3

Greece

THE MOST FREQUENTLY MENTIONED PLACE-NAMES of mainland Greece include Phthia, Argos, Pylos, Thebes, Sparta, Ithaka, Mycenae, and the islands of Lesbos, Lemnos, Skyros, and Crete.[1] Given that each of these toponyms is closely associated either with a single Iliadic hero or with a specific phase of this hero's mythical saga, I have decided to examine them separately. From a methodological point of view, this approach aims at exploring the full range of interpretive ramifications of the principal Greek leaders' tendency to refer consistently to a wider space. Being attached to their general role in epic poetry, Greek heroes who systematically refer to a space that is constantly absent tend to employ it intertextually rather than intratextually.[2]

Phthia

Of the fourteen times that Phthia is mentioned in the *Iliad*, thirteen are in character text and only one in narrator text. Given that the latter attestation of this place name occurs in the Catalogue of Ships (*Iliad* II 683), which may be considered the "default mode" of the entire Iliadic system of proper names (both personal and place names), it can be claimed that the word *Phthia* is marked by being present only in speeches. Since it is the birthplace and habitat of Achilles, it is only natural that he refers to it more often (seven times) than any other Iliadic figure (*Iliad* I 155, 169; IX 363, 395; XVI 13; XIX 323, 330). Phthia is also

---

[1] I will not consider places like Rhodes, which is mentioned only in the CS (*Iliad* II 654, 655, 667), and Kos, which (apart from its entry in the CS [II 877]) is mentioned twice with respect to Herakles (*Iliad* XIV 255; XV 28) but is irrelevant to the epic's plot.

[2] On intertextuality within the framework of oral epic traditions, see Pucci 1987; Pedrick 1994; Danek 1998:13–15; Pucci 1998:5–6; Danek 2002; Nagy 2003:9–10; Burgess 2006:148–189; Tsagalis 2008b, 2011. On intertextuality and self-referentiality from the point of view of a written epic, see Rengakos 2006a:158–180. On diachronically observed variations of rival oral traditions, see Aloni 1986:51–67; Burgess 2002:234–245; Marks 2002, 2003. Spatial intertextuality, i.e. intertextual references organized on permutations of mythically familiar space, has not to my knowledge been systematically studied.

mentioned three times (IX 439, 479, 484) by Phoinix, who raised Achilles, and once each by Odysseus (IX 253), Nestor (XI 766), and Briseis (XIX 299).

Phthia is particularly linked to the way Achilles, as a "cognizer," reconstructs an important part of his epic persona. He regularly brings up his fatherland in moments of emotional upheaval, over his quarrel with Agamemnon, his desire to leave Troy and return home, or recalling his aging father Peleus. These three interpretive ramifications of Phthia construct a poetics of nostalgia that is filtered by Achilles' idiosyncratic view of the heroic code. They also suggest to the audience a specific way of "reading" distant space, since they put in the limelight the notion of absence, of both people and places, a topic of paramount importance for Achilles' liminal situation in the *Iliad*.

The poetics of loneliness

Within the heated context of his quarrel with Agamemnon, Achilles remembers his native land:

> "οὐ γὰρ ἐγὼ Τρώων ἕνεκ᾽ ἤλυθον αἰχμητάων
> δεῦρο μαχησόμενος, ἐπεὶ οὔ τί μοι αἴτιοί εἰσιν·
> οὐ γὰρ πώ ποτ᾽ ἐμὰς βοῦς ἤλασαν οὐδὲ μὲν ἵππους,
> οὐδέ ποτ᾽ ἐν Φθίῃ ἐριβώλακι βωτιανείρῃ
> καρπὸν ἐδηλήσαντ᾽, ἐπεὶ ἦ μάλα πολλὰ μεταξύ,
> οὔρεά τε σκιόεντα θάλασσά τε ἠχήεσσα."

> "I for my part did not come here for the sake of the Trojan
> spearmen to fight against them, since to me they have done nothing.
> Never yet have they driven away my cattle or my horses,
> never in Phthia where the soil is rich and men grow great did they
> spoil my harvest, since indeed there is much that lies between us,
> the shadowy mountains and the echoing sea ..."

Iliad I 152–157

Achilles succinctly expresses his special position among the other Achaean leaders. By stating that neither he nor his possessions have been injured by the Trojans in the past, because his homeland lies far away from theirs,[3] Achilles

---

3 According to Kirk on *Iliad* I 154–156, "the suggested motives for fighting—to avenge cattle- or horse-rustling or the destruction of crops—are distinctively oversimplified, since the heroic code of gift-obligations must have compelled one chieftain to take up arms in another's quarrel" (1985:68–69). Oversimplification is not the right word. Achilles employs typical diction colored by his own special position among the community of Achaean leaders, since the term "Trojans" stands in this context for Paris and the harm done, by implication, not just to Menelaos but to all the suitors of Helen, of whom Achilles is not one.

emphasizes that this is not his war. He has come to Troy, after all, for the sake of the Atreidai, not because of personal interest or the desire for revenge. The function of Phthia in this context is threefold. First, it designates Achilles' homeland by using two distinct spatial aspects: size and distance. Second, it tacitly brings up a subtle irony, by using an argument that is readily applicable to almost every other Achaean leader: that is, the lack of any direct harm to their possessions by the Trojans. Third, it opens a window of allusion to the background of the Trojan War, and especially to the oath that Tundareos has made all the suitors take, by which they are bound to help Menelaos and Helen should any reason arise.

With respect to the spatial aspects of size and distance, Achilles' language is revealing. The epithets ἐριβώλακι 'of the rich soil' and βωτιανείρῃ 'nourishing great men',[4] combined with the references to cattle (βοῦς) and horses (ἵππους), suggest that Achilles describes his native land as a rich and prosperous place. The memory of the fatherland is here tailored to the needs and aims of the particular situation, but contextual boundedness should not prevent us from realizing that the speaker paints an idyllic picture of Phthia. If seen as a cognizer, that is, a focalizer whose accumulated experience determines his words and actions, Achilles' positive description of Phthia is typical of those who long to see their homeland. In such cases, mnemonic recall is characterized on the one hand by a constant and powerful tendency to repress negative memories, virtually burying them in the mental cemetery of past experiences, and on the other by conjuring up and strengthening positive images of the past, even to the extent of "prettifying" them. By combining the traditional theme of cattle or horse raids with that of destroying the crops,[5] Achilles implicitly suggests that his homeland is a place where all these resources are abundant.

Distance is another spatial aspect deftly employed by Achilles in his description of Phthia. By saying that "the shadowy mountains and the resounding sea" separate his homeland from Troy, he accentuates the unlikeliness of harm from the Trojans, but also indicates both the huge "divide" between his present situation and his past life, as well as the sacrifice he is making for the sake of Agamemnon and Menelaos: he has traveled from afar to an unknown land to fight a war he does not really want to fight. In this light, space becomes the measure of Achilles' longing to go home. Now that he has been insulted by Agamemnon, Achilles will let his nostalgia come out with growing intensity.

---

[4] See also Nagy 1979:185, who argues that the application of βωτιάνειρα to Achilles' homeland signifies that "Phthie is [his] local Earth, offering him the natural cycle of life and death as an alternative to his permanent existence within the cultural medium of epic."

[5] On conflicts involving cattle raids and their use as a motif in archaic Greek epic, see Raaflaub 1991:222–223 and n55; A. Jackson 1993:64–76. On cattle-rustling as *casus belli* in Homer, see *Iliad* XI 670–684; XVIII 523–539; *Odyssey* xi 288–293; xx 51. For Indo-European parallels, see West 2007:451–452.

Phthia thus becomes, slowly but steadily, a potential goal, a target Achilles will set for himself until it is finally abandoned after the death of Patroklos.

Spatial designations such as Phthia are also telling for the internal audience of Achilles' speech. In particular, the arguments he uses to exclude the possibility of any Trojan harm to his possessions are directly applicable to most Achaean leaders. In a remarkable display of irony, Achilles makes a covert political gesture toward his fellow kings: the only person harmed by the Trojans is Menelaos (and by implication Agamemnon). Given that the rest have possessions in Greece that have never been taken or destroyed by the Trojans and that they have all made the long journey across "shadowy mountains and resounding sea" to Troy, Achilles' words must have struck a powerful note in many Achaean hearts. I will not push this point further and suggest that Achilles is aiming at a revolt against Agamemnon. His reaction, though, and the emphasis he places on describing his homeland would have made others realize that there was much truth in a statement that every one of the leaders could have made for himself.

Spatial clues function differently according to the audience, internal or external, that receives them. Though a powerful intratextual gesture to the other Achaean leaders, Achilles' arguments are intertextually undermined by the external audience's knowledge of the background of the Trojan War.[6] According to the Hesiodic *Catalogue of Women*,[7] Tundareos made all the suitors take an oath and vow with a libation that

> ... μή τιν' ἔτ' ἄλλον [ἄ]νεν ἕθεν ἄλλα πένεσθαι
> ἀμφὶ γάμωι κούρης εὐ[ω]λ[ένο]ν· ὃς δέ κεν ἀνδρῶν
> αὐτὸς ἕλοιτο βίηι, νέμεσίν τ' ἀπ[ο]θεῖτο καὶ αἰδῶ,
> τὸν μέτα πάντας ἄνωγεν ἀολλέας ὁρμηθῆνα[ι
> ποινὴν τεισομένους. τοὶ δ' ἀπτερέως ἐπίθον[το
> ἐλπόμενοι τελέειν πάντες γάμον·

> no one other than himself should make other plans
> regarding the fair-armed maiden's marriage; any man
> who would seize her by force, and set aside indignation and shame,
> he commanded all of them together to set out against him
> to exact punishment. They swiftly obeyed,
> all hoping to fulfill the marriage themselves.[8]

---

[6]   Kirk 1985:68–69 on *Iliad* I 154–156 seems to miss the point.
[7]   The *Iliad* is probably aware of this story; see Bethe 1929:229–231; Kullmann 1960:137–138; West 2011:87 on *Iliad* I 152–168.
[8]   Fr. 204.80–85 (M-W). All Hesiodic translations are from Most 2007 (fr. 155).

Achilles' spatial language thus acquires an ironic tone, for the external audience (and even perhaps the internal) would immediately notice the difference by recalling the oath Tundareos made the suitors of Helen swear. The audience would also remember that Achilles was not bound by this oath, since he was not a suitor of Helen, for

> ... Χείρων δ' ἐν Πηλίωι ὑλήεντι
> Πηλείδην ἐκόμιζε πόδας ταχύν, ἔξοχον ἀνδρῶν,
> παῖδ' ἔτ' ἐόν[τ'·] οὐ γάρ μιν ἀρηΐφιλος Μενέλαος
> νίκησ' οὐδέ τις ἄλλος ἐπιχθονίων ἀνθρώπων
> μνηστεύων Ἑλένην, εἴ μιν κίχε παρθένον οὖσαν
> οἴκαδε νοστήσας ἐκ Πηλίου ὠκὺς Ἀχιλλεύς.

> Chiron on wooded Pelion
> was taking care of Peleus' swift-footed son, greatest of men,
> who was still a boy; for neither warlike Menelaus
> nor any other human on the earth would have defeated him
> in wooing Helen, if swift Achilles had found her still a virgin
> when he came back home from Pelion.[9]

Achilles' use of spatial diction and motifs in this particular passage (and context) seems to point to the Hesiodic version of the episode of Helen's suitors. In fact, both Phthia's wealth in cattle and horses and the "spatial" argument of distance separating Achilles' homeland from Troy are also employed in reverse in the Hesiodic episode. In particular, by the use of traditional formulas (fr. 198.30 ἄργυφα μῆλα καὶ εἰλίποδας ἕλικας βοῦς; fr. 204.50 εἰλίποδάς τε βόας καὶ ἴφια μῆλα), the Hesiodic narrator emphasizes that several suitors offered sheep and cattle as marriage gifts to make Helen their wife. Riches of this sort are directly connected to the land each suitor comes from or has under his control. Of Telamonian Ajax, for example, it is explicitly stated that he "would drive them together and give" (fr. 204.51 συνελάσας δώσειν), that is to say he would collect them from a rather extended area including Troizen, Epidauros, Aegina, Mases, Megara, Corinth, Hermione, and Asine. Animal offerings to win Helen are therefore employed in a different manner, namely as wedding gifts. Moreover, in the Hesiodic episode distance is used not as a boundary that separates but as a space that will be crossed. Idomeneus, we are told, was the only one who did not ask for Helen's hand by proxy,

---

[9] Fr. 204.87–92 (M-W) = fr. 155 (Most).

ἀλλ' αὐτὸς [σ]ὺν νηΐ πολυκλήϊδι μελαίγη[ι
βῆ ὑπὲρ Ὠγυλίου πόντου διὰ κῦμα κελαιγ[ὸν
Τυνδαρέου ποτὶ δῶμα δαΐφρονος, ὄφρ[α ἴδοιτο
Ἀ]ρ[γείην] Ἑλένην, μηδ' ἄλλων οἶον ἀκ[ούοι
μῦθον, ὃς] ἤδη πᾶσαν ἐπὶ [χθ]όνα δῖαν ἵκαγ[εν

but himself with a many-benched black ship
came over the Ogylian sea through the black waves
to valorous Tyndareus' mansion, so that [he could see
Argive] Helen, and not merely [hear what others
said,] what had already reached the whole godly earth.[10]

Whereas in Achilles' speech distance is a barrier that prevents the Trojans from harming his homeland, in the Hesiodic passage it becomes the proof of Idomeneus' determination. Seen from this vantage point, the strong spatial framework of Achilles' words is put into perspective within the much wider framework of epic poetry. It seems then that both the internal and the external audience would evaluate Achilles' arguments, and by comparing them with the episode of Helen's marriage would realize the limits and limitations of the hero's viewpoint: he is certainly right, but he is alone in this, perhaps tragically alone.[11]

Spatial misdirection

Phthia appears again in the coda of Achilles' speech:

"νῦν δ' εἶμι Φθίηνδ', ἐπεὶ ἦ πολὺ φέρτερόν ἐστιν
οἴκαδ' ἴμεν σὺν νηυσὶ κορωνίσιν, οὐδέ σ' ὀΐω
ἐνθάδ' ἄτιμος ἐὼν ἄφενος καὶ πλοῦτον ἀφύξειν."

"Now I am returning to Phthia, since it is much better
to go home again with my curved ships, and I am minded no longer
to stay here dishonoured and pile up your wealth and your luxury."

Iliad I 169–171

---

[10] Fr. 204.59–63 (M-W) = fr. 155 Most.

[11] This is a case where the traditional dichotomy of "argument" and "key function" collapses. Both the characters who take part in this scene (the Achaean leaders) and the members of the external audience (the narratees, in narratological terminology) interpret Achilles' words in the same way, i.e. against the backdrop of the fact that Achilles was the only one not bound by oath. Characters can, at least sometimes, share the same amount of mythical knowledge with the audience because of their mythically measured store of experience. Under these circumstances they function as "cognizers"; see Fludernik 1996; 2003a:382–400; 2003b:243–267; 2008:355–383.

Achilles ends his speech by revealing his intended departure for Phthia, since he is no longer willing to increase the wealth of Agamemnon in Troy. In order to explore the spatial dynamics of this powerful declaration, we need first to discuss in some detail the function of *misdirection* as a narrative mechanism. Next to the techniques of *retardation, gradual determination of the plot*, and *dramatic irony*, misdirection constitutes one of the key devices for creating suspense in Homeric epic.[12] With the term misdirection, I refer to anticipated events that are either completely nullified by being canceled, or fulfilled only partially and with important deviations from what was planned.[13]

Spatial misdirection can be defined as an anticipated change of location, temporarily or for a longer period of time, which a single individual or group of people make explicit but never carry out. This particular type of misdirection makes listeners revise their cognitive schemata:[14] the binary opposition between Greece and Troy ("home" vs. "out there") is time and again evoked by the Achaeans as a potential deviation from the plotline, a deviation that remains continuously suspended. Certain Achaean leaders, Achilles being by far the most notable, express their determination to leave Troy and return to mainland Greece. That return never materializes, and the audience, in an ongoing state of expectation, is encouraged to realize the endless suspense and drama produced by the overturning of such futile hopes.

In this respect, Shklovsky's dictum that "plot is defamiliarized story"[15] is also applicable to the embedded story space of the *Iliad*. The simple story-pattern "(1) city is besieged by an enemy coming from afar, (2) defenders do well for a long time, (3) in the end they are deceived and the enemy invades and sacks the city, (4) enemy returns home" is defamiliarized not only by the epic's presenting only a part of (2) but also by its systematic playing with the possibility of (4)'s occurring before (3), and thus canceling (3) for good. There are two important observations to be made here: (1) defamiliarization remains potential in the *Iliad*, that is, a scenario that the two chief figures of the poem's generative episode (μῆνις 'wrath'), Agamemnon (deceitfully)[16] and Achilles (systematically), seem to endorse but leave continuously suspended; and (2) defamiliarization is virtually spatial, since (returning to) Greece is a spatially expressed

---

[12] On suspense in epic poetry, see Duckworth 1933; Schadewaldt 1966; Hölscher 1939; Rengakos 2006a: 31–73 (= 1999:308–338). On misdirection, see Morrison 1992a, 1992b.

[13] See Rengakos 2006a:54 (= 1999:310).

[14] "Cognitive schemata are the means by which we construct a narrative in our minds"; Mittell 2007:168.

[15] 1965:12. This terminology may create confusion, since *story* stands here for what narratologists call *fabula*. In modern narratological terms, Shklovsky's motto could be rephrased as "the story is defamiliarized *fabula*."

[16] In *Iliad* II.

threat to heroic κλέος, and (staying at) Troy the prerequisite for the acquisition of such κλέος, and also for the *Iliad* itself.[17]

In this light, by declaring that he will now (νῦν) return to Phthia because he considers this a much better alternative than staying in Troy and increasing Agamemnon's wealth (*Iliad* I 169–171), Achilles creates a profound intratextual misdirection. He virtually makes the audience expect that he will depart from Troy and leave the Achaeans to fight the war without him. Reading this on the level of narrative discourse, we are entitled to interpret Achilles' statement about his permanent change of location as a threat to abandon the *Iliad* as soon as it has started. The audience, of course, knows perfectly well that this is a *credible impossibility*,[18] but for the rest of the Achaeans inside Agamemnon's hut Achilles' threat is real. In other words, we must distinguish between what the audience knows and what the characters of the plot are aware of. One may have the impression that this observation significantly weakens the effect of such a credible impossibility, since an *Iliad* without Achilles would be virtually unthinkable. Still, the Iliadic tradition, as I will show, employs a cumulative technique in presenting such credible impossibilities, which it both repeats and enriches, so as to make the audience reevaluate on their own this unfulfilled scenario that stands against the most elementary nucleus of Achilles' function in the Trojan War tradition, his fighting and dying at Troy. Moreover, the Iliadic tradition exploits at full length the fact that listeners tend to use cognitive schemata to fill in narrative gaps by making the most likely assumptions.[19] Having introduced its audience to its own defamiliarized plot, Achilles' wrath, the epic can now turn it into a learned schema that the audience is expected to absorb. Since the new cognitive grammar of the *Iliad* has taught the members of the audience that Achilles will withdraw from the war, it can now attempt to trick them by maximizing this withdrawal, by spatially extending it from his hut at the edge of the Achaean camp to his homeland in Phthia, across the vast sea. Muellner has argued that "*mênis* is an emotion that acts to change the world."[20] This powerful insight is all the more significant given that the defamiliarization of the story is only potential in the *Iliad*. Since the various "wraths" (Apollo's against the Achaeans, Zeus' that lurks in the background and surfaces only to support the μῆνις of Achilles, and finally Achilles' own μῆνις) are invoked against the breaking of cosmic rules, the credible impossibility of Achilles' return to Phthia

---

[17] On the poetics of κλέος in the *Iliad*, see Nagy 1979:16–18, 21–22, 28–29, 35–41, 94–106, 111–115, 175–177, 184–185, 188–189, 317–319.

[18] On *credible impossibilities*, see Scodel 1999:33–42, 49–57, 59–60, 63–65, 66–69, 70–74, 80–82; Rengakos 2002:97–98.

[19] On filling narrative gaps, see Mittell 2007:170–171.

[20] See Muellner 1996:194.

is the *ne plus ultra* of his μῆνις: he threatens not only to change the world, but to change this very epic, to annul the *Iliad* itself.[21] Achilles' threat to return to Phthia, therefore, is a spatial misdirection that the epic systematically exploits for both internal and external audiences. By recourse to an invisible and absent space, the *Iliad* engages its listeners in realizing the larger spatial framework of the Trojan War. Space works as a mechanism anchoring counternarratives that allow listeners to immerse themselves deep into heroic recognition and become participatory narratees, invited to continuously reconstruct the fragmented world of the epic's chief figures.[22]

In the name of the father: Phthia and Peleus

Achilles' withdrawal from the plot unavoidably results in the disappearance of Phthia from the *Iliad*'s spatial horizon.[23] It is only during the embassy in *Iliad* IX that Phthia is mentioned again, this time by Odysseus, Phoinix, and of course Achilles.

Odysseus:

> "ὦ πέπον, ἦ μὲν σοί γε πατὴρ ἐπετέλλετο Πηλεύς
> ἤματι τῷ, ὅτε σ' ἐκ Φθίης Ἀγαμέμνονι πέμπεν,
> 'τέκνον ἐμόν, κάρτος μὲν Ἀθηναίη τε καὶ Ἥρη
> δώσουσ', αἴ κ' ἐθέλωσι, σὺ δὲ μεγαλήτορα θυμὸν
> ἴσχειν ἐν στήθεσσι· φιλοφροσύνη γὰρ ἀμείνων·
> ληγέμεναι δ' ἔριδος κακομηχάνου, ὄφρα σε μᾶλλον
> τίωσ' Ἀργείων ἠμὲν νέοι ἠδὲ γέροντες.'"

> "Dear friend, surely thus your father Peleus advised you
> that day when he sent you away to Agamemnon from Phthia:
> 'My child, for the matter of strength, Athene and Hera will give it
> if it be their will, but be it yours to hold fast in your bosom

---

[21] There is a telling analogy between Achilles' threat to return to Phthia and the episode of the Sirens in the *Odyssey*, in which the Sirens with their seductive song lure Odysseus to the "Iliad." As Pucci has shown, if Odysseus abandons the metonymical ship of the *Odyssey*, the poem will abruptly end (1998:1–10). In both cases, a radical spatial shift associated, though antithetically, with a sea journey is employed as the vehicle for a powerful game of poetics.

[22] On invisible space and counternarratives, see Purves 2002:138.

[23] On the connotative semantics of Phthia (< φθι-), which is used at times as a symbol for Achilles' loss of κλέος within the world of the epic tradition, see Nagy 1979:174–187; C. Mackie 2002:1–11. According to Nagy, "the overt Iliadic contrast of *kléos áphthiton* with the negation of *kléos* in the context of *Phthíē* is remarkable in view of the element *phthi-* contained by the place name. From the wording of *Iliad* IX 412–416, we are led to suspect that this element *phthi-* is either a genuine formant of *Phthíē* or is at least perceived as such in the process of Homeric composition" (1979:185).

the anger of the proud heart, for consideration is better.
Keep from the bad complication of quarrel, and all the more for this
the Argives will honour you, both their younger men and their
elders.'"

Iliad IX 252–258

Achilles:

"νῦν δ', ἐπεὶ οὐκ ἐθέλω πολεμιζέμεν Ἕκτορι δίῳ,
αὔριον ἱρὰ Διὶ ῥέξας καὶ πᾶσι θεοῖσιν,
νηήσας εὖ νῆας, ἐπὴν ἅλαδε προερύσσω,
ὄψεαι, ἢν ἐθέλησθα καὶ αἴ κέν τοι τὰ μεμήλῃ,
ἦρι μάλ' Ἑλλήσποντον ἐπ' ἰχθυόεντα πλεούσας
νῆας ἐμάς, ἐν δ' ἄνδρας ἐρεσσέμεναι μεμαῶτας·
εἰ δέ κεν εὐπλοΐην δώῃ κλυτὸς Ἐννοσίγαιος,
ἤματί κε τριτάτῳ <u>Φθίην ἐρίβωλον ἱκοίμην</u>."

"But, now I am unwilling to fight against brilliant Hektor,
tomorrow, when I have sacrificed to Zeus and to all gods,
and loaded well my ships, and rowed out on to the salt water,
you will see, if you have a mind to it and if it concerns you,
my ships in the dawn at sea on the Hellespont where the fish swarm
and my men manning them with good will to row. If the glorious
shaker of the earth should grant us a favouring passage
on the third day thereafter *we might raise generous Phthia*."[24]

Iliad IX 356–363 (emphasis added)

Achilles:

"ἢν γὰρ δή με σαῶσι θεοὶ καὶ οἴκαδ' ἵκωμαι,
<u>Πηλεύς</u> θήν μοι ἔπειτα γυναῖκά γε μάσσεται αὐτός·
πολλαὶ Ἀχαιΐδες εἰσὶν ἀν' <u>Ἑλλάδα τε Φθίην τε,</u>
κοῦραι ἀριστήων, οἵ τε πτολίεθρα ῥύονται·
τάων ἥν κ' ἐθέλωμι φίλην ποιήσομ' ἄκοιτιν."

---

[24] The idea of being able to get home in three days with a good wind makes the space both far
and just close enough. From a larger epic perspective, it is interesting that Achilles speaks to
Odysseus in a way that would have been particularly ironic for the Odysseus of the *Odyssey*,
i.e. about having a swift journey home, especially since it is Poseidon whom Achilles imagines
providing the good passage. On the larger intertextual echoes of Achilles' speech to Odysseus in
Iliad IX, see Mitsis 2010.

"For if the gods will keep me alive, and I win homeward,
Peleus himself will presently arrange a wife for me.
There are many Achaian girls in the land of *Hellas and Phthia*,
daughters of great men who hold strong places in guard. And of
    these
any one that I please I might make my beloved lady."

Iliad IX 393–397

Phoinix:

"... σοὶ δέ μ' ἔπεμπε γέρων ἱππηλάτα Πηλεύς
ἤματι τῷ, ὅτε σ' ἐκ Φθίης Ἀγαμέμνονι πέμπεν
νήπιον, οὔ πω εἰδόθ' ὁμοιΐοο πτολέμοιο
οὐδ' ἀγορέων, ἵνα τ' ἄνδρες ἀριπρεπέες τελέθουσιν·
τούνεκά με προέηκε διδασκέμεναι τάδε πάντα,
μύθων τε ῥητῆρ' ἔμεναι πρηκτῆρά τε ἔργων."

"... Peleus the aged horseman sent me forth with you
on that day when he sent you from Phthia to Agamemnon
a mere child, who knew nothing yet of the joining of battle
nor of debate where men are made pre-eminent. Therefore
he sent me along with you to teach you all of these matters,
to make you a speaker of words and one who accomplished in
    action."

Iliad IX 438–443

Phoinix:

"φεῦγον ἔπειτ' ἀπάνευθε δι' Ἑλλάδος εὐρυχόροιο,
<u>Φθίην δ' ἐξικόμην ἐριβώλακα, μητέρα μήλων,</u>
<u>ἐς Πηλῆα ἄναχθ'</u>· ὃ δέ με πρόφρων ὑπέδεκτο
καί μ' ἐφίλησ', ὡς εἴ τε πατὴρ ὃν παῖδα φιλήσῃ
μοῦνον τηλύγετον πολλοῖσιν ἐπὶ κτεάτεσσι·
καί μ' ἀφνειὸν ἔθηκε, πολὺν δέ μοι ὤπασε λαόν,
<u>ναῖον δ' ἐσχατιὴν Φθίης, Δολόπεσσιν ἀνάσσων."</u>

"Then I fled far away through the wide spaces of Hellas
and *came as far as generous Phthia, mother of sheepflocks,*
and to lord Peleus, who accepted me with a good will
and gave me his love, even as a father loves his own son
who is a single child brought up among many possessions.

181

> He made me a rich man, and granted me many people,
> *and I lived*, lord over the Dolopes, *in the edge of Phthia*."

Iliad IX 478–484

As the above passages amply show, Phthia is systematically connected in *Iliad* IX with Peleus, since all the speakers link Achilles' homeland with his father. This pairing of space with a particular individual is revealing for the way the epic begins to unravel a new thread within the thick web of associations around Achilles and Phthia. The anchoring of Peleus to Phthia can be seen as an interpretive guide for the Homeric audience. Being in fact a subcategory of the larger topic of Phthia, it functions as a key that opens the door to a particular version of Achilles' homeland, one that is mainly characterized by the presence of the father.

The members of the embassy who refer to Phthia together with Peleus constantly point to the past, in an ongoing attempt to shed light on those aspects of Achilles' past life that suit the embassy's rhetorical goal, namely to persuade the great hero to return to battle.[25] In this respect they make constant reference to the authority of his father Peleus, by recalling instances of the past, snapshots of either their visit to Phthia (Odysseus) or the way their personal fate was linked with Phthia and Peleus (Phoinix).[26] Given that these narratives use traditional mythical material, the audience is expected to check on their validity and realize that for both Odysseus and Phoinix, important fissures created on the narrative surface reaffirm or contradict other epic versions of the same events.

The Iliadic version of the recruitment of Achilles in Phthia deviates from the *Cypria* tradition with respect to Odysseus' participation,[27] and of course his

---

[25] See Alden 2000:179–290.

[26] Phoinix's focalization in the *Iliad* is to some extent influenced by Achilles', since Phthia quickly becomes his "home," even though he is an outsider.

[27] According to *Iliad* III 205–224, Odysseus had visited Troy together with Menelaos to convince the Trojans to give Helen back. This is an Iliadic mirroring of the traditional role of Odysseus as a member of the embassy, who is sent to achieve difficult tasks, i.e. just as with the Iliadic version of Odysseus' and Nestor's visit to Phthia. Dictys Cretensis (*Ephemeridos belli Troiani libri* 1.4) includes a third member in the embassy sent to Troy for Helen before the war, namely Palamedes. The same is true for the embassy to Phthia: according to Tzetzes (*Allegoriae Iliadis Prolegomena* 455–458), Palamedes went to Phthia with Nestor and Odysseus to recruit Achilles. Palamedes as a rival of Odysseus for taking part in the embassy can be also seen in the episode of his journey to the island of Delos to bring to Troy the Oinotropoi, who would save the Achaean army from famine (which caused Odysseus' envy and resulted in Palamedes' drowning by Odysseus and Diomedes, *Cypria* fr. 30, PEG 1 = fr. 20, EGF [Pausanias 10.31.2 on Polygnotus' paintings at Delphi]). A different tradition is reported by the fourth-century rhetor Alcidamas (*Odysseus* 16.20.3–16.20.6), who says that Palamedes bribed Kinyras, king of Cyprus, and convinced him not to take part in the Trojan War; see P. Kakridis 1995:95. On Odysseus and Palamedes, see W. Kullmann 2002:166–167.

"verbatim" report of Peleus' words in *Iliad* IX 254–258, which is clearly an Iliadic αὐτοσχεδίασμα tailored to the epic's main theme and the aim of the embassy, namely to convince Achilles to stop his anger.[28]

The pairing of Phthia with a Peleus who is very willing to send Achilles to Troy must have keyed the Iliadic audience to the note of a *Cypria* tradition that may also have presented Achilles as eager to win glory, and his father as ready to offer his son to the Greek cause. By taking notice of the gap between this version and a rival one, according to which an Achaean embassy[29] had found Achilles disguised in women's clothes and hiding in Skyros, where he had been sent by Peleus to avoid being recruited to Troy,[30] the listeners of the *Iliad* would have realized that the pairing of Phthia with Peleus increases the dramatic weight of Achilles' lot. By depriving Peleus of the ability to know Achilles' fate and attempt to save his son, the Iliadic tradition on the one hand accentuated the irony of having the father send his son to his death, and on the other left the audience to evaluate on their own Odysseus' effort to convince Achilles to return to battle. Against the backdrop of Odysseus' fake madness[31] stands Achilles, who willingly went to the war; a true hero being advised by a swindler and trickster. To this extent, within the Homeric tradition the space delineated by Phthia becomes the direct opposite of that of Ithaka: Achilles who went to Troy willingly will not return home, while Odysseus who did not want to join the expedition finally will; the former will never see his father Peleus, who dies while the war is going on, the latter will see his father Laertes, who lives long enough to see his son return to Ithaka.

Another aspect of Phthia's pairing with Peleus can be seen if we compare Achilles' references to his homeland to those made by Phoinix. Whereas Achilles' misdirection about returning home (*Iliad* IX 356–363 and 393–397) becomes progressively concretized and enriched by details,[32] and therefore

---

[28] See W. Kullmann 1960:258–259.

[29] With respect to its members, we can only speak with certainty for Odysseus. On this issue, see Tsagalis (forthcoming in *RFIC*).

[30] See the D-scholium on *Iliad* XIX 326 (IV 222.29 Dind.) and (*Cypria*) fr. 19, PEG 1. See also the *scholia vetera* on *Iliad* IX 668b (Erbse) and Ptolemaeus Chennus *Kaine historia* in Photius *Library* 147a18 (III 53, 18 Henry) = 17.26 Chatzis.

[31] See Proclus Chrestomathy (§22 Kullmann = 119–121 Severyns = Allen 103.25–27): καὶ μαίνεσθαι προσποιησάμενον τὸν Ὀδυσσέα ἐπὶ τῷ μὴ θέλειν συστρατεύεσθαι ἐφώρασαν, Παλαμήδους ὑποθεμένου τὸν υἱὸν Τηλέμαχον ἐπὶ κόλασιν ἐξαρπάσαντες ("and they caught Odysseus pretending to be insane because he did not want to join up, after Palamedes advised them to seize his son Telemachus threateningly"; transl. by Burgess 2001). For a useful collection of ancient sources on the episode of Odysseus' madness, see Zografou-Lyra 1987:69–88.

[32] See Lynn-George 1988:142–143, who calls Achilles, the sacker of cities, "a seeker of security," and emphasizes the opposition between a marriage to one of Agamemnon's daughters and one to a girl Achilles chooses among those in Hellas and Phthia.

more dramatic, Phoinix (IX 438–443)[33] attempts to construct his own version of Achilles' past life in Phthia, so as to achieve his goal. Space (Phthia), therefore, not only constitutes a *chronotopic* entity, being linked to time, past and (false) future; it also begins to be associated with a person as the poem moves on, leading to the climactic scene between Priam and Achilles. Space is thus used as a vehicle for exploring the tormented psychology of Achilles, and Peleus becomes the thematic hook that the toponym *Phthia* is hung on.[34]

In line with Odysseus and Phoinix, who both use the motif of "paternal assent," Nestor adds Patroklos and his father Menoitios to the spatiotemporal reference to his and Odysseus' visit to Phthia to recruit Achilles.[35]

> "ὦ πέπον, ἦ μὲν σοί γε Μενοίτιος ὧδ' ἐπέτελλεν
> ἤματι τῷ ὅτε σ' ἐκ Φθίης Ἀγαμέμνονι πέμπεν·
> νῶϊ δέ τ' ἔνδον ἐόντες, ἐγὼ καὶ δῖος Ὀδυσσεύς,
> πάντα μάλ' ἐν μεγάροις ἠκούομεν, ὡς ἐπέτελλεν·"

> "Dear child, surely this was what Menoitios told you
> that day when he sent you out from Phthia to Agamemnon.
> We two, brilliant Odysseus and I, were inside with you
> and listened carefully to everything, all that he told you."

> *Iliad* XI 765–768

By reduplicating the motif of "paternal assent" that is now developed around the figure of Patroklos,[36] just as it was presented with reference to Achilles by Odysseus in *Iliad* IX, Nestor intensifies the importance of Phthia even more. Phthia therefore becomes a *spatiotemporal metonym* for the involvement of Achilles and Patroklos in the war, a chronotope where the two friends started their journey to Troy and death, but also to epic κλέος.

---

[33] See also *Iliad* IX 478–484, in which Phoinix implicitly compares Peleus' love for him with his (Peleus') love for his son Achilles.

[34] The pairing of Peleus with Phthia is so strong and pervasive in the *Iliad* that it is also reflected in the language Thetis employs for Achilles' cancelled return home; see e.g. XVIII 58–60 νηυσὶν ἔπι προέηκα κορωνίσιν Ἴλιον εἴσω / Τρωσὶ μαχησόμενον· τὸν δ' οὐχ ὑποδέξομαι αὖτις / οἴκαδε νοστήσαντα δόμον Πηλήϊον εἴσω ("'I sent him away with the curved ships into the land of Ilion / to fight with the Trojans; but I shall never again receive him / won home again to his country and into the house of Peleus'"). Notice the way Thetis presents herself as the one who has sent Achilles to Troy, because in other rival versions of the *Iliad* it was she, and not Peleus as in the D-scholium tradition, who tried to hide Achilles in Skyros.

[35] On the technique of *thematic reduplication*, see Tsagalis 2008b:252–266.

[36] Alden (2000:287–289) argues that given that the father figure is of great importance, we may assume that it must have been highly esteemed by the Iliadic audience.

Places of memory: Phthia as "anti-Troy"

To this point I have argued that Phthia is constructed by recourse to a set of features that make divisions of space "override" divisions of time: spatial remoteness "spills over" to temporal distancing as Phthia becomes the Iliadic synonym of Achilles' past and endlessly suspended future, while the nostalgic feeling of "home" is contrasted with his painful experience in the foreign—both literally and figuratively—and unfathomable world of Troy (*Iliad* XIX 324–325 ... ὃ δ' ἀλλοδαπῷ ἐνὶ δήμῳ / εἵνεκα ῥιγεδανῆς Ἑλένης Τρωσὶν πολεμίζω ["who now in a strange land / make war upon the Trojans for the sake of accursed Helen"]).[37]

In the following passages, Phthia is seen from a new perspective, as speakers use it as a means of reconstructing the past and expressing the total collapse of their expectations about the future:

Achilles:

> "τίπτε δεδάκρυσαι, Πατρόκλεις, ἠΰτε κούρη
> νηπίη, ἥ θ' ἅμα μητρὶ θέουσ' ἀνελέσθαι ἀνώγει
> εἱανοῦ ἁπτομένη, καί τ' ἐσσυμένην κατερύκει,
> δακρυόεσσα δέ μιν ποτιδέρκεται, ὄφρ' ἀνέληται;
> τῇ ἴκελος, Πάτροκλε, τέρεν κατὰ δάκρυον εἴβεις.
> ἠέ τι Μυρμιδόνεσσι πιφαύσκεαι ἢ ἐμοὶ αὐτῷ,
> <u>ἦέ τιν' ἀγγελίην Φθίης ἒξ ἔκλυες οἶος—</u>
> ζώειν μὰν ἔτι φασὶ Μενοίτιον Ἄκτορος υἱόν,
> ζώει δ' Αἰακίδης Πηλεὺς μετὰ Μυρμιδόνεσσιν,
> τῶν κε μάλ' ἀμφοτέρων ἀκαχοίμεθα τεθνηώτων—
> ἦε σύ γ' Ἀργείων ὀλοφύρεαι, ὡς ὀλέκονται
> νηυσὶν ἔπι γλαφυρῇσιν ὑπερβασίης ἕνεκα σφῆς;
> ἐξαύδα, μὴ κεῦθε νόῳ, ἵνα εἴδομεν ἄμφω."

> "Why then
> are you crying like some poor little girl, Patroklos,
> who runs after her mother and begs to be picked up and carried,
> and clings to her dress, and holds her back when she tries to hurry,
> and gazes tearfully into her face, until she is picked up?
> You are like such a one, Patroklos, dropping these soft tears.
> Could you have some news to tell, for me or the Myrmidons?
> *Have you, and nobody else, received some message from Phthia?*
> Yet they tell me Aktor's son Menoitios lives still

---

[37] See Tsagalis 2004:82–87.

and Aiakos' son Peleus lives still among the Myrmidons.
If either of these died we should take it hard. Or is it
the Argives you are mourning over, and how they are dying
against the hollow ships by reason of their own arrogance?
Tell me, do not hide it in your mind, and so we shall both know."

Iliad XVI 7–19

The series of ironic questions that Achilles throws at Patroklos constitutes a standard epic device for shedding light on the last item of a list (as is done, though by the use of negatives, with the priamel),[38] which the speaker already knows but dislikes.[39] J. Kakridis, who has stressed that this stylistic feature traces its origins in popular oral songs,[40] has also argued that

> in the beginning the audience, hearing the surmises of the person asking, is led to imagine mistaken solutions. But in the answer the explicit and striking refutation of these surmises follows immediately, so that the correct solution is heard at the end and is given its full weight. In this scheme the erroneous questions have no other purpose than to form a negative background from which the positive assertion will emerge, in full clarity, at the end.[41]

In this light, and taking a closer look at the wrong assumptions Achilles makes in the erroneous questions he has asked in the first place, we can see that they closely associate the news from Phthia with the imagined deaths of Menoitios and Peleus, the fathers of the two interlocutors Patroklos and Achilles. The two wrong assumptions, whose style echoes that of popular poetry,[42] do "form a negative background from which the positive assertion will emerge, in full clarity, at the end," but are also linked to the particular way Achilles constructs

---

[38] On the priamel, see Race 1982.

[39] See Janko 1992:316 on *Iliad* XVI 7–19.

[40] See J. Kakridis 1949:110–111, and on mistaken questions 108–120; Janko 1992:316 on *Iliad* XVI 7–19.

[41] J. Kakridis 1949:110–111.

[42] See e.g. the repetition of ζώειν/ζώει in verse-initial position (*Iliad* XVI 14–15), and cf. examples of modern Greek popular songs, where the repetition of the same word in verse-initial or half-verse position constitutes a stylistic feature of the motif of "mistaken questions": Αχός βαρύς ακούγεται, πολλά τουφέκια πέφτουν. Μήνα σε γάμο ρίχνονται, μήνα σε χαροκόπι; Μηδέ σε γάμο ρίχνονται, μηδέ σε χαροκόπι. Η Δέσπω κάνει πόλεμο με νύφες και μ' αγγόνια ("A great uproar is heard, many gunshots are fired. Is it at someone's wedding? Is it at someone's funeral? It is neither at a wedding nor at a funeral. Despo is waging war together with her daughters-in-law and her grandchildren").

the notion of his homeland.[43] The "news from Phthia" thus becomes a linchpin that keeps together fathers and sons, namely Menoitios and Peleus with Patroklos and Achilles respectively. That said, and given that this is the only example in the *Iliad* where the "right" answer to the erroneous questions asked is anticipated by the same person who asks the question, *before* it is confirmed by the addressee, Patroklos (*Iliad* XVI 21–24), it can be argued that Achilles employs Phthia as a hook on which to hang his personal outlook on the Trojan War. By stating at the end of his speech that the Achaeans are suffering because of their arrogance, Achilles draws a line between "home" and "Troy," between the pain that he feels for the potential death of both his own and Patroklos' father in Phthia as well as his indifference to the deaths of Achaean warriors at Troy. Phthia is thus elevated from a location to a "site of memory,"[44] albeit a constructed or imaginary memory that emphatically contrasts with the reality of Troy. Suffering for human losses is thus measured by spatial features, since Phthia allows Achilles to play with such perceptions as absence, privation, and estrangement.

Phthia is also mentioned in a highly pitched lament by Briseis, the slave girl Patroklos had promised to make Achilles' wife after their return home:

> "... ἀλλά μ' ἔφασκες Ἀχιλλῆος θείοιο
> κουριδίην ἄλοχον θήσειν, ἄξειν τ' ἐνὶ νηυσίν
> ἐς Φθίην, δαίσειν δὲ γάμον μετὰ Μυρμιδόνεσσιν.
> τώ σ' ἄμοτον κλαίω τεθνηότα μείλιχον αἰεί."

> "... but said you would make me godlike Achilleus'
> wedded lawful wife, that you would take me back in the ships
> to Phthia, and formalize my marriage among the Myrmidons.
> Therefore I weep your death without ceasing. You were kind always."

> *Iliad* XIX 297–300

The spatial grammar of Briseis' speech, with its annulled "futurity" (ἔφασκες ... θήσειν, ἄξειν, δαίσειν), points to the tension between the "canonical" and the "subversive."[45] By allowing herself to believe in Patroklos' promise concerning a future marriage to Achilles in Phthia, Briseis silently acknowledges that she has entertained the thought of a new life. The spatialization of cultural and social life makes her closely associate the unfulfilled promise of a new life with

---

[43] With respect to this last point, I disagree with J. Kakridis, who explicitly says that "the erroneous questions have no other purpose than to form a negative background" (1949:110).

[44] On "sites of memory," see Nora 1996.

[45] See Tsagalis 2004:82–86, 139–143.

Phthia, and therefore disentangle the cultural premises of this spatialization that bear on the grim reality of a slave woman living at Troy. Phthia becomes here a spatial metaphor, deftly employed in order to allow Briseis to fabricate an identity, or rather to "displace" her old identity and construct a new one. In this respect she follows the general practice of defining ownership (emotional, intellectual, or political) on the basis of familiarity: what is familiar (the status of a wife as in her past life) is "one's own," and what is unfamiliar (the status of a slave woman) belongs to "others." In this light, let us consider the following formulation by Said in his description of the poetics of space:

> The objective space of a house—its corners, corridors, cellar, rooms—is far less important than what poetically it is endowed with, which is usually a quality with an imaginative or figurative value we can name and feel: thus a house may be haunted or homelike, or prisonlike or magical. So space acquires emotional and even rational sense by a kind of poetic process, whereby the vacant or anonymous reaches of distance are converted into meaning for us here.[46]

In Briseis' speech there is no description of the objective space of Phthia: on the contrary, this space acquires an imaginative value, it becomes a toponymic metaphor for a better life. The death of Patroklos thus signifies for Briseis the cancellation of a promise that would have turned her journey to Phthia from exile into a return to the status of a married woman, and to all the respect derived from it. The fulfillment of such important cultural prerequisites as marriage turns Phthia into an "anti-Troy," through a process of adjusting the topography of identity into an emotional, rational, and cultural landscape[47] and allowing the slave woman to become once again a lawful wedded wife.

In Achilles' antiphonal lament to Briseis,[48] Phthia is incorporated into a geographical triptych involving Troy and Skyros, where Achilles' son Neoptolemos is growing up:[49]

"ἦ ῥά νύ μοί ποτε καὶ σύ, δυσάμμορε, φίλταθ' ἑταίρων,
αὐτὸς ἐνὶ κλισίῃ λαρὸν παρὰ δεῖπνον ἔθηκας
αἶψα καὶ ὀτραλέως, ὁπότε σπερχοίατ' Ἀχαιοί
Τρωσὶν ἐφ' ἱπποδάμοισι φέρειν πολύδακρυν ἄρηα·
νῦν δὲ σὺ μὲν κεῖσαι δεδαϊγμένος, αὐτὰρ ἐμὸν κῆρ

---

[46] Said 1995:55.

[47] See Gregory 2001:313–314.

[48] On these two antiphonal laments (γόοι), see Pucci 1998:97–112; Tsagalis 2004:139–143, 148–151.

[49] I do not agree with West, who brackets lines 326–337; for his point of view, see West 2011:359 on *Iliad* XIX 326–337. On this issue, see Tsagalis (forthcoming in *RFIC*).

ἄκμηνον πόσιος καὶ ἐδητύος, ἔνδον ἐόντων,
σῇ ποθῇ. οὐ μὲν γάρ τι κακώτερον ἄλλο πάθοιμι,
<u>οὐδ’ εἴ κεν τοῦ πατρὸς ἀποφθιμένοιο πυθοίμην,</u>
ὅς που νῦν Φθίηφι τέρεν κατὰ δάκρυον εἴβει
χήτει τοιοῦδ’ υἷος· ὁ δ’ <u>ἀλλοδαπῷ ἐνὶ δήμῳ</u>
εἵνεκα ῥιγεδανῆς Ἑλένης Τρωσὶν πολεμίζω.
ἠὲ τόν, ὃς Σκύρῳ μοι ἐνιτρέφεται φίλος υἷός,
εἴ που ἔτι ζώει γε Νεοπτόλεμος θεοειδής.
πρὶν μὲν γάρ μοι θυμὸς ἐνὶ στήθεσσιν ἐώλπει
οἶον ἐμὲ φθίσεσθαι ἀπ’ Ἄργεος ἱπποβότοιο
αὐτοῦ ἐνὶ Τροίῃ, <u>σὲ δέ τε Φθίην δὲ νέεσθαι,</u>
ὡς ἄν μοι τὸν παῖδα θοῇ σὺν νηΐ μελαίνῃ
Σκυρόθεν ἐξαγάγοις καί οἱ δείξειας ἕκαστα,
κτῆσιν ἐμὴν δμῶάς τε καὶ ὑψερεφὲς μέγα δῶμα.
ἤδη γὰρ Πηλῆά γ’ ὀΐομαι ἢ κατὰ πάμπαν
τεθνάμεν, ἤ που τυτθὸν ἔτι ζώοντ’ ἀκάχησθαι
γήραΐ τε στυγερῷ <u>καὶ ἐμὴν ποτιδέγμενον αἰεὶ</u>
<u>λυγρὴν ἀγγελίην,</u> ὅτ’ ἀποφθιμένοιο <u>πύθηται.</u>”

"There was a time, ill fated, o dearest of all my companions,
when you yourself would set the desirable dinner before me
quickly and expertly, at the time the Achaians were urgent
to carry sorrowful war on the Trojans, breakers of horses.
But now you lie here torn before me, and my heart goes starved
for meat and drink, though they are here beside me, by reason
of longing for you. There is nothing worse than this I could suffer,
not even if I were to hear of the death of my father
who now, I think, in Phthia somewhere lets fall a soft tear
for lack of such a son,[50] for me, who *now in a strange land*
make war upon the Trojans for the sake of accursed Helen;
or the death of my dear son, who is raised for my sake in Skyros
now, if godlike Neoptolemos is still one of the living.
Before now the spirit inside my breast was hopeful
that I alone should die far away from horse-pasturing Argos
here in Troy; I hoped *you would win back again to Phthia*
so that in a fast black ship you could take my son back
from Skyros to Phthia, and show him all my possessions,
my property, my serving men, my great high-roofed house.

[50] I have replaced Lattimore's "bereavement" with "lack of," since Peleus is presented as waiting
for the evil message of Achilles' death (*Iliad* XIX 336–337).

> For by this time I think that Peleus must altogether
> have perished, or still keeps a little scant life in sorrow
> for the hatefulness of old age and *because he waits ever from me*
> *the evil message*, for the day *he hears* I have been killed."

Iliad XIX 315–337

Achilles' vision of places is discursively constructed more or less like Foucault's and Said's emotional and genealogical geographies.[51] The "great divide" between "here" (Troy)[52] and "there" (Phthia) is verbalized by Achilles' brief mental journey with respect to his family. Along these lines, Skyros becomes a "stopover" bridging Troy and Phthia,[53] the two ends of the hero's spatialized identity (see Table 5).

Table 5: Spatial thematization of Achilles' family

Troy	foreign	Achilles
Skyros	foreign and familiar	Neoptolemos
Phthia	familiar	Peleus

By emphasizing the partial and incomplete nature of recollection, which is determined by a complex nexus of external stimuli, Achilles' former experiences are presented as "reawakened," not resurrected.[54] Achilles' recollections of Phthia are presented as dispersed bits of the past, a "subversive archipelago"[55] of scattered memories insularized in his emotional mapping of the heroic code, a series of connected interventions that simultaneously call into question the most fundamental tenets of Achaean heroic discourse and create deep ruptures in the surface of Agamemnon's and Menelaos' rhetoric about the justification of the Trojan War. For Achilles, Phthia and Skyros gradually lose their Trojan War coloring and are emotionally anchored to the space of his family, as they represent father and son respectively.[56] This shrinking of

---

[51] Foucault 1984; Said 1995.

[52] Notice the deictic force of αὐτοῦ 'here' in *Iliad* XIX 330.

[53] It is part of Achilles' past (*Cypria*, §27 Kullmann = 130–131 Severyns = Allen 104.8–9) and Neoptolemos' future (*Little Iliad*, §§76–77 Kullmann = 217–218 Severyns = Allen 106.29–31).

[54] On this approach to memory, see Halbwachs 1980:75, 1992:39.

[55] The expression "subversive archipelago" belongs to Hulme 1990, who used it to refer to Edward Said's work on postcolonial societies.

[56] Thus Achilles does not explicitly refer to his arriving at Skyros after the Teuthranian expedition (*Cypria*, §27 Kullmann = 130–131 Severyns = Allen 104.8–9) but *to Neoptolemus' growing up there,*

Achilles' spatial horizon is the next step in a process of diminishing his social and moral horizon. While in the beginning of the epic he cares about the entire Greek army and speaks for all of them,[57] he gradually narrows his concerns only to a small circle of warriors, his beloved Myrmidons, and then to a single person, Patroklos.[58] Achilles' mutilated recollections are filled with a longing that is not only psychological but also cultural.[59] His disillusionment at Agamemnon's behavior takes the form of a cultural melancholy, his own idiosyncratic polemic and criticism of the heroic code. Achilles does not resurrect the past; he rather reconstructs it in the present, and most importantly in a way that challenges the collective memory that the Achaeans, and predominantly the Atreidai, have framed. Agamemnon and Menelaos, being the ones who have practically organized the entire Achaean expedition to Troy, constantly promote their own version of the past, which is based on the unanimous rise of all Greece against the city of Priam, and thus they are able to construct a collective memory of the past that is selective, oversimplifying, and singular. In sociological terms, the Atreidai, to borrow Halbwachs's terminology, are turning memory that should be multiple and plural into a cohesive version of the past, that is, into history.[60] It is the very foundations of this "canonical" version of the past promoted by the Atreidai that Achilles profoundly shatters by excluding himself from the group of the other Achaean leaders who have been summoned to Troy. He therefore uses Phthia not as a mere topographical place, but as a "site of memory," a *lieu de mémoire* in Nora's words. Like the French *province*,[61] in Achilles' speech Phthia monopolizes a certain version of his past: it becomes an "anti-Troy," the opposite of the Achaeans' outlook on the entire war and its heroic rhetoric.

Argos

The word Ἄργος (Argos) denotes in the *Iliad* any of the following:[62] (1) the homeland of Diomedes in the Argolid,[63] (2) the homeland and kingdom of Agamemnon

---

though *Iliad* IX 668 (Σκῦρον ἑλὼν αἰπεῖαν, Ἐνυῆος πτολίεθρον ["when he took sheer Skyros, Enyeus' citadel"]) may be an Iliadic adaptation of what the *Cypria* says about his arrival there.

[57] See *Iliad* I 158–159 (... ἅμ' ἑσπόμεθ', ὄφρα σὺ χαίρῃς, / τιμὴν ἀρνύμενοι Μενελάῳ σοί τε, κυνῶπα ["we followed, to do you favour, / you with the dog's eyes, to win your honour and Menelaos' ..."]), when he replies to Agamemnon as a representative of the whole Achaean army.

[58] See Shay 1995:23–26.

[59] See Whitehead 2009:126.

[60] See Nora 1996:3.

[61] See Corbin 1996.

[62] The etymology of this word points to the notion of "field": see LfgrE s.v. Ἄργος; Frisk GEW I 132; Chantraine DELG 103–104.

[63] *Iliad* II 559 (narrator); IV 52 (Hera); VI 152 (Glaukos); XIV 119 (Diomedes); XV 30 (Zeus); XIX 115 (Agamemnon); XXIV 437 (Hermes).

in the Peloponnese,[64] (3) the homeland of Achilles (Pelasgian Argos) in Thessaly,[65] (4) the entire Peloponnese, (5) the whole of Greece. Of these five meanings of "Argos," only the second, fourth, and fifth are narratively exploited as spatial terms. Before I embark on an analysis of the relevant material and explore the use of Argos as thematized space within the discourse of Agamemnon and various other Homeric (not only Achaean but also Trojan) heroes, I shall dwell briefly on the wide use of this term and the narrative disinterest in connecting Diomedes and Achilles to Peloponnesian and Pelasgian Argos respectively.

The name *Argos* seems to be the default mode for denoting vague spatial references. Its etymology, indicating the notion of "field," explains effectively why it was widely used for different places and why, in a later phase, it was semantically expanded to designate larger geographical regions such as the entire Peloponnese or Greece as a whole. This semantic indeterminacy is also reflected in the Homeric use of the word *Argives* (Ἀργεῖοι),[66] on a par with Danaans (Δαναοί) and Achaeans (Ἀχαιοί), for all Greeks.[67] In the light of these observations, it is no wonder that the epic tradition of the *Iliad* has selected for narrative exploitation only those connotations of Argos that were closely associated with its subject matter. Hence Argos as the homeland of Diomedes was not appropriate as a thematized space, since Diomedes did not belong to the core of the Trojan War but was imported from the Theban epic tradition.[68] Likewise, Pelasgian Argos could only marginally be used as the homeland of Achilles,[69] since the *Iliad*, as I have shown, reserved the toponym Phthia for Achilles. Given the systematic narrative exploitation of such an important thematized space as Phthia, there was no room for a thematically neutral place-name such as Pelasgian Argos.

---

[64] According to Piérart, "Le découpage des royaumes ne réflète donc pas une réalité historique, mycénienne ou autre, mais un effort ... d'organisation de la matière épique" (1991:143); see also Wathelet 1992:115; Burkert 1998:175. Cf. Cingano 2004:67–68, who speaks of a "contesto epico-mitico" ("an epic-mythic context").

[65] *Iliad* II 681 (narrator).

[66] On the mythopoeic or even ritualistic aspects of Ἀργεῖοι, see Clader 1976: ch. 3, section 3, following Frame 1971; on Δαναοί, see Nagy 1990a:223–262.

[67] See Strabo 8.6.5 Ἀργείους γοῦν καλεῖ πάντας, καθάπερ καὶ Δαναοὺς καὶ Ἀχαιούς.

[68] On Diomedes, see Andersen 1978. See also Cingano 2004:61–62, who shows how the storyteller tried to accommodate certain Theban features, such as the obscure *hapax legomenon* Ὑποθῆβαι, to the framework of the Trojan epic tradition. Agamemnon is now considered a "late insertion" in the Argive mythology, his territory originally being located in Laconia: see Piérart 1992a:130; W. Kullmann 1993:140–142; Hall 1997:89–93; Cingano 2004:67.

[69] Only once (*Iliad* II 681), by the narrator.

Locating infamy

The *Iliad* uses space as a filter for the way Agamemnon "sees" his return home, in order to further deepen the gap between the Achaean commander and Achilles that has already been strong since the beginning of the poem.[70] Given that the crucial theme of μῆνις is introduced as soon as the epic begins, the narrator feels the need to provide his audience, at regular narrative intervals, with more information concerning the heroic *Weltanschauung* of these two great heroes. In fact, the *Iliad* capitalizes on the spatial representation of their conflict as early as the proem:

ἐξ οὗ δὴ τὰ πρῶτα διαστήτην ἐρίσαντε
Ἀτρείδης τε ἄναξ ἀνδρῶν καὶ δῖος Ἀχιλλεύς

since that time when first there stood in division of conflict
Atreus' son the lord of men and brilliant Achilleus.

Iliad I 6–7

This verbal spatialization of the conflict is covertly reflected even in what seems a random issue, namely the placement of the camps of Agamemnon and Achilles far apart, or to be more accurate the location of Achilles' hut at the far end of the Achaean camp.[71]

Achilles punctuates his past both by reference to his family and by calling into question the heroic rhetoric of the Atreidai, and especially Agamemnon. For Achilles, returning to Phthia means reuniting with his father and the end of his troubles. But in contrast with the way Achilles emotionally maps his homeland, Agamemnon constructs a profoundly opposite vision of Argos, one that erases all manner of discontinuities, aberrations, and deviations. Agamemnon envisions the past as "an uninterrupted chain of essentially contiguous occurrences flowing into one another like the successive musical notes that form legato phrases."[72] Whereas Achilles adopts a style of spatiotemporal discontinuity, punctuated by sharp breaks and deep ruptures, Agamemnon favors a continuous, almost etiological view of events that leads, almost unavoidably, to the present situation. It is exactly in this light that he excludes from his perception of "homeland" those events that are incompatible with the kind of

---

[70] See M. Reichel 1994:198–201; on Agamemnon, see Kalinka 1943; Whitman 1958:156–163; Donlan 1971–1972; Belloni 1978; Griffin 1980:70–73; L. Collins 1988:69–103; Taplin 1990.

[71] On the function of the spatial marginalization of Achilles' hut as a reflection of his social marginalization, see "The headquarters of Agamemnon and Achilles," chapter 2 above; on the placement of Achilles' hut, see Clay 2007:241. On space and society, see Soja 1989.

[72] Zerubavel 2003:82.

personality he wants to present to the army: "profound changes in consciousness, by their nature, bring with them characteristic amnesias."[73] Major watersheds like the sacrifice of Iphigenia, the state of his relation to Klutaimnestra, and his insulting of Achilles at the cost of enormous Achaean losses are thus repressed and filtered into a discourse featuring his fears about disgrace, infamy, and reproach should he return unsuccessful to Argos, on the one hand, and almost complete lack of reference to or consideration of his family on the other.[74]

In *Iliad* I, Agamemnon imagines himself at home, with Khruseis there as a slave:

"τὴν δ' ἐγὼ οὐ λύσω· πρίν μιν καὶ γῆρας ἔπεισιν
ἡμετέρῳ ἐνὶ οἴκῳ, ἐν Ἄργεϊ, τηλόθι πάτρης,
ἱστὸν ἐποιχομένην καὶ ἐμὸν λέχος ἀντιόωσαν."

"The girl I will not give back; sooner will old age come upon her
in my own house, in Argos, far from her own land,
going up and down by the loom and being in my bed as my
     companion."

Iliad I 29–31

His arrogant claim that he will not let her go before she grows old[75] indicates his legato formulation of time.[76] Agamemnon promotes Khruseis to high status and virtually erases the memory of Klutaimnestra, his queen.[77] Some of the ancient audience must have smiled or shaken their heads in disdain, in the light of their knowledge of the tradition reflected in the *Odyssey* and the cyclic *Nostoi*,

---

[73] Anderson 1991:204.

[74] See M. Reichel 1994:198–201, who states that Agamemnon's constant concern about a possible return to Argos is at odds with both his leading position among the Achaeans and his supposed obligation with respect to his brother Menelaos to sack Troy and take Helen back.

[75] The language Agamemnon uses reflects the way he regards Khruseis. The expression (*Iliad* I 31) ἱστὸν ἐποιχομένην καὶ ἐμὸν λέχος ἀντιόωσαν ("'going up and down by the loom and being in my bed as my companion'") pertains to the regular tasks of a housewife. Agamemnon's refusal to let her go until she grows old may allude to the lack of sexual activity, since Khruseis would then be of no use to him.

[76] See Zerubavel 2003:82.

[77] *Iliad* II 134–138 supplies Agamemnon with an argument for ending the war: he is not concerned though with his own family but with the family of each and every soldier. Scholars disagree on the function of this reference. W. Kullmann (1955), with whom I side, has argued in favor of the influence of a *Kyprienstoff*, in which the Achaeans, suffering from hunger, were incited by Agamemnon (who had no intention, as in the *Iliad*, of testing their morale) to return home. In that version, Achilles was the one who prevented them from embarking for Greece; see *Cypria* §42 Kullmann = 159–160 Severyns = Allen 105.9–10. M. Reichel (1994:200n5) is skeptical.

according to which Klutaimnestra murders Agamemnon upon his return to Argos with a slave woman at his side who is not the daughter of Apollo's priest but Kassandra, a priestess of Apollo.[78]

One of Agamemnon's main concerns is that he may become infamous and even be reproached if he returns to Argos without having accomplished his task:

> "Ζεύς με μέγα Κρονίδης ἄτη ἐνέδησε βαρείη,
> σχέτλιος, ὃς πρὶν μέν μοι ὑπέσχετο καὶ κατένευσεν
> Ἴλιον ἐκπέρσαντ' εὐτείχεον ἀπονέεσθαι,
> νῦν δὲ κακὴν ἀπάτην βουλεύσατο, καί με κελεύει
> <u>δυσκλέα Ἄργος ἱκέσθαι, ἐπεὶ πολὺν ὤλεσα λαόν.</u>

"Zeus son of Kronos has caught me fast in bitter futility.
He is hard; who before this time promised me and consented
that I might sack strong-walled Ilion and sail homeward.
Now he has devised a vile deception, and bids me *go back
to Argos in dishonour having lost many of my people.*"

Iliad II 111–115 (= IX 18–22)

> "καί κεν ἐλέγχιστος πολυδίψιον Ἄργος ἱκοίμην.
> αὐτίκα γὰρ μνήσονται Ἀχαιοὶ πατρίδος αἴης,
> κὰδ δέ κεν εὐχωλὴν Πριάμῳ καὶ Τρωσὶ λίποιμεν
> Ἀργείην Ἑλένην· σέο δ' ὀστέα πύσει ἄρουρα
> κειμένου ἐν Τροίῃ ἀτελευτήτῳ ἐπὶ ἔργῳ."

"And I must return a thing of reproach to Argos the thirsty,
for now at once the Achaians will remember the land of their fathers;
and thus we would leave to Priam and to the Trojans Helen
of Argos, to glory over, while the bones of you rot in the ploughland
as you lie dead in Troy, on a venture that went unaccomplished."

Iliad IV 171–175

> "οὕτω που Διὶ μέλλει ὑπερμενέϊ φίλον εἶναι,
> νωνύμνους ἀπολέσθαι ἀπ' Ἄργεος ἐνθάδ' Ἀχαιούς."

---

[78] On early knowledge of the killing of Kassandra, see *Odyssey* xi 421–423; *Nostoi* (fr. 10, PEG 1 = test. 2, EGF). In the art of the archaic period, there is just a single example of the death of Kassandra. Prag (1985:58 and no. G1: plate 37a) describes it as "a beautifully worked fragment of bronze sheathing found during the excavation of the small seventh-century shrine at the Argive Heraeum in 1927." The depiction seems to agree with Agamemnon's narration in *Odyssey* xi 411.

"then such is the way it must be pleasing to Zeus, who is too strong,
that the Achaians must die here forgotten and far from Argos."

Iliad XIV 69–70[79]

Agamemnon reads Argos not as simply a place, but as an evaluation[80] of his undertaking the whole enterprise of the Trojan War.[81] Regarding himself (together with his brother) as the main instigator of the expedition, Agamemnon sees his homeland not as the locus of his family or a happy life left behind, but as the measure of his success or failure. Argos exists for him only in the future tense, not in the past. The epithets δυσκλεής 'ill-famed, in dishonor' (*Iliad* II 115), ἐλέγχιστος 'a thing of reproach' (IV 171), and νώνυμνος 'nameless, forgotten' (XII 70 = XIII 227)[82] belong to the language of blame that runs high on every warrior's heroic agenda,[83] the more so that of the commander-in-chief of the entire Achaean army. Although the expression ἐπεὶ πολὺν ὤλεσα λαόν ("having caused the loss of many of my people"; II 115 = IX 22; my translation)[84] amounts to Agamemnon's remorse intensified by his preeminent role in recruiting the

---

[79] West omits this line, which is also attested in *Iliad* XII 70, XIII 227.

[80] The emphasis Agamemnon places on the importance of a glorious νόστος must have struck an ironic note in the audience's ears, for Agamemnon's return to Argos was coupled with murder. In fact, this is the only truly λυγρός νόστος, for the one other hero who dies after the sack of Troy, Locrian Ajax, does not have a complete νόστος since he does not manage to return home. The *Odyssey* (iv 496–497) designates both Agamemnon and Locrian Ajax as the only two Achaean leaders who perished ἐν νόστῳ, which must be interpreted as "in the process of accomplishing their return."

[81] The formula πολυδίψιον Ἄργος, which is attested in archaic epic poetry only here and in the first line of the Cyclic *Thebais* (fr. 1, PEG 1 = fr. 1, EGF: Ἄργος ἄειδε, θεά, πολυδίψιον, ἔνθα ἄνακτες ["Sing, goddess, of Argos the thirsty, from where the kings ..."]), opens an interesting possibility, further strengthened by Agamemnon's words that he is afraid lest he return home leaving Menelaos' bones in Troy and without having accomplished his task (*Iliad* IV 174–175 σέο δ' ὀστέα πύσει ἄρουρα / κειμένου ἐν Τροίῃ ἀτελευτήτῳ ἐπὶ ἔργῳ ["while the bones of you rot in the ploughland / as you lie dead in Troy, on a venture that went unaccomplished"]). Is it possible that when Agamemnon "invaded" Argolic myth, he acquired some of the features of one of the Seven who had departed from πολυδίψιον Ἄργος to sack Thebes? What he says to Menelaos in IV 171–175 echoes one of the typical motifs of the Theban war, namely the problem of burying the dead in Theban territory, far away from Argos. One cannot exclude the possibility that the tradition of the *Iliad* here fuses material from a lost Theban epic or song tradition with that of a *Nostoi* song tradition, or even a tradition concerned only with the return of the Atreidai (like the Ἀτρειδῶν Κάθοδος mentioned by Athenaeus 9.399a [*Nostoi*, fr. 11, PEG 1 = fr. 8, EGF], on which see Davies 1989:82–83).

[82] As the plot unfolds, Agamemnon gradually focuses on a smaller Achaean audience with the theme of returning home: in *Iliad* II 110–141 it was the entire Achaean army, in IX 17–28 the elders, and in XIV 65–81 Odysseus and Diomedes; see Janko 1992:157–158 on *Iliad* XIV 65–81; M. Reichel 1994:201.

[83] On the language of praise and blame in the *Iliad*, see Nagy 1979:222–242; Vodoklys 1992.

[84] The device of Agamemnon's testing the army in *Iliad* II restores the king's shattered status after his conflict with Achilles in *Iliad* I. On the *Diapeira*, see Owen 1946:17–26; von der Mühll 1946;

196

army and leading the expedition,[85] it is contradicted by his selfish insistence on being recompensed for the loss of Khruseis, a stance that was clearly inconsiderate of the interests of the army. In IV 171–175, Agamemon's fears that Menelaos might die are translated into his concern about both being reproached by the Achaeans and giving Priam and the Trojans a reason to boast.

In Agamemnon's discourse, his homeland is a highly thematized space that allows him to express his anxiety and fears. The Iliadic tradition is thus able to construct a continuous process, with an uninterrupted succession of events leading from Argos to Troy and back again. If this succession is interrupted by the failure to accomplish his goal, or by the death of his brother, which renders it pointless to continue the war, Agamemnon's fame is at stake. By favoring a discourse emphatically different from that of Achilles, who regards his potential return to Phthia as a salvation from unwanted troubles (even at the cost of his fame),[86] Agamemnon elevates Argos to the ultimate litmus test of his status as a hero.[87] Thus he moves away from Achilles' staccato poetics of discontinuous and multiple narratives and turns toward a legato spatialization of the items on his heroic agenda.[88]

In one of the rare occasions when Agamemnon refers to one of his family members, and the only time he mentions Orestes,[89] he remains emotionally uninvolved and even transforms his son into a potential brother-in-law of Achilles.

"εἰ δέ κεν Ἄργος ἱκοίμεθ' Ἀχαιϊκόν, οὖθαρ ἀρούρης,
γαμβρός κέν μοι ἔοι, τίσω δέ μιν ἶσον Ὀρέστῃ,
ὅς μοι τηλύγετος τρέφεται θαλίῃ ἔνι πολλῇ."

Lämmli 1948; W. Kullmann 1955; Katzung 1960; Reinhardt 1961:107–123; Kirk 1985:115–156; McGlew 1989; Knox and Russo 1989; M. Reichel 1994:198–199.

[85] Although it is not clear that both the Atreidai participated in actually recruiting the army (§§19–21 Kullmann = 112–119 Severyns = Allen 103.19–24), Agamemnon considers himself the main instigator and mastermind of the entire expedition to Troy.

[86] See *Iliad* IX 412–416 "εἰ μέν κ' αὖθι μένων Τρώων πόλιν ἀμφιμάχωμαι, / ὤλετο μέν μοι νόστος, / ἀτὰρ κλέος ἄφθιτον ἔσται· / εἰ δέ κεν οἴκαδ' ἵκωμι φίλην ἐς πατρίδα γαῖαν, / ὤλετό μοι κλέος ἐσθλόν, ἐπὶ δηρὸν δέ μοι αἰών / ἔσσεται, οὐδέ κέ μ' ὦκα τέλος θανάτοιο κιχείη" ("'If I stay here and fight beside the city of the Trojans, / my return home is gone, but my glory shall be everlasting; / but if I return home to the beloved land of my fathers, / the excellence of my glory is gone, but there will be a long life / left for me, and my end in death will not come to me quickly'").

[87] In contrast with Achilles, Agamemnon, who undoes all his family's ties to Argos, seems to be thinking Panhellenically, not locally, which of course fits the way that Phthia is treated as small and remote, and Argos often as all of Greece.

[88] For the terms staccato and legato with respect to space and time, see Zerubavel 2003:34–36.

[89] On problems concerning Homer's naming of Agamemnon's daughters, see Hainsworth 1993:77 on *Iliad* IX 145.

"And if we come back to Achaian Argos, pride of the tilled land,
he may be my son-in-law; I will honour him equally with Orestes
my growing son, who is brought up there in abundant luxury."

Iliad IX 141–143 (repeated by Odysseus in IX 283–285)

This single reference to Orestes must be read against the background of the ironic comments of Idomeneus to Othruoneus in *Iliad* XIII:[90]

"... ὃ δ' ὑπέσχετο θυγατέρα ἥν.
καί κέ τοι ἡμεῖς ταῦτά γ' ὑποσχόμενοι τελέσαιμεν,
δοῖμεν δ' Ἀτρεΐδαο θυγατρῶν εἶδος ἀρίστην
Ἄργεος ἐξαγαγόντες ὀπυιέμεν, εἴ κε σὺν ἄμμιν
Ἰλίου ἐκπέρσῃς εὖ ναιόμενον πτολίεθρον.
ἀλλ' ἔπε', ὄφρ' ἐπὶ νηυσὶ συνώμεθα ποντοπόροισιν
ἀμφὶ γάμῳ, ἐπεὶ οὔ τοι ἐεδνωταὶ κακοί εἰμεν."

"... who in turn promised you his daughter.
See now, we also would make you a promise, and we would fulfil it;
we would give you the loveliest of Atreides' daughters,
and bring her here from Argos to be your wife, if you joined us
and helped us storm the strong-founded city of Ilion.
Come then with me, so we can meet by our seafaring vessels
about a marriage; we here are not bad matchmakers for you."

Iliad XIII 376–382

Idomeneus' ironic comments play on Agamemnon's offer to Achilles: Agamemnon seems willing to give Achilles not only twenty Trojan slave women in case the Achaeans sack Troy, but even one of his daughters, without expecting any gifts in return (ἀνάεδνον), only Achilles' return to the battlefield with the ultimate purpose of sacking Troy; likewise, Othruoneus brings no gifts, and Priam is willing to give him the hand of Kassandra on the sole condition that he repel the Greeks. The comments of Idomeneus evoke Agamemnon's promise to Achilles, especially since Idomeneus uses language that explicitly refers to Agamemnon's daughters (δοῖμεν δ' Ἀτρεΐδαο θυγατρῶν εἶδος ἀρίστην / Ἄργεος ἐξαγαγόντες ὀπυιέμεν),[91] and ironically suggests to Othruoneus that he join the

---

[90] In the *Odyssey*, Orestes is mentioned six times (i 30; i 40; i 298; iii 306; iv 546; xi 461), and Agamemnon's fate is systematically opposed to that of Odysseus. On this topic, see D'Arms and Hulley 1946; Hommel 1958; Hölscher 1967.

[91] The one person who will take Kassandra with him as a mistress will be Agamemnon, after the end of the war (see *Odyssey* xi 421–423; *Nostoi*, fr. 10, PEG 1 [see also test. 4] = test. 2, EGF).

Achaean cause and help them sack Troy. In that case, he adds, they will bring one of Agamemnon's daughters from Argos and give her to him to marry. In other words, Idomeneus virtually says to Othruoneus that the Achaeans are desperately *looking for an Achilles*. In that case Othruoneus (whose name, like Orestes', means "mountainous" < ὄθρυς 'mountain') would, Achilles-like,[92] have become Orestes' brother-in-law. Moreover, Idomeneus' words must have struck a familiar chord with the audience, since they point also to Kassandra, who instead of becoming Othruoneus' wife would be brought back to Argos as Agamemnon's slave. The Iliadic storyteller is clearly building on both the scene in *Iliad* IX and the tradition of the *Nostoi* (where Kassandra will be murdered together with Agamemnon in Argos).

These two last passages show that Agamemnon's homeland, as thematized space, is gradually associated with Achilles and the possibility of their reconciliation and future kinship. Read against the ironic backdrop of Idomeneus' words to Othruoneus, Argos even hints at the fact that we are dealing with a *credible impossibility*, that Achilles will never marry one of Agamemnon's daughters[93] nor will he survive the war. Argos thus becomes a spatial metonym for the unbridgeable gap separating the two heroes, the epic antonym of Phthia in Iliadic lingo.[94]

The spatialized alias

When Argos designates the Peloponnese or the whole of Greece, it is used as an alias for each speaker's focalization of the entire Trojan War or a part of it. The Achaeans tend to refer to Argos as a thematized space that epitomizes their concerns about dishonor. Odysseus (*Iliad* II 287, IX 246),[95] Nestor (II 348,

---

[92] See *Iliad* IX 142 γαμβρός κέν μοι ἔοι, τίσω δέ μιν ἶσον Ὀρέστῃ ("he may be my son-in-law; I will honour him with Orestes ...").

[93] Cf. Euripides *Iphigenia in Aulis* 97–105, in which Agamemnon falsely promises to marry his daughter Iphigenia to Achilles.

[94] Phthia is also associated with the violation of Briseis' expectations about a future marriage with Achilles upon their return to Greece after the end of the war (*Iliad* XIX 297–300). Seen from this angle, both Phthia and Argos play with the false expectation of a marriage between Achilles and Briseis or one of Agamemnon's daughters respectively.

[95] *Iliad* II 284–288 "Ἀτρεΐδη, νῦν δή σε, ἄναξ, ἐθέλουσιν Ἀχαιοί / πᾶσιν ἐλέγχιστον θέμεναι μερόπεσσι βροτοῖσιν, / οὐδέ τοι ἐκτελέουσιν ὑπόσχεσιν ἥν περ ὑπέσταν / ἐνθάδ' ἔτι στείχοντες ἀπ' Ἄργεος ἱπποβότοιο, / Ἴλιον ἐκπέρσαντ' εὐτείχεον ἀπονέεσθαι" ("'Son of Atreus: now, my lord, the Achaians are trying / to make you into a thing of reproach in the sight of all mortal / men, and not fulfilling the promise they undertook once / as they set forth to come here from horse-pasturing Argos, / to go home only after you had sacked strong-walled Ilion'"); *Iliad* IX 244–246 "ταῦτ' αἰνῶς δείδοικα κατὰ φρένα, μή οἱ ἀπειλάς / ἐκτελέσωσι θεοί, ἡμῖν δὲ δὴ αἴσιμον εἴη / φθίσθαι ἐνὶ Τροίῃ, ἑκὰς Ἄργεος ἱπποβότοιο" ("'All this I fear terribly in my heart, lest immortals / accomplish all these threats, and lest for us it be destiny / to die here in Troy, far away from horse-pasturing Argos'").

XV 372),[96] Idomeneus (XIII 227),[97] and Agamemnon (XIV 70)[98] express their fears about dying away from home by employing the general meaning of Argos, without designating their particular homeland. Ithaka, Pylos, and Crete—the kingdoms of Odysseus, Nestor, and Idomeneus respectively—vanish from the epic horizon when the emphasis is on the collective function of the army. The threat of defeat and failure, therefore, acquires a spatial perspective, made possible by the semantic flexibility of Argos, which can expand into a geographically wider term encompassing the place of origin of each and every Achaean.

The Trojans for their part refer to Argos in the sense of "Greece" either in the context of a potential agreement between the two sides or with respect to their fears or hopes about the future. In the former case Paris,[99] expressing his intention to fight a duel against Menelaos, employs Argos and Achaea as mere synonyms for the whole of Greece and places them in emphatic opposition to Troy. By translating the antithesis between "they-Achaeans" and "us-Trojans" into the geographical pair "Argos-Troy," Paris spaces time: while the past and the future mean "Argos" for the Achaeans, the present equals their offensive presence at Troy. Paris' use of "Argos" points to his special status with respect to Trojan perceptions of space, since he alone of all the Trojans has been there,[100] when he abducted Helen. Given the dynamic aspect of the Achaean past and future space and its contrast to the static Trojan space, Paris' spatial exclusivity becomes even more significant, since in the eyes of the Trojans it is he, after all, who is responsible for the war. His determination to return the possessions he stole from Menelaos' palace but keep Helen (Iliad VII 363–364 κτήματα δ', ὅσσ' ἀγόμην ἐξ Ἄργεος ἡμέτερον δῶ, / πάντ' ἐθέλω δόμεναι, καὶ ἔτ' οἴκοθεν ἄλλ' ἐπιθεῖναι)[101] is expressed by replacing Sparta with Argos. Paris, who is

---

[96] Iliad II 348–349 "πρὶν Ἄργοσδ' ἰέναι, πρὶν καὶ Διὸς αἰγιόχοιο / γνώμεναι εἴτε ψεῦδος ὑπόσχεσις εἴτε καὶ οὐκί" ("'until they get back again to Argos without ever learning / whether Zeus of the aegis promises false or truly'"); Iliad XV 372–376 "Ζεῦ πάτερ, εἴ ποτέ τίς τοι ἐν Ἄργεΐ περ πολυπύρῳ / ἢ βοὸς ἠ' ὄϊος κατὰ πίονα μηρία καίων / εὔχετο νοστῆσαι, σὺ δ' ὑπέσχεο καὶ κατένευσας, / τῶν μνῆσαι καὶ ἄμυνον, Ὀλύμπιε, νηλεὲς ἦμαρ, / μηδ' οὕτω Τρώεσσιν ἔα δάμνασθαι Ἀχαιούς" ("'Father Zeus, if ever in wheat-deep Argos one of us / burning before you the rich thigh pieces of sheep or ox prayed / he would come home again, and you nodded your head and assented, / remember this, Olympian, save us from the day without pity'").

[97] Iliad XIII 225–227: "... ἀλλά που οὕτω / μέλλει δὴ φίλον εἶναι ὑπερμενέϊ Κρονίωνι, / νωνύμνους ἀπολέσθαι ἀπ' Ἄργεος ἐνθάδ' Ἀχαιούς" ("'but rather / this way must be pleasurable to Kronos' son in his great strength, / that the Achaians must die here forgotten, and far from Argos'").

[98] Iliad XIV 69–70: "οὕτω που Διὶ μέλλει ὑπερμενέϊ φίλον εἶναι / νωνύμνους ἀπολέσθαι ἀπ' Ἄργεος ἐνθάδ' Ἀχαιούς" ("'then such is the way it must be pleasing to Zeus, who is too strong, / that the Achaians must die here forgotten and far from Argos'").

[99] Cf. Idaios' words in Iliad III 256–258.

[100] I.e. the Peloponnese.

[101] "'But of the possessions I carried away to our house from Argos / I am willing to give all back, and to add to these from my own goods.'"

here speaking in front of the Trojan assembly and wants to defend his behavior against the propositions of Antenor, implicitly reminds his internal audience that his personal actions against a single Achaean king, Menelaos, do not justify a massive expedition of the whole of Greece against Troy. The phrase ἡμέτερον δῶ 'to our house' (VII 363)[102] implicitly suggests that what he did was personal, and so should have been dealt with on an individual level. This being said, we see here how the *Iliad* has made spatial references integral to a hero's particular function within the trajectory of Trojan myth: Paris' moral deviation from Trojan norms in abducting Helen is reflected in his spatial mobility in myth, as opposed to the static spatiality of the other Trojans.

Hektor (*Iliad* VI 456–458)[103] and Pouludamas (XII 69–70)[104] use Argos to express their fears and hopes for the future. Where the former fears that Andromakhe may be enslaved in the event of his death and subsequent Achaean victory, the latter states his wish that the Achaeans will die νωνύμνους 'nameless', away from Argos.[105] This thematized use of Argos is intricately entwined with the unfolding of the Iliadic plot, since these two Trojans are associated with the fatal decision to invade the Achaean camp and stay too long away from the Skaian Gates and the protection of the city walls. In a masterful display of tragic irony, Hektor's spatialized fears about Andromakhe will begin to become true only when Pouludamas' spatialized hopes about the outcome of the war start to vanish: by having Hektor reject Pouludamas' prudent advice to bring the Trojan army back to the city (XII 211–229, XVIII 254–283), the tradition of the *Iliad* sets in motion a chain of events that will finally deprive Hektor of a return to the safe space of Troy and will ultimately lead Andromakhe to Greece as a slave.

Pylos

Pylos is attested twelve times in the *Iliad*, the majority (ten times) in character text.[106] Given that one of the chief Achaean leaders, the Gerenian horseman

---

[102] The plurality of ἡμέτερον 'ours' points rather to Menelaos and Helen than to the whole of Troy, for δῶ 'house' or 'chamber' can hardly bear this sense.

[103] "καί κεν ἐν Ἄργει ἐοῦσα πρὸς ἄλλης ἱστὸν ὑφαίνοις, / καί κεν ὕδωρ φορέοις Μεσσηΐδος ἢ' Ὑπερείης / πόλλ᾽ ἀεκαζομένη, κρατερὴ δ᾽ ἐπικείσετ᾽ ἀνάγκη" ("... and in Argos you must work at the loom of another, / and carry water from the spring Messeis or Hypereia, / all unwilling, but strong will be the necessity upon you").

[104] "ἦ τ᾽ ἂν ἐγώ γ᾽ ἐθέλοιμι καὶ αὐτίκα τοῦτο γενέσθαι, / νωνύμνους ἀπολέσθαι ἀπ᾽ Ἄργεος ἐνθάδ᾽ Ἀχαιούς" ("this is the way I would wish it, may it happen immediately / that the Achaians be destroyed here forgotten and far from Argos").

[105] Contrast Agamemnon's fear that the Achaean leaders will die "nameless" away from Argos (*Iliad* XIV 70 "νωνύμνους ἀπολέσθαι ἀπ᾽ Ἄργεος ἐνθάδ᾽ Ἀχαιούς"), where the same diction is employed.

[106] See Allen 1921:75–81.

Nestor, comes from that place, it is only natural that Pylos looms large in his speech.[107] In narrator text, Pylos is either modified by the formulaic epithets ἠγαθέη 'sacred' (I 252) and ἠμαθόεις 'sandy' (II 77), or is tied to a list of cities in the southwestern Peloponnese under Nestor's control (II 591–594). Speakers other than Nestor employ this place-name either with reference to Herakles' attack on the Pylians (V 397) or in the context of a list of neighboring cities offered by Agamemnon to Achilles (IX 149–153 = 291–295) as a recompense for the dishonor he suffered in *Iliad* I.[108]

Before exploring the function of Pylos in Nestor's speeches, I shall dwell for a moment both on *Iliad* II 595, where to the otherwise colorless reference to a series of cities is anchored a brief digression to the narrator Thamyris, and on *Iliad* V 397, where Dione's reference to Pylos is relevant to certain features pertaining to Nestor's epic past and Iliadic present. These two passages offer a background against which to locate the denser and more highly thematized use of Pylos by Nestor himself, for they help us reconsider topics like the authority of the ἀοιδός and the metaphorical function of Pylos.

Spatial metonymy

Although most commentators have focused their attention on the figure of the singer Thamyris in the brief digression that is appended to Dorion (*Iliad* II 594–600), the last city in the small list included in Nestor's catalogue, and on the role of Herakles in an attack against the Pylians (*Iliad* V 395–400) or against Hades, they have failed to observe that these two passages share a number of common features that stem from the metonymic function of Pylos in epic song: both Thamyris and Herakles,[109] who are the "protagonists" of these short excursuses, are related to the city of Oikhalia and king Eurutos. In particular, Thamyris is explicitly said to come from there, and Herakles, of course, is the one who sacked the city upon Eurutos' refusal to give him the hand of his daughter Iole after being defeated in marksmanship. Since the Oikhalia connection is an intriguing but also a troubling one, let us briefly discuss some of the problems connected with it:

The name Oikhalia is used for various cities in Greece (Thessaly [see *Iliad* II 730],[110] Euboea, and Messenia). Given that an epic tradition about the sack of Oikhalia by Herakles antedates the Homeric epics, the traditions of the *Iliad*

---

[107] On Nestor, see Vester 1956; Dickson 1995; Frame 2009.

[108] See M. Reichel 1994:204, who observes that the *Iliad* systematically builds on a discourse comparing the leader of the army, Agamemnon, with the wise counselor Nestor: "Keine andere Personenkombination wird in der *Ilias* so häufig realisiert."

[109] On the association between the Neleid saga and Herakles, see Vetta 2003:13–14n3.

[110] On Messenian and Thessalian Oikhalia, see Lenk, s.v. "Oichalia," RE XVII. 2:2099–2101.

and the *Odyssey* were confronted with the problem of adjusting this information to their subject matter. The result is a blurred picture, created by the older Thessalian lay and by certain changes that occurred when other figures of Thessalian origin were strongly tied to places in the south. This "mythical migration" of heroes and cities can certainly be seen in the case of Nestor, who was strongly tied to his Messenian kingdom (since the Homeric epics erased all relics of his grandfather Kretheus, king of Iolkos, who had gone south to Messenia from the area close to the Boebean lake in Thessaly). In *Iliad* II 591–596, we can see a clear manifestation of this fusing of two different lays: the Thracian singer Thamyris is explicitly said to be coming to the city of Dorion, which was situated in the Messenian kingdom of Nestor, from king Eurutos' palace in Oikhalia. This must be Thessalian Oikhalia, given (1) the probable confusion between Dorion in Messenia and Dotion in Thessaly,[111] (2) Hesiod's placing Thamyris' encounter with the Muses in the plain of Dotion close to the Boebean lake in Thessaly (*Catalogue of Women*, frr. 59.2 and 65 M-W), (3) Thessaly's being "a more likely place for bumping into the Muses than the south-western Peloponnese,"[112] and (4) that Iolkos (from where Nestor's grandfather Kretheus had descended to Messenia) is situated near the Boebean lake, both locations being under the control of Eumelos of Pherae (as explicitly mentioned in the Catalogue of Ships, *Iliad* II 711–715).[113] In *Odyssey* xxi 11–38, the preference for a Messenian Oikhalia is triggered by the need to trace Odysseus' bow to Eurutos. Odysseus meets Iphitos, Eurutos' son, in Ortilokhos' house in Messenia, where he has gone to recover the three hundred sheep some Messenians have stolen from Ithaka. It is only appropriate to discover Iphitos coming from Messenian Oikhalia, who was also going around in order to recover a dozen mares Herakles had stolen from Eurutos' palace. Given that Iphitos gives Odysseus the bow his father Eurutos bequeathed to him at his death, it becomes clear that the *Odyssey* not only transfers Oikhalia from Thessaly to Messenia but also takes Eurutos out of the picture altogether, making his son Iphitos the chief victim of Herakles. We need not postulate, as Schischwani does,[114] that the myth of the sack of Oikhalia by Herakles is post-Homeric, but simply that it did not suit the *Odyssey*'s plot requirements and perspective (for if Herakles had killed Eurutos and Iphitos after sacking Oikhalia, Iphitos would never have received the bow from his father, nor could he have passed it to Odysseus or offered hospitality to

---

[111] See Niese 1882:22–23; West 2011, 117 on *Iliad* II 594.

[112] Kirk 1985:216 on *Iliad* II 594–600.

[113] For all these arguments, see Kirk 1985:216 on *Iliad* II 594–600.

[114] Schischwani 1994:199–200 contra Krischer 1992. The view that the story of Iole and the sack of Oikhalia by Herakles were not known before Homer is a mistaken deduction from the information offered by some ancient and medieval authorities, see e.g. Eustathius in *Commentary on the Odyssey* 1593.29 and 1899.34.

Herakles; cf. *Odyssey* xxi 11–38).[115] It was for this reason that the tradition of the *Odyssey* opted for a Herakles as rustler rather than sacker of cities.

The digression on Thamyris, centered on the episode of his arrogant claims against the Muses, ends in the loss of his sight and his singing ability. Scholars have argued that this Thracian singer,[116] who resembles Thracian Orpheus, functions as a negative example of the fact that what the gods give, they can also take away.[117] This is certainly true, but it does not explain why this digression has been appended to a Messenian city under the control of Nestor in the Catalogue of Ships. This is an awkward extension of a subentry in the Catalogue, and moreover one that points to a link between Thamyris and Herakles, both connected to Thessalian Oikhalia. This connection is further strengthened by the fact that they were both (together with Orpheus) students of the mythical Linus, who taught the art of song and κιθάρα. According to Diodorus Siculus (*Library* 3.67), Herakles' musical education did not thrive, since he attacked his master who was continually trying to improve his student's skills. Although the information comes from a late author, we may wonder why Herakles, who is known not for his musical excellence but for his strength, formed part of a group of music students together with the two famous Thracians, Orpheus and Thamyras/Thamyris. Diodorus' text clearly associates Thamyras/Thamyris and Herakles through their improper conduct towards their musical masters. In Sophocles' *Thamyras*, the Thracian singer and musician suffers a breakdown and literally breaks his lyre, the symbol of his vocal and musical ability. Likewise, in

---

[115] See also *Odyssey* viii 223–228, where there is no mention of the sack of Oikhalia by Herakles, although this would have been an extremely appropriate place for it: "ἀνδράσι δὲ προτέροισιν ἐριζέμεν οὐκ ἐθελήσω, / οὔθ' Ἡρακλῆϊ οὔτ' Εὐρύτῳ Οἰχαλιῆϊ, / οἵ ῥα καὶ ἀθανάτοισιν ἐρίζεσκον περὶ τόξων. / τῷ ῥα καὶ αἶψ' ἔθανεν μέγας Εὔρυτος, οὐδ' ἐπὶ γῆρας / ἵκετ' ἐνὶ μεγάροισι· χολωσάμενος γὰρ Ἀπόλλων / ἔκτανεν, οὕνεκά μιν προκαλίζετο τοξάζεσθαι" ("'I should not care to compete with the men of the past, with Herakles, for instance, or Eurytus of Oechalia, who as bowmen even challenged the gods. In fact that was why the great Eurytus came to a sudden end and never lived to see old age in his home, but was killed by Apollo, whom he had offended by challenging him to a match'"). For the *Odyssey*, I am using the translation by Rieu (2003).

[116] So Willcock 1984:21. Despite the testimony of Heracleides Ponticus (fr. 157 Wehrli) that there was a *Titanomachy* assigned to Thamyris, it is much more likely that "Thamyris" is nothing more than a personification of a festal song, "an ancient Aeolic name for a special form of communal gathering, for supra-local meetings at a religious centre," as P. Wilson argues (2009:50–51). On the semantics of Thamyris, see Hesychius θ 90 θάμυρις· πανήγυρις, σύνοδος, where the meaning is "festal assembly or gathering," and θ 91 θαμυρίζει· ἀθροίζει, συνάγει; given that Hesychius used the adjective θαμυρός to describe highways (καὶ ὁδοὺς θαμυρὰς τὰς λεωφόρους· ἔστι δὲ καὶ κύριον ὄνομα), P. Wilson (2009:50–51) has argued that it suggests the "centripetal force of song, the gathering into union and collectivity," whereas the term οἴμη points to centrifugal paths of *aoidic* performance; on Thamyris, see also Kirk 1985:216 on *Iliad* II 595; Grandolini 1996:48–50; Brügger et al. 2003:192 on *Iliad* I 595; P. Wilson 2009:50n9.

[117] On Thamyris as a negative example, with emphasis on the function of his wandering as a cultural or *epistemic* process, see Dickson 1995:7–9.

Diodorus' narrative (3.67) Herakles uses his κιθάρα as a weapon with which he kills his master Linus, who had punished him with rods in the first place.[118] In fact, as Nagy has argued, Thamyris/Thamyras and Herakles represent examples of a "disintegration of identity," a "shattering of the self."[119] This "poetics of refraction"[120] is all the more significant in the case of Thamyris/Thamyras and Herakles, for these two figures represent two opposing cases with respect to musical skill, the former being the epitome of the talented singer-musician, the latter the paragon of the slow-to-learn and artistically incompetent hero. This observation is strengthened when we turn our attention to the way they use their musical instruments: in Sophocles' *Thamyras*, the gifted singer-musician himself breaks his lyre, whereas Herakles (in Diodorus' account) uses his κιθάρα as a weapon to kill Linus. Thamyras/Thamyris and Herakles are a case of *coincidentia oppositorum*. What is important for my argument is that there seems to have been some branch of a tradition that connected Thamyris with Herakles,[121] both through Oikhalia and through their arrogance, to be seen here in their shared negative behavior in the context of music and song. Perhaps the answer is that it is not only Thamyris and Herakles who are wandering as mythical figures, but also Oikhalia itself. Given that these wandering Oikhalias belong to regions within the Aeolian sphere,[122] one is tempted to interpret the entire digression as an abbreviated note on a rival epic tradition, whose figure-head Thamyris has been defeated by the Olympian Muses, the mouthpiece of Homeric epic.[123] We are in no position to decide about how this subtradition developed, but we can take our analysis a step further.

---

[118] Fr. **244, TrGF 4 [Radt].

[119] See Nagy 2009d:69–71, who traces this topic also in Sappho fr. 31 (Voigt).

[120] Nagy 2009d:69.

[121] According to Durante 1976:195–202, there was a religious association of Thamyridai or Thamuradai in Boeotia, and inscriptional evidence (SEG 32, no. 503, fourth century BC) makes it abundantly clear that there was a cult at Thespiae. In the same city, a statue of Thamyris (Pausanias 9.30.2 "already blind and holding a broken lyre") was erected in the third century BC by Philetaerus, son of Eumenes of Pergamon (BCH 26, 1902–1908:155–160); see P. Wilson 2009:51n17. An epigram by Honestus was added later (first century BC–first century AD), which featured Thamyris' rivalry and subsequent punishment by the Muses, as well as his confession of his mistake. Herakles is also at home in Boeotia, and especially, in Thebes; see Der Neue Pauly, s.v. "Herakles," 389.

[122] The reference to a Euboean Oikhalia is much later, since it was made by the νεώτεροι (cf. Aristonicus on *Iliad* II 596, vol. I, p. 311 [Erbse]), but see Pausanias 4.2.2., who refers to the rivalry over the location of Oikhalia by stating that the Thessalians place it at Eurution, whereas the Euboeans locate it in Skios, part of Eretria (on the basis of Creophylus' *Heraclea* and Hecataeus of Miletus); see Wilson 2009:53n21 and n24.

[123] See P. Wilson 2009; see also Martin 1989:229–230; Vetta 2003:21.

It is now time to turn our attention to the other passage in question, Dione's comforting speech to Aphrodite (*Iliad* V 382–400), and in particular to Herakles' Pylian war (*Iliad* V 395–400):

"τέτλαθι, τέκνον ἐμόν, καὶ ἀνάσχεο κηδομένη περ.
πολλοὶ γὰρ δὴ τλῆμεν Ὀλύμπια δώματ' ἔχοντες
ἐξ ἀνδρῶν, χαλέπ' ἄλγε' ἐπ' ἀλλήλοισι τιθέντες.
τλῆ μὲν Ἄρης, ὅτε μιν Ὧτος κρατερός τ' Ἐφιάλτης
παῖδες Ἀλωῆος, δῆσαν κρατερῷ ἐνὶ δεσμῷ·
χαλκέῳ δ' ἐν κεράμῳ δέδετο τρισκαίδεκα μῆνας.
καί νύ κεν ἔνθ' ἀπόλοιτο Ἄρης ἆτος πολέμοιο,
εἰ μὴ μητρυιή, περικαλλὴς Ἠερίβοια,
Ἑρμέᾳ ἐξήγγειλεν· ὃ δ' ἐξέκλεψεν Ἄρηα
ἤδη τειρόμενον, χαλεπὸς δέ ἑ δεσμὸς ἐδάμνα.
τλῆ δ' Ἥρη, ὅτε μιν κρατερὸς πάϊς Ἀμφιτρύωνος
δεξιτερὸν κατὰ μαζὸν ὀϊστῷ τριγλώχινι
βεβλήκει· τότε καί μιν ἀνήκεστον λάβεν ἄλγος.
τλῆ δ' Ἀΐδης ἐν τοῖσι πελώριος ὠκὺν ὀϊστόν,
εὖτέ μιν ωὑτὸς ἀνήρ, υἱὸς Διὸς αἰγιόχοιο,
ἐν Πύλῳ ἐν νεκύεσσι βαλὼν ὀδύνησιν ἔδωκεν·
αὐτὰρ ὃ βῆ πρὸς δῶμα Διὸς καὶ μακρὸν Ὄλυμπον
κῆρ ἀχέων, ὀδύνῃσι πεπαρμένος, αὐτὰρ ὀϊστός
ὤμῳ ἔνι στιβαρῷ ἠλήλατο, κῆδε δὲ θυμόν·"

"Have patience, my child, and endure it, though you be saddened.
For many of us who have our homes on Olympos endure things
from men, when ourselves we inflict hard pain on each other.
Ares had to endure it when the strong Ephialtes and Otos,
sons of Aloeus, chained him in bonds that were too strong for him,
and three months and ten he lay chained in the brazen cauldron;
and now might Ares, insatiable of fighting, have perished,
had not Eëriboia, their stepmother, the surpassingly lovely,
brought word to Hermes, who stole Ares away out of it
as he was growing faint and the hard bondage was breaking him.
Hera had to endure it when the strong son of Amphitryon
struck her beside the right breast with a tri-barbed arrow,
so that the pain he gave her could not be quieted. Hades
the gigantic had to endure with the rest the flying arrow,
when this self-same man, the son of Zeus of the aegis,
struck him among the dead men at Pylos, and gave him to agony;

but he went up to the house of Zeus and to tall Olympos
heavy at heart, stabbed through and through with pain, for the
  arrow
was driven into his heavy shoulder, and his spirit was suffering."

Iliad V 382–400

The role of Herakles in this passage is crucial, for we not only have ample early evidence of his involvement in a war in Pylos, but we are in a position to see that these verses were later on particularly associated with him in a fifth-century epic, Panyassis's *Heracleia* (fr. 16 Matthews = fr. 3, PEG 1):[124]

τλῆ μὲν Δημήτηρ, τλῆ δὲ κλυτὸς ἀμφιγυήεις,
τλῆ δὲ Ποσειδάων, τλῆ δ' ἀργυρότοξος Ἀπόλλων
ἀνδρὶ παρὰ θνητῶι †θητευσέμεν[125] εἰς ἐνιαυτόν,
τλῆ δὲ <καὶ> ὀβριμόθυμος Ἄρης ὑπὸ πατρὸς ἀνάγκης.

Demeter had to endure it and the famous cripple,
Poseidon had to endure it and Apollo of the silver bow
to spend a long year at the service of a mortal man
and Ares had to endure it ...

In *Iliad* V 397, the wounding of Hades is placed at Pylos, though it is not clear what the occasion was. Various explanations have been offered: (1) an attack on the Pylians, who had supported the city of Orkhomenos against Thebes (scholia T on *Iliad* XI 690–693), or when Herakles killed the sons of Neleus (cf. what Nestor says at *Iliad* XI 690–693 and the scholia bT on *Iliad* V 392–394), who were assisted by Poseidon, Hera, and Hades (D-scholia at *Iliad* XI 690); (2) a violent penetration into the Underworld, when Hades removed Kerberos (a view that Aristarchus may have supported, since he interpreted Πύλος as "gate [to the Underworld]").[126] The occasion's obscurity is irrelevant to our argument, for in both cases what is important is that Dione uses a paranarrative as an example of the ultimate destruction of the θεομάχοι.[127] Just as Herakles would be punished for his impiety towards the gods,[128] so, at some point, will Diomedes.[129]

In the *Iliad*, Thamyris and Herakles are associated not by way of their improper behavior in the field of musical ability, but through their arrogance

---

[124] See W. Kullmann 1956:13n1; Erbse 1961:162n10; Matthews 1974:93.

[125] θῆσαι μέγαν: Meineke 1843:363. Apollo serves Admetos for eight years, a μέγας ἐνιαυτός indeed.

[126] See Kirk 1990:101–102 on *Iliad* V 396–397.

[127] Alden 2000:126.

[128] See *Iliad* V 403–404.

[129] West 2011:160 on *Iliad* II 395–397; see also *Iliad* V 405–409.

towards the gods (Muses or Olympians). The *Iliad* attempts to present this behavior against the backdrop of Pylos,[130] which has a secondary, metonymic function in early epic as a "gate to the Underworld," given that Nestor's original function may have been "to restore mortals to life and light."[131] This figurative function of Pylos accords with Nestor's extremely positive presentation in the *Iliad*. Here is the great Pylian, whose sweet voice (λιγὺς ἀγορητής) and excellent speaking skills, his narrative authority and function as an ἀοιδός,[132] and his wisdom and moderation[133] are contrasted with the negative paradigms of Thamyris and Herakles,[134] who both stand for the sudden shift from dexterity and ability to arrogance and punishment and are treated as relics of a vanished rival tradition. Pylos is thus employed as a spatial metonym pointing to Nestor, the only son of Neleus who survived Herakles' attack on Pylos,[135] and the restrained and shrewd counselor whom the Muses respect.

Spacing the epic past

> The *Iliad* plays out the opposition between the two ideologies for its audience in proper epic fashion, through a paradigmatic story about the epic past, for, considered in context, the views that Nestor and Priam have of the past become the choice Achilles faces between *kleos* and *nostos* (return home).[136]

Turkeltaub's apt phrasing sheds light on the fact that Nestor not only "resurrects" the epic past but also creates the necessary background for Achilles' eventual choice. This is true, but I maintain that Nestor's special access to the epic past has a further role to play, especially since the paranarratives he systematically unravels are directly relevant to the exigencies of the Iliadic plot. What matters is not simply his ability to recall the epic past, but mainly, and tellingly so, *the kind of epic past* he systematically evokes. In other words, we need

---

[130] Notice that Oikhalia (as its name suggests) is a city destined "to be gone" (οἴχεσθαι); see Bölte, RE XVII 2:2099 s.v. "Oichalia"; P. Wilson 2009:54–55.

[131] See Frame 1978:93 passim. On Nestor's name, see also Mühlestein 1987:4–5, and Dickson 1995:25–38 on Nestor's name and on the formula λιγύς ἀγορητής.

[132] See Dickson 1995:47–100.

[133] See Dickson 1995:101–156.

[134] The "relation" between Nestor and Herakles goes much deeper, as Frame 2009:304–309 has shown. Their association in the Catalogue of Heroines in *Odyssey* xi is effected via the theme of the "separation between twins": Neleus-Pelias/Nestor-Periklumenos/Herakles-Iphikles/Castor-Pollux.

[135] See *Iliad* XI 692–693 "δώδεκα γὰρ Νηλῆος ἀμύμονος υἱέες ἦμεν, / τῶν οἶος λιπόμην, οἳ δ' ἄλλοι πάντες ὄλοντο" ("'For we who were the sons of lordly Neleus had been twelve, and now / I alone was left of these, and all the others had perished'"); see also Frame 1978:93, 2009:9–21.

[136] Turkeltaub 2010:149.

to study the particular kind of paranarrative he develops, but also to consider the effect that calling upon his epic past may have on the Iliadic narrative.[137] As we shall see, Pylos plays a particular role in this process, a role that is relevant to the poetics of space that the *Iliad* employs for other chief characters to whom Nestor's speech is addressed, directly or indirectly. Let us consider his first intervention in the quarrel between Agamemnon and Achilles:

"ὦ πόποι, ἦ μέγα πένθος Ἀχαιΐδα γαῖαν ἱκάνει.
ἦ κεν γηθήσαι Πρίαμος Πριάμοιό τε παῖδες,
ἄλλοι τε Τρῶες μέγα κεν κεχαροίατο θυμῷ,
εἰ σφῶϊν τάδε πάντα πυθοίατο μαρναμένοιιν,
οἳ περὶ μὲν βουλὴν Δαναῶν, περὶ δ᾽ ἐστὲ μάχεσθαι.
ἀλλὰ πίθεσθ᾽· ἄμφω δὲ νεωτέρω ἐστὸν ἐμεῖο.
ἤδη γάρ ποτ᾽ ἐγὼ καὶ ἀρείοσιν ἠέ περ ὑμῖν
ἀνδράσιν ὡμίλησα, καὶ οὔ ποτέ μ᾽ οἵ γ᾽ ἀθέριζον.
οὐ γάρ πω τοίους ἴδον ἀνέρας, οὐδὲ ἴδωμαι,
οἷον Πειρίθοόν τε Δρύαντά τε ποιμένα λαῶν
Καινέα τ᾽ Ἐξάδιόν τε καὶ ἀντίθεον Πολύφημον
Θησέα τ᾽ Αἰγεΐδην, ἐπιείκελον ἀθανάτοισιν·[138]
κάρτιστοι δὴ κεῖνοι ἐπιχθονίων τράφεν ἀνδρῶν·
κάρτιστοι μὲν ἔσαν καὶ καρτίστοις ἐμάχοντο,
φηρσὶν ὀρεσκῴοισι, καὶ ἐκπάγλως ἀπόλεσσαν.
καὶ μὲν τοῖσιν ἐγὼ μεθομίλεον ἐκ Πύλου ἐλθών,
τηλόθεν ἐξ ἀπίης γαίης· καλέσαντο γὰρ αὐτοί.
καὶ μαχόμην κατ᾽ ἔμ᾽ αὐτὸν ἐγώ· κείνοισι δ᾽ ἂν οὔ τις
τῶν οἳ νῦν βροτοί εἰσιν ἐπιχθόνιοι μαχέοιτο.
καὶ μέν μεο βουλέων ξύνιεν πείθοντό τε μύθῳ.
ἀλλὰ πίθεσθε καὶ ὕμμες, ἐπεὶ πείθεσθαι ἄμεινον·
μήτε σὺ τόνδ᾽ ἀγαθός περ ἐὼν ἀποαίρεο κούρην,
ἀλλ᾽ ἔα, ὥς οἱ πρῶτα δόσαν γέρας υἷες Ἀχαιῶν·
μήτε σύ, Πηλείδη, ἔθελ᾽ ἐριζέμεναι βασιλῆϊ
ἀντιβίην, ἐπεὶ οὔ ποθ᾽ ὁμοίης ἔμμορε τιμῆς
σκηπτοῦχος βασιλεύς, ᾧ τε Ζεὺς κῦδος ἔδωκεν.
εἰ δὲ σὺ καρτερός ἐσσι, θεὰ δέ σε γείνατο μήτηρ,
ἀλλ᾽ ὅδε φέρτερός ἐστιν, ἐπεὶ πλεόνεσσιν ἀνάσσει.

---

[137] See Alden 2000:76–82.

[138] With respect to *Iliad* I 265, which is considered an interpolation by West (1998–2000 ad loc.; 1999:186) and Latacz (2002:108 on *Iliad* I 265), see W. Kullmann's convincing remarks (2002:164–165) about the *Iliad*'s knowledge of Theseus. W. Kullmann explains the absence of this line in the *vulgata* and the papyri as due to the influence of Aristarchus (165).

Ἀτρείδη, σὺ δὲ παῦε τεὸν μένος· αὐτὰρ ἐγώ γε
λίσσομ' Ἀχιλλῆϊ μεθέμεν χόλον, ὃς μέγα πᾶσιν
ἕρκος Ἀχαιοῖσιν πέλεται πολέμοιο κακοῖο."

"Oh, for shame. Great sorrow comes on the land of Achaia.
Now might Priam and the sons of Priam in truth be happy,
and all the rest of the Trojans be visited in their hearts with gladness,
were they to hear all this wherein you two are quarrelling,
you, who surpass all Danaans in council, in fighting.
Yet be persuaded. Both of you are younger than I am.
Yes, in my time I have dealt with better men than
you are, and never once did they disregard me. Never
yet have I seen nor shall see again such men as these were,
men like Peirithoös, and Dryas, shepherd of the people,
Kaineus and Exadios, godlike Polyphemos,
or Theseus, Aigeus' son, in the likeness of the immortals.
These were the strongest generation of earth-born mortals,
the strongest, and they fought against the strongest, the beast men
living within the mountains, and terribly they destroyed them.
I was of the company of these men. Coming from Pylos,
a long way from a distant land, since they had summoned me.
And I fought single-handed, yet against such men no one
of the mortals now alive upon earth could do battle. And also
these listened to the counsels I gave and heeded my bidding.
Do you also obey, since to be persuaded is better.
You, great man that you are, yet do not take the girl away
but let her be, a prize as the sons of the Achaians gave her
first. Nor, son of Peleus, think to match your strength with
the king, since never equal with the rest is the portion of honour
of the sceptred king to whom Zeus gives magnificence. Even
though you are the stronger man, and the mother who bore you was
    immortal,
yet is this man greater who is lord over more than you rule.
Son of Atreus, give up your anger; even I entreat you
to give over your bitterness against Achilleus, he who
stands as a great bulwark of battle over the Achaians."

Iliad I 254–284

Nestor's narrative about his participation in the war between the Lapithai and the
Centaurs, which started because of the rape of Hippodameia and other women

by the Centaurs during her wedding with Peirithous, bears striking similarities to the situations in both *Iliad* I and *Iliad* IX. Given that the same story is referred to in *Odyssey* xxi 295–304, we need to deal with all three passages as forming the mythical backdrop against which Nestor's paranarrative is developed:

> "ὦ γέρον, οὔ τι ψεῦδος ἐμὰς ἄτας κατέλεξας.
> ἀασάμην, οὐδ' αὐτὸς ἀναίνομαι. ἀντί νυ πολλῶν
> λαῶν ἐστιν ἀνὴρ ὅν τε Ζεὺς κῆρι φιλήσῃ,
> ὡς νῦν τοῦτον ἔτισε, δάμασσε δὲ λαὸν Ἀχαιῶν.
> ἀλλ' ἐπεὶ ἀασάμην φρεσὶ λευγαλέῃσι πιθήσας,
> ἂψ ἐθέλω ἀρέσαι δόμεναί τ' ἀπερείσι' ἄποινα."

> "Aged sir, this was no lie when you spoke of my madness.
> I was mad, I myself will not deny it. Worth many
> fighters is that man whom Zeus in his heart loves, as now
> he has honoured this man and beaten down the Achaian people.
> But since I was mad, in the persuasion of my heart's evil,
> I am willing to make all good, and give back gifts in abundance."

Iliad IX 115–120

> "οἶνος καὶ Κένταυρον, ἀγακλυτὸν Εὐρυτίωνα,
> ἄασ' ἐνὶ μεγάρῳ μεγαθύμου Πειριθόοιο,
> ἐς Λαπίθας ἐλθόνθ'· ὁ δ' ἐπεὶ φρένας ἄασεν οἴνῳ,
> μαινόμενος κάκ' ἔρεξε δόμον κάτα Πειριθόοιο·
> ἥρωας δ' ἄχος εἷλε, διὲκ προθύρου δὲ θύραζε
> ἕλκον ἀναΐξαντες, ἀπ' οὔατα νηλέϊ χαλκῷ
> ῥῖνάς τ' ἀμήσαντες· ὁ δὲ φρεσὶν ᾗσιν ἀασθείς
> ἤϊεν ἣν ἄτην ὀχέων ἀεσίφρονι θυμῷ.
> ἐξ οὗ Κενταύροισι καὶ ἀνδράσι νεῖκος ἐτύχθη,
> οἳ δ' αὐτῷ πρώτῳ κακὸν εὕρετο οἰνοβαρείων."

"Remember Eurytion the famous Centaur! It was the wine that stupefied him in brave Peirithous' palace, during his visit to the Lapithae. Stupefied with drink he perpetrated that outrage in Peirithous' very home. His hosts leaped up in anger, dragged him to the porch and threw him out of doors; but not before they had ruthlessly sliced his ears and nose off with a knife. He staggered away stupefied, carrying the burden of his folly in his darkened mind. That was the beginning of the feud between Centaurs and men. But he was the first to suffer, and he brought his troubles on himself by getting drunk."

Odyssey xxi 295–304

The story told by Nestor in *Iliad* I 254–284 has been regarded as an ad hoc invention, an αὐτοσχεδίασμα the poet of the *Iliad* made up in order to supply Agamemnon and Achilles with an example of Nestor's authority and status, and thus persuade them to listen to his advice and put an end to their quarrel. Conversely, Kirk seems to consider the possibility that this paranarrative may be due to Nestor's Thessalian origins,[139] a view that is further supported by two points that have escaped scholarly attention:

First, the relevant episode in *Odyssey* xxi 295–304 plays on Eurution's drunkenness (295 οἶνος, 304 οἰνοβαρείων), which led to his ἄτη (296 ἄασ(ε), 297 ἄασεν, 301 ἀασθείς, 302 ἄτην), and is significant not only because Nestor's traditional epithet (λιγύς) is a term of sweetness, often employed together with the term ἡδυεπής,[140] whose first part (ἡδυ- 'sweet') is regularly used for wine (οἶνος),[141] but also because this is the kind of diction employed in the quarrel between Agamemnon and Achilles in *Iliad* I 225 (οἰνοβαρές) and in *Iliad* IX 116 and 119, when Agamemnon acknowledges his ἄτη to Nestor (ἀασάμην).

Second, since the diction employed in *Odyssey* xxi 303–304 is reminiscent of the beginning of an epic poem: ἐξ οὗ Κενταύροισι καὶ ἀνδράσι νεῖκος ἐτύχθη, / οἳ δ' αὐτῷ πρώτῳ κακὸν εὕρετο οἰνοβαρείων,[142] it can be argued that Nestor is about to point to a song tradition that is similar to the Trojan one (which also began with strife at a wedding and is based on the rape or abduction of a woman), but in which the side he supported was not suffering from internal strife. In other words, evoking Nestor's coming from Pylos to assist the Lapithai makes it relevant to the situation of Achilles, who was not bound by oath but whose arrival and presence in Troy is of crucial importance for winning the war. In Nestor's parable in *Iliad* I, Pylos becomes an "anti-Phthia," a space he never explicitly says that he wishes to return to, Achilles-like, but one that he left to participate in various exploits and so build up his heroic persona. In this

---

[139] Nestor is the grandson of Kretheus, who immigrated from Thessaly to the southwestern Peloponnese; see Cauer 1895:233 ff.; Valeton 1915:90–93.

[140] E.g. *Iliad* I 248–249 ἡδυεπὴς ἀνόρουσε, λιγὺς Πυλίων ἀγορητής, / τοῦ καὶ ἀπὸ γλώσσης μέλιτος γλυκίων ῥέεν αὐδή ("the fair-spoken rose up, the lucid speaker of Pylos, / from whose lips the streams of words ran sweeter than honey"). The adjective ἡδύς may point to a kind of diction used by the type of wise man Nestor embodies. His language after all contains multiple features of the language of seers; cf. Hesiod *Melampodia* fr. 273 M-W ἡδὺ δὲ καὶ τὸ πυθέσθαι, ὅσα θνητοῖσιν ἔνειμαν / ἀθάνατοι, δειλῶν τε καὶ ἐσθλῶν τέκμαρ ἐναργές ("and it is sweet too to learn the clear distinguishing mark / of bad and good things that the immortals have assigned to mortals"; fr. 210 Most), fr. 274 M-W [ἡδύ ἐστιν] ... ἐν δαιτὶ καὶ εἰλαπίνηι τεθαλυίηι / τέρπεσθαι μύθοισιν, ἐπὴν δαιτὸς κορέσωνται ("[it is sweet] ... in the feast and blooming banquet / to take pleasure in stories, when they have their fill of the feast"; fr. 209 Most), and Löffler 1963:40–41.

[141] See Dickson 1995:27–35.

[142] The prepositional phrase ἐξ οὗ and the numeral πρῶτος are used in the proem of the *Iliad* (I 6 ἐξ οὗ δὴ τὰ πρῶτα διαστήτην ἐρίσαντε) to define a point of departure for the epic plot; νεῖκος is a standard epic term for "quarrel," almost a synonym for ἔρις.

way, Pylos functions as Nestor's epic past, which the Iliadic tradition deftly employs in order to counterbalance Achilles' Phthia. Yet in a supreme manifestation of unity, the *Iliad* makes both Phthia and Pylos stand for a "menace" to its unfolding plot, the former representing the place Achilles threatens to return to, the latter the place Nestor offers as a "narrative temptation" that lures the tradition of the *Iliad* toward the narrative realm of a "regular" Trojan War epic— one that features a compromised Achilles, and not the epic of his unappeasable wrath. Nestor's role in *Iliad* II, as mediator between the army and Agamemnon, is consistent with his support for a Trojan War epic that would have ended at once in the event of an Achaean mutiny.

Nestor's compromising tactics will of course fail,[143] but given his supreme knowledge of the past, they become a kind of threat to the Iliadic plot.[144] Seen within the wider perspective of typical motifs that permeate archaic epic, Nestor is trying to deprive Agamemnon and Achilles, and by extension the *Iliad*, of its most elementary motif of νεῖκος 'strife'. In other words, a potential compromise between Agamemnon and Achilles *at such an early point in the plot* would have brought the *Iliad* to an end and given its place to another epic song about the Trojan War. The memory of the epic past that Nestor summons to the *Iliad* is a threat to the continuation of the Iliadic tradition and to the development of its plot.[145] By endowing Nestor with the ability to return to his epic past,[146] the Iliadic tradition creates the illusion of a potential "return" to a song about the Trojan War not based on the theme of Achilles' unquenchable wrath that is so crucial for Iliadic poetics, a song that is not and could never have been endorsed by the *Iliad*.

Wandering epic

In contrast with other paranarratives that Nestor regularly employs as examples, his long digression about the war against the Epeians (*Iliad* XI 670–761) is not, at least entirely, linked to the situation at hand.[147] Bölte argues for the

---

[143] On the relationship between Nestor and Agamemnon, one of those most frequently employed in the *Iliad*, and the constant failure of Nestor's advice, see M. Reichel 1994:204–206.

[144] On misdirection, see Morrison 1992a; 1992b:61–71; Rengakos 1999.

[145] In this light, one can see that the strong poetological overtones of Nestor's embedded narratives are employed either in support of the Iliadic tradition, when rival singers like Thamyris are involved, or against it, when his epic past is reconstructed as the backdrop for evaluating the choice of Achilles. Since metapoetic allusions and epic cross-references are almost the default mode of Nestor's epic diction, it comes as no surprise that Pylos, with which he is so closely associated, is used as metapoetic space.

[146] Cf. the derivation of his name from the root *νεσ- 'to return home' (: νέομαι).

[147] W. Kullmann 1960:96. On the so-called *Nestoris, see also Schadewaldt 1966:17–20.

existence of a Pylian epic ("ein Stück Heldendichtung"),[148] featuring a now lost version of a "border war" between Pylians and Epeians.[149] In his view, the detailed knowledge of topographical features implies the existence of a local epic lay, which may have *migrated* together with the Pylians from Messenia to Colophon in Asia Minor, "where the memory of their old home always remained alive."[150] Traditional themes like that of the "cattle raid"[151] were then combined with the Iliadic story line,[152] and Nestor together with his father Neleus became associated with the old lay, so that Pylos could represent the contrast with Achilles' Phthia. In particular, Nestor presents himself as keen to fight by leaving Pylos even against his father's will, and ties this reminiscence of the past to his visit to Phthia with Odysseus to bring Achilles to Troy. He is thus able to offer a counternarrative to the way Achilles refers to Phthia in the *Iliad*. Nestor's Pylos becomes, so to speak, inscribed on his version of Phthia, as a space that the epic hero has to leave in order to win κλέος.

All this being said, it can be argued that Nestor uses Pylos as Achilles' anti-Phthia, a polar opposite to the way Achilles interprets and imagines his homeland. By fostering a narrative that promotes the idea that the epic hero must leave his homeland to undertake heroic exploits, Nestor constructs his distant past in a way that runs counter to Achilles' spatial grammar. Seen from the vantage point of the homeland as an epic figure's notional *origo*, Nestor's heroic deixis is spatialized centrifugally, whereas Achilles' is mapped centripetally.[153]

Since the name *Nestor* originally meant "the one who brings [the war-folk] safely home,"[154] we find further support for the claim that the *Iliad* systematically employs the spaces of Phthia and Pylos in a way that reverses the fate of the two heroes. Achilles, who initially desires to return home since he bears no grudge against the Trojans, who have never stolen his cattle, will die at Troy (deprived of a νόστος comparable to that of Odysseus and Nestor), whereas

---

[148] Bölte 1934:345.

[149] See A. Lang 1906:287.

[150] Bölte 1934:346.

[151] On cattle raiding, see Lincoln 1976 and 1981. The wider implications of cattle raiding can be better grasped when set against the importance of cattle wealth. According to McInerney, "cattle wealth is acceptable since it activates a set of institutions that establish good relations with the gods (sacrifice) and between humans, whether as a community (feast) or even with strangers (*xenia*)" (2010:90).

[152] Bölte (1934:345) thinks that Herakles, Augeias, Agamede, etc. were added to the older Pylian lay at a later stage, but their ties to Elis and even older material pertaining to the theme of "stealing the Sun's cattle" point in the opposite direction; see Frame 1978:88–90.

[153] See Felson 2004:257n11.

[154] On Achilles and "return," see Frame 1978:116–124; on the etymology of Nestor's name, see Frame 1978:93 passim; Mühlestein 1987:4–5; Dickson 1995:25–38. Frame (2009:23–102) summarizes previous bibliography and offers new insights.

Nestor, who constantly unfolds narratives of an epic past (in which he features as an epic hero who leaves his homeland, though he does not need to, and wins κλέος) and in the *Iliad* never wishes to return home, will finally be the one who will have a safe and untroubled return.

The theme of βοηλασίη 'cattle-raid' constitutes a typical motif in archaic epic.[155] In *Iliad* XI 670–761, Nestor refers to the cattle-raid he led against the Eleans, in retaliation for their unpaid debts to the Pylians. Nestor presents himself as participating in the Pylians' defensive stand against the counter-attacking Epeians. The motif of the "father preventing his son from going to war" that Nestor employs (*Iliad* XI 717–718) would probably have helped an ancient audience realize that his epic past stands against that of Achilles (as presented in the *Iliad*), whom Peleus[156] sent to Troy wholeheartedly. As noted earlier,[157] this version, which was also that of the *Cypria* tradition, deviates from another one, which we may call the D-scholium tradition, which features Thetis' (and in one version Peleus') effort to hide Achilles in Skyros at the palace of king Lukomedes. Given that the tradition fostered by the *Iliad* presents Nestor's epic past in contrast to Achilles' present and past (with respect to his father), and that Nestor's role in the cattle-raid against the Epeians and the subsequent defense of Pylos reflects his figurative role as "rescuer of the Sun's cattle,"[158] it supplies us with a reasonable explanation for the kind of narrative the king of Pylos presents. In fact, the cattle-raiding motif that is built into the deep structure of Nestor's mythical persona, owing to his metaphorical role of rescuer,[159] becomes closely associated with Pylos, just as Achilles' doom is intertwined with Phthia. Although both of them are somehow linked to death—the former coming from a geographical area suggesting the gates of Hades (Πύλαι < πύλος 'gate'), the latter from the land of "perishing" (Φθία < φθίνω 'perish')[160]—they are treated differently.

Space is thus individually thematized and replete with strong Iliadic overtones: the "out there" of locations in Greece is thus brought into the "here" of the characters in Troy, and is further grafted onto the Iliadic presentation of their epic personas. Pylos, therefore, spatializes Nestor's past and becomes the emblem of a heroic narrative that stands in contrast to Achilles' position in the *Iliad*, and especially his ironic illusion of return.

---

[155] See Harrauer 1999.

[156] *Iliad* IX 252–258; IX 438–443; XI 783–784.

[157] See the section "In the name of the father: Phthia and Peleus," above.

[158] Frame 1978:86–95.

[159] See McInerney 2010:99, who argues that the presentation of Nestor as part of "an unending cycle of cattle thefts" is also used by Homer as an effective means for exploring "the limitations of the heroic code" that is set against a vicious circle of "tit-for-tat violence."

[160] See Nagy 1979:174–185.

Boeotian Thebes

The antiquity and significance of the city of Thebes in Boeotia is mainly responsible for its enormous importance in early Greek myth and archaic epic poetry. Thebes was closely associated with both the story of Oedipus and the great Theban wars (the expedition of the Seven and the sack of Thebes by the Epigonoi) and with Herakles, the son of Zeus and Alkmene and a major hero with an entire saga of his own.[161] While a whole part of the Epic Cycle was devoted to Thebes (*Oedipodia, Thebais, Epigoni*), in the case of Herakles' mythic past we may postulate that he was not particularly associated with a single epic tradition. This being said, we can see that we are dealing with two separate branches of myth, a Theban one "inserted" into the plot of the *Iliad* (and the Homeric epics in general) by means of a song tradition in epic form,[162] and another known to Homeric epic not necessarily, or solely, through epic but from the large storehouse of mythical material pertaining to the legend of Herakles, which was widely diffused during the archaic period. The variety of sources, of course, explains only partly why Thebes looms large in the *Iliad* mainly through the Theban wars, and not through Herakles. Other possible reasons for this deliberate Homeric choice may be that Thebes was considered in the archaic period a "first Troy," and that the core of its myth, twice involving the recruitment and expeditions of entire armies, as well as the lack of a single protagonist, activated strong analogies with the Trojan War saga.[163] Moreover, and as early as Hesiod (*Works and Days* 156–165), the Greeks regarded these two great war traditions (Thebes and Troy) as the ones that had shaped their past in a truly emblematic way, culminating in the end of the generation of heroes:

> αὐτὰρ ἐπεὶ καὶ τοῦτο γένος κατὰ γαῖα κάλυψεν,
> αὖτις ἔτ' ἄλλο τέταρτον ἐπὶ χθονὶ πουλυβοτείρη
> Ζεὺς Κρονίδης ποίησε, δικαιότερον καὶ ἄρειον,
> ἀνδρῶν ἡρώων θεῖον γένος, οἳ καλέονται
> ἡμίθεοι, προτέρη γενεὴ κατ' ἀπείρονα γαῖαν.
> καὶ τοὺς μὲν πόλεμός τε κακὸς καὶ φύλοπις αἰνή

---

[161] Although Thebes was also the birthplace of Dionysus, the extremely limited references to this god in the Homeric epics have rendered any epic exploitation of this mythical aspect marginal; on Dionysus in the Homeric epics, see Privitera 1970; Davies 2000; Tsagalis 2008b:1–29.

[162] According to Burkert 1981:32, "a Theban tale in oral poetry [existed], besides and sometimes interfering with the Trojan tales."

[163] On the possible influence of the *Thebais* (and the *Oedipodia*) on the Homeric epics, see Torres-Guerra 1995; W. Kullmann 2002:167–169, 2011:19n16, 24. On Theban traces in Homer, see Barker and Christensen 2008; Ebbott 2010; Slatkin 2011:99–119. On a metapoetic reading of the race of heroes, see Tsagalis 2009:146–147. See also Scodel 2012, who argues that a poet (like Hesiod) criticizes other traditions "only when such criticism suits his other purposes" (502).

τοὺς μὲν ὑφ' ἑπταπύλῳ Θήβῃ, Καδμηίδι γαίῃ,
ὤλεσε μαρναμένους μήλων ἕνεκ' Οἰδιπόδαο,
τοὺς δὲ καὶ ἐν νήεσσιν ὑπὲρ μέγα λαῖτμα θαλάσσης
ἐς Τροίην ἀγαγὼν Ἑλένης ἕνεκ' ἠυκόμοιο.

When the earth covered up this race too, Zeus, Cronus' son, made another one in turn upon the bounteous earth, a fourth one, more just and superior, the godly race of men-heroes, who are called demigods, the generation before our own on the boundless earth. Evil war and dread battle destroyed these, some under seven-gated Thebes in the land of Cadmus while they fought for the sake of Oedipus' sheep, others brought in boats over the great gulf of the sea to Troy for the sake of fair-haired Helen.

Hesiod *Works and Days* 156–165[164]

Thebes is thus used in the *Iliad* as a spatiotemporal linchpin, bridging mainly the epic past of the Theban tradition with the Trojan War myth. In the case of the weaker connection with Herakles, Thebes becomes synonymous with a tradition of deception and bewilderment that serves as a useful parallel to the theme of μῆνις that stands at the very core of the *Iliad*.

Rival spaces

The Iliadic tradition consistently employs the expedition of the Seven as a backdrop for the Achaean expedition against Troy. In particular, heroes who belong exclusively to the Trojan War tradition (Agamemnon) accuse heroes who have migrated to this tradition from the Theban one (Diomedes) of being inferior to their fathers (Tudeus). The sons of the Seven (Sthenelos) respond by reminding the audience that it was the Epigonoi who sacked Thebes, and not the Seven, who "died of their own headlong stupidity" (*Iliad* IV 409 κεῖνοι δὲ σφετέρῃσιν ἀτασθαλίῃσιν ὄλοντο).[165]

---

[164] Translation by Most 2006.

[165] The strong metapoetic tone of this passage may be seen in the emblematic use of the same expression for Odysseus' comrades in *Odyssey* i 7. Diomedes refers to his father Tudeus in *Iliad* VI 222–223 by saying that he does not remember him, since he left when Diomedes was very young for Thebes, where the Achaean army was defeated ("'Τυδέα δ' οὐ μέμνημαι, ἐπεί μ' ἔτι τυτθὸν ἐόντα / κάλλιφ', ὅτ' ἐν Θήβῃσιν ἀπώλετο λαὸς Ἀχαιῶν'"). This may be one more manifestation of the traditional motif of "father goes to war and leaves behind his very young son," which is constantly employed in epic tradition: Odysseus and Telemakhos, Agamemnon and Orestes, Achilles and Neoptolemos. I do not see any reason to believe that this motif is particularly filtered by the Theban tradition or that an ancient audience would have associated it with a single epic hero.

In *Iliad* IV 376–379, Agamemnon explicitly links Thebes with the Theban wars, and in particular with the recruitment of the army by Poluneikes. Given that his speech is addressed to Diomedes, Agamemnon carefully selects an early phase of the first Theban war, in which Diomedes' father Tudeus arrived at Mycenae with Poluneikes to recruit forces for the expedition.

"ἤτοι μὲν γὰρ ἄτερ πολέμου εἰσῆλθε Μυκήνας
ξεῖνος ἅμ' ἀντιθέῳ Πολυνείκεϊ λαὸν ἀγείρων·
οἳ δὲ τότ' ἐστρατόωνθ' ἱερὰ πρὸς τείχεα Θήβης,
καί ῥα μάλα λίσσοντο δόμεν κλειτοὺς ἐπικούρους."

"Once on a time he came, but not in war, to Mykenai
with godlike Polyneikes, a guest and a friend, assembling
people, since these were attacking the sacred bastions of Thebe,
and much they entreated us to grant him renowned companions."

Iliad IV 376–379

Agamemnon's criticism of Diomedes by alluding to his father's Theban past is answered again in Theban terms, since Sthenelos reminds him of the second Theban war, the successful expedition of the Epigonoi:

τὸν δ' υἱὸς Καπανῆος ἀμείψατο κυδαλίμοιο·
"Ἀτρεΐδη, μὴ ψεύδε', ἐπιστάμενος σάφα εἰπεῖν.
ἡμεῖς τοι πατέρων μέγ' ἀμείνονες εὐχόμεθ' εἶναι·
ἡμεῖς καὶ Θήβης ἕδος εἵλομεν ἑπταπύλοιο,
παυρότερον λαὸν ἀγαγόνθ' ὑπὸ τεῖχος ἄρειον,
πειθόμενοι τεράεσσι θεῶν καὶ Ζηνὸς ἀρωγῇ·
κεῖνοι δὲ σφετέρῃσιν ἀτασθαλίῃσιν ὄλοντο."

But the son of Kapaneus the glorious answered him, saying:
"Son of Atreus, do not lie when you know the plain truth.
We two claim we are better men by far than our fathers.
We did storm the seven-gated foundation of Thebe
though we led fewer people beneath a wall that was stronger.
We obeyed the signs of the gods and the help Zeus gave us,
while those others died of their own headlong stupidity."

Iliad IV 403–409

In Sthenelos' reply, Thebes becomes the litmus test for the excellence of the younger generation of the Epigonoi. This time, though, there are five important differences from the earlier expedition undertaken by their fathers: (1) success versus failure;[166] (2) smaller versus larger army; (3) stronger versus weaker walls; (4) yielding to divine advice and accepting Zeus' help; (5) not committing any wrongdoings. According to Sthenelos, these five features show that the Epigonoi were far better (*Iliad* IV 405 ἡμεῖς τοι πατέρων μέγ' ἀμείνονες εὐχόμεθ' εἶναι).

What we see at work here is that different speakers focalize Thebes according to their own points of view, so as to promote their importance as heroes and refute any claims made against their warrior skills. Given that the first and second Theban wars, that is, the expeditions of the Seven and the Epigonoi, were emblematically represented by the *Thebais* and the *Epigoni*, it can be plausibly argued that the tradition of the *Iliad* reminds its audience that some of its principle heroes, like Diomedes and Sthenelos, have come to the *Iliad* from another epic tradition.[167] Seen from this perspective, Agamemnon's accusations against Diomedes acquire a metaliterary tone, since the king of Mycenae becomes, temporarily, the spokesman for the Iliadic tradition, which complains that the "Theban" heroes it has welcomed into its plot are not showing themselves to be the kind of warriors they should. By blaming Diomedes and praising his father Tudeus, Agamemnon lets the audience entertain the possibility that the Achaeans would be better off if Tudeus had come to Troy, that is, if the great heroes of the *Thebais* were alive and had accompanied him to the war. Like Nestor,[168] Agamemnon points to a more remote past, to a generation that has now disappeared from the face of the earth, and was better than the present one.

Sthenelos' reaction is equally telling. His five arguments are directed not only toward the tradition of the Seven but also, and significantly so, against Agamemnon and the *Iliad*: (1) unlike the Seven and the Achaeans (at least until now), the Epigonoi succeeded and sacked Thebes; (2) unlike the Seven and Agamemnon, they mustered not a huge army but a smaller and more effective one; (3) unlike the Seven and the Achaeans, they attacked a city whose walls had been improved and made stronger; (4) unlike Agamemnon's arrogance (and his

---

[166] Diomedes (*Iliad* XIV 114) is aware of the death of his father Tudeus in Thebes.

[167] See also Slatkin 2011:112.

[168] The superiority of the heroes of the past to those of the present, which Nestor systematically exploits, reiterates within the race of heroes the very tenets of the generational decay that features in the Hesiodic myth of the five races (*Works and Days* 109–201). What was there an intergenerational distinction operates here on an intragenerational level, i.e. within the race of heroes. This internally determined decay of the heroes is defined not only temporally but also spatially. As Nestor's various embedded narratives make clear, none of these heroes of the past belongs to the mythical geography of Homeric tradition or of the previous generation of heroes from whom the Homeric heroes were born. Nestor's narrative digressions evoke or reconstruct for all audiences, internal and external alike, a whole nexus of epic traditions rivaling Homeric epic, traditions which the *Iliad* has effectively erased.

quarrel with Achilles), they heeded the signs sent by the gods and thus gained the help of Zeus; and finally, (5) unlike Agamemnon they did not perish by their own wrongdoing. The intertextual force of Sthenelos' answer is enormous, since he is virtually telling Agamemnon and the audience that the tradition of the *Epigoni*, in which he truly belongs, outdoes not only that of the *Thebais* but also that of the *Iliad*.[169]

The two Theban wars and the poetic traditions embodying them provided the backdrop against which the Iliadic tradition could place its own subject matter. Thebes delineated a twofold space symbolizing failure, arrogance, and divine disregard (*Thebais*) on the one hand, and success, moderation, and respect for the gods (*Epigoni*) on the other. Since the epic oscillated between these two traditions, epitomized in certain heroic figures that the Iliadic tradition constantly referred to (Tudeus, Diomedes, and Sthenelos), Thebes was especially appropriate for intertextual cross-referencing and subsequent evaluation of the *Iliad*'s narrative choices and status of its heroes, against a double backdrop summarizing what *could* and what *would* happen in an expedition.

In *Iliad* V 801–808 and X 283–290 respectively, Athena and Diomedes refer to Thebes in the context of Tudeus' embassy to the Kadmeians, which ends with Tudeus' double victory, first within Thebes and then in an ambush set against him on his way home, by fifty Thebans under the command of Maion and Poluphontes. The same topic appears in XXIII 677–680, where we are told that Mekisteus, one of the Seven, having visited Thebes for the funeral of Oedipus,[170] defeated all the Kadmeians.

> "Τυδεύς τοι μικρὸς μὲν ἔην δέμας, ἀλλὰ μαχητής·
> καί ῥ' ὅτε πέρ μιν ἐγὼ πολεμίζειν οὐκ εἴασκον
> οὐδ' ἐκπαιφάσσειν, ὅτε τ' ἤλυθε νόσφιν Ἀχαιῶν
> ἄγγελος ἐς Θήβας πολέας μετὰ Καδμείωνας·
> δαίνυσθαί μιν ἄνωγον ἐνὶ μεγάροισιν ἔκηλον,
> αὐτὰρ ὃ θυμὸν ἔχων ὃν καρτερόν, ὡς τὸ πάρος περ,
> κούρους Καδμείων προκαλίζετο, πάντα δ' ἐνίκα
> ῥηϊδίως· τοίη οἱ ἐγὼν ἐπιτάρροθος ἦα."

---

[169] See Slatkin 2011:114–115, who argues that in his final speech in the poem, Diomedes tries to restore the importance of Tudeus by emphasizing his genealogy and military prowess (*Iliad* XIV 110–127).

[170] According to Hesiod's *Catalogue of Women* (fr. 192 M-W = scholium T on *Iliad* XXIII 679b [Erbse]), Argeia, the daughter of Adrastos, went together with others (the ἄλλοις of the scholium indicates that men were certainly among them, and this information may be compatible with *Iliad* XXIII 679–680 about Mekisteus; contrast Erbse's note in the critical apparatus: "fort. melius σὺν ταῖς ἀδελφαῖς") to the funeral of Oedipus at Thebes.

"Since Tydeus was a small man of stature, but he was a fighter.
Even on that time when I would not consent to his fighting
nor drawing men's eyes, when he went by himself without the
    Achaians
as a messenger to Thebe among all the Kadmeians,
then I invited him to feast at his ease in their great halls;
even so, keeping that heart of strength that was always within him
he challenged the young men of the Kadmeians, and defeated all of
    them
easily; such a helper was I who stood then beside him."

Iliad V 801–808

δεύτερος αὖτ' ἠρᾶτο βοὴν ἀγαθὸς Διομήδης·
"κέκλυθι νῦν καὶ ἐμεῖο, Διὸς τέκος, Ἀτρυτώνη·
σπεῖό μοι ὡς ὅτε πατρὶ ἅμ' ἕσπεο Τυδέϊ δίῳ
ἐς Θήβας, ὅτε τε πρὸ Ἀχαιῶν ἄγγελος ἤει,
τοὺς δ' ἄρ' ἐπ' Ἀσωπῷ λίπε χαλκοχίτωνας Ἀχαιούς,
αὐτὰρ ὃ μειλίχιον μῦθον φέρε Καδμείοισιν
κεῖσ'· ἀτὰρ ἂψ ἀπιὼν μάλα μέρμερα μήσατο ἔργα
σὺν σοί, δῖα θεά, ὅτε οἱ πρόφρασσα παρέστης."

Diomedes of the great war cry spoke in prayer after him:
"Hear me also, Atrytone, daughter of great Zeus.
Come with me now as you went with my father, brilliant Tydeus,
into Thebes, when he went with a message before the Achaians,
and left the bronze-armoured Achaians beside Asopos
while he carried a word of friendship to the Kadmeians
in that place; but on his way back he was minded to grim deeds
with your aid, divine goddess, since you stood in goodwill beside
    him."

Iliad X 283–290

Εὐρύαλος δέ οἱ οἶος ἀνίστατο, ἰσόθεος φώς,
Μηκιστῆος υἱὸς Ταλαϊονίδαο ἄνακτος,
ὅς ποτε Θήβασδ' ἦλθε δεδουπότος Οἰδιπόδαο
ἐς τάφον· ἔνθα δὲ πάντας ἐνίκα Καδμείωνας.

Alone Euryalos stood up to face him, a godlike
man, son of lord Mekisteus of the seed of Talaos;
of him who came once to Thebes and the tomb of Oidipous after
his downfall, and there in boxing defeated all the Kadmeians.

Iliad XXIII 677–680

We are dealing here with the motif "visit to Thebes by one of the Seven and subsequent victory over the Kadmeians." Given that this motif is hardly reflected in Diomedes' role in the *Iliad*[171] and serves no paradigmatic purpose,[172] it may be reflecting older epic material stemming from the Theban tradition. W. Kullmann[173] has convincingly argued that the presence of Diomedes, Sthenelos, and Eurualos in the *Iliad* points both to an Epigoni- and an Alcmaeonis-lay, since Eurualus is named as one of the Epigonoi only in the *Alcmaeonis* and not in the *Epigoni*. In like manner, the bulk of the references to Tudeus in the *Iliad* come from the tradition of the *Thebais*, though the episode of his visit to Thebes and his heroic exploits there probably reflects an initially distinct heroic song about Tudeus, part of which was later incorporated in the tradition of the Seven.[174]

Both cases show that Thebes is evoked as a rival epic space, a spatial backdrop against which the exploits and heroism of double-identity warriors is measured. At times, this contrast amounts to an implicit *laudatio* of certain "Theban" heroes who take part in the *Iliad*, but the comparison may also work against them. The decisive factor is the point of view taken by each speaker or the narrator, whose focalization is based on the epic space he is alluding to. Thebes can thus be the space of either the first or the second Theban war, and each speaker may tailor his evaluation of the present by reference to the epic space Thebes occupied in different song traditions of the *Thebais*, the *Epigoni*, or the *Alcmaeonis*. Athena reminds Diomedes, who excels in *Iliad* V, of the greatness of his father, thus evoking the epic space of the *Thebais*. Likewise Diomedes prays to Athena *before entering Troy* in *Iliad* X, and asks her to help him as she did his father Tudeus when he entered Thebes. In these two cases Diomedes is evaluated positively, as he is presented as a hero of equal rank and status with his father. With Eurualos, things are different. Eurualos takes part in the Trojan expedition, and subsequently in the funeral games in honor of Patroklos, *because* his father Mekisteus participated in the expedition of the Seven against Thebes and visited Thebes for the funeral of Oedipus.[175] Since Eurualos—unlike

---

[171] The situation is very different in the *Doloneia*, where there is no embassy, only a spy mission undertaken by Odysseus and Diomedes. The same is true, *mutatis mutandis*, for the Palladion (*Little Iliad* §83 Kullmann = 228–229 Severyns = Allen 107.7–8).

[172] On the importance of distinguishing between genuine borrowings and adaptations on the one hand and ad hoc inventions for paradigmatic purposes on the other, see Davies 1989:22–23.

[173] 1960:149–151.

[174] This can be seen from certain significant details pertaining to Tudeus' myth: the only person whom Tudeus spares in the ambush the Thebans organized against him is Maion, son of Haimon. Maion belongs to the older phase of Theban myth, before the advent of Oedipus and certainly long before the expedition of the Seven, and Haimon is presented as a husband-to-be of Antigone. When Tudeus was incorporated into the myth of the Seven, he dragged with him earlier material that was closely associated with his independent lore.

[175] See Friedländer 1914:319–320.

his father who emerged victorious over the Kadmeians—will be defeated by Epeius in the boxing match, we can see that the *Iliad* lets its audience entertain the thought that he is inferior to his father. Whereas one of the Epigonoi (Diomedes) excels in the epic space of the *Iliad*,[176] another (Eurualos) is clearly outdone.[177] Thebes is thus measured in terms of epic space, as a locus bestowing varying levels of excellence on its heroes, according to the epic tradition the *Iliad* decides to focus on each time.

Spacing deception

After the "Theban lay" of the *Iliad* is exhausted in the ἀριστεία of Diomedes, Thebes begins to be "anchored" to Herakles. Both Zeus and Agamemnon remember Herakles' birth, in different contexts which are connected by the theme of deception: like Zeus, who was deceived by Hera in *Iliad* XIV, Agamemnon, who was taken in by Ate, points to Zeus' deception by Hera at the birth of Herakles:

> "οὐδ' ὅτε περ Σεμέλης, οὐδ' Ἀλκμήνης ἐνὶ Θήβῃ,
> ἥ ῥ' Ἡρακλῆα κρατερόφρονα γείνατο παῖδα,
> ἢ δὲ Διώνυσον Σεμέλη τέκε, χάρμα βροτοῖσιν·"

> "not when I loved Semele, or Alkmene in Thebe,
> when Alkmene bore me a son, Herakles the strong-hearted,
> while Semele's son was Dionysos, the pleasure of mortals."

Iliad XIV 323–325

> καὶ γὰρ δή νύ ποτε Ζεὺς ἄσατο, τόν περ ἄριστον
> ἀνδρῶν ἠδὲ θεῶν φασ' ἔμμεναι· ἀλλ' ἄρα καὶ τόν
> Ἥρη θῆλυς ἐοῦσα δολοφροσύνης ἀπάτησεν
> ἤματι τῷ, ὅτ' ἔμελλε βίην Ἡρακληείην
> Ἀλκμήνη τέξεσθαι ἐϋστεφάνῳ ἐνὶ Θήβῃ.
> . . . .
> ὣς ἔφατο· Ζεὺς δ' οὔ τι δολοφροσύνην ἐνόησεν,
> ἀλλ' ὄμοσεν μέγαν ὅρκον, ἔπειτα δὲ πολλὸν ἀάσθη.

> Yes, for once Zeus was deluded, though men say
> he is the highest one of gods and mortals. Yet Hera
> who is female deluded even Zeus in her craftiness

---

[176] As he excels in the horse race in the funeral games for Patroklos. For a metapoetic interpretation of this whole episode and the self-reflexivity of the *Iliad*, see Rengakos 2006a:17–30.

[177] Eurualos has a brief ἀριστεία in *Iliad* VI 20–28.

on that day when in strong wall-circled Thebe Alkmene
was at her time to bring forth the strength of Herakles.

. . . .

So Hera spoke. And Zeus was entirely unaware of her falsehood,
but swore a great oath, and therein lay all his deception.

Iliad XIX 95–99, 112–113

Herakles is regularly mentioned in archaic Greek epic in connection with Thebes, which is his standard birthplace.[178] The question to be asked here is whether the reference to Thebes is simply typological, and if not what is its function. One could argue that the point of the analogy in both passages is the theme of deception linked to a mythological reference to Herakles, and that Thebes plays no role in it whatsoever. Conversely, deception is linked in both cases to *a particular incident or episode* in Herakles' widely known saga, namely his birth. In other words, deception is not associated, for example, with his death, although Herakles "died" by means of deception and not heroic defeat. The insistence on his birth necessarily leads us directly to Thebes. Given that his birth was closely associated with Zeus' deception by Hera, Thebes (which in *Iliad* XIV 325 is also the birthplace of another "illegal" son of Zeus, Dionysus, who was born to Semele) and birth are turned into a single semantic pair. The birth of a great son, Herakles, from the union of a mortal and a god is of course particularly appropriate to the *Iliad*, given that one of its major heroes, Achilles, was born to a mortal (Peleus) and a goddess (Thetis). Galinsky has convincingly argued that "Herakles is cited as a parallel to the central hero of the *Iliad*, Achilles" mainly because they both break the "noble code of behaviour" and are constantly presented as two famous misfits.[179] In the light of these observations, we can see that Agamemnon's reference to Herakles' birth in Thebes as an example of the workings of Ate, who blinded Zeus as she blinded him in Troy,[180] reinforces the analogy even more: in the framework of his argument, Herakles and Achilles are intricately interwoven with Thebes and Troy respectively, the places where Ate can twist the minds of the most eminent leaders—the shepherd of men and the father of men and gods.[181] Uttered at a point in the plot where Agamemnon openly acknowledges his fault and Achilles is ready to return to battle, the

---

[178] Hesiod *Theogony* 530, *Catalogue of Women*, fr. 195.55–60 [= *Shield* 48–53]; *Homeric Hymn to Heracles* (15.1–3).

[179] Galinsky 1972:14.

[180] See *Iliad* XIX 87–136, where Agamemnon responds to Achilles with an extended etiological speech on the workings of Ate (which is repeated in various verbal and substantival forms no fewer than twelve times); see Louden 2006:118.

[181] Agamemnon constantly welcomes the analogy between himself and Zeus; see Tsagalis 2008b:209–238.

implicit analogy between Thebes and Troy becomes the spatial vehicle for a temporary assimilation of Herakles and Achilles, who are called "dearest of all to lord Zeus"[182] and "dearer to the immortals"[183] respectively.

Minor Places

Minor places are treated either as simple geographical references that do not attain the status of space, or as thematized spaces that form a network of associations around the figure of Achilles. Sparta,[184] Ithaka,[185] Crete,[186] and Mycenae[187] are not thematically or narratively exploited in the *Iliad*, for reasons about which we may only speculate.

The first three of these place-names delineate spaces of huge thematic importance for the tradition of the *Odyssey*. Telemakhos' visit to Menelaos' palace, Odysseus' home, and Crete, the unifying thread of most of Odysseus' false tales and the trademark of his fictive Cretan persona, make us wonder whether in the treatment of these places in the Iliadic and the Odyssean traditions we are dealing with a purely coincidental antithesis. Before taking sides, we should clarify that Pylos, which is thematically fertile in both epic traditions, should not be used as an argument in favor of this idea, for the narratives Nestor unravels in the *Iliad* are of a very different nature than those he unfolds in the *Odyssey*, since in the former he situates himself in pre–Trojan war saga, but in the latter he places himself within the tradition of the *Nostoi*. My main argument here is that during the formative period of Homeric poetry, Sparta, Ithaka, and Crete had acquired a clearly non-Iliadic character, since they were related to the tradition of the Returns that followed the sack of Ilion. The *Iliad* could hardly incorporate them in its subject matter by means of embedded analeptic narratives, since they had become gradually associated with the post-war tradition. Moreover, events antedating the subject matter of the *Iliad*, like Menelaos' marriage to Helen, her abduction, Odysseus' fake madness, or Idomeneus' departure from Crete were neglected by the tradition of the *Iliad*, since they were unsuitable to its plot.

---

[182] *Iliad* XVIII 118.

[183] *Iliad* XX 334. See Galinsky 1972:14.

[184] *Iliad* II 582 (narrator); IV 52 (Hera). It is worth noting that Helen never uses the word *Sparta* for her homeland.

[185] *Iliad* II 632 (narrator); III 201 (Helen).

[186] *Iliad* II 649 (narrator); III 233 (Helen); XIII 450–453 (Idomeneus). Crete is simply associated with Idomeneus, the leader of the Cretans, who is often accompanied in battle by Meriones.

[187] *Iliad* II 569 (narrator); IV 52 (Hera); IV 376 (Agamemnon); VII 180 (τις-speech); IX 44 (Diomedes); XI 46 (narrator). Mycenae is one of the beloved cities of Hera and the royal city of the "golden" king Agamemnon.

Conversely, the three Aegean islands of Skyros, Lemnos, and Lesbos[188] constitute highly thematized spaces, since they present a spatiotemporal triptych that epitomizes Achilles' fate: Lemnos is associated with events further back in time, namely the Achaean fleet's sojourn there while sailing to Troy, and stands for a space that is friendly to Achilles.[189] Lesbos (*Iliad* IX 129 and 271) represents hostile space,[190] and is connected to the more recent past, since it is one of the cities sacked by Achilles after the Achaeans arrived at Troy.[191] Skyros, again sacked by Achilles, points both to his marriage to Deidameia there and to a non-Iliadic future centered around the coming of Neoptolemos to Troy after his death.[192] Seen from a different angle, these three islands present the audience with an ascending climax in the process of Achilles' estrangement and gradual isolation:[193] Skyros, close to mainland Greece, stands for the place where his dearest son is, an island close to Phthia where his beloved father is located; Lemnos is still a friendly place, because of king Jason, Hypsipyle's father, who

---

[188] Since Lesbos looms large in Aeolic lyric poetry (both Alcaeus and Sappho), certain scholars have argued for the existence of a branch of heroic epic tradition in local dialect; see Gentili 1972:72; Pavese 1974:36; West 1973:189–191; West 2002b.

[189] See *Iliad* VII 467–475 (narrator), VIII 229–232 (Agamemnon), XXI 40 and 46 (narrator), XXI 58 (Achilles), XXI 79 (Lukaon). W. Kullmann (1960:270) argues that these passages show that the Achaeans had stopped at Lemnos on their way to Troy.

[190] Linguistic (Janko 1982:89–93) and literary arguments (Nagy 1974:134–139), as well as historical-political conflicts between Lesbos's most important city, Mytilene, and Athens in the Peisistratid era (Aloni 1986:51–67; Nagy 2009c II 6–41) indicate that Lesbos is the key element in the Aeolic phase of the *Iliad*'s transmission, preceding the final Ionic phase. Dué (2002:59–65) postulates an Aeolic epic narrative about Briseis and Achilles based on the sack of the island that was associated with beautiful queens, whom Achilles took captive. This tradition is shared by both the *Iliad* (IX 129, 271) and the poetry of Alcaeus (fr. 130b32–35 [Voigt]). In fact, the capture of Lurnessos, Pedasos, and various cities on Lesbos by Achilles may well reflect an Aeolic epic tradition concerning the Troad and its outlying islands. See Carpenter 1946:56–59; Nagy 1979:140–141, 272–273; 1990a:75n114; 2009c II 301–325.

[191] On Lesbos, see West 2002b.

[192] On Skyros as a link between Phthia and Troy with respect to the fate of Achilles, see "Places of memory: Phthia as 'anti-Troy,'" above. On *Iliad* IX 666–668 (narrator), see W. Kullmann 1960:196, who argues that Enueus was the founder of the city (like Erekhtheus in the expression δῆμος Ἐρεχθέως, used for Athens), whereas Lukomedes was known as the native king. This episode must reflect a sack of Skyros by Achilles (W. Kullmann 1960:197), but not the one mentioned in Proclus' summary of the *Cypria*, when Achilles married Lukomedes' daughter Deidameia (§27 Kullmann = 130–131 Severyns = Allen 104.8–9 Ἀχιλλεὺς δὲ Σκύρῳ προσχὼν γαμεῖ τὴν τοῦ Λυκομήδους θυγατέρα Δηϊδάμειαν); on the distinction between three separate versions concerning Achilles on Skyros, of which two are reflected in the *Iliad*, see Marin 2008–2009:24; Fantuzzi (forthcoming); Tsagalis (forthcoming in *RFIC*). On Neoptolemos, see *Iliad* XIX 326–333 (Achilles).

[193] According to Valeton (1915:41–54), Achilles' leading role in all these raids and exploits stems from a separate epic tradition about him.

offered hospitality to the Achaean army on its way to Troy;[194] Lesbos is a pro-Trojan island, lying close to the shore of Asia Minor and under the general control of Priam.[195] What we see here is an almost hodological mapping of Achilles' fate: the further he moves from Phthia, the more he leaves behind what is dear to him. These three islands represent three steps in Achilles' gradual movement from the world of endearment and happiness to that of cruelty and death.

---

[194] On Lemnos: (1) as a place connected with divine activity, see *Iliad* I 592–594 (fall of Hephaistos), XIV 229–232 (Hera goes to Lemnos and meets with Sleep), 278–282 (Hera swears an oath to all the gods who are in Tartaros); (2) in the tradition of the *Cypria*, see *Iliad* II 721–723 (Philoktetes); (3) as a place where Achilles sells Trojan captives, see *Iliad* XXI 40, 46, 58, 76–79 (Lukaon) and XXIV 751–753 (Hekabe).

[195] On Lesbos as a place sacked by Achilles and a source of captive women, see *Iliad* IX 128–130 (Agamemnon = IX 271–273 Odysseus), IX 664 (narrator); as an area under the control of Priam, see XXIV 544–546 (Achilles). W. Kullmann (1960:287) argues that this information coincides with the plot of the *Cypria* (§44 Kullmann = 160–162 Severyns = Allen 105.11–12 καὶ Λυρνησσὸν καὶ Πήδασον πορθεῖ καὶ συχνὰς τῶν περιοικίδων πόλεων), and that Lesbos must have been one of the περιοικίδας πόλεις sacked by Achilles. With respect to the slave girl lying at his side in *Iliad* IX 663–665, we cannot decide whether she formed part of the source used by the *Iliad*.

4

The Troad and Lycia

Since the Trojans are fighting in their own country, it is hardly surprising that places in Asia Minor are less often narratively exploited than specific areas of mainland Greece. A few places in the wider Troad, though, are thematized, as they are either tied to the fate of specific heroes or belong to the central core of the epic's plot. Apart from some less important areas in Asia Minor that are briefly mentioned, the *Iliad* has at its disposal an extremely fertile field for spatial thematization: Lycia. Among the chief allies of the Trojans are some heroes of high esteem and significance for the *Iliad*, such as Sarpedon, Glaukos, and Pandaros, who are narratively exploited at great length. These two categories of space (Troad and Lycia) with respect to Asia Minor will be the subject of the two following sections, since they represent distinct spaces that the tradition of the *Iliad* constantly uses for different purposes.

The Troad

The Troad includes a number of rather small cities, some of which the Achaeans have sacked during the Trojan War, and certainly before the events narrated in the *Iliad*.[1] The *Iliad* treats these cities more or less in the same way they are presented in the *Cypria*, as targets of small-scale expeditions or raids led by the Achaeans during the nine long years of the war. I begin my investigation by looking at the relevant material from the plot of the *Cypria*, according to the summary offered by Proclus' *Chrestomathy*:

---

[1] Places like Killa, Pedaios, Thumbre, Dardania, and Egyptian Thebes are mere locations with no role at all in the plot. Arisbe, Tenedos (*Iliad* I 38, 452; XI 625; XIII 33), and Imbros do not constitute thematized spaces but are occasionally associated with Achilles' exploits in the wider region surrounding Troy. Arisbe is the last place in Lukaon's troubled life: taken captive by Achilles while in his father's gardens, he was then sold as slave in Lemnos, bought by the son of Jason, and subsequently redeemed by Eëtion of Imbros and sent to Arisbe, from where he returned to Troy (XXI 34–44). Nestor's slave girl, the wise Hekamede, was taken captive by Achilles during the sack of Tenedos (XI 624–627). Imbros (together with Samos and Lemnos) is mentioned as a place where Achilles sold Hekabe's sons (XXIV 752–753).

ἔπειτα τὴν χώραν ἐπεξελθόντες πορθοῦσι καὶ τὰς περιοίκους πόλεις
Then setting out, they plunder the land and surrounding cities.

§40 Kullmann = 155–156 Severyns = 105.6–7 Allen

καὶ Λυρνησσὸν καὶ Πήδασον πορθεῖ [sc. Ἀχιλλεὺς] καὶ συχνὰς τῶν
περιοικίδων πόλεων.
[Achilles] sacks Lurnessos, Pedasos, and many of the surrounding
cities.

§44 Kullmann = 160–162 Severyns = Allen 105.11–12

According to the *Iliad*, the Achaeans have sacked four cities in the Troad
(Hypoplakian Thebes, Lurnessos, Pedasos, and Khruse). Each of these cities
is linked to the plot mainly by a single character, whom the epic will narratively exploit more or less at length. In particular, Andromakhe comes from
Hypoplakian Thebes,[2] Briseis from Lurnessos,[3] and Lukaon from Pedasos,[4] while
Khruseis, who was taken captive during the sack of Hypoplakian Thebes,[5] is
narratively anchored to the city of Khruse through the famous episode with her
father in *Iliad* I.[6]

This one-to-one correspondence is of paramount importance for comprehending the function of these locations within the Iliadic plot, the more so since
they seem to have been selected in preference to other variants. According to
a scholium (T) on *Iliad* XVI 57, Briseis was captured during the sack of Pedasos
in the *Cypria*, but during the sack of Lurnessos in the *Iliad*: Τὴν Πήδασον οἱ
τῶν Κυπρίων ποιηταί, αὐτὸς δὲ Λυρνησ<σ>όν ("The poets of the *Cypria* [refer]
to Pedasos, but he [Homer] [refers] to Lurnessos"). Moreover, Aineias, who
seems to have his personal epic tradition in the Troad,[7] declares that Achilles

---

[2] See *Iliad* VI 396–397 and 415–416; cf. scholium on *Iliad* VI 397a about Heracles' founding and
naming of Thebes after the king's daughter Thebe: †Ἀνδράμυς τις Πελασγὸς ἀφικόμενος εἰς
τὴν Ἴδην τὴν ἐν Κιλικίᾳ κτίζει πόλιν †ἀδραμύστειαν† καλουμένην. ἔχων δὲ θυγατέρα Θήβην
ἔπαθλον δρόμου αὐτὴν ὥρισε τῷ βουλομένῳ. Ἡρακλῆς δὲ ταύτην λαβὼν ὑπὸ τῷ Πλάκιον τῆς
Κιλικίας πόλιν κτίσας Θήβην αὐτὴν ὠνόμασεν.
[3] *Iliad* II 688–693.
[4] On Lukaon's pedigree, see *Iliad* XXI 84–89.
[5] *Iliad* I 365–369.
[6] Notice the emphasis that Khruseis' father Khruses places on the city of Khruse, which is
mentioned first in his prayer to Apollo in *Iliad* I 37–38 (= I 451–452); see also I 97–100, 387–390,
428–431.
[7] See *Iliad* XX 188–194; Aloni 1986:62–64, 76–98; Dué 2002:25; West 2003b:15–16, 2011:371 on
Iliad XX 291–340. On Poseidon's prophecy concerning the future rule of the Aineiadai over the
Trojans, see the "Little Aeneid" in *Iliad* XX 307–339 (especially 307–308) and the *Homeric Hymn to
Aphrodite* 196–199. Conversely, the context (*Iliad* XX 307–317) indicates that Τρώεσσιν ἀνάξει 'will
rule over the Trojans' does not refer to the old city of Troy, which will be razed to the ground.
The relocation of Aineias' descendants from Troy was later associated with conflicting claims on

has sacked both Lurnessos and Pedasos (*Iliad* XX 87–92). Dué argues that the Panhellenic tradition of the *Iliad* systematically downplays local versions,[8] and fosters a narrative where Achilles looms large, not as a person who gets emotionally involved with various slave-girls, but one who treats them, and especially Briseis, as the emblem of his heroic status among the Achaean army. In fact, the *Iliad* deliberately employs for the raids made by Achilles in the cities surrounding Troy the same subthemes that Achilles himself has verbalized in *Iliad* I 152–157, where he explicitly says for the Trojans:

> "οὐ γὰρ ἐγὼ Τρώων ἕνεκ' ἤλυθον αἰχμητάων
> δεῦρο μαχησόμενος, ἐπεὶ οὔ τί μοι αἴτιοί εἰσιν·
> οὐ γὰρ πώποτ' ἐμὰς βοῦς ἤλασαν οὐδὲ μὲν ἵππους,
> οὐδέ ποτ' ἐν Φθίῃ ἐριβώλακι βωτιανείρῃ
> καρπὸν ἐδηλήσαντ', ἐπεὶ ἦ μάλα πολλὰ μεταξύ,
> οὔρεά τε σκιόεντα θάλασσά τε ἠχήεσσα."

> "I for my part did not come here for the sake of the Trojan
> spearmen to fight against them, since to me they have done nothing.
> Never yet have they driven away my cattle or my horses,
> never in Phthia where the soil is rich and men grow great did they
> spoil my harvest, since indeed there is much that lies between us,
> the shadowy mountains and the echoing sea ..."

> *Iliad* I 152–157

The opposition between the proximity of the cities surrounding Troy and the remoteness of Phthia, as well as between the destructiveness of Achilles and the harmlessness of the Trojans, is strongly thematized by the Iliadic tradition, which turns these locations in the Troad into the backdrop for measuring Achilles' dramatic function in the epic. Hypoplakian Thebes, Lurnessos, Pedasos, and Khruse are not simply places on a notional mythical map, but variations on the emotional turbulence of Achilles, who fights a war against a people who have never harmed him.

Apart from the interplay between the remoteness of Phthia and the proximity of these cities, the *Iliad* exploits the spatial aspect of size, in order to hint at the difference between the ease with which Achilles sacks all these small cities in the Troad and his failure to take the great city of Troy. Moreover, although the

---

Homer: the Aineiadai were considered to be Aeolians or Ionians depending on the identity of the city they settled in; see Nagy 2009c, part II, 181–188.

[8] Dué 2002:23–25.

Achaeans take various women captive, they cannot succeed in getting Helen,[9] the one person for whom this whole expedition was organized. This emphatic contrast reveals that space is used here with respect to both distance and size, in order to deepen our understanding of the situation Achilles has been facing in the epic.

Furthermore, these cities supply the poem with rather secondary characters, who are either linked to other prime figures of the epic or represent distinct phases in the development of the plot. To be more specific, the four figures mentioned earlier—Khruseis, Briseis, Andromakhe, and Lukaon—encapsulate Achilles' role in the *Iliad*. Khruseis is the reason for all the Achaeans' troubles, Briseis symbolizes the "apple of discord" between Agamemnon and Achilles,[10] Andromakhe is closely associated with the presentation and drama of Hektor, and Lukaon's encounter with Achilles is a dramatic reenactment of his first captivity during the sack of Pedasos. Four different cities in the Troad are thus linked to four distinct characters who thematically epitomize the evolution of Achilles within the poem.

The small cities of the Troad are therefore thematized spaces within a larger framework. They spatially contextualize Achilles and dramatize his own role: ironically but tellingly, the great Achaean warrior is also a captive, not of some mighty hero, but of the *Iliad*'s perception and thematic exploitation of space. He will neither return to Phthia nor sack Troy, but remains the figurative prisoner of the very tradition that depends so much on his unsurpassed fighting skills.

Lycia

Lycia is mentioned eighteen times in character text and only twice in narrator text.[11] The sheer size of this difference shows that Iliadic characters use Lycia mainly as an embedded story space. Its function differs according to ethnic group (Lycians, Trojans,[12] Achaeans) and the mortal/divine dichotomy that epic regularly exploits.

---

[9] On the Achaeans' failure to "reabduct" Helen, see Jamison 1994.

[10] *Iliad* II 688–694; XIX 56–60.

[11] *Iliad* II 877 and XVI 683. Given that the first is part of the Catalogue of Ships and the second a mere repetition of Zeus' orders to Apollo (who is commanded to send the twins Hupnos and Thanatos to carry the corpse of Sarpedon to Lycia), I do not treat them separately.

[12] See Louden 2006:28, who argues for the existence of a story pattern that "positions the best of the Akhaians *in duels* with leaders of each of the three Trojan contingents: the Trojans, the Dardanians, and the allies" (emphasis added).

Coming from afar: Sarpedon and Glaukos

One of the main features of Lycian identity in the *Iliad* is conditioned by the geographical location of Lycia. Described as the land of the "swirling river Xanthos" (*Iliad* II 877 Ξάνθου ἄπο δινήεντος), Lycia is placed far away from the Troad (877 τηλόθεν ἐκ Λυκίης), which is, of course, the theater of all war operations. This important point often passes unnoticed, but as I argued above, the *Iliad* capitalizes on the antithesis between less important Trojan allies coming from the nearby Troad and first-rank Lycians coming from faraway Lycia. In fact, the geographical location of Lycia filters the identity and function of Lycians in the Iliadic plot to such an extent that it becomes the measure of their bravery. The interpretive implications of this narrative strategy are far-reaching, for the chief Lycian heroes constitute an indispensable and crucial part of the Iliadic plot. Since the death of Sarpedon at the hands of Patroklos corresponds to the killing of Memnon by Achilles, as neoanalysis showed long ago,[13] it is likely that the "coming from afar" motif pertaining to the Lycians in the *Iliad* was modeled upon an *Aethiopis* tradition that featured Memnon coming from distant Aethiopia and being killed by Achilles.[14]

As is often the case, the tradition of the *Iliad* transforms inherited material through dramatization and intensification. In V 478–481, the "coming from afar" motif is expanded by means of two distinct additions that lend the passage a clear Iliadic tone:

> "καὶ γὰρ ἐγὼν ἐπίκουρος ἐὼν μάλα τηλόθεν ἥκω·
> τηλοῦ γὰρ Λυκίη, Ξάνθῳ ἔπι δινήεντι,
> ἔνθ᾽ ἄλοχόν τε φίλην ἔλιπον καὶ νήπιον υἱόν,
> κὰδ δὲ κτήματα πολλά, τὰ τ᾽ ἔλδεται ὅς κ᾽ ἐπιδευής."

> "I have come, a companion to help you, from a very far place;
> Lykia lies far away, by the whirling waters of Xanthos;
> there I left behind my own wife and my baby son, there
> I left my many possessions which the needy man eyes longingly."

> *Iliad* V 478–481

---

[13] Pestalozzi 1945:13–15; Schadewaldt 1965:169; Howald 1946:85–90; W. Kullmann 1960:318 n2; Clark and Coulson 1978:70–73; for a different view, see Aceti 2008:231–262; Burgess 2009:77–78.

[14] The motif "far from home" is typical, as can be seen in its ample use for various heroes in the *Iliad* (see Griffin 1980:106–110), but its application to the Lycian Sarpedon is closely associated with its climactic phase, the transfer of his body to Lycia by the twins Hupnos and Thanatos. The same is so, *mutatis mutandis*, with Memnon in the *Aethiopis*, who is given immortality. These two cases stand out from the general pattern as specific and interrelated.

Sarpedon adds two important details to the "coming from afar" motif: First, his reference to his wife and children echoes Hektor, and thus portrays Sarpedon as a tragic hero who has left his family behind.[15] The mention of a son is a dramatic tour de force on the part of the *Iliad*, since having only a single son intensifies the tragedy of a father's not coming back home alive, adding to the grief of loss the further sufferings awaiting an orphan, as they are eloquently described for Astuanax in Andromakhe's γόος (*Iliad* XXII 484–506).[16] Second, the detail about Sarpedon's wealth (V 481 κὰδ δὲ κτήματα πολλά) creates an antithesis to the formula concerning Menelaos' possessions that Paris stole from Sparta (III 91 ἀμφ' Ἑλένῃ καὶ κτήμασι πᾶσι μάχεσθαι). The point is effectively made by means of similar diction: in contrast with the Trojan prince who stole Menelaos' treasures and his wife, who for her part abandoned her own daughter (III 174–175 υἱέϊ σῷ ἑπόμην, θάλαμον γνωτούς τε λιποῦσα / παῖδά τε τηλυγέτην καὶ ὁμηλικίην ἐρατεινήν), Sarpedon has left behind his wife and baby son (V 480 ἔνθ' ἄλοχόν τε φίλην ἔλιπον καὶ νήπιον υἱόν), and his possessions *which have been eyed by other men in need*, to come to Troy and fight a war that is not his.[17] Thus we see that Sarpedon uses Lycia as a thematized space that allows him to occasionally accuse the Trojans, more or less in the way Achilles uses Phthia and the life he has left behind to help Agamemnon, whom he accuses similarly in *Iliad* I. Both heroes employ distant space, Lycia and Phthia respectively, to promote a rhetoric of space that highlights their participation and excellence in a war that is not really their own. In terms of the wider analogy between the *Aethiopis* tradition and the Iliadic tradition, it becomes plausible that this feature was not taken from the former and used in the latter, since in the *Aethiopis* Memnon is clearly the chief anti-Achaean warrior and foremost enemy, and there is no Trojan of Hektor's stature against whom Memnon's potential accusation could be directed. This is firm evidence, I maintain, that the tradition of the *Iliad* has *expanded* the "coming from afar" motif by dramatizing it around two of the main figures of the epic's plot, Sarpedon and Achilles. Distant space thus becomes a vehicle both for expressing complaints or accusations against one's comrades-in-arms and for evaluating heroic κλέος in terms of human sacrifice and loss.

---

[15] See Aceti 2008:21, who observes that the very diction employed in this passage recalls an epitaph for a fallen hero (λείπω + accusative amounts to a formula used in epitaphs), and in this respect foreshadows the death of Sarpedon. Typical funerary diction is thus deftly used to add pathos to this scene. See Griffin 1980:103–143.

[16] On this passage, see Tsagalis 2004:129–133.

[17] See *Iliad* V 482–484 "ἀλλὰ καὶ ὣς Λυκίους ὀτρύνω καὶ μέμον' αὐτός / ἀνδρὶ μαχέσσασθαι· ἀτὰρ οὔ τί μοι ἐνθάδε τοῖον / οἷόν κ' ἠὲ φέροιεν Ἀχαιοὶ ἤ κεν ἄγοιεν" ("'Yet even so I drive on my Lykians, and myself have courage / to fight my man in battle, though there is nothing of mine here / that the Achaians can carry away as spoil or drive off'"). Sarpedon speaks like Achilles in *Iliad* I 152–157 (and also XIX 325); see "The Poetics of Loneliness," chapter 3, above.

At the same time, remote space like Lycia and Phthia allows the *Iliad* to present as emotionally close to its audience's feelings what is geographically remote and distant: the beloved members of Sarpedon's and Achilles' families who are located in areas far from Troy are the ones who awaken the audience's sympathy and compassion.

Raum macht Leute: Sarpedon's sociology of space

Sarpedon's exhortation to Glaukos in *Iliad* XII 310–328 is one of the rare glimpses offered by the epic at a specific geographical location.[18] Lycia is described not by its landscape, but in terms of social space, through a brief description of the life and status of Lycian princes. The most telling part of Sarpedon's speech are the following lines:

"Γλαῦκε, τίη δὴ νῶϊ τετιμήμεσθα μάλιστα
ἕδρῃ τε κρέασίν τε ἰδὲ πλείοις δεπάεσσιν
ἐν Λυκίῃ, πάντες δὲ θεοὺς ὣς εἰσορόωσιν,
καὶ τέμενος νεμόμεσθα μέγα Ξάνθοιο παρ' ὄχθας,
καλὸν φυταλιῆς καὶ ἀρούρης πυροφόροιο;
τὼ νῦν χρὴ Λυκίοισι μέτα πρώτοισιν ἐόντας
ἑστάμεν ἠδὲ μάχης καυστειρῆς ἀντιβολῆσαι,
ὄφρά τις ὧδ' εἴπῃ Λυκίων πύκα θωρηκτάων·
'οὐ μὰν ἀκλεῖς Λυκίην κάτα κοιρανέουσιν
ἡμέτεροι βασιλῆες ἔδουσί τε πίονα μῆλα
οἶνόν τ' ἔξαιτον μελιηδέα· ἀλλ' ἄρα καὶ ἲς
ἐσθλή, ἐπεὶ Λυκίοισι μέτα πρώτοισι μάχονται.'"

"Glaukos, why is it you and I are honoured before others
with pride of place, the choice meats and the filled wine cups
in Lykia, and all men look on us as if we were immortals,
and we are appointed a great piece of land by the banks of Xanthos,
good land, orchard and vineyard, and ploughland for the planting of
	wheat?
Therefore it is our duty in the forefront of the Lykians
to take our stand, and bear our part of the blazing of battle,
so that a man of the close-armoured Lykians may say of us:
'Indeed, these are no ignoble men who are lords of Lykia,
these kings of ours, who feed upon the fat sheep appointed

---

[18]   On Sarpedon and Glaukos, see M. Reichel 1994:261–263.

and drink the exquisite sweet wine, since indeed there is strength
of valour in them, since they fight in the forefront of the Lykians.'"

Iliad XII 310–321

By reminding Glaukos of the privileges Lycian kings possess and enjoy in Lycia
(honorary places in symposia, best portion of food, cups full of wine, special
piece of land along the banks of Xanthos), Sarpedon offers an internal picture of
royal life in Lycia in terms of the social space occupied by kings. This brief but
impressive list of privileges demarcates a space that exercises its own influence
on the unique heroic attitude of Sarpedon.[19] Despite Hainsworth's use in this
connection of the term "social contract," since honor can be achieved through
manhood,[20] little attention has been paid to its constituent parts. Sarpedon's list
of privileges can be divided into smaller groups, pertaining to the banquet on
the one hand and to the τέμενος on the other.

The banquet is often used as the symbolic locus where the ἄριστοι, or the
leaders of the army in the *Iliad,* reaffirm their participation in the ideology of the
heroic society. The inherent theatricality of the symposium,[21] with the importance assigned to setting, food, and drink, makes an effective metaphor for the
representation and reenactment of status and authority. The banquet, with its
tightly choreographed framework, can be considered an emblem of society—
a society Sarpedon returns to after his "temporary" sojourn in the bestialized
world of the simile that precedes it, where he is compared to a ferocious lion
whose "valiant heart [*Iliad* XII 300 θυμὸς ἀγήνωρ] incited him to attack a well-
built stable [301 πυκινὸν δόμον] just as the king's heart excites him to attack
the Achaean wall," who is "willing to be wounded in the front ranks [306 ἐν
πρώτοισι] just as he is ready to do now [315, 321, 324 Λυκίοισι μέτα πρώτοισι; ἐνὶ
πρώτοισι]," and who "was needing meat, just as he, as a king, consumes abundant meat [300 κρειῶν, 311 κρέασιν]." Sarpedon's "return" to the main narrative
has not lost all of its leonine echoes,[22] but it is their reappropriation within the
context of human civilization that gives to this passage its own distinctive tone.[23]

---

[19] See Carlier 1984:172: "Tous les rois homériques n'ont pas de leur devoir militaire une idée aussi
exigeante."

[20] Hainsworth 1993:352 on *Iliad* XII 310–321; see also Adkins 1960:34–36.

[21] On the symposium, see Detienne and Vernant 1979; Grottanelli and Parise 1979; Vetta 1983;
Lissarague 1987; O. Murray 1990; Slater 1991; Schmitt–Pantel 1992; Scheid–Tissinier 1994.

[22] Pucci 1998:52.

[23] Within the framework of archaic epic traditions, let us recall that the banquet occurs at an early
stage in the troubles that afflict the houses of Atreus (Aeschylus *Agamemnon* 1096–1097, 1220–
1222, 1242–1244, 1501–1505, 1593–1602; Sophocles *Ajax* 1291–1294; Euripides *Electra* 637–638,
Iphigenia in Tauris 195–197, 812–813, *Orestes* 11–15, 812–818, 996–1000) and Oedipus (*Thebais*, frr. 2
and 3, PEG 1). In both cases, food and drink play a crucial role. See Nagy 1979:130–131, 218–219,
311.

According to Durkheim, society at large is a huge organization based on the principle of classification, which is nothing else than a manifestation of space.[24] Sarpedon's strong emphasis on the special place reserved for the Lycian kings in the symposium (a communal activity par excellence), as well as the offering of the best portion of food and drink, for all its conventionality,[25] reveals that the banquet is a miniature of society at large, since it reaffirms and solidifies classification and priority even during one of the most relaxed human activities.[26] Being reserved for the elite, the banquet mirrors class structure, dividing individuals into upper classes and commoners. Sarpedon's specific description of a banquet, though, accentuates an internal, intraconvivial dichotomy between the kings and the other members of the elite. This intensification of the class division reflects a clear spatialization of authority and status,[27] which is immediately paralleled by the spatialized presentation of authority and valor between those fighting in the first ranks and those standing behind, among the mass of warriors.[28] The same is the case, *mutatis mutandis*, with the apportioning of choice meat and the detail about the kings' full wine cups. Within the universe of Greek myth, meat constitutes a means of recognizing authority that goes back to older beliefs about sacrifice.[29] By offering a look inside Lycia, and in particular at the secluded and privileged world of a banquet,[30] Sarpedon associates royal identity and obligations (*noblesse oblige*) not with territory at large (as he has done in the past when he used the motif of "coming from afar"), but with a specific activity of a given social group. Seen from this angle, banquet and war are presented as two parallel and complementary aspects of heroic and royal identity: since the Lycian kings occupy a privileged social space in the former, they also have to occupy an equivalent military space in the latter.

The same is true of the τέμενος (*Iliad* XII 313–314 καὶ τέμενος νεμόμεσθα μέγα Ξάνθοιο παρ' ὄχθας, / καλὸν φυταλιῆς καὶ ἀρούρης πυροφόροιο ["'and

---

[24] Durkheim 1984:592; see also Schroer 2006:48–51.

[25] Pucci 1998:53.

[26] Sometimes, though, this special group of people meeting in a special space exerts such an enormous influence on the kind of discourse developed that it becomes a world of its own, a "spettacolo a se steso" in the words of Rossi (1983:41–50).

[27] On sympotic space, see O. Murray 1990:37–101.

[28] On fighting in the first rank, see chapter 1 above, passim.

[29] See Burkert 1985:57.

[30] The exclusivity of the banquet can be seen as a working metaphor for the idea of the state: according to Simmel (1995), space can sometimes bestow uniqueness, individuality, and distinctiveness on a given structure. As with the state territory that is thought of as the mechanism connecting individuals, so the closed space of the banquet reaffirms the social links of the elite. This *Ausschließlichkeit des Raums* ("exclusivity of space") results, unavoidably, in the construction of a specific identity by the individuals who pertain to this social space. See also Schroer 2006:65–67.

we are appointed a great piece of land by the banks of Xanthos, / good land, orchard and vineyard, and ploughland for the planting of wheat'"]). It may be that locating the τέμενος along the banks of Xanthos results from the *Iliad*'s identification of Lycia with the Xanthos region, that is, by the only landscape feature it is aware of from this geographical area. We should not forget that a τέμενος, like cult in general,[31] is defined locally,[32] and that (as the etymology of the word indicates) these are pieces of land "cut off" and demarcated by boundary stones to keep out the βέβηλοι, literally and metaphorically. In this light, the τέμενος situated along the banks of the river Xanthos, that is, in a fertile area so that it may be used as an "orchard and vineyard, and ploughland for the planting of wheat," reinforces the notion of exclusive space that we have seen before, translating the traditional diction with which Sarpedon describes the privileged place reserved for the kings in Lycian society into an epic sociology of space.

Pandaros: Associative space

Compared with Sarpedon and Glaukos, the famous archer Pandaros represents a special case of Lycian identity. How are we to explain his claim that he has come to Troy from distant Lycia (*Iliad* V 105), even though he has been presented (II 824–827) as the leader of the Trojans coming from Troy's neighboring city of Zeleia?

Historical interpretations[33] have tried to explain Pandaros' double identity as reflecting a more general perplexity, stemming from an incomplete conflation of older and more recent traditions linked to a southward movement of a population group coming from the northeast.[34] In this light, the Iliadic tradition may reflect the existence of a small pocket of Lukka people near Troy (in Zeleia), who later moved towards Lycia and were associated with the Lycians.

---

[31] On τέμενος, see Burkert 1985:84–87.

[32] Sarpedon's words "and all men look on us as if we were immortals" (*Iliad* XII 312 πάντες δὲ θεοὺς ὣς εἰσορόωσιν) work well with his reference to a τέμενος in the next two lines. Only gods and heroes have their own τεμένη. Τέμενος is used in a profane sense in Linear B and in the following passages from the Homeric epics: *Iliad* VI 194 (for Bellerophon in Lycia), IX 578 (for Meleager in Calydon), XII 313 (for Sarpedon and Glaukos in Lycia), XVIII 550 (for a king on the shield of Achilles), XX 184 (for Aineias in Troy), XX 391 (for Iphition, son of Otrunteus, in the Gugaian lake, close to the rivers Hullos and Hermos); *Odyssey* vi 293 (for Alkinoös in Skheria), xi 185 (for Odysseus in Ithaka), xvii 299 (for Odysseus in Ithaka); see also Burkert 1985:84–87 and 382n37.

[33] On the use of peoples and places in both Homeric epics to determine their relative chronology, see Dickie 1995:29–56. This kind of approach is not relevant to my research.

[34] See Strabo 12.4.6. Bryce (2006:137) argues that this population movement may have happened around the end of the Bronze Age (in the manner of the Leleges, who also moved to the southeast corner of Caria).

Later on, when "original" Lycians like Sarpedon and Glaukos were introduced in the Trojan saga, they dragged along with them the Trojan-Lycian Pandaros, whose inconsistent[35] identity in the *Iliad*—involving an older, stronger Zeleian and a weaker, more recent Lycian connection—reflects the dynamic nature and function of oral song. The conflation of various lays led to a new form of symbiosis, in which the adaptation of older material to later beliefs and practices is only partial, leaving ruptures on the surface of the epic text.[36] It is likely that the Greek oral traditions knew, probably from as early as the late Bronze Age, the ancestors of the Lycians, the Lukka people, who were dispersed in a vast area of western Anatolia and had become for the Greeks a by-word for other Luwian-speaking populations.[37]

Despite its appeal, this theory is unfounded for a number of reasons: First, it is based on the argument that "Lukka" appears first in a list of western Anatolian states that formed the so-called Assuwa Confederacy, an alliance stretching from Lycia in the south to the Troad in the north. This list, though, which has come down to us through the Hittite annals of Tudhaliya I (c. 1420–1400 BC), mentions not Lukka but the "[country of Artu]cca."[38] Second, the Luwian language is so widespread in the second millennium BC that any special connection with the Lycians is biased, as Lycian is only one dialect of Luwian, next to hieroglyphic Luwian, cuneiform Luwian, and Milyan. Finally, although it is likely that in early Greek poetic memory the Lukka people and the Lycians were associated, at least on the grounds of the similarity of their names, Pandaros' double identity in the *Iliad* can be effectively explained internally, with respect to the plot of this epic and the Trojan War saga in general.[39] The important question, though, with respect to our topic is whether, and if so how, the tradition of the *Iliad* has used Pandaros' double origin to poetic effect. In other words, it is worth exploring whether Pandaros' role in the plot is conditioned by his ambiguous identity.

Pandaros features as the leader of the contingent from Zeleia in *Iliad* II 824–827, where it is explicitly stated that he is in charge of the Trojans who

---

[35] Pandaros is not presented as belonging to the Lycian army in the Trojan catalogue of allies, nor is he anywhere in the *Iliad* linked to the Lycians par excellence, Sarpedon and Glaukos.

[36] See Tsagalis 2010b:109–110.

[37] See *Iliad* XII 330, where the expression "vast nation" (μέγα ἔθνος) designating the Lycians is more apt for their Lukka ancestors than for the limited region of historical Lycia. Expressions like κτήματα πολλά (V 481) and Λυκίης εὐρείης (VI 173) should be interpreted along the same lines. See Jenniges 1998:140; Aceti 2008:170–171.

[38] See Frei 1993; Brill's New Pauly 432–434 s.v. "Pandarus" and 916–920 s.v. "Lycii, Lycia."

[39] According to Bryce 1986:41 and Jenniges 1998:140, the *Iliad* offers a picture of Lycia and Lycians that combines features of their proto-Lycian Lukka ancestors at the end of the second millenium on the one hand, and those of their typically Lycian descendants, "permanently" located in southwestern Anatolia after the eighth century, on the other. For a recent overview of the whole matter of the Lycians, see Aceti 2008:167–172.

live in Zeleia, a city next to the river Aisepos, at the foot of Mount Ida. He is described as the son of Lukaon and the owner of a bow given to him by Apollo. In IV 100–103, Athena incites Pandaros to break the truce and be the first offender by shooting an arrow at Menelaos. She explicitly tells him that he should pray to the archer-god, Apollo the Lycian, promising to offer him a great sacrifice of lambs upon his return to sacred Zeleia. Pandaros follows her advice, and after praying to Apollo (IV 119–121) shoots an arrow and wounds Menelaos. As a result, the truce is broken, the Trojans being considered the offenders, and fighting resumes. In V 101–105, Pandaros, who has wounded Diomedes, tries to encourage the Trojans, and says explicitly that it was Apollo who brought him to Troy from Lycia. Finally, in *Iliad* V 169–178 Aineias praises Pandaros by reminding him that he is the best archer in Lycia, and they subsequently decide to attack Diomedes.

A careful examination of these passages shows that Pandaros is not associated with Lycia in general, but only when his excellence as an archer is emphasized. Bryce[40] argues that Apollo's epithet Λυκηγενής (*Iliad* IV 101, 119) means "wolf-born" or "light-born," and that contrary to the scholia (on *Iliad* IV 101b[1] [T] ἐν Λυκίᾳ γενομένῳ), if it were associated with Lycia it should have been Λυκιηγενής.[41] I disagree with this approach, since the false association works well on a poetic level, in both the figure of Pandaros and Lycia. In other words, the connection between Apollo the archer-god (see *Iliad* I),[42] Lycian excellence in archery,[43] the Apolline origin of Pandaros' own bow (minutely described in IV 105–111),[44] and the fact that Pandaros was sent to Troy by Apollo the Lycian and archer-god (V 101–105), constitute a whole nexus of associations pointing to one conclusion: the Iliadic tradition, through a series of historically inaccurate but poetically effective associations, stressed that Pandaros came from Lycia *when his skill as an archer was accentuated*.

This interpretive suggestion paves the way for one more, significant question: why, after all, did the tradition of the *Iliad* present Pandaros as an archer? The answer has been partly anticipated by some scholars, but I think we can add one more item to the already rich storehouse of arguments. It has been

---

[40] 1990–1991:144–145.

[41] See also Kirk 1985:340 on *Iliad* IV 101.

[42] See also Bacchylides *Epinicians* 13.147–148; Sophocles *Oedipus the King* 203–205; Euripides fr. 700 (TrGF 5.2 [Kannicht]).

[43] See e.g. Herodotus 7.77.3–5 Μιλύαι δὲ αἰχμάς τε βραχέας εἶχον καὶ εἵματα ἐνεπεπόρπεατο· εἶχον δὲ αὐτῶν τόξα μετεξέτεροι Λύκια, περὶ δὲ τῇσι κεφαλῇσι ἐκ διφθερέων πεποιημένας κυνέας ("The Milyans bore short spears, and had their garments fastened with buckles. Some of their number carried Lycian bows. They wore about their heads skull-caps made of leather" (translation by Rawlinson).

[44] The same is true of the description of the actual shooting of Pandaros in *Iliad* IV 116–126.

suggested[45] that Pandaros is a kind of Paris-like figure in the *Iliad*, whose poet is well known for his tendency to create partial doublets of certain figures.[46] Pandaros and Paris are associated through their skill as archers; they both receive the help of Apollo in fighting against the Achaeans, Pandaros in the *Iliad* by means of his bow (which is Apollo's gift and functions as a link between his own presentation in the Catalogue of Ships and the rest of the epic),[47] and Paris in the *Aethiopis* where he kills Achilles with the god's help (§62 Kullmann = 191–192 Severyns = Allen 106.7–9 τρεψάμενος δ' Ἀχιλεὺς τοὺς Τρῶας καὶ εἰς τὴν πόλιν συνεισπεσὼν ὑπὸ Πάριδος ἀναιρεῖται καὶ Ἀπόλλωνος); last, and most important, they both break oaths and laws: the former the truce, the later of hospitality. The episode presenting Pandaros breaking the truce and wounding Menelaos, who has almost defeated Paris, is a very strong argument for this interpretation. It is as if the *Iliad* deliberately creates the conditions for Menelaos' revenge for Paris' violation of the laws of hospitality in Sparta and the abduction of Helen, only to keep it suspended and entertain the possibility of reversing it by means of Paris' doublet, Pandaros, who nearly kills Menelaos. Moreover, when Pandaros and Aineias decide to attack Diomedes and the Achaeans, the picture is enlarged. In Taplin's words:

> As Pandarus' crime is a kind of re-enactment of the hospitality-breaking deed of Paris, so Aineias is the equivalent of the Trojans in the larger story. They go on with Paris in their midst, and they fail to renounce him. They are guilty by association; and in due course they will pay for it.[48]

In this light, the *Iliad*'s presentation of Pandaros as a famous archer (and famous archers come traditionally from Lycia) falls within the epic's larger aim of creating a partial doublet of Paris. In Pandaros, the Iliadic tradition has not just thematized geography: it has subordinated it to the larger goal of reenacting the beginning of the Trojan War, by recalling Paris' violation of the laws of hospitality. This time, Lycia is evoked as a second-level associative allusion, since it shaped the identity of a character (Pandaros) who was then used to conjure up another character (Paris), and in particular his insolent behavior in the events preceding the plot of the *Iliad*. Space is here the means that enables the association of Pandaros with archery; at a later stage, this association led to a new one

---

[45] Mette 1951; Schmitt 1990:82–84; Taplin 1992:104–109. See also Kirk 1978:18–40.

[46] See e.g. the nurses Eurukleia, Eurunome, and Eurumedousa, and Mentor and Mentes in the Odyssey.

[47] Brügger et al. 2003:271.

[48] Taplin 1992:109.

with another archer, whose name, and most of all whose role as a violator of oaths, was central to the Trojan War epic tradition.

Feeling uneasy: Trojans and Lycians

A certain uneasiness between the Trojans and the Lycians is evident both in the accusations of cowardice Glaukos makes against the Trojans and in Hektor's subsequent reply. In the midst of the fighting over Patroklos' body, when Ajax emerges as one of the chief Achaean leaders who struggle to save the corpse from the rage of its slayer, Glaukos rebukes Hektor (*Iliad* XVII 142–168), threatening to take the Lycians and return home:

> "τὼ νῦν, εἴ τις ἐμοὶ Λυκίων ἐπιπείσεται ἀνδρῶν,
> οἴκαδ' ἴμεν, Τροίη δὲ πεφήσεται αἰπὺς ὄλεθρος."

> "Therefore now, if any of the Lykian men will obey me,
> we are going home, and the headlong destruction of Troy shall be
>   manifest."

> *Iliad* XVII 154–155

This is the first time that Hektor will reply to the rebukes of the Lycian leaders. In both *Iliad* V 493 and XVI 548, he has refrained from responding to Sarpedon and Glaukos respectively. This time, things are very different, since Sarpedon is dead and Glaukos' accusations aim at exchanging the body and armor of Patroklos for those of Sarpedon (XVII 160–165). This is the only time a mutual exchange of bodies and armor is suggested.[49]

Hektor's reply begins by expressing his disappointment at Glaukos' rebukes:

> "ὢ πόποι, ἦ τ' ἐφάμην σὲ περὶ φρένας ἔμμεναι ἄλλων
> <u>τῶν ὅσσοι Λυκίην ἐριβώλακα ναιετάουσιν·</u>
> νῦν δέ σε' ὠνοσάμην πάγχυ φρένας, οἶον ἔειπες,
> ὅς τ' ἐμὲ φὴς Αἴαντα πελώριον οὐχ ὑπομεῖναι."

> "I am surprised. I thought that for wits you surpassed all the others
> *of those who dwell in Lykia where the soil is generous*; and yet
> now I utterly despise your heart for the thing you have spoken
> when you said I cannot stand in the face of gigantic Aias."

> *Iliad* XVII 171–174

---

[49] Edwards 1991:78 on *Iliad* XVII 160–165.

In this case, Lycia features in both Glaukos' and Hektor's speeches. While the former (as the sole Lycian leader alive after Sarpedon's death) threatens to take his Lycians and return home, the latter virtually says that he is let down by Glaukos' bitter words, the more so since he regarded him as the wisest man in Lycia. Both references to Lycia are inscribed within the larger framework of distant places employed as thematized space. Glaukos' words recall Achilles' speech in *Iliad* I, in which he too threatened Agamemnon with the possibility of taking his army and returning to Phthia. Both warriors and leaders of their own armies, the Myrmidons and the Lycians respectively, are (or at least feel) dishonored by their allies for whose sake the war is fought. Hektor is for Glaukos what Agamemnon is for Achilles, that is, the brother of the hero (Paris and Menelaos respectively) who claims Helen as his wife and for whose sake he (Glaukos and Achilles respectively) came to Troy. Both Glaukos and Achilles turn distance into an argument, place into space. Thus they offer a balanced presentation of remote places by tailoring them to their own rhetoric, the rhetoric of an ally who feels betrayed, or at least let down, by those for whom he is fighting this war. A closer look at Achilles' verbalization of his threat to Agamemnon yields interesting results:

> "ὦι μοι, ἀναιδείην ἐπιειμένε, κερδαλεόφρον,
> πῶς τίς τοι πρόφρων ἔπεσιν πείθηται Ἀχαιῶν,
> ἢ' ὁδὸν ἐλθέμεναι ἢ' ἀνδράσιν ἶφι μάχεσθαι;
> οὐ γὰρ ἐγὼ Τρώων ἕνεκ' ἤλυθον αἰχμητάων
> δεῦρο μαχησόμενος, ἐπεὶ οὔ τί μοι αἴτιοί εἰσιν·
> οὐ γὰρ πώποτ' ἐμὰς βοῦς ἤλασαν οὐδὲ μὲν ἵππους,
> οὐδέ ποτ' ἐν Φθίῃ ἐριβώλακι βωτιανείρῃ
> καρπὸν ἐδηλήσαντ' ..."

> "O wrapped in shamelessness, with your mind forever on profit,
> how *shall any one of the Achaians* readily *obey you*
> *either to go on a journey or to fight men strongly in battle?*
> I for my part did not come here for the sake of the Trojan
> spearmen to fight against them, since to me they have done nothing.
> Never yet have they driven away my cattle or my horses,
> *never in Phthia, where the soil is rich and men grow great* did they
> spoil my harvest ..."

Iliad I 149–156

> "νῦν δ' εἶμι Φθίηνδ', ἐπεὶ ἦ πολὺ φέρτερόν ἐστιν
> οἴκαδ' ἴμεν σὺν νηυσὶ κορωνίσιν, οὐδέ σ' ὀίω
> ἐνθάδ' ἄτιμος ἐὼν ἄφενος καὶ πλοῦτον ἀφύξειν."

"*Now I am returning to Phthia*, since it is much better
to go home again with my curved ships, and I am minded no longer
to stay here dishonoured and pile up your wealth and your luxury."

Iliad I 169–171

The similarities in the diction employed by both Achilles in *Iliad* I and Glaukos in *Iliad* XVII indicate that a common pattern is used, which includes the following elements: (1) spatial misdirection is temporarily entertained by means of *a potential return home* (νῦν δ᾽ εἶμι Φθίηνδ᾽, ἐπεὶ ἦ πολὺ φέρτερόν ἐστιν / οἴκαδ᾽ ἴμεν - νῦν ... / οἴκαδ᾽ ἴμεν); (2) both heroes play with the idea of *convincing the army* to act, although Achilles uses this theme to rebuke Agamemnon (πῶς τίς τοι πρόφρων ἔπεσιν πείθηται Ἀχαιῶν / ἢ ὁδὸν ἐλθέμεναι ἠ᾽ ἀνδράσιν ἶφι μάχεσθαι), whereas Glaukos employs it with respect to himself (τὼ νῦν, εἴ τις ἐμοὶ Λυκίων ἐπιπείσεται ἀνδρῶν, / οἴκαδ᾽ ἴμεν).

Given that Achilles' rebuke of Agamemnon is based on his losing his war-prize (γέρας), and by extension his heroic honor, and that Glaukos' accusations hurled at Hektor stem from his fear of losing the body and armor of Sarpedon, it becomes clear that Lycia, as the spatialized doublet of Phthia, thematizes heroic concerns and also functions as an "anti-Troy." This being said, the audience, ancient and modern alike, is invited to realize the sophisticated construction of the Iliadic plot: the initial theme of the epic is so intricately interwoven into its texture that it has almost come full circle.

From this perspective, the idea of exchanging Sarpedon's body with that of Patroklos reminds the listeners that Glaukos threatens to be a Lycian Achilles, who will abandon his Trojan allies and return home. But just as Achilles' threat was only a spatial misdirection, so Glaukos' menace will soon be forgotten. The audience should not fail to remember that although Glaukos has lost his companion Sarpedon, just as Achilles has lost his companion Patroklos, he also lost Sarpedon *because of* Patroklos and *before* expressing his threat. The doublet or mirror story is tellingly misleading. Lycia may be considered another Phthia, but Hektor (as the addressee of Glaukos' rebuke) is not Agamemnon; and certainly Glaukos, who will not even abstain from war, is not a second Achilles. Μῆνις does not become the Lycians.

Lycia deauthorized: Tlepolemos and Sarpedon

The episode between Tlepolemos and Sarpedon in *Iliad* V 627–698,[50] together with a scholium on V 639.1 (bT) referring to the continuous enmity between the Lycians and the Rhodians, has given rise to the theory of a lost Lycian-

---

[50] On this episode, see Kelly 2010.

Rhodian source, a pre-Homeric epic featuring a war between the Lycians and the Rhodians. The theory has numerous and eminent supporters,[51] despite the problems of chronology that stem from it.[52] The Lycian-Rhodian epic saga may well satisfy scholarly excitement concerning the "discovery" of lost sources or even epics, but hardly has a bearing on the function of this episode within the Iliadic plot. Aceti has made this point quite strongly with respect to the importance of the Lycians in the entire *Iliad*:[53]

> Non è necessario, infatti, ipotizzare che per avere conoscenza di alcuni elementi appartenenti alle leggende locali i poetici greci avessero dovuto operare *in* Licia, tanto più dal momento che ci è noto come molti dei dettagli del mito che nelle fonti greche risultano associati a questo paese o ambietati in esso fossero frutto di un'invenzione degli stessi poetici greci ... [I] due eroi del poema [i.e. Sarpedon and Glaukos] sono collegati per via genealogica alla Grecia e dunque, come già rilevava Bassett, "their prowess and unstained fame reflect glory *on the Greek race.*"[54]

I do not disagree with a possible Lycian-Rhodian source, though serious difficulties arise when we try to describe it. I simply reiterate Aceti's observation that the emphasis on both the genealogical link between Sarpedon and Tlepolemos on their paternal side (the former being the son of Zeus, the latter his grandson) and their connection to the city of Ephura on their maternal side (the former through his uncle Bellerophon, the latter through his mother)[55] shows that the Lycian-Rhodian source, if it existed, had been epicized to such an extent that Sarpedon could be incorporated into the Greek heroic world.[56]

---

[51] Valeton 1915:125; Malten 1944; W.-H. Friedrich 1956; Frei 1978; W. Kullmann 1960; Peppermüller 1962. Glaukos' presence in the *Post-Homerica* is an indication that the catalogue of Trojan allies is based on a source to which Sarpedon was added at a later stage; see W. Kullmann 1960:175, who leaves this possibility open, and W.-H. Friedrich 1956:108–109.

[52] See Aceti 2008:180n463.

[53] Aceti 2008:180–181.

[54] Bassett 1938:219, italics added by Aceti.

[55] Frei 1978; Hiller 1993; Aceti 2008:182–183. See *Iliad* II 658–659 (and the scholium on *Iliad* II 659, which may go back to Aristarchus) and VI 152–155. The digression concerning the story of Tlepolemos points in the direction of an independent saga featuring Herakles' affair with Astuokheia in Ephura (which may well be the one in Thesprotia); the birth of Tlepolemos there; the departure and arrival of Herakles and Astuokheia to Rhodes after the sack of many cities; the murder of his mother's brother Likumnios by Tlepolemos, who subsequently gathered his supporters and left for Rhodes, where he arrived after having troubles at sea (II 667 ἀλώμενος, ἄλγεα πάσχων); and last his governing of the Rhodians by means of a system of tripartite division of the island's population based on tribes (in a Doric manner, according to Valeton 1915:22).

[56] See Valeton 1915:124, who argued that the Ionian storytellers knew from the Lycians a god Sarpedon, son of Zeus and Europa, who had come to Lycia from Crete and was governing the

This being said, Tlepolemos' address to Sarpedon is revealing:

"Σαρπῆδον, Λυκίων βουληφόρε, τίς τοι ἀνάγκη
πτώσσειν ἐνθάδ' ἐόντι μάχης ἀδαήμονι φωτί;
ψευδόμενοι δέ σέ φασι Διὸς γόνον αἰγιόχοιο
εἶναι, ἐπεὶ πολλὸν κείνων ἐπιδεύεαι ἀνδρῶν
οἳ Διὸς ἐξεγένοντο ἐπὶ προτέρων ἀνθρώπων.
ἀλλ' οἷόν τινά φασι βίην Ἡρακληείην
εἶναι, ἐμὸν πατέρα θρασυμέμνονα θυμολέοντα,
ὅς ποτε δεῦρ' ἐλθὼν ἕνεχ' ἵππων Λαομέδοντος
ἐξ οἴης σὺν νηυσὶ καὶ ἀνδράσι παυροτέροισιν
Ἰλίου ἐξαλάπαξε πόλιν, χήρωσε δ' ἀγυιάς.
σοὶ δὲ κακὸς μὲν θυμός, ἀποφθινύθουσι δὲ λαοί,
οὐδέ τί σε Τρώεσσιν ὀΐομαι ἄλκαρ ἔσεσθαι
ἐλθόντ' ἐκ Λυκίης, οὐδ' εἰ μάλα καρτερός ἐσσι,
ἀλλ' ὑπ' ἐμοὶ δμηθέντα πύλας Ἀΐδαο περήσειν."

"Man of counsel of the Lykians, Sarpedon, why must you
be skulking here, you who are a man unskilled in the fighting?
They are liars who call you an issue of Zeus, the holder
of the aegis, since you fall far short in truth of the others
who were begotten of Zeus in the generations before us:
such men as, they say, was the great strength of Herakles,
my own father, of the daring spirit, the heart of a lion:
he came here on a time for the sake of Laomedon's horses,
with six vessels only and the few men needed to man them,
and widowed the streets of Ilion and sacked the city;
but yours is the heart of a coward and your people are dying.
And I think that now, though you are come from Lykia, you will
bring no help to the Trojans even though you be a strong man,
but beaten down by my hands will pass through the gates of Hades."

Iliad V 633–646

Tlepolemos' rhetoric follows a carefully constructed plan: after quickly defaming
his opponent's fighting skills (*Iliad* V 633–634), he attempts to reject Sarpedon's
divine parentage on the grounds of his enemy's cowardice (635–637). He then

---

winds, and turned him into a mortal hero. It was only at a later stage (after colonizing Rhodes)
that the Dorians became aware of a Lycian king named Sarpedon.

switches from Sarpedon to himself, boasting of his father Herakles[57] who sacked the city of Ilion[58] because of the horses Laomedon had promised but failed to give him (638–642). In the third and last part of his speech, the Rhodian prince adds one important feature to the negative portrait of Sarpedon: he will not be able to save the Trojans, though he comes from Lycia, but will soon be killed at his opponent's hands (643–646).

The reference to Sarpedon's coming from Lycia must be interpreted within both the immediate context of the reference to the Trojans and the framework of the antithesis Tlepolemos paints between his own and his enemy's pedigrees. The phrase ἐλθόντ᾽ ἐκ Λυκίης is not a mere line-filler, but aims to be heard in contrast with the help Sarpedon was supposed to give to the Trojans. It is as if Tlepolemos is telling Sarpedon that for all his Lycian origin, he cannot help his allies. This line of thought accords with the contrast between the two heroes' genealogical status in the previous part of the speech. Tlepolemos' rhetoric aims at the very heart of the Iliadic conception and presentation of the chief Lycian leaders Sarpedon and Glaukos, who as we saw have been "dragged" into the Greek heroic world by virtue of their genealogy and their connection to the city of Ephura. By casting doubt on his opponent's divine parentage, while emphasizing his own, Tlepolemos tries to deauthorize Sarpedon's status and prestige: "he cannot possibly be the son of Zeus, since he behaves as a coward." It is in this context that Lycia is brought into the picture, in an attempt to deprive Sarpedon of his other heroic argument, the one that the Lycians systematically use to praise themselves: namely that they are coming from afar and are fighting not for their own country but for their Trojan allies.

Tlepolemos meticulously rejects all the components of Lycian heroic rhetoric and deauthorizes Sarpedon's claim to self-esteem and honor. From the Rhodian's point of view, Lycia is not a thematized space, not a source of pride and glory, not even an argument for heroic valor, but a mere topographical detail, a simple point of geography.

Merging spaces: Lycia as part of a mythical landscape

The encounter between Diomedes and Glaukos in *Iliad* VI includes the most noteworthy reference to Lycia, as the location of part of the embedded story of Bellerophon.[59] Being only a single place within the large mythical landscape

---

[57] Tlepolemos' view is a reversal of Sthenelos' arguments in *Iliad* IV 405–410: whereas Tlepolemos acknowledges the superiority of his father Herakles, Sthenelos has highlighted the preeminence and success of his own generation during the sack of Thebes. See "Rival Spaces," chapter 3, above.

[58] On Herakles' Trojan episode, see also *Iliad* XX 145–147.

[59] Part of this section is taken from Tsagalis 2010b:87–113.

delineated by Bellerophon's hodologically determined adventures, Lycia has to be examined within the complex nexus of this locale's associations. This being said, attention should be also paid to the general role of space, which seems to play a key role in this episode for two reasons: first because it is clearly inscribed within a genealogical framework, and second because it is marked by the strong antithesis between a limited physical space (the particular area of the battlefield where Diomedes and Glaukos meet) and a vast embedded story space. Given that both Diomedes' and Glaukos' insistence on their genealogical pedigrees is a way to acquire authority and legitimization,[60] the extended embedded story space they delineate may be seen as an effort to designate their proper historical space. Genealogies, after all, are maps of both time and space, since they allow the organization of collective memory into temporal and spatial terms and help communities reconsider their identity and shape it in social terms.[61]

The embedded narratives of Diomedes and Glaukos map out a mythical geography extending from Thrace to Ephura, then to Lycia and finally to Aetolia. In particular, the mythological paradigm employed by Diomedes refers to Lukourgos, and takes place on Mount Nuseion in Thrace; the first part of Bellerophon's story occurs in horse-pasturing Argos and the second part in faraway Lycia;[62] and finally, Diomedes' reference to the hospitality offered by Oineus to Bellerophon is placed at Kaludon in Aetolia.

The placement of the mythological paradigm of Lukourgos in Mount Nuseion (Νυσήϊον: *Iliad* VI 133) in Thrace stems both from the studied alliteration of this word with the epic form of Dionysus' name (Διωνύσοιο) mentioned in the previous verse (*Iliad* VI 132) and from the general staging of the meeting between Diomedes and Glaukos. Thrace, which (like Phrygia) represents one of the most typical areas from where the cult of Dionysus was diffused in Greece, points to an *otherness* symbolizing danger and peril, since for the Greeks this region stood metonymically for the unknown, the unexplored, and the irrational. In cases like this, space must be perceived in terms of cultural topography rather than geographical accuracy. In the story of Lukourgos, the landscape emphasizes the notion of *otherness* even further: the internal setting where Lukourgos' persecution of Dionysus and his maenads takes place is that of the mountain, of wild, untamed nature, far from the civilized world of the city. The embedded story of Lukourgos sheds light on a peripheral, marginalized, and

---

[60] On the paradigmatic function of genealogies, see Alden 2000:153–178, who states that "Glaucus is saved by his genealogy from fighting with Diomedes."

[61] On genealogies as time maps, see Zerubavel 2003; as means of bestowing legitimization, explanation, and obligation or duty, see Grethlein 2006:65–84; for Grethlein, though, the case of the genealogy of Glaukos in his meeting with Diomedes is different, as in this episode it is the distance between gods and men that is emphasized, and the latter's dependence on the former.

[62] In the larger sense of the northeastern Peloponnese.

inhospitable world,[63] from which the haunted god is saved by plunging into the sea, into the welcoming embrace of Thetis.

Seen from this angle, the embedded story space delineated in the parable offered by Diomedes stands in contrast to the story space of the entire scene: the absence of landscape markers in the narrator text has given way to specific markers in character text; these markers pertain both to the Greeks' notion of cultural geography and to a metonymic polarity between mountain and sea.[64]

The embedded story narrated by Glaukos is divided into two parts, the former taking place in mainland Greece,[65] the latter in Lycia. These two distinct parts are organized around the figure of Bellerophon, who is the common thread among these three different mythical lays which seem to have been imperfectly conflated. The first refers to a king who decided to exile from his kingdom a young hero who could potentially become a threat to his throne; the second is a variant of the well-known story of Potiphar's wife:[66] the wife of the king falls in love with a younger man, who in some versions is a potential usurper of the throne, and systematically slanders him after he rejects her love offers; the third lay refers to the contests and dangers a hero must overcome in order to be allowed to marry the king's daughter. The clearly pleonastic explanation of Bellerophon's exile from Argos (for reasons pertaining to both the first and the second lays), as well as his reward upon his arrival in Lycia, indicate that all three lays have been imperfectly merged into the Iliadic version. The final punishment of Bellerophon is a strong antiphonal echo of the punishment of Lukourgos, both being expressed in a similar formulaic manner: *Iliad* VI 140 ... ἐπεὶ ἀθανάτοισιν ἀπήχθετο πᾶσι θεοῖσιν; VI 200 ... καὶ κεῖνος ἀπήχθετο πᾶσι θεοῖσιν.[67]

---

[63] On the opposition between city and countryside, see Rosen and Sluiter 2006.

[64] For the leap into the sea as a metaphor for a transition into another state, see Nagy 1990a:223–262.

[65] There are a number of cities named Ephura. I am following the view of Frei (1973:823) that Homer is referring to Thesprotian Ephura (see also the scholium on *Iliad* II 659), so the term Argos is employed here in the sense of "the Achaean world"; see Graziosi and Haubold 2010:119 on *Iliad* VI 152. Differently West (1998–2000:381 s.v. Ἐφύρη [1]; 2011:177–178 on *Iliad* VI 152), who thinks that the "original Ephura was perhaps in Thessaly, in the Pelasgic Argos," but "in the sixth century the name with its associated mythology was appropriated by Corinth." Thesprotian Ephura is first mentioned by Thucydides (1.46.4).

[66] The Near Eastern elements in the story of Bellerophon are numerous (Khimaira; the theme of Potiphar's wife; the letter of Proitos to Iobates, king of Lycia, inscribed on the πίναξ πτυκτός; the wanderings of Bellerophon); see Strömberg 1961; Peppermüller 1962; West 1997:365–367.

[67] The word καί in *Iliad* VI 200 has caused both trouble and speculation: some scholars take it as a direct comparison between Lukourgos and Bellerophon, while others maintain that the two paradigms have been "excerpted" from an earlier catalogue-poem. For the relevant bibliography, see Scodel 1992:78n13, who argues that "the point lies in the contrast between the two [Lukourgos and Bellerophon]" (78), since in the former the favor of the gods is presented as subject to human control, while in the latter divine favor in the beginning of the story, with

In the first part of Bellerophon's story, embedded story space is designated by means of the typologically established opening of an embedded tale:
ἔστι πόλις Ἐφύρη μυχῶι Ἄργεος ἱπποβότοιο (*Iliad* VI 152).[68] As soon as specific
geographical features have been given, a genealogy follows, starting from
Sisuphos, continuing with Glaukos (the grandfather of the Iliadic Glaukos) and
then with his son Bellerophon, who is characterized as favored by the gods with
beauty and manhood.[69] The designation of space, which is done by means of
place-names, is invigorated by Bellerophon's pedigree, and especially by the
designation of Sisuphos, son of Aiolos (*Iliad* VI 154 Σίσυφος Αἰολίδης), as his
great-grandfather.[70]

The mention of Proitos recalls one of the three royal families of Argos,[71]
the Proitids/Anaxagorids, from whom Sthenelos descends (the other two being
the Melampodids and the Biantids, from whom come Eurualos and Diomedes).
In Glaukos' embedded narrative, Argos is more or less the domestic space of
the palace of Proitos, from which Bellerophon is exiled. In the second part,
space is designated through a series of changes: first the dangerous countryside of Lycia (after a brief scene of ξενία in the palace of the Lycian king, who
remains deliberately unnamed) where Bellerophon fights against Khimaira,[72]
the Solumoi, the Amazons (the symbol of untamed, savage female nature), and
an ambush organized against him by the king of Lycia himself with a group of

---

Bellerophon's πομπή in Lycia, and divine anger at the end, with the hero's wandering, are
left unexplained. See Webster 1958:186; Gaisser 1969:157–158; G. Murray (1907:197–199) has
postulated a relation between the stories of Lukourgos and Bellerophon going back to the epic
Corinthiaca by Eumelus.

[68] "There is a city, Ephyre, in the corner of horse-pasturing Argos ..." See H. Mackie 1996:68–69,
who draws attention to *Iliad* II 811, XI 711, and XIII 32, where the expression "there is a hill/city/
cave" is employed, and argues that "the line beginning with ἔστι marks a transition to a new
setting and the start of a new episode ... The examples show that the phrase ἔστι δέ τις ('there is a
...') functions as a narrative marker, equivalent to the camera's shift to a new frame in cinematic
narrative."

[69] *Iliad* VI 156–157 τῷ δὲ θεοὶ κάλλός τε καὶ ἠνορέην ἐρατεινήν / ὤπασαν ("To [Bellerophontes] the
gods granted beauty and desirable / manhood").

[70] In Pindar (*Olympians* 13.49–52), Sisuphos is presented as coming from Corinth, but it seems
that this identification is based on the interpretation of the relevant Homeric passage in *Iliad*
VI 150–211, with which *Olympian* 13.49–92 shares a number of common themes. Eumelus
(*Corinthiaca*, frr. 1–4, PEG 1 = frr. 1, 12, 2, 3a, 5, EGF = frr. 15–19 West) is probably the first who
identified Ephura with Corinth, so as to promote local Corinthian interests.

[71] Notice that Bellerophon has to obey Proitos' will to leave the city, given the power of the king
(*Iliad* VI 158 ἐπεὶ πολύ φέρτερος ἦεν). For the motif "he is (by far) mightier" which is attested
twenty-seven times in the *Iliad*, see Kelly 2007:173–174.

[72] On the possible link between Khimaira and the place-names of Lycia, see Kirk 1990:182–183;
between Khimaira and population movements, see Bryce 2006:148–149.

elite warriors;[73] then, upon Bellerophon's victory and subsequent marriage to the king's daughter, the hero moves to friendly space, the best τέμενος offered to him by the people of Lycia;[74] finally, Bellerophon is found, without any explanation on the part of Glaukos who narrates the story, wandering alone in the field of Aleion.[75]

The two parts of the story of Bellerophon constitute a bipolar organization of embedded story space: on the one hand, the historical and mythical geography of mainland Greece and Lycia, and on the other the systematic interplay between friendly and enemy space that continuously alternate: Proitos' palace—Lycian countryside—fertile τέμενος—Aleion field.

With Diomedes' final story we are brought back to the civilized world of the palace, though not this time in the Peloponnese, but in the city of Kaludon in Aetolia, in the palace of Diomedes' grandfather Oineus, who is also known to the Iliadic tradition from the famous mythological example of Meleager. The shift of the action to the palace positively accentuates the theme of ξενία offered to Bellerophon by Oineus, and highlights the importance of the gifts of hospitality (ξεινήϊα), which foreshadow the exchange of gifts between Diomedes and Glaukos at the end of the episode.[76]

Lycia's function in this episode is conditioned by its integration in a chain of locations comprising a mythical landscape, which connotes a shift of narrative settings on the basis of the following polar opposites:

Lukourgos	mountain	sea
Bellerophon	palace (Proitos'— Lycian king's)	countryside (Lycia— τέμενος—Aleion field)
	palace of Oineus	

The staging of the entire meeting of Diomedes and Glaukos is organized on the basis of the interaction between simple story space and embedded story space, which allows for the intersection of two basic themes of the entire

---

[73] The use of the preposition ἀντί by both Diomedes (*Iliad* VI 127 ἀντιόωσιν) and Glaukos (VI 160 Ἄντεια, VI 186 ἀντιανείρας) is intriguing. Both place-names, Nuseion and Aleion, are acoustically exploited through interpretive alliterations (132–133 Διώνυσος-Νυσήϊον, 201 Ἀλήϊον-ἀλᾶτο); see West 1997:367.

[74] See Karavites 1992:134–135, who draws attention to the fact that (1) a τέμενος does not always belong to the king but also to other preeminent citizens, and (2) the owner of the land may be the people as a collective entity.

[75] On the wandering of Bellerophon and the motif of the "the suffering of the Erring," see White 1982 and D'Alfonso 2008, who offers plenty of material on its oriental provenance.

[76] On the exchange of gifts in this episode, see Scodel 1992.

episode: the relation between gods and men, and hospitality. Although the mythological example narrated by Diomedes focuses on the predictability and rationalization of divine-human interaction, by implying that divine penalties are imposed on mortals for their disrespect towards the gods, whereas that of Glaukos emphasizes the unpredictability of divine favor and anger, they have as a common denominator the motif of ξενία (hospitality), which is a prerequisite for the establishment of long-term relations and whose violation results in divine punishment. Given that the motif of ξενία[77] is implicitly linked to the place where hospitality will take place, the sophisticated interaction between simple story space and embedded story space in this episode results in their narrative merger, and explains the paradox of a friendly encounter on the field of combat. In particular, the limited simple story space is expanded by the extended embedded story space to such a degree that the former merges with or is even absorbed by the latter, so that the entire scene can end with a ξενία, through the exchange of gifts, and not with a formal duel. The meeting between Diomedes and Glaukos in *Iliad* VI marks the transformation of the primary military space of the battlefield into the vicarious, secondary space of a ξενία. This transformation, not surprisingly, will be short-lived. When Lycia features outside the mythical landscape of an embedded story, as with Glaukos' rebuke of Hektor in *Iliad* XVII 142–168, then things are dramatically different: there is no exchange of weapons or of the corpses of the two fallen heroes Sarpedon and Patroklos. The mythical landscape has given way to the physical reality of the battlefield, where warriors come close only to kill.

Cultic space: Sarpedon returns home

The transfer of Sarpedon's corpse to Lycia by Hupnos and Thanatos is one of the highlights of the *Iliad*, although one of the most influential schools of Homeric criticism, neonalysis, has argued that it was transferred to the *Iliad* from the story of Memnon, whose body was also removed from the battlefield by Hupnos and Thanatos, and the Aethiopian hero was subsequently immortalized. This view is based partly on iconographic evidence,[78] though the picture seems to be rather blurred, as Hupnos and Thanatos are shown in iconography sometimes with Sarpedon and sometimes with Memnon.[79] Neoanalysts unanimously argue for the priority of the Memnon story, based on both the fact that Hupnos and Thanatos signify that the deceased's body will awaken from its sleep and

---

[77] On ξενία and φιλότης (within the framework of the making of agreements in the *Iliad*) and their relation to Near Eastern concepts of "brotherhood" or "fraternity," see Karavites 1992:47–55; on the typology and aesthetics of the hospitality scene, see Reece 1993:5–39.

[78] See Holland 1894–1897:2676–2679; Bothmer 1981:72, 76–77.

[79] See Burgess 2009:77.

become immortalized (which is true only of Memnon) and the genealogy of Hupnos and Thanatos, who are brothers of Eos, Memnon's mother. This is sufficient proof of the priority of the *Aithiopisstoff*,[80] where Hupnos and Thanatos are brothers of Eos and therefore their role is primary, not secondary as with Sarpedon in the *Iliad*.[81] Clarke and Coulson also favor the same interpretation,[82] arguing that since a number of vases depict the removal of Sarpedon's body by Hupnos and Thanatos in a manner that does not follow the *Iliad* (they add other figures not present in the Iliadic rendering of this episode), then it may be that they are following the Memnon story.[83] Burgess, on the other hand, is skeptical, since the genealogy of Hupnos and Thanatos is not unanimous in our sources[84] and the iconographic material does not favor one or the other interpretation.[85] Davies is equally skeptical of the argument supporting the priority of the motif in Memnon's story, since he thinks that Memnon is already immortalized and hence the removal of his body by Thanatos is paradoxical.[86] There is also another line of reasoning, put forward by West, who argues that Memnon is "a new-comer to mythology, with no accomplishments to his name before he came to Troy and met his death,"[87] and so his story could not have influenced that of Sarpedon. On the contrary, Nagy favors the idea of parallel stories that have grown independently; in this interpretation their similarities are due to the fact that they are thematic variants, each one being what Nagy has labeled, in oralist terminology, a multiform.[88] Aceti argues that similarities detected between certain Iliadic episodes and some elements in the Memnon story should be explained not as the result of imitation of a lost *Memnonis* by the *Iliad*, but as a by-product of the links between the narrative sequences pertaining to the fate of Achilles after the duel with Hektor.[89]

One of the crucial questions surrounding this thorny problem is the role of Lycia, to where Sarpedon's body is transferred. This aspect of the problem has not been studied before, but is directly relevant to the problem at hand. First,

---

[80] W. Kullmann 1960:319.
[81] See Schadewaldt 1965:165; W. Kullmann 1960:35–36. On the importance of specific uses of typical motifs, see W. Kullmann 1984; Burgess 2006.
[82] Arguing against Fenik 1968 and Dihle 1970.
[83] Clark and Coulson 1978:70–73.
[84] In Hesiod *Theogony* 758–759, Hupnos and Thanatos are children of Nux, while it is Eos who is a child of Nux in Quintus of Smyrna's *Posthomerica* 2.625–627.
[85] 2009:77–78.
[86] Davies 1989:57. But see Burgess 2009:76, who observes that "[Memnon] traditionally die[s], and death precedes most cases of heroic immortality"; see also Burgess 2009:98–110.
[87] West 2003a:9.
[88] See Nagy 1990a:130–131.
[89] Aceti 2008:256–262.

let me reiterate an argument that has passed unnoticed by those who argue for the priority of the Sarpedon story.

J. Kakridis has shown that the delay in the burning of Patroklos' pyre in *Iliad* XXIII, which is resolved by Iris' journey to the Winds, who finally decide to blow, reflects an episode in a pre-Homeric epic tradition (a lost **Achilleis*) where the Winds (as children of Eos) refused to burn Achilles' pyre, since Achilles had killed their brother Memnon (§60 Kullmann = 189 Severyns = Allen 106.5–6). In this epic, "Zeus' action would be fully justified when 'to honour Thetis' he sends a messenger—either Hermes[90] or Iris—and orders the Winds not to leave unburnt the body of the great hero who was the son of a goddess and loved by the gods."[91] This is a strong argument pointing to the motif of "Eos receiving help from two assistants," both her sons, the Winds Boreas and Zephuros, and her brothers Hupnos and Thanatos: the former with Achilles' pyre, the latter with the removal of Memnon's body. W. Kullmann, in fact, has shown that since we are dealing with the goddess of Dawn (Eos), Hupnos and Thanatos may be representing her temporal aspect, while Boreas and Zephuros her spatial or cosmological one (they are hardly ever placed in the East, where Eos' seat is).[92] Finally, with respect to the confusing genealogy of Hupnos and Thanatos, Kullmann suggests[93] that we are dealing with the contamination of two distinct mythological ways of thinking: Eos is the daughter of Nux, when the idea of the "course of time" is emphasized, whereas Hupnos and Thanatos are the children of Nux when the notion of "human fate" is highlighted.[94]

If the motif of the removal of Sarpedon's corpse by Hupnos and Thanatos is secondary to the *Iliad* and primary to a pre-Homeric epic tradition about Memnon, then the same should be true of the place where the corpse is to be finally deposited. In other words, where was Memnon's body placed after being removed by Hupnos and Thanatos in the Memnon story? Quintus of Smyrna (*Posthomerica* 2.585–591) explicitly says that the body was placed along the banks of the river Aisepos, in the beautiful grove of the Nymphs, where the daughters of Aisepos later made a huge σῆμα. This detail becomes all the more interesting given that in the *Posthomerica* the entire Aethiopean army is removed from the battlefield and covered in divine mist, so as to follow the corpse of their dead king to the streams of the river Aisepos. This last is obviously a late feature of the story, which is reflected in the future metamorphosis of the Aethiopians

[90] Hermes is not a good guess; Kakridis may have been misled, though he does not decide between Hermes and Iris, by Quintus of Smyrna (*Posthomerica* 3.699–701). Iris is the typical messenger of the gods in the *Iliad*; on this point, see W. Kullmann 1960:35n3.

[91] J. Kakridis 1949:82–83.

[92] W. Kullmann 1960:35.

[93] 1960:36.

[94] See Hesiod *Theogony* 211–212.

into birds (*Posthomerica* 2.643–655).[95] Still, the removal of Memnon's body to the nearby site of the river Aisepos may indicate that the older mythical material at Quintus' disposal designated only the place to where Memnon was removed by Eos: a wooded area not far from the battlefield, where she washes his body and anoints and dresses him,[96] as can be seen in the kylix of Pamphaios. This view may be surmised by considering that in contrast with Sarpedon, whose tomb is always located in his homeland Lycia, later sources disagree on the placement of Memnon's grave on the river Aisepos in Asia Minor, the river Badas in Syria, in Belas, or even in Susa. Some authors say either that there was no grave for Memnon (Philostratus *Imagines* I 7.2) or that his tomb on the Aisepos is a ceno-taph (Aelian *On the Nature of Animals* V 1). What matters here is the antithesis between the way later sources speak of the graves of two mythical heroes, so closely linked by the motif of the removal of their corpses from the battlefield by Hupnos and Thanatos.

There is, though, one more point to be considered. Given that the place where the first part of the lamentation and caring for the deceased's body had to be close to the battlefield, Quintus followed the tradition of both the **Memnonis/Aethiopis* and the *Iliad* that the corpses of Memnon and Sarpedon respectively were removed first to a neighboring wooded and watered area (a river). This is a significant detail: it seems that what was done in both the **Memnonis* and in the *Iliad* in two phases—first a transfer by Eos and Apollo respectively to a nearby watered area for the initial caring for the body, and then the same gods' calling on Hupnos and Thanatos to carry the bodies of Memnon and Sarpedon respectively—has been combined in a single transfer of two groups of people (Memnon and the Aethiopes).[97] In his reconstruction of the plot of the **Memnonis*, Schadewaldt suggests that Hupnos and Thanatos transferred Memnon's corpse to his homeland of Aethiopia, although he does not cite even a single source. He obviously thinks that this would be the only reasonable place for Memnon's body after his death. Such a view cannot explain the divergence between the unanimous agreement of later sources as to the location of Sarpedon's grave and the wide disagreement over Memnon's tomb. Nor does it take into account that the name Sarpedon was known in the Lycian language as *zrppudeine*[98] and that there was a local tradition narrating the death of Sarpedon at the hands of Tlepolemos in Lycia.[99] In other words, the transfer

---

[95]   See P. Kakridis 1962:35.
[96]   See Lung 1912:51, 57–58 and the kylix of Pamphaios. On this topic, see Schadewaldt 1965:160.
[97]   Moreover, Hupnos and Thanatos had been replaced by the Winds, who were Memnon's brothers.
[98]   Bryce 1986:26; Janko 1992:370–373 on *Iliad* XVI 489–683.
[99]   Valeton 1915:126. According to this view, Tlepolemos replaced Herakles, who in an older version killed Sarpedon. When the myth was taken up by storytellers of Doric descent, then the son

of Sarpedon's body to Lycia and the funeral it receives there together with the building of a tomb and a stele is more linked to Sarpedon's hero-cult than to Memnon's story. This is because Memnon was immortalized in the *Memnonis, while Sarpedon was not in the *Iliad*. It was Hera who suggested, against Zeus' entertaining the possibility of averting Sarpedon's death, that his body be transferred to Lycia and buried there. Since "hero-cult is a localized phenomenon in archaic Greek religion"[100] and Sarpedon is closely associated in the *Iliad* with the δῆμος of the Lycians (*Iliad* XVI 455; 673, cf. XVI 683), it may be that the motif of his transfer by Hupnos and Thanatos does after all reflect the *Memnonis, but the emphasis on Lycia where Sarpedon's relatives and comrades will give him a proper burial is due to a local tradition. The fate of Memnon's body is obscure: it apparently had to be transferred somewhere by Hupnos and Thanatos, but the hero's immortalization (cf. §61 Kullmann = 189–190 Severyns = Allen 106.6–7 καὶ τούτῳ μὲν Ἠὼς παρὰ Διὸς αἰτησαμένη ἀθανασίαν δίδωσι) excludes his homeland, for one cannot be immortalized among the living. In the light of the *Aethiopis* (§66 Kullmann = 199–200 Severyns = Allen 106.14–15), where Thetis snatches Achilles' body from the pyre and brings it to the White Island (Λευκὴ νῆσος), it may be that Hupnos and Thanatos carried Memnon's body beyond the borders of the human world, though I am hesitant about the possibility that both Memnon and Achilles would be immortalized on the White Island. Perhaps the Islands of the Blessed (Μακάρων νῆσοι) are a good alternative.[101]

In the scene of the transfer of Sarpedon's body by the twins Hupnos and Thanatos, Lycia plays a role determined by Sarpedon's hero-cult, and reflects a tradition about his burial in Lycia after his death at the hands of the Rhodian Tlepolemos, in a local epic lay featuring the struggles between Lycians and Rhodians.[102] Lycia in this scene is the space of a hero's future cult, the space where sleep and death, that is, fainting and dying, will cease to operate not by the immortalization of Zeus' son, as with Memnon and Achilles, but through a cultural process, namely the tomb and σῆμα that his countrymen will built for him. The removal of a hero's body after his death does not guarantee immortalization; it is the difference between human and semidivine space that does.

Having explored the function of place-names in the *Iliad*, we can summarize the results of our analysis briefly as follows:

(Tlepolemos) took the place of the father (Herakles), while subsequently Sarpedon became the one who killed Tlepolemos.

[100] Nagy 1990a:132.

[101] See Hesiod *Works and Days* 171 (ἐν μακάρων νήσοισι παρ' Ὠκεανὸν βαθυδίνην) and Nagy 1990a:141.

[102] Valeton 1915:126.

1. The CS and the CT&A represent the main section of the epic in which the narrator reserves the use of place-names for himself. In this globalizing view of the Greek and Trojans-and-allies worlds, he offers a programmatic outlook in the *Iliad* by associating heroes with specific geographical regions. By combining two mental processes, the *map* and the *tour*, the storyteller is able to present a panorama of the forces involved in the war at the lowest possible cognitive cost.

2. Having accomplished this task, the storyteller lets the characters of the plot, much more often than he does himself, employ place-names in their speeches. Embedded story space is thus left to the various heroes, who function as *cognizers*, thinking agents whose epic storage determines the way they act in the story-world. In this light, place-names are transformed from mere locations on a map into thematized spaces by means of which each hero's epic-mythical agenda is channeled into the *Iliad*. Phthia, Argos, Pylos, and Boeotian Thebes on the one hand, and the Troad and Lycia on the other are not just places linked to key figures of the plot. To a large extent, they constitute an integral part of the personalities of Achilles, Agamemnon, Nestor, Diomedes-Sthenelos, Hektor, Sarpedon, and Glaukos respectively. Being embedded in typical dichotomies of κλέος and νόστος and praise and blame, geography is turned into space that represents each hero's "epic home," the notional center around which his past, present, and future constantly evolve.

PART THREE

PARATOPIC SPACE

SIMILES AND VISUAL IMAGERY

I N THIS PART OF THE BOOK I examine the Homeric simile, which constitutes both a defining feature of Homeric epic and a hallmark of a mature stage in the development of oral song-making. Similes have been studied either from a taxonomic point of view,[1] or with respect to their diction,[2] or from a purely literary perspective.[3] Recently, in one of the most thorough and innovative analyses of Homeric similes, Elizabeth Minchin has begun to examine the simile within the complex network created by image and memory.[4] By adopting a cognitive approach, Minchin is able to place the simile in a much wider context that transcends the limits of literary aestheticism, exploring "how a storyteller who is performing before a listening audience works with the resources of memory to generate this kind of comparative material, which draws on both imagery and language."[5] One of the strongest conclusions reached in her study of similes is their *pictureability*, which unites them with respect to storyteller, audience, and song itself, thus making a moment recognizable and memorable. The results of Minchin's analysis can be applied to further investigations concerning one of the most powerful and effective mechanisms used in memory recall: space. My purpose is to bring to the fore this rather neglected aspect of imagery and memory, which is paramount not only in the light of cognitive approaches to the Homeric simile but also in its complex and often problematic connection to the Iliadic story-world.

The term *paratopic space* (from Greek παρά 'next to, beyond' + τόπος 'place') has been coined to denote space that exists "next to" and "beyond" story space. By combining two of the three syntactical uses of the preposition παρά when it takes the accusative (meaning either "beside, next to, near" or "past, beyond"), the term *paratopic* suggests that the space of the simile is a τόπος that exists next to or in parallel with the space of the main narrative, or story space, to which it is often attached, but also beyond, over, and above the regular story space. In fact, the Greek term that comes closer to the meaning of "simile" is not παρομοίωσις 'assimilation' but παραβολή 'illustration, analogy', the first part of which points to the meaning of "beside, next to, side by side," and the second indicates a movement, a dynamic delineation of space. Among the wealth of ancient rhetorical theories on simile and comparison,[6] various discussions illuminate the relevant terminology and offer valuable insights into the particular

---

[1]   See D. Lee 1964; Scott 1974; Moulton 1977.
[2]   Shipp 1972.
[3]   Fränkel 1921; Bowra 1952:266–280; Coffey 1957; Edwards 1987:102–110; Nimis 1987:23–95; Petegorsky 1982:9–74; Edwards 1991:24–41; Scott 2009. This brief list does not include studies of individual similes or groups of similes.
[4]   Minchin 2001:132–160.
[5]   Minchin 2001:133.
[6]   See McCall 1969.

kind of comparison that constitutes the simile: in particular by Aristotle, the author of the *Rhetorica ad Herennium*, the author of *On Style*, and Trypho in his handbook *On Tropes* (Περὶ τρόπων).

Aristotle mainly explores two forms of comparison, παραβολή and εἰκών. According to his approach, παραβολή is a subcategory of the *manufactured example*, which is in itself one of the two divisions of παράδειγμα (the other being the *actual* or *historical example*). Let us consider the following passage from *Rhetoric* 2 (1393b4–8):

> παραβολὴ δὲ τὰ Σωκρατικά, οἷον εἴ τις λέγοι ὅτι οὐ δεῖ κληρωτοὺς ἄρχειν· ὅμοιον γὰρ ὥσπερ ἂν εἴ τις τοὺς ἀθλητὰς κληροίη μὴ οἳ δύνανται ἀγωνίζεσθαι ἀλλ' οἳ ἂν λάχωσιν, ἢ τῶν πλωτήρων ὅντινα δεῖ κυβερνᾶν κληρώσειεν, ὡς δέον τὸν λαχόντα ἀλλὰ μὴ τὸν ἐπιστάμενον.

> The illustrative parallel is the sort of argument Socrates used: e.g. "Public officials ought not to be selected by lot. That is like using the lot to select athletes, instead of choosing those who are fit for the contest; or using the lot to select a steersman from among a ship's crew, as if we ought to take the man on whom the lot falls, and not the man who knows most about it."[7]

The important observation here is that the παραβολή is a form of comparison made to serve another purpose and not required on its own account, a point made explicitly in Aristotle's *Topics* (156b25–27).[8] Although the illustrative parallel is employed to persuade or prove, it is fair to say that its core aspect is *analogy* based on knowledge, even knowledge of potential and recognizable situations, devoid of any historical element.

As for the εἰκών, or stylistic comparison, which Aristotle treats in considerable detail in *Rhetoric* 3, he observes that the elements of one of its subdivisions, namely the "successful or popular similes" (εὐδοκιμοῦσαι εἰκόνες) and "proportional metaphor" (ἡ ἀνάλογον μεταφορά), are alike in that they always involve two relations:[9] in expressions like "a shield is the drinking-bowl of Ares" (ἡ ἀσπὶς ... ἐστι φιάλη Ἄρεως) and "a bow is a chordless lyre" (τὸ τόξον φόρμιγξ ἄχορδος), the only difference between successful simile and proportional metaphor is the

---

[7] The translation by Roberts (ed. Ross) is used for all passages from Aristotle's *Rhetoric*.

[8] καὶ τὸ ὡς ἐν παραβολῇ προτείνειν· τὸ γὰρ δι' ἄλλο προτεινόμενον καὶ μὴ δι' αὐτὸ χρήσιμον τιθέασι μᾶλλον ("Formulate your premiss as though it were a mere illustration: for people admit the more readily a proposition made to serve some other purpose, and not required on its own account"; translation by W. A. Pickard-Cambridge, cited in McCall 1969:28).

[9] Aristotle *Rhetoric* 1412b34–1413a3.

presence or absence of a term of comparison (e.g. ὡς or ὥσπερ).[10] Aristotle, therefore, treats similes as the most refined type of εἰκών, which shares with proportional metaphor the aspect of *analogy*. In both the illustrative parallel and the successful simile, analogy is created through the comparison not of subjects but of *situations*. Public officials are not compared with athletes or steersmen, but the process of selecting public officials is presented as like that of competing athletes or choosing a steersman from among the ship's crew. Situational analogy of this sort presupposes implicit second-level comparisons: the governing of a city resembles either a race or contest between rival athletes, or the piloting of a ship, which needs experience and skill. Likewise for successful similes: the comparison is not simple, for neither is the shield compared to a drinking-bowl nor the bow to a lyre; the shield is like the drinking-bowl of the god of war, for whom the shield is what a drinking-bowl is to a man participating in a symposium; along the same lines, the bow is like a lyre deprived of its chords, that is, one that produces not sonorous sounds but the grim twang of death. Thus situational analogy evokes a whole nexus of associations that activates more than a single set of relations.[11] In this type of comparison, every part of the situational analogy has to be in a one-to-one relation with the corresponding comparandum: public officials and athletes, city and athletic contests, shield and drinking-bowl, warrior and Ares. In fact, it is the direct analogy between the multiple constituent parts of the simile that creates the nexus of associations that I have called situational analogy. We should bear this point in mind, for it will be directly applicable to the Homeric simile.

In the *Rhetorica ad Herennium* we come across a detailed examination of comparison (4.45.59–4.48.61). The anonymous author of this treatise distinguishes four types of comparison (by *contrast*, by *negation*, by *concision*, and by *detailed comparison*), the last two of which are relevant to my discussion. In this context, conciseness is used as a method of elucidation, while detailed comparison aims at creating vividness. What matters here is that the former refers "both to the condensing of separate descriptions of subject and comparison into one and to the consequent brevity of the comparison itself,"[12] whereas the latter "achieves its purpose of vividness through the extensive embellishment of both of its parts and that method of presentation is *per conlationem* ['by detailed parallel'] because ... *all the corresponding items of the subject and comparative parts are expressed and correlated*."[13] Although in his view, very much unlike Aristotle's, no type of comparison is correlated with metaphor, the author of

---

[10] See Jürgensen 1968:53–54.
[11] See McCall 1969:45.
[12] McCall 1969:72.
[13] McCall 1969:73. The italics are mine.

the *Rhetorica ad Herennium* makes two important points: brevity in comparisons enhances clarity, and vividness presupposes extensive correspondence between the various comparative parts of the simile. When combined with Aristotle's insights, these two observations allow us to reconsider certain aspects of the Homeric simile: the situational analogy we encounter there (expressed in the form of condensed visual snapshots, with correspondence and correlation of all constituent elements of the two parts of the simile) asks for an interpretation. First, however, I would bring into the picture some other aspects of ancient discussions of simile and comparison.

The *auctor incertus* of the treatise *On Style* goes a step further than Aristotle, distinguishing between two types of literary comparison, εἰκασία and παραβολή. Whereas the former is brief and can be employed freely in prose, the latter is long (or longer) and constitutes a poetic figure (89–90):

(89) Ἐπὰν μέντοι εἰκασίαν ποιῶμεν τὴν μεταφοράν, ὡς προλέλεκται, στοχαστέον τοῦ συντόμου, καὶ τοῦ μηδὲν πλέον τοῦ ὥσπερ προτιθέναι, ἐπεί τοι ἀντ' εἰκασίας παραβολὴ ἔσται ποιητική, οἷον τὸ τοῦ Ξενοφῶντος· ὥσπερ δὲ κύων γενναῖος ἀπρονοήτως ἐπὶ κάπρον φέρεται, καὶ ὥσπερ ἵππος λυθεὶς διὰ πεδίου γαυριῶν καὶ ἀπολακτίζων· ταῦτα γὰρ οὐκ εἰκασίαις ἔτι ἔοικεν, ἀλλὰ παραβολαῖς ποιητικαῖς. (90) Τὰς δὲ παραβολὰς ταύτας οὔτε ῥᾳδίως ἐν τοῖς πεζοῖς λόγοις τιθέναι δεῖ, οὔτε ἄνευ πλείστης φυλακῆς. καὶ περὶ μεταφορᾶς μὲν <τοσαῦτα> ὡς τύπῳ εἰπεῖν.

(89) When we turn a metaphor into a simile in the way I described, we must aim at conciseness, and do no more than prefix "like," or else we shall have a poetic comparison instead of a simile. Take, for example, "like a gallant hound which recklessly charges a boar" (from Xenophon) and "like a horse let loose, kicking and proudly prancing over the plain." Such descriptions no longer seem similes but poetic comparisons, (90) and poetic comparisons should not be used freely in prose nor without the greatest caution. This concludes my outline on the subject of metaphor.[14]

Although this description of εἰκασία and παραβολή is included in the discussion of "grand" style (μεγαλοπρεπὴς χαρακτήρ), it is also applicable to "elegant" style (γλαφυρὸς χαρακτήρ), while παραβολή also pertains to "plain" style (ἰσχνὸς χαρακτήρ) and εἰκασία to "forceful" style (δεινὸς χαρακτήρ).[15] The main point

---

[14] Translation by Innes 1995, Loeb Classical Library.
[15] See McCall 1969:150–155.

made by the author of *On Style*, despite reasonable objections concerning his omitting any discussion of εἰκασία from the plain style and treating παραβολή as unsuitable for the forceful style, is that he has brought into the picture the features of length and poetic suitability of the παραβολή.[16] In fact, some of his arguments, like the one that "the comparison owes its vividness to the fact that all the accompanying circumstances are mentioned and nothing is omitted" (209 τὸ γὰρ ἐναργὲς ἔχει ἐκ τοῦ πάντα εἰρῆσθαι τὰ συμβαίνοντα, καὶ μὴ παραλελεῖφθαι μηδέν),[17] draw on specific Homeric examples of extended similes,[18] which silently shows that the author set out to discuss not the single feature of simile but two distinct types of literary comparison, εἰκασία and παραβολή.[19]

In Trypho's *On Tropes*,[20] the main term for "comparison," ὁμοίωσις, is subdivided into εἰκών, which pertains to the comparison of objects that share visible or physical similarities;[21] παράδειγμα, which involves events that have taken place in the past;[22] and παραβολή,[23] which highlights vividness and action in the comparison of similar objects.[24] In this light, let us consider the following definition of παραβολή 'simile':

παραβολὴ δέ ἐστι λόγος δι' ὁμοίων καὶ γινωσκομένων εἰς ὄψιν ἄγειν πειρώμενος τὸ νοούμενον.

The simile is speech that attempts to make visible by means of similar and known things what exists in the mind.

Rhetorica anonyma "περὶ ποιητικῶν τρόπων" 3.212.19

---

[16] In this respect, there is partial overlap with the observations in the *Rhetorica ad Herennium* (see above).

[17] See McCall 1969:152–153.

[18] 209 οἷον "ὡς δ' ὅτ' ἀνὴρ ὀχετηγὸς" [*Iliad* XXI 257] καὶ πᾶσα αὕτη ἡ παραβολή ("an instance is the Homeric simile which begins 'as when a man draws off water by a runnel.'") See McCall 1969:152–153.

[19] Neither *On Literary Composition* by Dionysius of Halicarnassus nor *On the Sublime* by Pseudo-Longinus are of any help, the former due to its apparent lack of interest in illustrative comparison (there is only a single mention, in chapter 11, echoing pre-Aristotelian views on εἰκών); the latter because of a famous lacuna in chapter 37, exactly where the unknown author was about to explore our two key terms of comparison, εἰκασία and παραβολή.

[20] 200.4–6 Ὁμοίωσίς ἐστι ῥῆσις, καθ' ἣν ἕτερον ἑτέρῳ παραβάλλομεν, εἴδη δὲ αὐτῆς εἰσι τρία, εἰκών, παράδειγμα, παραβολή.

[21] 200.6–8 εἰκών ἐστι λόγος ἐναργῶς ἐξομοιοῦν πειρώμενος διὰ τοῦ παραλαμβανομένου, πρὸς ὃ παραλαμβάνεται.

[22] 200.21–23 παράδειγμά ἐστι τοῦ προγεγονότος πράγματος παρένθεσις καθ' ὁμοιότητα τῶν ὑποκειμένων πρὸς παραίνεσιν προτροπῆς ἢ ἀποτροπῆς ἕνεκεν.

[23] 201.12–13 παραβολή ἐστι λόγος διὰ παραθέσεως ὁμοίου πράγματος τὸ ὑποκείμενον μετ' ἐνεργείας παριστάνων.

[24] See McCall 1969:256.

The very language of this definition shows that the simile aims at helping listeners or readers to "visualize" mental images by means of what is familiar, and therefore easily retrieved by the mind's eye, as well as what is pictureable. While testifying to one of the principal functions of the simile, the expressions εἰς ὄψιν ἄγειν 'lead into one's sight'[25] and δι' ὁμοίων καὶ γινωσκομένων 'by means of similar and known things' accentuate the importance of visual representation through what is identifiable and common to human experience. To return briefly to the term *paratopic space*, I suggest that the delineation of simile space *in parallel with* but also *beyond* that of ordinary story space is based on these two elements of the definition of the simile, that is, "visualization of mental images" and "familiarity or knowledge." As we will now see, it is the kind of "knowledge" employed in such mental representations that plays a crucial role in creating the paratopic space of the simile. In this light, let us see how ancient rhetorical theory distinguished between two kinds of such "literary" knowledge:

> Τί διαφέρει τὸ παράδειγμα παραβολῆς; ὅτι τὸ μὲν παράδειγμα ἀπὸ <u>προγεγονότων πραγμάτων</u> παραλαμβάνεται· ἡ δὲ παραβολὴ <u>ἐξ</u> <u>ἀορίστων καὶ ἐνδεχομένων</u> γενέσθαι· παραβολὴ γάρ ἐστι πράγματος οἵου γενέσθαι ἀπομνημόνευσις εἰς ὁμοίωσιν τοῦ ζητουμένου.

> What is the difference between example and simile? That the example comes from things which *have happened before*, whereas the simile [comes from things] which are *indefinite and can happen*; for the simile refers to a thing which is memorized so as to resemble what is sought.

> *Rhetorica anonyma* "Prolegomena in artem rhetoricam"
> 6.34.26 (emphasis added)

Unlike the "example" or παράδειγμα, which refers to things that have happened before, the simile is based on "indefinite things and things that can happen." In other words, whereas in the example "knowledge" and familiarity are the result of past action, in the simile they stem from both its timeless aspect and its "potentiality." This is because the simile employs *memorization* (ἀπομνημόνευσις) of things that "look like" what is to be represented. In other words, the "past time" of the "example" gives way to the spatialization of experience, to the visual representation through memory of an indefinite "body" of possibilities. In this mental world of space, the subject, which in the example is the prevailing entity, is replaced by, or at least reshaped into, a *site* of

---

[25] Cf. the expression εἰς ὄψιν τινὸς ἥκειν 'come into view', with various verbs of motion (μολεῖν, ἐλθεῖν, περᾶν).

experience.[26] The spatialization of the subject within the realm of the simile was advocated by the ancient grammarian Trypho:

παραβολή ἐστι λόγος διὰ παραθέσεως ὁμοίου πράγματος <u>τὸ ὑποκείμενον</u> <u>μετ' ἐνεργείας παριστάνων</u>, οἷον κινήθη δ' ἀγορή, ὡς κύματα μακρὰ θαλάσσης / πόντου Ἰκαρίοιο· γίνονται δὲ αἱ παραβολαὶ τετραχῶς, ἤτοι πάθους πάθει ἢ διαθέσεως διαθέσει ἢ φύσεως φύσει ἢ πράξεως πράξει. πάθους μὲν οὖν πάθει, ὡς δ' ὅταν ἀσπασίως· διαθέσως δὲ διαθέσει, ὡς δ' ὅτε τίς τε δράκοντα ἰδὼν παλίνορσος ἀπέστη, ... / ὣς αὖθις καθ' ὅμιλον ἔδυ Τρώων ἀγερώχων. φύσεως δὲ φύσει, οἷον οἵη περ φύλλων γενεή, τοιήδε καὶ ἀνδρῶν. πράξεως δὲ πράξει, οἱ δ' ὡς ἀμητῆρες ἐναντίοι ἀλλήλοισι.

The simile is speech that refers to a similar thing and *represents the subject while performing some activity*, like "the assembly moved, like the long waves of the Icarian sea"; similes function in four ways, i.e. [similes] of feelings by feeling or [similes] of representation by representation or [similes] of nature by nature or [similes] of action by action. So, [similes] of feeling by feeling: "as when dearly"; [similes] of representation by representation: "as a man who has come on a snake in the mountain valley suddenly steps back ... / lost himself again in the host of the haughty Trojans"; [similes] of nature by nature, like "as is the generation of leaves, so is that of humanity"; [similes] of action by action "and the men, like two lines of reapers who, facing each other."

Trypho *On Tropes* (ed. L. Spengel) 3.201.17–26
(emphasis added)

One of Trypho's most important observations concerns the presentation of the subject within the simile as "performing some activity." The very formulation of the term "activity" (ἐνέργειά ἐστι φράσις ὑπ' ὄψιν ἄγουσα τὸ νοούμενον, οἷον μυρίοι, οὐκ ἄνδρεσσιν ἐοικότες, ἀλλὰ Γίγασιν· ἔχονται δὲ τῆς ἐνεργείας καὶ αἱ τοῦ Ὁμήρου παραβολαί)[27] suggests that Trypho is here describing a type of illustrative comparison based on the subject's performing some action, and that this kind of situational comparison based on extended analogy "brings thoughts before the mind's eye."[28] Trypho therefore suggests that Homeric similes (αἱ τοῦ Ὁμήρου παραβολαί), which are marked by this type of illustrative comparison, enhance the "imaging" of mental pictures by presenting the audience with

---

[26] See West-Pavlov 2009:104, who discusses such spatial issues in Kristeva's work.
[27] *On Tropes* 199.22–25.
[28] On Aristotle's use of ἐνέργεια, see Jürgensen 1968:41.

vivid visualizations of νοούμενα. But what else can these νοούμενα be than the narrative scenes or events that the storyteller decides to present by means of extended similes?

In spite of some differences, ancient accounts of simile create a functional framework that can be summarized as follows: similes like those we encounter in Homer (extended similes) refer to a situational analogy, featuring illustrative comparisons of scenes where all the corresponding items of the subject and comparative parts are expressed and correlated. Illustrative comparison takes the form of brief and elliptical narrative snapshots whose compressed form is balanced by extensive correspondence between the various comparative parts of the simile, through vivid presentation of a subject or subjects in the performance of some activity. This last observation, though not developed further by ancient grammarians, opens a window of interpretive opportunity, since situational analogy based on a subject's (or subjects') activity that is not temporally bound (unlike the "example" or παράδειγμα, which presupposes historical precedence) has by definition to be located somewhere. This "somewhere" in the case of Homeric similes is a locus independent of the spatial coordinates of the main narrative, a place that works as a background onto which, by means of illustrative comparison, the storyteller deposits the images of the narrative he desires to recall. The situational aspect of the brief and yet extended narrative snapshots that the storyteller presents through the similes is based on a body of indefinite possibilities that takes "past sites of experience and elaborate[s] them into spaces of sensual immediacy. The spatialization of each past site engenders a global work of metonymic creation: expansions of space compensate the shrinking of temporal possibility."[29]

Homeric similes do not "invent" a new story-world that is simply different from that of the narrative, but are characterized by a complex combination of density and gradual zooming in on details. The very form of the alleged "extended" simile suggests a reconsideration and reappraisal of spatial coordinates. On the one hand, the use of the term "extended" for Homeric similes is valid only from the viewpoint of and in comparison to the short simile, in which tenor and vehicle are expressed with the utmost density and are bound together by a single *tertium comparationis*.[30] The so-called *nuclear* simile consists of a *target domain* or *tenor*, a *similarity marker* (e.g. "like" or "as"), and the *base domain* or *vehicle*.[31] On the other hand, Homeric similes are a compressed type of imagery, containing a narrative snapshot whose compactness does not hinder its ability

[29] West-Pavlov 2009:103 on Kristeva.
[30] On the applicability of the terms "tenor" and "vehicle" to the Homeric simile, see Silk 1974:14–15.
[31] Or *source domain*, see Minchin 2001:133 with bibliography.

to shrink or expand minutiae at the right spot and for the right reason.[32] The dual spatial nature of the Homeric simile tends to defy characterization of its size or extent. This flexibility of the epic simile as presented in Homer lies at the very heart of a "spatial turn" that I have decided to explore under the two headings of "Simile Space and Narrative Space" (chapter 5) and "The Cognitive Aspect of the Homeric Simile" (chapter 6).

---

[32]   This point has been emphasized by Muellner 1990.

5

Simile Space and Narrative Space

IN THE *ILIAD*, place is most often delineated within the context of the Homeric similes, rather than in narrative.[1] Previous scholarship has emphasized two distinct but equally important aspects of Iliadic *Gleichnisorte* ("simile spaces"): their use as a way of making intratextual references, and their function within the wider framework of the epic's plot. With respect to the former, Elliger has detected two further uses. When the narrative context is that of the Trojan plain, then the *Gleichnisort* may be that of a plain (*Iliad* V 597; VI 507) or a garden (XXI 257–258; 346). At other times, the correspondence can refer overtly to a geographical feature not belonging to the landscape of the Troad, as in II 461, where the famous simile of the geese, cranes, and long-throated swans is set "in the Asian meadow beside the Kaüstrian waters."[2] As far as the functional use of the *Gleichnisort* is concerned, Elliger has argued that its relation to narrative scenery "causes ... a different distribution of the simile landscapes in the distinct phases of the Iliadic plot,"[3] and concludes by suggesting that the rhythm of the entire Iliadic epic can also be traced in the rhythm of the various simile sceneries. The choice of mountains and sea as the two most frequent *Gleichnisorte* reflects both the "outer zone" of the Iliadic setting—the mountain of Ida and the sea—and the "inner zone" of the Trojan plain.[4]

Although he was not interested in the Homeric similes' spatial aspect, Moulton made a number of acute observations on their function as a whole. He highlighted their connection with narrative structure,[5] argued convincingly for the existence of networks of similes that intensified events and themes, and claimed that vehicles were associated and simile-generated major images were coordinated across substantial narrative segments in order to

---

[1]   See Storch 1957:69; Elliger 1975:81.
[2]   Ἀσίω(ι) ἐν λειμῶνι Καϋστρίου ἀμφὶ ῥέεθρα.
[3]   "... bedingt ... eine unterschiedliche Verteilung der Gleichnislandschaften in den einzelnen Phasen der Iliashandlung" (Elliger 1975:83).
[4]   Elliger 1975:85.
[5]   Moulton 1977:49.

create consistent characterization.[6] In accord with other studies that suggested explicitly or implicitly that similes must be interpreted within a wider nexus of interconnections permeating (and sometimes extending beyond) epic poetry,[7] Moulton's research broke new ground.

Minchin's study of the Homeric similes marked what we may call a "cognitive turn,"[8] since she was the first who systematically focused her attention on "the interactive relationship between imagery, which is at the heart of the simile, and memory—the way in which memory prompts an image, the way in which imagery and memory guide the expression of the simile, and the way in which imagery promotes recall—and the working out of this relationship in the Homeric simile."[9]

In discussing the way ancient authors studied the simile, I suggest that the notion of *situational analogy*, which lies at the very heart of the Homeric simile, is closely associated with the creation of background images, on which the storyteller is able to "hang" various scenes of his narrative. I also emphasize the fact that these background images are presented as a coherent whole, which takes the form of a narrative snapshot that may be called "paratopic," in the sense that it lies outside the space delineated by the main narrative. The principle underlying this approach is that what is familiar and easily recognized lends force and clarity to what is unknown and hard to visualize, and that narrative images pertaining to a scene and corresponding to individual background images are effectively recalled when they are "deposited" along a clear mental pathway, which the storyteller readily "tours" when performing the simile. In order to make this point clear, let us review the following evidence.

One of the most remarkable modern examples of strong memory recall is that reported by the neuropsychologist A. R. Luria, who studied the case of Solomon Venyaminovich Shereshevsky (1886–1958), a highly gifted man who became famous for his astounding feats of memory. Shereshevsky used Gorky Street in Moscow as a background framework on which to place images he wanted to recall. Shereshevsky devised a method that allowed him to walk mentally along Gorky Street and actually "see" in his mind the various images he had stored in different locations along it. This does not mean that the gifted mnemonist did not make mistakes. What is remarkable is that these mistakes resulted from "misplacing" certain images, storing them in the "wrong" locations, a problem he was able to solve "by inserting a streetlamp into his

---

6 Moulton 1977:87, 116.
7 See Petegorsky 1982; Nimis 1987.
8 2001:132–160.
9 Minchin 2001:133.

memorized scene for illumination or by adding in a contrasting background."[10] The case of Shereshevsky is telling, for it allows us to verify the arguments presented above. Like the Homeric storyteller, this Russian mnemonist organized the various background images into a coherent whole by *spatializing* them, that is, positioning them in locations that were all placed along Gorky Street. The selection of Gorky Street is not very different from the setting of the Homeric similes in nature. As Gorky Street was a familiar place for Shereshevsky, so the natural background of the Homeric similes was well known to, and therefore easily visualized by the Homeric narrator. Likewise, as Gorky Street facilitated a mental tour by Shereshevsky, who could easily walk down it and encounter the various images he had deposited in front of or next to familiar background locations, so the Homeric storyteller can easily follow the constant movements of the subjects of his similes, who are constantly presented as performing some activity. Trypho's formulations that "the simile is speech that refers to a similar thing and *represents the subject while performing some activity*"[11] and "the simile is speech attempting to 'make visible' by means of similar and known things what exists in the mind"[12] find strong confirmation and ample support in the case of Shereshevsky.

It now becomes clear that for both Shereshevsky and the Homeric storyteller, space is the determining factor in the mental organization and retrieval of images. There is, though, one more point to be made, regarding the principle of analogy. As we have noted, Luria observed that Shereshevsky's mistakes were due to "misplacement" of certain images, and that the famous mnemonist resorted to mechanisms of further "mental illumination" by creating a shining effect (street lamp) or a strong contrast. Let us review a Homeric simile that employs the same technique:

τῇ ῥά μιν οὖτα τυχών, διὰ δὲ χρόα καλὸν ἔδαψεν,
ἐκ δὲ δόρυ σπάσεν αὖτις. ὃ δ' ἔβραχε χάλκεος Ἄρης,
ὅσσόν τ' ἐννεάχιλοι ἐπίαχον ἢ δεκάχιλοι
ἀνέρες ἐν πολέμῳ ἔριδα ξυνάγοντες Ἄρηος.
τοὺς δ' ἄρ' ὑπὸ τρόμος εἷλεν Ἀχαιούς τε Τρῶάς τε
δείσαντας· τόσον ἔβραχ' Ἄρης ἆτος πολέμοιο.
οἵη δ' ἐκ νεφέων ἐρεβεννὴ φαίνεται ἀήρ
καύματος ἔξ, ἀνέμοιο δυσαέος ὀρνυμένοιο,

---

[10] Whitehead 2009:28.
[11] παραβολή ἐστι λόγος διὰ παραθέσεως ὁμοίου πράγματος <u>τὸ ὑποκείμενον μετ' ἐνεργείας παριστάνων</u>; see discussion above.
[12] παραβολὴ δέ ἐστι λόγος δι' ὁμοίων καὶ γινωσκομένων εἰς ὄψιν ἄγειν πειρώμενος τὸ νοούμενον; see discussion above.

τοῖος Τυδείδη Διομήδεϊ χάλκεος Ἄρης
φαίνεθ᾽ ὁμοῦ νεφέεσσιν, ἰὼν εἰς οὐρανὸν εὐρύν.

Picking this place she stabbed and driving it deep in the fair flesh
wrenched the spear out again. Then Ares the brazen bellowed
with a sound as great as nine thousand men make, or ten thousand,
when they cry as they carry into the fighting the fury of the war god.
And a shivering seized hold alike on Achaians and Trojans
in their fear at the bellowing of battle-insatiate Ares.
As when out of the thunderhead the air shows darkening
after a day's heat when the stormy wind uprises,
thus to Tydeus' son Diomedes Ares the brazen
showed as he went up with the clouds into the wide heaven.

Iliad V 858–867

While Athena and Diomedes are unleashing a fierce attack against Ares, the god
of war, Athena is presented as driving Diomedes' bronze spear into the depth
of Ares' belly. It is at this moment that the narrator cannot visualize the situation clearly, for Ares is a god and so he cannot be killed.[13] Given that Ares has
to escape, the storyteller has to create a familiar background, marked by a situational analogy with what Ares and Diomedes are facing. For this he uses two
spatial mechanisms in succession: the bellowing of the god of war is like the
bellowing of nine or ten thousand men, while Ares' ascension to Olympos is
presented by the illustrative analogy of the darkening of the sky "after a day's
heat when the stormy wind uprises."[14] The storyteller is careful to tell his audience that this was how Diomedes saw Ares ascending to the sky, because this
is the background image he has stored in his mind, watching the darkening
sky after a warm day. The two successive similes correspond to two successive
narrative scenes: they are organized by means of spatial mechanisms (sound and
color), and both deal with different kinds of activity (shouting and ascending),
thus bringing before the storyteller's and the audience's eyes "what exists in the
mind" (τὸ νοούμενον). Moreover, in both similes the visual framework is characterized by the principle of absolute correspondence and pictorial economy:

[13] Ares, who will soon return to Olympos, is presented as "grieving in his spirit" (*Iliad* V 869 θυμὸν
ἀχεύων). Emphasis on divine suffering is very often accompanied by the gods' easy allevia-
tion from pain. See Neal 2006:160, who makes the important point that "this is underlined by
the fact that *they* [gods] *can leave the mortal sphere, the apparently exclusive locus of their suffering*"
(the emphasis is mine). On how divine injury draws a line between immortal and mortal fate
(with special attention to Ares and Aphrodite, the two wounded pro-Trojan gods), see Neal
2006:152–167.
[14] *Iliad* V 864–865.

when the narrative space changes, then the simile space changes too. In other words, each narrative space corresponds to a single simile space. Ares' ascent to Olympos pertains to a different spatial mechanism than his bellowing, and so a different spatial framework has to be employed.

Having discussed pictorial correspondence between unfamiliar and familiar images, I turn now to the use and function of *visual units,* the larger components of narrative scenes and similes, and *visual frames,* the smaller building blocks grouped together in the simile snapshots. A visual unit can be defined as a *eusynoptic* mental view of a narrative or simile scene that contains a coherent action by one or more subjects, with a beginning and an end. A visual frame is a subdivision of the visual unit, that is, the larger image collection that forms a coherent whole, be it a narrative scene or a simile. Visual frames do not emphasize segmentation, however, but are orchestrated into a coherent visual tableau that works "as a model for the integration of description and action."[15] With this notion of visual frames, we have a truly *eusynoptic* view of a narrative or simile scene, that is, one that is easily taken in at a glance by the storyteller,[16] as it is by the internal spectator Diomedes, from one point of view and *im selben Augenblick,* to recall Zielinski's apt expression.[17]

In the example above, the visual frames forming the narrative and the second simile are organized in correlated pairs (Table 6):

Table 6: Narrative-simile pairs in *Iliad* V

Narrative	Simile
Visual Frame A	*Visual Frame A*
a. Ares the brazen showing ... with the clouds (χάλκεος Ἄρης / φαίνεθ' ὁμοῦ νεφέεσσι)	a. air showing darkening out of the thunderhead after a day's heat (οἴη δ' ἐκ νεφέων ἐρεβεννὴ φαίνεται ἀήρ / καύματος ἔξ)
a1. Ares (Ἄρης)	a1. air (ἀήρ)
a2. showing (φαίνεθ')	a2. showing (φαίνεται)
a3. with the clouds (ὁμοῦ νεφέεσσιν)	a3. out of the thunderhead (ἐκ νεφέων)
a4. brazen (χάλκεος)	a4. darkening (ἐρεβεννή)

---

[15] Purves 2010a:45.
[16] On Zielinski's "moving landscape," see the discussion by Purves 2010a:41–45.
[17] 1901:409.

Narrative	Simile
Visual Frame B b. Diomedes (Τυδεΐδῃ Διομήδεϊ)	*Visual Frame B* b. Narrator (understood from φαίνεται)
Visual Frame C c. as he went up ... into the wide heaven (ἰὼν εἰς οὐρανὸν εὐρύν)	*Visual Frame C* c. when the stormy wind uprises (ἀνέμοιο δυσαέος ὀρνυμένοιο)

The darkening thunderhead after a day's heat (οἵη δ᾽ ἐκ νεφέων ἐρεβεννὴ φαίνεται ἀήρ / καύματος ἔξ) constitutes the first "visual frame," which matches the narrative's correlated visual frame of Ares rising with the clouds into the wide heaven. The illustrative analogy is markedly expressed by almost full correspondence of all its constituent elements: the air that is compared to Ares bears such a close aural similarity (ἀήρ, Ἄρης) that it facilitates correlation; the "showing" (φαίνεται, φαίνεθ᾽) underscores the visual parallel between the moving air and Ares, the clouds (ἐκ νεφέων, ὁμοῦ νεφέεσσιν) function as a smaller orientation point that enhances the clarity of the suggested visualization, and finally the contrast between the darkening (ἐρεβεννή) of the air and the shining (χάλκεος) of Ares' armor further reinforces the entire illustration.

In the second visual frame, the internal observer of Ares' ascent to the sky is Diomedes, whereas the unstated observer of the scene in the simile is obviously the narrator (and also the audience). They are both able to capture the corresponding narrative and simile vistas with a single glance, in a truly eusynoptic way, as the simile's inherent pictureability encourages an equivalent mental visualization of its correlated narrative scene.[18]

In the third visual frame, Ares' ascent is compared with the rising wind. There are no smaller constituent parts here, as there were in the first visual frame. The key point is that the moving air in the simile widens the visual field of the mind's eye and brings before it the action of Ares in the narrative. The moving landscape of the simile "ensures that the plot-image keeps moving"[19] as well, and that this movement is visualized with clarity and ease.

---

[18] See bT scholia on *Iliad* V 866–867: γραφικῶς ἔχει Διομήδης τὴν ἄνοδον θεώμενος Ἄρεος ("Diomedes is imaginative in his perception of Ares going upwards"); see de Jong 1987a:135.

[19] Purves 2010a:45.

This system of visual frames confirms astute observations concerning the "art of memory" that were first explored by ancient authors.[20] In fact, visual frames allow the Homeric narrator to exploit at full length the two fundamental aspects of the process of mnemonic recall, both of which are subdivisions of the concept of space: namely the place system and the arrangement of places. As argued by both the *Rhetorica ad Herennium* (3.17–24) and by Cicero in *On the Orator* (354), association is enhanced not only by using the place system, but also by arranging the selected visual images in an orderly fashion. If the order of the localities corresponds to the order of things (as in the first visual frame of the simile discussed above), then the narrator will be able to move easily along his mental pathway and retrieve them, more or less as Quintilian's speaker (*Institutio oratoria* 11.2.18–22), who moves in his memory within an imaginary building, visiting the various rooms and looking at the furniture and ornaments on which various images have been fixed.[21] It is now clear that visual frames are the building blocks of the visual snapshots encountered in the correlated narrative-simile pairs, and equally importantly that they are *fundamentally spatial.*

In this light, and drawing on both Minchin's research on cognitive factors enhancing memorability and the pioneering work of Rubin on memory and oral traditions (such as epic, ballad, and counting-out rhymes), I argue that *the storyteller uses homologous visual mappings for the space of narrative scenes and corresponding similes.* This technique, which is clearly a result of the process of mnemonic association enhanced by spatial unity, and has been recognized in cognitive psychology as a powerful cue to recall,[22] has far-reaching consequences for the storyteller's mode of performance or composition in performance.

This is not to suggest that recall is the only reason, or even the main reason, for the use of hundreds of extended similes in the *Iliad.* Besides enhancing memorability,[23] foregrounding, and informing, a full list of the similes' multiple functions in the Homeric epics would include explaining and modeling, reconceptualizing, filling lexical gaps, expressing emotional attitude, decoration and hyperbole, cultivating intimacy, textual structuring, and extending the audience's pleasure.[24] What is clearly significant, though, is that *the spatial component of the similes is stronger than the spatial indicators of the battle narrative,* and *the similes are by far more frequent in the main narrative than in the speeches.* By analyzing a representative number of extended similes in the *Iliad* and consid-

---

[20] On ancient evidence concerning memory and recall, see Blum 1969:41–46. For a discussion of the role of literacy in the "art of memory," see Small 1997.

[21] See Yates 1966:18; Whitehead 2009:31.

[22] Bahrick 1974; Bellezza 1983; Rubin 1995:51.

[23] See Bahrick 1974; Bellezza 1983; Rubin 1995:51.

[24] Minchin 2001:138–139.

ering their spatial coordinates within their specific contexts, I will maintain that *Gleichnisorte* are organized with respect to *narrative space*. To be sure, the simile is called up in the process of visualizing the events of the narrative, but it is done on the basis of *the visual space of the narrative,* which is organized around whole *visual units* with their respective *visual frames,* the mental building blocks of similes. The correspondence is not one-to-one, but is based on the spatial representation of entire scenes or episodes.

A key aspect in understanding this process is the *partial overlap* between the common mental structure underlying every simile and its particularized expression, adapted to meet the contextual restrictions of a given scene. Taking a cue from Scott's recent work on the Homeric similes, I suggest that we should distinguish between what he calls the *simileme,* that is, "the mental structure underlying each simile—in itself not fully expressible but composed of repeated actions and objects and alternative modes of expression, all of which have become associated through frequent usage" and the "individual simile [that] is the single poet's particularized composition shaped by poet and audience."[25] In fact, the nonverbal background of the *simileme* that Scott speaks about is *profoundly pictorial.*[26] It pertains to the deep structure of the simile, which has through frequent usage become part of the tradition's (the poet's and the audience's) cultural memory. The regularity with which individual features appear in distinct families of similes in the Homeric epics is both impressive and suggestive. Given that their phrasing is not necessarily the same, it is perhaps advisable to recall that as there are clusters of meaning, there are also constellations of images, grouped together in the form of a mental gallery, shaped by "the lifeblood of generations of poems and performances."[27] Returning to my point of departure, I would claim that the Homeric epics' version of Shereshevsky's Gorky Street is a *metonymic pathway,* stemming from the notion of traditional referentiality, and embracing a context far wider than that of the individual performance. The epic storyteller is able to recall, by means of traditional referentiality, not only foci of meaning but also clusters of background images.

This approach elucidates two widely recognized features of the Homeric simile: its limited use of formulas and its much more frequent occurrence in the main narrative than in the speeches.[28] As far as the low degree of formulaic repetition in the similes is concerned, it can be plausibly argued that it is

---

[25] Scott 2009:19.

[26] In similes, the storyteller's mind works with nonverbal collections of elements. By using the simileme, that is, the most basic system of features that make up a traditional simile family, he is able to create brief visual snapshots consisting of flexible and variable visual units.

[27] See Foley 1991:7, 22–29; Scott 2009:20.

[28] See Appendix 2.

because similes pertain to the recall of images rather than words—for which the place system we have described does not work effectively, as observed by both the author of the *Rhetorica ad Herennium* and Alexander Luria, who noticed that Shereshevsky had serious problems when challenged to recall words or whole passages of text.[29] With respect to the greater frequency of similes in the main narrative of the *Iliad*,[30] the limitation of most of the action to a single theater of activity[31] is balanced by the wealth of locations that the system of similes can offer.[32]

I now turn my attention to how the narrator uses homologous visual mappings for the spaces of narrative scenes and corresponding similes, in four books of the *Iliad* (II, V, XI, and XVI).[33] First, I briefly discuss the thematic structure of each book; then I cite all the relevant passages and divide the book's similes, based on their homologous visual mappings, into visual units comprising one or more similes; and last I explore the interaction between narrative and simile space, on the levels of both the larger visual units and the smaller visual frames.[34] My selection of these books of the *Iliad* is based both on the wealth of similes attested in each of them and on the fact that—scattered as they are over a large part of the epic—they offer a general outline of the developing plot.

Iliad II

Iliad II comprises two large narrative sections: (1) attempts to organize the Greek army (1–483) and (2) the Catalogue of Ships and the Catalogue of Trojans

---

[29] See Whitehead 2009:30.

[30] On similes in Iliadic speeches, see Appendix 2. The speeches, with the exception of those containing extended embedded narratives (e.g. by Phoinix in *Iliad* IX and Nestor in *Iliad* XI) virtually lack a place system, since they do not indicate nor are they accompanied by a change of location.

[31] This observation is implicitly supported by the fact that in the *Odyssey*, which unlike the *Iliad* takes place in multiple locations, the distribution of similes between the main narrative and the speeches is almost even: of 136 similes and comparisons, 69 occur in narrator text and 67 in speech; see de Jong 2001:105 ad *Odyssey* iv 333–340.

[32] Contrast what happens in the main narrative: at certain narrative junctures there is almost a "need" for similes; see Scott 2009:22, 31.

[33] In Appendix 1 below, I offer charts with an equivalent analysis of the entire *Iliad*.

[34] In what follows, the abbreviation *N* is used for narrative space, *S* for simile space. Numbers refer to the particular narrative or simile space. When the narrative or its corresponding simile context contain a movement from one place to another, this is indicated by the symbol >. Commas and dashes separate multiple smaller spaces within the same narrative or simile context. I have not included the space of similes attested in speeches, because there the focalization is that of the particular character delivering the actual speech and not that of the narrator. Moreover, a number of common themes and features shared by narrative and similes (motion, entering the battle, pursuit, death, atittudes and emotions, and avoidance of abstract thought), but not by speeches, indicate that the speeches should be treated separately; see Hogan 1966:202.

and their Allies (484–877). The main theme in this book is the challenge to Agamemnon's leadership when he deliberately misinforms the army, with almost disastrous consequences that put the entire expedition in peril. The action unfolds around the area where the first and second Achaean councils take place, and then in the plain not far from the Achaean camp, as the troops march to battle.

Iliad II contains ten extended similes,[35] which are for the most part concentrated in the first narrative section (Iliad II 1–483), before the Catalogue of Ships, and are divided into two visual units, the first comprising the first and second Achaean councils, the second the army's marching into battle. Simile subjects vary widely, but spatial mappings are rather limited, since they correspond to the specific locations presented in the equivalent narrative sections. In the second visual unit, most of the similes occur just before the important narrative juncture of the final marshaling of the troops before the Catalogue of Ships. This cluster will be discussed in detail after the analysis of the relevant visual units.

Visual unit 1

First Achaean council:

   87–93: (N1) huts > seashore (ἀγορή) / (S1) rock > springtime flowers

   144–146: (N2) seashore > huts / (S2) sea waves

   147–149: (N3) seashore (ἀγορή) > ships / (S3) cornfield

Second Achaean council:

   207–210: (N4) ships (ἀγορή) / (S4) seashore, πόντος

   394–397: (N5) ἀγορή > ships / (S5) cliff jutting out (sea)

   ἠΰτε ἔθνεα εἶσι μελισσάων ἀδινάων
   πέτρης ἐκ γλαφυρῆς αἰεὶ νέον ἐρχομενάων,
   βοτρυδὸν δὲ πέτονται ἐπ' ἄνθεσιν εἰαρινοῖσιν·
   αἳ μέν τ' ἔνθα ἅλις πεποτήαται, αἳ δέ τε ἔνθα·
   ὣς τῶν ἔθνεα πολλὰ νεῶν ἄπο καὶ κλισιάων
   ἠϊόνος προπάροιθε βαθείης ἐστιχόωντο
   ἰλαδὸν εἰς ἀγορήν·

   Like the swarms of clustering bees that issue forever
   in fresh bursts from the hollow in the stone, and hang like
   bunched grapes as they hover beneath the flowers in springtime

---

[35] The overall number of similes (brief and extended) in *Iliad* II is twenty. I discuss only the extended ones that are relevant to my investigation.

fluttering in swarms together this way and that way,
so the many nations of men from the ships and the shelters
along the front of the deep sea beach marched in order
by companies to the assembly ...

Iliad II 87–93

κινήθη δ' ἀγορὴ φὴ κύματα μακρὰ θαλάσσης.
πόντου Ἰκαρίοιο· τὰ μέν τ' Εὖρός τε Νότος τε
ὦρορ' ἐπαΐξας πατρὸς Διὸς ἐκ νεφελάων.

And the assembly was shaken as on the sea the big waves
in the main by Ikaria, when the south and south-east winds
driving down from the clouds of Zeus the father whip them.

Iliad II 144–146

ὡς δ' ὅτε κινήσῃ Ζέφυρος βαθὺ λήϊον ἐλθών,
λάβρος ἐπαιγίζων, ἐπί τ' ἠμύει ἀσταχύεσσιν,
ὣς τῶν πᾶσ' ἀγορὴ κινήθη· ...

As when the west wind moves across the grain deep standing,
boisterously, and shakes and sweeps it till the tassels lean, so
all of that assembly was shaken, ...

Iliad II 147–149

ὣς ὅ γε κοιρανέων δίεπε στρατόν· οἳ δ' ἀγορήνδε
αὖτις ἐπεσσεύοντο νεῶν ἄπο καὶ κλισιάων
ἠχῇ, ὡς ὅτε κῦμα πολυφλοίσβοιο θαλάσσης
αἰγιαλῷ μεγάλα βρέμεται, σμαραγεῖ δέ τε πόντος.

So he went through the army marshalling it, until once more
they swept back into the assembly place from the ships and the
 shelters
clamorously, as when from the thunderous sea the surf-beat
crashes loudly[36] upon the beach, and the whole sea is in tumult.

Iliad II 207–210

ὣς ἔφατ', Ἀργεῖοι δὲ μέγ' ἴαχον, ὡς ὅτε κῦμα
ἀκτῇ ἔφ' ὑψηλῇ, ὅτε κινήσῃ Νότος ἐλθών,

---

[36] Here I have replaced Lattimore's "upon the great beach," reading μεγάλῳ as μεγάλα in accordance with West's edition of the *Iliad*.

281

προβλῆτι σκοπέλῳ· τὸν δ' οὔ ποτε κύματα λείπει
παντοίων ἀνέμων, ὅτ' ἂν ἔνθ' ἢ' ἔνθα γένωνται.

So he spoke, and the Argives shouted aloud, as surf crashing
against a sheer ness, driven by the south wind descending,
some cliff out-jutting, left never alone by the waves from
all the winds that blow, as they rise one place and another.

Iliad II 394–397

In visual unit 1, the movement of the kings and troops who leave their ships and huts and gather at the seashore (II 92 ἠϊόνος προπάροιθε βαθείης) is illustrated by bees flying from a hollow rock (88 πέτρης ἐκ γλαφυρῆς) to the springtime flowers (89 ἐπ' ἄνθεσιν εἰαρινοῖσιν). When the meeting is over and both kings and troops return to their ships, the narrator employs two successive similes, which share the same simileme by their pictorial association of wind and waves.[37] Although the visual spaces of sea and cornfield are different, they are linked through the blowing wind that makes the waves rise and the ears of grain bob. The same associative principle is employed for the second Achaean council: the movement of the troops to their meeting place by the seashore is illustrated by the simile of the roaring waves of the sea, and the army's noisy return to their ships and huts is presented as a wave against a high cliff (394–397). Although there is no "base" form for all these similes, as Scott observes,[38] I maintain that quite a different principle explains their selection by the storyteller: namely size. The multitude of bees (87 μελισσάων ἀδινάων), the long sea waves (144 κύματα μακρὰ θαλάσσης), the depth of the field of grain (147 βαθὺ λήϊον), the wave of the much-sounding sea (209 κῦμα πολυφλοίσβοιο θαλάσσης), and the wave against a high cliff (394–395 κῦμα / ἀκτῇ ἔφ' ὑψηλῇ) do not belong to the same simile family, but share the same simileme. This is the guiding principle in the selection of familiar mental images by the narrator, who organizes this pictorial material on the basis of homologous spatial mappings. As long as the narrative scene he is describing is located at a given spot, the space delineated by the simile does not change: when the space where the troops are placed shifts, then different spatial coordinates are "summoned" within the simile space. The use of the same simileme (size) becomes the mental pathway that allows the storyteller to correlate narrative and simile space, while particular visual frames help him reinforce these associations. The designation of both the bees and the troops as ἔθνεα 'swarms' (87) and 'nations' (91), and the emphasis on sound in both narrative and simile (209 ἠχῇ and 210 αἰγιαλῷ μεγάλα βρέμεται,

---

[37] See Scott 2009:46.
[38] 2009:48.

σμαραγεῖ δέ τε πόντος) when the second meeting begins, constitute effective visual frames. The tremendous visual force of spatial mappings is best seen in the very last of the similes in this first visual unit. The simile in 394–397 is anticipated in the narrative by the impression that this comparison will be based on sound (394 Ἀργεῖοι δὲ μέγ' ἴαχον).[39] After the simile, though, the narrative goes on to emphasize the troops' being scattered among the ships. Surprisingly, in the simile itself "the only support for the scattering of the Greeks is the winds that blow 'from this side and that.'"[40] In my view, this is a key example of the impact of space on the organization and presentation of simile material. The storyteller began his narrative, after the end of Agamemnon's speech (370–393), with the approbation of the Argive troops, which he attempted to illustrate through an extended simile. Such was the influence of the spatial mappings of the previous similes, within the same visual unit and along the lines of the same simileme (size), that the comparison that started with an emphasis on sound, with the simile of "a wave,"[41] soon turned into the illustrative analogy of "a wave and a wind," which owing to its "false" start did not materialize properly. This visual spilling over of space due to the impact of simileme-reinforced pictorial illustrations "corrects" the double focus of the simile in the narrative by a process of visual and spatial contextualization:[42] the audience can easily interpret this narrative-simile cluster.[43]

Let us now turn our attention to the second visual unit:

Visual unit 2

> 455–458: (N1) plain (distance) / (S1) mountains > air
>
> 459–466: (N2) plain of Skamandros / (S2) flying above the Asian meadow of Kaüstros
>
> 469–473: (N3) plain / (S3) flying hither and thither about the stalls of a sheepfold
>
> 474–477: (N4) battlefield / (S4) pasture

---

[39] Scott (2009:48) argues that "in the simile there is no word for sound," although ἰάχει is easily understood from the preceding ἴαχον in the narrative.

[40] Scott 2009:48.

[41] In the manner of *Iliad* II 207–210.

[42] This is a good lliustration of the fact that, as Minchin (2001:29) has put it, "professional storytellers work not so much *from* memory, but *with* memory."

[43] Note e.g. how this last simile of visual unit 1 ends with the expression ὅτ' ἂν ἔνθ' ἢ' ἔνθα γένωνται (397), which builds on a visual frame first encountered in the initial simile of the same visual unit: αἵ μέν τ' ἔνθα ἅλις πεποτήαται, αἳ δέ τε ἔνθα (90). The spatial vista of the first simile is still "in effect" until the very end of the last simile of the same visual unit, because the space, a powerful cue to recall, has not changed.

480–483: (N5) battlefield / (S5) pasture

780–785: (N6) plain / (S6) land of the Arimoi

ἠΰτε πῦρ ἀΐδηλον ἐπιφλέγει ἄσπετον ὕλην
οὔρεος ἐν κορυφῇς, ἕκαθεν δέ τε φαίνεται αὐγή,
ὣς τῶν ἐρχομένων ἀπὸ χαλκοῦ θεσπεσίοιο
αἴγλη παμφανόωσα δι' αἰθέρος οὐρανὸν ἷκεν.

As obliterating fire lights up a vast forest
along the crests of the mountain, and the flare shows far off,
so as they marched, from the magnificent bronze the gleam went
dazzling all about through the upper air to the heaven.

Iliad II 455–458

τῶν δ', ὥς τ' ὀρνίθων πετεηνῶν ἔθνεα πολλά,
χηνῶν ἢ γεράνων ἢ κύκνων δουλιχοδείρων,
Ἀσίω(ι) ἐν λειμῶνι Καϋστρίου ἀμφὶ ῥέεθρα
ἔνθα καὶ ἔνθα ποτῶνται ἀγαλλόμενα πτερύγεσσιν,
κλαγγηδὸν προκαθιζόντων, σμαραγεῖ δέ τε λειμών,
ὣς τῶν ἔθνεα πολλὰ νεῶν ἄπο καὶ κλισιάων
ἐς πεδίον προχέοντο Σκαμάνδριον· αὐτὰρ ὑπὸ χθών
σμερδαλέον κονάβιζε ποδῶν αὐτῶν τε καὶ ἵππων.

These, as the multitudinous nations of birds winged,
of geese, and of cranes, and of swans long-throated
in the Asian meadow beside the Kaÿstrian waters
this way and that way make their flights in the pride of their wings,
    then
settle in clashing swarms and the whole meadow echoes with them,
so of these the multitudinous tribes from the ships and
shelters poured to the plain of Skamandros, and the earth beneath
    their
feet and under the feet of their horses thundered horribly.

Iliad II 459–466

ἠΰτε μυιάων ἀδινάων ἔθνεα πολλά,
αἵ τε κατὰ σταθμὸν ποιμνήϊον ἠλάσκουσιν
ὥρῃ ἐν εἰαρινῇ, ὅτε τε γλάγος ἄγγεα δεύει,
τόσσοι ἐπὶ Τρώεσσι κάρη κομόωντες Ἀχαιοί
ἐν πεδίῳ ἵσταντο, διαρραῖσαι μεμαῶτες.

Like the multitudinous nations of swarming insects
who drive hither and thither about the stalls of the sheepfold
in the season of spring when the milk splashes in the milk pails:
in such numbers the flowing-haired Achaians stood up
through the plain against the Trojans, hearts burning to break them.

Iliad II 469–473

τοὺς δ’, ὥς τ’ αἰπόλια πλατέ’ αἰγῶν αἰπόλοι ἄνδρες
ῥεῖα διακρίνωσιν, ἐπεί κε νομῷ μιγέωσιν,
ὣς τοὺς ἡγεμόνες διεκόσμεον ἔνθα καὶ ἔνθα
ὑσμίνηνδ’ ἰέναι …

These, as men who are goatherds among the wide goatflocks
easily separate them in order as they take to the pasture,
thus the leaders separated them in this way and that way
toward the encounter …

Iliad II 474–477

ἠΰτε βοῦς ἀγέληφι μέγ’ ἔξοχος ἔπλετο πάντων
ταῦρος, ὃ γάρ τε βόεσσι μεταπρέπει ἀγρομένῃσιν,
τοῖον ἄρ’ Ἀτρεΐδην θῆκε Ζεὺς ἤματι κείνῳ,
ἐκπρεπέ’ ἐν πολλοῖσι καὶ ἔξοχον ἡρώεσσιν.

like some ox of the herd pre-eminent among the others,
a bull, who stands conspicuous in the huddling cattle;
such was the son of Atreus as Zeus made him that day,
conspicuous among men, and foremost among the fighters.

Iliad II 480–483

οἳ δ’ ἄρ’ ἴσαν ὡς εἴ τε πυρὶ χθὼν πᾶσα νέμοιτο,
γαῖα δ’ ὑπεστονάχιζε Διὶ ὣς τερπικεραύνῳ
χωομένῳ, ὅτε τ’ ἀμφὶ Τυφωέϊ γαῖαν ἱμάσσῃ
εἰν Ἀρίμοις, ὅθι φασὶ Τυφωέος ἔμμεναι εὐνάς.
ὣς ἄρα τῶν ὑπὸ ποσσὶ μέγα στοναχίζετο γαῖα
ἐρχομένων· μάλα δ’ ὦκα διέπρησσον πεδίοιο.

But the rest went forward, as if all the earth with flame were eaten,
and the ground echoed under them, as if Zeus who delights in
        thunder
were angry, as when he batters the earth about Typhoeus,
in the land of the Arimoi, where they say Typhoeus lies prostrate.

> Thus beneath their feet the ground re-echoed loudly
> to men marching, who made their way through the plain in great
>> speed.

Iliad II 780–785

The second visual unit, consisting of six similes and their corresponding narrative contexts, is visually localized through nature (mountains, pasture-lands) and the plain of Troy. The narrator mentally takes six distinct snapshots in the course of the fighting, and enhances his recall and the audience's visualization of them by grouping an equal number of similes on the basis of their spatial placement.

Of these six extended similes, the first five are presented successively, just before the beginning of the second part of *Iliad* II, the famous Catalogue of Ships, followed by the smaller Catalogue of the Trojans and their Allies. I will discuss first the thorny question regarding the narrator's decision to use a cluster of similes, and second the role of "transitional" similes attached to two of this cluster's extended similes. I will then go on to explore the function of the similes in this visual unit as a whole.

The question concerning this larger clustering of similes in the entire *Iliad* is closely linked to both larger narrative issues, such as the placing of extended similes at cardinal points of the plot,[44] and cognitive aspects of image organization and recall. The clustering of extended similes, which is characterized by the storyteller's attempt to offer multiple image-mappings of basically the same narrative scene (the marshaling of the Achaean troops), shows that there was some strongly felt need for such a grand undertaking.[45] The narrator wanted to make it clear that the impending Catalogue of Ships was a major watershed for his epic, a large-scale presentation of the Achaean army in all its splendor and grandeur; as Scott has neatly put it, "this display of the Greek forces provides a moment of order from which the maelstrom of the *Iliad* will be generated; only in book 23 will the characters of the Greek heroic world be regathered."[46] The storyteller was well aware that the strong pictorial input of a series of extended similes would have marked this moment as of key importance, and make his audience focus even greater attention on the ensuing narrative section. Along

---

[44] "*Hauptpunkten der Handlung*"; see Schadewaldt 1975:84.

[45] Attempts to link simile clustering with Iliadic book divisions and trace a certain pattern followed by the narrator are on the wrong track, since the question concerning the antiquity and origin of the division of the *Iliad* (and *Odyssey*) into twenty-four ῥαψῳδίαι is one of the thorniest in Homeric research. Even a cursory look at the debate presented in *Symbolae Osloenses* 1999, vol. 74 (where all the relevant bibliography can be found) in reaction to Minna Skafte Jensen's suggestions shows how contentious this issue is.

[46] 2009:49.

the same lines, this magisterial "parade" of images, impressive as it is by itself, would have somehow balanced the long and perhaps monotonous "parade" of Achaean forces that is to follow. The rather colorless Catalogue of Ships would thus be "prefaced" by a cornucopia of mental pictures that captivate the imagination. Aesthetic considerations of this kind may have been coupled, on the narrator's part, with his attempt to offer a background against which he wished his listeners to conceptualize the Catalogue of Ships. The similes' inherent pictureability would have helped put the Catalogue into the "right" perspective. The pictorial wealth of the similes, referring to multiple scenes of the natural world, is an excellent way of dynamically interpreting the illustrative analogy to the Catalogue that the storyteller is suggesting: the gathering of the Achaean army at Troy and its marshaling is silently compared to the behavior of a large part of the natural world, presented not in its menacing aspect—as it is often with simile families pertaining to fire, birds, and pasture—but as harmonious cooperation.[47]

I have decided to treat separately the two similes of the troops that are as numerous as leaves or springtime flowers and of Agamemnon, whose appearance is compared to that of Zeus, Ares, and Poseidon, because they are "transitional" similes, attached to two of the extended similes of this cluster in order to facilitate the mental leap to the next narrative-simile pair. The term *transitional* describes extended similes that are not fully developed according to the typical structure of the Homeric simile and are used as "bridging" devices within a cluster of similes.[48] A closer look at these two similes shows that they both lack the standard expansive relative clause that turns the initial comparative statement into a brief pictorial snapshot. In 467–468 ἔσταν δ' ἐν λειμῶνι Σκαμανδρίῳ ἀνθεμόεντι / μυρίοι, ὅσσά τε φύλλα καὶ ἄνθεα γίνεται ὥρῃ,[49] the initial "anaphoric" ὅσσα clause is never developed by the accumulation of other anaphoric expansions, paratactically juxtaposed according to common simile practice, but is abruptly replaced by another extended simile. Likewise in 477–479 μετὰ δὲ κρείων Ἀγαμέμνων, / ὄμματα καὶ κεφαλὴν ἴκελος Διὶ τερπικεραύνῳ, / Ἄρεϊ δὲ ζώνην, στέρνον δὲ Ποσειδάωνι,[50] Agamemnon's anatomical comparison to three different gods is carried out by the typical means of a brief comparison (ἴκελος + dative). Both these similes are attached to their simile contexts: in 467–468 the expressions ἐν λειμῶνι Σκαμανδρίῳ and γίνεται ὥρῃ look toward

---

[47] This point was made convincingly by Scott 2009:49–57.
[48] On the transitional aspect of similes, see Martin 1997:146; Clay 2011:21, 65.
[49] "They took position in the blossoming meadow of Skamandros, / thousands of them, as leaves and flowers appear in their season."
[50] "... and among them powerful Agamemnon, / with eyes and head like Zeus who delights in thunder, / like Ares for girth, and with the chest of Poseidon ..."

the previous and the following similes respectively, where similar expressions are used (465 ἐς πεδίον προχέοντο Σκαμάνδριον and 471 ὥρῃ ἐν εἰαρινῇ), and in 477–479 the highlighting of Agamemnon's preeminence among the other ἡγεμόνες that is expressed rather implicitly (477 μετὰ δὲ κρείων Ἀγαμέμνων) becomes explicitly and emphatically stated in the following simile (481 μεταπρέπει). Considering that the role of these two similes is to aid the transition from one narrative-simile pair to another, let us dwell for a moment on the mental process that determined the storyteller's choice. Put differently, why did the narrator use these "undeveloped" similes instead of other extended ones? The answer to this question can only be of a cognitive nature, that is, his choice was determined by mental factors of image organization and recall. During the performance of the extended simile in 459–466, the spatial designation ἐς πεδίον προχέοντο Σκαμάνδριον (465), further reinforced by its creeping up toward the end of the simile, created a "pictorial response," a visual *saut du même au même*, to use an expression from the field of textual criticism. The force of the spatial designation of Skamandros was doubled by a new image that the narrator began to develop in his mind's eye. By the time he started to visualize the new simile, though, the storyteller happened to employ familiar images that activated other, stronger simile families, like the "insect" similes. In particular, visualizing the meadow of Skamandros as "full of flowers" (ἀνθεμόεντι) triggered the simile of "leaves and flowers" (φύλλα καὶ ἄνθεα), which evoked in its turn the stronger simile family of insects (μυιάων ἀδινάων). We can even trace certain aural by-products of this process of "visual rebounding," like the reverse alliteration of the cluster νθ/θν in ἀνθεμόεντι, ἄνθεα/ἔθνεα. Through a similar process, as soon as the pastoral simile in 477–479 was completed, the narrator added Agamemnon to the concluding "deictic" part (476–477 ὡς τοὺς ἡγεμόνες διεκόσμεον ἔνθα καὶ ἔνθα / ὑσμίνηνδ' ἰέναι). In this case two factors determined the final result: First, the pressure exercised by the clustering of similes, and in particular of the two previous pastoral similes which directed the storyteller's mind toward a new pastoral simile, centered on the figure of Agamemnon. This was a rather expected outcome, for the great king of Mycenae had been dictionally fossilized in epic idiom by the formula ποιμὴν λαῶν 'shepherd of the people', and in this respect it was only natural for him to be described as such visually as well, just before the presentation of the Achaean forces *in toto*, among whom he was preeminent. Second, his brief anatomical comparison to three different gods, which was nontraditional and rather innovative (there is no other example in Homer), had few chances to be expanded within the pictorial series of these concatenated pastoral similes. It may have been created by the narrator's effort to help his audience mentally see Agamemnon among the multitude of warriors marching to battle. Such were the crowds of men on the battlefield that the narrator had to resort to a handy epic mechanism for allowing his audience to visualize Agamemnon: a "disguised" epiphany, the sudden impressive appearance of a god to mortal men.[51] Agamemnon's anatomical assimilation to three different gods through the accumulation of familiar mental images was an eye-catching technique that distinguished the king of Mycenae from the other warriors. It was destined to be short-lived, however, for the force of the pastoral similes' imagery was soon to take over.

Apart from its relevance to the following scene, a cluster of extended similes belonging to the same visual unit and marked by their built-in pictorial abundance would have created extremely strong background images for visualizing the marshaling of the troops from multiple angles. As we will see, the narrator aimed to offer his audience a visualization of the gathering of Achaean forces that was as complete as possible. To this end, he accumulated similes whose spatial aspect let him visualize the marshaling of the troops from different points of view. In particular, we will see how the concatenation of simile space was made possible in his mind by means of *pictorial dovetailing*, mentally selecting each simile on the grounds of a spatial aspect highlighted in the previous narrative-simile pair. In fact, the two transitional similes I have analyzed above serve exactly this purpose, each one functioning as a bridge that enables the visual crossing from one narrative-simile pair to the next.

A careful reading of this scene shows that the storyteller's eye follows the marshaling of the army in various steps, and gradually zooms in. He visualizes the army as it moves to the plain and takes its fighting position, dividing this process into various steps, each of which he mentally illustrates by means of the homologous visual mappings of concatenated similes. In particular, he first watches the troops moving from a distance; at this point he can see only the gleaming of their bronze armor, which he visualizes through the simile of the fire blazing on mountain peaks and rising to the sky. Although the fire similes depict fire as destructive, the expression "destructive fire" (455 πῦρ ἀΐδηλον) is not activated, and the fire's menacing aspect is left unexplored.[52] This weakening or deactivation of the simileme allows us to glimpse the narrator at work, as he visually recontextualizes his simile subject matter. We can also see how he lets himself be guided by his simile's strong spatial coordinates: the gleam going up and "dazzling all about through the upper air to the heaven," which is the last visual frame of the first simile, evokes another visual frame in the beginning of the second simile that is marked by a homologous image-mapping: the spatial

---

[51] The storyteller can employ epiphanic conventions to create not only intratextual (as here), but also intertextual associations; see Pucci 1998:81–96.

[52] Cf. the simile in *Iliad* XI 155–159, where fire is presented as a threat. This point is strongly made by Scott 2009:49–50.

aspect of height triggers the image of the birds flying noisily this way and that above the meadow of Kaüstros. This is not to say that the storyteller did not plan on depicting the second phase of the army's marshaling as the Achaean troops flood the plain of Skamandros, but the particular visualization of this phase is effected by an initial mental cue given by the last, spatially oriented visual frame of the previous simile. This *pictorial dovetailing* goes on, since the storyteller, who next sees the numerous warriors standing close to one another, employs the illustrative analogy of the numerous flies. Here, the spatial aspect denoted by the flying birds in the previous simile, particularized by the reference to spring-time in the transitional simile of lines 467–468, has been visually combined in the extended simile of the flies "who drive hither and thither about the stalls of the sheepfold / in the season of spring when the milk splashes in the milk pails." The introduction of a pastoral simile belonging to an extremely strong simile family generates a series of three successive extended similes, based on specific visual frames of a clearly spatial nature. In particular, visualizing the troops as they now take their fighting positions presupposes a mental "zooming in," since the troops no longer move but stand still in the plain. Therefore, the pastoral simile of the goatherds separating and sorting the herd is based on the same visual frame of pastoral life. A further zooming in is then possible, by selecting a single hero among the Achaean leaders, who like the goatherds tries to place the troops in the right positions. By focusing on Agamemnon "standing conspic-uous among men," the narrator can visualize further details of the larger scene he has mentally pictured. The widely represented simile family of pastoral life is presented no longer in a menacing framework (with some carnivorous predator attacking helpless sheep or cattle), but through the dominating presence of a single animal, the bull, whose prominence among the rest of the cattle effec-tively brings before the audience's eyes Agamemnon standing out among the troops.

I have used the term *pictorial dovetailing* to describe the process of concate-nating visually interlocked simile images through spatially oriented enmeshing. The impressive simile cluster in *Iliad* II is telling, since it shows how important space is as a mental cue for image recall and organization of narrative-simile pairs in narrative junctures placed at turning-points of the plot. Within the system of epic song, memorization and traditionality go hand in hand with innovation and originality, to such an extent that Lord's saying that "the singer is the tradition"—with all its flexibility and rigor, one might add—acquires its true meaning.

Despite being separated from the cluster of similes discussed above, the last extended simile, in *Iliad* II 780–785, still falls within the same visual unit as the previous ones in lines 455–483. The narrator has kept in his mind several spatial features, such as the blazing fire and the loud echoing of the earth, that occur in different similes but belong to the same long simile cluster before the Catalogue of Ships. This time, though, when the battle is about to begin, the recalled spatial features of the earth as well as noise acquire their traditional menacing role. The majestic grandeur of the whole scene is further reinforced by the visualization of a mythical event, the fighting between Zeus and Typhoeus after the Titanomachy. Although the mythical reference weakens the pictorial openness of the simile by attaching it to a specific "event," the mechanism of spatial association through homologous visual mappings between narrative and simile still works. When leaving the register of catalogic poetry to come back to that of narrative poetry, the storyteller returns to the same spatial coordinates, facilitating recall and allowing him to remember where he left off when he began to sing the Catalogue of Ships.

Iliad V

Iliad V comprises four thematic sections:

1–165: Diomedes' entering battle and killing of Trojans

166–459: his episode with Aineias and Aphrodite

460–710: the intervention of Ares, who regroups the Trojan troops

711–909: Diomedes' wounding of Ares by means of Athena's and Hera's help

Iliad V contains twelve extended similes, mentally organized in seven visual units, which are unequally distributed in these four thematic sections. Most of the similes refer, quite understandably, to Diomedes, who prevails by means of his truly extraordinary military exploits. Most of these visual snapshots allow the storyteller to place Diomedes' activity in space, whereas the rest enable him to mnemonically "locate" several phases or incidents that have different protagonists. Space, therefore, becomes a means by which the general theme "Diomedes excels in battle" is mentally visualized by narrator and audience alike. *Iliad* V has been called a "fragile mixing of unmixable locales and characters,"[53] which focuses on the ineffectiveness of Diomedes' ἀριστεία and his fighting against the gods. In the following analysis, I will deal with the way the storyteller employs the spatial mappings of a number of extended similes with respect to these two main themes, in his effort to view the protagonist's action as belonging to a single trajectory and to create a continuous action space.

---

[53] Scott 2009:102–112.

Visual unit 1

5–8: (N1) Diomedes' first entrance on the battlefield / (S1) shining star
rising from the ocean

87–94: (N2) Diomedes' second entrance on the battlefield / (S2) strong-
compacted dikes and mounded banks of blossoming vineyards

136–143: (N3) Diomedes' third entrance on the battlefield / (S3) wild
lands, fence of the fold, sheep pens, deep yard

161–165: (N4) two Trojans in a chariot / (S4) wooded places

ἀστέρ' ὀπωρινῷ ἐναλίγκιον, ὅς τε μάλιστα
λαμπρὸν παμφαίνῃσι λελουμένος Ὠκεανοῖο.
τοῖόν οἱ πῦρ δαῖεν ἀπὸ κρατός τε καὶ ὤμων,
ὦρσε δέ μιν κατὰ μέσσον, ὅθι πλεῖστοι κλονέοντο.

like that star of the waning summer who beyond all stars
rises bathed in the ocean stream to glitter in brilliance.
Such was the fire she made blaze from his head and his shoulders
and urged him into the middle fighting, where most were struggling.

Iliad V 5–8

θῦνε γὰρ ἂμ πεδίον ποταμῷ πλήθοντι ἐοικώς
χειμάρρῳ, ὅς τ' ὦκα ῥέων ἐκέδασσε γεφύρας,
τὸν δ' οὔτ' ἄρ τε γέφυραι ἐεργμέναι ἰσχανόωσιν
οὔτ' ἄρα ἕρκεα ἴσχει ἀλωάων ἐριθηλέων
ἐλθόντ' ἐξαπίνης, ὅτ' ἐπιβρίσῃ Διὸς ὄμβρος,
πολλὰ δ' ὑπ' αὐτοῦ ἔργα κατήριπε κάλ' αἰζηῶν·
ὣς ὑπὸ Τυδείδῃ πυκιναὶ κλονέοντο φάλαγγες
Τρώων, οὐδ' ἄρα μιν μίμνον πολέες περ ἐόντες.

since he went storming up the plain like a winter-swollen
river in spate that scatters the dikes in its running current,
one that the strong-compacted dikes can contain no longer,
neither the mounded banks of the blossoming vineyards hold it
rising suddenly as Zeus' rain makes heavy the water
and many lovely works of the young men crumble beneath it.
Like these the massed battalions of the Trojans were scattered
by Tydeus' son, and many as they were could not stand against him.

Iliad V 87–94

δὴ τότε μιν τρὶς τόσσον ἕλεν μένος, ὥς τε λέοντα,
ὅν ῥά τε ποιμὴν ἀγρῷ ἐπ' εἰροπόκοις ὀΐεσσιν
χραύσῃ μέν τ' αὐλῆς ὑπεράλμενον, οὐδὲ δαμάσσῃ·
τοῦ μέν τε σθένος ὦρσεν, ἔπειτα δέ τ' οὐ προσαμύνει,
ἀλλὰ κατὰ σταθμοὺς δύεται, τὰ δ' ἐρῆμα φοβεῖται·
αἳ μέν τ' ἀγχηστῖναι ἐπ' ἀλλήλῃσι κέχυνται,
αὐτὰρ ὃ ἐμμεμαὼς βαθέης ἐξάλλεται αὐλῆς·
ὣς μεμαὼς Τρώεσσι μίγη κρατερὸς Διομήδης.

Now the strong rage tripled took hold of him, as of a lion
whom the shepherd among his fleecy flocks in the wild lands
grazed as he leapt the fence of the fold, but has not killed him,
but only stirred the lion's strength, and can no more fight him
off, but hides in the steading, and the frightened sheep are forsaken,
and these are piled pell-mell on each other in heaps, while the lion
raging still leaps out again over the fence of the deep yard;
such was the rage of strong Diomedes as he closed upon the Trojans.

Iliad V 136–143

ὡς δὲ λέων ἐν βουσὶ θορὼν ἐξ αὐχένα ἄξῃ
πόρτιος ἠὲ βοός, ξύλοχον κάτα βοσκομενάων,
ὣς τοὺς ἀμφοτέρους ἐξ ἵππων Τυδέος υἱὸς
βῆσε κακῶς ἀέκοντας, ἔπειτα δὲ τεύχε' ἐσύλα,
ἵππους δ' οἷς ἑτάροισι δίδου μετὰ νῆας ἐλαύνειν.

As among cattle a lion leaps on the neck of an ox or
heifer, that grazes among the wooden places, and breaks it,
so the son of Tydeus hurled both from their horses
hatefully, in spite of their struggles, then stripped their armour
and gave the horses to his company to drive to their vessels.

Iliad V 161–165

Iliad V begins with an impressive presentation of its protagonist,[54] Diomedes, who is visually singled out by being compared to a star of the waning summer or early autumn that "rises bathed in the ocean stream to glitter in brilliance" (6). In his mind's eye, the narrator sees Diomedes entering battle for the first time by means of a blaze of fire rising from his head and shoulders. The simileme of

---

54 On the epic law of concentration on a "leading character," see Olrik 1992:48.

the shining star is particularly apt for visualizing Diomedes, since it is accompanied by a short but effective visual frame of the ocean, which renders the rising star mentally clearer since it presents it as a single object against the backdrop of a massive amount of water. To put it a different way, the star is not visualized as a separate entity, but is "tagged" to a location of an impressive size. Perceiving a single very bright object against a larger background enhances visualization and memorability.[55] *Iliad* V thus begins with a clear look at Diomedes, moving toward the enemy troops. To visualize him penetrating the Trojan phalanxes two more times,[56] the storyteller employs two extended similes, while one more simile brings the whole scene to a close.[57] He does not change visual units, but organizes his material in successive phases, each of which is mentally mapped to an equivalent simile space. In particular, Diomedes' second violent assault on the Trojans is compared to a "winter-swollen river" that destroys the "strong-compacted dikes" and "mounded banks" of the vineyards which can hold it no longer. The visual frame of the rain "making heavy the water" particularizes this rather common simileme, and adds force to the mental picture of the Trojan troops' scattering hither and thither as Diomedes unleashes his fierce attack.[58] The third extended simile depicts Diomedes as a lion entering the pens where the sheep are kept. The shepherd cannot stop it, and the sheep in utmost fear "are piled pell-mell on each other in heaps, while the lion / raging still leaps out again over the fence of the deep yard." Although the spatial coordinates of the simile and the deep structure of the simileme are the same—they represent the impressive, unstoppable, and destructive activity of a physical phenomenon or animal—individual spatial frames create variation. Whereas in the previous simile the dikes and mounded banks of the vineyards are destroyed, here the sheep are heaped one upon the other. The shift of visual frames not only in theme but also in function is illustratively analogous to the activity of the Trojans, who are scattered and grouped together in the

---

[55] See Rubin 1995:53.

[56] On the standard structure of scenes describing a warrior's entry into battle, see Fenik 1968:22–23. On the use of similes (both long and short) to describe a character's entrance in the narrative, see Scott 1974:38–41.

[57] The use of the pattern of three entrances on the battlefield abides by the epic law of "the three," which according to Olrik (1992:52) is typical of oral narratives. The first time, the hero is one among a group of Achaean warriors depicted slaying their Trojan opponents; his second entrance is particularized and singled out, as he is presented as the opponent of the Lycian archer Pandaros; the third time, his ἀνδροκτασία is presented on its own, rather than making him one of a list of Achaean leaders.

[58] From the standpoint of mnemonic recall and image processing, the visual frame of the ocean may (at least partly) have triggered the water imagery of the river that appears in the second simile. Pictorial association of this sort is typical in oral storytelling.

equivalent narrative units.[59] The fourth extended simile brings this initial visual unit to an end, as the narrative lens zooms in on Ekhemmon and Khromios, the sons of Priam, who are driving their chariot. Diomedes, who "hurls them from their horses,"[60] is compared to a lion jumping on "the neck of an ox or heifer that grazes among the wooden places."[61] The storyteller's mind still holds the picture of wild nature, where a ferocious carnivore makes his attack against powerless animals. By zooming in on a particular spot on the battlefield, he creates a visual analog that can only have the same spatial characteristics as the previous simile, since the narrative space has not changed.

We see here the importance of imagery in organizing and processing the material of separate narrative incidents.[62] To increase recall and visualize the action, the oral poet employs background information rich in pictorial features. Diomedes, who will be the book's protagonist, looms large in this initial visual unit of *Iliad* V. His aggressive attack on the Trojans and killing of various second-rank opponents is organized by a process of narrative segmentation, in which each of his three successive attacks is mentally tied to an extended simile, whose spatial features allow the storyteller to create strong mental links with his protagonist's different narrative snapshots. As long as Diomedes' narrative space remains the same, the narrator uses homologous simile space for material recall and visual clarity. When the storyteller decides to shift to a different scene, he employs an extended simile with analogous spatial coordinates to indicate completion (161–164). One of the oral poet's principal aims in *Iliad* V is *to view the protagonist's action as belonging to a single trajectory and create a continuous action space*. The spatial function of the similes facilitates this effect, because similes constitute *high-imagery* spatial units that require more visual imagery on the part of the narrator and audience than do the low-imagery visual units of narrative.[63] The similes thus become a series of spatial links, creating through high-density imagery a single *path* on which the activity of Diomedes can be placed. Thus by the time this visual unit is completed and the narrator breaks off, the similes with their vivid visual imagery and the powerful pictureability that has

---

[59] Cf. Scott 2009:229n58: "The wound increases the lion's wrath, and the shepherd no longer defends the sheep, but he (the shepherd) lurks around the sheep pens and fears the open areas. The sheep are heaped upon one another in piles, but the lion in his fury leaps out of the high enclosure. This version has the advantage of emphasizing the broader passage, both the lion and the shepherd; this double focus reflects the return of Diomedes as well as Pandaros, who is conscious of his failure." See also Kirk 1990:70–72.

[60] It is understood that the plural ἵππων 'horses' (*Iliad* V 163) refers to the chariot as a whole.

[61] See Moulton 1977:61.

[62] On imagery as a type of organizing material in oral traditions, see Rubin 1995:52–54 with bibliography.

[63] On high and low imagery, see Marschark and Paivio 1977; Marschark 1979.

so vividly highlighted the exploits of Diomedes have created high expectations for the action: the audience is invited to believe that something really great will come out of Diomedes' outstanding military performance. We shall now see how the listeners' horizon of expectations will be further broadened by the introduction of a new theme, Diomedes' fighting against the gods.

Section 2 (*Iliad* V 166–459) lacks extended similes, for Diomedes, who is still the protagonist, does not change location. The narrator does not need new image-mappings in order to visualize his leading character's further exploits against Pandaros, Aineias, and Aphrodite. Conversely, in section 3, where new scenes with protagonists other than Diomedes are introduced (Sarpedon and Hektor, the Ajaxes, Odysseus, and Diomedes defending the Achaean troops) the storyteller uses the spatial mapping of similes as a backdrop against which he can mentally locate and visualize the new action. The final simile of this section, with Diomedes drawing back on Ares, functions as a bridge that allows the narrator to return mentally to where he left Diomedes, for he will be the great protagonist of the book's fourth and final section.

The third part of *Iliad* V (460–710) includes four extended similes distributed among three visual units, the first containing two similes and the other two one each. Distribution of similes over a wide range of visual units shows a low level of dramatization of the plot, for segmentation and visual "bricolage" unavoidably diminish cohesion and leave little, if any, room for character exploitation. The narrator is at pains to create cohesion in a scene whose only central theme is Ares' intervention and rallying of the Trojans.

Visual unit 2

> 499–505: (N1) Achaeans standing firm against Trojan counterattack / (S1) *whitening of heaps of chaff blown by the wind*

> 522–527: (N2) Ajaxes, Odysseus, and Diomedes standing firm against Trojan counterattack / (S2) clouds *heaping up above* the mountaintops

ὡς δ' ἄνεμος ἄχνας φορέῃ ἱερὰς κατ' ἀλωάς
ἀνδρῶν λικμώντων, ὅτε τε ξανθὴ Δημήτηρ
κρίνῃ ἐπειγομένων ἀνέμων καρπόν τε καὶ ἄχνας,
αἳ δ' ὑπολευκαίνονται ἀχυρμιαί, ὣς τότ' Ἀχαιοὶ
λευκοὶ ὕπερθε γένοντο κονισάλῳ, ὅν ῥα δι' αὐτῶν
οὐρανὸν ἐς πολύχαλκον ἐπέπληγον πόδες ἵππων
ἂψ ἐπιμισγομένων· ὑπὸ δ' ἔστρεφον ἡνιοχῆες.

As when along the hallowed threshing floors the wind scatters
chaff, among men winnowing, and fair-haired Demeter
in the leaning wind discriminates the chaff and the true grain
and the piling chaff whitens beneath it, so now the Achaians
turned white underneath the dust the feet of the horses
drove far into the brazen sky across their faces
as they rapidly closed and the charioteers wheeled back again.

Iliad V 499–505

ἀλλ' ἔμενον, νεφέλῃσιν ἐοικότες, ἅς τε Κρονίων
νηνεμίης ἔστησεν ἐπ' ἀκροπόλοισιν ὄρεσσιν
ἀτρέμας, ὄφρ' εὕδῃσι μένος Βορέαο καὶ ἄλλων
ζαχρειῶν ἀνέμων, οἵ τε νέφεα σκιόεντα
πνοιῇσιν λιγυρῇσι διασκιδνᾶσιν ἀέντες·
ὣς Δαναοὶ Τρῶας μένον ἔμπεδον οὐδ' ἐφέβοντο.

but stayed where they were, like clouds, which the son of Kronos
stops in the windless weather on the heights of the towering
    mountains,
motionless, when the strength of the north wind sleeps, and the
    other
tearing winds, those winds that when they blow into tempests
high screaming descend upon the darkening clouds and scatter
    them.
So the Danaans stood steady against the Trojans, nor gave way.

Iliad V 522–527

Ares' entry on the battlefield after Aphrodite is wounded creates high expectations for the Trojans, since the god of war rallies them and prepares a fierce attack against the Achaeans. The narrator visualizes this attack in two steps, by means of two extended similes sharing the same simileme: in the first, he focuses on Hektor's and Sarpedon's attack, and in the second on that of Aineias, who has returned to the battlefield (to the great surprise and joy of the Trojans) and is led by Apollo, Ares, and Enuo. To see how the two similes' spatial coordinates help the storyteller organize his scene, we must note that the action is localized on the basis of a balanced presentation of the Trojans attacking and the Achaeans holding their ground. Having flirted with the idea of a successful Trojan counterattack under the leadership of the fiercest god, the god of war, the storyteller begins to undermine it, even from its beginning. Although he has reintroduced Aineias, one of the Trojan protagonists of section 2 (166–459),[64] and has also brought into the picture more reinforcements of the highest caliber and fighting skill, such as the preeminent Lycian leader Sarpedon and the best Trojan warrior Hektor, he makes it clear that the Achaeans will hold their positions and fight back. For the time being, he can concentrate on this scene, leaving Diomedes' triumph for later. One can see here how the narrator uses the motif of "ineffective fighting" in developing and organizing his material. Violation of expectations and narrative suspension are key terms for *Iliad* V. Both of the extended similes in this visual unit offer strong illustrative analogies: in the first, the whitening (from the dust raised by the horses' feet) of the heads and shoulders of the Achaeans, who refuse to withdraw, is compared with the whitening of heaps of chaff blown by the wind, while in the second the Achaeans are likened to clouds *piling high* on mountaintops when the winds are asleep. Wind similes are often employed to denote imminent destruction,[65] and are associated with some change that *may happen* in the plot.[66] In this visual unit the emphasis is on the spatial markers of *density* (piling up) and *verticality* (depth and height): the blowing wind whitens heaps of chaff underneath the true grain in the threshing floor (first simile), while its absence allows the clouds to pile up over the mountain peaks (second simile). This pictorial movement along a vertical axis in the same visual unit indexes two separate yet associated phases in the narrative: the Achaeans, massing in their ranks like the chaff and the clouds, will hold their ground. The similes the storyteller employs replay on a different spatial register the same game of creating and then violating the audience's expectations: for the listeners, the family of the wind simile would no doubt have created the impression of a destructive result. By draining these similes of their typical, expected force as images[67] and linking them by means of the spatial markers of density and verticality (below: chaff and high up: clouds), the narrator created for his audience a new visual situation, that of the Achaeans standing firm one close to the other, just as with the piling up of chaff and clouds in the two extended similes. In this way, he was able to exploit at full length the high-imagery spatial dynamics of the similes and mentally almost "impose" their spatial horizon on the main narrative.[68]

---

[64] The other main Trojan figure of this section is Pandaros. The chief pro-Trojan deity of this part of *Iliad* V is Aphrodite.

[65] See Scott 1974:62–66; Moulton 1977:60–63.

[66] Purves 2010b:325.

[67] On this point, see the observations of Scott 2009:108.

[68] See Tsagalis 2008b:272–285.

Visual unit 3

554–560: (N1) battlefield (sons of Diokles) / (S1) high places in the
    mountains

οἵω τώ γε λέοντε δύω ὄρεος κορυφῇσιν
ἐτραφέτην ὑπὸ μητρὶ βαθείης τάρφεσιν ὕλης·
τὼ μὲν ἄρ’ ἁρπάζοντε βόας καὶ ἴφια μῆλα
σταθμοὺς ἀνθρώπων κεραΐζετον, ὄφρα καὶ αὐτώ
ἀνδρῶν ἐν παλάμῃσι κατέκταθεν ὀξέϊ χαλκῷ·
τοίω τὼ χείρεσσιν ὑπ’ Αἰνείαο δαμέντε
καππεσέτην, ἐλάτῃσιν ἐοικότες ὑψηλῇσιν.

These, as two young lions in the high places of the mountains,
had been raised by their mother in the dark of the deep forest,
lions which as they prey upon the cattle and the fat sheep
lay waste the steadings where there are men, until they also
fall and are killed under the cutting bronze in the men's hands;
such were these two who beaten under the hands of Aineias
crashed now to the ground as if they were two tall pine trees.

Iliad V 554–560

Aineias' attacking and killing Diokles' twin sons seems to tip the scales in favor
of the Trojans, just as Diomedes' killing of the two sons of Dares in the beginning
of *Iliad* V signaled Achaean victory. The narrator exploits this parallel in order
to play with his audience's expectations. To this end, he also uses secondary
features, such as the wealth of their father[69] and their skill in war,[70] which reinforce the analogy. A long, high-imagery simile with vivid spatial features marks
the narrative event as important. The twins are compared to two lions that lay
waste the farmstead, prey upon cattle and sheep, and are subsequently killed at
the hands of shepherds. The deep structure of a lion simile includes the human
protection of otherwise powerless sheep and cattle against the attack of this
fierce and persistent predator, but the brief snapshot usually remains suspended,
as no end result is stated. Conversely, this simile ends with the death of the
two lions, which are killed by the shepherds, just as the sons of Diokles are by
Aineias. The narrator has used the simile's rich spatial imagery, with its typical
locations of farmsteads and mountains, as a background image to suggest a
comparison with Diomedes' previous activity. For a moment, Aineias seems to be
an anti-Diomedes, who this time returns to the battlefield in triumph. Members

---

[69] *Iliad* V 9 ἀφνειὸς ἀμύμων, 544 ἀφνειὸς βιότοιο.
[70] *Iliad* V 11 = V 549 μάχης εὖ εἰδότε πάσης.

of the audience may have even expected a second encounter between the two, a replay of their initial conflict, cut short by Aphrodite's intervention. Since the narrative circumstances are analogous and the spatial coordinates have not changed, the storyteller reemploys the same simileme of the lion *attacking sheep and cattle in wild, wooded places* that has already been applied twice to Diomedes, in V 136–143, when he entered the Trojan phalanxes for the third time, and later in 161–164, when he killed Priam's sons Ekhemmon and Khromios. Exactly at the point when Diomedes fades into the background and Aineias prevails, the storyteller uses spatial imagery that evokes Diomedes' earlier exploits.[71] In this way, the narrator is able to devise an internal organizing mechanism that "guides" him and his listeners and creates effective mnemonic associations between different narrative scenes.

Visual unit 4

597–600: (N1) Diomedes draws back / (S1) river

ὡς δ' ὅτ' ἀνὴρ ἀπάλαμνος, ἰὼν πολέος πεδίοιο,
στήῃ ἐπ' ὠκυρόῳ ποταμῷ ἅλαδε προρέοντι,
ἀφρῷ μορμύροντα ἰδών, ἀνά τ' ἔδραμ' ὀπίσσω,
ὣς τότε Τυδεΐδης ἀνεχάζετο

and like a man in his helplessness who, crossing a great plain,
stands at the edge of a fast-running river that dashes seaward,
and watches it thundering into white water, and leaps a pace
       backward,
so now Tydeus' son gave back ...

Iliad V 597–600

Visual unit 4 is marked by the same phenomenon observed in the previous visual unit: a simileme employed earlier on (in visual unit 1) for Diomedes is repeated under analogous spatial coordinates but for a different narrative situation. Diomedes, who was then compared to a "river in spate that scatters the dikes in its running current, / one that the strong-compacted dikes can contain no longer, / neither the mounded banks of the blossoming vineyards hold it"[72] is now like a man faced with a rushing river. The storyteller employs equivalent

---

[71] At the completion of the simile the narrator appends a short comparison of the falling warriors to fallen fir trees. For tree similes describing fallen warriors, see *Iliad* IV 482, XIII 178, XIII 389–390 (= XVI 482–483), XIV 414, and XVII 53. There are important observations in Fenik 1968:58; Scott 1974:70–71; Lonsdale 1990:55; and Scott 2009:108 and 229–230n67. On brief necrological vignettes of second-rank heroes such as the sons of Diokles, see Tsagalis 2004:179–192.

[72] *Iliad* V 88–90.

image-mappings to visualize reverse narrative situations occurring in the same narrative space. This spatial homology cues recall and facilitates thematic interconnections. The space delineated by the imagery of the river is evoked again when the storyteller returns to Diomedes, although this time he is retreating instead of attacking the Trojans. With this simile, the storyteller completes a separate visual unit that brings the entire third section to an end. The four similes he has used have allowed him to organize disparate scenes (Sarpedon's and Hektor's attack; the resistance of the two Ajaxes, Odysseus, and Diomedes who hold their ground; the killing of Diokles' twin sons by Aineias; Diomedes' withdrawal at the attack of Ares) and coordinate them with earlier narrative scenes *by means of simile space*. From this point of view, he has created for his audience a mechanism for observing and evaluating internal thematic correlations, as his narrative unfolds with the tide turning to the Trojan side and Ares prevailing, albeit temporarily.

Visual unit 5

770–772: (N1) stride of divine horses between earth and sky / (S1) lookout–sea

ὅσσον δ᾽ ἠεροειδὲς ἀνὴρ ἴδεν ὀφθαλμοῖσιν
ἥμενος ἐν σκοπιῇ, λεύσσων ἐπὶ οἴνοπα πόντον,
τόσσον ἐπιθρῴσκουσι θεῶν ὑψηχέες ἵπποι.

As far as into the hazing distance a man can see with
his eyes, who sits in his lookout[73] gazing on the wine-blue water,
as far as this is the stride of the gods' proud neighing horses.

Iliad V 770–772

The last thematic section of *Iliad* V (711–909) includes four extended similes, organized in three visual units. As noted before, wide distribution of similes and lack of accumulation within a single visual unit is a sign of a low level of dramatization. The storyteller aims mainly at presenting Diomedes' counterattack and wounding of Ares, thus interweaving the two threads he has been unraveling since the beginning of *Iliad* V, that is, the suspended results of the action and the problematic interference of the gods in human affairs. In this visual unit, an extended simile is employed to introduce divine action on the Achaean side. The arrival of the goddesses Athena and Hera is visualized by means of the stride of their horses, which is compared to the distance seen by a man sitting

---

[73] I have changed Lattimore's "eyrie" to "lookout," since the word σκοπιή does not indicate an eagle's nest or any other bird's nest.

in his lookout. The simile, which is based on distance, an aspect of space, aims at imagining the divine chariot of Athena and Hera approaching at high speed.[74] Their arrival at the place where the rivers Simoeis and Skamandros meet reinforces the visualization.[75] Taking the form of doves, they will now approach the Achaean troops and try to instill courage in their hearts. The storyteller, who has decided to use the divine advent as a turning point in the plot of *Iliad* V, needs a strong prop for his audience, a sign marking this shift in the course of the action. He therefore employs the spatial aspect of distance as a way to introduce a new scene. Once this is done, he has to change visual units and focus his mind's eye again on the battlefield, but this time when Diomedes inflicts a serious wound on Ares himself.

Visual unit 6

859–863: (N1) sound (Ares' roar) / (S1) sound

864–867: (N2) color, clouds (Ares) / (S2) color, clouds

ὃ δ' ἔβραχε χάλκεος Ἄρης,
ὅσσόν τ' ἐννεάχειλοι ἐπίαχον ἢ δεκάχειλοι
ἀνέρες ἐν πολέμῳ ἔριδα ξυνάγοντες Ἄρηος·
τοὺς δ' ἄρ' ὑπὸ τρόμος εἷλεν Ἀχαιούς τε Τρῶάς τε
δείσαντας· τόσον ἔβραχ' Ἄρης ἆτος πολέμοιο.

Then Ares the brazen bellowed
with a sound as great as nine thousand men make, or ten thousand,
when they cry as they carry into the fighting the fury of the war god.
And a shivering seized hold alike on Achaians and Trojans
in their fear at the bellowing of battle-insatiate Ares.

Iliad V 859–863

οἵη δ' ἐκ νεφέων ἐρεβεννὴ φαίνεται ἀήρ
καύματος ἔξ, ἀνέμοιο δυσαέος ὀρνυμένοιο,
τοῖος Τυδείδῃ Διομήδεϊ χάλκεος Ἄρης
φαίνεθ' ὁμοῦ νεφέεσσιν, ἰὼν εἰς οὐρανὸν εὐρύν.

---

[74] See Scott 1974:20, who observes that poets measured space by employing the principle: "Use approximate measurements when the use of precise figures does not serve a poetic purpose and will merely bore or distract the audience." Scott distinguishes between two types of similes indicating measurement: those suggesting "meaningful approximation" and those expressing the notion of "infinite extent" (24). The simile in *Iliad* V 770–772 belongs to the second type: "Since no hearer could make a meaningful approximation of such a measure, Homer merely means that the horses bounded an unimaginable distance, an idea well suited to divine horses."

[75] See W. Kullmann 1956:91.

As when out of the thunderhead the air shows darkening
after a day's heat when the stormy wind uprises,
thus to Tydeus' son Diomedes Ares the brazen
showed as he went up with the clouds into the wide heaven.

Iliad V 864–867

The fighting between Diomedes (aided by Athena) and Ares is presented by means of two extended similes focusing on two different spatial aspects, sound and color, and (as noted above) correspond to two successive narrative scenes. Although they both deal with different kinds of activity (shouting and ascending), their visual frameworks show absolute correspondence between narrative space and simile space: when the former changes, then the latter changes too. Ares' ascent to Olympos belongs to a different spatial mechanism than that of his bellowing, and so a different spatial framework has to be employed.

Both similes highlight the strong divine element of this last section of *Iliad* V. The audience will now have realized that Ares' intervention and the false expectation of a Trojan victory that it created are interwoven with a complex nexus of associations between gods and men, and that in the end, the narrative suspension of the plot is a feature that permeates the whole of *Iliad* V. Neither can the pro-Trojan gods prevail (for both Aphrodite and Ares are wounded and withdraw from the fighting), nor will Diomedes achieve any solid results.

Visual unit 7

902–904: (N1) Ares' wound / (S1) white milk

ὡς δ' ὅτ' ὀπὸς γάλα λευκὸν ἐπειγόμενος συνέπηξεν
ὑγρὸν ἐόν, μάλα δ' ὦκα περιτρέφεται κυκόωντι,
ὡς ἄρα καρπαλίμως ἰήσατο θοῦρον Ἄρηα.

As when the juice of the fig in white milk rapidly fixes
that which was fluid before and curdles quickly for one who
stirs it; in such speed as this he healed violent Ares.

Iliad V 902–904

Iliad V ends with an extended simile referring to the *swift* healing of Ares' wound by Paion. The emphasis here is on the speed, another aspect of space, with which Ares is healed. The illustrative analogy of "curdling milk" belongs to a completely different simileme, one that has not been used before. The story-teller, therefore, employs a different spatial aspect to coordinate narrative and simile. The effect of this last simile can be appreciated only when it is seen as the last in a series of extended similes that frame the entire book. *Iliad* V ends with the *quick* healing of a god,[76] a sure hint at the unbridgeable gulf separating the divine from the human world, but also with the implicit indication to the audience that no progress has really been achieved with respect to the developing plot. We are basically at the same place[77] where we were when Diomedes first entered the battlefield, "like that star of the waning summer who beyond all other stars / rises bathed in the ocean stream to glitter in brilliance."[78]

Iliad XI

Iliad XI is one of the richest books of the epic in both extended similes (sixteen) and the visual units to which they belong (nine). Clustering is limited to half (five) of the total number of visual units, but the repetition of simile subjects shows that the storyteller used them to suggest lines of association and cross-references for his audience.[79] *Iliad* XI is marked by its tight structure and thematic cohesion as well as its key function in the unfolding of the Iliadic plot. Given that a fair number of themes developed here "are absorbed into over-riding structures and play on our imagination as a set,"[80] it is important to explore how a dense array of similes has allowed the storyteller to elaborate characterization and organize the development of his plot.[81]

The book's structure is as follows:

1–283: Agamemnon's ἀριστεία

284–596: Hektor's entry into battle (310–440: wounding of Diomedes; 401–488: wounding of Odysseus; 489–596 fighting of Ajax)

597–848: the Nestor-Patroklos episode[82]

The first section comprises four visual units containing six similes, and the second five visual units including nine similes, whereas the last section lacks any extended similes. From these data it becomes clear that the storyteller has concentrated most on the similes in the central battle section of this book, and has created a strong antithesis between the first and third sections. The reason may be that the last and final section is for the most part occupied by

---

[76] Mortals are also healed in the *Iliad*, but never swiftly or easily.

[77] Seen from a different angle, the poet is able to adopt a truly eusynoptic view of the narrative space of such a very long book as *Iliad* V. On the eusynoptic aspect of Iliadic space and Aristotle's observations, see Purves 2010a:24–64.

[78] *Iliad* V 5–6.

[79] Scott 2009:78.

[80] Fenik 1986:21.

[81] On the role of *Iliad* XI in the overall structure of the *Iliad*, see Schadewaldt 1966.

[82] See Scott 2009:80–81.

the *Nestoris*, the long digression by the great king of Pylos on his heroic past. Speeches, as we have argued, are notoriously lacking in extended similes, the more so since Nestor's embedded narrative displays high-density imagery, but of a different quality than that found in similes: the thematized space of Pylos is so rich in itself, and so spatially differentiated from the story space of the Iliadic narrative, that the narrator had no need or reason to employ extended similes.

Iliad XI is a good example of the technique of *visual progression on the run* that the narrator is employing. He begins his narrative with the two armies preparing for battle (visual units 1 and 2); he then focuses his attention on Agamemnon, whose ἀριστεία stamps *Iliad* XI (visual unit 3); turns his mind's eye to the wounding and withdrawal of Agamemnon (visual unit 4) and then to the attacks of the Trojans (visual unit 5) and Hektor (visual unit 6); visualizes the brief counterattack by Diomedes and Odysseus (visual unit 7); and devotes much narrative space to Odysseus' perils (visual unit 8) and Ajax's retreat (visual unit 9). In particular, the storyteller uses a technique of *visual exhaustion* of a character: when Agamemnon is out of his sight (because he withdraws), he visualizes Hektor and the Trojans (who attack); when Diomedes and Odysseus fight back, he visualizes Odysseus, who is now in danger; and when Odysseus is saved by Ajax, he watches Ajax until he retreats. *Iliad* XI amply shows how space, as a powerful cue for recall, allows the oral composer to *tour* the notional area where his narrative takes place by means of the vivid and solid space of the extended similes, the mental GPS that allows him to navigate effectively from one character to the next across the vast space of the Iliadic battlefield.

Visual unit 1

> 62–65: (N1) rise in the plain, first and last ranks of the Trojans / (S1) sky and clouds

> οἷος δ' ἐκ νεφέων ἀναφαίνεται Αὔλιος ἀστὴρ
> παμφαίνων, τοτὲ δ' αὖτις ἔδυ νέφεα σκιόεντα,
> ὣς Ἕκτωρ ὀτὲ μέν τε μετὰ πρώτοισι φάνεσκεν,
> ἄλλοτε δ' ἐν πυμάτοισι κελεύων·

> as among the darkened clouds the rustic[83] star shows forth
> in all its shining, then merges again in the clouds and the darkness.
> So Hektor would at one time be shining among the foremost,
> and then once more urging on the last ...

> *Iliad* XI 62–65

---

[83] I.e. the star that leads the sheep and cattle to their pens or folds. For Αὔλιος instead of the reading οὔλιος, see the critical apparatus in West 1998–2000 on *Iliad* XI 62 and West 2001:211.

Visual unit 1 refers initially to the placement of the Trojans around Hektor at the rise in the plain (56 ἐπὶ θρωσμῷι πεδίοιο), and then to his movement among the first and last ranks of the army (64–65 μετὰ πρώτοισι / ἐν πυμάτοισι). The simile of the star shining when it emerges *out of* the clouds and then disappearing when it merges *back into* the clouds creates a twofold space that effectively captures Hektor's movement. The storyteller here employs the reference to the rise in the plain (one of the few landmarks on the battlefield) to create for his audience a location around which the Trojans are placed. But since the rise in the plain pertains to the stationing of the troops and not to the movement of Hektor in and out of the ranks of his men, he resorts to the familiar space of the aforementioned simile. Although both Hektor and the Trojan troops are positioned at the rise in the plain, the narrator still has trouble seeing them *separately* from this landmark. In other words, as soon as the storyteller has to refer to the *internal connection* of Hektor and the troops, he resorts to the space of a simile in order to "see" them apart from the rise.[84] Whereas the θρωσμός delineates a space with reference to the entire battlefield, the space of the simile creates a mental hook on which further positionings can be visually hung.

Visual unit 2

67–71: (N1) plain (Achaeans and Trojans approaching each other) / (S1) a field of wheat or barley

οἳ δ', ὥς τ' ἀμητῆρες ἐναντίοι ἀλλήλοισιν
ὄγμον ἐλαύνωσιν ἀνδρὸς μάκαρος κατ' ἄρουραν
πυρῶν ἢ κριθῶν, τὰ δὲ δράγματα ταρφέα πίπτει,
ὣς Τρῶες καὶ Ἀχαιοὶ ἐπ' ἀλλήλοισι θορόντες
δῄουν ...

And the men, like two lines of reapers who, facing each other,
drive their course all down the field of wheat or of barley
for a man blessed in substance, and the cut swathes drop showering,
so Trojans and Achaians driving in against one another
cut men down ...

Iliad XI 67–71

Although the spotlight is close to where Hektor was just before, the narrator tries to mentally chart a different location on the plain as he visualizes the Achaean and Trojan troops approaching each other. To visualize further the two armies of the Achaeans and Trojans fighting each other "somewhere there,"

---

[84] See Fenik 1968:80: "It is a regular function of the simile to describe masses of men, or armies ... and a simile also frequently describes two armies marching against each other."

between the rise in the plain and the ditch, the storyteller resorts to the spatial framework offered by another extended simile. The field of wheat or barley constitutes a solid visual space where narrator and audience can place the two groups of reapers facing each other.[85] Now, the hazy "somewhere there" of the narrative can become a clear mental picture. The space of the simile thus helps the narrator to move on to a different spot on the battlefield, but also enables his listeners to follow this move and see with their mind's eye the forward movement of the Trojans, previously set next to the rise in the plain, and the Achaeans coming close for a dreadful battle that will soon begin. This gradual preparation for the battle exploits of various individuals who will be the focus and organizing principle of most of *Iliad* XI reflects a law of oral narrative, according to which the storyteller's mind moves from the general and collective to the individual and personal. Having laid the groundwork for an undertaking of truly epic proportions, the narrator will soon focus his attention to Agamemnon, whose ἀριστεία will be presented in a single visual unit loaded with four extended similes.

Visual unit 3

> 86–90: (N1) plain / (S1) mountain glens
>
> 113–121: (N2) plain / (S2) lair of a deer, forests
>
> 155–159: (N3) plain / (S3) timbered forest
>
> 172–178: (N4) middle of the plain, Ilos' tomb / (S4) pasture

> ἦμος δὲ δρυτόμος περ ἀνὴρ ὡπλίσσατο δεῖπνον
> οὔρεος ἐν βήσσῃσιν, ἐπεί τ' ἐκορέσσατο χεῖρας
> τάμνων δένδρεα μακρά, ἄδος τέ μιν ἵκετο θυμόν,
> σίτου τε γλυκεροῖο περὶ φρένας ἵμερος αἱρεῖ,
> τῆμος σφῇ ἀρετῇ Δαναοὶ ῥήξαντο φάλαγγας

> But at the time when the woodcutter makes ready his supper
> in the wooded glens of the mountains, when his arms and hands
>   have grown weary
> from cutting down the tall trees, and his heart has had enough of it,
> and longing for food and for sweet wine takes hold of his senses;
> at that time the Danaans by their manhood broke the battalions
> calling across the ranks to each other.

Iliad XI 86–90

[85] On this simile, the ancient grammarian Trypho observed that action (fighting) is paired with action (reapers facing each other); see *On Tropes* (ed. L. Spengel) 3.201.15–26.

ὡς δὲ λέων ἐλάφοιο ταχείης νήπια τέκνα
ῥηϊδίως συνέαξε λαβὼν κρατεροῖσιν ὀδοῦσιν,
ἐλθὼν εἰς εὐνήν, ἁπαλόν τέ σφ' ἦτορ ἀπηύρα·
ἢ δ' εἴ πέρ τε τύχῃσι μάλα σχεδόν, οὐ δύναταί σφιν
χραισμεῖν, αὐτὴν γάρ μιν ὑπὸ τρόμος αἰνὸς ἱκάνει,
καρπαλίμως δ' ἤϊξε διὰ δρυμὰ πυκνὰ καὶ ὕλην
σπεύδουσ', ἱδρώουσα κραταιοῦ θηρὸς ὑφ' ὁρμῆς·
ὣς ἄρα τοῖς οὔ τις δύνατο χραισμῆσαι ὄλεθρον
Τρώων, ἀλλὰ καὶ αὐτοὶ ὑπ' Ἀργείοισι φέβοντο.

And as a lion seizes the innocent young of the running
deer, and easily crunches and breaks them caught in the strong teeth
when he has invaded their lair, and rips out the soft heart from them,
and even if the doe be very near, still she has no strength
to help, for the ghastly shivers of fear are upon her also
and suddenly she dashes away through the glades and the timber
sweating in her speed away from the pounce of the strong beast;
so there was no one of the Trojans who could save these two
from death, but they themselves were running in fear from the
    Argives.

Iliad XI 113–121

ὡς δ' ὅτε πῦρ ἀΐδηλον ἐν ἀξύλῳ ἐμπέσῃ ὕλῃ,
πάντῃ τ' εἰλυφόων ἄνεμος φέρει, οἱ δέ τε θάμνοι
πρόρριζοι πίπτουσιν ἐπειγόμενοι πυρὸς ὁρμῇ,
ὣς ἄρ' ὑπ' Ἀτρείδῃ Ἀγαμέμνονι πίπτε κάρηνα
Τρώων φευγόντων· ...

As when obliterating fire comes down on the timbered forest
and the roll of the wind carries it everywhere, and bushes
leaning under the force of the fire's rush tumble uprooted,
so before Atreus' son Agamemnon went down the high heads
of the running Trojans ...

Iliad XI 155–159

οἳ δ' ἔτι κὰμ μέσσον πεδίον φοβέοντο βόες ὥς,
ἅς τε λέων ἐφόβησε μολὼν ἐν νυκτὸς ἀμολγῷ
πάσας, τῇ δέ τ' ἰῇ ἀναφαίνεται αἰπὺς ὄλεθρος,
τῆς δ' ἐξ αὐχέν' ἔαξε λαβὼν κρατεροῖσιν ὀδοῦσιν
πρῶτον, ἔπειτα δέ θ' αἷμα καὶ ἔγκατα πάντα λαφύσσει·

ὣς τοὺς Ἀτρεΐδης ἔφεπε κρείων Ἀγαμέμνων,
αἰὲν ἀποκτείνων τὸν ὀπίστατον· οἳ δ' ἐφέβοντο.

while others still in the middle plain stampeded like cattle
when a lion, coming upon them in the dim night, has terrified
the whole herd, while for a single one sheer death is emerging.
First the lion breaks her neck caught fast in the strong teeth,
then gulps down the blood and all the guts that are inward;
so Atreus' son, powerful Agamemnon, went after them
killing ever the last of the men; and they fled in terror.

Iliad XI 172–178

In his desire to move one step further than the previous visual unit, where he visualized the two armies approaching each other, the narrator begins his mental "localization" of Agamemnon's triumph by using the spatial coordinates of a new simile, set in the wooded mountain glens (lines 86–90). In this way, he is able to offer an impressive visualization of the first clash of Achaeans and Trojans. His choice of the space of the mountains is crucial for the visual unfolding of the rest of Agamemnon's ἀριστεία. By employing the technique of *associative composition*,[86] the storyteller reactivates the same simile space every time he wants to mark a different step in Agamemnon's outstanding performance. To organize his material, he mentally follows Agamemnon as he first kills Isos and Antiphos, the sons of Priam.[87] The lack of landmarks to which he can anchor this scene is here counterbalanced by the vivid space of the simile, which visualizes both the lair where the innocent fawns (Isos and Antiphos) are located[88] and the forest where their mother finds refuge, as she is unable to fight the lion attacking them.[89] The latter spatial reference (the forest) is then narratively exploited, as the audience finds out that the Trojans, being unable to help Isos and Antiphos, are running away like deer. The simile of the lion seizing the innocent young of the fleeing deer that does not dare even to try to save them is powerful, since it sets the tone for the kind of ἀριστεία the storyteller will present to his audience. Picking up the thread of the fighting from

---

[86] See Moulton 1977:98.

[87] It is a typical feature of an ἀριστεία to present a hero's military exploits through his killing (or facing) of a series of opponents fighting in pairs. See Fenik 1968:82 and chapter 1 above. Cf. also *Iliad* V 10, 144, 148, 152, 159, and 239, where Diomedes does the same thing in his own ἀριστεία.

[88] If pressed a bit more, the mention of the lair where the doe's newly born young are attacked by the lion may be pointing to the helplessness of Priam's sons; see D. Lee 1964:23.

[89] Lion similes are in general the standard type for presenting the movement and mood of a single warrior, whereas the wind and wave similes seem more visually appropriate for group scenes. See Scott 1974:65.

the end of *Iliad* VIII, and after the "interlude" of the embassy and the *Doloneia*,[90] Agamemnon is pictured as a ruthless warrior who kills, tellingly, the two sons of Priam whom Achilles[91] had spared in the past.[92] The storyteller plays with the idea of an Achaean triumph brought about by Agamemnon, whose gifts Achilles has just refused (*Iliad* IX) and whose insolent behavior is beginning to create problems for the army. Since the narrator is determined to keep his attention focused on Agamemnon, he will resort to the same simile space when the son of Atreus leads the Achaean troops forward. Leaving the spot where he kills the two sons of Antimakhos (148–149), the storyteller turns to a comparison of Agamemnon with a destructive forest fire (155–159).[93] Critics have emphasized the completeness of the destruction that this simile expresses,[94] but have failed to notice that the storyteller, despite changing similemes, is mentally visualizing Agamemnon's ruthless and destructive activity "on the run," as if he is following his hero as he moves over the plain. This coordination of narrative and simile space creates strong mental links that tighten the developing action and enhance memorability.[95] The third and last extended simile of this visual

---

[90] On the problems of authenticity of *Iliad* X, see two contrasting views in Danek 1988 and Dué and Ebbott 2010.

[91] *Iliad* XI 104–106 ὤ ποτ' Ἀχιλλεύς / Ἴδης ἐν κνημοῖσι δίδη μόσχοισι λύγοισιν, / ποιμαίνοντ' ἐπ' ὄεσσι λαβών, καὶ ἔλυσεν ἀποίνων ("Before this Achilleus / had caught these two at the knees of Ida, and bound them in pliant / willows as they watched by their sheep, and released them for ransom.")

[92] Likewise, Agamemnon will attack and eventually kill, for all their pleas, the sons of Antimakhos, Peisandros and Hippolokhos (*Iliad* XI 122–147). Associative composition is also at work here, for the narrator carefully notes that—as with Isos and Antiphos—Antimakhos has been bribed by Alexandros to oppose the return of Helen to Menelaos. This apparently trivial point is nicely made: Agamemnon successively kills pairs of brothers whose brief stories remind the audience of his role as the rival of Achilles and avenger of the wrong done to his brother Menelaos; see Strasburger 1954:70; Fenik 1968:84.

[93] Partly reminiscent of another simile used for the Achaean army as a whole in II 455–458; see Moulton 1977:97. Fire similes are used for gleaming objects, warriors in battle, and anger. With respect to heroes, only the preeminent ones are given such similes (Agamemnon and Idomeneus in *Iliad* XI, Hektor in *Iliad* XI and XV, Achilles in *Iliad* XX and XXI). See Scott 1974:66–68.

[94] See Scott 2009:147, who points to a possible connection with the atrocity of Hippolokhos' decapitation (*Iliad* XI 146–147).

[95] Notice the use of repetitive language before and after the similes in *Iliad* XI 155–159 (153–154 ἀτὰρ κρείων Ἀγαμέμνων / <u>αἰὲν</u> ἀποκτείνων <u>ἕπετ'</u> Ἀργείοισι κελεύων; 165 Ἀτρεΐδης δ' <u>ἕπετο</u> σφεδανὸν Δαναοῖσι κελεύων) and XI 172–178 (168–169 ὃ δὲ κεκληγὼς <u>ἕπετ'</u> αἰεί / Ἀτρεΐδης· λύθρῳ δὲ παλάσσετο χεῖρας ἀάπτους; 177–178 ὣς τοὺς Ἀτρεΐδης <u>ἔφεπε</u> κρείων Ἀγαμέμνων / <u>αἰὲν</u> ἀποκτείνων τὸν ὀπίστατον). See Schadewaldt 1966:52, who calls this repetition a *Kehrreim* 'refrain'. See also Fenik, who is able to discern the following pattern (observable also in *Iliad* XX 455–489) that is, interestingly and perhaps tellingly, applied to both Agamemnon and Achilles: "(1) *aristeia* with quick and grisly slaughter of many Trojans; (2) unhindered pursuit of the Trojans described by a fire simile; (3) further description of the charging Greek, plus another simile, and the descriptive detail of the bloodstained hands; (4) return to the account of the slaughter" (1968:84–85).

unit is again a lion simile, which shares the same spatial coordinates with the two previous similes of the same visual unit. When the Trojan troops retreat, passing the tomb of Ilos[96] and the wild fig tree, they arrive at the Skaian Gates and the oak tree, a thematized landmark on the Trojan plain.[97] Seen from this angle, the simile space's mnemonic function may seem redundant, since both storyteller and audience may readily employ these same landmarks for the Trojans. In other words, they can easily use the signposts of the tomb of Ilos and the fig tree as place-markers to facilitate visualization. But the point is not *where* the second group of Trojans is placed, but *which part* (space) of their ranks Agamemnon attacks. To create a further mental image for this purpose, the storyteller resorts to a timely expressed simile of a lion attacking a group of cows by breaking the neck of one of them. Although the wider space of the simile is not indicated *expressis verbis*, the audience can call to mind the familiar space of the pasture where the cattle are. The lion's attack on the neck of one—that is, from behind—can be then visualized together with Agamemnon's wreaking havoc and killing the last of the retreating Trojan army.[98]

Visual unit 4

269–272: (N1) woman in labor / (S1) wound on Agamemnon's body

ὡς δ' ὅτ' ἂν ὠδίνουσαν ἔχῃ βέλος ὀξὺ γυναῖκα,
δριμύ, τό τε προϊεῖσι μογοστόκοι Εἰλείθυιαι,
Ἥρης θυγατέρες πικρὰς ὠδῖνας ἔχουσαι,
ὣς ὀξεῖ' ὀδύνη δῦνεν μένος Ἀτρείδαο.[99]

As the sharp sorrow of pain descends on a woman in labour,
the bitterness that the hard spirits of childbirth bring on,
Hera's daughters, who hold the power of the bitter birthpangs,
so the sharp pain began to break in on the strength of Atreides.

Iliad XI 269–272

Visual unit 4 contains an extended simile comparing the sharp pain experienced by the wounded Agamemnon to that of a woman in labor. The wordplay[100] between ὀδύναι/ὀδύνη 'pain(s)' (268, 272), ὠδίνουσαν 'in labor' (269), and

---

[96] *Iliad* XI 166–168 οἳ δὲ παρ' Ἴλου σῆμα παλαιοῦ Δαρδανίδαο / μέσσον κὰπ πεδίον παρ' ἐρινεὸν ἐσσεύοντο / ἱέμενοι πόλιος. On the tomb of Ilos as a "site of memory," see Grethlein 2008.

[97] On the function of the wild fig tree and the oak tree in the *Iliad*, see "Protection and danger: the oak tree of Zeus and the fig tree," chapter 1 above.

[98] See Moulton 1977:96–99.

[99] For the reading ὀξεῖ' ὀδύνη δῦνεν, see West 1998–2000 on *Iliad* XI 272 and West 2011:211–212.

[100] On sound as a form of organization that cues recall and constitutes one of the three main classes of constraints in oral traditions (alongside imagery and meaning), see Rubin 1995:65–89.

ὠδῖνας 'birth pangs' (271) and the repetition of ὀξύ-ὀξεῖ'(α) 'sharp' (269–272) no doubt strengthen the link between Agamemnon's pain and that of a woman in labor, but the particular way space is visualized is also important. The story-teller uses the image of the "sharp arrow" sent by the daughters of Hera down into the body of a pregnant woman as a foil for the same descending movement of the spear inside Agamemnon's body.[101]

Complementing the theme of a warrior's entering battle, similes marking a hero's withdrawal and denoting a reversal in the action indicate the completion of a narrative scene. Where both the beginning and the end of a narrative section are indicated by the entrance and withdrawal of a character, the story-teller may resort to the use of similes as a highlighting device that delineates openings and closures.[102]

Visual unit 5

292–295: (N1) Hektor leads the Trojans in the plain / (S1) a hunter drives his hounds against a beast

ὡς δ' ὅτε πού τις θηρητὴρ κύνας ἀργιόδοντας
σεύῃ ἐπ' ἀγροτέρῳ συΐ καπρίῳ ἠὲ λέοντι,
ὣς ἐπ' Ἀχαιοῖσιν σεῦε Τρῶας μεγαθύμους
Ἕκτωρ Πριαμίδης, βροτολοιγῷ ἶσος Ἄρηϊ·

As when some huntsman drives to action his hounds with shining teeth against some savage beast, wild boar or lion,
so against the Achaians Hektor the son of Priam,
a man like the murderous war god, lashed on the high-hearted Trojans.

Iliad XI 292–295

In visual unit 5, the storyteller visualizes the movement of the Trojans and their allies on the battlefield, after Agamemnon is wounded and withdraws, through the space of the familiar simile of hounds chasing a wild beast. Although the simile space is not denoted in so many words, the simile's compressed nature allows for a "filling in" of the missing data by recourse to the deep structure

---

[101] Cf. *Iliad* XI 253 ἀντικρὺ δὲ διέσχε φαεινοῦ δουρὸς ἀκωκή.

[102] See Fenik 1968:86, who shows how Agamemnon's charge in *Iliad* XI 148–162 and 166–180 (both containing similes) alternates with Zeus' drawing Hektor out of the battle in two phases. This, as Fenik notes, is a stylistic feature of Homeric epic, according to which "an event which receives its full development at one point is first stated briefly, then dropped, only to return again where it is treated in full." In this perspective, similes may enhance the storyteller's ability to organize his material in the way described above; see also Scott 1974:41–42.

of the simileme. By assuming through traditional referentiality that the scene takes place in the mountains or in wild nature, that is, in a place that they can easily visualize, the audience can tie to it Hektor's reentering the battle and picture it vividly in their mind's eye. Having being absent from the narrative because of Agamemnon's ἀριστεία,[103] Hektor—whose initial entry into the battle in *Iliad* XI was accompanied by another extended simile (62–65)—looms large, for he will be the undisputed protagonist of the following visual unit.

Visual unit 6

> 297–298: (N1) Hektor (attacks) the first ranks of Achaeans / (S1) wind blowing over the sea
>
> 305–309: (N2) Hektor (attacks) the first ranks of Achaeans / (S2) wind blowing over the sea

ἐν δ' ἔπεσ' ὑσμίνῃ ὑπεραέϊ ἶσος ἀέλλῃ,
ἥ τε καθαλλομένη ἰοειδέα πόντον ὀρίνει.

and hurled himself on the struggle of men like a high-blown
      storm-cloud
which swoops down from above to trouble the blue sea-water.

Iliad XI 297–298

... ὡς ὁπότε νέφεα Ζέφυρος στυφελίξῃ
ἀργεστᾶο Νότοιο, βαθείῃ λαίλαπι τύπτων,
πολλὸν δὲ τρόφι κῦμα κυλίνδεται, ὑψόσε δ' ἄχνη
σκίδναται ἐξ ἀνέμοιο πολυπλάγκτοιο ἰωῆς·
ὡς ἄρα πυκνὰ καρήαθ' ὑφ' Ἕκτορι δάμνατο λαῶν.

... as when the west wind strikes in the deepening
whirlstorm to batter the clouds of the shining south wind,
so that the bulging big waves roll hard and the blown spume
scatters high before the force of the veering wind's blast.
So the massed high heads of the people were struck down by Hektor.

Iliad XI 305–309

The obvious question is why the storyteller has decided to shift from one visual unit to another, although we are clearly still dealing with Hektor, who has just been described as leading the Trojan troops into battle. Fenik draws a

---

[103] See Scott 1974:41, who shows that the *Iliad* regularly uses similes for "people who have been absent from the narrative, because hindered, and now return."

parallel with *Iliad* V 554–560, where a "long simile is followed by a very short and common one."[104] But the parallel is inaccurate, since the situation is not the same: whereas in V 554–560 the final short simile is embedded, so to speak, and forms part of the long lion simile, the simile in XI 297–298 is both (a) separate from the previous long one, since almost three lines intervene between the two, and (b) not a short simile but an extremely compressed and elliptical form of an extended simile belonging to the wind family. The tree simile in V 554–560 is a kind of pictorial reflex triggered by typical usage, since fallen warriors are often compared to downed trees. Conversely, in XI 297–298 a very specific reason has evoked in the storyteller's mind the imagery of "a high-blown storm-cloud / which swoops down from above to trouble the blue sea-water."[105] A careful look at the passage shows that Hektor is now presented as *changing locations*, albeit still within the general framework of the battlefield. While visualizing him as "hurling himself on the struggle,"[106] the storyteller evokes a simile belonging to the widely attested wind family. In this way, he can more readily visualize Hektor's movement and entry into battle,[107] since the background images of the simile will function as the necessary backdrop that enhances image recall. The extremely abbreviated form of this "extended" simile seems to have resulted from a new need that was even stronger than the one the simile addressed: namely the list of warriors killed by Hektor which the narrator was about to utter.[108] The list of Hektor's victims, which extends to a few lines, must have been such a high priority for the storyteller, who had to recite this series of names accurately, that the simile immediately preceding it was drained to its minimum. It is no accident that as soon as the list was over, the narrator mentally "returned" to an extended simile from the very same family, which he could now fully expand.

Visual unit 7

324–326: (N1 plain) / (S1) place of hunting

ὡς ὅτε κάπρω
ἐν κυσὶ θηρευτῆσι μέγα φρονέοντε πέσητον.
ὣς ὄλεκον Τρῶας πάλιν ὀρμένω·

---

[104] 1968:58.

[105] *Iliad* XI 297–298.

[106] *Iliad* XI 297.

[107] Although wind and wave similes (on which see Scott 1974:62–66) emphasize the movement of groups of people, they are rarely used for a single warrior, like Hektor when he enters the battlefield after Agamemnon is wounded and withdraws (XI 296).

[108] See W.-H. Friedrich 1956:62, who argues that there is nothing abnormal or colossal in the remarkable performance of Agamemnon, and later those of Diomedes and Odysseus. The small list of Agamemnon's victims will be "counterbalanced" by his future wounding and retreat from the battlefield.

> as when two wild boars
> hurl themselves in their pride upon the hounds who pursue them.
> So they whirled on the Trojans again and destroyed them.

> *Iliad* XI 324–326

This simile serves a twofold purpose: first, it marks the transition to a different visual unit, focusing on the joint activity of Diomedes and Odysseus, who try to stop Hektor's slaughter; second, it helps the storyteller shed light on a specific aspect of the current fighting by highlighting a spatial aspect of the situation at hand. By drawing on the rich pictorial force of the simile referring to *how* two wild boars hurl themselves upon the hounds,[109] that is, by emphasizing that the pursued boars turn around and counterattack the hunting dogs, the narrator helps his listeners vividly "picture" Diomedes' and Odysseus' turning around and killing the Trojans.[110] The introduction of a new visual unit is accompanied by a shift of simileme, underlining the change in the storyteller's mental course as he moves from the spot where Hector is to that of the two Achaean heroes. Now that Agamemnon is wounded and has withdrawn from the fighting, the storyteller's mind can turn to other central heroes so as to promote his narrative goal, which is nothing else than Trojan victory. To this end, other Achaean leaders need to be brought into the picture, only to be wounded and withdraw from battle so that Trojan success can be guaranteed. When Odysseus and Diomedes stand close to each other, kill Thumbraios and Molion, and attack the ranks of the Trojans, the need to locate their activity within the area of the fighting makes the storyteller use the space delineated by the movement of two wild beasts against a group of hounds. It seems that this part of the fighting has now, at least visually, come full circle, since visual units 5 and 7 spatially frame the two similes of unit 6: the wind-sea similes pertaining to Hektor's attack are enclosed by a visual ring of two hunting similes.

---

[109] Boars and lions are often "interchangeable" within the lion simile family, which is the largest in both the *Iliad* and the *Odyssey*; on lion similes that occur very often in fighting contexts, see Scott 1974:58–62. On patterns of interchangeability with respect to boars and lions, see the incisive observations of Muellner 1990:63–64. There are cases, though, in which lions and boars are not interchangeable, since the former are presented as aggressive predators, while the latter are depicted as aggressive defenders; see Scott 1974:58–60.

[110] The specific place where this event occurs is expressed in the simile not verbatim, but by means of traditional referentiality and experience listeners can easily fill in the spatial framework and localize the action. The storyteller refrains from offering any such reference here, because the stress is on the two boars' *turning around* and counterattacking the hounds who pursue them (325 θηρευτῆσι). It is the sudden change of direction in the mental picturing of this simile (from the hounds to the boars) that is the key factor.

A. *Visual unit 5*

    292–295: hunting simile

B. *Visual unit 6*

    297–298: wind-sea simile

    305–309: wind-sea simile

A´. *Visual unit 7*

    324–326: hunting simile

Visual unit 8

    414–420: (N1) ranks of Trojans falling on Odysseus / (S1) deep of a thicket

    474–484: (N2) ranks of Trojans falling on Odysseus / (S2) mountains and shaded glen

    492–497: (N3) Ajax approaches Odysseus and helps him / (S3) mountains

> ὡς δ' ὅτε κάπριον ἀμφὶ κύνες θαλεροί τ' αἰζηοί
> σεύωνται, ὃ δέ τ' εῖσι βαθείης ἐκ ξυλόχοιο
> θήγων λευκὸν ὀδόντα μετὰ γναμπτῇσι γένυσσιν,
> ἀμφὶ δέ τ' ἀΐσσονται, ὑπαὶ δέ τε κόμπος ὀδόντων
> γίγνεται, οἳ δὲ μένουσιν ἄφαρ δεινόν περ ἐόντα,
> ὥς ῥα τότ' ἀμφ' Ὀδυσῆα διίφίλον ἐσσεύοντο
> Τρῶες.

> as when closing about a wild boar the hounds and the lusty young
>   men
> rush him, and he comes out of his lair in the deep of a thicket
> grinding to an edge the white fangs in the crook of the jawbones,
> and these sweep in all about him, and the vaunt of his teeth uprises
> as they await him, terrible though he is, without wavering;
> so closing on Odysseus beloved of Zeus the Trojans
> rushed him.

Iliad XI 414–420

> ὡς εἴ τε δαφοινοὶ θῶες ὄρεσφιν
> ἀμφ' ἔλαφον κεραὸν βεβλημένον, ὅν τ' ἔβαλ' ἀνήρ
> ἰῷ ἀπὸ νευρῆς· τὸν μέν τ' ἤλυξε πόδεσσιν
> φεύγων, ὄφρ' αἷμα λιαρὸν καὶ γούνατ' ὀρώρῃ,

αὐτὰρ ἐπεὶ δὴ τόν γε δαμάσσεται ὠκὺς ὀϊστός,
ὠμοφάγοι μιν θῶες ἐν οὔρεσι δαρδάπτουσιν
ἐν νέμεϊ σκιερῷ· ἐπί τε λῖν ἤγαγε δαίμων
σίντην· θῶες μέν τε διέτρεσαν, αὐτὰρ ὃ δάπτει·
ὥς ῥα τότ' ἀμφ' Ὀδυσῆα δαΐφρονα ποικιλομήτην
Τρῶες ἕπον πολλοί τε καὶ ἄλκιμοι, αὐτὰρ ὅ γ' ἥρως
ἀΐσσων ᾧ ἔγχει ἀμύνετο νηλεὲς ἦμαρ·

                         as bloody scavengers in the mountains
crowd on a horned stag who is stricken, one whom a hunter
shot with an arrow from the string, and the stag has escaped him,
     running
with his feet, while the blood stayed warm, and his knees were
     springing beneath him.
But when the pain of the flying arrow has beaten him, then
the rending scavengers begin to feast on him in the mountains
and the shaded glen. But some spirit leads that way a dangerous
lion, and the scavengers run in terror, and the lion eats it;
so about wise, much-devising Odysseus the Trojans
crowded now, valiant and numerous, but the hero
with rapid play of his spear beat off the pitiless death-day.

                                  Iliad XI 474–484

ὡς δ' ὁπότε πλήθων ποταμὸς πεδίονδε κάτεισιν
χειμάρρους κατ' ὄρεσφιν, ὀπαζόμενος Διὸς ὄμβρῳ,
πολλὰς δὲ δρῦς ἀζαλέας, πολλὰς δέ τε πεύκας
ἐσφέρεται, πολλὸν δέ τ' ἀφυσγετὸν εἰς ἅλα βάλλει,
ὣς ἔφεπε κλονέων πεδίον τότε φαίδιμος Αἴας,
δαΐζων ἵππους τε καὶ ἀνέρας·

As when a swollen river hurls its water, big with rain,
down the mountains to the flat land following rain from the sky god,
and sweeps down with it numbers of dry oaks and of pine trees
numbers, until it hurls its huge driftwood into the salt sea;
so now glittering Aias cumbered the plain as he chased them,
slaughtering men and horses alike;

                                  Iliad XI 492–497

In visual unit 8, three extended similes are employed as the narrator aims at pinning down Odysseus as he is surrounded by the Trojans. The depth of a thicket, the glens in the mountains, and last the movement of water in a river from the mountains, oaks, and pines to the sea constitute a vivid spatial framework intended to locate Odysseus on the battlefield. Although the last simile refers to Ajax, the storyteller does not change visual units, for Ajax approaches Odysseus and drives the Trojans away. In fact, by turning the spotlight on Ajax, the storyteller prepares to concentrate his attention on him in the following visual unit.

This visual unit is a typical example of what I have called above the *visual exhaustion* of a character: the storyteller, like his heroes in *Iliad* XI, is "on the run": he moves his mind's eye from one hero to the next and refuses to look back. When Agamemnon is wounded he turns to Hektor, then to Diomedes; after Diomedes is injured to Odysseus, and after Odysseus to Ajax; he then changes direction and focuses his attention on the Nestor-Patroklos episode that brings *Iliad* XI to a close. Scholars who have studied the similes of this long Iliadic book have observed two important features: first, that many of them are organized as a dispersed sequence stretching from the extended middle section and overlapping the beginning of *Iliad* XII,[111] and second, that if seen as a whole, the similes picture Agamemnon, who dominates the first section, and Hektor, who seems to be the common thread of the second section (since he leads the Trojans against various Achaean leaders), as stronger and weaker figures respectively.[112] Given that both of these arguments are explicitly or implicitly linked to the visual unit at hand, I would like to briefly explore some relevant issues.

The first claim, about the dispersed sequence of similes, is based on their "defensive emphasis,"[113] which is visually expressed by their belonging, for the most part, to the same or equivalent subject matter, namely that of animal similes (featuring boars, stags, lions, a donkey, and insects). This approach indicates that the storyteller has decided to employ subject matter of a given type to picture the same narrative theme. In other words, the storyteller has organized his material on the basis of narrative relevance. In this light, my own suggested classification of the similes in visual units on the basis of the cognitive factors of mental recall and homologous image-mappings allows for a further interpretive step. In particular, the formation of the dispersed simile sequence observed by Moulton is facilitated by the techniques of visual exhaustion of a character and spatial correlation of narrative and simile: as long as the action takes place in a given spot or area of the battlefield, the space referred to in the similes does not change. To restrict myself to *Iliad* XI, it can be plausibly argued that in the dispersed sequence of similes in lines 324–565, the storyteller has visually

---

[111] Moulton 1977:46–48.
[112] Scott 2009:86.
[113] Moulton 1977:46.

concatenated a series of similes on the basis of the spatial correlation of their images, since they all take place in the mountains or the fields.

> 292–295: (N1) Hektor leads the Trojans in the plain / (S1) a hunter drives his hounds against a beast
>
> 297–298: (N1) Hektor (attacks) the ranks of Achaeans / (S1) wind blowing over the sea
>
> 305–309: (N2) Hektor (attacks) the ranks of Achaeans / (S2) wind blowing over the sea
>
> 324–326: (N1 plain) / (S1) place of hunting
>
> 414–420: (N1) ranks of Trojans falling on Odysseus / (S1) deep of a thicket
>
> 474–484: (N2) ranks of Trojans falling on Odysseus / (S2) mountains and shaded glen
>
> 492–497: (N3) Ajax approaches Odysseus and helps him / (S3) mountains
>
> 548–557: (N1) Ajax retreats / (S1) mid-fenced ground
>
> 558–565: (N2) Ajax retreats / (S2) cornfield

In fact, of all those similes Moulton[114] calls "interspersed," because they interrupt his "dispersed" sequence as non–hunting similes, the first two (297–298 and 305–309) precede the chain of similes that share a "defensive" emphasis (so they do not really interrupt it); while the third (492–497), which has a clearly "defensive" theme (as Ajax approaches Odysseus to offer his help), and is a river- and not an animal or hunting simile, is left unexplained, provided that we adopt only the logic of thematic association. On the contrary, subject-matter relevance is a secondary associative mechanism, occurring alongside the primary associative mechanism of spatial correlation, which is based on cognitive factors. From this perspective, spatial imaging shows itself to be the driving force and unifying mechanism in this dispersed sequence of similes.

The second claim, that the simile sequences pertaining to Agamemnon and Hektor in sections 1 and 2 present the former as dominating and the latter as weak, needs to be elaborated and modified. According to Scott, "the poet uses his similes to show the undiminished power of the Greek warriors, who thus retain sufficient strength to reverse the direction of the battle in books 13–15."[115] This is certainly true, but again—as in the previous claim by Moulton—subject

---

[114] 1977:47.
[115] 2009:87.

matter is neither the sole nor the primary correlating factor. Apart from the fact that the wind-sea similes used for Hektor in XI 297–298 and 305–309 picture him as a tremendous force of nature and not at all as frail, the "weak" aspect of the Trojans is rather a by-product of the whole system of animal and hunting similes that dominates most of *Iliad* XI. Narrative themes have indeed shaped and determined the specific verbalization of most (but not all) of the animal and hunting similes pertaining to the Trojans in the central section of *Iliad* XI, but only within the much broader framework of the primary pictorial correlation between narrative and simile space. The fact that according to the constraints of the system of Iliadic simile images, dogs, oaks, and pines or small boys are not used "to describe impressive power" is a secondary development of the system, since the use of the above subjects in quite different similemes indicates that the storyteller can employ them for various purposes.

Visual unit 9

548–557: (N1) Ajax retreats / (S1) mid-fenced ground

558–565: (N2) Ajax retreats / (S2) cornfield

ὡς δ' αἴθωνα λέοντα βοῶν ἀπὸ μεσσαύλοιο
ἐσσεύαντο κύνες τε καὶ ἀνέρες ἀγροιῶται,
οἵ τέ μιν οὐκ εἰῶσι βοῶν ἐκ πῖαρ ἑλέσθαι
πάννυχοι ἐγρήσσοντες· ὃ δὲ κρειῶν ἐρατίζων
ἰθύει, ἀλλ' οὔ τι πρήσσει· θαμέες γὰρ ἄκοντες
ἀντίον ἀΐσσουσι θρασειάων ἀπὸ χειρῶν
καιόμεναί τε δεταί, τάς τε τρεῖ ἐσσύμενός περ,
ἠῶθεν δ' ἀπὸ νόσφιν ἔβη τετιηότι θυμῷ·
ὣς Αἴας τότ' ἀπὸ Τρώων τετιημένος ἦτορ
ἤϊε, πόλλ' ἀέκων· περὶ γὰρ δίε νηυσὶν Ἀχαιῶν.

as when the men who live in the wild and their dogs have driven
a tawny lion away from the mid-fenced ground of their oxen,
and will not let him tear out the fat of the oxen, watching
nightlong against him, and he in his hunger for meat closes in
but can get nothing of what he wants, for the raining javelins
thrown from the daring hands of the men beat ever against him,
and the flaming torches, and these he balks at for all of his fury
and with the daylight goes away, disappointed of desire;
so Aias, disappointed at heart, drew back from the Trojans
much unwilling, but feared for the ships of the Achaians.

Iliad XI 548–557

ὡς δ᾽ ὅτ᾽ ὄνος παρ᾽ ἄρουραν ἰὼν ἐβιήσατο παῖδας
νωθής, ᾧ δὴ πολλὰ περὶ ῥόπαλ᾽ ἀμφὶς ἐάγη,
κείρει τ᾽ εἰσελθὼν βαθὺ λήϊον· οἳ δέ τε παῖδες
τύπτουσιν ῥοπάλοισι, βίη δέ τε νηπίη αὐτῶν,
σπουδῇ τ᾽ ἐξήλασσαν, ἐπεί τ᾽ ἐκορέσσατο φορβῆς·
ὣς τότ᾽ ἔπειτ᾽ Αἴαντα μέγαν Τελαμώνιον υἱόν
Τρῶες ὑπέρθυμοι πολυηγερέες τ᾽ ἐπίκουροι
νύσσοντες ξυστοῖσι μέσον σάκος αἰὲν ἕποντο.

As when a donkey, stubborn and hard to move, goes into a cornfield
in despite of boys, and many sticks have been broken upon him,
but he gets in and goes on eating the deep grain, and the children
beat him with sticks, but their strength is infantile; yet at last
by hard work they drive him out when he is glutted with eating;
so the high-hearted Trojans and companions in arms gathered
from far places kept after great Aias, the son of Telamon,
stabbing always with their spears at the centre of the great shield.

Iliad XI 558–565

In the next and last visual unit (9), two similes, one using the space of the "mid-fenced ground" and the other of a cornfield, help the storyteller locate Ajax as he retreats from the swarms of opponents moving against him. Scholars have argued that these two successive similes picture two distinct and rather contrasting aspects of the unifying theme of Ajax's stubborn resistance against superior force.[116] In both of them, Ajax's stubbornness is illustrated in *spatial* terms. A careful look at the lion and donkey similes shows that both lion and donkey finally retreat, although in the first the lion does so without having achieved its goal (551–552), whereas in the second the donkey gets out of the cornfield only after having satisfied its desire for food (562). In other words, both similes play with the intrusion of an animal into a place of human activity, be it herding or farming, and its stubborn refusal to be driven out of this place. The storyteller visualizes Ajax's obstinate opposition to the Trojans in terms of space, since the great Achaean hero refuses to withdraw, and even when he does so he turns back for a while (547 ἐντροπαλιζόμενος, ὀλίγον γόνυ γουνὸς ἀμείβων;[117] 566–568 Αἴας δ᾽ ἄλλοτε μὲν μνησάσκετο θούριδος ἀλκῆς / αὖτις ὑποστρεφθείς, καὶ ἐρητύσασκε φάλαγγας / Τρώων ἱπποδάμων· ὁτὲ δὲ τρωπάσκετο φεύγειν[118]).

---

[116] Moulton 1974:386–387; 1977:48–49. See also Fenik 1968:110.
[117] "... turning on his way, shifting knee past knee only a little ..."
[118] "And now Aias would remember again his furious valour / and turn upon them, and beat back the battalions of Trojans, / breakers of horses, and then again would turn and run from them."

The shift from the traditional lion simile[119] to the hapax of the donkey has often been noticed, and explained by means of the two different aspects of Ajax's stubbornness.[120] From the point of view of cognitive theory, imagery variation in the illustrative presentation of one and the same event reflects the story-teller's effort to limit and control his audience's image-mappings.[121] By doing so—though he can never succeed completely—and by piling up details that lead to particularization and hence greater levels of involvement for his listeners, the storyteller leaves room for the discovery of a profound and hidden meaning which he consistently refuses to state.[122] This meaning lies in the fact that since in their respective similes both lion and donkey are pictured as intruders, the audience is invited to realize that Ajax is also an intruder, this time in a space that is not his own. The narrator, therefore, tries to cultivate the notion of "proper" space that the Trojans now possess on the plain, and that Ajax represents a warrior who is retreating from an area that is no longer controlled by the Achaean army. This point accords with the gradually developed idea of a Trojan victory that will result in complete control of the plain, after the Achaeans have been pushed back to their ships. The multiple image-mappings offered by the lion and donkey similes, with their rich pictureability and abundance of detail, help the audience realize a far-reaching consequence for the Iliadic plot: now that Zeus is clearly on the Trojan side,[123] the Achaeans will continually lose ground, until they are threatened with the loss of the only "proper" space left to them, their camp by the ships.

Iliad XVI

Iliad XVI can be divided into the following four thematic units:

> 1–256: Patroklos persuades Achilles to lend him his armor and let him enter the battle with the Myrmidons
>
> 257–418: Patroklos pushes back the Trojans
>
> 419–683: Sarpedon is killed by Patroklos
>
> 684–867: Patroklos is killed by Apollo, Hektor, and Euphorbos

Iliad XVI contains more extended similes than any other book of the epic, with no fewer than twenty similes, organized in ten visual units. Simile grouping

---

[119] On Zenodotus' omission of the lion simile and a defence of the succession of similes, see Fenik 1968:110–111 and Hainsworth 1993:283 on *Iliad* XI 548–557.

[120] Fenik 1968:110; Hainsworth 1993:284 on *Iliad* XI 558–562.

[121] See Lakoff and Turner 1989:91; Minchin 2001:145.

[122] See Edwards 1987:104.

[123] See Scott 2009:89.

occurs in seven units, mainly as a result of the action's concentration around the fighting activity of major heroes like Sarpedon, Patroklos, and Hektor.[124] Given its importance for the development of the plot—since Patroklos' death is the major turning point in the epic, as it will lead to the return of Achilles—*Iliad* XVI displays not only the largest number of extended similes, but also a remarkably concentrated range of simile-generated spatial imagery, which speaks for the strongly dramatic coloring of the narrative's subject matter. The storyteller visualizes the various events in *Iliad* XVI in the light of their impact on the epic as a whole.

Visual unit 1

3–4: (N1) Patroklos *next to* Achilles / (S1) impassable rock (spring of dark-running water)

[7–11: Speech]

156–166: (N2) *along* the shelters / (S2) mountains, spring of dark-running water

δάκρυα θερμὰ χέων ὥς τε κρήνη μελάνυδρος,
ἥ τε κατ' αἰγίλιπος πέτρης δνοφερὸν χέει ὕδωρ.

... and wept warm tears, like a spring dark-running
that down the face of a rock impassable drips its dim water;

Iliad XVI 3–4

οἳ δὲ λύκοι ὥς
ὠμοφάγοι, τοῖσίν τε περὶ φρεσὶν ἄσπετος ἀλκή,
οἵ τ' ἔλαφον κεραὸν μέγαν οὔρεσι δῃώσαντες
δάπτουσιν, πᾶσιν δὲ παρήϊον αἵματι φοινόν,
καί τ' ἀγεληδὸν ἴασιν, ἀπὸ κρήνης μελανύδρου
λάψοντες γλώσσῃσιν ἀραιῇσιν μέλαν ὕδωρ
ἄκρον, ἐρευγόμενοι φόνον αἵματος· ἐν δέ τε θυμὸς
στήθεσιν ἄτρομός ἐστι, περιστένεται δέ τε γαστήρ·
τοῖοι Μυρμιδόνων ἡγήτορες ἠδὲ μέδοντες
ἀμφ' ἀγαθὸν θεράποντα ποδώκεος Αἰακίδαο
ῥώοντ'·

And they, as wolves
who tear flesh raw, in whose hearts the battle fury is tireless,

---

[124] The only exception is visual unit 1.

who have brought down a great horned stag in the mountains, and
then feed
on him, till the jowls of every wolf run blood, and then go
all in a pack to drink from a spring of dark-running water,
lapping with their lean tongues along the black edge of the surface
and belching up the clotted blood; in the heart of each one
is a spirit untremulous, but their bellies are full and groaning;
as such the lords of the Myrmidons and their men of counsel
around the brave henchman of swift-footed Aiakides
swarmed, and among them was standing warlike Achilleus
and urged on the fighting men with their shields, and the horses.

Iliad XVI 156–166

In unit 1, the storyteller visualizes Patroklos and Achilles in their part of the camp through the simile of the flowing spring. The two instances seem different because in the first Patroklos is standing next to Achilles, whereas in the second the Myrmidons begin taking their positions inside Achilles' headquarters. In the first, the target domain of the simile is the picture of Patroklos' tears; in the second, it is the Myrmidons, who are like wolves satisfying their thirst. This is certainly true, but the space where these two activities are placed in the narrative is the same, that is, Achilles' camp, and the storyteller has every reason to link two different activities in his mind by means of their location: the spring is their common mental hook.

The beginning of *Iliad* XVI is telling in this respect, for the initial simile of the spring (3–4) seems to have been cut short by the storyteller's speedy transition to character speech, which soon takes the form of an extended simile, one of the few attested in direct speech. The whole matter becomes even more intriguing since, although Achilles asks Patroklos why he is crying, he employs a different kind of simile altogether: that of a girl holding her mother's dress and asking to be taken in her arms (7–11).

At the beginning of *Iliad* IX, the distraught Agamemnon is compared to a "spring of dark-running water." What is significant, though, is that in both cases the spring simile is never fully developed, for the storyteller cuts it short by giving the floor to one of the main characters of the surrounding narrative, in *Iliad* IX to Agamemnon, in *Iliad* XVI to Achilles. Similarities between books IX and XVI have made critics entertain the thought that the spring simile in *Iliad* XVI is a conscious reminiscence and internal allusion to the beginning of *Iliad* IX, since the storyteller wanted to draw a parallel between the situations the Greeks were and are facing. The association is further strengthened by the fact that the fountain similes are interrupted by the speeches of the same two characters, Agamemnon and Achilles, whose initial disagreement has brought the Achaean army to this difficult situation.[125] In my view, this parallel does exist, but we need not resort to speculations about compositional priority—the more so since the repetition of the spring simile is not an isolated phenomenon, but intricately entwined with its highly compressed character. *Visual abbreviation of this sort is mental*: the storyteller used the spatial coordinates of the spring simile to picture Achilles and Patroklos. The fact that the same simile was employed for Agamemnon in *Iliad* IX shows that the storyteller has thematized not only narrative but also simile space:[126] the dark spring symbolized in his pictorial metalanguage "distress" in the face of a difficult situation.[127] In this light, the compressed nature of this simile, which has become standardized in the process of shaping pictorial material, may have resulted from built-in mental factors and not from the "phantom" of interruption by the speeches of Agamemnon and Achilles. In other words, what is at work here is a form of compact mental picture that has acquired contextual significance not through parallel verbal input but through association by theme: the mental image of "the distraught hero in his hut" has been so closely anchored to the imagery of a fountain, with its water looking like a black streak flowing over a cliff, that it can be employed under similar circumstances.

With respect to the simile of the young girl that Achilles employs in his speech (7–11), the change of register is mainly responsible for the change in the simile's spatial coordinates. Even though Achilles is situated in the same place where the storyteller mentally placed him in the previous narrative, when he begins to speak he cancels the previous visualization and creates a very different one. Similes of this family "describe a character acting strangely or foolishly and illustrate the protection given by a strong ally,"[128] and sometimes, especially when men are about to enter fighting space, "make the change to active combat all the more striking."[129] This is generally correct, and one would not be wrong in stating that Patroklos has been associated with some feminine tasks and traits (like preparing food and being gentle),[130] but other reasons as well may

---

[125] See Whitman 1958:279; cf. Webster 1958:236 and Scott 1974:130–131.

[126] On the function of the conventional context of similes that have certain features in common, see Muellner 1990.

[127] See Dué 2010:291, who argues that the spring simile in *Iliad* IX 14–16 "recalls the iconic lamenter of Greek myth, Niobe, whose example is invoked by Achilles as he and Priam mourn for fathers and sons in the lament-filled *Iliad* 24. Niobe in her grief for her twelve children was transformed into just such a weeping rock."

[128] Scott 1974:74.

[129] Scott 1974:104.

[130] These should in no way be exaggerated or used to suggest an innuendo of homosexual activity; see Monsacré 1984:91–92; Crotty 1994:55n13; Scott 2009:241n83.

have influenced the choice of this simile.[131] The narrator carefully constructs a Patroklos who cannot live up to the Achaeans' expectations: he is not and will never be a second Achilles. There are numerous instances where the *Iliad* makes this quite clear, and I see no reason why the storyteller cannot make even Achilles himself (or perhaps especially Achilles), now that his friend's death is approaching, tragically allude to Patroklos' unwarlike nature.[132]

Visual unit 1 also includes the simile of the Myrmidons, who will accompany Patroklos in his doomed entry into the battle. The storyteller sees them standing beside the shelters and evokes the illustrative analogy of wolves that have killed a stag in the mountains. The visual unity of the spaces occupied by Patroklos and the Myrmidons is reflected in the way the animal simile of the wolves is swiftly absorbed by the fountain simile (160–166). The spatial coordinates of the spring simile cue the narrator's mind to a homologous image-mapping that "erases," or at least subordinates, the initial spatial aspect of the wolf simile. Image coding reveals the storyteller's aim: Patroklos and the Myrmidons are visualized similarly, for they are and always will be together throughout *Iliad* XVI.

Visual unit 2

212–217: (N1) lines of Myrmidons / (S1) house-wall, stones

ὡς δ' ὅτε τοῖχον ἀνὴρ ἀράρῃ πυκινοῖσι λίθοισι
δώματος ὑψηλοῖο, βίας ἀνέμων ἀλεείνων,
ὣς ἄραρον κόρυθές τε καὶ ἀσπίδες ὀμφαλόεσσαι.
ἀσπὶς ἄρ' ἀσπίδ' ἔρειδε, κόρυς κόρυν, ἀνέρα δ' ἀνήρ,
ψαῦον δ' ἱππόκομοι κόρυθες λαμπροῖσι φάλοισιν
νευόντων· ὣς πυκνοὶ ἐφέστασαν ἀλλήλοισιν.

And as a man builds solid a wall with stones set close together
for the rampart of a high house keeping out the force of the winds, so
close together were the helms and shields massive in the middle.
For shield leaned on shield, helmet on helmet, man against man,
and the horse-hair crests along the horns of the shining helmets
touched as they bent their heads, so dense were they formed on each
          other.

Iliad XVI 212–217

---

[131] I am skeptical of the argument put forward by Schoeck (1961:89), who suggests that since Achilles will be—like his mother Thetis in the *Memnonis*—a helpless spectator of the death of Patroklos, his assuming the role of his mother in the simile is quite effective. Even if we were to accept the debatable possibility that the simile's subject matter was chosen on the basis of the role Achilles' mother played in another epic poem or tradition, his rebuking tone can stand on its own.

[132] See J. Armstrong 1958; Scott 2009:158–159. See also scholia (B[BCE³E⁴]T) on *Iliad* XVI 7–10.

Visual unit 2 focuses on the Myrmidons' preparation for battle: the story-teller views them standing close to each other and compares them to stones in a house-wall. This is the second of three "camera shots" of the Myrmidons,[133] each one visualized with the help of an extended simile: XVI 156–166, 212–217, and 259–267. The emphasis on density or closeness between the ranks of the troops works very well for the storyteller's visualization and organization of the ensuing battle; as I have shown in chapter 1 above, it will be Patroklos' transgression of spatial borders and his moving away from the safety of the closely packed ranks of his companions that will lead him to his death.

Visual unit 3

259–267: (N1) the Myrmidons start moving from the ships / (S1) street

αὐτίκα δὲ σφήκεσσιν ἐοικότες ἐξεχέοντο
εἰνοδίοις, οὓς παῖδες ἐριδμαίνωσιν ἔθοντες,
αἰεὶ κερτομέοντες, ὁδῷ ἔπι οἰκί' ἔχοντας,
νηπίαχοι· ξυνὸν δὲ κακὸν πολέεσσι τιθεῖσιν·
τοὺς δ' εἴ περ παρά τίς τε κιὼν ἄνθρωπος ὁδίτης
κινήσῃ ἀέκων, οἳ δ' ἄλκιμον ἦτορ ἔχοντες
πρόσσω πᾶς πέτεται καὶ ἀμύνει οἷσι τέκεσσιν.
τῶν τότε Μυρμιδόνες κραδίην καὶ θυμὸν ἔχοντες
ἐκ νηῶν ἐχέοντο· βοὴ δ' ἄσβεστος ὀρώρει.

The Myrmidons came streaming out like wasps at the wayside
when little boys have got into the habit of making them angry
by always teasing them as they live in their house by the roadside;
silly boys, they do something that hurts many people;
and if some man who travels on the road happens to pass them
and stirs them unintentionally, they in heart of fury
come swarming out each one from his place to fight for their
    children.
In heart and in fury like these the Myrmidons streaming
came out from their ships, with a tireless clamour arising.

Iliad XVI 259–267

The second thematic section of *Iliad* XVI begins with an impressive extended simile from the insect family. In order to visualize the movement of

---

[133] See Scott 1974:38. The visual interplay between Patroklos and the troops is rewarding, for the storyteller will soon capitalize on their interaction during the actual fighting. Simile space allows the narrator to enhance memorability, and thereby create dramatic effects.

the Myrmidons from the camp to the battlefield, the storyteller has employed the illustrative analogy of a swarm of wasps streaming out at the wayside when little boys have made them angry. Scholars have argued about the "authenticity" of this simile, since they have tended to regard it as the conflation of two initially independent similes, one of the children destroying the nests of wasps and one of a passer-by irritating them as they try to protect their own children.[134] From the point of view of cognitive theory, a crucial observation supports the authenticity of the simile as we have it. The simile's spatial unity—since both "parts" describe activities occurring at the same place where the wasps' nests are situated—shows that we are dealing with one and the same spatial imagery, and by extension with one and the same simile. No extended simile is spatially divided into smaller parts:[135] spatial unity means imagery unity within the simile snapshot. The mental factors of image organization and recall must capture the continuity and connectedness of space, which is "an important ingredient in spatial representation."[136]

Visual unit 4

297-302: (N1) (Danaans try to push back the fire) along the ships / (S1) peak of mountain

352-357: (N2) in front of ships / (S2) mountains

364-367: (N3) from the ships / (S3) Mount (Olympos)

---

[134] The main "problems" with respect to this simile are two: Aristophanes of Byzantium's and Aristarchus' athetesis of *Iliad* XVI 261 on the grounds that κερτομεῖν (261 κερτομέοντες) is employed for words and not deeds (as here), and the "parallel" similes of *Iliad* XVI 259 + 260–262 and 259 + 263–265. See Ameis-Hentze 1908:21 on *Iliad* XVI 259–262; Wilamowitz 1920:127n1; Fränkel 1921:72; von der Mühll 1952:245n25; Jachmann 1958:329 and n112. With respect to the first objection, Janko's suggestions (1992:353 on *Iliad* XVI 261) that *Iliad* XVI 261 "explains in chiastic order the rare words ἔθω, 'be wont' (9.540, cf. εἴωθα), ἐριδμαίνω (next in Hellenistic verse, cf. Risch, *Wortbildung* 290) and εἰνόδιος (*Cat.* 23.26, cf. 6.15)" and that κερτομεῖν can mean "tease non-verbally, e.g. Eur. *Helen* 619 (J. Jackson, *Marginalia Scaenica*, Oxford 1955, 26)" are persuasive. On Homer's tendency to explain compound words, see Rank 1951:74–84 (and add to the example noted by Janko *Iliad* XVIII 54, which is explained in XVIII 55–60). As far as the "parallel" similes are concerned, the authenticity of our text has been strongly defended by Marcovich 1962:290 and J. Kakridis 1971:138–140. Recent scholarship unhesitatingly favors retaining the text as we have it; see Janko 1992:352–353; Erbse 2000:266–268; Scott 1974:158–159 and 2009:160–161.

[135] Spatial frames are of a different kind, for they constitute the most elementary subdivisions of the visual unit, that is, of the larger image collection that forms a coherent whole. Visual frames neither accentuate segmentation nor do they pertain to different spatial coordinates. On visual units and visual frames, see the discussion at the beginning of this chapter.

[136] Pylyshyn 2007:172.

ὡς δ᾽ ὅτ᾽ ἀφ᾽ ὑψηλῆς κορυφῆς ὄρεος μεγάλοιο
κινήσῃ πυκινὴν νεφέλην στεροπηγερέτα Ζεύς,
ἔκ τ᾽ ἔφανεν πᾶσαι σκοπιαὶ καὶ πρώονες ἄκροι
καὶ νάπαι, οὐρανόθεν δ᾽ ἄρ᾽ ὑπερράγη ἄσπετος αἰθήρ,
ὣς Δαναοὶ νηῶν μὲν ἀπωσάμενοι δήιον πῦρ
τυτθὸν ἀνέπνευσαν· πολέμου δ᾽ οὐ γίγνετ᾽ ἐρωή·

And as when from the towering height of a great mountain Zeus
who gathers the thunderflash stirs the cloud dense upon it,
and all the high places of the hills are clear and the shoulders
   out-jutting
and the deep ravines, as endless bright air spills from the heavens,
so when the Danaans had beaten from the ships the ravening
fire, they got breath for a little, but there was no check in the
   fighting;

Iliad XVI 297–302

ὡς δὲ λύκοι ἄρνεσσιν ἐπέχραον ἠ᾽ ἐρίφοισιν
σίνται, ὕπεκ μήλων αἱρεόμενοι, αἵ τ᾽ ἐν ὄρεσσιν
ποιμένος ἀφραδίῃσι διέτμαγεν, οἳ δὲ ἰδόντες
αἶψα διαρπάζουσιν ἀνάλκιδα θυμὸν ἐχούσας,
ὣς Δαναοὶ Τρώεσσιν ἐπέχραον· οἳ δὲ φόβοιο
δυσκελάδου μνήσαντο, λάθοντο δὲ θούριδος ἀλκῆς.

They as wolves make havoc among lambs or young goats in their
   fury,
catching them out of the flocks, when the sheep separate in the
   mountains
through the thoughtlessness of the shepherd, and the wolves seeing
   them
suddenly snatch them away, and they have no heart for fighting;
so the Danaans ravaged the Trojans, and these remembered
the bitter sound of terror, and forgot their furious valour.

Iliad XVI 352–357

ὡς δ᾽ ὅτ᾽ ἀπ᾽ Οὐλύμπου νέφος ἔρχεται οὐρανὸν εἴσω
αἰθέρος ἐκ δίης, ὅτε τε Ζεὺς λαίλαπα τείνῃ,
ὣς τῶν ἐκ νηῶν γένετο ἰαχή τε φόβος τε,
οὐδὲ κατὰ μοῖραν πέραον πάλιν.

> As when a cloud goes deep into the sky from Olympos
> through the bright upper air when Zeus brings on the hurricane,
> so rose from beside the ships their outcry, the noise of their terror.
> In no good order they went back.

Iliad XVI 364–367

When the storyteller passes to a new thematic section, featuring Patroklos' advancing into battle and repelling the Trojans from the ships, he employs three extended similes that allow him to coordinate narrative action with the content of his similes' snapshots. Helping his audience "see" the unexpected reversal of the almost desperate situation the Achaeans were facing and the intense rhythm of the fighting upon Patroklos' entry into the battle, the narrator chooses three similes that take place on high ground (mountains and even Olympos), to which he attaches the image of fighting in front of the ships. In imagining a spatial layout, the storyteller uses labels,[137] one for each imagined location, that allow him to keep the mentally indexed individual locations apart and create patterns between them. The embedding of the imagery contained in these three similes within the same visual unit reflects their sharing of the spatial label of "high ground." Having said this, I would postulate a process in which the storyteller selects a "target" space (the high ground of a mountain) where a brief snapshot is visualized.[138] In fact, the removal of a cloud and the appearance of the hills, out-jutting shoulders and glens in the first simile (297–302) visually replays the gradual revealing of space in the narrator's mind. His target space becomes clearer as the pictorial load of the simile begins to make its presence felt. As the simile's imagery unfolds, the target space increases in visual force and memorability. It can now be pictured with ease, even when it has temporarily disappeared from the mnemonic horizon of the storyteller, who returns to his main narrative once the simile is over. As long as he is mentally situated within the borders of the same visual unit, the target space can be readily accessed, although it can now activate a different set of images. This is exactly the case with the next simile (352–357): since the narrative space has not changed, the storyteller retrieves from his memory the same target space, that of the mountains, which now becomes the setting of an animal imagery. The Myrmidons are once more compared to wolves attacking lambs or young goats not properly protected by their shepherd,[139] as Hektor fails to protect his Trojan troops

---

[137] See Pylyshyn 2007:178.
[138] On target space, see Pylyshyn 2007:182–191.
[139] See *Iliad* XVI 156–166.

against the fierce attack of Patroklos and his army.[140] The role of spatial factors in the function of this visual unit's next and last simile is observable in the way the storyteller pictures his selected target space. Having given his audience a hint at the role of Hektor, on whose advice the Trojans have invaded the Achaean camp, the narrator briefly but selectively describes how the hero holds his position against all odds in his attempt to save his comrades. As the force of the preceding simile "spills over" to the narrative, the storyteller visually reactivates once more the target space of "high ground" and introduces a new simile. This time, he visualizes the noise of terror rising from the ships by means of "a cloud going deep into the sky from Olympos / through the bright upper air when Zeus brings on the hurricane" (364–365). In spatial mental imagery, the property of continuity and connectedness of space leads the narrator one more time to activate the target space of "high ground." As the simile evokes imagery that begins to resemble that used in the first simile of this visual unit, the storyteller realizes that he does not need to say more. His target space has done the work for him.

Visual unit 5

384–393: (N1) noise of horses / (S1) noise of sky, rivers, glens, sea,
      mountains

ὡς δ' ὑπὸ λαίλαπι πᾶσα κελαινὴ βέβριθε χθών
ἤματ' ὀπωρινῷ, ὅτε λαβρότατον χέει ὕδωρ
Ζεύς, ὅτε δή ἄνδρεσσι κοτεσσάμενος χαλεπήνῃ,
οἳ βίῃ εἰν ἀγορῇ σκολιὰς κρίνωσι θέμιστας,
ἐκ δὲ Δίκην ἐλάσωσι, θεῶν ὄπιν οὐκ ἀλέγοντες,
τῶν δέ τε πάντες μὲν ποταμοὶ πλήθουσι ῥέοντες,
πολλὰς δὲ κλειτὺς τότ' ἀποτμήγουσι χαράδραι,
ἐς δ' ἅλα πορφυρέην μεγάλα στενάχουσι ῥέουσαι
ἐξ ὀρέων ἐπικάρ, μινύθει δέ τε ἔργ' ἀνθρώπων,
ὣς ἵπποι Τρῳαὶ μεγάλα στενάχοντο θέουσαι.

As underneath the hurricane all the black earth is burdened
on an autumn day, when Zeus sends down the most violent waters
in deep rage against mortals after they stir him to anger
because in violent assembly they pass decrees that are crooked,

---

[140] See Janko 1992:361–362 on *Iliad* XVI 352–355. Scott 2009:155 aptly describes the generalized tendency of *Iliad* XVI to create expectations that are violated and to impose on the audience sequences of events that are suddenly and violently overturned as "a house of mirrors," where actions often have double images, one the reverse of the other.

and drive Righteousness from among them and care nothing for
  what the gods think,
and all the rivers of these men swell current to full spate
and in the ravines of their water-courses rip all the hillsides
and dash whirling in huge noise down to the blue sea, out of
the mountains headlong, so that the works of men are diminished;
so huge rose the noise from the horses of Troy in their running.

Iliad XVI 384–393

This is one of the most problematic similes in the entire *Iliad*: its moralizing tone, the meaning of Δίκη,[141] seemingly at odds with standard Homeric use, and the Hesiodic echoes of the passage are the main source of trouble for a large number of scholars.[142] I would add a new perspective, that of cognitive theory, to the ongoing discussion of this vexing problem.

Classifying this simile in one of the standard families is difficult, since its paratactic expansion, which adds new blocks of lines, extends the simile's borders so much that its beginning is almost forgotten. The fact that these additions have clear-cut boundaries, since only one (the second) of its nine lines is not coterminous,[143] is on a cognitive level a hint at the pictorial comprehensiveness of its visual frames. In other words, from the standpoint of cognitive theory, most of the "problems" detected by scholars who doubt the authenticity of this simile can be translated into the phenomenon of image accumulation. Let us first review the simile's six visual frames:

(1) 384–385 ὡς δ' ὑπὸ λαίλαπι πᾶσα κελαινὴ βέβριθε χθών / ἤματ' ὀπωρινῷ, ὅτε λαβρότατον χέει ὕδωρ (earth burdened by hurricane—size and noise)

(2) 386–388 Ζεύς, ὅτε δή ἄνδρεσσι κοτεσσάμενος χαλεπήνῃ, / οἳ βίῃ εἰν ἀγορῇ σκολιὰς κρίνωσι θέμιστας, / ἐκ δὲ Δίκην ἐλάσωσι, θεῶν ὄπιν οὐκ ἀλέγοντες· (men in violent assembly—location)

(3) 389 τῶν δέ τε πάντες μὲν ποταμοὶ πλήθουσι ῥέοντες (rivers—size)

(4) 390 πολλὰς δὲ κλειτὺς τότ' ἀποτμήγουσι χαράδραι (hillsides—movement)

(5) 391 ἐς δ' ἅλα πορφυρέην μεγάλα στενάχουσι ῥέουσαι (sea—noise)

---

[141] See Janko 1992:364–365 on *Iliad* XVI 384–393 with all the relevant bibliography. I am following West 1998–2000 ad loc., who takes it as a proper name and prints it as Δίκην. See also his commentary (2011:320) on *Iliad* XVI 387–388.

[142] For a discussion of the various problems of this simile, see Scott 1974:155–156; Moulton 1977:35–37; Janko 1992:364–365 on *Iliad* XVI 384–393; Scott 2009:160.

[143] See Scott 1974:155.

(6)   392 ἐξ ὀρέων ἐπικάρ, μινύθει δέ τε ἔργ' ἀνθρώπων· (mountains—movement)

What we see here is one of the conditions of active spatial representation, according to which space can sometimes be multimodal. Spatial features that are initially perceived and represented in one modality can be remapped onto other modalities.[144] Seen from the standpoint of image processing and the organization of spatial representation, the simile at hand displays exactly this crossover between modalities, as its sequence of six visual frames shows that the narrator has continuously shifted from one modality to another: the size and noise made by the hurricane is interrupted by the visualization of the assembly place, which is followed by the emphasis on the size of the flowing rivers, then by the movement of the water on the hillsides, its noise as it falls into the sea, and retrospectively its flowing from the mountains. Movement, placement, noise, and size are all different modalities of spatial representation that constitute the visual frames, that is, the building blocks of this extended simile. What scholars have called a "paratactic expansion of smaller units"[145] is better explored in terms of a crossing over of modalities in active spatial representation. The dispersed sequence of cloud/rain similes in 297–302 and 364–366 was so strong in the storyteller's mind that it activated relevant images in line 384; this time, though, as the narrative frame has changed and the combat is taking place at the ditch (and not by the ships), the flow of images changes fast and produces a multimodal spatial representation that captures our attention.[146]

Visual unit 6

> 406–410: (N1) between ships, river, and Achaean wall / (S1) jutting rock
> next to the sea
>
> 428–430: (N2) between ships, river, and Achaean wall / (S2) high rock

ὡς ὅτε τις φώς
πέτρῃ ἔπι προβλῆτι καθήμενος ἱερὸν ἰχθύν

---

[144] See Spence and Driver 2004; Pylyshyn 2007:171.

[145] Rhyming patterns observed at verse-ends (388 ἀλέγοντες/389 ῥέοντες; 391 ῥέουσαι/393 θέουσαι) and repetition of participles of the same verb again at verse-end (389 ῥέοντες/391 ῥέουσαι) are dictional traces indicating the completion of visual frames. See also Scott's observations on the use of δέ, and his assertion that "when [the poet] was called upon to extend his simile beyond a few lines, the paratactic structure began to dominate and the unconnected nature of the poet's thinking became more and more evident" (1974:155–156).

[146] In visual unit 5, the noise of horses is compared to the sound of virtually the whole of nature: sky, rivers, glens, sea, and mountains participate in the making of a huge noise that creates a feeling of proximity to storyteller and audience. Sound is a powerful aspect of space, one that enhances participation by giving the impression of "being there."

ἐκ πόντοιο θύραζε λίνῳ καὶ ἤνοπι χαλκῷ·
ὣς ἕλκ᾽ ἐκ δίφροιο κεχηνότα δουρὶ φαεινῷ,
κὰδ δ᾽ ἄρ᾽ ἐπὶ στόμ᾽ ἔωσε· πεσόντα δέ μιν λίπε θυμός.

　　　　　　　　　　　　　　　　as a fisherman
who sits out on the jut of a rock with line and glittering
bronze hook drags a fish, who is thus doomed, out of the water.
So he hauled[147] him, mouth open to the bright spear, out of the
　　　chariot,
and shoved him over on his face, and as he fell the life left him.

Iliad XVI 406–410

οἳ δ᾽, ὥς τ᾽ αἰγυπιοὶ γαμψώνυχες ἀγκυλοχεῖλαι
πέτρῃ ἔφ᾽ ὑψηλῇ μεγάλα κλάζοντε μάχωνται,
ὣς οἳ κεκλήγοντες ἐπ᾽ ἀλλήλοισιν ὄρουσαν.

They as two hook-clawed beak-bent vultures
above a tall rock face, high-screaming, go for each other,
so now these two, crying aloud, encountered together.

Iliad XVI 428–430

While the fighting is taking place somewhere between the ships, the Achaean wall, and the river (396–397), the storyteller facilitates visualization by recourse to the same pictorial space, that of a jutting or high rock (visual unit 6). The actual corresponding scenes may be different (Patroklos kills Thestor and then dismounts his chariot and is ready to face Sarpedon), but the spatial cue for recall is the same. Storytellers often employ a *map* strategy, according to which "space is represented panoramically from a perspective ranging from the disembodied god's-eye point of view of pure vertical projection to the oblique view of an observer situated on an elevated point."[148] Elevated places, corners, or outjutting peaks, rocks, and so on are effective mental vantage points that facilitate pictureability, for they enhance visual isolation and distinctiveness, which assist the narrator in his effort to visualize space.

The use of the same visual unit for the beginning of the Sarpedon-Patroklos encounter (419–683) helps the narrator make the transfer smoothly, since he will now have to change the tone from Patroklos' "easy" victories against second- or

---

[147] In *Iliad* XVI 409, I have chosen the unaugmented form ἕλκ᾽ that is offered by Aristarchus and some mss, instead of the augmented εἷλκ᾽ given by another group of mss. West (1998:xxvii) opts for the augmented form.

[148] Ryan 2003:218.

third-rate opponents to a dangerous duel versus the Lycian prince Sarpedon. The emphasis on the "two hook-clawed beak-bent vultures" (428) screaming at each other invites the audience to visualize the two opponents on an equal footing.[149] The storyteller creates for his audience the illusion that the narrative game of *Iliad* XVI is replayed or even intensified in the visually richer register of the similes, since the ease with which the fisherman catches the fish matches the apparent equality between Sarpedon and Patroklos. But while the fisherman's easy success remains unchanged, the equality between the two heroes will be painfully overturned: Patroklos will kill his Lycian opponent anything but easily, and he will continue to prevail on the battlefield, but not for long. The storyteller gradually moves his hero to an unfamiliar space which Achilles has explicitly told him not to enter, a space that will bring his death. The simile space paves the way for this violation of boundaries by cueing the audience to the possibility that nothing is as it seems—especially Patroklos, who can never be a second Achilles.

Visual unit 7

482–486: (N1) (Sarpedon falls) in front of horses and chariot / (S1) mountains

487–491: (N2) in front of horses and chariot / (S2) unspecified (among other cattle)

ἤριπε δ' ὡς ὅτε τις δρῦς ἤριπεν ἢ ἀχερωΐς
ἠὲ πίτυς βλωθρή, τήν τ' οὔρεσι τέκτονες ἄνδρες
ἐξέταμον πελέκεσσι νεήκεσι νήϊον εἶναι·
ὣς ὃ πρόσθ' ἵππων καὶ δίφρου κεῖτο τανυσθείς,
βεβρυχώς, κόνιος δεδραγμένος αἱματοέσσης.

He fell, as when an oak goes down or a white poplar,
or like a towering pine tree which in the mountains the carpenters
have hewn down with their whetted axes to make a ship-timber.
So he lay there felled in front of his horses and chariots
roaring, and clawed with his hands at the bloody dust.

Iliad XVI 482–486

ἠΰτε ταῦρον ἔπεφνε λέων ἀγέληφι μετελθών
αἴθωνα μεγάθυμον ἐν εἰλιπόδεσσι βόεσσιν,

[149] See Baltes 1983:37–38; Scott 2009:162. See also the scholion (b[BCE³E⁴]T) on *Iliad* XVI 428: πρὸς τὸ ἰσοδυναμοῦν τῶν ἀντιμαχομένων τῇ εἰκόνι κέχρηται, ἐνδείξασθαι βουλόμενος ὅτι ὅμοιοι ἦσαν ("He has used this imagery to indicate the equal matching of the opponents, because he wanted to show that they were similar").

ὤλετό τε στενάχων ὑπὸ γαμφηλῇσι λέοντος,
ὣς ὑπὸ Πατρόκλῳ Λυκίων ἀγὸς ἀσπιστάων
κτεινόμενος μενέαινε

or as

a blazing and haughty bull in a huddle of shambling cattle
when a lion has come among the herd and destroys him
dies bellowing under the hooked claws of the lion, so now
before Patroklos the lord of the shield-armoured Lykians
died raging ...

Iliad XVI 487–491

Sarpedon's death at the hands of Patroklos is of course the major event in this thematic section of *Iliad* XVI. The narrator caps the narrative of the actual duel with a cluster of two extended similes: Sarpedon's falling in front of his horses and chariot is visualized by means of two familiar scenes: the felling of a tall tree by men who wish to use its wood for shipbuilding,[150] and a lion attacking a bull among a herd of cattle. Both similes are very traditional, for they belong to two widely attested families, the tree and lion similes.[151] Yet they both display a certain aberration from regular usage with respect to their structure, which comprises two visual frames. In the tree simile, the first visual frame of the falling of a tall tree (an oak or a white poplar or a tall pine) is coupled with a second one of its being felled in the mountains by men's "whetted axes to make a ship's timber." Likewise in the lion simile, the lion's attack on the bull among the herd is followed by a zooming in on the bull held under its hooked claws. The mental construction of imagery by means of visual framing should be seen not as segmentation, but as a method for building and organizing data. In fact, the double visual framing of each simile reveals the exact process the storyteller follows in dealing with mental imagery. In the first, he moves from a general mental picture to a detail initially contained in this picture but stated separately. The image of the falling tree is particularized by a spatial specification, namely the mountains, where the storyteller later sees men felling the tree with their axes. In the second simile, he follows a different course: from the spatial specification of the lion attack (ἀγέληφι 'among the herd'), he zooms in on an even smaller spot in his mental image, the snapshot of the bull being

---

[150] This simile is identical to the one used in XIII 389–393, after Asios' death at the hands of Idomeneus. This verbatim repetition strengthens the cognitive analysis presented above, for the narrator seems to be using standard techniques for the mental processing of images. On repeated similes in the Homeric epics, see Scott 1974:127–140.

[151] On tree and lion similes, see Scott 1974:70–71 and 58–61 respectively.

held by the hooked claws of the lion. This visual *particularization of space* reflects the storyteller's very process of constructing mental images, as he first reconnoiters in his mind's eye the territory in which he will place his simile's snapshot, and then mentally plunges himself into it by focusing on a particular spot. In this way, the storyteller can shed light on special aspects of his similes that allude to hidden aspects of his narrative: the emphasis on "men's progress and purposefulness"[152] in felling the tree to make a ship's timber in the first simile, and the absence of any reference to "protecting shepherd, men, dogs, and sheltering farmstead"[153] in the second allude to the lack of planning and calculation that will eventually lead Patroklos to his death.[154]

Visual unit 8

> 582–585: (N1) (Patroklos moves) among the πρόμαχοι / (S1) struggle between a hawk and other birds (measure: "so straight")
>
> 589–592: (N1) retreat (of Trojans and Hektor) / (S1) contest or battle (measure)

> ἴθυσεν δὲ διὰ προμάχων ἴρηκι ἐοικώς
> ὠκέϊ, ὅς τ' ἐφόβησε κολοιούς τε ψῆράς τε·
> ὣς ἰθὺς Λυκίων, Πατρόκλεις ἱπποκέλευθε,
> ἔσσυο καὶ Τρώων, κεχόλωσο δὲ κῆρ ἑτάροιο.

> He steered his way through the ranks of the front fighters, like a flying
> hawk who scatters into flight the daws and the starlings.
> So straight for the Lykians, o lord of horses, Patroklos,
> you swept, and for the Trojans, heart angered for your companion.

> *Iliad* XVI 582–585

> ὅσση δ' αἰγανέης ῥιπὴ ταναοῖο τέτυκται,
> ἥν ῥά τ' ἀνὴρ ἀφέῃ πειρώμενος ἢ ἐν ἀέθλῳ,
> ἠὲ καὶ ἐν πολέμῳ δηΐων ὕπο θυμοραϊστέων,
> τόσσον ἐχώρησαν Τρῶες, ὤσαντο δ' Ἀχαιοί.

---

[152] Scott 2009:162. Minchin (2001:146–147), commenting on the identical simile employed for Asios' death in *Iliad* XIII 389–393, suggests that one of the reasons the storyteller may have used the apparently irrelevant detail of the carpenters' cutting the tree to make a ship's timber is the contrast between the purposefulness of their act and the purposelessness of Asios' death. This observation is also applicable to the simile in *Iliad* XVI 482–486.

[153] Scott 2009:163.

[154] See Scott 2009:162–163.

As far as goes the driving cast of a slender javelin
which a man throws making trial of his strength, either in a contest
or else in battle, under the heart-breaking hostilities,[155]
so far the Trojans gave way with the Achaians pushing them.

Iliad XVI 589–592

After the death of Sarpedon, Glaukos tries to stir Hektor to launch a counterattack in order to save Sarpedon's corpse from the Achaeans. Hektor is convinced and the Achaeans are initially pushed back (569 ὦσαν δὲ πρότεροι Τρῶες ἑλίκωπας Ἀχαιούς). The storyteller zooms his narrative lens in on the death of Epeigeus, son of Agakles and one of the Myrmidons, whose head is smashed by a stone thrown by Hektor just at the moment when he is about to remove Sarpedon's corpse. By concentrating on the killing of a Myrmidon by Hektor, the narrator paves the way for the deadly encounter with Patroklos, who at once moves among the first ranks (the πρόμαχοι) and kills, again by throwing a stone, Sthenelaos, son of Ithaimenes. Both events are presented through parallel actions:[156]

A. Hektor leads the Trojans and Lycians straight against the Achaeans

B. Hektor throws a stone and kills Epeigeus

A′. Patroklos enters the ranks of the πρόμαχοι

C. Simile for Patroklos

B′. Patroklos throws a stone and kills Sthenelaos

C′. Simile for Hektor and the Trojans

The ABA′B′ structure is interrupted by two extended similes. Having turned his mind's eye to a new visual unit, the storyteller visualizes the movement of Patroklos and the retreat of Hektor and the Trojans by means of two similes of measurement. Although the sweeping down of a hawk straight against other birds and the cast of a javelin belong to different families of similes, they are both presented here in terms of measuring. The aggressive advance of Patroklos and the speedy retreat of Hektor and the Trojans are viewed through the space covered by the hawk and by a javelin throw respectively. Cognitive psychologists have convincingly shown that the larger the mental drawing of imagery,[157]

---

[155] West brackets line 591 on the basis of the arguments of Leaf 1900–1902:197 on *Iliad* XVI 591; but see Janko 1992:388–389 on *Iliad* XVI 588–592.

[156] See Fenik 1968: 206–207.

[157] The mental image of Patroklos' spear being cast far away is large, since storyteller and audience alike follow the entire course of the spear. Visualizing the space delineated by the distance covered by this moving object requires a significant mental input.

the faster the information included in the verbal output will be processed.[158] In other words, visualizing the speed by which Patroklos moves forward and the spear "travels" in the two extended similes facilitates the mental following up or parallelism with the situation described in the narrative.[159] The audience is thus able to see Patroklos' speedy advance and the Trojan retreat in similar terms. Once more, the narrator with utmost precision and efficiency plays the game of mirrors,[160] where appearances are regularly misleading, since Hektor's counterattack is deliberately cut short by the response of Patroklos, who seems to prevail, but only for a while. The throwing of the stones, like the speedy movement of the two warriors in the front ranks of their troops, shows how the storyteller singles out his two future opponents, almost as soon as the duel between Patroklos and Sarpedon is over.

Visual unit 9

633–637: (N1) plain / (S1) mountains

641–644: (N2) plain (around Sarpedon) / (S2) sheepfold

τῶν δ᾽, ὥς τε δρυτόμων ἀνδρῶν ὀρυμαγδὸς ὀρώρει
οὔρεος ἐν βήσσῃς, ἕκαθεν δέ τε γίγνετ᾽ ἀκουή,
ὣς τῶν ὄρνυτο δοῦπος ἀπὸ χθονὸς εὐρυοδείης
χαλκοῦ τε ῥινοῦ τε βοῶν τ᾽ εὐποιητάων,
νυσσομένων ξίφεσίν τε καὶ ἔγχεσιν ἀμφιγύοισιν.

As the tumult goes up from men who are cutting
timber in the mountain valleys, and the sound is heard from far off,
such was the dull crashing that rose from earth of the wide ways,
from the bronze shields, the skins and the strong-covering ox-hides
as the swords and leaf-headed spears stabbed against them.

Iliad XVI 633–637

ὡς ὅτε μυῖαι
σταθμῷ ἔνι βρομέωσι περιγλαγέας κατὰ πέλλας
ὥρῃ ἐν εἰαρινῇ, ὅτε τε γλάγος ἄγγεα δεύει·
ὣς ἄρα τοὶ περὶ νεκρὸν ὁμίλεον.

---

[158] See Shepard 1978.
[159] See Clay 2011:8n17: "Similarly, the mind of the poet can dart across time and space and, despite temporal and spatial distance, can convey his audience to the Trojan plain where his drama unfolds."
[160] On the "mirror design" of this thematic section of *Iliad* XVI, see Scott 2009:162–163.

> as flies
> through a sheepfold thunder about the pails overspilling
> milk, in the season of spring when the milk splashes in the buckets.
> So they swarmed over the dead man.

> *Iliad* XVI 641–644

In visual unit 9, the fighting in the plain around the body of Sarpedon is visualized with the help of the familiar space of a pair of mountain scenes (as in unit 7).[161] Timber-cutting and flies belong to two very different similemes, and yet they are joined in the narrator's imagination through two spatial features: noise and placement. By evoking two pictorial snapshots placed at mountain locations, and highlighting the noise produced by the activity of these two groups of actants (men and flies), the storyteller creates a solid visual background against which he is able to inscribe noise, a rather neglected but quite important aspect of active spatial representation. The emphasis on the sound produced during the fierce fighting over Sarpedon's body creates the impression of "being there," of coming close to the actual hubbub of battle. By recourse to spatial mechanisms that the universe of the similes contains in abundance, the narrator can thus turn his listeners into spectators and then back into listeners: they listen to his song about the death of Sarpedon, see the actual fighting in their mind's eye, and even mentally hear the clamor of battle against the spatial backdrop of the similes, which offer familiar image-mappings that enhance mental representation and aesthetic pleasure.[162]

Visual unit 10

752–754: (N1) plain (next to Hektor's chariot) / (S1) sheepfolds

756–761: (N2) plain (next to Hektor's chariot) / (S2) peaks of mountain

765–771: (N3) plain (next to Hektor's chariot) / (S3) valleys of mountains

823–828: (N4) plain (next to Hektor's chariot) / (S4) peaks of mountains

---

[161] Sheepfolds are typically placed in the mountains in Homeric epic. Traditional referentiality allows both narrator and audience to fill in the missing details even when they are not explicitly stated. Dictional ellipsis is often counterbalanced in traditional oral epic by the almost built-in *pars pro toto* thematic principle. To recall Nagy's famous terminology, the reference to the mountains in the above similes is *synchronically* absent but *diachronically* present.

[162] On the importance of sound as a spatial feature, see my discussion of the shield of Achilles in chapter 8 below.

οἶμα λέοντος ἔχων, ὅς τε σταθμοὺς κεραΐζων
ἔβλητο πρὸς στῆθος, ἑή τέ μιν ὤλεσεν ἀλκή·
ὣς ἐπὶ Κεβριόνῃ, Πατρόκλεις, ἆλσο μεμαώς.

with the spring of a lion, who as he ravages the pastures
has been hit on the chest, and his own courage destroys him.
So in your fury you pounced, Patroklos, above Kebriones.

Iliad XVI 752–754

τὼ περὶ Κεβριόναο λέονθ' ὣς δηρινθήτην,
ὥ τ' ὄρεος κορυφῇσι περὶ κταμένης ἐλάφοιο,
ἄμφω πεινάοντε μέγα φρονέοντε μάχεσθον·
ὣς περὶ Κεβριόναο δύω μήστωρες ἀϋτῆς,
Πάτροκλός τε Μενοιτιάδης καὶ φαίδιμος Ἕκτωρ,
ἵεντ' ἀλλήλων ταμέειν χρόα νηλέϊ χαλκῷ.

and the two fought it out over Kebriones, like lions
who in the high places of a mountain, both in huge courage
and both hungry, fight together over a killed deer.
So above Kebriones these two, urgent for battle,
Patroklos, son of Menoitios, and glorious Hektor,
were straining with the pitiless bronze to tear at each other.

Iliad XVI 756–761

ὡς δ' Εὖρός τε Νότος τ' ἐριδαίνετον ἀλλήλοιιν
οὔρεος ἐν βήσσῃς βαθέην πελεμιζέμεν ὕλην,
φηγόν τε μελίην τε τανύφλοιόν τε κράνειαν,
αἵ τε πρὸς ἀλλήλας ἔβαλον τανυήκεας ὄζους
ἠχῇ θεσπεσίῃ, πάταγος δέ τε ἀγνυμενάων,
ὣς Τρῶες καὶ Ἀχαιοὶ ἐπ' ἀλλήλοισι θορόντες
δῄουν, οὐδ' ἕτεροι μνώοντ' ὀλοοῖο φόβοιο.

As east wind and south wind fight it out with each other
in the valleys of the mountains to shake the deep forest timber,
oak tree and ash and the cornel with the delicate bark; these
whip their wide-reaching branches against one another
in inhuman noise, and the crash goes up from the splintering timber;
so Trojans and Achaians springing against one another
cut men down, nor did either side think of disastrous panic.

Iliad XVI 765–771

ὡς δ' ὅτε σῦν ἀκάμαντα λέων ἐβιήσατο χάρμῃ,
ὥ τ' ὄρεος κορυφῇσι μέγα φρονέοντε μάχεσθον
πίδακος ἀμφ' ὀλίγης, ἐθέλουσι δὲ πιέμεν ἄμφω,
πολλὰ δέ τ' ἀσθμαίνοντα λέων ἐδάμασσε βίηφιν,
ὣς πολέας πεφνόντα Μενοιτίου ἄλκιμον υἱόν
Ἕκτωρ Πριαμίδης σχεδὸν ἔγχεϊ θυμὸν ἀπηύρα.

As a lion overpowers a weariless boar in wild combat
as the two fight in their pride on the high places of a mountain
over a little spring of water, both wanting to drink there,
and the lion beats him down by force as he fights for his breath, so
Hektor, Priam's son, with a close spear-stroke stripped the life
from the fighting son of Menoitios, who had killed so many.

Iliad XVI 823–828

After Sarpedon, the storyteller turns his gaze to the area where Hektor stands, since that is the one hero he has to bring close to Patroklos for their fatal encounter. Hektor's position, somewhere next to his chariot, is visualized through no fewer than four similes, all of which contain small narratives occurring in mountain settings. The cornucopia of imagery displayed for the mental mapping of Hektor's location in the plain reflects his importance for the rest of *Iliad* XVI,[163] since the narrator intends to dwell for a while on the climactic duel that will end with Patroklos' death at his hands. For this, the storyteller (and his audience) need to have a clear view of the space where this fighting will take place.

The first (752–754) and last (823–828) of the four similes of this last visual unit refer to the deaths of Kebriones and Patroklos respectively, while the two others (756–761 and 765–771) pertain to the actual fighting between Patroklos and Hektor over the body of the slain charioteer Kebriones. The importance of Kebriones for this whole episode has been explained by neoanalytical scholars in terms of the "dependence" of the *Patrokleia* on the so-called *Memnonis*, but we are in no position to ascertain the *Iliad*'s debt to this particular episode in terms of the pictorial richness reflected in the use of similes. On the contrary, the overflow of images that marks this scene as of utmost importance shows how the Iliadic storyteller was able to coordinate narrative emphasis with simile-oriented pictorial wealth. Moreover, he made full use of a visual grammar

---

[163] There is, of course, no causal link between the mountains and the duel between Patroklos and Sarpedon. The storyteller repeatedly employs similes featuring action that occurs in *the same place* (mountains), in order to allow his audience to mentally anchor to it the uncharted spot on the battlefield where the fatal encounter between these two first-rank heroes will take place.

he seems to have devised especially for *Iliad* XVI, the turning point in his exposition of the plot. The simile cross-reference with respect to the dark spring, creating a ring that denotes the opening and closing of *Iliad* XVI,[164] the systematic clustering of similes, and the use of simile sequences constitute effective mechanisms for creating cohesion and dramatic effect, in a book that is characterized by a continuous movement from one episode to the other. This strung-on style is strongly supported by the simile system as employed in *Iliad* XVI. Active spatial representation by means of rich imagery enhances visualization and reinforces internal associations, keying the audience to the special weight of the interconnected deaths of Sarpedon, Kebriones, and Patroklos.

In the first part of this chapter I attempted to offer a comprehensive mapping of the distribution of all the extended similes and their narrative context in four books of the *Iliad*, on the basis of what I termed "visual units," the building blocks of the mental representation of the plot. These optical groupings allow the storyteller to *tour* the Iliadic landscape, and especially the spatially uncharted (and for this reason δυσμνημόνευτον) area of the vast Trojan plain, and turn it into an εὐσύνοπτον (and therefore εὐμνημόνευτον[165]) whole, which he can see in "one glance" (to stick to the famous Zielinskian expression)[166] but can also *tour* with ease. Seeing vividly with the mind's eye requires the use of effective mnemonic tools, such as imagery, which combined with another powerful cue to recall, space, allows the narrator to create vivid mental representations of unknown areas. The spatial aspect of strong forms of imagery such as the similes satisfies this need in a remarkably successful manner. Simile space provides the mental signposts for tagging narrative space and turning the vague Iliadic landscape into clear and vivid visual snapshots.

Gleichnisorte are organized with respect to narrative space. The narrator composes his similes in visual units that correspond to the spatial organization of his narrative. Being concerned with the deployment of the similes throughout the plot, the examination of their sequence or relevance to the context has not dealt at all with the actual process by which the narrator mnemonically recalls or constructs them. This is partly due to the lack of interest in the means by which memory recall or mental visualization is enhanced. Cognitive psychology has stressed the importance of space as a cue to recall: people tend to use spatial elements, coordinates, and features as mnemonic anchors on which series of images are based and developed. Within the medium of oral performance, the

---

[164] For other examples of cross-references between the similes in *Iliad* XVI, see Scott 2009:170.

[165] On these terms with respect to memory and recall, see Aristotle Poetics 1450b34–1451a6; see also the analysis by Purves 2010a:46–49.

[166] See Zielinski 1901:409; Rengakos 1995; Nünlist 1998; Scodel 2008; Clay 2011:30–36.

system has to be economical: when the visual setting of a given narrative unit does not change, then the space delineated in an extended simile has to be the same or at least of the same sort. If we try to reconstruct this mental process, we see that the narrator creates in his mind a visual image of the story he sings. He follows the process of a visual tour of the mental space of the places he refers to in his story. When he interrupts his narrative by inserting a simile or similes, he consistently does not change the spatial framework as long as he remains within the same narrative unit. In other words, he represents each spatial framework in the narrative by a single spatial framework within the corresponding simile or similes. When the space of a narrative unit changes, then the space of the equivalent simile or similes changes too. This correspondence is to be explained neither by some deeper narrative plan nor by the content of the similes, as has been done in the past, but by a mental process of recall through space.

Similes are much more frequent in battle scenes, not only because they allow the narrator to present his audience with something familiar in their own experience (since their subject matter is drawn from daily life), which stands in contrast to the unfamiliar (and hard to map) battle scenes, but also because similes are organized on the basis of solid spatial constraints that allow the storyteller to "find his way" amid the spatial vagueness created by continuous fighting. Nowhere is this clearer than in *Iliad* XV. In this light, a comparison with *Iliad* XVI is noteworthy: in *Iliad* XV there are thirteen visual units for seventeen similes, whereas in *Iliad* XVI there are ten visual units for twenty similes—in other words, there is a significantly higher grouping of similes in *Iliad* XVI than in *Iliad* XV. This is because most of the fighting in *Iliad* XVI is concentrated on the activity of a single man, Patroklos, who confronts two major heroes, Sarpedon (two similes in a single visual unit) and Hektor (four similes in a single visual unit). The storyteller's mental concentration on Patroklos' spatial activity is therefore more condensed than in *Iliad* XV, where the narrator, given that there is no major protagonist, needs to visualize first one hero and then another and another, and so changes visual snapshots more frequently. From this perspective, it can be plausibly argued that *the higher the dramatic pitch in the fighting books of the Iliad, the stronger is the tendency of the similes to be mentally charted by the storyteller in groups on the basis of spatial markers which function as cues to recall.*

Another aspect of the changing *Gleichnisorte* that has not been dealt with by scholars in the past concerns what I would call *imagery splitting*. In order to grasp the meaning and function of this phenomenon, let us consider the fact that although "there are no one-scene epics,"[167] most of the action of the Homeric *Iliad* is carried out in a rather confined area between the city of Troy

---

[167] Rubin 1995:62.

and the Achaean ships by the sea.[168] This almost built-in difficulty stemming from the poem's subject matter is effectively compensated for by the constantly changing location of battles and other events.[169] Even when the storyteller narrates continuous fighting taking place in an uncharted, rather vague area "somewhere by the Achaean ships" or "somewhere in the plain," and although he lacks any other means to locate and narrate the action, he adopts a strategy of visual segmentation, by creating sublocations within the larger area of the plain or the Achaean camp. One of the most powerful means at his disposal to achieve this segmentation is the extended simile. This is because the pictorial output of the simile is much greater than that of a simple scene or episode. What we call the extended or Homeric simile is a strong pictorial snapshot, characterized more intensely than simple narrative by its spatial nature: the emphasis on movement and spatial references that are constantly found in Homeric similes transform what seems, at least initially, like a simple form of comparison into an intense and vigorous, albeit short-lived, story-world existing within a known and recognizable space. By dividing an event, like the death of Patroklos, into smaller scenes leading up to the hero's end and placing each of them in a different location, made clearer by its pictorial attachment to a spatially stronger extended simile, the narrator is able to mentally orient himself and find his way amid the confusion of battle. In this way, the oral tradition's spatial nature becomes plainly evident: similes are the spatial hooks on which visual imagery is hung, making memory recall "on the run" a reality of the performance.

---

[168] Purves (2010a:31–32 and n16) draws attention to the astute observations of Aristotle, who insisted on seeing the plot as a whole (συνορᾶσθαι, εὐσύνοπτον); cf. Poetics 1459b19–20.

[169] Rubin 1995:62.

6

The Cognitive Aspect of the Homeric Simile

Ontological Boundaries

T HE TERM *ONTOLOGICAL BOUNDARY* refers to (a) the creation of vivid
mental imagery that transports the audience from the world of the plot to
different visual spheres, and (b) a boundary-crossing experience that enables
the narrator to create a further spatial division of the typical dichotomy
between the mental world of the narrative and the ontological and corporeal
habitat of the real world.[1]

Multiple space

Homeric similes are about a different mental universe, one that does not belong
to any single plotline but is fragmented, in the sense that the mental pictures it
allows the audience to visualize are like images seen from a window that opens
and closes very fast. Given that this universe is not one, but differs every time
the simile-window opens, it becomes clear that we are dealing with multiple
different worlds, each accessed by the audience only for a very brief time. One of
the trademarks of this different register seems to be its multiformity: it not only
applies to the simile-system as a whole, but also works internally, that is, within

---

[1] See Ben-Porat 1992. Ben-Porat belongs to the second generation of scholars of the Tel Aviv School
of Narrative Poetics, who have made a serious impact on narrative theory on an international
scale. Founded by Benjamin Hrushovski (later Harshav) in 1966–1967, this school, which ten
years later became the theoretical mouthpiece of the Porter Institute for Poetics and Semiotics,
exercised a considerable influence on literary theory, mainly through the journal *Poetics Today*.
The school's three main contributions to narrative theory, which are all relevant to the following
analysis of the epic simile, can be summarized as follows: (1) units of meaning are linked through
patterns, whether intraliterary (sound, analogy) or pertaining to reality-reflecting templates
(scripts, schemata, etc.); (2) the role of the reader, who forms hypotheses and fills in gaps based
on patterns and analogy, is of crucial importance in the narrative process; and (3) formalism
and structuralism are important, but mainly to the extent that they help determine functional
orientation (the study of the motivation of forms). On the Tel Aviv School, see McHale and Ron
2008.

the framework of a single simile. It actually takes the forms of *bilaterality, complex expansions, mapping inconsistency of the target domain and base domain,*[2] *nontransferability of the simile marker and its replacement by a spatial framework,*[3] and the *multiplied simile*, or the "elliptical combination of two superimposed comparative structures ... violating all four requirements of the standard epic simile."[4] In this way, the simile achieves an approximation and equation of elements, conditions, and people, by *presenting parts of some specific and highly selective activity*, that is, of situating them in space.

Bilaterality

Bilaterality is a spatial aspect par excellence that is particularly associated with the expanded Homeric simile. In what follows, I will explore the question: *Why do epic similes tend to be bilateral, and what is the function and effect of their spatial split?*

The term *bilaterality* describes the split of the simile marker into two domains, the base domain and the target domain. I have opted for these terms instead of the traditional "vehicle" and "tenor," or the even more traditional "anaphoric" and "deictic" parts, which are based on Fränkel's *Wie-* and *So-Satz.*[5] New terms imply novel perspectives, and since these have been employed only by Ben-Porat in an article published in a non–classical journal, they need some preliminary remarks.

The split of the simile marker is a phenomenon so closely, and perhaps so intimately connected with the Homeric simile that it is fair to say that it belongs to its deep structure, or even to its ontogeny, its coming into being. If we endorse this scenario, then it may be argued that what we see as a split of the simile marker is only due to our literary perspective and our familiarity with written literature, which has accustomed us as readers only to the nuclear simile of the type "A is *like* B." Reading the *Iliad*, instead of listening, and writing poetry instead of composing it and performing it orally, have shaped our understanding of the simile as a form of comparison. They have virtually deprived us of the ability to comprehend the simile as imagery, whose dynamic nature can be seen in its constantly changing perspective. Unlike the nuclear simile, which is characterized by its stillness and presents the two terms of comparison as motionless, that is, as expressing fixed identities, the Homeric simile invites

---

[2] For this terminology (with a slight variation between "base" and "source" domain), see Lakoff and Turner 1989:63–64.

[3] This kind of multiformity is also known as the *open* simile, where the narrator does not provide his listener with all the information needed to interpret it; see Ben-Porat 1992:746–748.

[4] Ben-Porat 1992:748.

[5] Introduced in Homeric scholarship with his 1921 monograph on Homeric similes.

the audience on a mental journey, following a visual path that takes the listener in various directions. Visual motion is a powerful mnemonic tool, the more so if associated with imagery that is suited to transformational thinking, which requires "moving rapidly from one situation to another."[6] From this perspective, what we see as the split of a single simile marker acquires a completely different meaning. The oral storyteller does not work with a given verbal model consisting of a single anchoring mechanism, the simile marker, which has been broken or divided into two parts. He composes by following a path with his mind's eye: this path he searches "on the run," without deciding beforehand which aspect of the narrative he will highlight through his use of a simile. He may initially have used an aspect of the narrative as a mental link to begin the simile, but he does not depend solely on this; in fact he often forgets it and moves on to a new image. The introduction of the target domain *after* the completion of the base domain is a surface effect of the process of composing the simile "on the run," since it stems from the storyteller's decision to return to his narrative.

Having discussed the theoretical underpinnings of this cognitive approach, let us perform a litmus test on an Iliadic simile:

> ὣς ἔφατ', Ἀτρείδης δὲ παρῴχετο γηθόσυνος κῆρ·
> ἦλθε δ' ἐπ' Αἰάντεσσι κιὼν ἀνὰ οὐλαμὸν ἀνδρῶν.
> τὼ δὲ κορυσσέσθην, ἅμα δὲ νέφος εἵπετο πεζῶν·
> ὡς δ' ὅτ' ἀπὸ σκοπιῆς εἶδεν νέφος αἰπόλος ἀνὴρ
> ἐρχόμενον κατὰ πόντον ὑπὸ Ζεφύροιο ἰωῆς,
> τῷ δέ τ' ἄνευθεν ἐόντι μελάντερον ἠΰτε πίσσα
> φαίνετ' ἰὸν κατὰ πόντον, ἄγει δέ τε λαίλαπα πολλήν,
> ῥίγησέν τε ἰδών, ὑπό τε σπέος ἤλασε μῆλα,
> τοῖαι ἅμ' Αἰάντεσσι διοτρεφέων αἰζηῶν
> δήϊον ἐς πόλεμον πυκιναὶ κίνυντο φάλαγγες
> κυάνεαι, σάκεσίν τε καὶ ἔγχεσι πεφρικυῖαι.
> καὶ τοὺς μὲν γήθησεν ἰδὼν κρείων Ἀγαμέμνων,
> καί σφεας φωνήσας ἔπεα πτερόεντα προσηύδα·

So he spoke, and Atreides, cheerful at heart, went onward.
On his way through the thronging men he came to the Aiantes.
These were armed, and about them went a cloud of foot-soldiers.
As from his watching place a goatherd watches a cloud move
on its way over the sea before the drive of the west wind;
far away though he be he watches it, blacker than pitch is,
moving across the sea and piling the storm before it,

---

6   Rubin 1995:48; on transformational thinking, see Paivio 1971:28–33.

and as he sees it he shivers and drives his flocks to a cavern;
so about the two Aiantes moved the battalions,
close-compacted of strong and god-supported young fighters,
black, and jagged with spear and shield, to the terror of battle.
Agamemnon the lord of men was glad when he looked at them,
and he spoke aloud to them and addressed them in winged words.

Iliad IV 272–284

This extended simile cannot be reduced to a nuclear simile of the type *target domain + simile marker + base domain*. The split of the simile marker into ὡς δ' ὅτε and τοῖαι, coupled with two hypothesized domains, a base domain in the first part and a target domain in the second, transforms the epic simile into a bilateral one. The use of multiple images (a goatherd in his lookout, a black cloud over the sea piling a storm around it, the goatherd driving his flock to a cavern), the shifting perspectives (goatherd-cloud-goatherd-cloud), the elliptical nature of the landscapes evoked, the technique of paratactic visual syntax (analogous to the λέξις εἰρομένη), and finally the vividness of the colors (an essential aspect of space),[7] all suggest that this is a universe of revisited landscapes, comprising multiple memory images stored in the mind, which the narrator and audience know from common experience. This is not only the result of the inbuilt picture-ability of the Homeric simile; it also reenacts a mental process of transformational thinking that is typical of oral traditions, where the storyteller's mind constantly changes visual locations. When he decides to rein in his pictorial overabundance, he returns to his narrative, indicating the change of register to his audience by introducing the target domain. Bilaterality is indeed present, but it transcends the verbal constraints of its native register and amounts to a split between two paths of visual representation, traditionally known as narrative and extended simile.

Together with this, I would argue that bilaterality must be interpreted within the framework of transformational thinking, which requires a swift movement from one visual snapshot to another. The use of space as a cue for recall is inherently associated with the process the narrator's mind follows in visualizing the micronarrative of a Homeric simile. By beginning always *in medias res*, he makes full use of traditional imagery with which he and his audience are familiar; by leaving his "miniature" unfinished, he opts for suspension and ellipsis instead of cohesion and completeness. In the realm of transformational thinking, that is, visualizing the world of the narrative by transposing oneself into another register, most, if not all, of the rules of narrative collapse:

---

[7]   *Iliad* IV 277 μελάντερον ἠΰτε πίσσα 'blacker than pitch'.

there is no protagonist, no time, no plot; only vivid vistas of another world, where the mind's eye can temporarily wander before it is summoned back to the main narrative.

Complex expansions

In contrast with the nuclear simile, which is virtually a "closed" simile, Homeric poetry makes ample use of the *extended* simile, which is characterized by its openness. The typical structure of the nuclear simile, consisting of a base item, a target item, and a simile marker, assumes that storyteller and audience will be able to extract the most salient feature of the base item and extend it to the target item, even if this characteristic (the *tertium comparationis*) is not expressed. In this closed form of utterance or comparison, stating that the target item (e.g. Achilles) is like the base item (a lion), listeners are expected to realize that the most typical feature of the lion in this context is its ferocity, and apply it to Achilles. Ben-Porat has criticized this approach, arguing that its main deficiency lies in its reductiveness, since those endorsing it "must posit an earlier stage in the generation of such incomplete utterances by their authors, a stage in which the unexpressed attribute is present."[8]

In the world of the extended simile, openness is the rule. We should make clear from the beginning that we are dealing more with simile utterances, involving a search for transferable attributes and a mapping of whole domains,[9] than with selecting a single relational attribute on which the whole comparison relies. Viewed from this angle, internal expansions of the base domain create multiple domains that storyteller and listeners need to scan with their mind's eye, resulting—unavoidably but also tellingly—in the activation of many irrelevant features. In both narrative and extended similes, traditional referentiality is present not only on the formulaic but also on the thematic level. This "mnemonic flood" carries with it a number of details or aberrant features that deviate from the visual framework of the epic simile. It is exactly at this point that referential incompatibility becomes part of the very nature of the Homeric simile, whose openness reminds us of the importance of asymmetry and "estrangement" in tracing the cognitive process of interpreting it. Given that aberration and complex expansions constitute integral parts of the open simile, we shall now explore their function in a complex Iliadic example:

> Τρῶες δὲ προύτυψαν ἀολλέες, ἦρχε δ' ἄρ' Ἕκτωρ
> ἀντικρὺ μεμαώς, ὀλοοίτροχος ὣς ἀπὸ πέτρης,

---

[8] Ben-Porat 1992:745.
[9] Ben-Porat 1992:746.

ὅν τε κατὰ στεφάνης ποταμὸς χειμάρροος ὤσῃ,
ῥήξας ἀσπέτῳ ὄμβρῳ ἀναιδέος ἔχματα πέτρης,
ὕψι δ᾽ ἀναθρῴσκων πέτεται, κτυπέει δέ θ᾽ ὑπ᾽ αὐτοῦ
ὕλη· ὃ δ᾽ ἀσφαλέως θέει ἔμπεδον, ὄφρ᾽ ἂν ἵκηται
ἰσόπεδον· τότε δ᾽ οὔ τι κυλίνδεται, ἐσσύμενός περ.
ὣς Ἕκτωρ εἵως μὲν ἀπείλει μέχρι θαλάσσης
ῥέα διελεύσεσθαι κλισίας καὶ νῆας Ἀχαιῶν
κτείνων· ἀλλ᾽ ὅτε δὴ πυκινῇς ἐνέκυρσε φάλαγξιν,
στῆ ῥα μάλ᾽ ἐγχριμφθείς. οἳ δ᾽ ἀντίοι υἷες Ἀχαιῶν
νύσσοντες ξίφεσίν τε καὶ ἔγχεσιν ἀμφιγύοισιν
ὦσαν ἀπὸ σφείων, ὃ δὲ χασσάμενος πελεμίχθη.

The Trojans came down on them in a pack, and Hektor led them
raging straight forward, like a great rolling stone from a rock face
that a river swollen with winter rain has wrenched from its socket
and with immense washing broken the hold of the unwilling rock
    face;
  the springing boulder flies on, and the forest thunders beneath it;
  and the stone runs unwavering on a strong course, till it reaches
  the flat land, then rolls no longer for all its onrush;
  so Hektor for a while threatened lightly to break through
the shelters and ships of the Achaians and reach the water
cutting his way. But when he collided with the dense battalions
he was stopped, hard, beaten in on himself. The sons of the Achaians
against him stabbing at him with swords and leaf-headed spears
thrust him away from them so that he gave ground backward,
    staggering.

Iliad XIII 136–148

This extended simile is a typical example of how expanding the base domain can create a level of complexity that virtually defies compactness and imme-diate directionality. The base domain comprises three smaller domains, which are better examined as they come into existence instead of being seen as parts of a coherent whole.

The base domain begins by offering a view of Hektor, leading his army (a) "like a great rolling stone from a rock face / that a river swollen with winter rain has wrenched from its socket / and with immense washing broken the hold of the unwilling rock face."[10] Next, the base domain expands in another

---

[10] *Iliad* XIII 137–139 ὀλοοίτροχος ὣς ἀπὸ πέτρης, / ὅν τε κατὰ στεφάνης ποταμὸς χειμάρροος ὤσῃ, / ῥήξας ἀσπέτῳ ὄμβρῳ ἀναιδέος ἔχματα πέτρης.

direction by mentally mapping a different spatial aspect: from the sight of a stone breaking away from a cliff under the pressure of a swollen river, the story-teller now turns (b) to the forest thundering from the noise ("the springing boulder flies on, and the forest thunders beneath it").[11] He subsequently sees (c) the stone running "unwavering on a strong course, till it reaches / the flat land, then roll[ing] no longer for all its onrush."[12] The expansion of the base domain has not only created multiple visual domains which the audience is invited to view, but also led to a rather unpredicted result for the narrative to follow: when the narrator began uttering his simile, he had probably visualized the steady movement of a rolling stone; but since his visualization was done "on the fly," it generated other visualizations in succession. "Carried away" from his point of departure (the rolling stone), the storyteller mentally arrived at a different destination, namely the stone's stopping on the flat land. The complex expansion of the base domain led unavoidably to the need for a new mapping of the target domain, whence its expansion by the storyteller to six whole lines (*Iliad* XIII 143–148).

Details are also important not only as traces of incompatibility but also as signs of asymmetry and visual "estrangement." Let us consider the beginning of the base domain. What is the function of the visualization of Hektor not simply as a rolling stone but "as a rolling stone wrenched from its socket and broken from an unwilling rock face because of the immense washing of a river swollen with winter rain"? Why is the rock "unwilling," the river "swollen with winter rain," the stone part of "a rock face"? In order to answer these questions, we could engage, as scholars have often done, in sophisticated interpretive techniques and innovative literary interpretations. It is not my purpose to deny all that, but to shed light on a different aspect of this issue. Details may also, at least at times and at least some of them, be *irrelevant*. Their irrelevance, not to speak of pure incompatibility, stems from the constraints exerted upon us by our belief that the nuclear simile represents the default mode of comparison, that its closedness and compactness, its stillness and solidity, represent the idea of perfection. In Homeric epic, asymmetry is relevant from the perspective of oral poetics. The details of the unwilling rock, the river swollen with winter rain, and the rolling stone that forms part of a rock face are spatial elements of the narrator's visualization of a rolling stone. They come up in the process of his mental imaging of the stone, because it has to be "placed" somewhere in his mind's eye. Like all human beings, he recalls images of familiar things not on their own, but *within a given space*. In this light, the rolling stone is mentally

---

[11]   *Iliad* XIII 140–141 ὕψι δ' ἀναθρῴσκων πέτεται, κτυπέει δέ θ' ὑπ' αὐτοῦ / ὕλη.
[12]   *Iliad* XIII 141–142 ὃ δ' ἀσφαλέως θέει ἔμπεδον, ὄφρ' ἂν ἵκηται / ἰσόπεδον· τότε δ' οὔ τι κυλίνδεται, ἐσσύμενός περ.

"anchored" both to a rock face, which resists ("unwilling") the breaking off of the stone, and to a river, not any river but one that exerts enormous force to break the stone from the rock, because it is swollen by the rain. All these details that particularize and concretize space stem from its role as a cue for recall and visualization. They may be, or seem, asymmetrical with the kernel of the comparison, but our simile utterance extends well beyond that level of inter-pretation. Spatial minutiae of the sort described above are strong evidence of the storyteller's *eusynoptic* view, and testify to the vividness and clarity of visual imagery.

Mapping inconsistency between the target and base domains

The extended Homeric simile or simile utterance, as we have seen, has specific comparative features, but "is not necessarily consistent when it comes to the process of mapping its domains."[13] Let us consider the following example, and then attempt to explain the origins and function of inconsistency between the target domain and base domain:

> οἵη δ' ἐκ νεφέων ἐρεβεννὴ φαίνεται ἀήρ
> καύματος ἔξ, ἀνέμοιο δυσαέος ὀρνυμένοιο,
> τοῖος Τυδείδῃ Διομήδεϊ χάλκεος Ἄρης
> φαίνεθ' ὁμοῦ νεφέεσσιν, ἰὼν εἰς οὐρανὸν εὐρύν.

> As when out of the thunderhead the air shows darkening
> after a day's heat when the stormy wind uprises,
> thus to Tydeus' son Diomedes Ares the brazen
> showed as he went up with the clouds into the wide heaven.

> *Iliad* V 864–867

This simile has puzzled interpreters. Its lack of clarity has been effectively summarized by Moulton:

> The dark air rising after a day's heat and the stirring wind almost lead us to expect a storm; yet the departure of Ares represents the passing of a threat to Diomedes and the Greeks, from whose point of view the description is given. The best way to understand the comparison is probably to equate Ares' disappearance with the dissolution of the clouds in the sky after a thunderstorm; this is supported by the detail of Ares surrounded with clouds at 867. If we compare the image with the simile at 522, we note the following: Diomedes is connected with

---

[13]   Ben-Porat 1992:748.

both (519 and 866); in the first the clouds are stationary and the winds calm (522–525), while in the second the wind is rising (865) and Ares moves up into the sky with the clouds (867); both images allude to dark clouds of storm (525–526, 864). Variation of the same motifs, and the placement of the similes in the narrative movement, warrant consideration of these images as an associated pair.[14]

Moulton's line of argument abides by the interpretive approach he takes in his monograph. Association of images obscures simile-internal inconsistencies. As I have argued, similes operate in visual blocks, on the basis of common mnemonic anchors like spatial references, but as far as their internal consistency is concerned they tend to defy macroscopic connections of the sort Moulton points to. Conversely, it could be plausibly argued that first, it is not only "Diomedes [who] is connected with both (519 and 866)," as Moulton argues, since in the first case it is the two Ajaxes, Odysseus, and Diomedes who are compared to stationary clouds, and second, the wind-cloud simile of 522–527 belongs to the same visual unit as a preceding wind–threshing floor simile (499–505), both of them visualizing the Achaeans' standing firm against the Trojan onslaught.

The simile under discussion is a typical example of mapping inconsistency between the base domain (which comes first) and the target domain, based on the fact that "the formal simile compares the *heads* of the respective parts explicitly, by using the split simile marker"[15] and not the base and target domains. What is really assimilated is the darkening air and brazen Ares, that is, the semantic topics of the base domain and target domain. The heads of these two domains reflect the base item and target item of a nuclear simile. In other words, were we to reduce this extended simile to a nuclear simile, it would have the form "brazen Ares" (target item) is like (simile marker) "darkening air" (base item). What would have been the target and base items of a nuclear simile that would function as a complete comparative structure have now become heads of entire spatial domains that appear in reverse order, the target domain coming first and the base domain following. This is not to say that extended similes have come into being from nuclear similes by the generative process of expansion. I have simply referred to the nuclear simile in order to show the limited comparative scope of the epic simile.[16]

---

14   Moulton 1977:63.
15   Ben-Porat 1992:748.
16   Critics have emphasized that a successful simile may compare in one aspect only, and that is all we need to achieve an effective comparison.

The question of the origins of this mapping inconsistency can be answered only by considering the way visual imagery evolves. The storyteller has visually paired the space of this simile on the basis of the blowing wind, which constitutes an effective cue to recall that is frequently used in Iliadic similes, for the wind combines various spatial aspects such as sound, movement, and color (since it often changes the color of the clouds or the sea). The narrator, who has kept in his mind's eye the image of "Ares the brazen" (V 859, 866 χάλκεος Ἄρης), aims at creating equivalent spatial cues in both similes of the same visual unit. He therefore resorts to two spatial features, sound (859–860 "Ares the brazen bellowed with a sound as great as nine thousand men make, or ten thousand") and color (864: "as when out of the thunderhead the air shows darkening"), in order to see the god of war in his mind's eye. In fact, both these spatial features create the illusion of proximity, of "being there" on the battlefield like Diomedes and the rest of the Achaeans, listening to the great sound and looking at the darkening figure of Ares. Seen from this angle, the inconsistency between base and target domains in this wind simile is caused by the dynamic spatial nature of visual imagery, which evolves freely and transcends the fixed identities of the heads of the base and target domains.

The term "inconsistency" is useful mainly in discussing the dynamic spatial nature of the extended simile as a form of visual imagery. Visual imagery does not operate in a linear manner. Its telling combination of a low degree of compactness and consistency with a high degree of vividness and visual richness[17] may violate the rules of symmetry and complete relevance under which modern readers have been trained to read written literature, but it is the natural outcome of the visual cornucopia of imagery created and recalled in the mind's eye of the storyteller while performing his song.

Multiplied simile

The *multiplied simile* is a variant form of the epic simile, whose elliptical nature results from the blurring of target and base domains and the nontransferability of the simile marker.[18] By superimposing comparative structures, the oral storyteller creates a type of simile that defies almost all the rules governing the formal or nuclear simile. The role of key principles of recall, such as spatial organization and mental association and ordering of material, is paramount for the multiplied simile.[19]

---

[17] Ben-Porat 1992:750.

[18] See Ben-Porat 1992:748.

[19] On these principles, see Aristotle *On Memory and Reminiscence* 452a17–24; on order in image recall, see 451b10.

To explore in detail the form and function of superimposed space in multi-plied similes, let us focus our attention on an Iliadic example:

ὡς δ᾽ ὅτε πῦρ ἀΐδηλον ἐν ἀξύλῳ ἐμπέσῃ ὕλῃ,
πάντῃ τ᾽ εἰλυφόων ἄνεμος φέρει, οἳ δέ τε θάμνοι
πρόρριζοι πίπτουσιν ἐπειγόμενοι πυρὸς ὁρμῇ,
ὣς ἄρ᾽ ὑπ᾽ Ἀτρείδῃ Ἀγαμέμνονι πίπτε κάρηνα
Τρώων φευγόντων·

As when obliterating fire comes down on the timbered forest
and the roll of the wind carries it everywhere, and bushes
leaning under the force of the fire's rush tumble uprooted,
so before Atreus' son Agamemnon went down the high heads
of the running Trojans ...

Iliad XI 155–159

Every interpreter of this simile is vexed by the asymmetrical comparison between the heads of the anticipating base domain and the target domain that follows:[20] ὡς δ᾽ ὅτε πῦρ ἀΐδηλον—ὣς ... πίπτε κάρηνα / Τρώων φευγόντων· ("As when obliterating fire ... so ... the high heads / of the running Trojans"). When a listener hears the beginning of the extended simile, he starts to visualize the head of the base domain, the "obliterating fire," doing something ("coming down on the timbered forest": ἐν ἀξύλῳ ἐμπέσῃ ὕλῃ). By analogy, he expects the head of the target domain to be mapped onto it—that is, to be doing something similar. Surprisingly enough, and despite the use of the same verbal form that was employed for the head of the base domain (πίπτε κάρηνα / Τρώων φευγόντων), the head of the target domain is different altogether, namely the actual heads (κάρηνα) of the running Trojans instead of Agamemnon's. The heads of the simile's two spatial domains, the base domain and the target domain, "should" normally be symmetrical with respect to syntactic position and meaning, being as they are, figuratively speaking, at equal distance from the simile marker. In this case, there is a clear blurring between heads, which unavoidably results in the tempting illusion of fusion between spatial boundaries. Since members of the audience must have readily assumed that Agamemnon, who was emphatically mentioned just before the beginning of the simile (lines 153–154), is to be compared with "obliterating fire," it is plausible to say that their subsequent confusion may have resulted from the fact that the inconsistency of the two heads has generated the chiastic connection between two nuclear similes included in this multiplied simile:

---

[20]   I follow the type of analysis of Ben-Porat 1992.

Target Domain	Simile Marker	Base Domain
(1) Agamemnon is	like	fire
(2) the heads of the Trojans are	like	bushes

Because of the chiastic connection of the two verbalized spatial domains (the "fire" that is the base domain of the first nuclear simile with the "heads of the Trojans" that are the target domain of the second), listeners are inclined to cross-link the other two spatial domains ("Agamemnon" and the "bushes"), which are half-verbalized but readily hypothesized due to analogy.[21] The result is a striking paradox: the listeners are tempted to assume that the comparison is between the verbalized heads of a single simile containing one base domain and one target domain, the fire and the heads of the Trojans. They are, therefore, confused by the illogical assumption that "the heads of the Trojans are like fire," and the even more illogical inference that "Agamemnon is like bushes."

The spatial blurring of the domains of different nuclear similes, accompanied by the inconsistent spatial mapping of their respective heads, is caused by the fact that the narrator is "carried away" in the process of visualization. In particular, the mental image that comes last (the bushes as a base domain) guides the storyteller in visualizing its corresponding target domain (the heads of the Trojans), to which is subordinated the symmetrically and logically equivalent target domain (Agamemnon) that corresponds to the first mental image (fire) of the base domain. In other words, the last image contained in the first spatial domain, the base domain "fire" (θάμνοι / πρόρριζοι πίπτουσιν ἐπειγόμενοι πυρὸς ὁρμῇ ["bushes / leaning under the force of the fire's rush tumble uprooted"]), creates a mental route that leads the storyteller to a semantically, syntactically, and grammatically (plurals) analogous target domain, despite the fact that the latter belongs to a different nuclear simile.

Having suggested a possible explanation for the blurring of target and base domains belonging to different similes within the structure of a multiplied simile, we may now explore some of its functions; for whatever the mental process of its creation, it represents a prominent trademark of the poetic grammar of Homeric poetry, and as such it belongs to the deep structure of the epic.

In order to interpret analogical reasoning, which stands at the basis of similes, people are expected to make judgments based on symmetry. To this

---

[21] This link is made smoother by the use of the same verb (ἔπιπτον) for the bushes, the fire in the forest (ἐμπέσηι), and the heads of the Trojans (πίπτε).

end, they select what Tversky[22] calls a "feature space" or a "frame of reference," and then assume a resemblance between the subject and its referent. Notwithstanding such one-to-one analogies, the Homeric narrator selects a space where the referent is placed, and then associates the referent with other shifting spaces. Space is thus conceived as a way of mentally contextualizing a referent that is presented by means of specific manifestations of its existence or activity. But what is it that determines which features or aspects of the referent the narrator selects? Its applicability to the subject, Tversky says, though this is not really valid for the extended Homeric similes, since their general comparative structure involves not a subject and a referent, but particular activities or situations of the subject and the referent, or as with the multiplied simile a chiastic relation between subjects and referents.[23] In fact, the whole process is even more complicated: not only a single activity or situation of the subject is compared, and not only a single activity or situation of the referent is evoked. Situational multifariousness is accentuated by pictorial multiformity and an ongoing processing of mental images in ever-shifting spatial frames.

In *Iliad* XI 155–159, the audience is helped to visualize Agamemnon's killing Trojans through the movement of obliterating fire carried everywhere by the wind in a timbered forest. Then, the simile captures a part of the forest and some bushes, leaning under the force of the fire. The reference to the timbered forest and the uprooted bushes takes any listener on a short visual tour of the place where this snapshot occurs. The storyteller does not provide his audience with information about the cause of the fire, nor will he inform them of its end result. He has only captured a snapshot, a given moment or series of moments of what could have been a plotline. In other words, we are suddenly situated in the middle of a brief story, not knowing how it began or how it will end. What matters is *suspense, incompleteness,* and *indeterminacy.* As if this were not enough, the narrator shuns the symmetrical mapping of the heads of his two nuclear similes, adding confusion, asymmetry, and inconsistency to the mental tableau he has painted for his audience. From this perspective, multiplied similes present snapshots of a world that takes human attention by storm. By defying most of the rules of epic narrative, it challenges the audience, who are temporarily faced with an alternative mode of expression within the set of constraints imposed by epic song. An almost lyric tone emerges,[24] as if the

---

[22]   Tversky (quoted in Ortony 1979a:189).

[23]   Cf. the remark of the ancient grammarian Trypho (*On Tropes* [ed. L. Spengel] 3.201.17–26: παραβολή ἐστι λόγος διὰ παραθέσεως ὁμοίου πράγματος <u>τὸ ὑποκείμενον μετ' ἐνεργείας παριστάνων</u> ("The simile is speech that refers to a similar thing and *represents the subject while performing some activity*").

[24]   On detecting a number of formal features common to Homeric similes and lyric poetry with respect to diction and meter, see Martin 1997. Martin's suggestion can be further strengthened

storyteller "turns on the switch," and the space of the battlefield disappears while the audience visualizes a space more akin to that of lyric poetry. I am not suggesting that the audience experiences this phenomenon as a generic shift, but that the register of the Homeric simile is tuned to a lyric instead of an epic note. By introducing snapshots of potential narratives *in medias res*, where beginning and end are systematically lacking[25] and pictorial richness blurs spatial levels, the narrator performs at the level of visualization what he does at the level of diction, and as has been suggested even of meter:[26] he marks his similes as special kind of song within the supergenre of Homeric epic, a song imbued with lyric overtones, and thus memorable and strongly pictureable for both himself and his audience.

Metaleptic space

The Homeric simile allows for a boundary-crossing experience,[27] into a different world that is visualized in vivid snapshots of action suspended *in medias res*. The similes enable the narrator to create a further spatial division of the typical dichotomy between the mental world of the narrative and that of the onto-logical and corporeal habitat of the real world. This time, the song itself intro-duces a new distinction, between the world of the narrative and that of the similes. Keeping the former dichotomy in mind, we can see the latter as its internal reflection: the audience is invited on a new journey, a novel mental *iter* to a new "space," the universe of the simile. The clear-cut demarcation of the simile, whose beginning and end are carefully delineated by deictic markers, bears a striking similarity to the very performance of epic song. The storyteller informs his audience that he is going to begin his song by invoking the Muse and asking for inspiration. In tandem with this explicit acknowledgment of

---

by revisiting a neglected, but very important, observation made by Hogan, according to whom forty hapaxes in the Iliadic similes are attested one or more times in the narrative parts of the *Odyssey* (1966:228–233). Unfortunately, Hogan interpreted this feature as a result of the tradi-tionality of Homeric diction. In my view, this observation may well be seen within the frame-work of the diffusion or dissemination of lyric features from Iliadic similes to the more "lyrical" Odyssean narrative. In other words, the lyrical tone that Martin detects in the similes tends to spread to the narrative of the more "lyrical" Odyssean version of epic song, which steadily moves away from the martial epic of the *Iliad*.

25 See Maehler 2004:21: "He [Bacchylides] tends to begin the narration in the middle of a myth, at a point from where its progression to the dramatic climax can already be anticipated."

26 See Martin 1997.

27 On the history and use of the term μετάληψις 'sharing' by ancient rhetoricians and grammar-ians, see F. Wagner 2002:235–237; de Jong 2009:88 and n5. On modern discussions of metalepsis, see Genette 1980:234–237, 1988:58–59; McHale 1987; Herman 1997; Nelles 1997; F. Wagner 2002; Fludernik 2003a; Genette 2004; Pier and Schaeffer 2005; on metalepsis in Homeric epic, see de Jong 2009.

the metaliterary aspect of oral song-making, the narrator attempts to liberate his listeners from the spatiotemporal bonds of their ontological life and transport them to a different mental world. Likewise, when introducing a simile, the storyteller changes register: he temporarily stops referring to the world of the plot, carries his listeners over the mental boundaries[28] that he has constructed for them while performing his epic song, and attempts to create a new spatiotemporal framework, a mental landscape which they are invited to explore. By following this strategy he is able to put the process of "escapism" in the limelight. "Estrangement" is not only the result of the blurring of the spatial domains of two nuclear similes within the visual framework of a multiplied simile, but also the by-product of realizing the dichotomy between the world of the narrative and that of the similes. The latter of course evoke familiar mental images, but at the same time they remind the audience of the gap that separates the realm of the narrative from the ontological sphere of the real world. While the very performance of epic song carries the listeners to a distant world (both temporally and spatially), that of the epic heroes of Troy, the internal mirroring of this technique on the shifting registers of narrative and simile allows the narrator to invite his audience to return to the mental images of the natural world, the world they inhabit ontologically. This metaleptic effect of the simile is not so much author- but performance-oriented. In the oral universe of Homeric poetry, audience immersion, for all its resemblance to readerly immersion, taps into the very nature of performance: the simile capitalizes on the fundamental realities of oral singing and mirrors internally the basic dichotomy between reality and song, allowing the audience to comprehend and evaluate for themselves the futile "escapism" of the art of epic poetry. By relativizing the medium, the narrator engages his listeners in a process of revealing the fact that like the simile, the poetry of the *Iliad* enhances the sameness, or at least the approximation, of human nature and human fate.

The crucial role of space in the metaleptic aspect of the Homeric simile can be better evaluated by considering the following observations:

---

[28] See Ryan 1990:874: "The narrative can cross a boundary, by selecting the 'here' and 'now' of the other side as points of reference, or can simply look through boundaries, by revealing what is beyond the line from the perspective of this side of the line. In this second case, the crossing of the boundary is only virtual." Addison applies this observation to the Homeric simile: "This distinction is helpful in indicating what happens to the reader's central focus as similes are extended. Whereas many short similes invite only a 'virtual' crossing of their boundaries, longer, especially Homeric-type, similes attempt to seduce the reader into a 'real' crossing, one that reorientates him/her into a different universe from that of the main story or discourse. Just as 'literalness' and 'figurativeness' are variable qualities, so some crossings may be 'more real' or 'more virtual' in comparison with others" (Addison 2001:499). See also Addison 1993.

(1) Extended similes have more space to develop, allowing for "more real" boundary crossings by listeners, in richer and more developed worlds of the base domain, where the audience can mentally stay longer.

(2) When the simile is introduced, there is a moment of oscillation, of spatial hesitation[29] between the space of the main narrative and the location of the short narrative included in the base domain.[30] As the base domain evolves, the piling up of "modifiers" enhancing specificity and contextuality weakens narrative echoes, in an ongoing effort to immerse the audience in a spatially new visual realm.[31] Despite the effect of these modifiers, the transition from narrative to simile is strongly felt, not so much sequentially as spatially.

(3) The digressive aspect of the Homeric simile constitutes a narrative strategy, according to which extradiegetic base domains can "expatiate freely." The term "digression," of course, is based on the narrative sequence and evolution of the plot. It presupposes a notion of linearity, from which there can be deviations. But the simile can hardly have such an effect, for its register is distinct from that of the narrative. Unlike other aspects of Homeric narrative, such as the mythological example,[32] the simile does not have protagonists nor does it refer to myth: it is devoid of names and distinctive "individualized" agents. It constitutes not a paranarrative but a paratopic space, a place to which the narrator invites his audience, a universe without all the mental images created for the Iliadic narrative. Its clearly demarcated boundaries are not just a surface element of how the pictorial world of the simile is verbalized, but also, and significantly so, a metaleptic hint to the very performance of the song.[33]

The metaleptic aspect of the Homeric simile is sometimes alluded to by its very content. In *Iliad* XV 80–84, the swift journey of Hera to Olympos is compared with the speed of thought in the mind of a traveler, who "sees" places before actually going there. This is a very interesting example of the relationship between space and mental visualization, the more so since it is attested

---

[29] On hesitation, see the discussion at "*Androktasiai*" in chapter 1 above; see also Fränkel 1921:104.

[30] See Fränkel 1921:104: "Wenn der Sänger neben ein Stück der epischen Erzählung ein Gleichnis stellte, so schwebte seine Phantasie in einem Spannungszustand zwischen zwei verschiedenen, aber ähnlichen Bildern."

[31] See Addison 2001.

[32] On the difference between the strongly temporal aspect of the example and the spatial dimension of the simile, see *Rhetorica anonyma*, "Prolegomena in artem rhetoricam" 6.34.26, and the discussion at the beginning of part 3 above.

[33] On the poetics of the Homeric simile, see Nimis 1987:23–95.

in an oral epic like the *Iliad*. Given that "Homeric epic refers to itself as a *path* (οἴμη),"[34] this simile has an almost metapoetic coloring, since the traveler resembles the epic storyteller who travels along the path of song and "thinks of things in the mind's awareness, 'I wish I were this place, or this,' and imagines many things" (XV 81–82). Another illustration of the epic simile's metaleptic effect is that of the "spearcast." Cognitive psychologists have proved that "measuring"[35] distance or size by way of drawings is faster and more effective than by means of words.[36] Moreover, as the storyteller's constant recourse to the image of the spearcast in "measuring" similes shows (e.g. XV 358–359), performance can achieve greater precision and clarity by repeatedly creating a mental image of an event or action.[37] In other words, the reiterated imaging of the distance covered by a spearcast is not only an effective way of visualizing an action presented in the narrative, but also may have helped the narrator improve his performance by picturing the course of his narrative in advance.[38]

Despite appearances reinforced by sets of formulaic and metrical constraints, epic song is a multilayered web, characterized by various interwoven registers. The extended simile, like ecphrasis and catalogue, is an example of how the mental organization of space may also have a metaleptic aspect, reminding the audience of the fictionality of the epic song during the long hours of its performance.

Hypertextual Space

Hypertext facilitates access to material in any order and in various forms (auditory, graphic, textual, or a combination of all three), challenging hierarchy and promoting multilinearity.[39] By allowing for a number of effects that simple

---

[34]   Rubin 1995:62.
[35]   On similes and measurement, see Scott 1974:20–24.
[36]   Paivio 1975.
[37]   See also Shepard 1978.
[38]   See Neisser 1983. Improved performance is a desideratum for singers in oral traditions. This is a vast topic, the study of which requires a careful consideration of both ends of the communicative process. Singers no doubt measured their own performance skills and tried to improve them, but the choices they made, or at least some of them, may have been determined by audience expectations. Although the Panhellenic scope of Homeric epic would tend to obscure local differences, considering the "needs" of particular audiences may have guided the storyteller in making some choices. Oral corrections are often a feature of song, stemming from the storyteller's need for positive evaluation from his audience. Improvement of performance is also a key aspect of rhapsodic competition; see D. Collins 2001.
[39]   On hypertext and literary theory, see Delany and Landow 1991; Hawisher and Selfe 1991; Joyce 1991; Kaplan 1991; Landow 1997; Kveim 1998; Gibson and Oviedo 2000; Joyce 2000; Joyce 2002; on "Homeric hypertextuality," see Kahane 1997; Bakker 2001; Landow 2006:69–124; Tsagalis 2008b:272–285, 2010a.

narrative is unable to offer, the Homeric simile displays some of these hyper-textual features. In order to make this point clearer, I will explore a series of aspects of hypertextual space, through various examples comparing the effects of narrative segments with those of their accompanying similes.[40]

Aural hypertextuality

Hypertext editions of books now contain even audio links, which allow readers to listen to a song or a performance of a whole musical composition. For example, an e-book on Beethoven may contain, apart from information about his life and music, actual performances of some of his symphonies and other musical pieces in the form of links that can be activated by the reader with a simple click of the mouse. It should be noted that such a hypertext edition is different from a modern printed book on the same topic that may be accompanied by a CD of Beethoven's music. The difference lies in the fact that the auditory material is hypertextually linked, and in this way built in to the e-book, whereas it is exter-nally added to the printed book.[41]

Similarly, sound as a spatial aspect of the Homeric simile may function as a "hypertext link" for the audience. The clamor and hubbub of battle, the shouting of the troops and other sound effects of the narrative, can be linked in the listeners' minds to more familiar sounds from the world of nature. The latter work in the manner of hypertext nodes that activate audio segments: the audience can thus "hear" the sound of battle by imagining the sound of the sea waves; they can listen to the noise made by the body of a falling warrior by recalling the sound of a falling tree. As with hypertext editions, spatial sound-links are only partly under the author's control. In oral verse-making, although the narrator decides where to insert such links, and to this extent predeter-mines for his audience the material available to them, listeners decide for them-selves about the particulars of their mental representation of sound:[42] some may hear in their minds a louder sound, others a longer one, while others may even keep this spatial aspect in their minds long after the completion of the simile, reactivating it at will in other similar narrative circumstances, even without recourse to any other such simile. This overriding of narrative constraints is due to the effective function of the spatial aspect of sound, both a strong cue for memory recall and a dynamic means of aural hypertextuality, at the disposal of both storyteller and audience.

---

[40] On space and hypertextuality, see Bolter 1991; Strate 2000.
[41] On orality and electronic editions, see Foley 2005.
[42] See J. Lee 1996.

Tagging and annotating narrative space

Similes help listeners mentally visualize, and therefore comprehend, what is going on in the narrative, as if reading an encyclopedia or dictionary. Mental viewing of narrative snapshots is "visually explained" by examples of vivid imagery contained in the similes. To this extent, the example offered by a modern dictionary is valid. Let us take the entry "crew" from Oxford's *Advanced Learner's Dictionary*:

> **crew** /kruː/ n [CGp] **1(a)** all the people working on a ship, an aircraft, etc: *The ship had a crew of 60.* / *All the passengers and crew survived the crash.* **(b)** all these people except the officers: *the officers and crew of the SS Neptune.* **(c)** a rowing team: *a member of the Cambridge crew.* **2** a group of people working together: *a camera/film crew* / *an ambulance crew.* **3** (usu *derog*) a group of people: *The people she'd invited were a pretty **motley** crew.*

The entry contains information organized in multiple levels: headword and pronunciation, classification of the word *crew* according to traditional grammatical categories (noun), and meanings separated by numbers or, when closely related, by letters. Sometimes (though not in this example) the standard American pronunciation and spelling of the entry are given (when different from British English), as well as cross-references to related or contrasted words. Let us now consider a series of extended similes belonging to the same visual unit:

ὡς δ' ὅτ' ἀφ' ὑψηλῆς κορυφῆς ὄρεος μεγάλοιο
κινήσῃ πυκινὴν νεφέλην στεροπηγερέτα Ζεύς,
ἔκ τ' ἔφανεν πᾶσαι σκοπιαὶ καὶ πρώονες ἄκροι
καὶ νάπαι, οὐρανόθεν δ' ἄρ' ὑπερράγη ἄσπετος αἰθήρ,
ὣς Δαναοὶ νηῶν μὲν ἀπωσάμενοι δήιον πῦρ
τυτθὸν ἀνέπνευσαν· πολέμου δ' οὐ γίνετ' ἐρωή·

> And as when from the towering height of a great mountain Zeus
> who gathers the thunderflash stirs the cloud dense upon it,
> and all the high places of the hills are clear and the shoulders
>   out-jutting
> and the deep ravines, as endless bright air spills from the heavens,
> so when the Danaans had beaten from their ships the ravening
> fire, they got breath for a little, but there was no check in the
>   fighting.

Iliad XVI 297–302

ὡς δὲ λύκοι ἄρνεσσιν ἐπέχραον ἠ' ἐρίφοισιν
σίνται, ὕπεκ μήλων αἱρεόμενοι, αἵ τ' ἐν ὄρεσσιν
ποιμένος ἀφραδίῃσι διέτμαγεν, οἳ δὲ ἰδόντες
αἶψα διαρπάζουσιν ἀνάλκιδα θυμὸν ἐχούσας,
ὣς Δαναοὶ Τρώεσσιν ἐπέχραον· οἳ δὲ φόβοιο
δυσκελάδου μνήσαντο, λάθοντο δὲ θούριδος ἀλκῆς.

They as wolves make havoc among lambs or young goats in their
fury,
catching them out of the flocks, when the sheep separate in the
mountains
through the thoughtlessness of the shepherd, and the wolves seeing
them
suddenly snatch them away, and they have no heart for fighting;
so the Danaans ravaged the Trojans, and these remembered
the bitter sound of terror, and forgot their furious valour.

Iliad XVI 352–357

ὡς δ' ὅτ' ἀπ' Οὐλύμπου νέφος ἔρχεται οὐρανὸν εἴσω
αἰθέρος ἐκ δίης, ὅτε τε Ζεὺς λαίλαπα τείνῃ,
ὣς τῶν ἐκ νηῶν γένετο ἰαχή τε φόβος τε,
οὐδὲ κατὰ μοῖραν πέραον πάλιν.

As when a cloud goes deep up in the sky from Olympos
through the bright upper air when Zeus brings on the hurricane,
so rose from beside the ships their outcry, the noise of their terror.

Iliad XVI 364–367

These three extended similes constitute a single visual unit, which employs
the space of the mountains to help audience and storyteller specify and mentally
visualize the fierce fighting next to the ships between Achaeans and Trojans.
Particular details constitute a form of visual annotation of the "spatial entry"
"fighting next to the ships." The use of three similes accompanying the action
in the same location sheds light on distinct levels of the same visual entry and
clarifies all its different aspects.

Like the headword and pronunciation at the beginning of all entries in a
standard dictionary, all three similes begin by indicating the head of their base
domain (cloud/wolves/cloud). Moreover, as a dictionary intended for speakers
of both American and British English also gives the standard American pronunciation and spelling when it differs from British English, the similes try to cater

to different audiences and even different members of the same audience; for this reason they aim at widening the scope of potential visualizations by presenting their audience with alternatives. In this light, the shift between cloud/wolves/cloud in the heads of the three similes and the alternatives lambs/young goats in the second stand for different simile-visualizations of the same location in the narrative, just as differences in spelling represent morphological or phonological variations of the same verbal item.

Similes include visual classification according to space, just as dictionaries classify entries according to traditional grammatical categories ("crew": noun). All three similes cited above, offering mental views of the space of the mountains, belong to a larger category of similes, usually accompanying fighting scenes that take place in the mountains.

In a typical dictionary entry, meanings are separated by numbers, or when closely related by letters. Such grouping of meaning is paralleled in the similes by grouping of space: the mountains function like the letter-based division in a dictionary entry, indicating that these three similes are spatially and visually related. The entry "crew" quoted above contained a number of examples of the various senses or nuances of the word "crew." What examples regularly do is to encapsulate a new term within a verbal chain consisting of easily recognizable words that the reader is expected to know. Examples where the new term is placed next to other difficult terms, potentially unknown to readers, would be unsuitable, and for this reason dictionary compilers systematically avoid them. Likewise, the three aforementioned similes rely on the familiar space of nature, and employ images that can be visualized with clarity and precision by the audience. In this way the mental viewing of a new scene occurring in the narrative (the fighting by the ships) begins to become clear in the listeners' minds.[43]

Sometimes similes contain visualizations of related locations or aspects of a given scene, more or less in the manner of dictionary entries that include cross-references to related words. In the simile of the wolves cited above, the "thoughtlessness of the shepherd" and the lack of resistance on the part of the sheep attacked by wolves constitute visual cross-references to other "visual entries" where the same kind of scene is presented. One such case may be the following:

ὄφρα μὲν αἰγίδα χερσὶν ἔχ' ἀτρέμα Φοῖβος Ἀπόλλων,
τόφρα μάλ' ἀμφοτέρων βέλε' ἥπτετο, πῖπτε δὲ λαός·

---

[43] Sometimes dictionary entries are accompanied by visual illustrations in order to clarify a given term to the reader. To this extent, space-familiar images in the similes seem to correspond to the visual illustrations in standard dictionaries.

αὐτὰρ ἐπεὶ κατ' ἐνῶπα ἰδὼν Δαναῶν ταχυπώλων
σεῖσ', ἐπὶ δ' αὐτὸς ἄϋσε μάλα μέγα, τοῖσι δὲ θυμόν
ἐν στήθεσσιν ἔθελξε, λάθοντο δὲ θούριδος ἀλκῆς.
οἳ δ' ὥς τ' ἠὲ βοῶν ἀγέλην ἢ πῶϋ μέγ' οἰῶν
θῆρε δύω κλονέωσι μελαίνης νυκτὸς ἀμολγῷ
ἐλθόντ' ἐξαπίνης σημάντορος οὐ παρεόντος,
ὣς ἐφόβηθεν Ἀχαιοὶ ἀνάλκιδες· ἐν γὰρ Ἀπόλλων
ἧκε φόβον, Τρωσὶν δὲ καὶ Ἕκτορι κῦδος ὄπαζεν.

So long as Phoibos Apollo held stilled in his hands the aegis,
so long the thrown weapons of both took hold, and men dropped
  under them.
But when he stared straight into the eyes of the fast-mounted
  Danaans
and shook the aegis, and himself gave a great baying cry, the spirit
inside them was mazed to hear it, they forgot their furious valour.
And they, as when in the dim of black night two wild beasts
stampede a herd of cattle or big flock of sheep, falling
suddenly upon them, when no herdsman is by, the Achaians
fled so in their weakness and terror, since Apollo drove
terror upon them, and gave the glory to the Trojans and Hektor.

Iliad XV 318–327

Note how the expressions ποιμένος ἀφραδίῃσι ("through the thoughtlessness of the shepherd"; XVI 354) and οἳ δὲ φόβοιο / δυσκελάδου μνήσαντο, λάθοντο δὲ θούριδος ἀλκῆς ("and these remembered / the bitter sound of terror, and forgot their furious valour"; 356–357) represent cross-references to the "visual entries" σημάντορος οὐ παρεόντος ("when no herdsman is by"; XV 325) and τοῖσι δὲ θυμόν / ἐν στήθεσσιν ἔθελξε, λάθοντο δὲ θούριδος ἀλκῆς ("the spirit / inside them was mazed to hear it, they forgot their furious valour"; XV 321–322) in the narrator's mind.

In this respect, the similes constitute a highly dynamic, hypertextual dictionary, which aims at creating visual annotations of mentally uncharted locations mentioned in the narrative. The storyteller, and to a large extent the tradition he represents, have compiled this interactive system of tags and references by means of mental spatial paths. Seen from this angle, the extended simile paves the way for continuous navigation within a rich referential system of vistas that can be superimposed on the main narrative, and therefore activated and deactivated, at the storyteller's will.

Reclaiming authority: Space, similes, and the hypertext

> By keying the audience on a narrative register distinct from the
> external narrative, the similes allow the audience to participate in a
> dynamic interplay with their own experiential universe, which consists
> of multiple image-mappings, both converging on and diverging from
> the visualization suggested by any given simile. As a set of allusions to
> and comments on the story, similes constitute an elaborate, memory-
> oriented cognitive mechanism, allowing the audience to "look" outside
> the narrative window and to enjoy the imagistic richness of their own
> ability to construct pictures.[44]

This is how I have summarized in a recent work the hypertextual function of
similes, which allow the audience to "*erase* and *(re)write* the oral palimpsest of
epic song."[45] The heavy experiential load of the extended simile, allowing for
multiple image-mappings and leading more often to an implicit (rather than
explicit) form of hypertextuality, sets the framework for reconsidering the
boundaries separating storyteller and audience.[46] Whereas the omniscient
external narrator retains complete authority over his narrative, similes present
the listener with the ability to visually *rewrite* space, and in this sense to claim
authorship.[47]

In order to explore the multiple ways this is effected within the delineated framework of the Homeric simile, I have adopted the following method: I
consider the various means the storyteller employs to create integration, specificity, and familiarity as indicative of his effort to control the audience's mental
navigation, to restrict and guide their imagination to the particular visualizations of space he actualizes in his similes.

One such method is that of *mapping alternatives*.[48] Plurality operates here as
visual disjunction, and therefore equilibrium, not as hypertextual multiplicity.
The storyteller maps alternative visualizations of some subentries of the base
domain, in order to limit his listeners' tendency to create their own mental

---

[44] Tsagalis 2008b:284–285.
[45] Tsagalis 2008b:285.
[46] See S. Richardson 1990:66; Minchin 2001:43.
[47] On "writing" space and hypertext, see Bolter 1991.
[48] Although *mapping alternatives* refers to different attributes, i.e. predicates with a single attribute (e.g. shape, size, color) and not to relations, i.e. predicates with two or more attributes (in
the manner of metaphors), similes also "feature rich source domain images which map onto or
match up with complex relations in the target," as Israel et al. emphasize (2004:131). On structure-mapping in similes, see Aisenman 1999.

images and thus deviate from the visual spaces he tries to chart for them. If he does not feel able to completely control their visualization, he resorts to limiting it to two or at most three alternatives. Let us consider the following examples:

ἠΰτε πορφυρέην ἶριν θνητοῖσι τανύσσῃ
Ζεὺς ἐξ οὐρανόθεν, τέρας ἔμμεναι ἢ πολέμοιο
ἢ καὶ χειμῶνος δυσθαλπέος, ὅς ῥά τε ἔργων
ἀνθρώπους ἀνέπαυσεν ἐπὶ χθονί, μῆλα δὲ κήδει,
ὣς ἡ πορφυρέη νεφέλη πυκάσασα ἓ᾽ αὐτήν
δύσετ᾽ Ἀχαιῶν ἔθνος, ἔγειρε δὲ φῶτα ἕκαστον.

As when in the sky Zeus strings for mortals the shimmering
rainbow, to be a portent and sign *of war, or of wintry
storm*, when heat perishes, such storm as stops mortals'
work upon the face of the earth, and afflicts their cattle,
so Athene shrouded in the shimmering cloud about her
merged among the swarming Achaians, and wakened each man.

Iliad XVII 547–552

οἴμησεν δὲ ἀλεὶς ὥς τ᾽ αἰετὸς ὑψιπετήεις,
ὅς τ᾽ εἶσιν πεδίονδε διὰ νεφέων ἐρεβεννῶν
ἁρπάξων ἢ ἄρν᾽ ἀμαλὴν ἢ πτῶκα λαγωόν·
ὣς Ἕκτωρ οἴμησε τινάσσων φάσγανον ὀξύ.

... he made his swoop, like a high-flown eagle
who launches himself out of the murk of the clouds in the flat land
to catch away *a tender lamb or a shivering hare*; so
Hektor made his swoop, swinging his sharp sword ...

Iliad XXII 308–311

In both these examples, the narrator aims at limiting his audience's multiple image-mappings by offering two alternatives for visualizing a rainbow "to be a portent and a sign" and the victims of the attack of an eagle respectively. In the first example, he indicates which of the two alternatives he would prefer them to visualize. By extending only the last of the alternatives (the wintry storm but not the war), he implicitly designates his preference, since it is this alternative that he further develops and furnishes with details, thus reinforcing its vividness and visualization. This technique can also involve visual variants of the head of the simile's base domain, especially where interchangeability has been conditioned by conventional context, a shared framed of reference for both audience and storyteller.[49]

Let me now turn to a single simile, one of the pictorial highlights of the entire *Iliad*, where three other techniques aimed at controlling image-mappings can be pinpointed and discussed:

τὸν δ' ὁ γέρων Πρίαμος πρῶτος ἴδεν ὀφθαλμοῖσιν,
<u>παμφαίνονθ' ὥς τ' ἀστέρ' ἐπεσσύμενον πεδίοιο,</u>
ὅς ῥά τ' ὀπώρης εἶσιν, ἀρίζηλοι δέ οἱ αὐγαί
φαίνονται πολλοῖσι μετ' ἀστράσι νυκτὸς ἀμολγῷ,
ὅν τε <u>κύν' Ὠρίωνος ἐπίκλησιν καλέουσιν·</u>
λαμπρότατος μὲν ὅ γ' ἐστί, κακὸν δέ τε σῆμα τέτυκται,
καί τε φέρει πολλὸν πυρετὸν δειλοῖσι βροτοῖσιν·
ὣς τοῦ χαλκὸς ἔλαμπε περὶ στήθεσσι θέοντος.

The aged Priam was the first of all whose eyes saw him
as he swept across the flat land in full shining, like that star
which comes on in the autumn and whose conspicuous brightness
far outshines the stars that are numbered in the night's darkening,
the star *they give the name of Orion's Dog*, which is brightest
among the stars, and yet is wrought as a sign of evil
and brings on the great fever for unfortunate mortals.
Such was the flare of the bronze that girt his chest in his running.

Iliad XXII 25–32

In order to limit variation and hypertextual activation of multiple spatial domains, the narrator insists on details that enhance specificity. Achilles is not like a star, but like a specific star that the storyteller presents in detail: it comes out in the autumn; its brightness surpasses all other stars in the darkest part of the night (νυκτὸς ἀμολγῷι);[50] finally it is a sign of great heat for mortals. Details such as these narrow the hypertextual horizon of image-mappings that the reference to a shining star opens to the audience, who would no doubt have conjured up many different images of a bright star in the night sky. These mental vistas are so familiar and powerful that they would tend to shape the listeners' perception of the given spatial imagery according to their own store

---

[49] See Muellner 1990:61–73 on two- and three-member groupings of simile-heads like "bees or wasps," "lions or boars," "geese, cranes, and swans," "eagle, vulture, or falcon," and "jackdaws, starlings, or rock-dove."

[50] On this formula, see Tsagalis 2008b:153–187.

of experiential details. It is exactly the direction of such pictureability that the storyteller intends to place under his control.

A less effective mechanism, employed only occasionally, is the use of proper names designating visually incontestable identities that are generally lacking in pictorial variations according to individual mnemonic ability and experience. A constellation evokes multiple mental icons in an individual's mind, but a specific star, Orion's Dog, would narrow the possibilities for visual variation significantly.[51]

Last, the storyteller avails himself of generalizing mechanisms from the simile's traditional dictional inventory. 'Ρα 'you see' and τε 'as you know', which are not often rendered in English by translators, channel the listeners' attention to the performance of epic song and remind them of their familiarity with the storyteller's suggested image-mapping. Their strong metaleptic effect accentuates their role as devices that create vividness (ἐνάργεια) and promote intimacy between storyteller and audience. In this way, the storyteller attempts to bring his listeners to the reality of the performance and keep them away from the distracting visual pathways created by the hypertextually plural world of their familiar mental space, with which the extended similes are replete.

Operating on a special spatial register that fully exploits the audience's knowledge of the natural world, the extended simile immerses listeners in a different mental cartography, where the narrator's suggested view does not necessarily coincide with the visualization of space evoked in each member of the audience, depending on his individual mnemonic inventory. Given the mental accessibility of the simile's content, listeners tend to follow their own navigational maps in the process of visual imaging. From the narrator's vantage point, the simile embodies his attempt to enrich the audience's view of the action, by adding to the description of the epic past an analogous, atemporal imagery that is shared by the average listener. This dissonance between the view suggested by the narrator and the multiple image-mappings of members of the audience creates a critical juncture that relativizes perspective: the simile, although it is an attempt to assimilate story space with a *paratopic space*, through its built-in pictureability leads to the creation of multiple mental spheres. Similes, after all, unlike their performers, cannot really be challenged.[52]

---

[51] The use of proper names is not the rule; cf. the following observations concerning the difference between example and simile (*Rhetorica anonyma* "Prolegomena in artem rhetoricam" 6.34.26): ὅτι τὸ μὲν παράδειγμα ἀπὸ προγεγονότων πραγμάτων παραλαμβάνεται· ἡ δὲ παραβολὴ ἐξ ἀορίστων καὶ ἐνδεχομένων γενέσθαι ("... that the example comes from things which *have happened before*, whereas the simile [comes from things] which are *indefinite and can happen*").

[52] This phrase plays upon Ong's claim, following Plato, that "books, unlike their authors, cannot really be challenged"; see Landow 1997:83.

PART FOUR

DESCRIPTIVE SPACE

DESCRIPTION CONSTITUTES A RATHER RESTRICTED MODE of discourse within Homeric poetry, where narration is preeminent.[1] In the *Iliad*, this unequal distribution between narration and description becomes even more obvious than in the *Odyssey*,[2] since descriptive passages, around twenty-four in number, refer to various objects that the characters of the plot have in their possession. It has been argued that "because the poet's descriptions of these small treasures render the items themselves memorable, the occasions with which they are associated remain in our memories also."[3] By offering his audience a description of these prized possessions, the poet brings the plot to a standstill, so as to bestow on his tale vividness, authenticity, and dramatic tension by temporarily prolonging or suspending its development.[4]

Taking my cue from the work of Elizabeth Minchin, who has emphasized the role of both visual memory and implicit knowledge in the way Homeric epic deals with descriptive segments, and was even able to identify a rough format (*summary description, workmanship, material, size/value, memorable feature, history*) that the oral storyteller employs in describing such valued objects, I will attempt to explore the function of perspective with respect to object-description and the method of organizing mnemonic formats. I will further argue that it is *spatial memory* that plays a pivotal role in activating specific mental formats, and that among other things the *size, color,* and *shape* of the object, or its *history,* constitute forms of spatial organization. I will also treat in detail, by focusing my attention on the shield of Achilles, the issue of ecphrastic space, which needs to be approached according to the framework of oral story-telling and the techniques employed by storytellers within the context of the performance. I will argue, therefore, that in this case the narrator uses the same technique he employs in the Homeric similes. The transition here from description into narration is similar to that from a simple comparison into a developed, extended simile. It is the workings of visual memory that enhance this shift, and in particular it is spatial memory, a powerful cue to recall, that creates the rich visual panorama of the shield of Achilles. In particular, I will maintain that the

---

[1]   See Genette 1969, who tried to overcome the dichotomy between narration and description by arguing that narration deals with objects and people in motion, while description with those in stasis. This approach has been strongly disputed; for a recent survey of previous research, see Dennerlein 2009:13–47 and 115–163. See also Riffaterre (1981:25), who has argued that description's "primary purpose is not to offer a representation, but to dictate an interpretation." Bal (1997:42–43) distinguishes six types of description: referential-encyclopaedic, referential-rhetorical, metaphorical metonymy, systematized metaphor, metonymic metaphor, and series of metaphors.
[2]   On hodological descriptions in the *Odyssey*, see Byre 1994b.
[3]   Minchin 2001:102.
[4]   See Tannen 1989:138–140; Rubin 1995:56 with further bibliography.

individual narrative snapshots of the shield are all drawn, more or less, from the same rich pictorial storehouse as the similes, and that they are based on equivalent devices of spatial memory.

7

Described Objects

IN THIS CHAPTER I will deal with the various spatial aspects of object description in the *Iliad*. The selected examples are chosen because these objects are described at some length, and are therefore most suitable for analysis and interpretation. In order to avoid unnecessary repetition, I have opted to discuss the different spatial aspects and techniques employed in describing objects, rather than examining each object separately. By adopting a "horizontal" rather than a "vertical" method of presenting and exploring the relevant material, I aim both at drawing some general conclusions about the function of "descriptive" passages within the medium of oral song and at exploring the role of spatial memory in the descriptive segments of the *Iliad*.

Drawing on the enormous progress that has been made in the fields of both cognitive science[1] and narratology of space,[2] I will adopt a working method that examines the following set of spatial aspects:

1. Position of the beholder (explicitly or implicitly expressed)

2. Diagrammatic iconicity

    A. Dynamic spatial description (movement of the object)

    B. Static spatial description

        i. Extrinsic perspective (stemming from its use)

        ii. Intrinsic perspective (unchangeable, e.g. a column, which always points to the notion of "verticality")

3. Mixed description

The list of objects that will be the litmus test of these categories includes the scepter of Agamemnon (*Iliad* I 234–239 and II 100–108), Helen's tapestry (III 125–128), Pandaros' bow (IV 105–111), the chariot of Hera (V 722–732), the aegis of Athena (V 738–742), the robe of Athena (VI 288–295), the helmet Meriones

---

[1]   See Zoran 1984; Minchin 2001:100–131.
[2]   See Wenz 1997; Dennerlein 2009:13–47, with further bibliography.

gives to Odysseus (X 261–271), the arms of Agamemnon (XI 16–46), the cup of Nestor (XI 628–635), the shield of Sarpedon (XII 294–297), the chest and cup of Achilles (XVI 221–227), Andromakhe's headdress (XXII 468–472), Asteropaios' breastplate (XXIII 560–562), Achilles' silver κρατήρ, given as second prize in the funeral games for Patroklos (XXIII 741–749), Priam's cup (XXIV 234–237), and the door-bolt of Achilles' hut (XXIV 453–456).

The thrust of my argument lies in the fact that in constructing descriptive passages, what the storyteller is doing is simply an extension of what we all do in everyday life. By exploring the function of spatial memory, we refrain from giving complete descriptions. On the contrary, we provide our audience with only that amount of information that will help them differentiate the described object from others of the same kind and picture it clearly in their minds. Homer, more or less like us, includes brief narrative chunks in his descriptions, so as to highlight the described object by bringing to the fore its manufacture or its history, that is, to give life to it.

The Position of the Beholder

The description of a prized object is presented from the position of either the narrator or a character. Position is important, for it often determines how the description will unfold. If the narrator or character is looking at an object from up close, as often with Iliadic prized objects, he can adopt a perimetrical description, since he is able to move (in his mind's eye) the object around itself or look at it from different angles; perimetrical visualization of an object can be enhanced by the use of deictic markers (*deixis ad oculos*) that accentuate the fact that the given object is described *in praesentia*, that is, while the narrator visualizes it as part of the scene he is narrating (and not as background setting), or while a character is actually using it, instead of just observing.

Agamemnon's scepter is described for the first time by Achilles in *Iliad* I:

> "ναὶ μὰ <u>τόδε</u> σκῆπτρον· τὸ μὲν οὔ ποτε <u>φύλλα καὶ ὄζους</u>
> φύσει, ἐπεὶ δὴ πρῶτα τομὴν <u>ἐν ὄρεσσι</u> λέλοιπεν,
> οὐδ' ἀναθηλήσει· περὶ γάρ ῥά ἑ χαλκὸς ἔλεψεν
> <u>φύλλά τε καὶ φλοιόν·</u> νῦν αὖτέ μιν υἷες Ἀχαιῶν
> <u>ἐν παλάμῃς</u> φορέουσι δικασπόλοι, οἵ τε θέμιστας
> πρὸς Διὸς εἰρύαται· ὁ δέ τοι μέγας ἔσσεται ὅρκος·"

> "In the name of *this* sceptre, which never again will bear *leaf nor branch*, now that it has left behind the cut stump *in the mountains*, nor shall it ever blossom again, since the bronze blade stripped

> *bark and leafage,* and now at last the sons of the Achaians
> carry *it in their hands* in state when they administer
> the justice of Zeus. And this shall be a great oath before you. "

Iliad I 234–239

By offering a visual tour of a precious object he holds in his hands (τόδε) as his eye moves around it, Achilles virtually *spaces time* by means of two distinct techniques: *perspective* and *chronotope*,[3] that is, a framework in which time and space not only constitute integral parts of the whole but also "read" one another. With respect to perspective, Achilles' eye follows a visual tour of the outer parts of the scepter, where there were leaves, branches, and bark before they were stripped by the bronze blade; as far as the chronotope is concerned, the scepter's past and present are "spaced" by being anchored respectively to the mountains, where the wood it is made of was first cut, and to the palms of the kings' hands that now hold it.

These two complementary spatial strategies stem from general mnemonic techniques that the storyteller employs, and are connected with spatial memory, but they also have a specific bearing on the actual context they are placed in. Spatial memory uses points as a background on which data are stored: perimetrically visualizing the scepter allows the storyteller's description to follow a certain path,[4] while the spatial markers employed for the object's history (mountains and kings' hands) function like mental hooks, on which stages in the scepter's "life" are hung. Moreover, these mental strategies have a powerful effect through their immediate referentiality and contextualization. Achilles' perimetrical visual tour of the scepter, with its strong emphasis on its "natural" aspect (leaves, branches, bark), is a "reading" of its past life; its changed use, that is, its transformation into a cultural object, is accompanied by a spatial shift, from the mountains to the hands of the kings. The combination of these two spatial mechanisms paves the way for an action of paramount importance that is about to happen: the scepter's being thrown on the ground (*Iliad* I 245).[5] Achilles does not dispute the scepter's symbolic importance; he actually accentuates

---

[3] See Bakhtin 1981; Riffaterre 1996; Pier 2005a.

[4] See Wenz 1997:28–31, who employs the term *diagrammatische Ikonizität* ("diagrammatic iconicity") and distinguishes, with respect to static descriptions of space, between *egozentrische Perspektive* (near-far, foreground-background, center-periphery, etc.) and *intrinsische Perspektive* (principle of topographical contiguity or proximity).

[5] The detail that the scepter is studded with golden nails, which is also based on perimetrical vision, ironically surfaces at the very point where this prized object will be "relocated" from the kings' hands to the ground (*Iliad* I 245–246).

it by suggesting that Agamemnon is not worthy of it.[6] The spatial strategies employed in describing the scepter set the background against which the throwing of it should be placed. The scepter is not a static object but a dynamic one.[7] Like the mind's eye, it travels in time and space, yet is a symbol of continuity, since neither its shape nor its power will change:[8] it is first visualized by means of Achilles' mental tour, and then follows its course in an ever downward movement, from the mountains into human hands and finally to the ground.[9] As with the similes, which use imagery to add things that are not mentioned in the narrative, so in descriptive segments, where the storyteller switches from direct narrative to "narrative" through imagery, dynamic description is not a pause or slowdown, but the continuation of the action, sometimes in the form of a comment, on a different interpretive level.[10]

The narrator can also assume the position of a "mobile" beholder, who describes an object by moving his mind's eye in a certain direction or along a visual path. In his description of the chariot of Hera, the narrator organizes the relevant material in six units, corresponding to the six parts of the chariot, which he tours by moving in his imagination from the lower to the central and then the front parts:

> ἣ μὲν ἐποιχομένη χρυσάμπυκας ἔντυεν ἵππους
> Ἥρη πρέσβα θεά, θυγάτηρ μεγάλοιο Κρόνοιο·
> Ἥβη δ' ἀμφ' ὀχέεσσι θοῶς βάλε καμπύλα κύκλα
> χάλκεα ὀκτάκνημα σιδηρέῳ ἄξονι ἀμφίς·
> τῶν ἤτοι χρυσέη ἴτυς ἄφθιτος, αὐτὰρ ὕπερθεν
> χάλκε' ὁπίσσωτρα προσαρηρότα, θαῦμα ἰδέσθαι·
> πλῆμναι δ' ἀργύρου εἰσὶ περίδρομοι ἀμφοτέρωθεν·
> δίφρος δὲ χρυσέοισι καὶ ἀργυρέοισιν ἱμᾶσιν
> ἐντέταται, δοιαὶ δὲ περίδρομοι ἄντυγές εἰσιν.

---

[6] See Bouvier 2002:275.

[7] See also Perrone-Moisès 1980, who draws a line between "static" and "dynamic" description, and Lyne 1989:68.

[8] See Nagy 1979:180; Grethlein 2008.

[9] On the scepter as a mirror of Achilles, see Lynn-George 1988:48–49.

[10] Scholars have used terms like *narrativized description* for descriptions containing narrative elements and *descriptivized narration* for narratives displaying formal features of the text-type of description; see Kittay 1981; Sternberg 1981:76; Chatman 1990:6–37; Mosher 1991. I am skeptical about the use of these terms, since sometimes the blurring or fusion between the boundaries of narration and description is so pervasive that it almost defies the underlying principle of priority that these terms take for granted. In other words, mixed narration and description, or description and narration, operates as a third text-type or mode, one that aims neither at concealing narration behind descriptive formats nor hiding description in the disguise of pseudonarration (see "Descriptivized Narration," below). It is with these thoughts that I opt for Bakhtin's *chronotope*, a nexus of interactive and coexistent modes.

τοῦ δ' ἐξ ἀργύρεος ῥυμὸς πέλεν· αὐτὰρ ἐπ' ἄκρῳ
δῆσεν χρύσειον καλὸν ζυγόν, ἐν δὲ λέπαδνα
κάλ' ἔβαλε χρύσει'· ὑπὸ δὲ ζυγὸν ἤγαγεν Ἥρη
ἵππους ὠκύποδας, μεμαυῖ' ἔριδος καὶ ἀϋτῆς.

... But Hera, high goddess, daughter of Kronos
the mighty, went away to harness the gold-bridled horses.
Then Hebe in speed set about the chariot the curved wheels
eight-spoked and brazen, with an axle of iron both ways.
Golden is the wheel's felly imperishable, and outside it
is joined, a wonder to look upon, the brazen running-rim,
and the silver naves revolve on either side of the chariot,
whereas the car itself is lashed fast with plaiting of gold
and silver, with double chariot rails that circle about it,
and the pole of the chariot is of silver, to whose extremity
Hebe made fast the golden and splendid yoke, and fastened
the harness, golden and splendid, and underneath the yoke Hera,
furious for hate and battle, led the swift-running horses.

Iliad V 720–732

The description of the chariot falls into the following six units:

(1) the wheels (κύκλα): 722–726

(2) the chariot-board (δίφρος): 727–728

(3) the rim surrounding the chariot-board (ἄντυγες): 728

(4) the pole (ῥυμός): 729

(5) the yoke (ζυγόν): 730

(6) the straps fastening the yoke (λέπαδνα): 730–731

Of these six units, corresponding to the six parts of the chariot, the first is described in greater detail as its various constituent parts are mentioned one by one: the axle (ἄξων): 723, the fellies of the wheel (ἴτυς): 724, the tires (ὀπίσσωτρα): 725, and the hubs or naves (πλῆμναι): 726.

The narrator's eye follows first a centrifugal and then a centripetal course in the description of the various parts of the wheels. Beginning with the axle (723),[11] the narrator moves from the center out to the fellies (724), then to the

---

[11] I do not treat the spokes (κνῆμαι [723 ὀκτάκνημα]) as a separate part because the way they are referred to (as an adjective modifying the wheels: καμπύλα κύκλα, ὀκτάκνημα) shows that they rather denote a type of wheel than being a description in their own right.

tires surrounding them (725), and finally back again to the center of the wheel, the hub into which the axle is inserted. Each part of the wheel is modified by one or more adjectives that always (but not solely) refer to the kind of metal used for its construction (axle *of iron*, *golden unbreakable* fellies, *bronze* tires, *circular* hubs *of silver*). Such hypertrophy of demarcation stems from the very nature of descriptive passages, since description, much unlike narration, tends to "advertise" its own mode to the audience. The use of the spatial adjectives referring to color or metal reflects the almost inbuilt tendency of description to privilege the use of a grammatical device or a syntactic construction (like the reiterated prepositional phrases ἀμφίς, ὕπερθε, ἀμφοτέρωθεν, or the verbal adjective περίδρομοι indicating space) that signals the passage's descriptive mode.[12]

In the description of the six parts of the chariot, the narrator moves from the lower and outer parts to the central (chariot–board and rim) and then the front parts (pole, yoke, and horses). He also opts for a strong descriptive demarcation, capitalizing on spatial markers like placement, color, number, and paratactic juxtaposition. The chariot-board (727–728 δίφρος), made of *golden* and *silver* straps or thongs, is *surrounded* (περίδρομοι) by two rims (728 ἄντυγες), and *from it* (τοῦ δ' ἐξ) the pole comes out; *on the pole's edge* (ἐπ' ἄκρῳ) Hebe tied a beautiful *golden* yoke, and *on it* (ἐν δὲ) she placed the beautiful *golden* straps. The entire description closes with one more spatial marker, as Hera places the swift-footed horses *under* the yoke (ὑπὸ δὲ ζυγόν).

The "mobility" of the narrator, whose viewpoint is reflected in this descriptive passage's spatial demarcations, erases the sequentiality of the various actions of Hebe and Hera as they prepare the chariot, and allows the audience to concentrate on the remarkable chariot of Hera, whose various parts are a θαῦμα ἰδέσθαι (725) as they glitter in gold, silver, and bronze. This prized object is therefore spatially presented to the listeners in all its detail, so that its magnificence "spills over" to the narrative sequence and can be transferred to what Hera is about to do. Apart from creating vividness and celebrating the object in question,[13] such spatial *amplificatio* prolongs the dramatic moment and functions as a proleptic signal within its immediate context.

Diagrammatic Iconicity

The term *diagrammatic iconicity* was employed by Wenz to describe analogies or similarities between the code used for perceiving space and the principles of organization of spatial description.[14] Scholars have distinguished between

---

[12] For a typology of descriptive markers in literature, see Hamon 1993:64–72.
[13] See Minchin 2001:101.
[14] Wenz 1997:28–31.

two modes of diagrammatic iconicity: a *dynamic* one, which iconizes the spatial orientation of an object, especially one characterized by its mobility, and a *static* mode, which is further divided into the categories of *extrinsic* and *intrinsic* perception—the former stemming from the object's use, the latter from its inherent function. For example, an amphora is perceived extrinsically, on the basis of its particular use in a given situation, since it can be a centerpiece in a museum gallery, or be made of gold, or be placed on the table where the characters of the plot are having dinner; whereas the walls of an ancient city are regularly perceived through the intrinsic feature of their *verticality* (requiring a further specification of direction[15]).

Dynamic spatial description

In this kind of iconicity, there is no description of the various properties of an object, but an iconization of its movement in space. A notable example of this form of diagrammatic iconicity is the description of Agamemnon's scepter by means of a catalogue format:

> ἀνὰ δὲ κρείων Ἀγαμέμνων
> ἔστη σκῆπτρον ἔχων· τὸ μὲν Ἥφαιστος κάμε τεύχων·
> Ἥφαιστος μὲν δῶκε Διὶ Κρονίωνι ἄνακτι,
> αὐτὰρ ἄρα Ζεὺς δῶκε διακτόρῳ Ἀργεϊφόντῃ,
> Ἑρμείας δὲ ἄναξ δῶκεν Πέλοπι πληξίππῳ,
> αὐτὰρ ὃ αὖτε Πέλοψ δῶκ' Ἀτρέϊ ποιμένι λαῶν·
> Ἀτρεὺς δὲ θνῄσκων ἔλιπεν πολύαρνι Θυέστῃ,
> αὐτὰρ ὃ αὖτε Θυέστ' Ἀγαμέμνονι λεῖπε φορῆναι,
> πολλῇσιν νήσοισι καὶ Ἄργεϊ παντὶ ἀνάσσειν.

> Powerful Agamemnon
> stood up holding the sceptre Hephaistos had wrought him carefully.
> Hephaistos gave it to Zeus the king, the son of Kronos,
> and Zeus in turn gave it to the courier Argeïphontes,
> and lord Hermes gave it to Pelops, driver of horses,
> and Pelops again gave it to Atreus, the shepherd of the people.
> Atreus dying left it to Thyestes of the rich flocks,
> and Thyestes left it in turn to Agamemnon to carry
> and to be lord of many islands and over all Argos.

> *Iliad* II 100–108

---

[15] That is to say, top-to-bottom or bottom-to-top.

In contrast with Achilles, the narrator employs a cataloguing type of organization, one that builds on the history of Agamemnon's scepter. By tracing its origins to the divine craftsman Hephaistos, the narrator capitalizes on its tremendous power as a symbol, while by listing all its previous holders and owners he underscores both its royal aspect and its temporariness, the former stemming from the fact that it has belonged only to kings, the latter that it has "moved" in time. Scholars have recently talked about *an archaeology of the past*[16] that is embodied in certain material objects in Homeric epic. The term *biography of things*,[17] though first used a century ago,[18] has become important again in descriptions of phases or stages in a thing's life. Biographies of material objects, however, especially those organized in catalogues, may determine not only temporal relations but also spatial ones, as part of the tracing of a given object's history. Before exploring this aspect of Agamemnon's scepter, I will try briefly to explain a frequent misunderstanding in discussions of the cataloguing principle of organization, which stems from a confusion between the terms "catalogue" and "list." The following formulation by Sammons sets things in the right order:[19]

> A catalogue is a list of items which are specified in discrete entries; its entries are formally distinct and arranged in sequence by anaphora or by a simple connective, but are not put into any subordinating relation to one another, and no explicit relation is made between the items except for their shared suitability to the catalogue's specified rubric.... By rubric I mean the stated category or class which legitimates the inclusion or exclusion of potential items; by entry I mean the component which is marked off by anaphora or connective and contains the specified item; by item I mean that person, thing, place etc. which is specified in the entry and whose specification is sufficient to render the entry intelligible under the rubric. All content of the entry not necessary to render the entry intelligible under the rubric, I will call *elaboration*. For the sake of this definition I will assume that a catalogue has at least three entries.[20]

---

[16] See Grethlein 2008.

[17] For the "biography of things," see the survey in *World Archaeology* 31.2 (1999) and Grethlein 2008:35–43; also Kopytoff 1986:66–67.

[18] Rivers 1910:3–12.

[19] 2010:9. Various terms have been employed to describe the entries or items of a list or catalogue. See Beye 1964; Powell 1978; Edwards 1980; Barney 1982:191–192; Thalmann 1984:23–26; Minchin 1996:4–5, 2001:74–76; Tsagalis 2010a.

[20] See Matz 1995 for three entries. Minchin (2001:75) argues for a minimum of four entries.

In this light, it becomes clear that what makes *Iliad* II 100–108 a catalogue, instead of a list, is *elaboration*, the means by which items are turned into entries. In particular, we are dealing with a catalogue organized under the heading "past owners of the scepter," containing six entries, each entry including two items, one following a right-dislocation (subject) and one a left-dislocation (object). Individual entries are metrically coterminous (they end at verse-end) and have a standard structure: *item 1 + (modifier 1) + verb "to give or leave to" + (modifier 2) item 2 + (modifier 2).*[21] This structuralist digression aims at highlighting the fact that the catalogue is a "narrativized" list, a special register that contains elements pertaining to narrative proper and not a simple enumeration of items. It is very important that the narrator organized the various owners of the scepter into a schema marked by a very specific poetic grammar. Such mechanisms privileging repetition[22] no doubt enhance memorability, since they embed the individual items into larger constructions (the *entries*) and further concatenate them, thus reinforcing their mental association and facilitating their recall. On a different level, though, this grouping of names turns them from mere references into parts of a chain that, apart from its mnemonic suitability, produces links, interdependences, and finally motion. If repetition of names is seen as a token of continuity, then the scepter surpasses consanguinity and geographical proximity, the two "natural" aspects of connectedness, and replaces a blood lineage with a social function. The scepter becomes endowed with an intergenerational transitivity, one that goes beyond divine-human dichotomies and generates in our minds the image of a continuous historical line.[23] Through the use of the verbs "to give" (δῶκεν) and "to leave to" (ἔλιπεν, λεῖπε), the narrator translates the history of the scepter into a series of transfers from one person to another. In other words, he sees time, the scepter's "biography," as space, as he follows the prized object passing from one king to the next until it finally reaches Agamemnon. By linking the scepter's archaeology not to any given time frame but to its transfer from the divine craftsman Hephaistos to the king of Mycenae, the narrator turns its biography into a movement in space.[24] The catalogue format employed in this passage effectively erases all traces of the individual histories of the scepter's various owners, or their potential conflicts, and presents them *qua* scepter in a highly compressed small story. In this way,

---

[21] Modifiers are substantives or adjectives modifying the subject or object; they are optional (hence the parenthesis) and may either precede or follow the item they refer to.

[22] Within the whole catalogue, each *item* acts as both subject and object. This double function of the individual items underscores the cohesion of the whole construction.

[23] Zerubavel 2003:57–58.

[24] The paratactic organization of the whole catalogue, and in particular the δέ particles, "indicate[s] the shifting focus in the ... field of vision, rather than any inherent temporal quality of events in the narrative," as Bakker notes (1997:68).

distance is decreased and the scepter's divine origins are set not in the remote past but only "six transfers away."

In the techniques they employ for describing this prized material object, therefore, the two Iliadic passages referring to Agamemnon's scepter both draw on space. Despite the importance they attribute to spatial factors, they deal with them in very different ways: while the first emphasizes perspective, the second focuses on transferability; whereas in the one, Achilles' mental eye guides the audience to a perimetrical visualization of the scepter, in the other the narrator emphasizes its mobility. These differences in spatial aspect have their own bearing on the particular functions the scepter fulfills: for Achilles, the focus on its lack of leaves and branches hints at the invincible power of his oath, while for the narrator the emphasis lies in the scepter's "royal pedigree," which is "transferred" to its last owner, Agamemnon.

Static spatial description

Static spatial description is subdivided into the types of *extrinsic* and *intrinsic* description. While the former results from principles like an object's perceptual significance and spatial pairs like *near-far, foreground-background,* and *center-periphery,* the latter is organized on the principle of *topographical contiguity,* stemming from a given object's inherent function as a point of orientation (*origo*).[25]

This classification is important not only because it allows us to evaluate the spatial means employed for description, but also because these two different perspectives are sometimes juxtaposed, in the transition from a descriptive to a narrative section.[26] In fact, it turns out that the *Iliad* at times plays on the differences between extrinsic and intrinsic space, in order to highlight for its audience the distance that separates the world of objects from that of men.

Extrinsic perspective

Diagrammatic iconicity can take the form of static spatial description, which in the case of Helen's web involves the antithesis between extrinsic and intrinsic perspective. Let us first consider the relevant lines:

> Ἶρις δ' αὖθ' Ἑλένῃ λευκωλένῳ ἄγγελος ἦλθεν,
> εἰδομένη γαλόῳ, Ἀντηνορίδαο δάμαρτι,
> τὴν Ἀντηνορίδης εἶχε κρείων Ἑλικάων,
> Λαοδίκην, Πριάμοιο θυγατρῶν εἶδος ἀρίστην.
> τὴν δ' εὗρ' ἐν μεγάρῳ· ἣ δὲ μέγαν ἱστὸν ὕφαινεν,

---

[25] See Dennerlein 2009:156.
[26] See "Extrinsic perspective," below.

δίπλακα πορφυρέην, πολέας δ' ἐνέπασσεν ἀέθλους
Τρώων θ' ἱπποδάμων καὶ Ἀχαιῶν χαλκοχιτώνων,
οὓς ἕθεν εἵνεκ' ἔπασχον ὑπ' Ἄρηος παλαμάων.

Now to Helen of the white arms came a messenger, Iris,
in the likeness of her sister-in-law, the wife of Antenor's
son, whom strong Helikaon wed, the son of Antenor,
Laodike, loveliest looking of all the daughters of Priam.
She came on Helen in the chamber; she was weaving a great web,
a red folding robe, and working into it the numerous struggles
of Trojans, breakers of horses, and bronze-armoured Achaians

Iliad III 121–128

In interpreting this passage, it is crucial to determine who the focalizer is—that is, through whose eyes the scene of Helen working at her loom is presented. The use of a verb of "finding" (εὖρε) indicates that we are invited to visualize this scene through Iris' eyes. If Iris finds Helen "weaving a great web ... and working into it the numerous struggles of Trojans ... and Achaians," then it becomes probable that space works either from a horizontal or a sagittal viewpoint, but surely not from a vertical one. This observation may seem trivial, but it is of key importance in understanding the function of spatial description in this passage. In fact, it is exactly the opposition between this horizontal or sagittal perspective of Iris looking at Helen's tapestry and the vertical viewpoint that is inherent in Helen's "looking from the walls" scene which is about to follow that is interpretively paramount.[27]

The web and the walls where Helen will soon be transferred are types of extrinsic and intrinsic space respectively: a tapestry does not by itself have a horizontal, vertical, or sagittal aspect, whereas the walls are marked in visual imagination by their verticality. By describing Iris' entrance into Helen's quarters, the narrator underscores the fact that she is looking at Helen weaving the tapestry from a position that is *the exact opposite* of the one Helen will shortly assume. The emphasis on the nonverticality of the tapestry's extrinsic space becomes a backdrop against which the audience should evaluate Helen's future role in the τειχοσκοπία proper, where she will assume a "vertical" perspective while looking at the Trojan and Achaean armies on the battlefield. The reiteration of similar vocabulary by the narrator and Iris (*Iliad* III 127–128 and 131–132[28])

---

[27] See Purves 2010a:24–64.
[28] *Iliad* III 127 (= 131) Τρώων θ' ἱπποδάμων καὶ Ἀχαιῶν χαλκοχιτώνων / οὓς ἕθεν εἵνεκ' ἔπασχον ὑπ' Ἄρηος παλαμάων (128) - οἳ πρὶν ἐπ' ἀλλήλοισι φέρον πολύδακρυν ἄρηα (132) ("of Trojans, breakers of horses, and bronze-armoured Achaians, / struggles that they endured for her sake at

points to the narrative exploitation of the tapestry's spatiality through a telling interplay with the view from the walls:[29] the *Iliad* will let Helen's gaze fall on the world of heroes fighting for her sake on the battlefield,[30] the very same world she has memorialized on the mini-ecphrasis of her weaving.[31] The narrator has opted for the nonvertical aspect of the tapestry's extrinsic space simply because he intends to use it as a backdrop for the vertical spatiality of the intrinsic space of the walls in the τειχοσκοπία episode that is about to follow.[32]

Iliad XI 628–635 contains a description of Nestor's table, with special emphasis on his cup. Although the majority of scholars have discussed this cup in detail, little attention has been paid to its connection to the whole description of Nestor's table, of which it represents the most amplified part.

> ἥ σφωϊν πρῶτον μὲν ἐπιπροΐηλε τράπεζαν
> καλὴν κυανόπεζαν ἐΰξοον, αὐτὰρ ἐπ' αὐτῆς
> χάλκειον κάνεον, ἐπὶ δὲ κρόμυον ποτῷ ὄψον,
> ἠδὲ μέλι χλωρόν, παρὰ δ' ἀλφίτου ἱεροῦ ἀκτήν,
> πὰρ δὲ δέπας περικαλλές, ὃ οἴκοθεν ἦγ' ὁ γεραιός,
> χρυσείοις ἥλοισι πεπαρμένον· οὔατα δ' αὐτοῦ
> τέσσαρ' ἔσαν, δοιαὶ δὲ πελειάδες ἀμφὶς ἕκαστον
> χρύσειαι νεμέθοντο, δύω δ' ὑπὸ πυθμένες ἦσαν.

> First she pushed up the table in front of them, a lovely
> table, polished and with feet of cobalt, and on it
> she laid a bronze basket, with onion to go with the drinking,

---

the hands of the war god ... who [Trojans and Achaeans] just now carried sorrowful war against each other"). This point is further strengthened by the fact that the expression employed in III 128 (ὑπ' Ἄρηος παλαμάων) is a hapax.

[29] See Becker 1995:56–57, who refers to the "concinnity between the language used to describe a depiction of these contests (127) and that which describes the contests themselves (131)," in order to argue that "epic formulaic language here discourages a differentiation between the representational capabilities of the verbal and the visual media."

[30] See scholia BT on *Iliad* III 126–127: ἀξιόχρεων ἀρχέτυπον ἀνέπλασεν ὁ ποιητὴς τῆς ἰδίας ποιήσεως· ἴσως δὲ τούτῳ τοῖς ὁρῶσιν ἐπειρᾶτο δεικνύναι τὴν Τρώων βίαν καὶ τὴν Ἑλλήνων δικαίαν ἰσχύν ("the poet shaped a worthy model of his own poetry; perhaps he was trying to show to those who see it the strength of the Trojans and the just force of the Greeks"). The literature on the implicit connection between Helen's tapestry and the storyteller's song is immense: Whitman 1958:117–118; Austin 1975:127–128; Snyder 1981; Schein 1984:23; Thalmann 1984:27, 153, 166; G. A. Kennedy 1986; Lynn-George 1988:29; Bergren 2008:43–55; Clay 2011:7. Nünlist (2009:132n51) maintains that this is a case of "*implicit* self-referentiality" that should be distinguished from instances in which characters represent the poet explicitly.

[31] Any discussion of how the "struggles" between Trojans and Achaeans may have been depicted on the tapestry is entirely speculative; see Kirk 1985:280.

[32] See Bergren 2008:47, who points to the link between these two scenes by accentuating the mixture of "the suspension of historical temporality with otherwise realistic narration."

and pale honey, and beside it bread, blessed pride of the barley,
and beside it a beautifully wrought cup which the old man brought
    with him
from home. It was set with golden nails, the eared handles upon it
were four, and on either side there were fashioned two doves
of gold, feeding, and there were double bases beneath it.

Iliad XI 628–635

Hekamede prepares a beautiful table, on which she places a bronze basket with onion and honey beside the bread, and next to it the exquisite cup of Nestor. Before turning our attention to this outstanding cup, let us first consider how the description unfolds. The dark-footed table sets the general spatial background against which the individual objects will be described. The three adjectives (καλὴν κυανόπεζαν ἐΰξοον) in asyndeton create what Hamon has felicitously called an *effet de liste*,[33] the tendency of descriptive passages to accumulate adjectives, creating a *syncopated, staccato rhythm* and a notable *augmentative particularization* of the individual items of the list.[34] Such series of adjectives "expand" the meaning of a given object by extending it in space: from the denomination "table", we move to the descriptive system "beautiful, dark-footed, well-polished table" which becomes the "proper name" or *pantonym* of this descriptive passage.[35] The descriptive system of this particular table is therefore the framework in connection with which the other objects will be described. In fact, we will see that their description, and especially that of Nestor's cup, acquires its full meaning only against the backdrop of the "beautiful, dark-footed, well-polished table" upon which they are all placed.

After describing the table, the narrator turns his attention to various objects or foods placed on it: a bronze basket or plate, onion, fresh honey, and bread. Most commentators and translators do not indicate whether the three edibles are placed within the basket or plate, or next to it.[36] If ἐπὶ δέ (630) means "upon it" (= ἐπ' αὐτῆς [sc. τῆς τραπέζης]), then we have a *non sequitur*, since παρὰ δ'

---

[33] 1993:66.

[34] Hamon 1993:67.

[35] By *pantonym* I refer to the notional center of a given description. According to Hamon, whom I follow, the *pantonym* can become "the center of reference within a whole system of anaphoric markers and by means of simple repetition it can economize the sum of an object's innumerable parts ..., the sum of its qualities ..., or both at the same time. The expansion of the *pantonym* can take the form of an inventory either of the object's individual parts (*configuration* of a referent) or of the various distinctive features of a term or notion (*definition*)" (1993:127; author's translation).

[36] With the notable exception of Ameis and Hentze 1906:82, who take ἐπὶ δέ (XI 630) as referring to the table (= ἐπ' αὐτῆς) and print a comma after κρόμυον.

389

in the next verse cannot possibly refer to the table, meaning "beside it [sc. the table]." It would have been extremely awkward (a) to have the bread placed not on the table but next to it, but all the rest of the food and objects on the table, (b) to juxtapose a useless bronze basket or plate to three different types of food without any reason, and finally (c) to have a second πὰρ δέ (XI 632) referring to the table. It is much more sound, I think, to take ἐπὶ δέ, παρὰ δ᾽, and πὰρ δέ as referring to their syntactic antecedents, the basket or plate, the honey, and the bread respectively. The narrator is simply listing all the edibles placed inside the χάλκειον κάνεον by concatenating them on the basis of their position with respect to the last item he has recalled from his memory: basket or plate > onion and honey > bread. This discussion may seem trivial, but it is necessary in order to explore the way the narrator works with space in this descriptive segment. Once we have clarified that the various edibles are placed within the bronze basket or plate and are described in terms of spatial association, then we can see that the χάλκειον κάνεον constitutes a second visual image that facilitates the transition from the spatial framework of the table to that of Nestor's cup, which will be the center of the narrator's attention.

The passage devoted to Nestor's cup begins with a single adjective empha-sizing the cup's beauty and a brief reference to its history (*Iliad* XI 632 ὃ οἴκοθεν ἦγ᾽ ὁ γεραιός), which soon give way to the actual description of this prized object. The cup's description is marked by what I would call, for lack of a better term, *visual ring composition*: the narrator uses the impression of gleaming gold, which strengthens mnemonic recall,[37] to frame his mental tour of the cup. In fact, the golden nails and the golden doves that begin and end the perimetrical description of the cup (the reference to the double bases is rather an addition) not only enhance memorability, but also function as a contrast with the visual background of the dark-footed table and the "intermediate" brightness of the bronze basket or plate. Moreover, the emphasis on the plurality of the cup's various decorative elements (four handles, two doves on each of them, double bases) reflects an *expansion aesthetic*,[38] which stems from the tendency of descrip-tive passages to schematize an object in space, the more so if this is an excep-tional object. The emphasis on the cup's plethora of various parts generates the mental image of this special cup with increasing intensity and allows the audience, as well as the narrator's imagination, to place it in space. The multiple nails, handles, doves, and bases are ancillary images that shape its visualiza-tion and bring about its spatialization, its positioning *in space*. Description thus becomes, in the words of Hamon,[39] "a meta-classification," a type of taxonomy

---

[37] See Rubin 1995:57.
[38] On the term *expansion aesthetic*, see Martin 1989:196, 206–230.
[39] Hamon 1993:56.

that pigeonholes a form of material already individualized in other discourses. The almost inherent *découpage*[40] that characterizes the description of any given object, as it does Nestor's cup, plays on the illusion of *insularization*,[41] only to suggest a spatialization that makes the object part of a larger narrative reality.

Seen from this angle, Nestor's cup is spatialized by both the emphasis on its constituent parts and the visual interplay between the dark-footed table and the bronze basket or plate: from a rather dark background, the narrator moves to a brighter foreground (that of the χάλκειον κάνεον), before visualizing an even brighter object, the golden-nailed cup, its handles decorated with golden doves.[42] The transition from a darker background to an ever brighter central point or focus helps the narrator extend his description by bringing in more details. Color and brightness are mentally perceived spatial markers, which correspond in this case to the descriptive space the narrator bestows on his target domain.

A significant number of prized objects are described in the *Iliad* from the extrinsic perspective of one or two noteworthy features that they possess. The storyteller does not follow a point-by-point photographic description,[43] but assuming that his audience will supplement all the missing details on their own, he focuses his attention on what he regards as remarkable. Sometimes these characteristics of the described objects are presented, overtly or implicitly, in opposition to others of the same kind.[44] The description of a prized object is a *selection* of something worth describing, imbued with features pertaining to comparisons and their special register in Homeric poetry, the simile. The temporary emphasis on the extrinsic, situation-oriented perspective in static spatial description is relevant to the nature and function of the Homeric similes, which "may begin in descriptive terms, but ... will slip into the narrative mode."[45]

The description of Athena's robe (*Iliad* VI 288–295) begins with a brief history of the object, but ends by highlighting its brightness and placement. After an *effet de liste* created by the adjectives "loveliest" (294 κάλλιστος) and "largest" (294 μέγιστος), the narrator underscores both the garment's brightness (295 ἀστὴρ δ᾽ ὣς ἀπέλαμπεν) and its placement beneath all the other robes stored in the chamber (295 ἔκειτο δὲ νείατος ἄλλων).

---

[40] On *découpage*, see Barthes 1964:213–220.
[41] On this term, see Bakhtin 1978:254 passim.
[42] On the "bright-dark" interplay as a basis for the organization of extrinsic static space, see Dennerlein 2009:156–157.
[43] Minchin 2001:106.
[44] See below on the robe of Athena.
[45] Minchin 2001:117n34.

αὐτὴ δ' ἐς θάλαμον κατεβήσετο κηώεντα,
ἔνθ' ἔσάν οἱ πέπλοι παμποίκιλοι, ἔργα γυναικῶν
Σιδονίων, τὰς αὐτὸς Ἀλέξανδρος θεοειδὴς
ἤγαγε Σιδονίηθεν, ἐπιπλοὺς εὐρέα πόντον
τὴν ὁδόν, ἣν Ἑλένην περ ἀνήγαγεν εὐπατέρειαν.
τῶν ἕν' ἀειραμένη Ἑκάβη φέρε δῶρον Ἀθήνῃ,
ὃς κάλλιστος ἔην ποικίλμασιν ἠδὲ μέγιστος,
ἀστὴρ δ' ὣς ἀπέλαμπεν· ἔκειτο δὲ νείατος ἄλλων.

... while she descended into the fragrant store-chamber.
There lay the elaborately wrought robes, the work of Sidonian
women, whom Alexandros himself, the godlike, had brought home
from the land of Sidon, crossing the wide sea, on that journey
when he brought back also gloriously descended Helen.
Hekabe lifted out one and took it as gift to Athene,
that which was the loveliest in design and the largest,
and shone like a star. It lay beneath the others.

Iliad VI 288–295

The robe's preeminence is pointed out by means of a technique I will describe as *partitive spatialization*: the storyteller refers to a group of objects of the same kind, only to draw attention to one of them that is exceptional for one or two of its features. From the background of the multitude of robes stored in the fragrant chamber, the narrator brings the garment of Athena into the limelight, and accentuates its special status through spatial markers such as brightness and placement. The repetition of similar diction for the other robes (*Iliad* VI 289 παμποίκιλοι) and that of Athena (294 ποικίλμασιν) facilitates the *insularization*[46] of the latter and paves the way for a further selection of two spatial features that are also accentuated by an explicit comparison to the other robes stored in the chamber.[47]

The single-feature technique is especially observable in brief descriptive passages for two reasons: first, the narrator must counterbalance the description's brevity by emphasizing a single characteristic, and second, he can easily create a mental link between the single feature highlighted in the descriptive passage and a detail from a narrative segment either immediately following or found in a previous reference to the same object or its owner. A noteworthy case is Asteropaios' breastplate:

[46] On the term *insularization*, see Bakhtin 1978:254 passim.
[47] As indicated by the superlatives κάλλιστος and μέγιστος (*Iliad* VI 294).

"δώσω οἱ θώρηκα, τὸν Ἀστεροπαῖον ἀπηύρων,
χάλκεον, ᾧ πέρι χεῦμα φαεινοῦ κασσιτέροιο
ἀμφιδεδίνηται· πολέος δέ οἱ ἄξιος ἔσται."

"I will give him that corselet I stripped from Asteropaios;
it is bronze, but there is an overlay circled about it
in shining tin. It will be a gift that will mean much to him."

Iliad XXIII 560–562

Diagrammatic iconicity is here centered on a single feature of Asteropaios' breastplate: its being fitted close in shining tin. The emphasis on this single feature counterbalances the brevity of the description by drawing attention to a remarkable feature of the breastplate that the listeners can effectively keep in their minds.[48] At the same time, and given that Achilles declares that he will offer to the winner of the spear contest the silver-fitted sword of Asteropaios (*Iliad* XXIII 807–808), the emphasis on a single feature seems to imply that this object's brief description acquires its importance not by its beauty, size, or some other characteristic of its own, but mainly by being associated with Achilles' defeat of Asteropaios. By isolating and therefore accentuating the importance of a single feature, the narrator can use it as a cue for recalling an important narrative incident that has taken place. It is of course quite fitting that in both XXIII 560–562 and 807–808 the speaker is Achilles, since it is he, after all, who has kept his previous exploits vividly in his memory.

But there is more to it. Rengakos, who has highlighted the fact that Achilles smiles just before promising to give Eumelos the breastplate of Asteropaios (*Iliad* XXIII 555 μείδησεν), has interpreted Achilles' reaction as a *mise-en-abyme*. From this point of view, it is not only Achilles who is smiling, because he realizes that here (in contrast to the situation in *Iliad* I, where the conflict was about the spoils of war) it is about an athletic prize, but together with him the poet of the *Iliad* himself, who alludes to the fact that his own narrative is, after all, a kind of intellectual game.[49] Along this line of interpretation, we can move one

---

[48]   The brevity of descriptive segments (between two or three and seven or eight lines of text) is due to the needs of both audience and poet. Listeners find narrative a more engaging medium, because, according to cognitive science, it expresses the sequential nature of all human experience. The storyteller knows that narrative is easier to call to mind and to perform because it comprises logical chains of events based on cause and effect. That is one reason why the longer set-piece descriptions, like that of the shield of Achilles, are expanded in narrative sections: limited descriptive material is augmented by longer narrative chunks. "Just as when the poet sings a catalogue-song, which includes fragments of stories, so it is with descriptive passages: it appears to be difficult for the poet to resist the pull of narrative" (Minchin 2001:117).

[49]   Rengakos 2006a:30.

step further and explore the possibility that the highlighting of a single feature of Asteropaios' breastplate may be also due to the narrator's desire to use this brief description as a backdrop against which to place the previously detailed conflict between Achilles and Asteropaios. A plethora of descriptive details would have eclipsed Asteropaios and accentuated his breastplate, whereas the emphasis on a single feature of the breastplate draws attention to Asteropaios himself, and especially to the narrative of the event that led Achilles to acquire his armor. This line of argument is supported by the fact that the poet is so eager to help his audience make this connection that he can even refer to an object *not mentioned at all* during the actual fighting between the two heroes in XXI 139–204: namely the sword that Achilles promises to give to the winner of the spear fight in XXIII 807–808,[50] which played no role at all in the actual duel between Achilles and Asteropaios. The two warriors fought basically with spears; in fact Asteropaios threw two of them at Achilles (XXI 162–168), who also threw his own spear at his opponent but missed his target (169–172). Why then does the poet refer to Asteropaios' sword in *Iliad* XXIII 807–808? My argument is that it is exquisitely apt for Achilles, as the speaker, who in the final scene of the duel with Asteropaios in *Iliad* XXI killed his opponent *with his own sword* (XXI 173–182).[51] In the realm of mnemonic recall, the sword is thus "transferred" from Achilles to Asteropaios, since the brief description of a single spatial feature becomes an *ancilla memoriae* that brings to the foreground of Achilles' emotional universe the profound antithesis between the cruelty of war and the jocular festivity of the games. Once more, accuracy is effectively sacrificed for the sake of dramatic effect.

Another descriptive passage that capitalizes on the single-feature technique involves Priam's cup (*Iliad* XXIV 234–237), which is placed last in a list of gifts that the aged king of Troy is determined to offer Achilles in exchange for Hektor's corpse:

ἦ, καὶ φωριαμῶν ἐπιθήματα κάλ' ἀνέῳγεν.
ἔνθεν δώδεκα μὲν περικαλλέας ἔξελε πέπλους,
δώδεκα δ' ἁπλοΐδας χλαίνας, τόσσους δὲ τάπητας,
τόσσα δὲ φάρεα λευκά, τόσους δ' ἐπὶ τοῖσι χιτῶνας,
χρυσοῦ δὲ στήσας ἔφερεν δέκα πάντα τάλαντα,
ἐκ δὲ δύ' αἴθωνας τρίποδας, πίσυρας δὲ λέβητας,
ἐκ δὲ δέπας περικαλλές, ὅ οἱ Θρῆκες πόρον ἄνδρες

---

[50] The spear fight ends in a draw, but the sword is awarded to Diomedes (*Iliad* XXIII 824–825).

[51] That is to say, Achilles' sword. This whole scene concludes when the narrator highlights Asteropaios' death on Achilles' sword (*Iliad* XXI 208 χέρσ' ὕπο Πηλείδαο καὶ ἄορι ἶφι δαμέντα ["gone down by force under the sword and the hands of Peleïdes"]).

ἐξεσίην ἐλθόντι, μέγα κτέρας· οὐδέ νυ τοῦ περ
φείσατ' ἐνὶ μεγάροις ὁ γέρων, περὶ δ' ἤθελε θυμῷ
λύσασθαι φίλον υἱόν.

He spoke, and lifted back the fair covering of his clothes-chest
and from inside took out twelve robes surpassingly lovely
and twelve mantles to be worn single, as many blankets,
as many great white cloaks, also the same number of tunics.
He weighed and carried out ten full talents of gold, and brought forth
two shining tripods, and four cauldrons, and brought out a goblet
of surpassing loveliness that the men of Thrace had given him
when he went to them with a message, but now the old man spared
    not
even this in his halls, so much was it his heart's desire
to ransom back his beloved son.

Iliad XXIV 228–237

This passage displays a number of typical elements of descriptive taxonomy. *Effet de liste*, plurality (through insistence on numbers), and the emphasis on visuality (colors and brightness) are all at work, but it seems that in this case they also serve the principal purpose of marking the last item of the list, Priam's beautiful cup, as special. This type of *descriptive priamel*,[52] where the list of objects described first functions as a foil to introduce and oppose the last object (the climax), is based on the single-feature technique that singles out one element of Priam's cup: that it is a μέγα κτέρας.[53] Unlike Asteropaios, the single feature is not a characteristic of this prized object, as it has to do not with its size, brightness, etc., but its use. Priam's cup acquires its special status and value because it becomes a measure of how much Priam values the return of the body of Hektor.[54] This interpretation is confirmed by the fact that the descriptive priamel is mapped onto the subsequent narrative: just as Priam's cup is a μέγα κτέρας,[55] a prized object that stands out among the multitude of other gifts

---

[52] On the priamel, see Race 1982.

[53] Lattimore 1951 leaves this expression untranslated.

[54] *Iliad* XXIV 235–237: οὐδέ νυ τοῦ περ / φείσατ' ἐνὶ μεγάροις ὁ γέρων, περὶ δ' ἤθελε θυμῷ / λύσασθαι φίλον υἱόν ("… but now the old man spared not / even this in his halls, so much was it his heart's desire / to ransom back his beloved son").

[55] See Minchin 2001:114–117, who discusses this and other passages by emphasizing that the poet often chooses to render descriptive passages through narration. I tend to regard this kind of narration as "pseudonarrative," for the boundaries between the two modes are intentionally blurred.

he intends to bring to Achilles,[56] so Hektor stands out among the rest of Priam's sons, whom the old king will rebuke in lines 239–246.[57]

A similar, but not identical, case is that of the brief description of Achilles' hut:

> ἀλλ' ὅτε δὴ κλισίην Πηληϊάδεω ἀφίκοντο
> ὑψηλήν—τὴν Μυρμιδόνες ποίησαν ἄνακτι
> δοῦρ' ἐλάτης κέρσαντες, ἀτὰρ καθύπερθεν ἔρεψαν
> λαχνήεντ' ὄροφον λειμωνόθεν ἀμήσαντες·
> ἀμφὶ δέ οἱ μεγάλην αὐλὴν ποίησαν ἄνακτι
> σταυροῖσιν πυκινοῖσι· θύρην δ' ἔχε μοῦνος ἐπιβλής
> εἰλάτινος, τὸν τρεῖς μὲν ἐπιρρήσσεσκον Ἀχαιοί,
> τρεῖς δ' ἀναοίγεσκον μεγάλην κληῖδα θυράων,
> τῶν ἄλλων, Ἀχιλεὺς δ' ἄρ' ἐπιρρήσσεσκε καὶ οἷος—

> But when they had got to the shelter of Peleus' son: a towering
> shelter the Myrmidons had built for their king, hewing
> the timbers of pine, and they made a roof of thatch above it
> shaggy with grass that they had gathered out of the meadows;
> and around it made a great courtyard for their king, with hedgepoles
> set close together; the gate was secured by a single door-piece
> of pine, and three Achaians could ram it home in its socket
> and three could pull back and open the huge door-bar; three other
> Achaians, that is, but Achilleus all by himself could close it.

Iliad XXIV 448–456

From the very beginning of this description, the storyteller carefully draws attention not only to various aspects of the hut, such as its size (449 ὑψηλήν) and the material used in making all its parts (walls, roof, hedgepoles), but also to the contribution of the Myrmidons to its construction. The audience is repeatedly told that it was Achilles' companions who cut the trees and provided the

---

56 See Woronoff 1983.

57 "ἔρρετε, λωβητῆρες, ἐλεγχέες· οὔ νυ καὶ ὑμῖν / οἴκοι ἔνεστι γόος, ὅτι μ' ἤλθετε κηδήσοντες; / ἦ ὀνόσασθ' ὅτι μοι Κρονίδης Ζεὺς ἄλγε' ἔδωκεν, / παῖδ' ὀλέσαι τὸν ἄριστον; ἀτὰρ γνώσεσθε καὶ ὔμμες / ῥηΐτεροι γὰρ μᾶλλον Ἀχαιοῖσιν δὴ ἔσεσθε / κείνου τεθνηῶτος ἐναιρέμεν. αὐτὰρ ἐγώ γε, / πρὶν ἀλαπαζομένην τε πόλιν κεραϊζομένην τε / ὀφθαλμοῖσιν ἰδεῖν, βαίην δόμον Ἄϊδος εἴσω" ("'Get out, you failures, you disgraces. Have you not also / mourning of your own at home that you come to me with your sorrows? / Is it not enough that Zeus, son of Kronos, has given me sorrow / in losing the best of my sons? You also shall be aware of this / since you will be all the easier for the Achaians to slaughter / now he is dead. But, for myself, before my eyes look / upon this city as it is destroyed and its people are slaughtered, / my wish is to go sooner down to the house of the death god'").

wood (449–450), who covered the hut's roof with grass they gathered from a meadow (450–451), and who finally built a large yard around it for their king using stakes closely fitted together (452–453). The narrator has organized the largest part of his description by means of a twofold list of the various parts of the hut and the materials used in their construction, which are tied together through the pseudonarrative of the work of a group of men, the Myrmidons.[58] When the description continues, attention is focused on one part of the hut, the single door-bolt made of pine. This single feature of the hut is accompanied by the contrast between the abilities of the Myrmidons and those of Achilles: the listeners are explicitly told that whereas three Myrmidons were needed in order to remove the bolt, Achilles could do the same thing on his own (456 οἶος).[59]

The audience is invited to realize that the single feature stressed at the end of the description of the hut is effectively coupled with the emergence of Achilles as a special figure among the Myrmidons. In other words, the difference in descriptive importance between the various parts of the hut and the door-bolt is mirrored in the difference between the Myrmidons and Achilles. The single-feature device becomes the means of drawing attention to a wider antithesis that is about to be fully exploited in the ensuing scene. Despite the fact that Priam has come to the Myrmidons' camp, the whole episode will be centered on his interaction with a single hero, Achilles. The son of Thetis is singled out in the description of the hut by his special ability with respect to a single spatial feature, because he will be isolated in the subsequent encounter with Priam. In turn, the door-bolt is equally singled out, because Achilles *alone* can remove it, as he *alone* can also remove some of the sorrow from Priam's heart by allowing the aged king to take the corpse of his beloved son back to Troy.

---

[58] See de Jong 2001:xvii on "scenery": "In Homer scenery is never described systematically or for its own sake; rather, we find descriptions or brief references when the story needs them; they derive almost exclusively from characters, in embedded focalization or a speech. Scenery descriptions either consist of a list of items connected via refrain composition (ἔνθα or ἐν) or have some form of spatial organization, or are a combination of the two." On scenery in Homer, see also Arend 1933:28; Müller 1968:123–137; Friedrich 1975:57; de Jong 1987a:107–110; Richardson 1990:51–57; Byre 1994a, 1994b:4–5; de Jong 2001:128–129 on *Odyssey* v 63–75.

[59] The description of one's abode is a standard element of the "arrival" type-scene. See Arend 1933:31–32, 37–38, 42–43, etc., and *Iliad* VI 242–250, 313–317; *Odyssey* v 55–75; vii 81–133; xiv 5–22. There are practical reasons that justify the huge size of Achilles' hut (washing and anointing Hektor's body without Priam's being able to watch, since the old king as well as Idaios are sleeping at some distance from Achilles and Briseis, though they all are in a single hut), but at the same time the narrator aims at offering his audience the focalization of Priam (XXIV 235–237) and paving the way for the emotional encounter to follow. In descriptive passages of embedded focalization the past tense is regularly employed instead of the present or gnomic aorist.

Diagrammatic iconicity is also built around the static perspective of extrinsic spatial pairs like *inside-outside, foreground-background, top-bottom*. A typical example of this technique is the description of Sarpedon's shield:

αὐτίκα δ' ἀσπίδα μὲν πρόσθ' ἔσχετο πάντοσ' ἐΐσην,
καλήν, χαλκείην ἐξήλατον, ἣν ἄρα χαλκεύς
ἤλασεν, ἔντοσθεν δὲ βοείας ῥάψε θαμειάς
χρυσείης ῥάβδοισι διηνεκέσιν περὶ κύκλον·

Presently he held before him the perfect circle of his shield,
a lovely thing of beaten bronze, which the bronze-smith hammered
out for him, and on the inward side had stitched ox-hides
in close folds with golden staples clean round the circle.

Iliad XII 294–297

Despite its terseness, this description of Sarpedon's shield reflects the typology of descriptive sections in general: it is framed by a "visual ring-composition" (294 πάντοσ' ἐΐσην; 297 περὶ κύκλον) and is also marked by the so-called *effet de liste* (295 καλήν, χαλκείην ἐξήλατον). These general features aside, the narrator focuses his attention on the spatial opposition between the shield's outward and inward sides, the former made of bronze, the latter of ox-hides stitched together and fastened with golden staples. The highlighting of this spatially determined antithesis strikes a dissonant note against the monumental description of Achilles' shield in *Iliad* XVIII, since in this case there is no tour of the various parts of the shield, but only a brief look at the outside and inside. In addition to its visual speed, the storyteller uses this technique to create a link with the ensuing narrative.[60] In fact, the emphasis on the marked opposition between the "beaten bronze" of the outer side and the closely folded ox-hides of the inner part functions as a visual backdrop against which the narrator, in the following simile, will emphasize not only the interplay between "outside" and "inside" in the lion's attack on the *strongly built* stable where the sheep are kept, but also the antithesis between Sarpedon's attack and the Achaeans' defense of their wall. It is of no importance that the initial spatial opposition pertains only to an object owned by the aggressor, whereas it is then split between aggressor and defender in both simile and narrative. This *"domino effect"* is based on the visual association of contiguous mental spaces that determines the course followed by the

---

[60] See scholia (b[BCE³]T) on *Iliad* XII 297b: προπαρασκευάζει δὲ ἀεὶ τοὺς ἀριστεύοντας, ἐξαίρων ἡμᾶς εἰς προσοχήν ("he always prepares [us] for those who are excelling [in battle] by drawing our attention"). See also Hainsworth 1993:350 on *Iliad* XII 294–296: "The short description of Sarpedon's equipment is an instance of what the scholia call αὔξησις; it enhances the standing of the warrior in the eyes of the poet's audience."

narrator's mind. Thus descriptive space can be mapped onto the space of the simile and then again onto its immediate narrative space, effectively allowing the storyteller to cross over to other registers by means of *concatenated visual units*.

The spatial pair *top-bottom* is also pertinent to static diagrammatic iconicity, the more so since its inherent verticality plays upon the illusion of concealed importance that humans regularly attribute to hidden objects. The description of Achilles' chest is a representative example of this technique:

αὐτὰρ Ἀχιλλεύς
βῆ ῥ' ἴμεν ἐς κλισίην, χηλοῦ δ' ἀπὸ πῶμ' ἀνέῳγε
καλῆς δαιδαλέης, τήν οἱ Θέτις ἀργυρόπεζα
θῆκ' ἐπὶ νηὸς ἄγεσθαι, ἐῢ πλήσασα χιτώνων
χλαινάων τ' ἀνεμοσκεπέων οὔλων τε ταπήτων·
ἔνθα δέ οἱ δέπας ἔσκε τετυγμένον, οὐδέ τις ἄλλος
οὔτ' ἀνδρῶν πίνεσκεν ἀπ' αὐτοῦ αἴθοπα οἶνον
οὔτέ τεῳ σπένδεσκε θεῶν, ὅτε μὴ Διὶ πατρί.

But meanwhile Achilleus
went off into his shelter, and lifted the lid from a lovely
elaborately wrought chest, which Thetis the silver-footed
had put in his ship to carry, and filled it fairly with tunics
and mantles to hold the wind from a man, and with fleecy blankets.
Inside this lay a wrought goblet, nor did any other
man drink the shining wine from it nor did Achilleus
pour from it to any other god, but only Zeus father.

Iliad XVI 220–227

As in *Iliad* VI 293-295, the most precious object is mentioned at the end of the actual description, and is singled out in stark contrast to the plurality of other, rather "transitional" objects (such as tunics, mantles, and blankets) placed either upon or next to it.[61] This time the *effet de liste* applies to both the description of Achilles' chest (XVI 222 καλῆς, δαιδαλέης) and the various other gifts placed in it. When the narrator refers to the cup of Achilles, he has already guided his listeners to the contents of the chest by means of a *mental tour*, following initially a vertical course from the lid as it is lifted to the tunics, mantles, and blankets, and then a horizontal one, by visualizing the cup *somewhere there* (ἔνθα),

---

[61] By the term *transitional* I refer to the function of these objects as a "bridge" that allows both narrator and audience to cross over from the narrative to the key object inside the chest, the prized cup of Achilles. The warm clothing gives a nice emotional touch; see Griffin 1980:17.

probably next to or beneath them. The top-bottom spatial pair is particularly effective, since the audience is mentally following the narrator in the course of his description: they are lifting the chest's lid and looking at its contents together with him, moving from a multitude of trivial objects to a prized cup devoted to a special god, Zeus himself, for whose sake it is used in libations.

This gradual process by which the narrator mentally arrives at the focus of his description builds on details that suggest to the audience a particular visualization of the chest's contents. The phrase ἐῢ πλήσασα χιτώνων (XVI 223) invites the listeners to visualize a scene in which Thetis herself is both filling (πλήσασα) the chest with tunics, wind-resisting mantles, and fleecy blankets (223–224) that will keep Achilles warm during the war, and placing them on the ship that will carry him to Troy (223 θῆκ' ἐπὶ νηὸς ἄγεσθαι). In the light of the mythic agenda that underlies the entire Iliadic plot, the audience may use the background information of Thetis' preparing Achilles' chest and putting it on board, as well as the highlighting of the cup inside the box (the only item whose placement by Thetis is not syntactically emphasized), as a cue for recalling the special connection between Thetis, Achilles, and Zeus within the *Iliad*. The hidden importance of the cup is then linked to its special use for the father of gods and men, whose help Achilles has sought through his mother's mediation in the beginning of the Iliadic plot. The audience follows the storyteller's visual tour to the contents of the chest, where a special object is placed, an object prized for its literal and symbolic importance in the *Iliad*. This elaborate interplay between description and wider narrative context is even imbued with a certain irony, for Achilles is about to ask Zeus for almost the opposite of what he asked for in *Iliad* I, when he requested through Thetis that the supreme god grant victory to the Trojans until his honor among the Achaeans was restored (365–427, 503–530). Zeus may be Achilles' privileged god, as the choice cup indicates,[62] but he is no longer willing to listen as he did in *Iliad* I. The cards cannot be reshuffled; Patroklos will not return to the ships.[63]

Sometimes the *top-bottom* spatial pair can be tellingly inverted, as it is with Andromakhe's various headdresses in *Iliad* XXII:

> τῆλε δ' ἀπὸ κρατὸς βάλε δέσματα σιγαλόεντα,
> ἄμπυκα κεκρύφαλόν τε ἰδὲ πλεκτὴν ἀναδέσμην
> κρήδεμνόν θ', ὅ ῥά οἱ δῶκε χρυσῆ Ἀφροδίτη

---

[62] See also *Iliad* XI 632–637 and 774–775, where reference is made to the prized cups of Nestor and Peleus respectively.

[63] See Griffin 1980:18: "The special cup, which exists only for this moment, marks the occasion as important, and also, as with the sceptre of Agamemnon in *Iliad* 2, has a bitterly ironical overtone, for Zeus, the god invoked and honoured with the precious cup, has already decided on Patroclus' death (15.65)."

ἤματι τῷ, ὅτε μιν κορυθαίολος ἠγάγεθ' Ἕκτωρ
ἐκ δόμου Ἠετίωνος, ἐπεὶ πόρε μυρία ἔδνα.

[She] threw from her head the shining gear that ordered her
    headdress,
the diadem and the cap, and the holding-band woven together,
and the head-veil,[64] which Aphrodite the golden once had given her
on that day when Hektor of the shining helmet led her forth
from the house of Eëtion, and gave numberless gifts to win her.

                    Iliad XXII 468–472

Andromakhe, who has been in her chamber since *Iliad* VI, after meeting with Hektor on the walls, is preparing a hot bath for her husband, who is expected to return from the battlefield. Hearing the cries of pain and lamentation, she decides to run to the walls, like a maenad (XXII 460 μαινάδι ἴσῃ). At the crucial moment, when she looks at the battlefield and sees Hektor's corpse being dragged by Achilles' chariot, she almost faints. It is at this point that the narrator undertakes a brief description of the headgear that falls from her head.

    Scholars have suggested that since the κρήδεμνον is placed last in the list of Andromakhe's headdresses, it must have been worn under the ἄμπυξ, κεκρύφαλος, and πλεκτὴ ἀναδέσμη that precede it in the text.[65] One would be easily inclined to accept this approach and argue that the storyteller is moving from top to bottom: he starts with the upper parts of Andromakhe's headdress and follows a downward course, from the diadem (ἄμπυκα) to the cap (κεκρύφαλον) to the "holding-band woven together" (πλεκτὴν ἀναδέσμην) to the κρήδεμνον (which scholars have misread as "fillet").[66] There are three problems with this kind of interpretation: first, κρήδεμνον is very likely to mean "head-veil that hung from the back part of the head and covered the back and the shoulders of the wearer,"[67] and so it cannot have been placed under the other head-coverings, but must have been on top of them; second, there are other cases in which a hero is presented as putting on first his outer robe and then his

---

[64] I have changed Lattimore's rendering of κρήδεμνον as "circlet" to "head-veil."

[65] See Studniczka 1909. I owe this reference to Llewellyn-Jones 2003:39n48.

[66] Iconographic representations where the very names of given objects are attested confirm beyond doubt that the ἄμπυξ is a diadem (in the form of a metal strip or band) for holding the hair; see e.g. a sixth-century black-figured Attic skyphos (Martin von Wagner Museum in Würzburg) in Paoletti-Neumann 2003:90 fig. 4, 95 fig. 7, 101. See also Marinatos 1967:B21–22; Llewellyn-Jones 2003:30–33; 2011; van Wees 2005. For a useful general introduction to ancient Greek hairstyles, see Blanck 1996:67–71.

[67] Llewellyn-Jones 2003:30.

tunic;[68] and third, we do not expect Andromakhe, being in a state of maenadic frenzy, to have taken off her headdresses in an orderly fashion.[69] The point of this description is exactly that: the top-to-bottom spatial principle is tellingly annulled because the situation Andromakhe is facing is about uncontrolled pain. By having her throw off her head-coverings all together, the Homeric storyteller translates mental turmoil into physical disarray.

The dramatic effect is further strengthened by the particular poetic grammar of the term κρήδεμνον. Nagler has observed that Greek epic employs the word for both a woman's headdress and the battlements of a walled city,[70] and that it exploits this rich symbolism to parallel the military violation of a city with the sexual violation of a woman, of which "the sad events of ancient history have recorded for posterity that the one followed all too naturally on the other."[71]

If this is so, then it can be plausibly argued that the violation of the top-to-bottom spatial description of the shining gear that ordered Andromakhe's headdress capitalizes on both the immediate context of her maenadic frenzy and the epic semantics of κρήδεμνον. By activating its twofold function as both headdress and symbol of a city's battlements, the narrator visually reenacts the gradual destruction of the city walls. Just as Andromakhe's headgear falls down, so the city's walls will figuratively fall down. The narrator seems to have been guided in his description of an act of grief by the "symbolic association between the citadel of a city and the physical head of its protective monarch."[72] Having not only just used the symbolic interplay between the head of Hektor in the dust and Hekabe throwing her λιπαρὴ καλύπτρη from her head (*Iliad* XXII 405–411),[73] but also having spelled out their association by explicitly stating that τῷ δὲ μάλιστ' ἄρ' ἔην ἐναλίγκιον, ὡς εἰ ἄπασα / Ἴλιος ὀφρυόεσσα πυρὶ σμύχοιτο κατ' ἄκρης (410–411),[74] the storyteller now exploits traditional and immediate referentiality in describing the most emotionally heated throwing off of the headgear by Andromakhe (468–472).[75] If the contrast between Hekabe's single headband and Andromakhe's multiple headgear reflects the latter's greater

---

[68] See *Odyssey* xvi 173, xxiii 155. I owe these examples to Llewellyn-Jones 2003:39n49.

[69] See Llewellyn-Jones 2003:31.

[70] 1974:10–11, 44–60.

[71] Reece 2009:249.

[72] Reece 2009:256.

[73] Hekabe's rather thrifty use of headbands (she is wearing only a καλύπτρη) is due to her old age; see Marinatos 1967:B22. In rural Greece of the present day, women tend, after having their first child, to take off all the parts of their headdress apart from the καλύπτρη; see Korre-Zografou 1991:17.

[74] "It was most like what would have happened, if all lowering / Ilion had been burning top to bottom in fire."

[75] See Foley 1991:24; Danek 2002; Tsagalis 2008b:123, 154, 187–188.

involvement in Hektor's loss,[76] then it may not be off the mark to argue that what has been spelled out in 405–411 is expressed with even more intensity in 468–472. By visualizing the narrator's violation of spatial order in the throwing off of Andromakhe's headgear (the actual κρήδεμνον falling down to the shoulders, almost like a veil), the audience, being familiar with epic poetic grammar, is invited to imagine the destruction of the city κατ' ἄκρης 'from top to bottom', through Andromakhe's throwing her headgear ἀπὸ κρατός 'from her head'.[77]

Intrinsic perspective

Since there are no descriptive segments in the *Iliad* that use the "intrinsic perspective" form of static diagrammatic iconicity, any discussion of this descriptive technique in this context may seem unfounded. However, a brief analysis of the reasons for this lack of intrinsic perspective in static spatial descriptions may help us understand much more about the way space works in descriptive passages. Intrinsic perspective reflects the particular, innate *origo* of a given object. In this case, the designation of spatial features in the text "is marked either through the movement from proximity to distance or through a radial structure, which makes a center the starting point of the description."[78] In an oral tradition such as that crystallized in our *Iliad*, there are at least two reasons why objects are not described from an intrinsic perspective.

First, this kind of description would have emphasized not *what* an object is, but *where* it is, since its innate *origo* would have rendered any reference to the particulars of the object at hand unnecessary: the audience would have known from the beginning that the narrator was referring to the "default" mode of a given object, whose visualization results from its standard form. Description would have been carried out, more or less, by means of *locational* instead of object, or visually patterned, imagery.[79] Iliadic epic, as shown above, employs

---

[76]   See also scholia vetera on *Iliad* XXII 468–472 [Erbse] ὅρα δὲ καὶ ἐν τοῖς λεπτοτάτοις τὴν παρατήρησιν τοῦ ποιητοῦ· ἐπὶ μὲν γὰρ τῆς Ἑκάβης διὰ συντόμων εἶπεν "ἀπὸ δὲ λιπαρὴν ἔρριψε καλύπτρην" (*Iliad* XXII 406) — ἑνὸς γὰρ ἔδει καλύμματος τῇ πρεσβύτιδι —, ἐπὶ δὲ ταύτης ὡς ἂν νέας καὶ γυναικὸς τοῦ μάλιστα εὐδοκιμοῦντος ἐπεξεργασίᾳ κέχρηται. b(BE³E⁴) T), which imply that Andromakhe's grief, as she is both young and the wife of the deceased, is more important.

[77]   *Iliad* XXII 468. The syntagm δέσματα σιγαλόεντα 'shining gear' seems to be reflecting λιπαρὰ κρήδεμνα 'shining diadem of towers' in *Odyssey* xiii 388, which is built on λιπαρὰ κρήδεμνα 'shining veil' in i 334 (= xvi 416, xviii 210, xxi 65).

[78]   Dennerlein 2009:156 (author's translation).

[79]   I use the term *locational* in order to avoid confusion and misunderstanding between what is often called *spatial* versus *object imagery*. Cognitive psychologists, in discussing the existence of two systems of imagery, as neuroanatomical studies have proved, do not "really mean spatial versus object imagery [but] the spatial system in humans that involves some parts of the posterior parietal cortex versus the complex visual-pattern system that involves some parts of the inferior temporal cortex" (Rubin 1995:58).

diagrammatic iconicity to present to its audience *what* an object is in terms of *how* and *what* its function is, not *where* it is placed. True, attention is paid to the actual placement of an object, but this aspect is used more or less as a background for its description, or to highlight a specific feature that marks it as valuable. Placement does not stem from the object's inherent *origo*, but is associated through antithetical pairs (near-far, foreground-background, top-bottom) with its function in a particular context.

Second, descriptions from an intrinsic perspective are notoriously lacking in multiple cues, since they are based on the object's standard and widely known function, which stems from the highlighting of its inherent role. On the other hand, both dynamic and static diagrammatic iconicity, in adopting an extrinsic perspective, employ multiple spatial cues for recall: material, workmanship, size, color, value, a special feature; all these belong to a rather typical format that the storyteller uses to increase mnemonic stability and facilitate the retrieval of information.[80] Having realized which particular set or sets of constraints are operating at a given point in the performance, such as in descriptive passages, we can understand the reasons why the narrator excludes description from an intrinsic perspective. He therefore uses prized objects, of the sort presented above, according to the constraints of oral-traditional song-making.

Mixed types

In the case of Agamemnon's scepter, we have seen that the *Iliad* not only employs two different descriptive techniques—the one based on the position of the beholder and the other on the object's "biography"—but also splits the presentation of the scepter into two passages, separated by significant textual space. Alternatively, the storyteller can also construct large descriptive segments, consisting of an initial static diagrammatic description followed by dynamic iconicity in the form of the object's history.[81] The following two cases are representative of this mixed type of description.

In *Iliad* X 260–271,[82] the narrator refers to the weapons Meriones gives to Odysseus. After a brief reference, in the typical list form, to a bow, a quiver, and

---

[80] Rubin 1995:304–305, with further bibliography; see also Havelock 1978.

[81] The history of most objects refers to events predating the Trojan War or the quarrel between Agamemnon and Achilles; see Minchin 2001:121. In the words of Lynn-George: "a distant past haunts the present" (1988:8).

[82] This is hardly the place to discuss the authenticity of *Iliad* X. Danek (1988) and Dué and Ebbott (2010) are the best accounts against and in favor of its authenticity respectively. Danek believes that the *Doloneia* was composed by a gifted poet other than Homer. This poet tried to develop a personal style, introduced linguistic colloquialisms, varied formulas, and made constant allusion to the *Iliad*. Dué and Ebbott argue that the *Doloneia* represents an alternative type of warfare,

a sword, he embarks on a description of a helmet,[83] which is expanded by the addition of a segment on the helmet's "biography":

Μηριόνης δ' Ὀδυσῆϊ δίδου βιὸν ἠδὲ φαρέτρην
καὶ ξίφος· ἀμφὶ δέ οἱ κυνέην κεφαλῆφιν ἔθηκεν
ῥινοῦ ποιητήν, πολέσιν δ' <u>ἔντοσθεν</u> ἱμᾶσιν
ἐντέτατο στερεῶς, <u>ἔκτοσθε</u> δὲ λευκοὶ ὀδόντες
ἀργιόδοντος ὑὸς θαμέες ἔχον ἔνθα καὶ ἔνθα
εὖ καὶ ἐπισταμένως, μέσσῃ δ' ἐνὶ πῖλος ἀρήρει·
τήν ῥά ποτ' ἐξ Ἐλεῶνος Ἀμύντορος Ὀρμενίδαο
ἐξέλετ' Αὐτόλυκος πυκινὸν δόμον ἀντιτορήσας,
Σκάνδειαν δ' ἄρα δῶκε Κυθηρίῳ Ἀμφιδάμαντι·
Ἀμφιδάμας δὲ Μόλῳ δῶκε ξεινήϊον εἶναι,
αὐτὰρ ὃ Μηριόνῃ δῶκεν ᾧ παιδὶ φορῆναι·
δὴ τότ' Ὀδυσσῆος πύκασεν κάρη ἀμφιτεθεῖσα.

while Meriones gave Odysseus a bow and a quiver
and a sword; and he too put over his head a helmet
fashioned of leather; on the *inside* the cap was cross-strung firmly
with thongs of leather, and on the outer side the white teeth
of a tusk-shining boar were close sewn one after another
with craftsmanship and skill; and a felt was set in the centre.
Autolykos, breaking into the close-built house, had stolen it
from Amyntor, the son of Ormenos, out of Eleon,
and gave it to Kytherian Amphidamas, at Skandeia;
Amphidamas gave it in turn to Molos, a gift of guest-friendship,
and Molos gave it to his son Meriones to carry.
But at this time it was worn to cover the head of Odysseus.

Iliad X 260–271

In lines 262–266, diagrammatic iconicity is built around the static perspective of the extrinsic spatial pair *outside-inside*, which finally brings the narrator's visual memory to the very center of the helmet, just when he is about to complete his description. Up to this point, the storyteller has dealt with the visual "mapping" of this special object. Why is he then expanding or supplementing it with a

---

the λόχος 'ambush', which was neither unheroic nor un-Homeric, but was endowed with its own system of traditional language and themes.

[83] On ivory helmets, see W. Reichel 1901:102; Lorimer 1950:212–219; Borchardt 1972:18–37, 47–52, 1977. On armor and arming in general, see Snodgrass 1999.

story-fragment whose time frame antedates Meriones' acquiring the helmet?[84] Is it significant, in this light, that the story-fragment textually follows but narratively precedes the beginning of the descriptive passage? It is my contention that the narrator employs this technique in order to offer his audience a *reconceptualization* of the described object, deepening their understanding of *what* the object *is* by telling them *how it was acquired* by its present holder. Had he stopped at the "pure" description of the helmet, the listeners would have assumed that it had been Meriones' since it was made. By following the helmet's transfer from one owner to the next, the storyteller puts the preceding description in perspective: the carefully delineated inside and outside parts of the helmet—its spatially conceived iconicity—and its history invite storyteller and audience not only to visualize the structure and material of this precious object but also to see how it has become part of the gesture Meriones is making toward Odysseus.[85] Having done this, the storyteller suggests that the entire description of the helmet should be interpreted in conjunction with its transfer[86] from one person to the other: *the helmet consists in not only what it is made of, but also how it was acquired.*[87]

In *Iliad* XXIII 740–749, the description of a silver bowl as first prize for the foot race during the funeral games for Patroklos is also capped by the object's "biography," from its manufacture by Sidonian men to its arrival in the hands of Achilles:

> Πηλείδης δ' αἶψ' ἄλλα τίθει ταχυτῆτος ἄεθλα,
> ἀργύρεον κρητῆρα τετυγμένον· ἓξ δ' ἄρα μέτρα
> χάνδανεν, αὐτὰρ κάλλει ἐνίκα πᾶσαν ἐπ' αἶαν
> πολλόν, ἐπεὶ Σιδόνες πολυδαίδαλοι εὖ ἤσκησαν,
> Φοίνικες δ' ἄγον ἄνδρες ἐπ' ἠεροειδέα πόντον,
> στῆσαν δ' ἐν λιμένεσσι, Θόαντι δὲ δῶρον ἔδωκαν·
> υἷος δὲ Πριάμοιο Λυκάονος ὦνον ἔδωκεν
> Πατρόκλῳ ἥρωϊ Ἰησονίδης Εὔνηος.

---

[84] The case of Ereuthalion's weapons in *Iliad* VII 136–149 is different, since there is no description of the armor at all.

[85] See Mitsi 1991:42, who argues that "since Autolykos is Odysseus's maternal grandfather, the stolen helmet signifies the passing of cunning to the heir."

[86] Hainsworth 1993:181 on *Iliad* X 267 thinks that the reference to the theft is ungracious, since the helmet will finally be given to his grandson, Odysseus. In my view, it is significant that it was with Odysseus' grandfather Autolukos that the "biography" of the helmet begins. The point is nicely made: the helmet is "fated" to go to Odysseus, following like human life a circular movement. The detail about the theft is secondary; what matters is the transfer and "travel" of the helmet from grandfather to grandson.

[87] Clay 1997:83–89 makes a compelling case for a deeper link between Meriones and Odysseus, a relation that "spills over" to Odysseus' Cretan tales in the *Odyssey*.

καὶ τὸν Ἀχιλλεὺς θῆκεν ἀέθλιον οὗ ἑτάροιο,
ὅς τις ἐλαφρότατος ποσσὶ κραιπνοῖσι πέλοιτο.

At once the son of Peleus set out prizes for the foot-race:
a mixing-bowl of silver, a work of art, which held only
six measures, but for its loveliness it surpassed all others
on earth by far, since skilled Sidonian craftsmen had wrought it
well, and Phoenicians carried it over the misty face of the water
and set it in the harbour, and gave it for a present to Thoas.
Euneos, son of Jason, gave it to the hero Patroklos
to buy Lykaon, Priam's son, out of slavery, and now
Achilleus made it a prize in memory of his companion,
for that man who should prove in the speed of his feet to run
    lightest.

Iliad XXIII 740–749

After a brief description of the mixing-bowl in terms of material (silver) and size ("it held only / six measures"), the storyteller makes an evaluative comment ("for its loveliness it surpassed all others / on earth by far"), which activates (ἐπεί 'for') a story-fragment on the bowl's "biography."[88]

The bowl was made by Sidonian men; the Phoenicians[89] carried it to Lemnos and gave it as a gift to Thoas, king of Lemnos and father of Hypsipyle, who married Jason and gave birth to Euneus (the gift was probably in return for the right to moor in a harbor of the island). The bowl remained there until Thoas' grandson, Euneus, gave it to Patroklos to buy Lukaon out of his slavery in Lemnos; thus the bowl came into Patroklos' and Achilles' hands. The mere mention of Lukaon triggers another mnemonic pathway concerning his own biography, which has already been presented in similar terms, as he was transferred as a slave from one place to another, until he was freed: Achilles had captured Lukaon and sold him to Euneus of Lemnos, whose ships brought wine to the Achaean camp at Troy and received bronze, cattle, and slaves in exchange (VII 467–475).[90] Eëtion from Imbros bought him and sent him to Arisbe; Lukaon left in secret and went to Troy, where he was subsequently killed by Achilles (XXI 34–48).[91]

The bowl's "biography" is a movement in space, which converges at a certain point with that of Lukaon, Priam's son. By translating the bowl's history

---

[88] See Minchin 2001:111.
[89] Sidonians and Phoenicians are often mentioned in Homer as skilled craftsmen and women as well as able merchants.
[90] See also *Iliad* XXI 79.
[91] On this passage, see Richardson 1993:249–252 on *Iliad* XXIII 740–749.

in terms of a change of place, that is, a "journey" from one place to another, and then inscribing it on the "transfer" of Lukaon, object-like, as a slave from one place to another, the narrator provides his audience with a profound reconceptualization of the bowl that he has described in the beginning of this passage. The message is clear: the value of the bowl stems not only from the aspects underscored in the "pure" description, but also from its link to the tragic fate of Lukaon. The prize Achilles sets for the foot race is presented to the audience in terms of both static and dynamic spatiality, since the storyteller's mind's eye tours not only the size and beauty of this prized object but also its history, translated into spatial associations.

Descriptivized Narration

Apart from the traditional dichotomy between narration and description, scholars have identified passages that represent a pair of text-types that are marked by a certain blurring of the boundaries between narration and description, and have been labeled *descriptivized narration,* or *pseudonarrative,*[92] and *narrativized description,* or *pseudodescription.*[93] By the term *descriptivized narration,* or *pseudonarrative,* scholars have defined a description "disguised as a narration,"[94] where the description remains in the background, concealed by minor elements of the narration. Conversely, *narrativized description,* or *pseudodescription,* describes a passage with formal qualities that mark it as description, but which is in fact a form of disguised narrative. Critics like Genette, Hamon, Sternberg, and Mosher,[95] to name a few of those who have immersed themselves in the study of these two intriguing text-types, have concentrated their attention on modern literature, with special emphasis on the novel, and so any attempt to apply their theoretical insights to ancient literary genres must be prepared to identify and explore their further ramifications.

In the *Iliad,* object descriptions at times show a certain fusing of boundaries between description and narration, but never by disguising a given section to conceal its true text-type or mode. Rather, a description of an object that begins in formal descriptive terms soon slips into a kind of pseudonarrative,[96] a form of descriptivized narration endorsed by the *Iliad,* in which a description is not concealed or disguised but blurred, either by a simile-like visual imagery or a

---

[92] See Hamon 1993:97–98, who refers in particular to Homeric description.
[93] See Sternberg 1981:76.
[94] See Kittay 1981:239–240, who argues that the making of the shield of Achilles by Hephaistos is a descriptivized narration.
[95] 1991.
[96] See Minchin 2001:114–117.

mini-ecphrastic format. These fused text-types blend description and narration both by expanding on given aspects of the description (*Iliad* IV 105–113) and by elaborating via mini-ecphrases one or more items in a list of briefly described objects that belong to a "whole" (V 733–742 and XI 16–46). These expansions do not constitute real narrative segments, but are a form of pseudonarrative that seems to sabotage the clearly demarcated frames within which narration and description normally operate.[97] These *glissements*, to use Hamon's apt term,[98] both remind the audience of the borders between description and narration and flirt with the idea of erasing them, at least temporarily. This blurring of the boundaries between description and narration has mainly been interpreted as a transition from space into time, but as we shall see, this point of view is based on examining "pure" narrative sections into which descriptive passages slip.[99] Instead, I will argue that we are dealing here with pseudonarrative that is so strongly anchored to its preceding descriptive "hooks" that it almost creates a new little universe, with different rules and tone: the narrator seems to jump from one mode into the other so as to create a new mixed mode, where description and narration conspire to suggest a reconceptualization of the given object. By building on the spatial description of some of the object's parts, pseudonarrative sections conjure up and subsequently activate equivalent narrative spaces and expand the object's spatial domain, which is no longer limited to the actual description of its parts but also includes its origin or its history, now conceived spatially.

Expanding certain aspects of the description

In *Iliad* IV 105–113, Athena stirs the archer Pandaros, who grabs his bow, made of polished horn from a wild goat, and prepares to shoot an arrow at Menelaos. Given the importance of this action for the development of the plot—as the Lycian archer virtually breaks the truce—the storyteller feels the need to focus on Pandaros' bow:

> αὐτίκ' ἐσύλα τόξον ἐΰξοον ἰξάλου αἰγός
> ἀγρίου, ὅν ῥά ποτ' αὐτὸς ὑπὸ στέρνοιο τυχήσας
> πέτρης ἐκβαίνοντα, δεδεγμένος ἐν προδοκῇσιν,
> βεβλήκει πρὸς στῆθος, ὃ δ' ὕπτιος ἔμπεσε πέτρῃ.

---

[97] According to Hamon 1993:114–115, differences between narration and description are played out by presenting the description through a character who describes an object or artifact to a listener, or through the view of a character, or through the narration of a craftsman making it. This astute observation fits very well the wider narrative context of the shield of Achilles.

[98] 1993:170.

[99] On this point, see Becker 1995:54; Minchin 2001:116–117.

τοῦ κέρα ἐκ κεφαλῆς ἑκκαιδεκάδωρα πεφύκει·
καὶ τὰ μὲν ἀσκήσας κεραοξόος ἤραρε τέκτων,
πᾶν δ' εὖ λειήνας χρυσέην ἐπέθηκε κορώνην.
καὶ τὸ μὲν εὖ κατέθηκε τανυσσάμενος, ποτὶ γαίῃ
ἀγκλίνας·

Straightaway he unwrapped his bow, of the polished horn from
a running wild goat he himself had shot in the chest once,
lying in wait for the goat in a covert as it stepped down
from the rock, and hit it in the chest so it sprawled on the boulders.
The horns that grew from the goat's head were sixteen palms'
    length.
A bowyer working on the horn then bound them together,
smoothing them to a fair surface, and put on a golden string hook.
Pandaros strung his bow and put it in position, bracing it
against the ground ...

Iliad IV 105–113

The description is divided into two parts,[100] each followed by a pseudo-narrative segment: in the first the storyteller narrates how Pandaros killed a wild goat, expanding the single descriptive detail that the bow was made from the horns of a wild goat; in the second, he narrates how the goat's horns were worked by a bowyer who turned them into a bow.[101] Each part of this passage is triggered by a single descriptive element. The adjectives ἰξάλου (*Iliad* IV 105)[102] and ἀγρίου (IV 106) become the driving force for the first part of the pseudo-narrative, which relates the killing of a wild goat as it steps or leaps down from a rock in the wild, and εὔξοον (105) activates the image of a bowyer polishing the horn of the same wild goat that Pandaros killed.[103]

In this example of a pseudo- or descriptivized narrative, the storyteller seems to be narrating events (the actual killing of the goat and the polishing of its horns by a bowyer) evoked by features of the "pure" description in the very beginning of the passage. This time, though, Hamon's *effet de liste* subordinates the narrative to the description: the narrative is embedded in the description and forms part of it, and becomes, so to speak, descriptivized. The narrator uses

---

[100] Becker (1995:58) treats the removal of the bow from its case (*Iliad* IV 105) as a framing action. Since I tend to regard it as a prelude to the actual description, I opt for a twofold division of the ensuing passage.

[101] For the Indo-European background of this technique, see West 2007:462.

[102] Pace Kirk 1985:341 on *Iliad* IV 105, who opts for the meaning "full-grown."

[103] See Becker 1995:58, who declares that "*euxoon* (well polished) refers to the activity of the craftsman in a way that, e.g. *megan* (large) would not."

all the object's features, which he presents in an initial list, as keys to unlock small pseudonarrative sections that refer both to Pandaros' acquiring the bow, stressing his personal involvement, and to the making of it from the goat's horns. Such a mixed mode blurs the clear-cut borders between narration and description, and by using spatial features (the speed of the goat and its living in the wild, the polished surface of the bow) it enables this object to be reconceptualized, as the audience is presented with the description not of a bow but of *Pandaros' bow*. Viewed from this perspective, the object's "biography" makes the description particular, personalized, and involved.[104]

Description and mini-ecphrastic expansion

A more or less brief description of an object can sometimes be expanded by, or focused on, a small-scale ecphrasis. In *Iliad* V 733–744, the narrator refers to Athena's preparation for battle by presenting one by one the various steps she takes. The beginning of this passage is based on the interplay between Athena's taking off her robe and putting on her χιτών and αἰγίς:

αὐτὰρ Ἀθηναίη κούρη Διὸς αἰγιόχοιο
πέπλον μὲν κατέχευεν ἑανὸν πατρὸς ἐπ’ οὔδει
ποικίλον, ὅν ῥ’ αὐτὴ ποιήσατο καὶ κάμε χερσίν,
ἣ δὲ χιτῶν’ ἐνδῦσα Διὸς νεφεληγερέταο
τεύχεσιν ἐς πόλεμον θωρήσσετο δακρυόεντα.
ἀμφὶ δ’ ἄρ’ ὤμοισιν βάλετ’ αἰγίδα θυσσανόεσσαν
δεινήν, ἣν περὶ μὲν πάντη Φόβος ἐστεφάνωται,
ἐν δ’ Ἔρις, ἐν δ’ Ἀλκή, ἐν δὲ κρυόεσσα Ἰωκή,
ἐν δέ τε Γοργείη κεφαλὴ δεινοῖο πελώρου,
δεινή τε σμερδνή τε, Διὸς τέρας αἰγιόχοιο·
κρατὶ δ’ ἐπ’ ἀμφίφαλον κυνέην θέτο τετραφάληρον
χρυσείην, ἑκατὸν πολίων πρυλέεσσ’ ἀραρυῖαν·

Now in turn Athene, daughter of Zeus of the aegis,
beside the threshold of her father slipped off her elaborate
dress which she herself had wrought with her hands' patience,
and now assuming the war tunic of Zeus who gathers
the clouds, she armed in her gear for the dismal fighting.

---

[104] This passage is replete with alliterative effects (δεδεγμένος ἐν προδοκῇσιν, ὃ δ’ ὕπτιος ἔμπεσε πέτρῃ. / τοῦ κέρα ἐκ κεφαλῆς ἑκκαιδεκάδωρα πεφύκει) that lend vividness to the whole section. Particularly strong is the alliteration of ξ (τόξον εὔξοον ἰξάλου), followed by the syllabic assonance of αἰγ-/ἀγ- (αἰγός, ἀγρίου), which is strengthened by placing all these syllables in the arsis of the relevant feet of the hexameter.

And across her shoulders she threw the betasselled, terrible
aegis, all about which Terror hang like a garland,
and Hatred is there, and Battle Strength, and heart-freezing
    Onslaught
and thereon is set the head of the grim gigantic Gorgon,
a thing of fear and horror, portent of Zeus of the aegis.
Upon her head she set the golden helm with its four sheets
and two horns, wrought with the fighting men of a hundred cities.

Iliad V 733–744

Athena's removing her robe, symbolizing her gradual transition from femininity to masculinity, is reinforced by the use of "a tactile and a visual adjective,"[105] namely ἑανόν 'pliant' and ποικίλον 'embroidered', whose spatiality brings Athena's garment before the audience's mind. The accumulation of more information with respect to the robe keys the listeners to the same note, since the robe was made by the goddess herself, a detail pointing to the traditional female task of weaving, and is now let slip to the floor, a nice touch recalling a familiar scene of a woman taking off her clothes.

The next step in Athena's change of state is preparing for battle. This process involves three subsections (putting on her father's tunic, placing her shield around her shoulders, and putting on her helmet),[106] which are symmetrically organized: a central ecphrasis concerning Athena's αἰγίς is flanked by two brief references to her tunic and helmet respectively. The fact that Athena wears Zeus' tunic builds on the previous reference to her letting her robe fall down in her father's house, but is not necessarily echoed in the depiction of the Gorgon's head on her shield, as a talisman from Zeus.[107] By putting on her father's tunic, Athena is clearly entering her warlike, nonfeminine nature: she steps into a world of fear, terror, and fright. This seemingly unimportant detail points to the most vital aspect of her preparation, her wearing the shield.[108]

---

[105] Becker 1995:62.

[106] I consider Athena's mounting Hera's chariot with a huge spear in her hand as "external" to her military preparation. At that moment she is already prepared for battle, but simply needs to enter the battlefield together with Hera.

[107] The Gorgon's head on Athena's αἰγίς reflects the myth in which Athena killed and skinned the monster Gorgo (Euripides *Ion* 987–997); it was from its skin that she made her shield. Burkert draws attention to the fact that "pictorial art turned the animal head into a Gorgon's head and bordered the *aegis* with snakes" (1985:140); see also *Iliad* II 447–449, where Athena's αἰγίς has golden tassels.

[108] Athena is often depicted in art with helmet, long robe, and raised spear; see Robertson 2001:41n27.

The two adjectives employed to describe the shield refer to a single feature (θυσσανόεσσαν 'betasseled') and its impact (δεινήν 'terrible') on someone looking at it.[109] As the narrator describes the various images of the shield depicting Terror, Hatred, Battle Strength, Onslaught, and the Gorgon's head, the audience is invited to visualize Athena's subsequent involvement in the actual fighting.[110] The scenes on the shield function as a kind of theoretical summary and comment on war: the αἰγίς of Athena is decorated with images of what war is about in its abstract form. The creatures on the shield explore one of the most frequently recurring issues in the entire *Iliad*, the pathology and nature of war.

Here the narrator has used a mixed text-type, starting with description and ending in an ecphrasis, to thematize and explore Athena's twofold nature as a goddess of female ἔργα and military exploits. This transition, which amounts to a general comment (almost a *mise-en-abyme*) about the *Iliad*, and is exploited at length in the case of the shield of Achilles, takes place with the description of Athena's change of clothing, and is intensified mainly by the longer ecphrasis on her shield and the shorter one on her helmet (decorated by the hundred cities' men-at-arms).[111] The spatial aspects of this descriptive section have been effectively orchestrated so as not to stress the pictorial richness of ecphrasis but to embed it within the epic's larger thematic agenda. Like Athena, who changes clothing to enter the battlefield, the storyteller is now ready to switch text-types and move from space to time, from description back to narration.[112]

The arming scene of Agamemnon in *Iliad* XI 15–46 is one of the most detailed in the entire epic. It includes short descriptions of seven different items (greaves, breastplate, sword, shield, belt, helmet, spears), three of which (breastplate, shield, and belt) are expanded by mini-ecphrastic sections:

> Ἀτρεΐδης δ' ἐβόησεν ἰδὲ ζώνυσθαι ἄνωγεν
> Ἀργείους· ἐν δ' αὐτὸς ἐδύσετο νώροπα χαλκόν.
> κνημῖδας μὲν <u>πρῶτα</u> περὶ κνήμῃσιν ἔθηκεν
> καλάς, ἀργυρέοισιν ἐπισφυρίοις ἀραρυίας·

---

[109] See Becker 1995:63.

[110] According to Burkert (1985:140 and n8), who points to *Iliad* XVI 100, "to conquer a city is [for Athena] to loosen her veils." This view is based on the twofold meaning of κρήδεμνα as "head-band" and "city walls": see scholia on *Iliad* XVI 100 (κρήδεμνα· νῦν τὰ τείχη, μεταφορικῶς· ἰδίως γὰρ κρήδεμνον τὸ τῆς κεφαλῆς κάλυμμα); scholia on *Odyssey* iii 392, xiii 388; Apollonius Sophista *Lexicon Homericum* s.v. κρηδέμνῳ; Hesychius s.v. κρήδεσμον; Eustathius on *Iliad* II 117, XVI 100; *Odyssey* i 335, iii 392, xiii 388; see also Nagler 1974:44–63; Reece 2009:257–258. I cannot see a specific connection with Athena in *Iliad* XVI 100, especially since Athena is not included in the list of goddesses wearing a κρήδεμνον in early Greek epic poetry (like Hera, Demeter, Rhea, Hekate, Thetis, Kharis, and Leukothea).

[111] See Reece 2009:257–258.

[112] See Mitsi 2007:9.

δεύτερον αὖ θώρηκα περὶ στήθεσσιν ἔδυνεν,
τόν ποτέ οἱ Κινύρης δῶκε ξεινήϊον εἶναι,
πεύθετο γὰρ Κύπρονδε μέγα κλέος, οὕνεκ' Ἀχαιοί
ἐς Τροίην νήεσσιν ἀναπλεύσεσθαι ἔμελλον·
τοὔνεκά οἱ τὸν δῶκε, χαριζόμενος βασιλῆϊ.
τοῦ δ' ἤτοι δέκα οἶμοι ἔσαν μέλανος κυάνοιο,
δώδεκα δὲ χρυσοῖο καὶ εἴκοσι κασσιτέροιο·
κυάνεοι δὲ δράκοντες ὀρωρέχατο προτὶ δειρήν
τρεῖς ἑκάτερθ', ἴρισσιν ἐοικότες, ἅς τε Κρονίων
ἐν νέφεϊ στήριξε, τέρας μερόπων ἀνθρώπων.
ἀμφὶ δ' ἄρ' ὤμοισιν βάλετο ξίφος· ἐν δέ οἱ ἧλοι
χρύσειοι πάμφαινον, ἀτὰρ περὶ κουλεὸν ἧεν
ἀργύρεον, χρυσέοισιν ἀορτήρεσσιν ἀρηρός.
ἂν δ' ἕλετ' ἀμφιβρότην πολυδαίδαλον ἀσπίδα θοῦριν,
καλήν, ἣν πέρι μὲν κύκλοι δέκα χάλκεοι ἦσαν,
ἐν δέ οἱ ὀμφαλοὶ ἦσαν ἐείκοσι κασσιτέροιο
λευκοί, ἐν δὲ μέσοισιν ἔην μέλανος κυάνοιο.
τῇ δ' ἐπὶ μὲν Γοργὼ βλοσυρῶπις ἐστεφάνωτο
δεινὸν δερκομένη, περὶ δὲ Δεῖμός τε Φόβος τε·
τῆς δ' ἐξ ἀργύρεος τελαμὼν ἦν, αὐτὰρ ἐπ' αὐτοῦ
κυάνεος ἐλέλικτο δράκων, κεφαλαὶ δέ οἱ ἦσαν
τρεῖς ἀμφιστρεφέες, ἑνὸς αὐχένος ἐκπεφυυῖαι.
κρατὶ δ' ἐπ' ἀμφίφαλον κυνέην θέτο τετραφάληρον
ἵππουριν· δεινὸν δὲ λόφος καθύπερθεν ἔνευεν.
εἵλετο δ' ἄλκιμα δοῦρε δύω, κεκορυθμένα χαλκῷ,
ὀξέα· τῆλε δὲ χαλκὸς ἀπ' αὐτόφιν οὐρανὸν εἴσω
λάμπ'. ἐπὶ δ' ἐγδούπησαν Ἀθηναίη τε καὶ Ἥρη,
τιμῶσαι βασιλῆα πολυχρύσοιο Μυκήνης.

And Atreus' son cried out aloud and drove the Achaians
to gird them, while he himself put the shining bronze upon him.
First he placed along his legs the beautiful greaves linked
with silver fastenings to hold the greaves at the ankles.
Afterwards he girt on about his chest the corselet
that Kinyras had given him once, to be a guest present.
For the great fame and rumour of war had carried to Kypros
how the Achaians were to sail against Troy in their vessels.
Therefore he gave the king as a gift of grace his corselet.
Now there were ten circles of deep cobalt upon it,
and twelve of gold and twenty of tin. And toward the opening

at the throat there were rearing up three serpents of cobalt
on either side, like rainbows, which the son of Kronos
has marked upon the clouds, to be a portent to mortals.
Across his shoulders he slung the sword, and the nails upon it
were golden and glittered, and closing about it the scabbard
was silver, and gold was upon the swordstraps that held it.
And he took up the man-enclosing elaborate stark shield,
a thing of splendour. There were ten circles of bronze upon it,
and set about it were twenty knobs of tin, pale-shining,
and in the very centre another knob of dark cobalt.
And circled in the midst of all was the black-eyed face of the Gorgon
with her stare of horror, and Fear was inscribed upon it, and Terror.
The strap of the shield had silver upon it, and there also on it
was coiled a cobalt snake, and there were three heads upon him
twisted to look backward and grown from a single neck, all three.
Upon his head he set the helmet, two-horned, four-sheeted,
with the horse-hair crest, and the plumes nodded terribly above it.
Then he caught up two strong spears edged with sharp bronze
and the brazen heads flashed far from him deep into heaven.
And Hera and Athene caused a crash of thunder about him,
doing honour to the lord of deep-golden Mykenai.

Iliad XI 15–46

After two introductory verses indicating that Agamemnon is preparing for battle, the narrator begins his description, following a *map* strategy, with the hero's greaves. In this mode, division into segments and their systematic presentation (left to right, north to south, front to back) is the rule.[113] Although the map creates the impression of a "disembodied and static perspective,"[114] the audience experiences what is described as a dynamic process, since the multiple short descriptions are anchored to the narration of Agamemnon's putting on the various parts of his armor. Knowing that the disclosure of spatial information is more effective when combined with narrative segments,[115] the narrator is free to decide where to pause for a longer period of time by expanding any of the armor's parts through the use of mini-ecphrastic units.

[113] See Ryan 2009:427, who follows Linde and Labov 1975 in distinguishing between a *map* strategy and a *tour*, which "represents space dynamically from a mobile point of view."

[114] Ryan 2003:218.

[115] Narrative facilitates recall and is a much stronger cue for keeping the audience's attention. See Rubin 1995:15–17, 56, 326.

There are at least two important questions to be asked with respect to this passage: first, why has the storyteller decided to expand some of the descriptive subsegments by mini-ecphrases, and second, why has not he done the same with all the parts of Agamemnon's armor? These two questions may seem trivial to those who are eager to explain all this as a random choice, but I will attempt to show that they lie at the very heart of the function of space in descriptive passages.

Let me then begin by saying that the entire passage could have had the abbreviated form of a list: "and Agamemnon put on his greaves, breastplate, sword, shield, belt, helmet, and spears." Instead of simply enumerating the individual parts of Agamemnon's armor, the storyteller could easily have turned this list into a catalogue, by expanding each item or entry with an extremely brief addition of the kind exemplified by the item "greaves": a short, one- or two-line, attributive addition. Why then has he opted for the use of a mini-ecphrastic type?

To answer this question, we need to revisit some of the basic aspects of ecphrasis. According to Krieger (1992), ecphrasis aestheticizes language, by shaping it into patterns that "translate" narrative temporality into spatial stillness. The "still moment," to use Krieger's apt expression,[116] freezes the unfolding of the narrative and creates pauses that allow the storyteller to shed light on what he describes. Ecphrasis sometimes raises questions about hidden aspects of the described object, as it can operate as a sort of commentary on its function, and it can also work proleptically by bringing into the limelight what will be employed later in the plot. From this perspective, ecphrasis can be also used to explore recurrent themes or issues within a larger framework—a point that will be of particular importance in the case of Agamemnon's armor.[117]

Agamemnon's breastplate is the first part of his armor that is doubly expanded, through its history and the use of a brief ecphrasis. The narrator informs his audience that it was a guest-gift to Agamemnon from Kinuras, king of Cyprus. The reference to Kinuras remains obscure, but the point may simply be that Agamemnon's fame had reached even far-off lands.[118] By beginning with the history of the breastplate, the storyteller tunes his description to a high note, which the narrative will effectively pick up once the description is over: Athena and Hera, as if they were witnessing—in the manner of an audience—Agamemnon's preparation for battle, thunder about him, "doing honour to the lord of deep-golden Mykenai" (*Iliad* XI 46). In fact, the digressive history of the breastplate posits a different kind of biography than the one used for

---

[116] 2003:91.
[117] On these aspects of ecphrasis, see Mitsi 2007.
[118] So Hainsworth 1993:218 on *Iliad* XI 20.

Agamemnon's scepter. Whereas Agamemnon's scepter is a symbol of continuity between generations and defines the king of Mycenae both in relation to its first recipient, Zeus, and to Agamemnon's heroic but also troubled human lineage in Argos (Pelops–Atreus–Thuestes),[119] the breastplate is a different kind of gift, one that does not identify Agamemnon with his ancestors but stems from his personal heroic fame.

The further expansion of the breastplate's description by a brief ecphrasis creates a "still moment," marked by the use of spatial features. Plurality ("twelve," "twenty," "three"), material ("gold," "tin," "cobalt"), positioning ("towards the opening of the throat," "on either side"), internal expansion by means of a simile that is embedded in the ecphrasis ("like rainbows, which the son of Kronos / has marked upon the clouds, to be a portent of mortals"); all these features create a vivid mental image of Agamemnon's breastplate and endow it with majestic grandeur. It is exactly this aspect of the breastplate that the storyteller wants to transfer from this prized object to its owner. Underscoring status is one aim of this double expansion, and especially of the brief ecphrastic format; pointing to human vanity is another. The audience, because of their familiarity with the plot of the epic, would no doubt have realized that for all the greatness of his armor, Agamemnon will never be Achilles' successful surrogate in the field of combat. Despite his initial success in *Iliad* XI, he will be wounded in the arm and retreat from the battlefield (*Iliad* XI 252–253 and 273–274). This bitterly ironic innuendo is confirmed by the fact that the narrator uses Hera, who (together with Athena) had thundered in honor of Agamemnon while he prepared for battle (XI 45–46), as the core of a simile comparing Agamemnon's pain from his wound to the birth pangs Hera's daughters bring upon a woman in labor (XI 269–272). The brief ecphrasis on the wide surface of the breastplate creates expectations of Agamemnon's ultimate victory, only to overturn them. This subversive function of the ecphrasis makes full use of the "still moment" to freeze the action, and by illusively highlighting authority and martial prowess to comment on Agamemnon's vanity and future failure. While temporal unraveling is at a rest, military greatness can be briefly aestheticized, since it will soon be cut short.

In the brief ecphrases on the shield and its strap, the narrator presents his audience with vivid depictions of terrifying creatures (Gorgon, Fear, Terror) and snakes respectively. Given that snakes were also depicted on Agamemnon's breastplate, it can be argued that the storyteller's aim is to aestheticize recurrent themes of martial epic like violence and war. Just before Agamemnon's ἀριστεία, which will be replete with the utmost cruelty of successive murders,

---

[119] See Mitsi 1991:42.

the narrator explores the theme of violence by using ecphrasis as a commentary on the nature of war. The presence of monsters, like the Gorgon, who are regularly excluded from Homeric narrative, and personified abstract entities like Fear and Terror lend the ecphrasis a generalized tone. Even though (or perhaps because) it forms part of Agamemnon's armor, it virtually amounts to a critical outlook on the nature of war. Making full use of standard mnemonic formats that exploit spatial cues such as the interplay between periphery[120] and center,[121] the narrator can easily append his brief descriptions of some of the individual parts of Agamemnon's armor through elaborate ecphrases, allowing his audience a glimpse into his own evaluation of the unfolding narrative. By creating a pause in his narration, the storyteller employs description and ecphrases tied to one of the two heroes around whom the theme of μῆνις has been unfolding since the beginning of the poem, in order to ponder the monstrosity, inhumanity, and cruelty of war.

As to the second question, referring to the narrator's selection of some parts of Agamemnon's armor for ecphrastic elaboration at the expense of others, the answer is twofold: given that ornamental depictions on works of art presuppose a surface on which the artwork will be placed, the breastplate and the shield with its strap are more suitable than the sword or the helmet. Space probably was the decisive criterion for this choice, but it was hardly the only one. Agamemnon's role in the *Iliad* was so deeply marked by his initial conflict with Achilles that it is not unthinkable that the narrator, having planned an ecphrasis on Achilles' shield on a massive scale in *Iliad* XVIII, wanted to endow Agamemnon with multiple but smaller ecphrases before his own ἀριστεία in *Iliad* XI. In this way the audience would realize, during the extended ecphrasis dedicated to a single part of Achilles' armor, that in contrast with Agamemnon, the son of Thetis will not be wounded but masterfully prevail on the battlefield, that his own single ecphrasis allusively outdoes the multiple short ecphrases for Agamemnon, just as his heroic prowess surpasses by far that of the king of Mycenae.

---

[120] *Iliad* XI 33–34: "There were ten circles of bronze upon it, / and set about it were twenty knobs of tin, pale-shining."

[121] *Iliad* XI 35–36: "... and in the very centre another knob of dark cobalt. / And circled in the midst of all was the blank-eyed face of the Gorgon."

8

Ecphrastic Space

B Y THE TERM *ECPHRASTIC SPACE*, I refer to: (1) the "external" or "physical" space or material on which the depiction is placed; and (2) the "internal" space or spaces mentioned in the various narrative snapshots of the ecphrasis, which consists of the individual locations of an imagined story-world (e.g. a city at peace or a dancing-floor) employed as spatial cues for information processing and mnemonic recall.[1]

External Space

The ecphrasis on the shield of Achilles (*Iliad* XVIII 478–608) describes the multiple depictions on the metal that covers the five folds of the shield.[2] Apart from highlighting the fact that the emphasis falls on the process of manufacturing this piece of pictorial art, classicists have not dealt with the "physical" space of the material on which Hephaistos' work appears.[3]

Working in metal rather than, say, on a tapestry or a woven fabric influences the end product of a skilled craftsman's labor. For in contrast to embroidering or weaving, the objects or figures depicted on metal tend to be bright

---

[1]   A good starting point is the relevant articles in Neue Pauly and OCD by Fantuzzi and Rusten; two useful collections of essays, accompanied by extensive bibliographies, are also provided by two special issues on ecphrasis published by Elsner in *Ramus* (2002) and by Bartsch and Elsner in *Classical Philology* (2007). For Homer, see Alden s.v. "Ekphrasis" in Finkelberg 2011, with further bibliography.

[2]   See Fittschen 1973:N5–N7. On the shield of Achilles in general, see the bibliographical guide by Arpaia 2010.

[3]   Becker (1995:84–85, 96–100) is an exception. He draws attention to *Iliad* XVIII 418 (χρύσειαι, ζωῇσι νεήνισιν ἐοικυῖαι ["these are golden, and in appearance like living young women"]) to argue that "through the naming of the material and the similetic comparison, the bard has assured that we remain aware of the medium (in this case sculpted metal) as well as the message." Becker points to defamiliarization and to the collapse of identity between the golden handmaids on the shield and real-world women, which increases the "admiration of the audience for the mimetic capabilities of the work of art" (85).

and gleaming,[4] intensifying the vividness of the images. In fact, this long ecphrasis contains so many references to the shining effect of the objects and figures depicted on the shield that it may be called an "exercise in *radiance*."[5] The storyteller makes this clear in a multitude of ways, through references to light (XVIII 492 δαΐδων ὕπο λαμπομενάων; 596 στίλβοντας ἐλαίῳ) and especially to shining metals (507 δύω χρυσοῖο τάλαντα; 510 τεύχεσι λαμπόμενοι; 517 ἄμφω χρυσείω, χρύσεια δὲ εἵματα ἔσθην; 522 αἴθοπι χαλκῷ; 529 ἀργεννέων ὀΐων; 548–549 ἣ δὲ μελαίνετ' ὄπισθεν, ἀρηρομένη δὲ ἐῴκει / χρυσείη περ ἐοῦσα; 560 λεύκ' ἄλφιτα; 561–562 ἀλωήν / καλήν, χρυσείην, μέλανες δ' ἀνὰ βότρυες ἦσαν; 563 κάμαξι διαμπερὲς ἀργυρέῃσιν; 564 κυανέην κάπετον; 564–565 περὶ δ' ἕρκος ἔλασσεν / κασσιτέρου; 574 χρυσοῖο τετεύχατο κασσιτέρου τε; 577 χρύσειοι δὲ νομῆες; 583 μέλαν αἷμα; 588 οἰῶν ἀργεννάων; 597–598 μαχαίρας / εἶχον χρυσείας ἐξ ἀργυρέων τελαμώνων).

Even a quick survey of all the above expressions makes clear that there is no great variety of *colors* used on the five folds of the shield. But this lack of variety is counterbalanced by intense brightness. The context may reinforce this point, to be sure, since we are in the middle of Hephaistos' workshop, where fire and metals are everywhere, but nevertheless brightness[6] facilitates and intensifies graphic quality (ἐνάργεια),[7] playing with the illusion that the figures on the shield are alive.[8] To this lack of color the images of the earth in the third fold

---

[4] On the importance and value the Greeks attributed to glitter and glow in art, see Neer 2010:74 and 76–77 (for examples from Homer).

[5] On the "aesthetics of radiance" and their association with the Near East, see Winter 1994; 1999. On radiance and statues, see D. Steiner 2001:97–98; on radiance in religion and cult, see Jameson 1999; Parisinou 2000.

[6] Brightness is a cue to recall; see "Internal Space," below.

[7] On the term "graphic quality" as a translation of ἐνάργεια, see Nünlist 2009:194. On ἐνάργεια (traditionally rendered as "vividness") in ancient criticism and poetry, see Römer 1879:xiii–xiv; Lehnert 1896:92; Zanker 1981; Rispoli 1984; Meijering 1987:29–52; Lausberg 1990:§810; Graf 1995; Dubel 1997; Bartsch 2007; Nünlist 2009:194–198; Webb 2009:87–106. On ἐνάργεια in Homer, see Bakker 1997:77–79. On ancient authors impressed by the vividness of Homeric discourse, see e.g. Gorgias *Helen* 9; Plato *Ion* 535b–e; Pseudo-Longinus *On the Sublime* 15; Quintilian *Institutio oratoria* 6.2.29. See also scholia vetera, e.g. on *Iliad* IV 154 (BT: χειρὸς ἔχων Μενέλαον, ἐπεστενάχοντο δ' ἑταῖροι: "and by the hand held / Menelaos, while their companions were mourning beside him"); ἄφελε τὸν στίχον καὶ οὐ βλάψεις τὴν σαφήνειαν, ἀπολέσεις δὲ τὴν ἐνάργειαν, ἥτις ἐμφαίνει τὴν Ἀγαμέμνονος συμπάθειαν καὶ τὴν τῶν συναχθομένων ἑταίρων διάθεσιν ("if you remove the verse, you will not harm the clarity, but you will destroy the vividness, which shows Agamemnon's sympathy and the disposition of his companions who share his grief"; I owe this example and the translation of the scholium to N. Richardson 2006:195). For more information, see Nünlist 2009:194–198. On the role of ἐνάργεια 'graphic quality, vividness' and σαφήνεια 'clarity'), which allow a beholder to "arrive at the same same inner vision—the same φαντασία— that the scene or object had originally brought to the mind's eye of the artist, speaker, or writer," see Squire 2011:327.

[8] The use of verbs like ποιεῖν, τιθέναι, τεύχειν, preceded by the strong spatial deixis of the preverb ἐν, shows how the "physical" space of the material on which the depictions are described

are no exception, as they constitute the backdrop on which human activity is presented—that is, they are a means to an end.

At the end of the ecphrasis on the shield, the narrator briefly mentions in list form the rest of Achilles' armor (*Iliad* XVIII 609–613), which is also characterized by its brightness (610 θώρηκα φαεινότερον πυρὸς αὐγῆς; 612 ἐπὶ δὲ χρύσεον λόφον ἧκεν; 613 κνημῖδας ἑανοῦ κασσιτέροιο).[9] In this way, the storyteller fully exploits the material on which the depictions are placed, by turning it from a mere accoutrement into an important spatial device that plays its own role in the visual brilliance of the epic's longer ecphrasis.

The radiance of the figures on the shield of Achilles points to an aesthetics of space that captures the listeners' imagination. The shield is a θαῦμα ἰδέσθαι in and of itself because it plays so masterfully with the relation between image and beholder.[10] Building on Prier's account of θαῦμα ἰδέσθαι[11] and Neer's analysis of the role of radiance in early and classical Greek sculpture, I would argue that the constant emphasis on both the shield's radiance and the glow and glitter of various figures and things depicted on it amount to "a phenomenology of the synapse, the 'joint' of presence and absence."[12] The shining effect refers to a dialectic of proximity and distance, of the gleaming "here" in Hephaistos' workshop and the radiant "there" of the mental beholders of the shield, the members of the external audience.[13] This interplay between "grasping sight and radiant light"[14] is a duality that occurs on both the level of the narrative and that of the discourse. The shining effect of the gleaming depictions on the shield is relevant to the grasping sight of both those looking at them and those who visualize this interaction in their mind's eyes. Grasping sight and radiant light are about spatial relationships of proximity and distance, of presence and absence, which are of prime importance for understanding that the wonder (θαῦμα) of the shield amounts to the interplay between medium and image, to the balance between subject and object. Perhaps it is not accidental that in the formula θαῦμα ἰδέσθαι the middle infinitive resists revealing its grammatical subject.[15]

---

determines some of the choices the narrator had to make with respect to the matter of vividness. On mechanisms that promote ἐνάργεια (like the emphasis on detail that makes the description seem authentic) according to ancient rhetoricians, see Meijering 1987:39–44; Nünlist 2009:194–195. See also Berardi 2010.

[9] See also τεύχεα μαρμαίροντα (*Iliad* XVIII 617).

[10] See Neer 2010:67.

[11] See also Mette 1961; Hunzinger 1994.

[12] Neer 2010:68.

[13] See Prier 1989:84–97; Neer 2010:66–67.

[14] Neer 2010:67.

[15] See Fränkel 1973:77–82, 524; Prier 1989:95; Neer 2010:67.

Internal Space

Most studies of the ecphrasis on Achilles' shield are either concerned with the conflict between narrative and description,[16] or seek to unlock some hidden pattern for interpreting the multiple, yet hard to classify scenes depicted on the five folds of the shield. The thrust of all these approaches is purely interpretive: it is informed by the standard opposition between time and space, which because of Lessing's seminal work[17] has been virtually equated in literature with the antithesis between narration and description. The limits and limitations of these interpretive tactics are multiple, but the thrust of the overall approach on ecphrasis has somehow convinced scholars that this is both the right way and the only way of tackling this issue.

Criticism requires strong supportive arguments, lest it slip into a sort of impressionistic academic vanity, seeking to persuade through far-fetched suggestions. It is in this light, and with the utmost respect and understanding for what previous approaches to the ecphrasis on the shield have contributed,[18] that I would like to follow a different tack. My take on this famous, albeit notoriously complex, ecphrasis forms part of a larger theoretical assumption concerning the medium within which it is placed and the broader framework it belongs to, that is, oral song. In order to begin to understand and evaluate the ecphrasis on the shield of Achilles, we first need to study how it came into being, the way it was composed, and of course the tenets and rules governing this particular kind of composition. I see two basic problems in many previous interpretations of Achilles' shield: First, by following a clear-cut division between description and narration, scholars have failed to realize that most of the scenes depicted on the shield operate on a special register, where the borders between pure narration and pure description are deliberately blurred. Second, the philological zeal with which classicists have struggled to unearth the single interpretive key[19]

---

[16] On this topic, see Fowler 1991.

[17] 1893 (1766).

[18] Stanley's attempt (1993:9–13) to draw attention to various verbal devices employed by the story-teller (refrain composition, ringing devices, interlocking form) to "emphasize the integration of individual elements" and point to associations between them is on the right track, though I disagree with the results of his analysis. A significant number of what he calls "ringing devices" are forced and seem to be the outcome of his effort to establish an overall organizing frame for the entire shield, on the basis of patterns of parallelism and contrast under the umbrella of the technique of ring-composition.

[19] The most significant attempts to interpret the shield of Achilles have been based on this principle: Marg (1957:20–37), Reinhardt (1961:401–411), and Schadewaldt (1965:361–367) have argued that the shield is an effort to represent the entire world, whether the stress is on everyday (Marg), aristocratic (Reinhardt), or civilized life (Schadewaldt); Ø. Andersen (1976) called attention to isolated aspects of the depicted scenes that he tried to connect to episodes of the main narrative; Gärtner (1976) highlighted the importance of the three agricultural scenes and maintained

to the entire shield not only reproduces, albeit on a different level, the ancient obsession with an allegorical reading of the multiple ecphrases on the shield,[20] but also falls into the trap of highlighting certain aspects of some scenes at the expense of others, in order to reach the desired interpretive conclusion. The crucial issue for the presentation of the various scenes on the shield is interlocked with their distribution on the five layers or folds, and must be approached by exploring the cognitive process adopted by the storyteller. Such a line of thought is unavoidably based on and colored by one's commitment to a specific school of criticism, which goes together with certain thorny issues concerning literacy and orality.[21] This kind of interpretation would postulate that the shield of Achilles may be suggesting (or even inviting) alternative ways of interpreting and arranging the material depicted on its surface.[22] Some may even entertain the thought that this is an essential part of its success, that it functions as a multiform that can appeal in different ways to different audiences. That said, my take on the shield differs from previous ones in two respects: (1) it does not posit any kind of orthodox reading that excludes alternative ones, and (2) it rather tries to follow the mental process of the composition of this long ecphrasis within the medium of oral song, by putting the stress—I hope not excessively—on the role of spatial organization and arrangement. Instead of deluding ourselves that there is a single interpretive key to the entire shield, the analysis I will propose suggests that the Iliadic narrator's aim may have been to alert his audience to possible ways of negotiating with the world: neither comprehensiveness nor pictorial *contrapposto* with the drama of the plot, but doubleness, and most of all the inducing of wonder.[23] In this light, I begin my approach to this complex matter by describing the framework within which this ecphrasis is born and breathes—that is, oral poetry.

In this medium, the narrator performs by following a mental path[24] that allows him to create strong visualizations of the contents of his song. This mental journey is so deeply built into the system of oral song-making that, as is widely known, it has been semantically epitomized by the telling meta-

---

that the king standing joyfully among the reapers is the central focus; Byre (1992), following Sheppard (1922:8), claimed that the scenes of conflict and discord stand out, since they bear a striking similarity to the thematic kernel of the *Iliad*. Apart from privileging a single interpretation, all these attempts are "plot-oriented," either by contrast (peaceful life versus the cruelty of war) or by similarity (conflict and discord).

[20] See Hardie 1985.

[21] See Ong 1982; Havelock 1986; Thomas 1992.

[22] With respect to this issue, Michael Squire has brought to my attention the case of the Iliac tablets.

[23] See Neer 2010:85.

[24] On mental paths versus real paths, see Giannisi 2006:75–90.

phor of the οἴμη,[25] the path the storyteller follows during the performance.[26] If we then try to envisage the actual process through which a narrator would describe to his audience the multiple depictions on the great shield of Achilles, we need to reconstruct the actual flow of images in his mind. This approach is very much in line with the fact that ecphrasis was described in late antiquity as λόγος περιηγηματικὸς ἐναργῶς ἄγων εἰς ὄψιν τὸ δηλούμενον ("a descriptive discourse bringing vividly/graphically[27] before the eyes what is expressed").[28] Although the ancient scholia on the shield of Achilles employ theatrical imagery for the vivid language of this extended descriptive passage,[29] "the adjective *periēgēmatikos* ... casts the speaker as a guide showing the listener around the sight to be described."[30] The metaphor of speech as a journey is not only frequent in Greek literature but also informs the technical vocabulary used. As I will try to show in the case of the shield of Achilles, it is as if the storyteller takes his listeners with him on a περιήγησις ("travelling around" or "winding path"). He intends not only to show his audience what is depicted on the shield, but also to direct and channel their attention. This kind of showing is about both seeing and understanding, about making visible and intelligible.[31]

Cognitive psychology and research on memory have shown that the human mind processes images by selecting details that it then configures and reconfigures according to preexisting schemata, patterns into which experience has been organized. The narrator, composing his song orally, works under multiple constraints. Some of these have to do with the generic features of his medium, such as diction and meter and the rules governing them; others with limits on how much innovation he can apply to the basic themes of his song within the larger framework of the tradition; while others are transgeneric and pertain to mental scripts available to him, which themselves interact with the reality of the performance. This complex system of constraints contextualizes meaning and sheds light on the importance of *how* images are produced. If we are allowed to use the term *pictorial artifact* for the ecphrastic universe of Achilles' shield,

---

25 *Odyssey* viii 74; viii 481; xxii 347.
26 See Rubin 1995:62, who cites Foley.
27 See Nünlist 2009:194.
28 Aelius Theon 2.118.7-8 [Spengel] on ἔκφρασις. For an almost verbatim repetition of this definition, see Hermogenes *Progymnasmata* 10.1-2 [Rabe], Aphthonius 10.36.22 [Rabe], Nicolaus 3.491 [Spengel]. See also Becker 1995:24-31.
29 Scholia on *Iliad* XVIII 476-477 (bT): δαιμονίως τὸν πλάστην αὐτὸς διέπλασεν, ὥσπερ ἐπὶ σκηνῆς ἐκκυκλήσας καὶ δείξας ἡμῖν ἐν φανερῷ τὸ ἐργαστήριον ("[Homer] presented the maker [Hephaistos] effectively, as if rolling him onto a stage and showing us his workshop in the open"); see Webb 2009:54.
30 Webb 2009:54.
31 See Webb 2009:54, who points to Pausanias' use of the term Περιήγησις for his traveling around Greece.

then we must be also permitted to argue that "artefacts are made possible by the spatial configurations which give rise to them, but artefacts in turn reconfigure spaces they inhabit."[32] In other words, what the storyteller describes in the ecphrasis on Achilles' shield is determined by a number of constraints on the material[33] on which the images are depicted; by generic limitations imposed by the diction, meter, and themes available to him; by the exigencies of the performance and the function of memory; and by the principle of *iconic solidarity*,[34] which views "the contradictory nature of images in sequence as both autonomous (meaningful in and of themselves) and dependent upon those around them (making meaning in juxtaposition to surrounding images)."[35] In fact, meaning emerges through a process of joining and ellipsis. The spatial linking and interlacing of certain elements placed on the various folds of the shield builds on a creative interplay between whole and fragment that is informed by the five folds' spatial seriality. The storyteller's choice to present Hephaistos as he makes the shield testifies to his aim of helping his listeners become spectators, who can visualize not just the end product but also the whole in all its parts. From this point of view, the ecphrasis on the shield of Achilles is not a depiction of human life in its various forms, but presents *the process of depicting* human life—not an image of the world but a negotiation with it.[36]

If we particularize these constraints with respect to the shield of Achilles, it becomes obvious that the five folds on which the depictions are placed constitute visual sections that operate on the basis of smaller visual panels, which with a slight addition to Groensteen's terminology[37] can be further divided into *frames, hyperframes, megaframes,* and *multiframes.* By the term *frame,* I refer to the minimal spatial unit, which sometimes may occupy the entire physical space of a *section* (a single fold of Achilles' shield). With the term *hyperframe,* I denote all of the frames included in a single panel,[38] while by *megaframe* I mean the total number of hyperframes in a section. Last, by *multiframe,* I designate the collection of frames comprising the entire shield.[39] In this light, the heavenly bodies in the central panel or fold of Achilles' shield constitute a frame, since they belong to a single visual unit, while the second section or fold contains the panels of the two cities, each of which includes in its turn other smaller visual frames.

---

[32] West-Pavlov 2009:23.

[33] For a similar approach to marble in Greek sculpture, see Neer 2010:71–77.

[34] Groensteen 2007:17–21, 57, 89, 113, 159.

[35] See K. P. Johnson 2008:2, who was the first (to my knowledge) to apply Groensteen's model to Achilles' shield.

[36] See Neer 2010:40–46.

[37] I.e. the term "mega-frame."

[38] A *panel* is a large visual unit (e.g. "city at peace") comprising one or more hyperframes.

[39] See Eisner 1990:38–99; K.P. Johnson 2008:4.

The frame, which represents the most elementary visual unit, is based on and coincides with spatial organization. In order to make this clear, I will use the following schema, which offers a detailed presentation of the entire ecphrasis on the shield according to this system of visual units I have described:

Section 1 (fold 1): 483–489

Panel 1 (Heavenly bodies)[40]

Section 2 (fold 2): 490–540

Megaframe (panels 1 and 2)

Panel 1 (city at peace)

Hyperframe 1 (weddings and symposia)

    Frame 1 (chambers)

    Frame 2 (dancing)

    Frame 3 (flute and phorminx playing)

    Frame 4 (among them women on doorsteps)

    Frame 5 (standing in wonder)

Hyperframe 2 (agora)

    Frame 1 (people, two men in dispute)

    Frame 2 (people speaking up on either side)

    Frame 3 (old men sitting on smooth stones in a circle)

    Frame 4 (heralds lifting their voices)

    Frame 5 (the two men rush before the heralds)

    Frame 6 (two golden talents placed in the middle)

Panel 2 (city at war)

Hyperframe 1 (walls of a city and plain)

    Frame 1 (dispute)

    Frame 2 (walls, old men, women, and children)

    Frame 3 (plain, army)

    Frame 4 (Athena and Ares in front)

---

[40] The first and last are presented without any expansion: see J. Kakridis 1971:112–113, who argues that the sky and stars occupy the first position in ecphrases in Modern Greek folk poetry.

Hyperframe 2 (river)

Frame 1 (two guards—two shepherds)

Frame 2 (εἰράων προπάροιθε and enemy forces)

Frame 3 (return to previous location with all actants together / ἐμάχοντο μάχην ποταμοῖο παρ' ὄχθας)

Section 3 (fold 3): 541–572

Megaframe (panels 1, 2, and 3)

Panel 1 (land)

Hyperframe 1 (sum of actions depicted in frames 1–3)

Frame 1 (many plowmen plowing)

Frame 2 (end of field, man comes)

Frame 3 (return to the previous sublocation (ἀν' ὄγμους) with its former actants (τοὶ δὲ)

Panel 2 (τέμενος)

Hyperframe 1 (sum of actions depicted in frames 1–6)

Frame 1 (ἔριθοι / ἤμων)

Frame 2 (μετ' ὄγμον ἐπήτριμα πῖπτον ἔραζε), new actant 1 (δράγματα δ' ἄλλα) motion (πῖπτον)

Frame 3 (ἐν ἐλλεδανοῖσι), new actants 2 (ἀμαλλοδετῆρες)

Frame 4 (ὄπισθεν), new actants 3 (παῖδες) doing something (ἐν ἀγκαλίδεσσι φέροντες, / ἀσπερχὲς πάρεχον)

Frame 5 (βασιλεὺς) standing in pleasure (γηθόσυνος κῆρ)

Frame 6 (new location: ἀπάνευθεν ὑπὸ δρυΐ), new actants 5 (κήρυκες) and 6 (αἱ δὲ γυναῖκες) doing something (5 δαῖτα πένοντο, / βοῦν δ' ἱερεύσαντες μέγαν ἄμφεπον and 6 δεῖπνον ἐρίθοισιν λεύκ' ἄλφιτα πολλὰ πάλυνον)

Panel 3 (vineyard, container-contents)

Hyperframe 1 (sum of actions depicted in frames 1–4)

Frame 1 (ἀμφὶ δὲ with actants (φορῆες ... παρθενικαὶ δὲ καὶ ἠΐθεοι) doing something (φέρον μελιηδέα καρπόν)

Frame 2 (περὶ δ' with actants (φορῆες ... παρθενικαὶ δὲ καὶ ἠΐθεοι) doing something (φέρον μελιηδέα καρπόν)

Frame 3 (ἀταρπιτὸς ἦεν ἐπ᾽ αὐτήν with actants (φορῆες ... παρθενικαὶ δὲ καὶ ἠΐθεοι) doing something (φέρον μελιηδέα καρπόν)

Frame 4 (τοῖσιν δ᾽ ἐν μέσσοισι) and a single actant is introduced (πάϊς) playing the phorminx

Frame 5 (τοὶ δὲ ῥήσσοντες ἁμαρτῇ / μολπῇ τ᾽ ἰυγμῷ τε ποσὶ σκαίροντες ἕποντο) dancing

Section 4 (fold 4): 573–606

Megaframe (panels 1, 2 and 3)

Panel 1 (cattle)

Hyperframe 1 (sum of actions depicted in frames 1–2)

Frame 1 (cattle ἐπεσσεύοντο ἀπὸ κόπρου νομόνδε)

Frame 2 (πὰρ ποταμὸν κελάδοντα, παρὰ ῥοδανὸν δονακῆα, actants νομῆες, κύνες, λέοντε, αἰζηοί, ἱστάμενοι)

Panel 2 (ἐν δὲ νομὸν)

Hyperframe 1 (sum of actions depicted in frames 1–2)

Frame 1 (ἐν καλῇ βήσσῃ μέγαν οἰῶν ἀργεννάων)

Frame 2 (σταθμούς τε κλισίας τε κατηρεφέας ἰδὲ σηκούς)

Panel 3 (dancing-floor)

Hyperframe 1 (sum of actions depicted in frames 1–3)

Frame 1 (χορὸν, ἔνθα), actants (ἠΐθεοι καὶ παρθένοι ἀλφεσίβοιαι) moving (ὠρχέοντ᾽, θρέξασκον)

Frame 2 (other actants around watching [πολλὸς δ᾽ ἱμερόεντα χορὸν περιίσταθ᾽ ὅμιλος], pleased (τερπόμενοι)

Frame 3 (κατ᾽ αὐτούς, κατὰ μέσσους) with addition of new actants and motion as part of a new piece of information (δοιὼ δὲ κυβιστητῆρε κατ᾽ αὐτούς / μολπῆς ἐξάρχοντες ἐδίνευον κατὰ μέσσους)

Section 5 (fold 5): 607–608

Panel 1 (ποταμοῖο μέγα σθένος Ὠκεανοῖο)

This classification is not based on structuralist taxonomic principles; it rather attempts to trace within the realm of ecphrasis the mechanism that created this impressive artifact. One of the underlying premises of this schema is its different levels of organization. It is clear that the narrator organizes his mental images by a triple process that can be summarized by the terms *segmentation, grouping,* and *interlacing*: the storyteller breaks down his pictorial tableau into separate segments, which he arranges into groups[41] that he can weave together at will. In fact, if we try to accommodate Groensteen's theoretical insights into the ecphrastic universe of Achilles' shield,[42] we will see that the narrator employs two types of "arthrology,"[43] or linkage, among the various groups of images: *restrained* and *general*.[44] Restrained linkage explicates the interconnection and interaction of panels *sequentially*, whereas general arthrology examines the ways panels are associated *nonsequentially*, through the echoes of earlier terms that recur in one or more nonadjacent panels. The key point for explicating the entire process of organizing mental images is the use of space,[45] which is a powerful cue for recalling and classifying material. The storyteller visualizes the various episodes depicted on the shield as "mini-tours,"[46] following a course that leads him from one spatial node or location to another. Spatial markers are used as mental hooks on which he hangs individual scenes. Even within each scene, elements are added "freely" but are tied to locations or motion.[47] Space and motion are effective means for mentally navigating an area that the main narrative leaves unexplored. From this perspective of *segmentation, grouping*, and *interlacing*, let us now see how these theoretical tenets explicate the creation of certain images on the shield of Achilles.

[41] I have deliberately used the word "groups" in order to make clear that I am referring to all types of classification explicated above: frame, hyperframe, megaframe, panel, and section.

[42] With some necessary modifications.

[43] From the Greek word ἄρθρον ("joint of a limb").

[44] Groensteen (2007) also refers to a spatio-topical system, which if applied to the shield of Achilles would pertain to the panels' physical size and placement within the sections or folds of the shield. Given that such a type of arthrology is based on the assumption that Achilles' shield is real, it is of no value to our study. Groensteen applied this kind of linkage to the very real size of a printed page on which the panels of a comic book are placed.

[45] In descriptions, space includes but is not restricted to location; see J. Kakridis 1971:120.

[46] In fact, mini-maps of spatial references are combined with mini-tours that unfold short stories; the suspended function of these narrative segments with no protagonists or mythical references has multiple roles: First, it comments on a different level, not that of the plot. Second, it constitutes a paratopic space, a place to which the narrator invites his audience, a universe devoid of all the mental images created for the Iliadic narrative. Its clearly demarcated boundaries are not merely a surface element, like the verbalizing of the pictorial world of the simile, but significantly also a metaleptic hint to the very performance of the song. The poet uses the rings of the shield as segmentation devices, a sort of iconic paragraphing; instead of a verbal format, he employs a visual one, based on pictorial snapshots placed on a mental map. Finally, the shield's multiformity, the lack of a single thread or pregnant moment in the visual spectacle, points to the decentralizing aspect of this particular form of ecphrasis. In this respect, the representations on the shield of Achilles mirror the technique the audience is familiar with from the pictorial plurality of the Homeric similes, where (in their extended form) there is no *tertium comparationis*, but a multiplicity of references and points of contact: images form a visual archipelago that the listener may mentally navigate at will.

[47] See Rubin 1995:278–279.

With respect to *segmentation*,[48] the narrator processes his material by dividing it into smaller, more easily managed visual shots. The scene of the city at peace, for example, is divided into two distinct panels, each of them further segmented into smaller units, the frames. Since the storyteller moves sequentially from one frame to the next, he tends to use material that is still active in his mind. This does not mean that he becomes repetitive; on the contrary, by employing what is still fresh in his memory, he is able to enhance vividness and surprise his audience by introducing unexpected topics, given the Iliadic narrative's traditional thematic agenda. Segmentation is a valid tool not only for mnemonic recall and handling, but also for the kind of *pictorial seriality* that marks Homeric ecphrasis. In the description of the city at peace, the two hyperframes (the weddings and symposia on the one hand and the litigation in the agora on the other) share a number of features, despite their very different themes (Table 7):

Table 7: Pictorial seriality in the city at peace

Section 2	Section 2
Panel 1 (city at peace)	Panel 1 (city at peace)
Hyperframe 1 (weddings and symposia)	Hyperframe 2 (litigation in the agora)
Frame 1: "the loud bride song was arising" (493 πολὺς δ' ὑμέναιος ὀρώρει)	Frame 1: "a quarrel had arisen" (497–498 νεῖκος / ὠρώρει)
Frame 2: "kept up their clamour" (495 βοὴν ἔχον)	Frames 2 and 4: "were speaking up" (502 ἐπήπυον), "who lift their voices" (505 ἠεροφώνων)
Frame 4: "women standing each at the door of her court" (495–496 αἱ δὲ γυναῖκες / ἱστάμεναι ... ἐπὶ προθύροισιν ἑκάστη)	Frame 3: "the elders / were in session on benches of polished stone in the sacred circle" (503–504 οἱ δὲ γέροντες /εἴατ' ἐπὶ ξεστοῖσι λίθοις ἱερῷ ἐνὶ κύκλῳ)

---

48   I use this term to refer to an operation or process conducted by the narrator, not by the audience (or reader, for which see Barthes's *découpage* [1964:213–220]). Groensteen maintains that "elementary relations, of the linear type [are] ... governed by the operation of breaking down (*découpage*), ... [and] put in place the sequential syntagms, which are most often subordinated to the narrative ends" (2007:22).

Since segmentation is a typical feature of *restrained arthrology*, it operates not only between hyperframes, that is, parts of a single panel, but also between panels, as can be seen in hyperframes 1 and 2 of panel 1 and hyperframes 1 and 2 of panel 2 in section 2 (Table 8):

Table 8: Restrained arthrology in the city at peace

Section 2	Section 2
Panel 1 (city at peace)	Panel 2 (city at war)
Hyperframe 2 (litigation in the agora)	Hyperframe 1 (walls of a city and plain)
Frame 1: "the people were assembled in the market place" (497 λαοὶ δ' εἰν ἀγορῇ ἔσαν ἀθρόοι) "two men" (498 δύο δ' ἄνδρες) "were disputing" (498 ἐνείκεον), "one man promised full restitution / ..., but the other refused ..." (499–500 ὃ μὲν εὔχετο πάντ' ἀποδοῦναι / ... ὃ δ' ἀναίνετο ...)	Frame 1: "sat in their councils" (531 εἰράων προπάροιθε καθήμενοι) "two men to watch" (523 δύω σκοποί), "two herdsmen" (525 δύω ... νομῆες) "counsel was divided, whether ... or share between both sides the property" (510–511 δίχα δέ σφισιν ἥνδανε βουλή, / ἠὲ ... ἢ ἄνδιχα πάντα δάσασθαι)
Frame 3: "the elders" (503 οἱ δὲ γέροντες)	Frame 2: "the men with age upon them" (515 ἀνέρες οὓς ἔχε γῆρας)
Frame 5: "rushed" (506 ἤϊσσον)	Frame 3: "went out" (516 οἳ δ' ἴσαν)
Frame 6: "two talents of gold" (507 δύω χρυσοῖο τάλαντα)	Frame 4: "These were gold, both, and golden raiment upon them" (517 ἄμφω χρυσείω, χρύσεια δὲ εἵματα ἕσθην)
Hyperframe 1 (weddings and symposia)	Hyperframe 2 (river)
Frame 3: "flutes and lyres" (495 αὐλοὶ φόρμιγγές τε)	Frame 2: "playing happily on pipes" (526 τερπόμενοι σύριγξι)

This table makes it clear that in his description of the city at war, the narrator uses visual units he has just employed in the previous panel, especially those which are freshest in his memory, the ones he used in the second hyperframe of the litigation in the agora. By reactivating what is at his disposal, the storyteller organizes "images in coherent, easy-to-recall sequences of narrative,"[49] or in the case of ecphrasis, of narrativized description. This argument agrees strongly with both the principles governing composition in performance and the workings of human memory, as revealed by cognitive psychology. What appears to be an incoherent whole is simply the result of the principles of pictorial seriality and iconic solidarity that govern the process of creating mental pictures during the oral performance of the song. Segmentation is one of the most important features of restrained arthrology, for it not only facilitates the organization and processing of information but also allows the storyteller to build freely without having a predetermined plan in mind.

Grouping of images is a mechanism by which the narrator tends to create small chains of images which seem to acquire a kind of traditional referentiality. As with formulaic material that has progressively acquired context-free meaning and anchors, at least at times, the secondary semantics of a given expression, so certain images have become part of a larger system of interconnections which when activated create mental chain reactions. The storyteller visualizes certain types of scenes in a rather limited number of ways, and tends to group individual images along a path that goes through a familiar chain of locations; in this way he can create strong nodes between places and actions and considerably increase mnemonic stability. In the ecphrasis on the shield of Achilles, grouping is observed both within a single panel and between panels.

In panel 1 (the city at peace) and after the reference to the wedding πομπή of the future brides, the storyteller visualizes a dancing scene (frame 2). The traditional referentiality of the image of a dance conjures up in his mind a number of other related images, which are anchored to the first one through pictorial seriality, determined not by any narrative plan but by the tradition-dependent linking of relevant images. The term "traditional referentiality," which has been used with respect to formulas,[50] can be effectively applied to mental images that constitute, within the traditional medium of oral song, a form of diachronically diffused intertextuality. Image chains do not represent any form of *quotation*, nor do they originate from any given source: they symbolize the iconic solidarity of mental pictures that form part of a system that crystallized during the shaping of the tradition. From this point of view, the dancing scene[51] triggers

---

[49] Rubin 1995:61.
[50] See Foley 1991:24; Danek 2002; Tsagalis 2008b:123, 154, 187–188.
[51] In section 2, panel 1, hyperframe 1, frame 2.

the following frames, which include the playing of the flute and the phorminx as well as the women spectators' standing and gazing in wonder. The initial visualization of the dancing has touched off an iconic chain-reaction in the storyteller's mind, facilitated by spatial links that pertain not only to location (496 ἐπὶ προθύροισιν) but also to sound (495 βοὴν ἔχον) and sight (496 θαύμαζον).[52]

Traditional referentiality is also at work in section 3, panel 3 (the vineyard). At the very end of this panel, the storyteller introduces a brief scene of a young man beautifully playing his phorminx, among other boys and girls who are described carrying the grapes in baskets. The reference to these boys and girls and the grapes has given the narrator a mental hint for continuing his song; thus he has visually "translated" this initial reference into a scene of festivity, which he then describes by the traditional means available to him: phorminx-playing (569–570 φόρμιγγι λιγείη / ἱμερόεν κιθάριζε), singing (570 λίνον δ' ὑπὸ καλὸν ἄειδεν), and dancing (571–572 τοὶ δὲ ῥήσσοντες ἁμαρτῇ / μολπῇ τ' ἰυγμῷ τε ποσὶ σκαίροντες ἕποντο). Here too, spatial markers have facilitated his recall: the young girls and boys are placed on the single path of the vineyard (565 μία δ' οἴη ἀταρπιτὸς ἦεν ἐπ' αὐτήν), the young man's playing the phorminx is tied to his standing in the middle of these boys and girls (569 τοῖσιν δ' ἐν μέσσοισι), the boy's singing is anchored to the sound he produces (571 λεπταλέῃ φωνῇ), and the dancing is connected with the noise produced by the singing and whistling of all the youths (572 μολπῇ τ' ἰυγμῷ τε).

Grouping of images can also be observed between different panels. In section 4, panel 2 (the sheep) has often bemused critics, whose rather negative reaction to what they regard as an addition to the larger and richer previous panel (cattle attacked by a lion) has even entertained thoughts of omitting lines 587–589.[53] This quite radical "solution" tends, I am afraid, to ignore some of the laws of oral epic verse-making. Repetition and doubling should not be regarded—as they arguably can in written composition—as deficiencies or signs of interpolation,[54] but should be explained as a result of the oral storyteller's different needs and methods of composition. Consider the following formulation by Olrik:

---

[52] See Squire, who speaks of "a prototypical dialectic (and slippage) between 'seeing' and 'hearing'—a phenomenon that ... would come to define ecphrasis as rationalized rhetorical trope" (2011:335).

[53] See e.g. Leaf 1900–1902 on *Iliad* XVIII 587–589; likewise Taplin 1980:9. Against this view, see Marg 1957:27, who highlights the fact that this brief scene creates a pause between the violent attack of the lions in the previous scene and the fast motion of the chorus of dancers in the following part. See also West 2011:353 on *Iliad* XVIII 490–606, who observes that the scene of the dancing-floor should possibly be regarded as part of the previous scene of pastoralism (587–589).

[54] See Krieger 2003:90: "a claim to form, to circular repetitiveness within the discretely linear, and this by the use of an object of spatial and plastic art to symbolize the spatiality and plasticity of literature's temporality."

Oral narrative composition does not know detailed description and thus cannot use it to express the nature and meaning of the plot. What must be shown to be important is depicted through repetition: in this way thought may dwell longer on the same subject.[55]

The brevity of panel 2, which lacks any expansion, is at odds not only with the pictorial wealth of the previous, simile-like panel (the cattle), but also with the way all the previous panels began. This is indeed the first time the skilled craftsman Hephaistos is mentioned in the line that introduces a panel.[56] Whereas previously the pattern employed was always ἐν μέν/δέ + *verb of making* (ἔτευξε, ποίησε, ἐτίθει) + *what he made*,[57] here the introductory formula takes the form ἐν δέ + *what he made* + *verb of making* + *periphrastic denomination for Hephaistos*. This may seem like mere quibbling, but the long panel of the dance that comes immediately after begins in virtually the same way (590 ἐν δὲ χορὸν ποίκιλλε[58] περικλυτὸς Ἀμφιγυήεις). Before I discuss this in detail, I will also draw attention to another crucial difference between lines 587–589 and all the other panels: these lines are the only ones that do not expand on what is being depicted (νομόν), but create a sudden pause by adding multiple spatial markers:[59]

ἐν δὲ νομὸν ποίησε περικλυτὸς Ἀμφιγυήεις
ἐν καλῇ βήσσῃ μέγαν οἰῶν ἀργεννάων,
σταθμούς τε κλισίας τε κατηρεφέας ἰδὲ σηκούς.

And the renowned smith of the strong arms made on it a meadow
large and in a lovely valley for the glimmering sheepflocks,
with dwelling places upon it, and covered shelters, and sheepfolds.

Iliad XVIII 587–589

---

[55] 1992:44 §61.
[56] Differently Becker 1995:142, who explains the oddity of lines XVIII 587–589 by comparing them to *Iliad* I 607–608, in which Hephaistos is again praised as a skilled craftsman, without describing the divine bedchambers. In my view, there is a crucial difference between the two passages: in *Iliad* I 607–608 there is no "expectation" of a description, whereas in *Iliad* XVIII 587–589 we are situated in the midst of descriptive passages on the various folds of the shield. In fact, the passage under discussion is flanked by long descriptive segments. The oddity, in other words, is determined by the context.
[57] There are slight modifications in the order of these features; cf. 573 ἐν δ' + *what he made* + *verb of making*.
[58] Notice that two manuscripts (see West's critical apparatus) offer the reading ποίησε instead of ποίκιλλε in *Iliad* XVIII 590.
[59] The shield of Achilles as an extended narrative pause has been emphasized by scholars time and again. Shorter, intraecphrastic pauses, such as the one under discussion, have escaped attention.

The meadow (νομόν) is not expanded but spatially overdetermined: it is located "in a lovely valley" (ἐν καλῇ βήσσῃ), and the sheep placed in it are "tied" to "dwelling places" (σταθμούς), "covered shelters" (κλισίας ... κατηρεφέας), and "sheepfolds" (σηκούς). Instead of presenting his audience with a narrative snapshot of the meadow, the narrator accumulates spatial references from the same thematic family as those in the previous panel. I would argue that the following panel shares the same pattern in its introductory formula, but not the brevity or the thematic range of content, as a result of *oral correction*. The storyteller begins to visualize a scene that shares the same or equivalent thematic content with the previous one (cattle), but soon decides to cut it short and move on to a different visualization. His initial task was to strengthen the effect of the previous panel by doubling it,[60] but he soon opted for a different goal. It is, of course, intriguing to wonder what may have changed his mind. The storyteller may have realized that the only images he could easily recall were so similar to the ones just presented in the previous panel that there was no room for variation, and therefore decided to undertake a wholesale shift in his topic. Using the same introductory formulaic pattern that was still very active in his mind, he tried to correct his false start and moved on to what is perhaps the crowning image of the whole shield, the dancing-floor. His grouping of images between the two panels may have been cancelled, but it has left traces of the very process by which it came into being.

Interlacing, which refers to the weaving together of nonsequential frames or panels, capitalizes on echoes or long-term links between individual or larger groups of visual units. The narrator occasionally reuses, or rather applies, frames previously used in other panels and sections. Frames 2 and 3 (section 2, panel 1), picturing the dancing and flute- and phorminx-playing, are interlaced with both frames 4 and 5 (section 3, panel 3; the youth playing the phorminx amid groups of dancing boys and girls) and frames 1–3 (section 4, panel 3; the entire panel of the dancing-floor). The progressively intensifying effect of this type of *expanding* or *strong interlacing* shows that we are dealing with a *pictorial gradation*: the initial frames (in section 2) did not become weaker in the process of the ecphrasis, but on the contrary were so strengthened that they could cover a whole panel. The dancing-floor, which some scholars have seen as the climactic scene of the entire ecphrasis,[61] and which verifies the "Law of Final Stress" that

---

[60] A herd of oxen and shining sheep have already featured in section 2, panel 2, hyperframe 2 (the city at war) of the shield (*Iliad* XVIII 528–529 ἀμφὶ βοῶν ἀγέλας καὶ πώεα καλά / ἀργεννέων οἰῶν). In this light, it may be plausibly argued that general arthrology (i.e. long-term linkage) is "responsible" for the selection of images the narrator conjured up in his mind when he began to enhance the vividness of the previous panel (section 4, panel 1) by doubling its content. For the link between herds of cattle and sheep flocks, see e.g. *Iliad* XI 678, 696.

[61] See J. Kakridis 1971:123: "The main scene is placed at the end of the description."

typifies oral literature,[62] shows that in presenting his ecphrastic material the storyteller is not so much following a given thematic blueprint, but employing recollections or echoes of previously used visual units to create, at times at least, new, surprising, but really unexpected visual compositions, like the impressive dancing-floor that crowns his description. There are also examples of *default interlacing*.[63] Frame 5 (section 2, panel 1), picturing the women who are standing in wonder (ἱστάμεναι θαύμαζον), is woven together with frame 5 (section 3, panel 2), depicting a king who is also standing (ἑστήκει), being pleased at heart (γηθόσυνος κῆρ), and frame 2 (section 4, panel 1), where the dogs stand their ground and bark at the lions as they try to chase them away from the cattle (ἱστάμενοι). Frame 3 (section 2, panel 1, hyperframe 2), describing the elders seated in the agora, is interlaced with frame 2 (section 2, panel 2, hyperframe 2), which depicts an army seated at the "place of the counsels." The number two is also a recurring device in the narrator's mind, since it appears in multiple panels of the ecphrasis (two men take part in a litigation, there are two options available for the besieged city, two gods lead the army outside the walls, there are two guards and two shepherds in the scene by the river, two lions attack the cattle in section 4, and finally there are two acrobats on the dancing-floor). These are only some of the manifestations of default interlacing. Finally, there are few cases of *weak interlacing*, where the initial visual unit is reproduced by means of a considerably less strong image. The heralds are an integral part of the litigation scene in the agora (section 2, panel 1, hyperframe 2, frame 4), although they are really ancillary and do not actually fit there, as they do not perform their usual task in the king's precinct (section 3, panel 2, hyperframe 1, frame 6). The storyteller has retained the visual image of the heralds in his memory, and he reproduces it less forcefully under different circumstances and at the expense of accuracy.

These are the three techniques the storyteller employs for image processing. By combining short- and long-term linkage (i.e. restrained and general arthrology), the narrator creates multiple associations within the rich pictorial universe of the ecphrasis, blending them with the pattern or story grammar of the individual snapshots to produce cohesion and meaning. This in fact amounts to a spatial grammar, endowed not only with specific structural features (which I have analyzed above) but also with a number of precise thematic traits:

(1) the snapshots lack a single center or focus

---

[62] Olrik 1992:52–54 §75.

[63] By "default interlacing," I refer to cases where the initial visual unit's vividness is neither intensified nor weakened.

(2)   most of the snapshots involve multiple actors[64]

(3)   they are based, mainly but not solely, on scenes from peaceful life

(4)   they pertain to public, not private life

(5)   they are, with minor exceptions, characterized by the absence of names of any sort[65]

(6)   most of the figures, humans, animals, and gods depicted on them are in motion[66]

(7)   they begin *in medias res*

(8)   they remain unfinished and suspended: there is no end in these short stories[67]

(9)   they are characterized by simile-like deixis and syntax (use of the indicative; no optative or generalizing subjunctive)

(10) they are organized mainly by parataxis (the number of secondary clauses is very limited)

(11) the snapshots contain information representing the narrator's own interpretation of what is depicted on the shield; the storyteller breaks the time perspective of the snapshots by referring to past and future events[68]

Taking my cue from this mapping of thematic features, I shall first suggest and then explicate the story grammar of the snapshots included in the shield of Achilles. These snapshots seem to follow a pattern that can be summarized this way:

[64]   See Byre 1992:39. These actors are certainly not the same individuals, as Byre notes, though I cannot agree with his assertion that the poet's words can be interpreted "as a synthesis and summary of different phases of the same action as they are performed by different actors on the represented scene before his mind's eye."

[65]   This is also a feature of spatial grammar. According to Dennerlein, "properties ascribed to spatial facts or objects can be typical events, positions, conditions or actions by collective or anonymous actors" (2009:141). Dennerlein calls this text-type *Beschreibung* ("description"); see Chatman 1978:141, who maintains that nameless, unimportant, and unrepeated characters belong to the setting.

[66]   See Schadewaldt 1965:363, who observes that "neben den Grundformen stehen die einfachen elementaren Geschehnisse. Sie entwickelt der Dichter, indem er ihre charakteristischen *Phasen* durchläuft"; see also Purves 2010a:46–47, who argues that "the animate picture is a common phenomenon within the tradition of ecphrastic description." Cf. Becker 1995:9–22.

[67]   See Byre 1992:39 on the use of iterative temporal constructions concerning the movement of people (XVIII 544–546, 566, 599, 602).

[68]   More or less in the manner of the Elder Philostratus in his *Imagines*; see Lesky 1966; J. Kakridis 1971:120–121; Webb 2009:187–190.

An actant or actants is/are doing something; secondary characters are watching or taking part in the action, which is progressively extended by the inclusion of other actants. Based on the movement of the first actant(s),[69] a different location or a different part of the first location is introduced, which brings with it new actants; each new addition is based on the visual image of a new place (the first actant's activity functions associatively, for it leads to a second activity tied to a new location).

The story grammar of the snapshots[70] is a spatial one: mini-maps of spatial references are combined with mini-tours[71] that reveal "abortive mini-narratives,"[72] or to put it differently, the narrator's mind, together with his moving subjects, moves from one visual shot to another, verbalizing them on the spatially juxtaposed sections or parts of the shield. This ecphrasis needs to be approached within the framework of oral storytelling and the techniques employed by storytellers within the context of the performance. Any attempt to reconstruct the shield of Achilles is off the mark, for the simple reason that it misses the illusion on which the visual imagery of the ecphrasis is being built. The shield of Achilles is governed by the same rules as a *simile of gigantic proportions:*[73] it func-

---

[69] See Webb 2009:187, who observes that the ecphrastic descriptions in the *Imagines* of the Elder Philostratus are "packed with concrete nouns, adjectives and verbs of movement, all denoting perceptible features."

[70] Critics have time and again wondered at the brief narrative snapshots that interrupt the description of the images on the shield of Achilles. But as Heffernan has argued, "ecphrastic literature reveals again and again this narrative response to pictorial stasis, this storytelling impulse that language by its very nature seems to release and stimulate" (1991:301). In order to avoid the pitfalls of description, Homer (as Lessing noted long ago) changed "das Coexistiriende" into "ein wirkliches Successives" (*Laokoon*, 128). But in contrast with other ecphrases, like that of Jason's mantle in *Argonautica* I, Homer does not create a continuous storyline, but follows separate spatial formats, based on implicit knowledge, by merging narrative and description, or continuing narrative in a different register. See also Heffernan 1993; Laird 1996; Putnam 1998; Bartsch and Elsner 2007; Francis 2009.

[71] See also Ryan 2003:219, who makes similar observations about Gabriel García Márquez's *Chronicle of a Death Foretold.*

[72] I owe this expression to Byre 1992:42. See also Palm's observation (1965–1966:119) that one has the impression that the scenes depicted on the shield describe events rather than things.

[73] See Rengakos 2006b, who has used the term *miniature-Ekphrasen* for the similes; see also Becker 1995:47–50, and Elsner 2002:4: "The shield's momentary raising of our eyes from the narrative flow of war to scenes of an idealised 'everyday' life set in something closer to the audience's world than the poem's main action, recalls the workings of the similes but on a much grander scale." See Byre 1992:37 and n9. The crossing of ontological boundaries that we explored earlier in the extended similes is also at work here: the figures in the snapshots begin to move, in an illusory effort to evolve into a plot and break free from the constraints and limitations imposed upon them by the medium they belong to. In the words of Ryan, observing the same phenomenon in the modern novel, "the world within the picture gradually emancipates itself

tions like a visual gallery,[74] presenting multiple images that the storyteller's rich imagination has created by means of spatial memory. There is no single thread or pattern running through these images, because we are not dealing with a *script* in cognitive terms (that refers to both form and content), but with a *story grammar* that refers only to form. In fact, the duplication that marks most of the snapshots included in the shield results from the fact that in oral storytelling "repeated pairings of ideas or words are noted as one way the individual words acquire traditional meanings within their genre."[75] Duality is a form of pairing, and pairing, at the most elementary level, is a sort of spatial association. The narrator does not divide each of the shield's central sections into two narrative snapshots; he duplicates visual images, and thereby associates and groups them together: a pictorial list has no clear structure; it is the associative imagination of the storyteller that imposes one.[76] The storyteller in this case uses the same technique he employs in the Homeric similes,[77] with one important addition. Here the slide from description into narrative[78] is similar to the shift from a simple comparison to a developed, extended simile. It is the workings of visual memory that enhance this smooth glide, and in particular it is spatial memory that creates this rich visual panorama of the shield. The individual narrative snapshots of the shield are all, more or less, drawn from the rich pictorial storehouse that also furnishes the similes,[79] and they are based on equivalent devices of spatial memory. What is new in the shield of Achilles is that the accumulation

---

from primary reality" (1990:875). See also Squire 2011:337, who observes that it is the oscillation between reality and representation that "makes the shield (like the ecphrasis mediating it) so wondrous."

[74] See Squire, who highlights the fact that the shield of Achilles "came to epitomize a dynamic both of intermediality (text as image and image as text), and of scale (the big in the small and the small in the big)," and draws a parallel with the Iliac tablets, whose wondrous mode consists in "a visual-cum-verbal, gigantic-cum-miniature, all-encompassing synopsis" (2011:303–304).

[75] Rubin 1995:31. On this topic, see also the work of F. Andersen 1985; Foley 1991, 1992.

[76] See Tulving 1962. See also Schadewaldt 1965:363.

[77] Motion is a basic spatial feature that functions as a cue to recall in both similes and ecphrasis; see Rubin 1995:304–305.

[78] See Byre 1992:37n11. Debray-Genette calls Achilles' shield a "description-récit" (1980:295).

[79] See Lyne 1989:68. The similes add things not mentioned in the narrative by means of the different, suggestive (not explicit) medium of imagery. As with the similes, so in ecphrasis, the author switches from direct narrative to narrative through imagery. See also Perrone-Moisès 1980, who draws a line between *static* and *dynamic* description, the former having a redundant, qualifying, explanatory, or emphatic function; the latter one of displacement, compensation, or instinct-liberating. Whereas static description refers to an already expressed narrative, dynamic description produces another narrative level. Description is not a pause or slowdown of the action, but the continuation of it on a different level. More or less along the same lines are the observations of Perutelli (1978), who distinguishes three modes of the description-narration relationship: (a) total subordination of description to narrative, (b) total independence, and (c) rhetorical relationship: the ecphrasis is used as "figure" (*inversione speculare*).

of mental pictures is organized not simply according to an associative pattern (as in simile-chains), but as successive pictures placed on successive levels of the shield. This ecphrastic gallery is a spatial tour of the world of the poet's imagination, a visit to a mental museum where listeners are turned into spectators and the poet's mind's eye is visually indexed on the massive shield of his chief hero Achilles.

I have deliberately left out of my analysis the inner and outer folds of the shield, since they are sharply distinguished from the three "intermediate" folds. Being empty of narrative snapshots, the inner and outer folds are marked by their stillness: no motion, no human figures, no shining effect expressed verbally, but a mere listing of heavenly bodies and the great ocean. This stillness, framing a world of human activity, is intended to induce wonder, based on polarity and antithesis. The shield's twofoldness, featuring a static and unchanging cosmos on the one hand and a vibrant, highly active, and shifting world of mankind on the other, reveals a contrast that is essential to the organization of space. This is neither a systemic impulse nor a structural formality, but a reflection on seeing. At the heart of this spatial arrangement lies the distinction between what the figures on the shield see and what we, the external beholders, look at. This point has been effectively made with respect to sculpture in classical pediments,[80] and with a certain degree of modification can be reiterated here: the human figures in the three intermediate but larger main folds of the shield are presented in the course of their various activities, unaware—as they are in the real world—of the unchanging framework of the static cosmos and ocean within which they are situated. The stillness of the vast space lying above (cosmos) and around them (ocean) is perceptible only to the external beholder. This effective disjunction of human activity and cosmic stillness amounts to a comment from the storyteller to his audience: the shield is not about the depiction of the world but about its denotation; not its comprehensiveness, but a way of dealing with it through space.[81]

The Metaleptic Aspect of Ecphrasis

Apart from the spatial story grammar of the ecphrasis on the shield of Achilles and the foregoing analysis of the cognitive process that brought it into being, space also emerges in the blurring of narrative levels. In fact, the description

---

[80] See Neer 2010:97–98.

[81] I generally agree with Squire, who draws attention to the fact that the most inner and outer zones of the shield of Achilles aim at highlighting the concentric design of the shield as a whole (2011:320). My take on this issue is based on *how* these "rings" help the viewer focus on the other three folds containing narrative snapshots.

of the shield of Achilles constitutes the earliest extended *metalepsis* in Greek literature. Μετάληψις (literally "sharing") is a term of ancient rhetoric[82] that denotes either "a particular status of a juridical case" or "figures of speech such as metonymy and metaphor, when one word is used for another."[83] Genette was the first to assign this term a narratological meaning, narrowing its use to the blurring or transcending of the distinction between narrative levels, as when the narrator enters the world of the characters, or the characters that of the narrator.[84] Recent narratological approaches have developed a more detailed typology of metalepsis, which like most narratological observations is very much at home in the genre of the novel. Given that the poetic reality of Homeric epic is profoundly different, I will restrict myself to a brief catalogue of the basic forms of metalepsis, without considering other types that are not applicable or are too jargon-oriented for archaic Greek epic. To this end, I will deliberately shy away from any sophisticated classification of metalepsis,[85] and instead opt for the simplest and most self-explanatory distinction, between passages where the narrator enters the world of the characters and those where the characters enter his, and also treat as a separate category instances where the narrator makes metanarrative comments and becomes not the reporter but the creator of the story.

The narrator enters the world of the characters

(1) the narrator takes the role of a narratee, who hears the song from a deity or deities, the Muses (*Iliad* II 484–486 ἔσπετε νῦν μοι, Μοῦσαι Ὀλύμπια δώματ' ἔχουσαι— / ὑμεῖς γὰρ θεαί ἐστε, πάρεστέ τε, ἴστέ τε πάντα, / ἡμεῖς δὲ κλέος οἶον ἀκούομεν, οὐδέ τι ἴδμεν—; *Odyssey* i 1 μοι ἔννεπε, i 10 εἰπὲ καὶ ἡμῖν)

(2) the view of a group of characters is presented by means of τις

(3) direct address to a character (e.g. Menelaos, Patroklos, Eumaios)[86]

Characters enter the world of the narrator: A character passes from an embedded to an embedding level

(1) third-person imaginary spectator

---

[82] See F. Wagner 2002:235–237; de Jong 2009:88n4. On metaecphrasis in descriptions of works of art, see Webb 2009:185–191.

[83] De Jong 2009:88.

[84] Genette 1980:234–237.

[85] See Pier 2009.

[86] On second-person apostrophe, see de Jong 2009:93–99, with further bibliography; Clay 2011:19–21.

(2) a character's words point explicitly to the story-world, but implicitly to the world of the narrator and the narratees

(3) implicit presentation of a character's viewpoint

Rhetorical or discourse metalepsis: The narrator intervenes with a metanarrative comment, or the narrator becomes the creator instead of the reporter of the story. Rhetorical metalepsis opens a small window and then quickly closes it, while boundaries are at the end reascertained

(1) evaluative comments (νήπιος, σχέτλιος) or judgmental words (οὐλομένην)

(2) rhetorical questions (what should I say first and what last?)

(3) if-not situations (X would have happened if it were not for person Y)

(4) the narrator acknowledges that he has orchestrated a specific outcome in the plot (*Iliad* XXII 328–329)

Given this classification of metalepsis within the framework of Homeric epic, it is now important to see what kinds of metaleptic effects we can trace in the shield of Achilles.[87]

In the ecphrasis on the shield, the narrator at times enters the world depicted on it, by assuming the standpoint of a figure in a given snapshot, and projecting that person's feelings or referring to his or her perceptions. This differs markedly from the narrator's reference to the feelings of any character in the narrated parts of the epic. Here, the characters are figures depicted by Hephaistos on the shield, not part of the plot; these figures-as-artifacts cannot possibly feel or perceive what is happening; they can be depicted as looking at something that is going on, but they cannot possibly hear a sound. It is the narrator who, as the sole witness of Hephaistos' forging the shield,[88] jumps into the brief snapshots to "share" the feelings of the sculpted figures. It is the narrator who enters the world of the snapshot, and hears the sound or clamor produced by the actions of other figures in a previous panel of the same section of the shield. In this way he creates the illusion of characters who are alive, who feel and perceive.

In *Iliad* XVIII 496 (the city at peace), the narrator refers to a group of women standing by the front doors of their houses and marveling (θαύμαζον) at the bridal procession.[89] These women are figures on the shield and cannot have feel-

---

[87] On comparing the shield with the storyteller's perspective, see Becker 1990:152–153; Hubbard 1992:17; Alden 2000:53.

[88] See de Jong 2011:5.

[89] As an artist may depict internal spectators in his work, thus mediating between the world of the picture and that of the beholder, so the internal spectators in the ecphrasis of Achilles' shield

ings, or to put it in another way the narrator is the one who can give them feelings and turn them into both living beings and active spectators of the action depicted there. This strategy of mirroring his own experience within the ecphrasis while visualizing the divine craftsman making the shield is, of course, a hint to the narratees who will also marvel at his presentation of this divine masterpiece.[90] Another instance of this metaleptic effect appears in lines 530 and 556. In the former, the enemy forces hear the great uproar of another army attacking the shepherds (ἐπύθοντο πολὺν κέλαδον), whereas in the latter the king stands in silence (σιωπῆι) with pleasure in his heart (557 γηθόσυνος κῆρ). In both instances, the narrator enters the world of the figures on the shield and attributes to them feelings and perceptions he, as a mortal, wants them to experience. The figures cannot hear any sound, nor does it make any sense to say that they remain silent or that they can be pleased. This is all about the narrator's leaping into the illusionary story-world of the ecphrasis. Marvel, pleasure, sound, and silence are all his own, but when transferred to the figures of the shield, they let him blur the boundaries between distinct narrative levels and make the ecphrasis come alive, a magnificent, (mainly) peaceful world that could have been real but is not.[91]

Of the second type of metalepsis (characters entering the world of the narrator), the scene just before the actual making of the shield provides a stunning example. Before Hephaistos begins to work, he says to Thetis:

"ὥς οἱ τεύχεα καλὰ παρέσσεται, οἷά τις αὖτε
ἀνθρώπων πολέων θαυμάσσεται, ὅς κεν ἴδηται."

"as there shall be fine armour for him, such as another
man out of many men shall wonder at, when he looks on it."

Iliad XVIII 466–467

---

allow the poet to duplicate (within the actual ecphrasis) the visual *mise-en-abyme* of his own gaze at the shield (see *Iliad* XVIII 549 θαῦμα τέτυκτο). The narrator emulates the craftsman's own technique of selectively highlighting certain figures. This may seem an arbitrary selection, but it is a rather effective one, since the narrator employs what was known as ὑποτύπωσις, the performative strategy of bringing a spectacle vividly to the mind's eye. The internal spectators both mirror the narrator's gaze at Hephaistos' work and point to the external audience's visualizing not only the master craftsman's workmanship and skill but also the narrator's gaze at this workmanship. Thus all three levels communicate metaleptically. Space is of crucial importance in this respect, for the means used to achieve this effect consist of spatial elements that create vividness. On implicit reference to "a feeling of admiration for what the artist can do," see Mitsi 1991:53.

90 See Squire 2011:334 and n74.

91 Cf. Elsner: "Although the first ecphrasis in ancient literature, it presents a narrative pause, where the text turns from its relentless obsession with the unfolding of war to a vision of war's other: scenes of peace, festival, agriculture, song and dance, as well as war. This microcosm … includes, indeed emphasizes, what the *Iliad* is not" (2002:3–4).

This "other man out of many men" is an intriguing expression, the more so since he is left nameless. Given that similar phrasing was employed in another passage where a character "announces the text in the text," as de Jong has neatly put it,[92] Hephaistos' words seem to refer only to the narratees' world, rather than that of the characters. First, let us examine a similar passage:

"οἷσιν ἔπι Ζεὺς θῆκε κακὸν μόρον, ὡς καὶ ὀπίσσω
ἀνθρώποισι πελώμεθ' ἀοίδιμοι ἐσσομένοισιν."

"us two, on whom Zeus set a vile destiny, so that hereafter
we shall be made into things of song for the men of the future. "

Iliad VI 357–358

Helen's words will undoubtedly make the narratees think of the *Iliad* itself, a song that will present the κλέος and the fate of heroes like Hektor and women like Helen. By entering a different narrative level, Helen, a character with such a profound role in the Trojan myth in general, announces the *Iliad* within the *Iliad*.

In *Iliad* XVIII 466–467, Hephaistos does not merely "announce the *Iliad* at large," but points to the gazing at the armor of Achilles (and by implication at the famous ecphrasis on the shield) by an anonymous person "among many other men." This cryptic expression acquires its full meaning only after the armor is completed and handed to Achilles:

Μυρμιδόνας δ' ἄρα πάντας ἕλε τρόμος, οὐδέ τις ἔτλη
ἄντην εἰσιδέειν, ἀλλ' ἔτρεσαν· <u>αὐτὰρ Ἀχιλλεύς</u>
<u>ὡς εἶδ'</u>, ὥς μιν μᾶλλον ἔδυ χόλος, ἐν δέ οἱ ὄσσε
δεινὸν ὑπὸ βλεφάρων ὡς εἰ σέλας ἐξεφάανθεν·
τέρπετο δ' ἐν χείρεσσιν ἔχων θεοῦ ἀγλαὰ δῶρα.
αὐτὰρ ἐπεὶ φρεσὶν ᾗσι τετάρπετο δαίδαλα λεύσσων,
αὐτίκα μητέρα ἣν ἔπεα πτερόεντα προσηύδα·

Trembling took hold of all the Myrmidons. None had the courage
to look straight at it. They were afraid of it. *Only Achilleus
looked*, and as he looked the anger came harder upon him
and his eyes glittered terribly under his lids, like sunflare.
He was glad, holding in his hands the shining gifts of Hephaistos.
But when he had satisfied his heart with looking at the intricate
armour, he spoke to his mother and addressed her in winged words.

Iliad XIX 14–20

---

[92] 2009:98–99.

The contrast between the multitude of Myrmidons, who are terrified of the armor and do not dare to look at it, and Achilles, who alone marvels at his divine weapons, is not only striking but also puzzling.[93] The Myrmidons' fear is left unexplained, which becomes even more strange given that there are no monsters or other fearful creatures depicted on the shield. Why, then, are the Myrmidons terrified and shy away from looking at the divine armor? The answer can be better expressed by two other, related questions: why is it that Achilles *alone* admires the shield,[94] and why is the making of the shield flanked by both Hephaistos' words pointing to an anonymous admirer and by Achilles' marveling at the it?

First, a word on gaze: *Iliad* XIX 14–20 makes clear the importance of the shining effect of Achilles' armor. This radiant, gleaming light, bearing the trademark of divine craftsmanship, is a wonder imbued with "otherness." Part of its duality lies in its being both visible and invisible to different viewers.[95] The fear the Myrmidons feel, which underscores their failure as beholders, highlights the contrast with Achilles' fearless and ecstatic gaze. The true beholder of the divine armor (and of course the shield) can be none other than its proper owner. There can hardly be a more emphatic assertion of ownership, of the special association between the divine armor and Achilles.[96] The storyteller enhances this fact by presenting a brief but powerful *aesthetics of light*. Fear makes the Myrmidons turn their eyes away, since a frontal look entails a level of confrontation and engagement with a reality that is foreign and "other" to the average warrior. In contrast, Achilles' look (XIX 16 ὡς εἶδ') is correlated with the "sinking of his anger" even deeper inside him (XIX 16 ὥς μιν μᾶλλον ἔδυ χόλος), which is followed by a "terrible glittering of his eyes under his lids, like sunflare" (XIX 16–17 ἐν δέ οἱ ὄσσε / δεινὸν ὑπὸ βλεφάρων ὡς εἰ σέλας ἐξεφάανθεν). This aesthetics of light is not about a viewed object and a viewer, but about the duality of seeing: the divine armor projects its brilliant light[97] and the beholder

---

[93] Notice the repetition of verbs and expressions pertaining to gaze: εἰσιδέειν, εἶδ', ὄσσε ... ἐξεφάανθεν, λεύσσων.

[94] See Becker, who argues that Achilles' twofold reaction (he first feels χόλος, then τέρψις) demonstrates "precisely the ability to respond to *both* the referent *and* the medium" (1995:149). In light of this observation, I find the author's claim (150) that Achilles does not pause to look upon the shield contradictory, since it is explicitly said that Achilles is the only one who looks at the entire divine armor (*Iliad* XIX 14–20).

[95] On the point that a single thing can be two things at the same time, see Neer's discussion (2010:63–68), with examples from various ancient authors.

[96] The same is the case with the huge spear of Achilles, the only weapon that Patroklos could not take with him to battle; see *Iliad* XVI 140–144, where it is explicitly stated that Achilles *alone* could brandish this spear made of Pelian ash, given to him by Kheiron.

[97] In *Iliad* XIX 18 it is described as ἀγλαὰ δῶρα 'shining gifts' offered by Hephaistos to Achilles via Thetis. On the association between ἀγλαός and light, see Neer 2010:87.

grasps sight by emitting an equally brilliant light from his own eyes. The point is subtle but effectively made: pleasure is an emotion that takes hold of Achilles only in the framework of the interaction created by two communicating sources of light: his gaze and the shining armor. Thetis' son is pleased only when the light reflected from the weapons he is holding in his hands shines on him (XIX 18 τέρπετο δ' ἐν χείρεσσιν ἔχων θεοῦ ἀγλαὰ δῶρα), and only when the light shining from his glittering eyes falls upon the divine armor (XIX 19 αὐτὰρ ἐπεὶ φρεσὶν ᾗσι τετάρπετο δαίδαλα λεύσσων). In this light (literally and figuratively), Achilles becomes the first mortal beholder of the divine armor,[98] a model spectator of the poet's own art.[99]

The character of Achilles is privileged by the poet, or the tradition, of the *Iliad*.[100] His diction and his way of thinking seem, at times, to reflect the authorial voice of the poet of this epic. From this point of view, it may be plausibly argued that the words of Hephaistos (*Iliad* XVIII 466–467), who is of course a character in the plot, are addressed overtly to Thetis but covertly to the narratees. At the same time, they point to Achilles' (the narrator's privileged hero and mirror image of his own persona within the story-world) future gaze and wonder. Hephaistos' statement cues the entire ecphrasis that will soon follow to a metaleptic note: by presenting the master craftsman creating the entire world on the shield of Achilles,[101] the tradition of the *Iliad* invites the audience to realize that Iliadic Achilles can temporarily become a mirror image of the narrator himself, looking in pure wonder at his wonderful artifact. *Achilles is pleased because Homer is pleased.*

In *rhetorical*, or *discourse metalepsis*, the narrator intervenes in the story-world with a metanarrative comment, or he becomes the creator instead of the reporter of the story.[102] Rhetorical metalepsis opens a small window for a very brief time, only to close it and reaffirm the traditional distinction between narrative levels. By becoming a viewer,[103] the narrator briefly comments on what Hephaistos is depicting on the shield at least three times:

---

[98] As the narrator is the only mortal eyewitness of Hephaistos' making the shield, so Achilles is the first mortal marveling at it.

[99] See also Squire 2011:367–368.

[100] Parry 1956; Martin 1989:196, 206–230; Rengakos 2006a:17–30.

[101] One of the key factors concerning the interpretation of the ecphrasis on the shield of Achilles is that it displays the master craftsman (Hephaistos) *at work*, i.e. in the process of manufacturing the shield, and not for example when it is handed to Achilles. This has been interpreted as a covert reference to the master poet himself, whose mirror in the text is the smith-god; see Marg 1957:36–37.

[102] See Pier 2005b, 2009; de Jong 2009:114–115.

[103] See de Jong 2011:4.

In *Iliad* XVIII 518–519, the narrator briefly interrupts his description of an army moving to battle by inserting his own comment on the huge size of Athena and Ares, who were leading the army, in contrast to the small human figures in this scene.

καλὼ καὶ μεγάλω σὺν τεύχεσιν, ὥς τε θεώ περ,
ἀμφὶς ἀριζήλω· λαοὶ δ' ὑπολίζονες ἦσαν.

... [and they were]
beautiful and huge in their armour, being divinities,
and conspicuous from afar, but the people around them were smaller.

Iliad XVIII 518–519

In *Iliad* XVIII 539, during the actual description of a battle, the narrator observes that the divine figures depicted on the battlefield looked like living men. This comment belongs not to the description, but to the world of the narrator who is gazing at what is depicted on the shield: ὡμίλεον δ' ὥς τε ζωοὶ βροτοὶ ἠδ' ἐμάχοντο ("All closed together like living men and fought with each other"). Finally, in *Iliad* XVIII 548–549 the narrator refers to his own perception of the dark-colored earth, which in his eyes looks like "earth that has been ploughed," and calls this image forged on the shield "a wonder."

ἣ δὲ μελαίνετ' ὄπισθεν, ἀρηρομένῃ δὲ ἐῴκει
χρυσείη περ ἐοῦσα· τὸ δὴ περὶ θαῦμα τέτυκτο.

The earth darkened behind them and looked like earth that has been
    ploughed
though it was gold. Such was the wonder of the shield's forging.

Iliad XVIII 548–549

These brief comments inserted by the narrator remind the audience that the various snapshots included in this extended ecphrasis represent a "subtle combination and blending of narration and description."[104] They are a warning to the listeners of the epic song, who may become so immersed in the magnificent description of the shield that they forget the illusory nature of this world "forged on metal."

---

[104] de Jong 2011:7. The ample use of various spatial means lets the narrator re-create some pictorial effects, such as the distribution of light and shade or the nuances of color, and play with the antithesis between light and shade. The interplay between gleaming and darkness is a sort of verbal *chiaroscuro*, the famous eighteenth-century device for creating the illusion of truth.

These three types of metalepsis represent varying degrees of dependence on and innovation in the typology of metalepsis employed in Homeric epic. With the first type (the narrator entering the world of the characters), the ecphrasis presents a unique case of metalepsis, unprecedented in the entire *Iliad*, that does not belong to any of the techniques commonly used. As far as the second type is concerned, Hephaistos and the narrator tend to merge, and the narrative levels they belong to become blurred.[105] The introductory formulas to the different sections of the shield recall the distinction, which is soon forgotten as the descriptivized narrative snapshots merge the boundaries between these two levels.[106] By fusing the action of Hephaistos with his own description, as he passes from a dependent construction to an independent one (ποίησε, ἐτίθει, ἔτευξε) and then to independent clauses, the narrator can authenticate his song and increase its authority.[107] His song is as good as the god Hephaistos' marvelous depictions on the shield of Achilles.[108] Seen from this angle, the metaleptic effect is still felt,[109] when Achilles the receiver of the armor (and mirror image of the narrator) marvels at his new weapons. By temporarily fusing the spatial boundaries of different narrative worlds, the narrator's comments, which belong to the third type of metalepsis, aspire at reminding the audience of the fictionality of what is depicted in the entire ecphrasis. It is against such a strong pictorial illusion of a fictive story-world, then,[110] that the listeners and narratees are invited to evaluate the story-world of the *Iliad*.

---

[105] See de Jong 2009:100–101.

[106] See also de Jong 2011:5–7, who offers a list of "forms of narration in the ecphrasis on the shield," though some of them, as she herself acknowledges, "suit both description and narration" (6).

[107] See de Jong 2009:99–106. The merging of the narrative voices of Demodokos and "Homer" in *Odyssey* viii 367 (ταῦτ' ἄρ' ἀοιδὸς ἄειδε περικλυτός) also appears in the equivalent phrasing ποίησε περικλυτὸς Ἀμφιγυήεις and ποίκιλλε περικλυτὸς Ἀμφιγυήεις in *Iliad* XVIII 587 and 590 respectively.

[108] On the ecphrasis on the shield of Achilles as a *mise-en-abyme*, see de Jong 2011:9–11.

[109] See also Purves 2010a:52–55. For discussion of whether the shield works as a *mise-en-abyme* for the entire *Iliad*, see Marg 1957:20–37; Schadewaldt 1965:367; Ø. Andersen 1976; Taplin 1980; Burkert 1985:168; Hardie 1985; Stanley 1993:3–38; Becker 1995:4–5; Alden 2000:52–53; Nagy 2003:72–87.

[110] As Diderot, in his review of Fragonard's "Coresus and Callirhoe" (Diderot 1765), used the myth of Plato's cave to alert his readers to the illusion Fragonard employed, so the epic narrator presents his audience with a detailed look at the workshop of Hephaistos and the preparation of his work, and only then proceeds to the actual making of the shield. The storyteller has in fact "recomposed" his entire world: not only has he systematically avoided presenting private scenes (all the scenes presented on the shield involve multitudes of men and refer to public life), but he has also made his figures participate in short stories that will remain endlessly suspended, since they do exist separately, in distinct short tableaux. By distributing his narrative in various brief stories, the narrator emphasizes the illusion of the ecphrasis on the shield for his audience. On illusion, Diderot, Fragonard's "Coresus and Callirhoe," and ecphrasis, see Dubost 1996 and Fort 1996.

Conclusion

THE AIM OF THIS BOOK has been to offer a systematic and comprehensive presentation of the function of space in the *Iliad*. To this end, and following Nünning's theoretical model, four different aspects of space were studied, of which the first two (*simple story space* and *embedded story space*) pertain to the classical division between narrator text and character text proper, while the other two (*similes* and *prized objects*) belong to such special registers as imagery and description.

My main argument was that story space in the *Iliad* is a *thematized* space, since the story is not happening "there" but "in the way 'there' is constructed."[1] Iliadic story space is an indispensable mechanism for both the organization of the plot and the promotion of a particular Iliadic *Weltanschauung*. Character drawing, gender, age, and authority are all aspects of the epic's thematic agenda that are heavily influenced by and reflect active spatial representation. Although story space gives the impression of lurking in the epic's background, static and unchanging, it is in fact remarkably dynamic. To a large extent it shapes the plot, and makes possible all sorts of covert but especially strong comments on the distance between gods and men, the grimness of war, and the irony of human fate.

Following Ryan's analysis of narrative space,[2] I opted for a twofold division of story space into *simple* and *embedded story space*, the former pertaining to the actions, the latter to the thoughts of characters. The aim of part 1, which was devoted to real topographies, as mapped by the actants of the plot, was to study the way simple story space is presented in the *Iliad*.

Given the epic's dramatic theatricality, I adopted a further twofold division of simple story space between the battlefield, as the *base-level setting* (chapter 1), and various *framing spaces*, such as the Achaean camp, the city of Troy, and the world of the immortals (chapter 2).[3] In this light, older classifications, such as

---

[1]   See Bal 1997:136–137.
[2]   Ryan 2009:421–422.
[3]   On such a distinction between base-level and framed or framing spaces, see Ronen 1986.

the tripartite, horizontal area of mortal activity (the plain, the city of Troy, the Achaean camp) and the double vertical division between areas of mortal and immortal space, were mapped onto the dynamic interaction between framed and framing spaces in the *Iliad*. The advantage of the proposed classification of simple story space lies in the way it allows the epic to capitalize on the action taking place on the battlefield. The interplay between these zones of martial and nonmartial activity determines the development of the plot so much that it accentuates the epic's dramatic outlook on the race of heroes.

In chapter 1, I studied how the battlefield is presented as either dynamic, martial or static, nonmartial space. For the former, I examined the entire range of fighting activity in the epic, and explored how space is organized when the context is martial. Instead of offering a description of the vast, uncharted area of the Trojan plain, the storyteller has used his characters' actions during the battle as his visual compass to create a clear mental picture of the base-level setting. The various forms of Iliadic combat (ἀνδροκτασίαι, fighting in small groups, pairs of warriors, groups of θεράποντες and ἑταῖροι, formal duels, and ἀριστεῖαι) constitute different, yet complementary ways of organizing space.

In the case of ἀνδροκτασίαι, space is viewed dynamically. The storyteller's mental camera constantly changes perspective, following first one group of warriors and then another. This *zigzag* technique, which is combined with frequent *close-ups* on second- and third-rank heroes, shows that the narrator can switch from a global, panoramic view when the Achaean and Trojan armies approach each other, to zoom in on the shocking details of actual combat that accentuate the sheer brutality of war.

With respect to fighting in small groups, either as pairs of warriors or as groups of θεράποντες and ἑταῖροι, space is miniaturized by *spotlighting*: the storyteller zooms in on specific warriors, whose position is determined not by some topographical sign but through their proximity to an ancillary group of heroes. Likewise, in the case of larger masses of the two armies, which are described as they fight behind the πρόμαχοι, the narrator builds on a binary opposition between *foreground* and *background*: elite warriors fight in the front ranks, while ordinary groups of soldiers fight behind them.

In the climactic triad of formal duels that lies at the core of the *Iliad's* plot, the storyteller introduces his audience to a spatial grammar that creates expectations which are initially met, but ultimately violated. From the separate viewing of Sarpedon and Patroklos attacking one another, to the focus on the disoriented retreat of Patroklos speared in the back by Hektor, and finally to the transformation of symmetrical dueling space into the asymmetrical space of a pursuit in the Achilles-Hektor encounter, the narrator presents a wide range of fighting possibilities. The gradual shift from spatial symmetry (Sarpedon-Patroklos), to disorientation (Patroklos-Hektor), and finally to nullifying all spatial protocols for a duel (Hektor-Achilles) enhances narrative associations and reveals a carefully constructed thematic blueprint. Narrative cohesion is further strengthened by means of associative visualization, in the form of an *internal preview*. By introducing the impending duel through a preliminary minor episode in which Patroklos kills the henchman (Thrasudemos) of his future victim (Sarpedon), and then the charioteer (Kebriones) of the man by whom he will be soon defeated (Hektor), the storyteller helps the audience visualize the space of the ensuing duel, so that when the main confrontation takes place, the emphasis can be on evaluating the duel itself. The lesson he teaches his audience is that the two duels are subtly and ironically interconnected: Patroklos will prevail in the first duel, but will perish in the second. Tellingly, when the duel is deprived of such a minor incident, as in the Achilles-Hektor confrontation, listeners can be turned into viewers, who see Hektor's complete isolation from the rest of the troops in their minds' eye.

The ἀριστεία represents a complex and fluid form of dynamic space that combines features of both the ἀνδροκτασίαι (successive killings) and the duel (emphasis on an individual warrior). The main technique employed here is that of a *continuous action space*, or a *single trajectory* to which the activity of an individual hero belongs. By focusing on the exceptional military performance of a protagonist who is constantly "on the move," the storyteller can visualize an expanding space in the form of a *trail*. In this case, narrative unity almost amounts to spatial unity.

These techniques (zigzag, close-ups, spotlighting, foreground-background, symmetrical viewing, disorientation, asymmetrical space, internal preview, trail) show that warriors are used as *space-organizers*, representing martial activity in its most appalling minutiae and helping the audience recognize a coherent narrative sequence instead of random fighting scenes.

In the section "Static Space," I explored how martial space is transformed into static, nonmartial space to accommodate other activities, such as swearing oaths, friendly meetings, and assemblies. In addition, I studied a series of locus-images, such as the oak tree of Zeus, the fig tree, the river and ford of Skamandros, the tombstone of Ilos, the tomb of Myrine, and the rise in the plain.

The transformation of martial space is always narratively exploited by the storyteller: in the case of oath-swearings, he creates a limited, carefully delineated ritual space, contrasting with the vast and uncharted martial space of the battlefield, in order to present his audience, both internal and external, with credible scenarios about the end of the war. By associating the violation of the ritual space of the oath-swearing with the collapse of false expectations about a potential end of hostilities, the narrator silently comments on the illusory and temporary transformation of martial space. Likewise, the reversal of the typological features of a formal duel so as to meet the requirements of a friendly meeting, such as that between Diomedes and Glaukos, points out to the audience the inevitable other side of heroic camaraderie: the sheer brutality of war and the relentless carnage will soon take over. In the case of assembly meetings, the storyteller takes pains to help his audience visualize small areas that are either free of corpses or have been mentioned before as the site of some hero's intense martial activity. In a remarkable crossing-over from the level of the story to the level of the discourse, the Homeric narrator creates for his characters a clear space for an assembly, more or less as he creates for his audience a new mental image of a clear space in which to picture it.

Locus-images have two functions, a cognitive and a thematic. They help the narrator construct his story on the fly and mentally orient himself among multiple elements that creep into his mind. They also evoke association through connotative meaning: the oak tree of Zeus, the fig tree, and the river Skamandros denote an interplay between protection and danger; the tombstone of Ilos and the tomb of Myrine constitute time-marks, as they indicate the transformation of place into space by reactivating emotionally charged experience; whereas the rise in the plain stands for a change in the course of the war, as the Achaeans rise victorious after the return of Achilles.

In chapter 2, I explored the function of various framing spaces, such as the Achaean camp, Troy, and the places from where the gods watch or enter into the human theater of action. The Achaean camp includes the headquarters of Agamemnon and Achilles, the seashore, the Achaean wall, and the ships. When the action is located within the hut or in the headquarters of an Achaean leader, whether Agamemnon in *Iliad* I or Achilles in *Iliad* IX and XXIV, the role of space becomes all the more important, since the particular location is used not only as a place where an event takes place but as a special *social space*, which shapes the particular events occurring there, and more significantly functions as a code for "reading" the episode at hand. The seashore constitutes a highly thematized area, a place of isolation and sadness, of prayer and lament. It is closely associated with Achilles, who meets his mother Thetis there in *Iliad* I, XVIII, and XXIV, but as the episode with Khruses shows (he prays to Apollo while walking along the shore), it is also a "breakaway" space where mortals and immortals communicate. The Achaean wall and ditch perform three functions: (1) they help the narrator pin down the various phases of both the Achaean retreat and the Trojan attack, as Zeus begins to fulfill the promise he made to Thetis in *Iliad* I; (2) they are a means of *intratextual misdirection*, creating the illusion of safety for the Achaeans; and (3) they delay the return of Achilles to the war. The area of the ships is sometimes used as a lookout, from where the Achaeans observe what is going on in another part of the camp. Like the area of the Achaean camp, this vaguely charted space undergoes an internal expansion and provides the necessary background against which specific narrative events are placed.

In the funeral games for Patroklos, the storyteller first pictures for his audience the place where the games will be held. He therefore transforms an area inside the Achaean camp into an ἀγών, a "contest space," both by keeping his mental lens on Achilles' action while he organizes the actual games, and by mentally separating a rather uncharted area, inside the Achaean camp but at some distance from the huts of the army. In the individual contests, he separates the chariot race, which is the most important event, from the other contests, which he presents by distinguishing between those involving physical contact between the participants (boxing, wrestling, running, and duels in armor) and throwing events (weight, archery, and javelin). This classification is reflected in the type of mental picturing that the narrator employs: whereas in the chariot race he uses both the zooming-in and *high-angle long* or *medium camera-shot* techniques, he applies the former to the physical contact events (including running), and the latter to the throwing events.

The city of Troy, with its various subsettings (walls, palace, and the entrance to the city), fufills four distinct functions: as a place for councils, observing the enemy, prayer, and lament. That said, the locale of Troy represents a cluster of activities that allows the audience to glimpse the "hidden" world of the city, with its own social dynamics. All the key scenes that occur inside Troy are essential both to the dramatic input of the plot and to relations of power, whether notions of control, heroism, family, or jurisdiction. The fixed setting of the walls becomes the showpiece of a *spatialization of conflict*, shedding light on the gap that separates the family from the heroic world, the two extremities around which the Iliadic storyteller unravels the tragic life stories of two of his most important characters, Helen and Hektor. By limiting the spatial representation of the city of Troy to the houses of Priam, Paris, and Hektor and the temple of Athena, the *Iliad* makes space reflect its main narrative blueprint, which is centered only on the principal figures of the plot. To this end, the palace is presented by means of brief descriptions that are expressed from the particular perspective of a given character, who functions as an internal focalizer.

The distinction between the worlds of mortals and immortals, and the former's inability to access the latter, underlines the unbridgeable gap between gods and men. Specific spatial features of the divine world skillfully call attention to the profound difference between it and the events taking place on the Trojan plain and the mortal world at large. Emphasizing the spatial aspects of divine intervention in the mortal realm signals distance as a form of irony, since the ease with which the immortals enter and leave the mortal world stands in marked contrast to humans' confinement and entrapment in a space, both literal and figurative, that they cannot escape.

Apart from the use of spatial memory to visualize Olympos, dynamic space creates associations of cognitive and hierarchical factors that take the form of social and axiological coding. The intentional distinction between higher and lower places within the realm of Olympos indicates the higher divine status of Zeus, first among all the Olympian gods. Along the same lines, the emphasis on both the (often) lonely figure of Zeus, whom divine travelers visit at Olympos, and the fact that Zeus never travels to meet with another god, connects the cognitive schema that stresses the importance of "one" versus "many" with the higher status of Zeus, who dominates Olympos. With respect to the function of Olympos, I have drawn a line between its thematic and its symbolic roles, the former pertaining to the evolution of the plot, the latter to *spatial theography*, translating the thematic aspect of divine travel into a symbolic one, based on standard antitheses of status such as high (gods) versus low (men), or even higher (the Olympians) versus lesser gods (Thetis, Iris). The depths of the sea, as the abode of Thetis, symbolize the place where crucial narrative shifts begin to happen: the three fundamental changes in Achilles' behavior are linked to his mother's involvement in the Iliadic plot, since she is always pictured as being in her underwater home when she listens to her son or to the other gods.

The *Iliad* avails itself of a number of locations used by the gods as observation posts. From there, immortals watch what is going on, either in the plain of Troy or in the Achaean camp, and decide to intervene and influence the action. That said, it should be noted that these locations are not lacking in symbolic function: the land of the Aethiopes stands for an idyllic, problem- and tension-free community of gods and men that is contrasted with the world of the *Iliad*. Mount Ida and the highest peaks of Samothrace, by facilitating the transfer of a panoramic, actorial, and fixed standpoint from the omniscient storyteller to Zeus, a figure in the plot, amount to a metaliterary comment on the traditional dichotomy between the viewer and the viewed object. The Wall of Herakles and the Hill of Kallikolone represent two symmetrical landmarks used by the gods as observation points within the plain of Troy. They are both highly thematized spaces, since their location is closely entwined with the gods who stand on them: the Wall of Herakles is occupied by the pro-Achaean gods, while the Hill of Kallikolone is used by the pro-Trojan ones. At the same time, the Wall of Herakles and the Hill of Kallikolone pertain to *an archaeology of space,* as they both refer to the past. Whereas the former was built by the Trojans and Athena in order to help Herakles escape from a sea beast, the latter was the hill where the Judgment of Paris took place.

454

Taking a cue from the traditional narratological division between narrator and character text, part 2 is devoted to the study of embedded story space, that is, the absent space constantly referred to by the characters of the Iliadic plot. The theoretical foundation of this chapter lies in Fludernik's theory of *natural narratology*, and in particular the notion of *experientiality*, according to which focalizing characters constitute *cognizers,* or in other words thinking agents whose stock of experience shapes their perception of what is going on in the story-world. According to this line of argument, the epic tradition uses heroes as independent mental entities, whose role in the *Iliad* is shaped by both general features of human consciousness at large and personal characteristics stemming from their "biographies" in the entire epic tradition.

Before exploring the function of place-names in character text, I discussed their use in the two extended passages of narrator text, the Catalogue of Ships (CS) and the Catalogue of Trojans and Allies (CT&A). In this comprehensive view of the Greek and Trojan-and-allies worlds, the narrator offers a programmatic view of the *Iliad* by "tagging" heroes to specific geographical regions. By making use of the mental processes of the *map* and the *tour,* the storyteller offers a panorama of the forces arrayed against each other in the war at the lowest possible cognitive cost.

With respect to embedded story space, I chose to present the relevant material on the basis of the geographical opposition between the two sides of the Aegean (chapter 3: Greece vs. chapter 4: the Troad and Lycia). Since each of the most frequently mentioned place-names in mainland Greece (Phthia, Argos, Pylos, Thebes, Sparta, Ithaka, Mycenae) and the islands of Lesbos, Lemnos, Skyros, and Crete is associated either with a specific Achaean hero or with a given phase of this hero's mythical lore, I set out to explore how space is employed as a filter that allows the tradition to measure an individual's role in the *Iliad.*

Phthia symbolizes the emotions, thoughts, and concerns of Achilles: in the beginning of his quarrel with Agamemnon in *Iliad* I, it figuratively embodies his loneliness, his marginalization and isolation in a war that is not his own. Later on, it becomes the means for a powerful spatial misdirection when Achilles declares that he will return to Phthia immediately, thus threatening to deprive not only the Achaean army of their best hero but also the Iliadic epic of its most necessary thematic prerequisite, the one of the two figures around whom the theme of μῆνις is centered. In *Iliad* IX, Phthia is evoked through Achilles' father Peleus, narratively activating his pre-Iliadic past in his stance towards his son's participation in the war. Through a web of intertextual references, the epic downplays or ignores versions in which Peleus did not send Achilles to the war, in favor of versions in which he willingly sent him to Troy. Along this line, the

Iliadic tradition applies the motif of "paternal assent" to Patroklos as well, and transforms Phthia into a spatiotemporal metonym for the involvement of both heroes in the war, and their figurative journey to death and epic κλέος. Last, Phthia is treated not as a mere topographical location but as a "site of memory." By excluding himself from the constellation of the other Achaean leaders who were summoned to Troy and by shattering the very foundations of a "canonical" version of the past promoted by the Atreidai, Achilles turns Phthia into the political space of an "anti-Troy," throwing the Achaeans' heroic rhetoric into sharp relief.

In contrast with Phthia, which is associated strictly with Achilles, the semantic range covered by "Argos" is wide: it designates variously the homeland of Diomedes in the Argolid, the homeland of Achilles (Pelasgian Argos) in Thessaly, the homeland and kingdom of Agamemnon in the Peloponnese, the entire Peloponnese, and the whole of Greece. Whereas the first two meanings are not frequently used—since the former lies outside the scope of the Trojan epic tradition and the latter has been superseded by Phthia as an emotionally loaded space for Achilles—Argos is invoked in the poem mainly as the homeland of Agamemnon. Whereas Achilles adopts for Phthia a discourse of spatio-temporal discontinuity, full of abrupt breaks and deep ruptures, Agamemnon constructs a different picture of Argos, one that erases all manner of irregularities, since he excludes from his perception of the homeland those events that are against the kind of personality he wants to present to the army: major dividing lines like the sacrifice of Iphigenia, the state of his relation to Klutaimnestra, and his insulting Achilles at the expense of enormous Achaean losses are thus erased or repressed, and filtered into a discourse that reveals his anxiety about disgrace and blame should he return to Argos unsuccessful on the one hand, and an almost complete lack of reference to or consideration of his family on the other. Argos becomes a vehicle for channeling into the epic typical dichotomies between κλέος and νόστος and praise and blame. Geography is thus turned into space that represents a hero's "epic home," the notional center around which his past, present, and future constantly revolve. When "Argos" designates the Peloponnese or the whole of Greece, it is used as an alias for each speaker's focalization of the entire Trojan War, or a part of it. The Achaeans tend to refer to Argos as a thematized space that epitomizes their concerns about dishonor, while the Trojans refer to it in the sense of "Greece," either in the context of a potential agreement between the two sides or with respect to their fears or hopes about the future.

Pylos functions as a spatial metonym for a *gate* or *passage* that points to narratives centered on human arrogance, against which Nestor, the only son of Neleus who survived Herakles' attack on Pylos, and who is associated with *light and life*, can prevail. Pylos' figurative function accords with the extremely positive presentation of Nestor in the *Iliad*. Being endowed with an almost emblematic sweet voice (λιγὺς ἀγορητής) and unsurpassed rhetorical skills, he possesses a narrative authority that is harmoniously matched with his wisdom and moderation: from this point of view, Nestor functions as the backdrop against which the audience is invited to evaluate the negative paradigms of Thamyris and Herakles, who both symbolize the sudden shift from skill and ability to arrogance and punishment. Stories and storytelling are particular to Nestor, and stand for his privileged field of Iliadic activity. The narrative about his journey from Pylos to Thessaly to assist the Lapithai helps the audience to contrast him with Achilles, who was not bound by oath but whose participation in the expedition was considered indispensable for winning the war. In Nestor's story in *Iliad* I, Pylos becomes an "anti-Phthia," a space where he never explicitly says that he wishes to return, like Achilles, but which he has deliberately left in order to participate in various exploits and so build up his heroic persona. In this way, Nestor's Pylos becomes the kind of epic past that the Iliadic tradition uses to counterbalance Achilles' Phthia.

Boeotian Thebes constitutes a spatiotemporal bridge between the Theban and Trojan War epic traditions. It is regularly invoked as the necessary background for measuring the exploits and heroism of warriors in both Theban and Trojan epic. The picture that is painted is rather vague: while sometimes it results in the implicit praise of certain "Theban" heroes who feature in the *Iliad*, other times the comparison works against them. Thebes, therefore, points to the first or the second Theban war, since its epic past spans two different expeditions and is represented by a series of epic song traditions, as the epic poems *Thebais*, *Epigoni*, and *Alcmaeonis* amply attest. As far as the much weaker Herakles connection is concerned, space signifies deception and bewilderment, which serves as a useful parallel to the Iliadic theme of μῆνις.

In contrast with most of the minor places (like Sparta, Ithaka, Crete, and Mycenae) that constitute simple geographical references, the three Aegean islands of Lemnos, Lesbos, and Skyros stand for highly thematized spaces that form a network of associations around the fate of Achilles. Lemnos points to events further back in time, namely the Achaean fleet's sojourn there while sailing to Troy, and represents a space that is friendly to Achilles; Lesbos (the Aeolic filtering of which should be noted) is associated with hostile space and is linked to the more recent past, since its sack by Achilles occurred only after the Achaeans arrived at Troy; whereas Skyros, also sacked by Achilles, is evoked in the *Iliad* through both his marriage to king Lukomedes' daughter Deidameia and a non-Iliadic future involving Neoptolemos' coming to Troy after his father's death.

Locations in Asia Minor are rarely thematized, since the Trojans, fighting in their own country, are by definition deprived of the typical polarity between κλέος and νόστος that marks the Achaean presence in Troy. The wider Troad, though, is often thematized through the association of certain places with the fate of specific figures whose life stories dramatically converge with the fate of Achilles. The antithesis between the proximity of the cities surrounding Troy and the remoteness of Phthia is mapped to Achilles' unprovoked destructive actions in the Troad. The Iliadic tradition employed these locations as a device for measuring Achilles' dramatic role in the epic. Hypoplakian Thebes, Lurnessos, Pedasos, and Khruse are turned into variations on the theme of Achilles' arrogance and brutality against a people who have never harmed him. The *Iliad* further exploits this narrative strategy by capitalizing on the spatial aspect of size: the stark difference between the great ease with which Achilles sacks all these small cities in the Troad, taking captive various women, and his failure to take the great city of Troy and get Helen back amounts to a profound critical statement about the situation he has been facing. On a complementary level, the cities sacked by Achilles supply a male-dominated epic either with female characters (Khruseis, Briseis, Andromakhe) who are linked to other first-rank heroes of the epic and represent distinct phases in the development of the plot, or with other male characters (Lukaon) whose fate will be associated with a particular phase of Achilles' reintegration in the warrior society.

Lycia is the most significant of all the locations in Asia Minor. As the place of origin of the most important Trojan allies, the Lycians, it is regularly employed to achieve various ends. It thematizes the motif of "coming from afar," which is used as an accusation against Trojan cowardice, more or less in the way Achilles uses Phthia and the life he has left behind to come and help Agamemnon, whom he blames in *Iliad* I; and it is presented as social space through a brief description of the life, status, and privileges Lycian kings possess and enjoy. In the case of Pandaros, Lycia is evoked in the manner of a second-level associative allusion: it shapes his identity through the traditional reference to Lycians as famous archers, so that it can conjure up another character (Paris) and create a link to his insolent behavior as a violator of unwritten law in the events preceding the plot of the *Iliad*. It is used by Tlepolemos from the point of view of a rival Rhodian tradition aimed at invalidating any Lycian claims to esteem and honor, and by Glaukos as part of a mythical landscape that explains and supports arguments about a common genealogy between enemies on the battlefield. Finally, Lycia is employed as the place of a hero's future cult, the space where sleep and death, that is, fainting and dying, will cease to operate, through the cultural process represented by the tomb and σῆμα that Sarpedon's countrymen will build for him.

Part 3 offered a detailed examination of what I have termed the *paratopic* space of the Homeric simile. This term describes how the space of the similes exists next to or in parallel with the space of the main narrative to which it is anchored, but also beyond and above the regular story space. Homeric similes do not invent a novel story-world, but aim at immersing the audience in a different visual universe, whose density is fully exploited as the storyteller's lens gradually zooms in on its details.

In chapter 5, I analyzed the distribution and function of simile space versus narrative space in *Iliad* II, V, XI, and XVI. Drawing on cognitive theory, which explores the role of space as a powerful and effective cue to recall, and Rubin's pioneering work on memory and oral traditions, I argued that the narrator organizes the visual space of similes by means of *visual units*, the mental building blocks of narrative scenes. Such a finding has sweeping consequences for the storyteller's mode of performance, since it stresses the importance of the technique of mental association, which is enhanced by spatial unity, a mnemonic aspect recognized in cognitive psychology as a cue to information retrieval. Within the medium of oral performance, the system displays a remarkable economy: as long as the visual setting of a given narrative unit remains the same, the space delineated in the corresponding extended simile also remains the same, or at least of the same sort.

Chapter 6 was devoted to the study of the cognitive aspect of the Homeric simile. In this light, I explored the simile's ontological boundaries, that is, both the transfer of the audience from the world of the plot to different visual spheres by means of mental imagery, and a boundary-crossing experience by which the narrator creates a further spatial dichotomy between the mental world of the narrative and that of the ontological and corporeal habitat of the real world. To this end, I explored several aspects of the multiformity of the extended simile, such as *bilaterality* (as a manifestation of transformational thinking), *complex expansions* (stemming from the simile's openness and traditional referentiality), *mapping inconsistency between the target and base domains*, and the *multiplied simile* (the elliptical combination of two superimposed narrative structures).

Keeping in mind that the Homeric simile allows for a boundary-crossing experience into a different world, visualized in vivid snapshots of suspended action occurring *in medias res*, it becomes clear that the audience is invited on a journey to the new mental space of the simile's pictorial universe. Reinforced by the simile's deictic demarcation, the narrator attempts to key his listeners to a distinct note, free them from the spatiotemporal constraints of the world of the plot, and transport them to a new chronotopic framework, a different mental landscape which they are invited to explore. At the same time, by relativizing the medium, the narrator engages his listeners in a revealing realization of the fact that like the similes, the poetry of the *Iliad* enhances the sameness, or at least similarity, of human nature and human fate. The paratopic space of the Homeric similes reflects the storyteller's effort to limit and control the audience's multiple image-mappings of familiar scenes of the natural world, which he can easily access by means of their mental stock of common experience. It is exactly at this critical juncture that the pictorial richness of the simile lies: the disparity between the different mental visualizations available to the narrator and the members of the audience results in a fascinating outburst of visual imagery.

Part 4 dealt with description, one of the principal areas of spatial representation. Given the absence of landscape description in the *Iliad*, I focused my attention on descriptions of prized objects (chapter 7), culminating in the monumental ecphrasis on Achilles' shield (chapter 8). Building on the work of Minchin, who has stressed the importance of visual memory and implicit knowledge in Homeric description, I explored both the function of perspective in object-description and the way mnemonic formats are organized. Thus I examined spatial aspects such as the *position of the beholder*, *diagrammatic iconicity*, both *dynamic* and *static* (subdivided into *extrinsic* and *intrinsic perspective*), and *mixed description*.

The position of the beholder plays a pivotal role, since it may determine the particular way the description will unfold. A character-viewer may offer a visual tour of a precious object, which can serve as a reminder of the object's history, or may assume the role of a mobile beholder who moves his mind's eye in a certain direction or along a visual path, whose spatial demarcations prolong the dramatic moment and transfer the object's magnificence to the narrative to follow.

Diagrammatic iconicity refers to analogies or similarities between the code used for space perception and the way spatial description is organized. *Dynamic* spatial description is about visualizing an object's movement in space. The object's transfer from one owner to another through a catalogue format removes all traces of their individual biographies and translates time into space, transforming the past into the distance that dictionally separates them. *Static* spatialization, which is subdivided into *extrinsic* and *intrinsic* perspectives, represents the most common form of spatial description in the *Iliad*. Extrinsic perspective refers to an object's perceptual significance, determined by spatial pairs like *near-far*, *foreground-background*, *dark-shining*, *center-periphery*. A significant number of prized objects are described in the *Iliad* from the extrinsic perspective of one or two noteworthy features they possess. The narrator eschews a point-for-point photographic description, but rather zooms in on what he considers to be truly noteworthy, assuming that his audience will supply all the missing details on their own. Given that occasionally these characteristics of the described objects are presented in contrast to others of the same kind, the description of a prized object becomes a sort of *selection* of details regarded as meriting description. It is in this light that the single-feature technique is especially observable in brief descriptive passages. The reason for this is twofold: first, the narrator must counterbalance the description's brevity by emphasizing a single feature, and second, he can easily create a mental link in his mind between the single feature highlighted in the descriptive passage and a detail found either in the narrative segment immediately following it, or in a previous reference to the same object or its owner. Diagrammatic iconicity is also built around the static perspective of other extrinsic spatial pairs like *outside-inside and top-bottom*. Here, spatially conceived contrasts bring what is important to the fore: they are used as both cues that help the storyteller visualize what he describes, and guides that allow the audience to evaluate the description during the performance of the song.

Unlike the widespread use of extrinsic spatial perspective, intrinsic perspective, which is organized according to the principle of *topographical contiguity* based on an object's inherent function, is absent from Iliadic epic, for two reasons: First, this kind of description would have emphasized not *what* an object is, but *where* it is, which would have been very much against the *Iliad*'s emphasis on presenting an object to its audience in terms of how it functions, not where it is placed. Second, descriptions from an intrinsic perspective are notoriously lacking in multiple cues, for they are based on the object's standard and widely known function, which stems from the highlighting of its inherent role. Mixed types do exist: the narrator can construct large descriptive segments consisting of an initial static diagrammatic description followed by dynamic iconicity in the form of the object's history.

Apart from the traditional dichotomy between narration and description, there are passages marked by a certain blurring of the boundaries between these two modes. The term *descriptivized narration* or *pseudonarrative* refers to description disguised as narration: in this case description remains in the background, concealed by narration. Such a fusing of boundaries in the *Iliad* is accompanied by an expansion of certain aspects of the description and the occasional use of a small-scale ecphrastic format. The main result of this technique of spatial description is to reconceptualize a given object, by activating certain narrative domains, and to enlarge its own spatial domain. Thus Agamemnon's role in the *Iliad* is so deeply marked by his initial conflict with Achilles that the narrator, having planned an ecphrasis on Achilles' shield on a massive scale in *Iliad* XVIII, decided to endow Agamemnon with multiple but smaller ecphrases before his own ἀριστεία in *Iliad* XI. In this way he invited his audience to realize, during the extended ecphrasis dedicated to a single part of Achilles' armor in *Iliad*

XVIII, that in contrast with Agamemnon, the son of Thetis will not be wounded but will masterfully prevail on the battlefield, and that his own single ecphrasis allusively outdoes the multiple short ecphrases of Agamemnon, just as his heroic prowess far surpasses that of the king of Mycenae.

Ecphrastic space (chapter 8), with respect to Achilles' shield, refers both to the "external" or "physical" space or material on which the depiction is placed and to the "internal" space or spaces included in the various narrative snapshots that make up the ecphrasis. Moreover, ecphrastic space fuses the distinction between narrative levels and the effective gambit orchestrated around the verbal-cum-visual syllepsis that the shield of Achilles offers.

In the section "External Space," I explored how the use of metal as the material upon which the ecphrasis is presented conforms to an *aesthetics of space* that is of key importance for Greek art. At the core of this approach lies the role of *light*, whose glowing radiance is closely associated with spatial factors such as proximity and distance. The emphasis on the gleaming effect of various figures and features on the shield is about a dialectic of the shining "here" in Hephaistos' workshop and the radiant "there" of the shield's mental beholders, the members of the external audience. This interplay between "grasping sight and radiant light,"[4] I argued, testifies to a duality that applies to both the level of the narrative and that of the discourse.

In contrast with most studies on the ecphrasis of Achilles' shield, which are either concerned with the conflict between narrative and description or seek to unlock some hidden pattern for interpreting the multiple scenes on the five folds of the shield, I argued that what is important is to reconstruct the actual flow of images in the narrator's mind. Building on cognitive psychology and research on memory, which have shown that the human mind processes images by selecting details which it then configures and reconfigures according to familiar schemata, I maintained that in composing his song orally the narrator works under multiple constraints: what the storyteller describes in the ecphrasis on Achilles' shield is determined by a whole range of factors, ranging from the material on which it is depicted, to generic limitations imposed by diction, meter, and the themes available to him, to the exigencies of the performance and the function of memory, which is facilitated by specific kinds of mental links or nodes, as well as to the principle of *iconic solidarity*, which expresses "the contradictory nature of images in sequence as both autonomous (meaningful in and of themselves) and dependent upon those around them (making meaning in juxtaposition to surrounding images)."[5]

---

[4] Neer 2010:67.
[5] Johnson 2008:2.

Building on Groensteen's innovative work on image and language in comics, I particularized these constraints with respect to the shield of Achilles and suggested a division of the five folds on which the depictions are placed into visual sections, on the basis of smaller visual panels which can be further divided into frames, hyperframes, megaframes, and multiframes. My analysis showed that the narrator organizes his mental images by a triple process of *segmentation, grouping,* and *interlacing.* He breaks down his pictorial material into separate segments, which he arranges into groups that he can weave together at will. He does this by employing both *restrained* and *general* linkage between the various groups of images: the former designates the interconnection and interaction of panels *sequentially,* whereas the latter refers to the *nonsequential* way panels are associated, by means of evoking or resonating terms used before and featuring again in one or more nonadjacent panels. In this context, space is of paramount importance for understanding the entire process of organizing mental images. The storyteller visualizes the various episodes depicted on the shield by means of "mini-tours," mentally leaping from one spatial node to another. Even within the framework of individual scenes, added elements are anchored to locations or movements that facilitate the retrieval of information and speed up mental navigation.

Finally, I studied how space in the description of the shield of Achilles constitutes the earliest extended *metalepsis* in Greek literature. The blurring or transcending of the distinction between narrative levels, as when the narrator enters the space of the characters or the characters invade that of the narrator, or the narrator intervenes with a metanarrative comment or becomes the creator instead of the reporter of the story, is particularly significant in the case of Achilles' shield. By means of these types of metalepsis, the ecphrasis assumes an all-encompassing perspective: it extends far beyond both its immediate context and the Iliadic plot in general, becoming an emblem of poetics and a hint to the audience, who are invited to evaluate the story-world of the *Iliad* against the impressive visual illusion of a fictive constellation of images and unfinished snapshots.

Appendix 1
Space in the Similes of the *Iliad*
The Visual Units

IN THIS APPENDIX I offer a presentation, with very brief comments, of the organization and function of the system of visual units in the similes of each Iliadic book (with the exception of *Iliad* II, V, XI, and XVI, which were analyzed in detail in part 3).

Iliad III

Visual unit 1

    2: (N1) plain / (S1) sky

    10: (N2) plain / (S2) mountains

    23: (N3) plain / (S3) [mountains]

    34: (N4) plain / (S4) mountains

    [60: Speech]

Visual unit 2

    151: (N5) walls / (S5) woods, tree

    [196: Speech]

Iliad III contains two visual units of extended similes: in the first, four distinct similes are grouped together, which correspond to four phases of the action that takes place on the plain. The space of the similes is that of height (sky and mountains). When the action is carried to the walls of Troy, then the simile used changes spatial coordinates as well. The Trojan elders are compared to cicadas sitting on a tree (152 δενδρέῳ ἐφεζόμενοι).

Iliad IV

Visual unit 1

74: (N1) Olympos > plain / (S1) sky > sea or land

Visual unit 2

130: (N2) the secluded χῶρος where the duel between Menelaos and Paris took place in *Iliad* III (Menelaos is still standing where the narrator left him in *Iliad* III) / (S2) room (where a baby's cradle is)

Visual unit 3

141: (N3) the same as previous / (S3) chamber

[243: Speech]

Visual unit 4

275: (N4) plain / (S4) lookout > sea

Visual unit 5

422: (N5) plain / (S5) beach, sea

Visual unit 6

433: (N6) plain (Trojans) / (S6) sheep pens

Visual unit 7

452: (N7) the secluded χῶρος where the battle will take place (see 130) / (S7) mountains > meeting of streams

Visual unit 8

482: (N8) banks of Simoeis / (S8) marsh, river-banks

Similes in *Iliad* IV are visualized in six groups, each containing a single simile for a single location in the narrative. The low percentage of pairings within the context of a "fighting" book makes it evident that the narrator visualizes different parts of the area where the battle takes place. In this respect, similes in *Iliad* IV contrast with those attested in *Iliad* III: whereas the latter, in the manner of their narrative context, were concentrated on the same space, the former display a considerable variety, perhaps reflecting the effort on the part of the storyteller to create ποικιλία and enhance ἐνάργεια in the first book of massive fighting in the epic.

Iliad VI

Visual unit 1

506: (N1) high chambers > city > place where Hektor stands / (S1) manger > plain > river with other horses

Iliad VI contains only one extended simile, which is striking for its inclusion of multiple places: Hektor is like a horse leaving the stable and running across the plain until it reaches the river where other horses are watered. The shifting locations of this simile allow the narrator to *tour* in his mind's eye the movement of Hektor inside the palace and the city. Movement, as an aspect of space, is also a strong cue to mental recall.[1] In this way, the storyteller is able to pin Hektor down to specific locations and "follow" him inside the vague and uncharted area of the palace, which he does not need to visualize in detail: the simile has performed this role on a different register.

Iliad VII

Visual unit 1

4: (N1) ranks of Trojans in the plain / (S1) sailors at sea

63: (N2) ranks of armies in the plain / (S2) sea

Visual unit 2

208: (N3) battlefield / (S3) battlefield

Iliad VII contains three extended similes organized in two visual units. In the first unit, the storyteller uses the image of the sea as a concrete location that will allow him to locate the action taking place in the ranks of the armies. Given that he has a rather vague idea about exactly where the ranks are, he resorts to the space of the simile, which is more easily pictureable than the narrative space. In the second visual unit, it is not only Ajax and Ares who are compared, but also, and significantly so, their proper actions, that is to say, their marching to war. Size, lying at the very center of this comparison, is another aspect of space,[2] which facilitates the mental coordination between narrative and simile by effectively straddling their notional border. Being familiarized with the

---

[1]   See Rubin 1995:61–62.
[2]   See Bal 1997:133–135.

image of the huge god of war moving fast on the battlefield, the audience can thus "view" Ajax doing the same thing in the plot.

Iliad VIII

Visual unit 1

306: (N1) head of Gorguthion / (S1) garden (head of a poppy)

Visual unit 2

338: (N2) behind / (S2) behind

Visual unit 3

555: (N3) watchfires of the Trojans between ships and streams of Xanthos / (S3) sky, around moon > high places, ravines

The three extended similes of *Iliad* VIII correspond to three separate visual units. In the first unit, the narrator helps the audience visualize Gorguthion's head falling to one side through the concrete and familiar image of the drooping of a poppy's head. In this case the storyteller follows a twofold process: he not only employs the imagery of the poppy's head, which is itself based on the exploitation of space, but also takes pains to locate the poppy "in space," within a garden. Encapsulating a smaller locus (head of a flower) into a larger locus (poppy) and then an even larger space (the garden) reinforces the clarity and mental visibility of the narrative context: now the mind's eye of the listener can discern, among the mass of warriors on the battlefield (first-level location), a single hero (second-level location), whose head droops to one side (third-level location). Space works here not only as a cue to visualization and recall, but also as an advance mention of a spatial factor that will be developed in the narrative. In fact, the storyteller refers to Gorguthion's head only *after* he has visualized the poppy's head.[3] In this light, it is fair to say that, in simile-based parlance, the vehicle (base domain) has spatially shaped the tenor (target domain).

In the second visual unit, space is organized on the basis of what I would call *relative positioning*. By this term I refer to the Iliadic storyteller's tendency to indicate space not in absolute terms, by designating a given place, but by a person's position or location with respect to another person. In this realm of spatial features belong such expressions as "on the left" (ἐπ' ἀριστερᾷ), "on the right" (ἐπὶ δεξιά), "in front of" (πρόσθεν), "behind" (ὀπίσσω), and "next to" (παρά). Hektor in the narrative and a dog in the corresponding simile are thus

---

3 On similes as *advance organizers*, see Mayer 1983; Minchin 2001:137.

visualized in terms of relative positioning, by being mentally located behind those they are chasing: the former the Achaeans, the latter a boar or a lion (VIII 338–342).

In the third unit, the storyteller visualizes the night sky and the moon and stars, with their light falling upon the high places of the hills, the out-jutting shoulders, and the deep ravines. These concrete and well-known images give both narrator and audience a clear view, just as in the simile, of the Trojan watchfires blazing in the area between the streams of Xanthos and the ships, in front of Ilion. The space of the simile effectively conveys the vagueness of the Trojan landscape. No member of the audience could have an accurate map of the Trojan plain in his mind, the more so since the Iliadic topography was rather hazy for the storyteller's listeners. The picture of the Trojan watchfires blazing between Xanthos and the city of Troy becomes clear as the space delineated by the vehicle of the simile shines strongly in their minds' eyes. Moreover, since cognitive psychologists have recognized light as an important aspect of recall, it becomes clear why the shining feature enhances memorability and facilitates performance in both simile and narrative.

Iliad IX

Visual unit 1

4: (N1) plain [Achaeans] / (S1) sea-water

14: / (N2) plain [Achaeans] / (S2) rock, spring-water

[323: speech]

[481: speech]

Iliad IX contains two extended similes presented in a single visual unit. To foreground the space where the Achaean army stands and holds an assembly, the storyteller uses two, almost consecutive,[4] similes in his effort to *fill a spatial gap* in the narrative.[5] Since the narrator has no clear image in his mind about the place where the assembly should be located, he resorts to the world of the similes, which readily supplies him with spatial coordinates that help him mentally anchor his narrative. It is important to observe that, as the second simile of the rock and spring-water indicates, the storyteller performs this task "on the fly":

---

[4] It must be observed that sometimes sequences of similes aim at drawing attention to a picture before the poet turns to the particulars of a new scene. This is the case with the Catalogue of Ships in *Iliad* II, which is preceded by a long sequence of successive similes (*Iliad* II 455–483) placed before the invocation to the Muses (484–493). On these similes, see Moulton 1977:27–33.

[5] On *filling lexical items* as a basic function of the Homeric similes, see Minchin 2001:138.

the spring-water in the second simile is, in all probability, a mental reflex of the powerful and more expanded image of the sea that dominates the first simile.

Iliad X

Visual unit 1

5: (N1) camp / (S1) sky, land, battlefield

Visual unit 2

183: (N2) place of the Achaean guard, Trojans in the distance / (S2) yard, mountains

Visual unit 3

351: (N3) area with corpses / (S3) harvest land

360: (N4) area with soldiers / (S4) spaces of the woods

485: (N5) area of Thracian soldiers / (S5) pasture land

The three visual units that organize the similes in *Iliad* X are of unequal length. The first is characterized by the multiple and shifting space of its vehicle. Sky, plowlands, and battlefield aim, within the pictorial vividness of the simile, at mapping the largest possible area, for the space of the narrative that the story-teller wants to locate must be expressed in terms of size and not of topographical accuracy. Thus the multiplicity and variability of the spaces contained in the vehicle leads to an effective visualization of a specific aspect of space, namely the size and extent of Agamemnon's emotional turmoil. The second visual unit operates on two spatial levels, as the vehicle of its single simile includes two locations: the yard where the dogs are protecting the sheep and the mountains where a wild beast is moving. Movement, one of the most effective aspects of space, mentally ties the two levels together, since both the dogs in the yard and the beast in the mountains are restless. This spatially twofold simile concretizes the vague space(s) where the Achaean sentries and the Trojan army are located. The double spatial pointers in the simile counterbalance the complete lack of any spatial marker in the narrative. From this point of view, the spatial register of the simile creates the necessary foreground for the developing action.[6] The third visual unit presents the audience with a solid mental image of the episodes of Dolon and the horses of Rhesos. To this end, three extended similes are employed, which focus on animal space, be it cropland, woods, or pasture land.

---

[6] On *foregrounding* as one of the basic functions of similes, see Minchin 2001:138–139.

The visual grouping of the first two similes (belonging to the Dolon episode) with the third one (the Rhesos scene) reflects the direct connection between their narrative contexts, since it is Dolon who informs Odysseus and Diomedes about the Thracian king's famous horses and chariot (X 436–438). Dolon's revelation of where on the plain the Thracians and their king Rhesos are stationed (434–435: Θρήϊκες οἵδ' ἀπάνευθε νεήλυδες, ἔσχατοι ἄλλων· ἐν δέ σφι Ῥῆσος βασιλεύς, παῖς Ἠιονῆος) is reflected in the spatial unity of their corresponding similes.

Iliad XII

Visual unit 1

    41: (N1) ditch and Achaean wall / (S1) hunting (mountains)

    132: (N2) Achaean wall / (S2) mountains

    146: (N3) Achaean wall / (S3) mountains

    156: (N4) Achaean wall > ground / (S4) sky > earth

    [167: Speech][7]

    278: (N5) Achaean wall > ground; ground > Achaean wall / (S5) sky > mountains, out-jutting shoulders, low lands, cultivated areas

    299: (N6) Achaean wall / (S6) mountains, sheep pens

Visual unit 2

    421: (N7) closer to the rampart / (S7) cornfield

    433: (N8) closer to rampart / (S8) scales

Visual unit 3

    451: (N9) Achaean wall breaks / (S9) sheepfold

The τειχομαχία looms large in *Iliad* XII. The first visual unit contains no fewer than six extended similes, whose aim is to create a strong image of height, which is of course suitable for visualizing the space of the fighting from a wall. The space of the mountains, which is evoked directly or indirectly in the vehicles of all six similes, allows both narrator and audience to imagine clearly the Achaean wall and the fighting taking place around it.[8] The second visual unit

---

[7]   This is one of the only four extended similes attested in character text in the *Iliad* that contain spatial references; see Appendix 2.

[8]   On the Achaean wall, the various problems linked to its presentation, and the great fighting in *Iliad* XII, see Clay 2007:234–250 passim. On related issues, with emphasis on mapping the battlefield, see W. Andrae (fig. 1) in Schuchhardt 1928; Cuillandre 1944; Mannsperger 2001. Clay observes that

contains two similes, which emphasize the measuring of a straight boundary line in a cornfield and of weighing wool on the scales. The oscillation of victory, now on the Achaean and then on the Trojan side as the armies fight fiercely around the rampart, acquires strong visual support, since it is tied to the spatial coordinates of the two similes that emphasize the idea of "even distance or space." Hektor's lifting a huge stone is visualized through the space delineated by a shepherd carrying a bundle of fleece. Height[9] is an aspect of space that allows the storyteller and the audience to see vividly what seems an almost superhuman effort, the lifting of a huge stone with great ease by a single man.

Iliad XIII

Visual unit 1

62: (N1) plain where Poseidon and the Ajaxes stand / (S1) rock > plain

[101: Speech][10]

Visual unit 2

137: (N2) plain > dense battalions of the Achaeans / (S2) rock (forest) > flat land

Visual unit 3

178: (N3) body of Imbrios falling down / (S3) crest of a mountain

198: (N4) high up (body of Imbrios) / (S4) high off the ground (in the dense underbrush)

Visual unit 4

242: (N5) out of shelter of Idomeneus / (S5) Olympos

298: (N6) out of shelter of Meriones / (S6) out of Thrace

Visual unit 5

333: (N7) by the sterns of the vessels / (S7) pathways

"critical to our understanding of the *Iliad*'s action is the realization that its orientation of right and left remains constant throughout and is always seen from the perspective of *a narrator situated in the center of the Greek camp facing the Trojan plain*" (2011:45; the emphasis is mine).

9   Height belongs to one of the three dimensions of human orientation that are reflected in the mental organization of space. These dimensions include *verticality* (above-below), *sagitallity* (front-back), and *laterality* (right-left). See Nöth 1996:604–605.

10 See Appendix 2.

Visual unit 6

389: (N8) (Asios) falls in front of his horses and chariot / (S8) tree

437: (N9) (Alkathoös) falling down / (S9) statue or tree

Visual unit 7

471: (N10) (Idomeneus) holding his ground alone against Aineias / (S10) mountain (deserted place)

492: (N11) companions leave crowded place and approach Aineias / (S11) leave pasture

571: (N12) Adamas trying to retreat into the crowd of his companions is killed by Meriones / (S12) mountains

Visual unit 8

588: (N13) hollow of Menelaos' corselet / (S13) threshing-floor

Visual unit 9

703: (N14) (Ajaxes) fighting together before the vessels / (S14) fallow land

Visual unit 10

795: (N15) Trojan ranks within the Achaean camp / (S15) sea

Like all the fighting books, *Iliad* XIII is replete with extended similes. The general picture that emerges from the visualization of the long-lasting fighting near the Achaean camp consists of many brief snapshots and a few prolonged views of some key figures in this particular phase of the plot. Visual unit 1 is about Poseidon, who flies away from the spot where the two Ajaxes stand. The simile of a hawk taking off from a high rocky crag (63 ἀπ' αἰγίλιπος πέτρης περιμήκεος ἀρθείς) makes the most of the spatial concreteness of the simile landscape, so that the audience can visualize the place where Poseidon and the two Ajaxes were standing until now. With the image of a stone rolling from a rock towards the flat land but being stopped in the forest (visual unit 2), the storyteller creates a solid image of Hektor trying to reach the Achaean ships and shelters but being stopped at the dense battalions. Visual unit 3 contains two similes that focus on the death of the Trojan Imbrios, and although the first one refers to his actual falling and the second to the lifting of his body by the two Ajaxes, they both use the space of "high ground," either the crest of a mountain or "high from the ground" (200 ὑψοῦ ὑπὲρ γαίης).[11] Another snapshot, this time of Idomeneus and Meriones, who fight as a pair, is pictured by means of two similes (visual unit 4) that extend the spatial aspect of "origin," that is, *where* somebody or something comes from. In order to visualize the two heroes emerging from their shelters, the storyteller refers first to a thunderbolt and then to two divinities (Ares and Terror) coming from Olympos and Thrace respectively. The concrete landscape of the similes intensifies the image of the two warriors as they enter battle. Visual unit 5 focuses on "picturing" the turmoil of battle: the simile of the clouds of dust uplifted by the winds *along the roads* creates a eusynoptic vision of the fighting, a compressed and memorable (εὐμνημόνευτον) image of the "fog of war."[12] Visual unit 6 aims at helping the audience envision Asios' and Alkathoös' fatal encounters with Idomeneus. In the absence of any landmark sign or definite spot where these killings take place, the narrator uses the "space" of a "towering" tree or stele (390 πίτυς βλωθρή; 437 στήλην ἢ δένδρεον ὑψιπέτηλον) to imprint the vision of height. The listeners are thus invited to visualize the two men killed by Idomeneus as seen "from above," and therefore experiencing their dramatic crash to the ground. Visual unit 7 is concerned with the battle of Idomeneus and his comrades against Aineias and a host of Trojans. Three similes make full use of the familiar images of mountains and pasture lands in order to locate the activity of the two fighting groups. When the storyteller's camera-eye turns in a different direction across the vast fighting area, leaving Idomeneus and Meriones out of its field, it "pictures" three separate moments in the fighting (a hollow on Menelaos' corselet, the Ajaxes struggling before the ships, and the masses of Trojans swarming the Achaean camp) by means of the spaces of three different similes (a threshing-floor, a fallow field, and the sea). If we follow the sequence of snapshots taken by the storyteller, it becomes obvious that *Iliad* XIII begins and ends with brief camera shots of different parts of the fighting area, whereas the central part of the book includes the activity of principal heroes on the battlefield.

Iliad XIV

Visual unit 1

16: (N1) two courses in Nestor's mind / (S1) open sea

Visual unit 2

148: (N2) Achaean camp / (S2) war cry in battle

---

[11] On *verticality*, see visual unit 3 in the same book, and Nöth 1996:604–605.
[12] See Purves 2010a:24–64.

Visual unit 3

> 394, 396, 398: (N3) in front of the sea and the Achaean vessels / (S3) dry land, hills, oaks

Visual unit 4

> 414: (N4) Hektor falling on the ground / (S4) oak tree falling

The four extended similes of *Iliad* XIV are organized in four visual units: although Nestor's pondering takes the form of a spatial metaphor, with two courses from which he has to choose, the storyteller uses the familiar image of the hesitant motion of the sea to create a clear mental picture and a solid location as a cue to recall (visual unit 1). Poseidon's war cry lets the storyteller use sound, an important aspect of space, to make his audience feel that, like Agamemnon, they are inside the Achaean camp (visual unit 2). For the vivid visualization of the savage struggle between Achaeans and Trojans in front of the Achaean vessels, the storyteller makes use of three different images within the same simile: dry land, hills, and oaks offer multiple image mappings of the same area that allow the listeners to see clearly the place where the fighting is taking place (visual unit 3). In the last visual unit (4), the view of Hektor falling to the ground after being hit by a rock thrown at him by Ajax is visually translated into the falling of an oak tree under the stroke of Zeus' thunderbolt. A global look at *Iliad* XIV verifies what we observed earlier: that the lack of a protagonist in the fighting scenes of any given book of the epic is reflected in the absence of simile-grouping under a single visual unit.[13]

Iliad XV

Visual unit 1

> 80: (N1) (Hera ascends to) Olympos / (S1) earth-journey

Visual unit 2

> 170: (N2) (Iris descends from) Ida > Ilion / (S2) cloud-journey (snow or hail falling)

Visual unit 3

> 263: (N3) (Hektor) entrance on plain / (S3) stall (river with other horses) > plain

---

[13] For the opposite effect, i.e. high simile-grouping under few visual units when the plot includes one or a few protagonists, see my analysis of *Iliad* XVI in chapter 5 above.

Visual unit 4

271: (N4) (Achaeans) retreat from plain / (S4) rock and woods

323: (N5) (Achaeans) retreat from plain / (S5) pasture

Visual unit 5

358: (N6) ditch / (S6) spear-cast (measure)

Visual unit 6

362: (N7) Achaean wall / (S7) pile of sand at the seashore

Visual unit 7

381: (N8) (Trojans mount) wall (and Achaeans fight by) the ships' sterns / (S8) waves on ship at sea

Visual unit 8

410: (N9) by the ships / (S9) carpenter's workshop (cutting of a ship's timber)

Visual unit 9

579: (N10) Antilokhos leaves the πρόμαχοι and moves forward / (S10) deer leaving its covert

586: (N11) Antilokhos retreats into the ranks of the Achaeans / (S11) pasture

Visual unit 10

605: (N12) mouth, eyes, and helmet of Hektor / (S12) mountains

Visual unit 11

618: (N13) place where the Achaeans stand / (S13) rock next to the sea

624: (N14) place where the Achaeans stand / (S14) sea

630: (N15) place where the Achaeans stand / (S15) marsh (watered place)

Visual unit 12

679: (N16) (Ajax) deck to deck / (S16) street

Visual unit 13

690: (N17) (Hektor) ships / (S17) river

Iliad XV contains seventeen extended similes, organized in thirteen visual units. Simile grouping is limited to units 4, 9 (two similes each), and 11 (three similes). In unit 1, the swift journey of Hera to Olympos is compared with the speed of thought in the mind of a traveler, who sees places with his mind's eye before actually going there. This is a very interesting example of the relationship between space and mental visualization, the more so as it is attested in an oral epic like the *Iliad*. Given that "Homeric epic refers to itself as a *path* (οἴμη),"[14] we can say that this simile has an almost metapoetic coloring, and that the traveler resembles the epic storyteller, who travels within the path of song and "thinks of things in the mind's awareness, 'I wish I were this place, or this,' and imagines many things" (81–82).[15] The descending movement of Iris from Ida to Ilion is visualized by means of the falling of snow or hail from the clouds onto the earth (visual unit 2). In visual unit 3, the storyteller uses the image of a horse leaving its stall near the river, where it is in the company of other horses, to view Hektor's entrance on the mentally vague plain. In visual unit 4, the Achaean retreat on the plain is mentally located by means of the space of wildlife (two similes). In visual unit 5, Apollo's bridging a pathway over the ditch is "measured" by the distance covered by a spear-cast, whereas in unit 6 the Achaean wall is viewed via the mental image of sand piled up by a boy at the seashore. As far as unit 5 is concerned, cognitive psychologists have proved that measuring distance or size through drawings is faster and more effective than by means of words.[16] Moreover, as the storyteller's constant reliance on the image of the spear-cast in "measuring similes" shows, the precision and clarity of a performance can be improved by repeatedly creating a mental image of an event or action.[17] In other words, repeatedly imagining the distance covered by a spear-cast is not only an effective way of viewing an action presented in the narrative, but also may have helped the narrator improve his performance by visualizing the course of his narrative in advance.[18] In visual unit 7, the massive Trojan attack on the wall is presented through the image of the waves covering ships at sea, while in unit 8, the balance between the two sides fighting in the narrative, that is, their inability to gain new space, is mentally mapped to the actions of a skilled carpenter who at the advice of Athena straightens the cutting of a ship's timber. When the storyteller turns his attention to visualizing a different snapshot altogether (the conflict between Antilokhos and Hektor over Melanippos), he makes use of the familiar space of nature (a deer having

---

[14] Rubin 1995:62.
[15] See "Metaleptic space" in chapter 6 above.
[16] Paivio 1975.
[17] See also Shepard 1978.
[18] See Neisser 1983.

left its covert and a pasture respectively) in order to facilitate the mental positioning of the two opponents on the battlefield (unit 9). In visual unit 10, the narrator employs the spatial aspect of "thickness" (by referring to the dense forests in the mountains) to create a clear mental image of the various parts of Hektor's head squeezed inside his helmet. Visual unit 11 is the largest in *Iliad* XV. The Achaeans are pictured standing "somewhere close to the ships and the sea" through three similes whose brief narratives take place in or close to watery places, the sea or a marsh. The fact that these similes are heard one after the other further reinforces the visual effect of their pictorial content.[19] The book ends with two new snapshots, of Ajax crossing from deck to deck and Hektor making his attack on the ships. Visual unit 12 employs the space of a street, while visual unit 13 uses that of a river. At this point the storyteller sees these two activities separately, that is, he visualizes Ajax in a different spot from Hektor, an effective prelude to the great clash that is going to follow.

Iliad XVII

Visual unit 1

4: (N1) area around Patroklos' body / (S1) pasture (mountains)

[20: Speech]

53: (N2) area around Patroklos' body / (S2) lonely place in nature

61: (N3) area around Patroklos' body / (S3) mountains

109: (N4) away from Patroklos' body / (S4) farmstead

133: (N5) area around Patroklos' body / (S5) woods

281: (N7) area around Patroklos' body / (S7) mountains

657: (N12) area around Patroklos' body / (S12) mid-fenced ground

725: (N14) area around Patroklos' body / (S14) woods

Visual unit 2

263: (N6) sound, area around Patroklos' body / (S6) mouth of a river next to the sea

Visual unit 3

389: (N8) a small space around Patroklos' body / (S8) circle

---

[19] On the function of successive similes, see Moulton 1977:27–33.

Visual unit 4

434: (N9) (Achilles') horses away from the battle / (S9) stele on a grave

Visual unit 5

520: (N10) back of Aretos / (S10) back of oxen

Visual unit 6

547: (N11) sky > ranks of the Achaeans / (S11) sky > earth

674: (N13) ranks of companions / (S13) sky, shaggy bush

Visual unit 7

737: (N15) war / (S15) city, houses on fire

Visual unit 8

742: (N16) from battle to the ships / (S16) from the mountains > steep stony trail

Visual unit 9

747: (N17) Ajaxes standing fast / (S17) dike on a plain

Visual unit 10

755: (N18) screaming of Danaans / (S18) screaming of birds

Iliad XVII contains the largest grouping of similes in a single visual unit (unit 1), one that views the space where the fierce fighting about Patroklos' body takes place.[20] This extremely powerful visual unit includes no fewer than eight extended similes, whose sequence is twice interrupted by the shift of the narrator's eye to different locations, only to return again to the same spot both in the narrative and in the special register of the similes. In this light, a series of five similes is interrupted by another visual unit (2: S6) focusing on the sound of fighting, but is then visually "renewed" (S7), then interrupted again by three separate visual units (3: S8; 4: S9; 5: S10) and a fourth (6: S11) that is internally interrupted by a "visual return" to visual unit 1 (657: S12), then interrupted again by the second part of visual unit 6 (674: S13), until it is completed (725: S14). This

---

[20] On the use of Patroklos' body as a focal point around which the fighting takes place, in sharp contrast with the multiple military fronts in *Iliad* XII–XIII, see Clay 2011:90–95. This spatial anchoring of the action is, of course, a vehicle for the necessary conceptual dramatization of the plot.

visual dovetailing[21] is the most complex and complicated type of imagery organization in the entire epic. Its effect is remarkable: by canceling and renewing the storyteller's interest in the fighting around the body of Patroklos, it increases suspense, creates expectations on the part of the audience, and keeps the end of the fighting for Patroklos' body postponed, reinforcing the dramatic tension. On the contrary, visualization is effected in single camera shots in the rest of this book, with four visual units containing four separate similes that mentally locate the activity of other warriors or groups of soldiers. From this perspective, *Iliad* XVII is a striking example of the close link between dramatic tension on the battlefield and the spatial organization of imagery.

Iliad XVIII

[110: Speech]

Visual unit 1

161: (N1) plain, around the body of Patroklos / (S1) pasture

Visual unit 2

207: (N2) Achilles' helmet / (S2) high in the air

Visual unit 3

219: (N3) Achilles' voice / (S3) high in the air

Visual unit 4

318: (N4) Achaean camp, around Patroklos' body / (S4) woods

Visual unit 5

600: (N5) palace of Hephaistos / (S5) potter's workshop

Iliad XVIII contains only five extended similes, organized in four visual units. This pictorial economy is effectively counterbalanced by the long ecphrasis on Achilles' shield that occupies (together with Thetis' journey) the second half of the book. It can also be explained by the fact that this is not a fighting book, but one of grief for the death of Patroklos. In visual unit 1, the space of a pasture, where herdsmen cannot chase a lion away from a carcass, helps the narrator imagine the spot where the two Ajaxes were standing, unable to scare Hektor. Visual unit 2 plays on height as a spatial cue: both the ascending movement

---

[21] I have coined the term *visual dovetailing* on the model of *metrical dovetailing*, for which see West 1982 (index).

of the smoke signal going up to the sky, as Athena's blazing fire shoots up from Achilles' helmet into the air, and the sound of the trumpet, like the clear, rising voice of Achilles, emphasize the same aspect of space.[22] In visual unit 3, the familiar space of the woods is used to visualize the place where Achilles is standing and speaking to the Myrmidons. Finally, visual unit 4 includes a simile that is placed within the ecphrasis on Achilles' shield. The light dancing of girls and boys in the wide spaces of Knossos is compared with the smoothly turning wheel in a potter's workshop.

Iliad XIX

Visual unit 1

357: (N1) helmets and shields by the ships / (S1) height

375: (N2) shield of Achilles by the ships / (S2) height (sheepfolds in mountains) seen from the sea

The two extended similes of *Iliad* XIX are organized in a single visual unit emphasizing height. The brightly shining helmets and shields of the warriors by the ships and the shield of Achilles are captured in the storyteller's imagination through activities that take place on high ground. This is because he intends to guide his listeners toward his own visualization of the way the helmets and armor are shining: what he wants them to imagine is the radiant, blazing light of armor rising high into the air.

Iliad XX

Visual unit 1

164: (N1) plain (Achilles against Aineias) / (S1) hunt

[252: Speech][23]

Visual unit 2

403: (N2) bellowing of bull / (S2) bellowing of Hippodamas

---

[22] Height belongs to the vertical dimension of space; see Nöth 1996:604–605. *Verticality* (above-below) is much more often used than *sagitallity* (front-back) or *laterality* (right-left) within the framework of a Homeric simile. The reason for this spatial imbalance may be that when dealing with imagery, storytellers show a preference for spatial *maps* (which employ vertical mental views) over spatial *tours* (which employ horizontal mnemonic strategies, such as sagitallity and laterality). On cognitive maps and narrative space, see Ryan 2003.

[23] See Appendix 2.

Visual unit 3

490: (N3) earth / (S3) deep wooded valleys on a dry mountainside

Visual unit 4

495: (N4) Achilles' chariot / (S4) threshing-floor

Iliad XX includes four extended similes, which are grouped in four separate and completely distinct visual units. In unit 1, the visual space of the hunt helps the narrator locate the encounter between Achilles and Aineias on the plain. Visual unit 2 employs sound, an important aspect of space, to create the illusion of proximity, of "being there," at the spot where Hippodamas is fatally wounded by Achilles. By aural reference to the heavy sound produced by the bellowing of a bull, the storyteller is able to reinforce the audience's participation. This social aspect of sound is crucial to oral performance, for sound exists "when it is going out of existence,"[24] that is, in the presence of a narrator and a group of listeners. Sound in oral performance is space *in absentia*. Achilles' sweeping movement on the battlefield is visualized by means of the mental image of fire sweeping through the deep ravines of a parched wooded mountainside. Here it is the number of valleys, situated within a wider framework (the mountain), that helps the storyteller picture the sweeping movement of Achilles on the plain. In visual unit 4, the area covered by the bodies and the dead men and shields lying on the ground is pictured in the narrator's mind as the space of a threshing-floor: the movement of the yoke that crushes the barley creates a concrete spatial background, whose analogy with Achilles' chariot trampling corpses and shields enhances visualization, and by extension emotional involvement, on the part of the audience.[25]

Iliad XXI

Visual unit 1

12: (N1) river / (S1) river

22: (N2) along the course of the river, bluffs / (S2) deepwater harbor

257: (N3) crest of the river / (S3) water rushing in a steep place

[282: Speech]

346: (N4) plain with corpses / (S4) watered garden becoming dry

---

[24] Ong 1982:32. On sound in oral traditions, see Lord 1960 [2000]; Havelock 1978; Ong 1982; Rubin 1995:65–89.
[25] On emotional involvement in epic similes, see Minchin 2001:137–139.

Visual unit 2

493: (N5) sky / (S5) rock hollow or cave

Visual unit 3

522: (N6) plain / (S6) burning city > sky

Visual unit 4

573: (N7) in front of the city / (S7) timbered cover

Although *Iliad* XXI includes seven extended similes organized in four visual units, only unit 1 is marked by a dense grouping of similes. Moreover, the space employed in the four similes of this first unit virtually duplicates the narrative space of their corresponding scenes. The visualization of the fighting in the river, which is the centerpiece of this Iliadic book, is mentally reinforced by being doubled, that is, by means of the same simile space that offers visual variants of river images.[26] Visual units 2, 3, and 4 are focused on different snapshots of the narrative, with no special interest. *Iliad* XXI is a good example of how simile-grouping reflects the storyteller's main narrative preoccupation: his need to create powerful visualizations of his events in terms of location and positioning results in multiple viewings of target areas through the rich spatial imagery of the similes.

Iliad XXII

Visual unit 1

22: (N1) plain / (S1) racehorse in plain

26: (N2) plain / (S2) sky

Visual unit 2

93: (N3) close to the jutting tower / (S3) hole in the mountains

139: (N4) plain, close to the jutting tower / (S4) mountains

---

[26] This *doubling* of space enhances memorability because the vehicle it refers to is not only readily pictureable, but a mirror image of the narrative space it is compared with. See Goatly 1997:164–165, who states that the economy of information carried by an item is reversely proportional to its predictability; in other words, the more conventional a comparison is, the more strongly it enhances the meaning of its corresponding narrative passage. In this light, *doubling* of space reinforces mnemonic recall and visual clarity. Goatly's findings concerning metaphor are also applicable to the simile, for—as the work of Ortony (1979b) has shown—similes and metaphors are more closely associated than was thought in the past.

Visual unit 3

162: (N5) plain / (S5) racehorses in plain

Visual unit 4

189: (N6) plain / (S6) covert in mountains

[262: Speech]

Visual unit 5

308: (N7) springs (Hektor attacks) / (S7) sky > plain

Visual unit 6

317: (N8) springs (Achilles attacks) / (S8) sky

Iliad XXII includes eight extended similes belonging to six visual units, two of which group together pairs of similes. The narrative space is the plain of Troy, where Achilles' pursuit of Hektor and the fatal encounter between these two heroes takes place. In visual unit 1, the narrator and audience view Achilles through images of a racehorse running on the plain and of the dog star, seen from the vantage point of men looking at it from the ground. In visual unit 2, while Achilles is chasing Hektor on the plain, close to the outthrust bastion of a tower, the storyteller sets his two similes on the mountains as a spatial cue that enhances clarity and precision. Referring to the space of nature, so familiar for fighting scenes, allows the storyteller to view the actual chase as a form of fighting, although the most elementary requirement for such a characterization, namely a common space, is not fulfilled. Visual units 3 and 4 testify to the basic tendency of the Iliadic account of war to be given in frame-by-frame visual shots, where one camera shot follows another. Visual unit 6 refers to Hektor's actual attack on Achilles. The storyteller constructs the penultimate phase of the duel through spatial *verticality*, since Hektor is presented as attacking from above, down onto the plain. Finally, in visual unit 6 the storyteller employs the spatial aspect of height by comparing the shining effect of Achilles' spearhead with the light of the star Hesperos in the sky.[27]

Iliad XXIII

Visual unit 1

222: (N1) Patroklos' funeral, Achaean camp / (S1) funeral

---

[27] For a detailed analysis of the similes in *Iliad* XXII, see Tsagalis 2008b:272–284.

Visual unit 2

431: (N3) horse-race / (S2) range of a discus (measure, athletic contest)

Visual unit 3

517: (N3) space between Menelaos and Antilokhos, horse-race / (S3) space between wheel and horse (measure, athletic contest)

Visual unit 4

598: (N4) Menelaos' heart / (S4) field

Visual unit 5

692: (N5) boxing place / (S5) beach-break by the sea

Visual unit 6

712: (N6) middle of a circle / (S6) roof of a high house

Visual unit 7

845: (N7) area of weight-throwing / (S7) entire field

Iliad XXIII contains six extended similes belonging to six visual units. Achilles, who does not participate in the funeral games, lacks extended similes, most of which belong to different visual snapshots centered around the various athletic contests in honor of Patroklos. What is worth noting here is that a significant number of these similes employ an aspect of space—namely measuring—that is rather rare, at least according to Iliadic practice. Within the athletic context of this book, it may be plausibly argued that the storyteller aims at helping both himself and his audience visualize the spatial features of distance and size by means of measuring. This does not mean that he does not also resort to more traditional simile spaces, as in visual unit 7, where the area of weight-throwing is viewed by reference to the image of a vast field.[28]

---

[28] On the importance of size in imagery as far as making judgments in other areas of perception is concerned, see Rubin 1995:41–46. Paivio's work (1975) has convincingly shown that the analog nature of imagery often involves size judgments. In this light, the space of a vast field employed in the last simile of *Iliad* XXIII allows both storyteller and audience to monitor very quickly the size of the area of weight-throwing referred to in the narrative.

Iliad XXIV

[41: Speech]

Visual unit 1

80: (N1) sea / (S1) sea floor

Visual unit 2

317: (N2) eagle's wings / (S2) door of a chamber (measure)

Visual unit 3

480: (N3) Achilles' hut / (S3) foreign land

Iliad XXIV contains three extended similes organized in three visual units. Iris' visit to Thetis' abode in the depths of the sea is visualized by the descending movement of "a lead weight which, mounted / along the horn of an ox who ranges the fields, goes downward / and takes death with it to the raw-ravening fish" (80–82). The spatial aspect that the storyteller uses as a mental "guide" in his aim to create a vivid image of Iris' movement is the descending course of the lead weight.[29] The next visual unit pictures the size of the wings of Zeus' eagle. While it is true that the image of an eagle occupying a huge space with its outspread wings should be known to the audience and that there was no real need for a simile, the crucial detail is that this eagle is Zeus' own. In fact, the storyteller, in trying to imagine the vast size of this divine eagle, devotes almost two lines to the bird's description: "he sent down the most lordly of birds, an eagle, / the dark one, the marauder, called as well the black eagle."[30] The familiar image of the size of a huge door in a man's house gives "the measure," that is to say, an aspect of space, for a clear mental image of the size of Zeus' divine eagle. The last unit offers a vivid visualization of the amazement Achilles and his comrades feel when Priam enters his hut. The simile of a murderer leaving his own land and coming to the land of others seems inaccurate—to say the least—for Priam, but the feeling of amazement is what really matters here. Part of this amazement is the new space Priam has entered, the forbidden space occupied by the murderer of his son. The reversal of roles expressed in the vehicle of the simile must be interpreted within the context of the point made above about the function of space: Priam, who has left his own world, has moved into "a new country," that of the hut of Achilles, whose comrades look at him in sheer

---

[29] Cf. *Iliad* XI 237 on Iphidamas' spear; see Leaf 1902:484 on *Iliad* XI 237–238; Moulton 1977:97.

[30] *Iliad* XXIV 315–316 αὐτίκα δ' αἰετὸν ἧκε, τελειότατον πετεηνῶν, / μόρφνον θηρητῆρ', ὃν καὶ πέρκνον καλέουσιν.

wonder, as the audience looks in amazement on the old Trojan king, carrying with him the spatial framework of the simile's vehicle.

Appendix 2
Space in Similes Attested in Character Text

IN PART 3, I studied the function of space in Iliadic similes attested in narrator text. I have excluded from the main body of this book all similes found in character text, after carefully considering a number of factors, which I will now present and elucidate. Since my topic is space, I will then briefly focus on the only four Iliadic similes attested in character text that use spatial markers.[1]

In the study of similes, definitions and statistics have at times played an important role. Depending on how we define comparisons and similes and what subdivisions we are willing to accept, numbers can differ significantly. That said, I would like to begin by reconsidering some of them, the more so since they have significant implications for the way we treat similes, and may easily create false impressions. In my view, the fullest and most updated account is that given by Larsen (2007:5–63), who argues that comparisons and similes are two different concepts (with respect to external form, content, and sensuousness)[2] and as such they should be kept distinct and treated separately. Her statistics are much more comprehensive than those offered by D. J. N. Lee[3] and Scott,[4] but she fails to include 7 more cases (3 of δέμας + genitive)[5] and 4 similes (2 short and 2 long).[6] Thus, the total number of comparisons and similes in the *Iliad* is 427, of which only 81 (19%) are found in character text. This number decreases considerably, though, when we examine only the similes: of the 288 Iliadic similes, only 48 (59.3%) are attested in the speeches. This last number can decrease even further if we consider only the Homeric similes par excellence, that is, the long

---

[1]   XII 167–172; XIII 101–106; XVI 745–750; XX 251–255.
[2]   Ready (2011:14–16) uses dissimilarity between tenor and vehicle as the basic feature of similes, while he argues that what marks comparisons is similarity between the compared terms. I would replace the terms *dissimilarity* and *similarity* with *situational analogy* and *analogy of subjects or heads*. Though I agree with Muellner (1990) and Minchin (2001:144) that the distinction between long and short similes is misleading from a compositional point of view, since long similes are in fact compressed narrative snapshots marked by ellipsis, it is important from a cognitive perspective. See below on the ancient scholiasts' use of the term παραβολή.
[3]   1964; see also de Jong 1987a:135.
[4]   1974:190–200.
[5]   XIII 673; XVII 366; XVIII 1.
[6]   V 487; XVI 745–750; XVI 752–754; XXII 126–128.

or extended ones. In a recent study, Ready draws a line between similes and comparisons, and discusses all the variations along a spectrum ranging from less to greater similarity.[7] This distinction is a valid one, but I think that there is one more element that needs to be brought into the wider picture: very much unlike the comparison, the simile "is speech that refers to a similar thing and represents the subject as performing some activity."[8] In contrast to the static nature of the comparison that is expressed in the default mode "A is like B," the simile is a dynamic phenomenon that can expand so as to become a complex illustrative analogy between two situations, expressed in the form of an unfinished narrative snapshot. In this light, we may even distinguish between short and long similes,[9] the latter being what we usually call "the Homeric simile." According to this classification, of the 48 similes attested in speeches in the *Iliad*, only 20 are long. In other words, among the 200 long ("Homeric") similes found in the *Iliad*, only 20 (10%) belong to character text. Table 9 presents statistical data concerning the distribution of similes in character and narrator text in the *Iliad* on the basis of Larsen's distinction between short and long comparisons and short and long similes. In parenthesis I also offer the relevant percentages:[10]

Table 9: Similes in the *Iliad*—character vs. narrator text

	SC	LC	SS	LS	Total
CT	31 (94%)	2 (6%)	28 (57.1%)	20 (41.7%)	
Subtotal	33 (40.8%)		48 (59.3%)		81 (19%)
NT	91 (85.8%)	15 (14.2%)	60 (25%)	180 (75%)	
Subtotal	106 (30.6%)		240 (69.4%)		346 (81%)
Total	139 (32.6%)		288 (67.5%)		427

---

[7]   2011:11–26.

[8]   παραβολή ἐστι λόγος διὰ παραθέσεως ὁμοίου πράγματος τὸ ὑποκείμενον μετ' ἐνεργείας παριστάνων (Trypho *On Tropes* [ed. L. Spengel] 3.20.17–18).

[9]   The scholia make a distinction between short and long similes, but only the latter is given a name (παραβολή); see Snipes 1988:205–208. What is important is that the scholia do not use the term παραβολή for a short simile or any form of comparison. Nünlist (2009:284) notes that of 81 attestations of the word in the scholia, 77 times it refers to the long simile. Short and long similes are explicitly distinguished in both the treatise *On Style* (80 and 89), ascribed to Demetrius, and in [Herodian] *On Figures* 63–64 (Hajdú). While in the former the terminology employed is εἰκασία and παραβολή, in the latter it is ὁμοίωσις and παραβολή. In Pseudo-Herodian, the decisive factor for the distinction between short and long similes is ἀνταπόδοσις, "a phrase which follows the παραβολή and connects it with the action [sc. of the surrounding narrative]" (ἀνταπόδοσις δὲ φράσις ἐπαγομένη τῇ παραβολῇ καὶ συνάπτουσα τοῖς πραττομένοις αὐτήν). See Nünlist 2009:283.

[10] Explanation of abbreviations: CT = character text, NT = narrator text, SC = short comparisons, LC = long comparisons, SS = short similes, LS = long similes.

What these statistics show is that comparisons and similes should not be treated in the same way, since they constitute after all two distinct forms,[11] and that long similes used in speeches are only a small fraction (10%) of the entire number of long similes attested in the *Iliad*. I stress this last point because long similes lie at the very center of my research, since it is in them that spatial markers are employed in abundance. With respect to space, it is exactly at this critical fulcrum that the difference between character and narrator text is observed: only four long similes of the twenty found in the speeches contain any spatial references. These are the following:

"οἳ δ', ὥς τε σφῆκες μέσον αἰόλοι ἠὲ μέλισσαι
<u>οἰκία ποιήσωνται ὁδῷ ἔπι παιπαλοέσσῃ,</u>
<u>οὐδ' ἀπολείπουσιν κοῖλον δόμον</u>, ἀλλὰ μένοντες
ἄνδρας θηρητῆρας ἀμύνονται περὶ τέκνων,
ὣς οἵδ' οὐκ ἐθέλουσι πυλάων καὶ δύ' ἐόντε
χάσσασθαι, πρίν γ' ἠὲ κατακτάμεν ἠὲ ἁλῶναι."

"But they, as wasps quick-bending in the middle, or as bees
will make their homes at the side of the rocky way, and will not
abandon the hollow house they have made, but stand up to
men who come to destroy them, and fight for the sake of their
children,
so these, though they are only two, are unwilling to give back
from the gates, until they have killed their men, or are taken."

Iliad XII 167–172

"οἳ τὸ πάρος περ
φυζακινῆς ἐλάφοισιν ἐοίκεσαν, αἵ τε <u>καθ' ὕλην</u>
θώων παρδαλίων τε λύκων τ' ἤϊα πέλονται
αὔτως ἠλάσκουσαι ἀνάλκιδες, οὐδ' ἔπι χάρμη.
ὣς Τρῶες τὸ πρίν γε μένος καὶ χεῖρας Ἀχαιῶν
μίμνειν οὐκ ἐθέλεσκον ἐναντίον, οὐδ' ἠβαιόν·"

"they who in time past,
were like fugitive deer before us, who *in the forests*
are spoil for scavengers and wolves and leopards, who scatter
in absolute cowardice, there is no war spirit within them.

---

[11] According to Ready 2011:150–260, comparisons and similes of both types are associated with a system of cross-references that allows speakers to compete either among themselves or with the narrator.

So before now the Trojans were unwilling to stand up
against the strength and hands of the Achaians, even for a little"

Iliad XIII 101–106

"ὢ πόποι, ἦ μάλ' ἐλαφρὸς ἀνήρ· ὡς ῥεῖα κυβιστᾳ.
εἰ δή <u>που καὶ πόντῳ ἐν ἰχθυόεντι</u> γένοιτο,
πολλοὺς ἂν κορέσειεν ἀνὴρ ὅδε τήθεα διφῶν,
νηὸς ἀποθρῴσκων, εἰ καὶ δυσπέμφελος εἴη·
ὡς νῦν ἐν πεδίῳ ἐξ ἵππων ῥεῖα κυβιστᾳ.
ἦ ῥα καὶ ἐν Τρώεσσι κυβιστητῆρες ἔασιν."

"See now, what a light man this is, how agile an acrobat.
If only he were *somewhere on the sea, where the fish swarm*,
he could fill the hunger of many men, by diving for oysters;
he could go overboard from a boat even in rough weather
the way he somersaults so light to the ground from his chariot
now. So, to be sure, in Troy also they have their acrobats."

Iliad XVI 745–750

"ἀλλὰ τίη ἔριδας καὶ νείκεα νῶϊν ἀνάγκη
νεικεῖν ἀλλήλοισιν ἐναντίον, ὥς τε γυναῖκας,
αἵ τε χολωσάμεναι ἔριδος πέρι θυμοβόροιο
νεικέουσ' ἀλλήλῃσι <u>μέσην ἐς ἄγυιαν</u> ἰοῦσαι
πόλλ' ἐτεά τε καὶ οὐκί, χόλος δέ τε καὶ τὰ κελεύει;"

"But what have you and I to do with the need for squabbling
and hurling insults at each other, as if we were two wives
who when they have fallen upon a heart-perishing quarrel
go out in the street and say abusive things to each other,
much true, and much that is not, and it is their rage that drives
    them."

Iliad XX 251–255

Of these four long similes, the one expressed by Poseidon in XIII 101–106
is a special case, since it constitutes an "analeptic" simile. Poseidon pictures in
his mind's eye and renders by means of a vivid image of a deer what the Trojans
were doing in the past, when the Achaeans had the upper hand in the fighting.
The spatial coordinates of this simile simply reproduce standard themes associated with deer similes. The nuclear image of bewildered frightened deer

drinking water from a spring in the forest "feeds" two short comparisons (XXI 29, XXII 1) and one short simile (IV 243–246).[12]

With respect to the other three long similes mentioned above, my point accords with the basic thesis of Ready, who in his recent study of (mainly) Iliadic similes has argued that similes in character text are mechanisms and sites of competition either between characters or between characters and narrator.[13] The same observation applies to those long similes found in speeches that use spatial coordinates, that is, that locate in a given space the action described in the brief narrative snapshot of the base domain or vehicle. When long similes attested in character text are spatialized, they reproduce (like other features) the spatial location of the last-mentioned simile in the narrator or character text.

The designation of the wasps or bees as protecting their hollow houses at the side of the rocky way (XII 168 οἰκία ποιήσωνται ὁδῷ ἔπι παιπαλοέσσῃ) reproduces on a different pictorial register the picture used just before the beginning of the last-mentioned long simile in the narrator text: in XII 155–156 the narrator refers to the Achaeans' fighting "in defense of themselves, and the shelters, / and the fast-running vessels" (... ἀμυνόμενοι σφῶν τ' αὐτῶν καὶ κλισιάων / νηῶν τ' ὠκυπόρων). Whereas Asios' simile in XII 167–172 appropriates the language of tenacity employed in a series of previous similes attested in the main narrative, it reproduces only the space of the last long simile, the one that the storyteller uses as a cue to effect an intricate interplay between narrative and speech.[14]

The diver simile used by Patroklos in *Iliad* XVI 745–750 is built on two interwoven pieces of imagery: the vertical movement of a diver and that of an acrobat or tumbler. As Ready has shown,[15] the first image capitalizes on beliefs concerning short-term transactions in which the diver engages, while the second relies on "connections between the dance of war and choral dancing and on the opposition between fighting and choral dancing."[16] The result is a remarkable simile, which surpasses the earlier short simile that presented

---

[12] On deer similes in Homer, see Scott 1974:71–72; on the traditional referentiality of this simile family, see Tsagalis 2008b:188–205.

[13] Ready 2011:2.

[14] See Ready 2011:190–192, who argues that Asios' simile comparing the two Lapithai to wasps or bees holding their ground appropriates the language of tenacity used in the previous similes in order to create an ironic innuendo of Zeus' trickery; for the notion of stalemate between the two armies in this simile, see Scott 2009:97.

[15] 2011:160–165.

[16] Ready 2011:165.

Kebriones vaulting "to earth like a diver / from the carefully wrought chariot" (XVI 742–743). Without the elaborated expansion of Patroklos' simile, the short simile employed by the narrator would have lost some of its expressive force. The highly elliptical nature of the image of a diver is presented in such a compressed way that the listener has to supply all the relevant information on his own. But at the very juncture between main narrative and the ensuing speech, the Iliadic storyteller indicates that he will bestow on Patroklos knowledge that only his listeners could possibly have. By apostrophizing him just before the beginning of his speech, the storyteller implicitly indicates that Patroklos—just for a moment—has been given the privileges of the external narratees, that is, the members of the external audience, who have heard the short diver-simile just employed by the main narrator. In a remarkable display of poetic technique, Patroklos listens and responds to the narrator's offer by creating a beautiful long simile that expands and enriches the storyteller's abbreviated imagery. Likewise with space: Patroklos builds on and expands the space of the sea (XVI 746 πόντῳ ἐν ἰχθυόεντι) that is unexpressed (but inherent in the imagery of the diver).[17]

In *Iliad* XX 251–255, Aineias uses a long simile referring to women who "go out in the street and say abusive things to each other" (254 νεικέουσ' ἀλλήλῃσι μέσην ἐς ἄγυιαν ἰοῦσαι). Scholars have noticed that the simile builds on the female space of the city (inherent in the mention of ἄγυια),[18] but have failed to observe that the space of "*the middle* of the street" (254 μέσην ἐς ἄγυιαν) reproduces the narrative space attached to the last short simile used by Aineias, who complains to Achilles for the third time (as he has already done in XX 200 and 211):

> "ἀλλ' ἄγε, μηκέτι ταῦτα λεγώμεθα νηπύτιοι ὥς
> ἑσταότ' ἐν μέσσῃ ὑσμίνῃ δηϊοτῆτος·"

> "But come, let us no longer stand here talking of these things
> like children, here *in the space between* the advancing armies."

> *Iliad* XX 244–245

The "space between the advancing armies" (ἐν μέσσῃ ὑσμίνῃ) has been deeply rooted in the mind of the storyteller, since it is there that he has mentally placed the two heroes for the presentation of this episode. As early as XX 158–160, he has visualized Aineias and Achilles moving and taking a position

---

[17] There have been various attempts to exploit the full interpretive potential of Patroklos' simile: Rabel 1993; Di Benedetto 1998:9–10; Buxton 2004:151; Scott 2009:170; Ready 2011:160–165.

[18] For the female space of the city, see Arthur 1981:27; Scully 1990:33–34, 64–68; Ready 2011:50.

between the two armies (δύο δ' ἀνέρες ἔξοχ' ἄριστοι / ἐς μέσον ἀμφοτέρων συνίτην μεμαῶτε μάχεσθαι, / Αἰνείας τ' Ἀγχισιάδης καὶ δῖος Ἀχιλλεύς). This "initial" space is subsequently employed by Aineias himself at the very juncture between a short simile νηπύτιοι ὥς 'like children' and the main narrative (XX 244–245). This last time the simile, which has been repeatedly used in the same speech, has gained so much pictorial force that it allows the speaker, Aineias, to make a bold leap to the preceding narrative and create a vivid image that interweaves narrator and character text.

In the extremely few cases where the fully fledged Homeric similes are used in character text, visual spatialization abides by a system of remarkable economy that facilitates recall and effectively promotes vividness. By locating the action in the same spatial framework used by the previous simile, the Iliadic characters employ this special register of pictorial representation as a site for communication and rivalry. The paratopic nature of the similes shows that even when they are used in the speeches, they "build up a picture of a world outside, a world alongside" and that their "parallel world ... is not entropic: its rhythms are there to stay."[19]

---

[19] Buxton 2004:152.

Bibliography

Aceti, C., D. Leuzzi, and L. Pagani. 2008. *Eroi nell'Iliade: Personaggi e strutture narrative.* Rome.

Addison, C. 1993. "From Literal to Figurative: An Introduction to the Study of the Simile." *College English* 55:402–419.

———. 2001. "'So Stretched Out Huge in Length': Reading the Extended Simile." *Style* 35:498–516.

Adkins, A. W. H. 1960. *Merit and Responsibility: A Study in Greek Values.* Oxford.

Aisenman, R. A. 1999. "Structure-Mapping and the Simile-Metaphor Preference." *Metaphor and Symbol* 13.1:45–51.

Alden, M. 2000. *Homer Beside Himself: Para-Narratives in the* Iliad. Oxford.

———. 2011. "Ekphrasis." In Finkelberg 2011:1.242–243.

Allen, T. W., ed. 1912. *Homeri Opera.* Vol. 5. Oxford.

———. 1921. *The Homeric Catalogue of Ships.* Oxford.

Aloni, A. 1986. *Tradizioni arcaiche della Troade e composizione dell'Iliade.* Milan.

Ameis, K. F., and C. Hentze. 1906. *Homers* Ilias. Vol. 4. 4th ed. Leipzig.

———. 1908. *Homers* Ilias. Vol. 6. 4th ed. Leipzig.

Andersen, F. G. 1985. *Commonplace and Creativity: The Role of Formulaic Diction in Anglo-Scottish Traditional Balladry.* Odense.

Andersen, Ø. 1976. "Some Thoughts on the Shield of Achilles." *Symbolae Osloenses* 51:5–18.

———. 1978. *Die Diomedesgestalt in der* Ilias. Oslo.

Andersen, Ø., and M. Dickie., eds. 1995. *Homer's World: Fiction, Tradition, Reality.* Bergen.

Anderson, B. 1991 [1983]. *Imagined Communities: Reflections on the Origin and Spread of Nationalism.* London.

Andersson, T. M. 1976. *Early Epic Scenery: Homer, Virgil, and the Medieval Legacy.* Ithaca, NY.

Arend, W. A. 1933. *Die typischen Scenen bei Homer.* Berlin.

Argyle, M. 1988. *Bodily Communication.* 2nd ed. London.

Armstrong, C. B. 1969. "The Casualty Lists in the Trojan War." *Greece and Rome* 16:30–31.

Armstrong, J. I. 1958. "The Arming Motif in the *Iliad*." *American Journal of Philology* 79:337–354.

Arpaia, M. 2010. "Bibliografia sullo scudo di Achille (1945–2008)." In *Lo scudo di Achille nell'Iliade: Esperienze ermeneutiche a confronto*, ed. M. d'Acunto and R. Palmisciano, 233–245. Pisa.

Arthur, M. B. 1981. "The Divided World of *Iliad* VI." In *Reflections of Women in Antiquity*, ed. H. Foley, 19–44. New York.

Austin, N. 1975. *Archery at the Dark Side of the Moon*. Berkeley.

———. 1994. *Helen of Troy and her Shameless Fantom*. Ithaca, NY.

Bachelard, G. 1957. *La poétique de l'espace*. Paris.

Bacher, L. 1978. *The Mobile Mise-en-scène: A Critical Analysis of the Theory and Practice of Long-Take Camera Movement in the Narrative Film*. New York.

Baddeley, A. 1990. *Human Memory: Theory and Practice*. London.

Bakhtin, M. M. 1978. *Esthétique et théorie du roman*. Trans. D. Olivier. Paris.

———. 1981. *The Dialogic Imagination: Four Essays*. Ed. M. Holquist. Trans. C. Emerson and M. Holquist. Austin.

———. 1984. *Rabelais and His World*. Trans. H. Iswolsky. Bloomington.

Bahrick, H. P. 1974. "The Anatomy of Free Recall." *Memory and Cognition* 2:484–490.

Bakker, E. J. 1993. "Discourse and Performance: Involvement, Visualization, and 'Presence' in Homeric Poetry." *Classical Antiquity* 12:1–29.

———. 1997. *Poetry in Speech: Orality and Homeric Discourse*. Ithaca, NY.

———. 2001. "Homer, Hypertext, and the World of Myth." In *Varieties and Consequences of Orality and Literacy/Formen und Folgen von Mündlichkeit und Schriftlichkeit: Franz Bäuml zum 75. Geburtstag*, ed. U. Schaefer and H. Spielmann, 149–160. Tübingen.

———. 2005. *Pointing to the Past: From Formula to Performance in Homeric Poetics*. Hellenic Studies 12. Washington, DC.

Bakker, E., and A. Kahane., eds., 1997. *Written Voices, Spoken Signs: Tradition, Performance, and the Epic Text*. Cambridge, MA.

Bal, M. 1997. *Narratology: Introduction to the Theory of Narrative*. 2nd ed. Toronto.

Baltes, M. 1983. "Zur Eigenart und Funktion von Gleichnissen im 16. Buch der Ilias." *Antike und Abendland* 29:36–48.

Bannert, H. 1988. *Formen des Wiederholens bei Homer*. Vienna.

Barker, E., and J. Christensen. 2008. "Oedipus of Many Pains: Strategies of Contest in the Homeric Poems." *Leeds International Classics Studies* 7:1–30. http://www.leeds.ac.uk/classics/lics/.

Barney, S. 1982. "Chaucer's Lists." In *The Wisdom of Poetry*, ed. D. Benson and S. Wenzel, 189–223. Kalamazoo.

Barthes, R., ed. 1964. *Essais critiques*. Paris.

———. 1989. *The Rustle of Language*. Trans. R. Howard. Berkeley.

Bartsch, S. 2007. "'Wait a Moment, Phantasia': Ekphrastic Interference in Seneca and Epictetus." *Classical Philology* 102:83–95.

Bartsch, S., and J. Elsner., eds. 2007. "Special Issue on Ekphrasis." *Classical Philology* 102:1–135.

Bassett, S. E. 1920. "Hector's Charioteer." *Classical Philology* 15:296–297.

———. 1938. *The Poetry of Homer*. Berkeley.

Becker, A. S. 1990. "The Shield of Achilles and the Poetics of Homeric Description." *American Journal of Philology* 111:139–153.

———. 1995. *The Shield of Achilles and the Poetics of Ekphrasis*. Lanham.

Bellezza, F. S. 1983. "The Spatial-Arrangement Mnemonic." *Journal of Educational Psychology* 75:830–837.

Belloni, L. 1978. "In margine alla regalità di Agamemnone." *Aevum* 52:45–57.

Ben-Porat, Z. 1992. "Poetics of the Homeric Simile and the Theory of (Poetic) Simile." *Poetics Today* 13:737–769.

Berardi, F. 2010. "La descrizione dello spazio: Procedimenti espressivi e tecniche di composizione secondo i retori greci." In *Topos-chôra: L'espai a Grecia I: Perspectives interdisciplinàries: Homenatge a Jean-Pierre Vernant i Pierre Vidal-Naquet*, ed. J. Carruesco, 37–48. Tarragona.

Bergold, N. 1977. *Der Zweikampf des Paris und Menelaos*. Bonn.

Bergren, A. 2008. *Weaving Truth: Essays on Language and the Female in Greek Thought*. Hellenic Studies 19. Washington, DC.

Bethe, E. 1907. "Eumelos." *Real Encyclopädie* 6.1:1080–1081.

———. 1929. *Homer: Dichtung und Sage*. Vol. 2. 2nd ed. Leipzig.

Beye, C. R. 1964. "Homeric Battle Narrative and Catalogues." *Harvard Studies in Classical Philology* 68:345–373.

Bierl, A., A. Schmitt, and A. Willi, eds. 2004. *Antike Literatur in neuer Deutung: Festschrift für Joachim Latacz anlässlich seines 70. Geburtstages*. Munich.

Blanck, H. 1996. *Einführung in das Privatleben der Griechen und Römer*. Darmstadt.

Blum, H. 1969. *Die antike Mnemotechnik*. Hildesheim.

Boardman, J. 2002. *The Archaeology of Nostalgia: How the Greeks Re-Created their Mythical Past*. London.

Bölte, F. 1934. "Ein Pylisches Epos." *Rheinisches Museum* 83:319–347.

———. 1937. "Oichalia in Messenien." *Real Encyclopädie* 17.2:2097–2099.

Bolter, J. D. 1991. *Writing Space: The Computer, Hypertext, and the History of Writing*. Hillsdale.

Bonifazi, A. 2008. "Memory and Visualization in Homeric Discourse Markers." In Mackay 2008:35–64.

Bonnafé, A. 1984. *Poésie, nature et sacré*. Lyon.

Borchardt, J. 1972. *Homerische Helme: Helmformen der Ägäis in ihren Beziehungen zu orientalischen und europäischen Helmen in der Bronze- und frühen Eisenzeit.* Mainz.

———. 1977. "Helme." In *Kriegswesen,* vol. 1 of *Archaeologia Homerica,* ed. H.-G. Bucholz and J. Wiesner, E:57–74. Göttingen.

Bordwell, D. 1977. "Camera Movement and Cinematic Space." *Cine-Tracts* 1–2:19–25.

Bothmer, D. von. 1981. "The Death of Sarpedon." In *The Greek Vase,* ed. S. Hyatt, 63–80. Latham.

Bourdieu, P. 1991. *Language and Symbolic Power.* Trans. G. Raymond and M. Adamson. Cambridge, MA.

Bouvier, D. 2002. *Le sceptre et la lyre: L'Iliade ou les héros de la mémoire.* Grenoble.

Bowra, C. M. 1938. "The Daughters of Asopus." *Hermes* 73:213–221.

———. 1952. *Heroic Poetry.* London.

———. 1963. "Two Lines of Eumelus." *Classical Quarterly* 12:145–153.

Brady, M. P. 2002. *Extinct Lands, Temporal Geographies: Chicana Literature and the Urgency of Space.* Durham, NC.

Bridgeman, T. 2007. "Time and Space." In Herman 2007:52–65.

Bruford, A., and N. Todd. 1996. "The Eye Behind the Mouth: The Contribution of Visual Memory to Oral Storytelling." In *Orality, Literacy, and Modern Media,* ed. D. Scheunemann, 7–14. Columbia.

Brügger, C., M. Stoevesand, and E. Visser. 2003. *Homers Ilias: Gesamtkommentar.* Vol. 2.2. Munich.

Bryce, T. 1986. *The Lycians in Literary and Epigraphical Sources.* Copenhagen.

———. 1990–1991. "Lycian Apollo and the Authorship of the *Rhesus.*" *Classical Journal* 86:144–149.

———. 2006. *The Trojans and their Neighbours.* London.

Buchholz, E. 1871. *Die homerischen Realien.* Vol. 1, *Welt und Natur.* Berlin.

Buchholz, S., and M. Jahn. 2005. "Space in Narrative." In Herman, Jahn, and Ryan 2005:551–555.

Buggie, S. E. 1974. *Imagery and Relational Variety in Associative Learning.* PhD dissertation, University of Oregon.

Burch, N. 1979. *To the Distant Observer: Form and Meaning in the Japanese Cinema.* Berkeley.

Burgess, J. S. 2001. *The Tradition of the Trojan War in Homer and the Epic Cycle.* Baltimore.

———. 2002. "Kyprias, the *Kypria,* and Multiformity." *Phoenix* 56:234–245.

———. 2006. "Neoanalysis, Orality, and Intertextuality: An Examination of Homeric Motif Transference." *Oral Tradition* 21:148–189.

———. 2009. *The Death and Afterlife of Achilles.* Baltimore.

Burkert, W. 1981. "Seven Against Thebes: An Oral Tradition Between Babylonian Magic and Greek Literature." In *I poemi rapsodici non omerici e la tradizione orale*, ed. C. Brillante, M. Cantilena, and C. O. Pavese, 29–48. Padua.

———. 1985. *Greek Religion*. Trans. J. Raffan. Cambridge, MA.

———. 1998. "La cité d'Argos entre la tradition mycénienne, dorienne et homérique." Kernos Supplement 8:47–59 (= *Kleine Schriften.* Vol. 1, *Homerica*, 166–177. Göttingen, 2001).

Buxton, R. 2004. "Similes and Other Likenesses." In Fowler 2004:139–155.

Byre, C. S. 1992. "Narration, Description, and Theme in the Shield of Achilles." *Classical Journal* 88:33–42.

———. 1994a. "The Rhetoric of Description in *Odyssey* 9.116–141: Odysseus and Goat Island." *Classical Journal* 89:357–367.

———. 1994b. "On the Description of the Harbor of Phorkys and the Cave of the Nymphs, *Odyssey* 13.96–112." *American Journal of Philology* 115:1–13.

Calame, C. 2006. *Pratiques poétiques de la mémoire: Représentations de l'espace-temps en Grèce ancienne*. Paris.

Calder, W. M. 1978. "Gold for Bronze: *Iliad* 6.232–36." In *Studies Presented to Sterling Dow on his Eightieth Birthday*, ed. K. Rigsby, 31–35. Durham, NC.

Callaway, C. 1993. "Perjury and the Unsworn Oath." *Transactions of the American Philological Association* 123:15–26.

Capovilla, G. 1957. "Colchica-Adriatica parerga: Da Eumelo di Corinto ad Apollonio Rodio." *Rendiconti Istituto Lombardo* 91:739–802.

Carlier, P. 1984. *La royauté en Grèce avant Alexandre*. Strasbourg.

Carlisle, M., and O. Levaniouk., eds. 1999. *Nine Essays on Homer*. Lanham.

Carpenter, R. 1946. *Folk Tale, Fiction, and Saga in the Homeric Epics*. Berkeley.

Cauer, P. 1895. *Grundfrage der Homerkritik*. Leipzig.

Chadwick, H. M. 1900. "The Oak and the Thunder-God." *Journal of the Anthropological Institute of Great Britain and Ireland* 30:22–44.

Chantraine, P. 2009. *Dictionnaire étymologique de la langue grecque: Histoire des mots*. Ed. J. Taillardat, O. Masson, and J.-L. Perpillou. Includes supplement "Chroniques d'étymologie grecque," ed. A. Blanc, C. de Lamberterie, and J.-L. Perpillou, 1–10. Paris. Abbreviated DELG.

Chapman, J. 1997. "Places as Timemarks: The Social Construction of Prehistoric Landscapes in Eastern Hungary." In *Semiotics of Landscape: Archaeology of Mind*, ed. G. Nash, 31–45. Oxford.

Chaston, C. 2010. *Tragic Props and Cognitive Function: Aspects of the Function of Images in Thinking*. Leiden.

Chatman, S. 1978. *Story and Discourse: Narrative Structure in Fiction and Film*. Ithaca, NY.

———. 1990. *Coming to Terms: Verbal and Cinematic Narrative*. Ithaca, NY.

Christians, H. 2010. "Landschaftlicher Raum: Natur und Heterotopie." In Günzel 2010:250–265.

Christodoulou, G. 1977. Τὰ ἀρχαῖα σχόλια εἰς Αἴαντα τοῦ Σοφοκλέους: Κριτικὴ ἔκδοσις. Athens.

Ciani, M. G. 1963–1964. "Le morti minori nell'*Iliade*." *Atti/Istituto Veneto di Scienze* 122:403–415.

Cingano, E. 2004. "Tradizioni epiche intorno ad Argo." In *La città di ARGO: Mito, storia, tradizioni poetiche*, ed. P. Bernardini, 59–78. Rome.

Clader, L. L. 1976. *The Evolution from Divine to Heroic in Greek Epic Tradition*. Leiden.

Clark, M. E., and W. D. E Coulson. 1978. "Memnon and Sarpedon." *Museum Helveticum* 35:65–73.

Clay, J. S. 1972. "The Planktai and Moly: Divine Naming and Knowing in Homer." *Hermes* 100:127–131.

———. 1997. *The Wrath of Athena: Gods and Men in the* Odyssey. 2nd ed. Lanham.

———. 2007. "Homer's Trojan Theater." *Transactions of the American Philological Association* 137:233–252.

———. 2011. *Homer's Trojan Theater: Space, Vision, and Memory in the* Iliad. Cambridge.

Coffey, M. 1957. "The Function of the Homeric Simile." *American Journal of Philology* 78:113–132.

Collins, D. 2001. "Homer and Rhapsodic Competition in Performance." *Oral Tradition* 16:129–167.

Collins, L. 1988. *Studies in Characterization in the* Iliad. Frankfurt.

Corbin, A. 1996. "Divisions of Time and Space." In Nora 1996:427–464.

Craig, J. D. 1967. "ΧΡΥΣΕΙΑ ΧΑΛΚΕΙΩΝ." *Classical Review*, n.s., 17:243–245.

Crisp, M. 1993. *The Practical Director*. Boston.

Crotty, K. 1994. *The Poetics of Supplication: Homer's* Iliad *and* Odyssey. Ithaca, NY.

Cuillandre, J. 1944. *La droite et la gauche dans les poèmes homeriques en concordance avec la doctrine pythagorienne et avec la tradition celtique*. Paris.

Culler, J. 1981. *The Pursuit of Sign: Semiotics, Literature, Deconstruction*. Ithaca, NY.

D'Alfonso, F. 2008. "La terra desolata: Osservazioni sul destino di Bellerophonte (*Il.* 6.200–202)." *Museum Helveticum* 65:1–21.

Danek, G. 1988. *Studien zur Dolonie*. Vienna.

———. 1998. *Epos und Zitat: Studien zu den Quellen der* Odyssee. Vienna.

———. 2002. "Traditional Referentiality and Homeric Intertextuality." In *Omero tremila anni dopo*, ed. F. Montanari and D. Asheri, 3–19. Rome.

Dannenberg, H. P. 2008. *Coincidence and Counterfactuality: Plotting Time and Space in Narrative Fiction*. Lincoln.

D'Arms, E. F., and K. K. Hulley. 1946. "The Oresteia Story in the *Odyssey*." *Transactions of the American Philological Association* 77:207–213.

Davies, M. 1989. *The Greek Epic Cycle*. London.

———. 2000. "Homer and Dionysus." *Eikasmos* 11:15–27.

Debiasi, A. 2004. *L'epica perduta*. Rome.

Debray-Genette, R. 1980. "La pierre descriptive." *Poétique* 43:293–304.

de Certeau, M. 1974. *The Practice of Everyday Life*. Trans. R. Rendell. Berkeley.

———. 1980. *L'invention du quotidien*. Vol. 1, *Arts de faire*. Paris.

de Jong, I. J. F. 1987a. *Narrators and Focalizers: The Presentation of the Story in the* Iliad. Amsterdam. 2nd ed. 2004.

———. 1987b. "Silent Characters in the *Iliad*." In *Homer: Beyond Oral Poetry; Recent Trends in Homeric Interpretation*, ed. J. Bremer, I. J. F. de Jong, and J. Kalf, 105–121. Amsterdam.

———. 2001. *A Narratological Commentary on the* Odyssey. Cambridge.

———. 2009. "Metalepsis in Ancient Greek Literature." In *Narratology and Interpretation: The Content of Narrative Form in Ancient Literature*, ed. J. Grethlein and A. Rengakos, 87–115. Berlin.

———. 2011. "The Shield of Achilles: From Metalepsis to Mise en Abyme." *Ramus* 40:1–14.

de Jong, I. J. F., and R. Nünlist. 2004. "From Bird's Eye View to Close Up: The Standpoint of the Narrator in the Homeric Epics." In Bierl, Schmitt, and Willi 2004:63–83.

de Jong, I. J. F., R. Nünlist, and A. Bowie. 2004. "Glossary." In *Narrators, Narratees, and Narratives in Ancient Greek Literature*, vol. 1 of *Studies in Ancient Greek Narrative*, ed. I. J. F. de Jong, R. Nünlist, and A. Bowie, xv–xviii. Leiden.

Delany, P., and G. Landow, eds. 1991. *Hypermedia and Literary Studies*. Cambridge, MA.

Deleuze, G. 1986. *Cinema 1: The Movement-Image*. Trans. H. Tomlinson and B. Habberjam. London.

———. 1989. *Cinema 2: The Time-Image*. Trans. H. Tomlinson and R. Galeta. Minneapolis.

Dennerlein, K. 2009. *Narratologie des Raumes*. Berlin.

Detienne, M. 1965. "En Grèce archaïque: Géometrie, politique et société." *Annales E.S.C.* 20:425–440.

Detienne, M., and J.-P. Vernant, eds. 1979. *La cuisine du sacrifice en pays grec*. Paris.

Dickie, M. 1995. "The Geography of Homer's World." In Andersen and Dickie 1995:29–56.

Dickson, K. 1995. *Nestor: Poetic Memory in Greek Epic*. New York.

di Benedetto, V. 1998. *Nel laboratorio di Omero*. 2nd ed. Turin.

Diderot, D. 1765. "Le grand-prêtre Corésus s'immole, pour sauver Callirhoé." *Salons* 253–264.

Diggle, J. 1973. "The *Supplices* of Euripides." *Greek, Roman and Byzantine Studies* 14:241–269.

Dihle, A. 1970. *Homer-Probleme*. Opladen.

Donlan, W. 1971–1972. "Homer's Agamemnon." *Classical World* 65:109–115.

———. 1989. "The Unequal Exchange between Glaucus and Diomedes in Light of the Homeric Gift-Economy." *Phoenix* 43:1–15.

Downs, R. M., and D. Stea. 1977. *Maps in Mind: Reflections on Cognitive Mapping.* New York.

Drews, R. 1976. "The Earliest Greek Settlements on the Black Sea." *Journal of Hellenic Studies* 96:18–31.

Dubel, S. 1997. "Ekphrasis et enargeia: La déscription antique comme parcours." In *Dire l'évidence*, ed. B. Lévy and L. Pernot, 249–264. Paris.

Dubost, J.-P. 1996. "Iconolâtrie et iconoclastie de l'écriture libertine." In Wagner 1996:43–57.

Duchan, J. F., A. G. A. Bruder, and L. E. Hewitt, eds. 1995. *Deixis in Narrative: A Cognitive Science Perspective*. Hillsdale.

Duckworth, G. E. 1933. *Foreshadowing and Suspense in the Epics of Homer, Apollonius and Vergil*. Princeton.

Dué, C. 2002. *Homeric Variations on a Lament by Briseis*. Lanham.

———. 2010. "Agamemnon's Densely-Packed Sorrow in *Iliad* 10: A Hypertextual Reading of a Homeric Simile." In Tsagalis 2010c:279–299.

Dué, C., and M. Ebbott. 2010. Iliad *10 and the Poetics of Ambush*. Hellenic Studies 39. Washington, DC.

Dunbabin, T. J. 1948. "The Early History of Corinth." *Journal of Hellenic Studies* 68:59–68.

Dünne, J., and S. Günzel, eds. 2006. *Raumtheorie: Grundlagentexte aus Philosophie und Kulturwissenschaften*. Frankfurt.

Durante, M. 1976. *Sulla preistoria della tradizione poetica greca*. Vol. 2. Rome.

Durgnat, R. 1968. "The Restless Camera." *Films and Filming* 15:14–18.

Durkheim, E. 1984. *Die elementaren Formen des religiösen Lebens*. Frankfurt.

Ebeling, K. 2010. "Historischer Raum: Archiv und Errinerungsort." In Günzel 2010:121–133.

Ebbott, M. 1999. "The Wrath of Helen: Self-Blame and Nemesis in the *Iliad*." In Carlisle and Levaniouk 1999:3–20.

———. 2010. "Error 404: Theban Epic Not Found." In Tsagalis 2010c:239–258.

Edwards, M. W. 1980. "The Structure of Homeric Catalogues." *Transactions of the American Philological Association* 110:81–105.

———. 1987. *Homer: Poet of the* Iliad. Baltimore.

————. 1991. *The Iliad: A Commentary.* Vol. 5 (Books 17–21). Cambridge.

Eisner, W. 1990. *Comics and Sequential Art: Principles and Practice of the World's Most Popular Art Form.* 2nd ed. Tamarac.

Elliger, W. 1975. *Die Darstellung der Landschaft in der griechischen Dichtung.* Berlin.

Elsner, J. 2002. "Introduction: The Genres of Ekphrasis." In *The Verbal and the Visual: Cultures of Ekphrasis in Antiquity,* ed. J. Elsner, *Ramus* 31:1–18.

Emlyn-Jones, C. 1992. "The Homeric Gods: Poetry, Belief and Authority." In *Homer: Readings and Images,* ed. C. Emlyn-Jones, L. Hardwick, and J. Purkis, 91–103. London.

Erbse, H. 1961. "Beobachtungen über das 5. Buch der *Ilias.*" *Rheinisches Museum* 104:156–189.

Erbse, H., ed. 1969–1988. *Scholia Graeca in Homeri Iliadem I–VII.* Berlin.

————. 1986. *Untersuchungen zur Funktion der Götter im homerischen Epos.* Berlin.

————. 2000. "Beobachtungen über die Gleichnisse der *Ilias* Homers." *Hermes* 128:257–274.

Erskine, A. 2001. *Troy between Greece and Rome: Local Tradition and Imperial Power.* Oxford.

Esrock, E. J. 1994. *The Reader's Eye: Visual Imaging as Reader Response.* Baltimore.

Fantuzzi, M. 2004. "Ekphrasis." In *Brill's New Pauly,* ed. H. Cancik and H. Schneider, 4:872–875. Leiden.

————. Forthcoming. *Achilles in Love.* Oxford.

Felson, N. 2004. "Introduction." In *The Poetics of Deixis in Alcman, Pindar, and Other Lyric,* ed. N. Felson, *Arethusa* 37:253–266.

Fenik, B. 1968. *Typical Battle Scenes in the* Iliad: *Studies in the Narrative Techniques of Homeric Battle Description.* Wiesbaden.

————. 1986. *Homer and the Niebelungenlied: Comparative Studies in Epic Style.* Cambridge.

Ferguson, E., and M. Hegarty. 1994. "Properties of Cognitive Maps Constructed from Texts." *Memory and Cognition* 22:455–473.

Finkelberg, M. 2011. *The Homer Encyclopedia.* Vols. 1–3. London.

Finley, M. I. 2002. *The World of Odysseus.* New York.

Fittschen, K. 1973. "Der Schild des Achilleus." In *Archaeologia Homerica,* ed. F. Matz and H.-G. Buchholz, chapter N, part 1. Göttingen.

Fludernik, M. 1996. *Towards a "Natural" Narratology.* London.

————. 2000. "Genres, Text Types, or Discourse Modes—Narrative Modalities and Generic Categorization." *Style* 34:274–292.

————. 2003a. "Scene Shift, Metalepsis, and the Metaleptic Mode." *Style* 37:382–400.

————. 2003b. "Natural Narratology and Cognitive Parameters." In Herman 2003:243–267.

———. 2008. "Narrative and Drama." In *Theorizing Narrativity*, ed. J. Pier and J. A. García Landa, 355–383. Berlin.

Foley, J. M. 1991. *Immanent Art: From Structure to Meaning in Traditional Oral Epic.* Bloomington, Ind.

———. 1992. "Word-Power, Performance, and Tradition." *Journal of American Folklore* 105:276–301.

———. 1997. "Traditional Signs and Homeric Art." In Bakker and Kahane 1997:56–82.

———. 1999a. *Homer's Traditional Art.* University Park.

———. 1999b. "What's in a Sign?" *In Signs of Orality: The Oral Tradition and its Influence in the Greek and Roman World*, ed. E. A. Mackay, 1–27. Leiden.

———. 2005. "From Oral Performance to Paper-Text to Cyber-Edition." *Oral Tradition* 20:233–263.

Fort, B. 1996. "Ekphrasis as Art Criticism: Diderot and Fragonard's 'Coresus and Callirhoe.'" In P. Wagner 1996:58–77.

Foucault, M. 1984 [1967]. "Des espaces autres." In *Dits et ecrits* 4:752–762. Paris.

———. 1986 [1984]. "Of Other Spaces." Trans. J. Miskowiec. *Diacritics* 16:22–27.

Fowler, D. P. 1991. "Narrate and Describe: The Problem of Ekphrasis." *Journal of Roman Studies* 81:25–35.

Fowler, R., ed. 2004. *The Cambridge Companion to Homer.* Cambridge.

Frame, D. G. 1971. *The Origins of Greek NOUS.* PhD dissertation, Harvard University.

———. 1978. *The Myth of Return in Early Greek Epic.* New Haven.

———. 2009. *Hippota Nestor.* Hellenic Studies 37. Washington, DC.

Francis, J. A. 2009. "Metal Maidens, Achilles' Shield, and Pandora: The Beginnings of Ekphrasis." *American Journal of Philology* 130:1–23.

Frank, J. 1963 [1945]. "Spatial Form in Modern Literature." In *The Widening Gyre: Crisis and Master in Modern Literature*, ed. J. Frank, 3–62. New Brunswick.

———. 1978. "Spatial Form: Some Further Reflections." *Critical Inquiry* 5:275–290.

Fränkel, H. 1921. *Die homerischen Gleichnisse.* Göttingen.

———. 1973. *Early Greek Poetry and Philosophy: A History of Greek Epic, Lyric, and Prose to the Middle of the Fifth Century.* Trans. M. Hadas and J. Willis. New York.

Frei, P. 1978. "Die Lykier bei Homer." In *Proceedings of the Xth International Congress of Classical Archaeology (Ankara-Izmir, 23-30.9.1973)*, ed. E. Akurgal, 819–827. Ankara.

———. 1993. "Solymer, Milyer, Termilen, Lykier: Ethnische und politische Einheiten auf der lykischen Halbinsel." In *Götter, Heroen, Herrscher in Lykien*, ed. J. Borchhardt, R. Jacobek, and A. Dinstl, 87–97. Vienna.

Friedländer, P. 1914. "Kritische Untersuchungen zur Geschichte der Heldensage." *Rheinisches Museum* 69:299–341. Berlin (= *Studien zur antiken Literatur und Kunst* 19–53).

Friedman, S. S. 1993. "Spatialization: A Strategy for Reading Narrative." *Narrative* 1:12–23.

———. 1996. "Spatialization, Narrative Theory, and Virginia Woolf's *The Voyage Out*." In *Feminist Narratology and British Women Writers*, ed. K. Mezei, 109–136. Chapel Hill.

———. 2005. "A Spatial Poetics and Arundhati Roy's *A God of Small Things*." In *A Companion to Narrative Theory*, ed. J. Phelan and P. J. Rabinowitz, 192–205. Oxford.

Friedrich R. 1975. *Stilwandel im homerischen Epos: Studien zur Poetik und Theorie der epischen Gesang*. Wiesbaden.

Friedrich, W.-H. 1956. *Verwundung und Tod in der* Ilias. Göttingen.

Frisk, H. 1954–1970. *Griechisches etymologisches Wörterbuch*. Heidelberg.

Fry, N. 1970. *The Trial: A Film by Orson Welles*. London.

Gärtner, H. A. 1976. "Beobachtunen zum Schild des Achilleus." In *Studien zum antiken Epos*, ed. H. Görgemanns and E. A. Schmidt, 46–65. Meisenheim.

Gaisser, J. H. 1969. "Adaptation of Traditional Material in the Glaucus-Diomedes Episode." *Transactions of the American Philological Association* 100:165–176.

Galinsky, K. G. 1972. *The Herakles Theme: The Adaptations of the Hero in Literature from Homer to the Twentieth Century*. Oxford.

Garcia, L. F. 2007. *Homeric Temporalities: Simultaneity, Sequence, and Durability in the Iliad*. PhD dissertation, University of California at Los Angeles.

Gehrke, H.-J. 1998. "Die Geburt der Erdkunde aus dem Geiste der Geometrie: Überlegungen zur Entstehung und zur Frühgeschichte der wissenschaftlichen Geographie bei den Griechen." In *Gattungen wissenschaftlicher Literatur in Antike*, ed. W. Kullmann, J. Althoff, and M. Asper, 163–192. Tübingen.

Geiselman, R. E., and J. M. Crawley. 1983. "Incidental Processing of Speaker Characteristics: Voice as Connotative Information." *Journal of Verbal Learning and Verbal Behavior* 22:15–23.

Genette, G. 1969. *Figures II*. Paris.

———. 1980 [1972]. *Narrative Discourse: An Essay in Method*. Trans. J. E. Lewin. Ithaca, NY.

———. 1988. *Narrative Discourse Revisited*. Ithaca, NY.

———. 1992. *Fiktion und Diktion*. Munich.

———. 2004. *Métalepse: De la figure à la fiction*. Paris.

Gentili, B. 1972. "Lirica greca arcaica e tardo arcaica." In *Introduzione allo studio della cultura classica*, vol. 1:57–105. Milan.

Geulen, E. 2010. "Politischer Raum: Öffentlichkeit und Ausnahmezustand." In Günzel 2010:134–144.

Giannisi, P. 2006. *Récits des voies: Chant et cheminement en Grèce archaïque*. Grenoble.

Gibson, S., and O. O. Oviedo, eds. 2000. *The Emerging Cyberculture: Literacy, Paradigm, and Paradox*. Cresskill.

Giddens, A. 1981. *A Contemporary Critique of Historical Materialism*. London.

———. 1984. *The Constitution of Society: Outline of the Theory of Structuration*. Cambridge.

———. 1995. *Politics, Sociology and Social Theory: Encounters with Classical and Contemporary Social Thought*. Cambridge.

Giovannini, A. 1969. *Étude historique sur les origines du catalogue des vaisseaux*. Bern.

Goatly, A. 1997. *The Language of Metaphors*. London.

Goetsch, P. 1977. *Bauformen des modernen englischen und amerikanischen Dramas*. Darmstadt.

Goldhill, S. 1996. "Refracting Classical Vision: Changing Cultures on Viewing." In *Vision in Context: Historical and Contemporary Perspectives on Sight*, ed. T. Brennan and M. Jay, 17–28. New York.

Graf, F. 1995. "Ekphrasis: Die Entstehung der Gattung in der Antike." In *Beschreibungskunst-Kunstbeschreibung: Ekphrasis von der Antike bis zur Gegenwart*, ed. G. Boehm and H. Pfotenhauer, 143–155. Munich.

———. 1998. "Herakles." In *Der Neue Pauly* (German edition), vol. 5:387–392.

Grandolini, S. 1996. *Canti e aedi nei poemi omerici: Edizione e commento*. Pisa.

Graziosi, B., and J. Haubold. 2010. *Homer: Iliad Book VI*. Cambridge.

Gregory, D. 2001. "Edward Said's Imaginative Geographies." In *Thinking Space*, ed. M. Crang and N. Thrift, 302–348. London.

Grethlein, J. 2006. *Das Geschichtsbild der Ilias: Eine Untersuchung aus phänomenologischer und narratologischer Perspektive*. Göttingen.

———. 2007. "Ritual and Epic Narrative: The Case of the Funeral Games in the *Iliad*." In *Literatur und Religion*, vol. 1, *Wege zu einer mythisch/rituellen Poetik bei den Griechen*, ed. A. Bierl et al., 151–177. Berlin.

———. 2008. "Memory and Material Objects in the *Iliad* and the *Odyssey*." *Journal of Hellenic Studies* 128:27–51.

Griffin, J. 1978. "The Divine Audience and the Religion of the *Iliad*." *Classical Quarterly* 28:1–22.

———. 1980. *Homer on Life and Death*. Oxford.

———. 1986. "Homeric Words and Speakers." *Journal of Hellenic Studies* 106:36–57.

Groensteen, T. 2007. *The System of Comics*. Trans. B. Beaty and N. Nguyen. Jackson.

Grottanelli, C., and N. F. Parise, eds. 1979. *Sacrificio e società nel mondo antico.* Rome.

Gunning, J. 1924. "Laomedon 1." *Real Encyclopädie* 23.2:747–755.

Günzel, S., ed. 2010. *Raum: Ein interdisziplinäres Handbuch.* Stuttgart.

Hainsworth, J. B. 1966. "Joining Battle in Homer." *Greece and Rome* 13:158–166.

———. 1993. *The Iliad: A Commentary.* Vol. 3 (Books 9–12). Cambridge.

Halbwachs, M. 1980. *The Collective Memory.* Trans. F. J. Ditter and V. Y. Ditter. New York.

———. 1992. *On Collective Memory.* Trans. L. A. Coser. Chicago.

Hale, T. 1998. *Griots and Griottes: Masters of Words and Music.* Bloomington.

Hall, E. 1997. *Ethnic Identity in Greek Antiquity.* Cambridge.

Haller, B. S. 2007. *Landscape and Description in Homer's* Odyssey. PhD dissertation, University of Pittsburgh.

Hallet, W., and B. Neumann, eds. 2009. *Raum und Bewegung in der Literatur: Die Literaturwissenschaften und der Spatial Turn.* Bielefeld.

Halliwell, S. 1995. "Aristotle: *Poetics*." In *Aristotle: Poetics, Longinus: The Sublime, and Demetrius: On Style*, ed. S. Halliwell, W. H. Fyfe, and D. Innes. Cambridge, MA.

Hamon, P. 1993 [1981]. *Du descriptif.* 4th ed. Paris.

Hardie, P. H. 1985. "Imago Mundi: Cosmological and Ideological Aspects of the Shield of Achilles." *Journal of Hellenic Studies* 105:11–31.

Harpole, C. H. 1978. *Gradients of Depth in the Cinema Image.* New York.

Harrauer, C. 1999. "Die Melampus-Sage in der *Odyssee*." In Kazazis and Rengakos 1999:132–142.

Haubold, J. 2005. "Heracles in the Hesiodic *Catalogue of Women*." In *The Hesiodic Catalogue of Women: Constructions and Reconstructions*, ed. R. Hunter, 85–98. Cambridge.

Havelock, E. A. 1963. *Preface to Plato.* Cambridge, MA.

———. 1978. *The Greek Concept of Justice: From its Shadow in Homer to its Substance in Plato.* Cambridge, MA.

———. 1986. *The Muse Learns to Write: Reflections on Orality and Literacy from Antiquity to the Present.* New Haven.

Hawisher, G. E., and C. L. Selfe, eds. 1991. *Evolving Perspectives on Computers and Composition Studies: Questions for the 1990s.* Urbana.

Heffernan, J. A. W. 1991. "Ekphrasis and Representation." *New Literary History* 22:297–316.

———. 1993. *The Museum of Words.* Chicago.

Heiskanen, B. A. 2004. *Fighting Identities: The Body in Space and Place.* PhD dissertation, University of Texas at Austin.

Hellmann, O. 2000. *Die Schlachtszenen der* Ilias. Stuttgart.

Hellwig, B. 1964. *Raum und Zeit im homerischen Epos*. Hildesheim.

Henderson, B. 1980. *A Critique of Film Theory*. New York.

———. 1986. *Classical Film Theory: Eisenstein, Bazin, Godard, and Metz*. PhD dissertation, University of California at Santa Cruz.

Herman, D. 1997. "Toward a Formal Description of Narrative Metalepsis." *Journal of Literary Semantics* 26:132–152.

———. 2001. "Spatial Reference in Narrative Domains." *Text* 21:515–541.

———. 2002. *Story Logic: Problems and Possibilities of Narrative*. Lincoln.

Herman, D., ed. 2003. *Narrative Theory and the Cognitive Sciences*. Stanford.

———. 2007. *The Cambridge Companion to Narrative*. Cambridge.

Herman, D., M. Jahn, and M.-L. Ryan, eds. 2005. *Routledge Encyclopedia of Narrative Theory*. London.

Heubeck, A. 1949/1950. "Die homerische Göttersprache." *Würzburger Jahrbücher für die Altertumswissenschaft* 4:197–218. Erlangen (= *Kleine Schriften zur griechischen Sprache und Literatur*, 94–114).

Higbie, C. 1995. *Heroes' Names, Homeric Identities*. New York.

Higonnet, M. R., and J. Templeton. 1994. *Reconfigured Spheres: Feminist Explorations of Literary Space*. Amherst.

Hiller, S. 1993. "Lykien und Lykier bei Homer und in mykenischer Zeit." In *Akten des II. internationalen Lykien-Symposions, Wien 6-12 Mai 1990*, ed. J. Borchhardt and G. Dobesch, 107–115. Vienna.

Hintzman, D. L. 1993. "Twenty Five Years of Learning and Memory: Was the Cognitive Revolution a Mistake?" *In Attention and Performance XIV: Synergies in Experimental Psychology, Artificial Intelligence, and Cognitive Neuroscience*, ed. D. E. Meyer and S. Kornblum, 359–391. Cambridge, MA.

Hirsch, E. 1995. "Introduction. Landscape: Between Space and Place." In *The Anthropology of Landscape*, ed. E. Hirsch and M. O'Hanlon, 1–30. Oxford.

Hirzel, R. 1902. *Der Eid: Ein Beitrag zur eine Geschichte*. Leipzig.

Hoffmann, G. 1978. *Raum, Situation, erzählte Wirklichkeit: Poetologische und historische Studien zum englischen und amerikanischen Roman*. Stuttgart.

Hogan, J. C. 1966. *The Oral Nature of the Homeric Simile*. PhD dissertation, Cornell University.

Holland, R. 1894-1897. "Memnon." In *Ausführliches Lexicon der griechischen und römischen Mythologie*, ed. W. H. R. Roscher, 2:2653–2687. Leipzig.

Hölscher, U. 1939. *Untersuchungen zur Form der* Odyssee. Berlin.

———. 1967. "Die Atridensage in der *Odyssee*." In *Festschrift für R. Alewyn*, ed. H. Singer and B. von Wiese, 1–16. Cologne.

———. 1989. *Die Odyssee: Epos zwischen Märchen und Roman*. 2nd ed. Munich.

Hommel, H. 1958. "Aigisthos und die Freier." *Studium Generale* 8:237–245.

Howald, E. 1946. *Der Dichter der* Ilias. Erlenbach.

Hubbard, T. K. 1992. "Nature and Art in the Shield of Achilles." *Arion* 2:16–41.

Hühn, P., J. Pier, W. Schmid, and J. Schönert, eds. 2009. *Handbook of Narratology.* Berlin.

Hulme, P. 1990. "Subversive Archipelagos: Colonial Discourse and the Break-Up of Continental Theory." *Dispositio* 15:1–23.

Hunzinger, C. 1994. "Le plaisir esthétique dans l'épopée archaïque: Les mots de la famille de *thauma.*" *Bulletin de l'Association Guillaume Budé* 1:4–30.

Huxley, G. L. 1969. *Greek Epic Poetry from Eumelos to Panyassis.* London.

Innes, D. 1995. "Translation of [Demetrius] *On Style.*" In *Aristotle: Poetics, Longinus: The Sublime, and Demetrius: On Style*, ed. S. Halliwell, W. H. Fyfe, and D. Innes. Cambridge, MA.

Irigaray, L. 1974. *Speculum de l'autre femme.* Paris.

———. 1977. *Ce sexe qui n'est pas un.* Paris.

Israel, M., , J. R. Harding, and V. Tobin. 2004. "On Simile." *Language, Culture, and Mind* 9:123–135.

Jachmann, G. 1958. *Der homerische Schiffskatalog und die* Ilias. Cologne.

Jackson, A. 1993. "War and Raids for Booty in the World of Odysseus." In *War and Society in the Greek World*, ed. J. Rich and G. Shipley, 64–76. London.

Jackson, J. 1955. *Marginalia scaenica.* Oxford.

Jameson, M. 1999. "The Spectacular and the Obscure in Athenian Religion." In *Performance Culture and Athenian Democracy*, ed. S. Goldhill and R. Osborne, 321–340. Cambridge.

Jamison, S. W. 1994. "Draupadí on the Walls of Troy: *Iliad* 3 from an Indic Perspective." *Classical Antiquity* 13:5–16.

Janko, R. 1982. *Homer, Hesiod and the Hymns: Diachronic Development in Epic Diction.* Cambridge.

———. 1992. *The Iliad: A Commentary.* Vol. 4 (Books 13–16). Cambridge.

Janni, P. 1984. *La mappa e il periplo.* Macerata.

Jebb, R. C. 1883. "A Tour in the Troad." *The Fortnightly Review* 39 (n.s. 33):514–529.

Jenkyns, T. 1999. "*Homêros ekainopoiêse*: Theseus, Aithra, and Variation in Homeric Myth-Making." In Carlisle and Levaniouk 1999:207–226.

Jenniges, W. 1998. "Les Lyciens dans l'*Iliade*: Sur les traces de Pandaros." In *Quaestiones Homericae: Acta colloqui Namurcensis, habiti diebus 7-9 mensis Septembris anni 1995*, ed. L. Isebaert and R. Lebrun, 119–147. Leuven.

Johnson, K. P. 2008. "Ideology through Images: A Comics Approach to the Shield of Achilles." Unpublished graduate paper, New York University, Department of Classics.

Johnson, M. 1987. *The Body in the Mind: The Bodily Basis of Meaning, Imagination, and Reason.* Chicago.

Johnson, V. T., and P. Graham. 1994. *The Film of Andrei Tarkovsky: A Visual Fugue.* Bloomington.

Jones, S. G. 2008. "Television." In Herman, Jahn, and Ryan 2005:585–589.

Joyce, M. 1991. *Of Two Minds: Hypertext Pedagogy and Poetics.* Ann Arbor.

———. 2000. *Othermindedness: The Emergence of Network Culture.* Ann Arbor.

———. 2002. "No One Tells You This: Secondary Orality and Hypertextuality." *Oral Tradition* 17:325–345.

Jürgensen, H. 1968. *Der antike Metaphernbegriff.* PhD dissertation, Christian-Albrechts University, Kiel.

Kahane, A. 1997. "Quantifying Epic." In Morris and Powell 1997:326–342.

Kajetzke, L., and M. Schroer. 2010. "Sozialer Raum: Verräumlichung." In Günzel 2010:192–203.

Kakridis, J. 1949. *Homeric Researches.* Lund.

———. 1971. *Homer Revisited.* Lund.

———. 1980. *Προομηρικά, Ὁμηρικά, Ἡσιόδεια.* Athens.

———. 1982. "Μετακένωσις." *Wiener Studien* 16, n.s, 5–12.

Kakridis, P. 1962. *Γενικὴ μελέτη τῶν 'Μεθ' Ὅμηρον' καὶ τοῦ ποιητῇ τους.* Athens.

———. 1995. "Odysseus und Palamedes." In Andersen and Dickie 1995:91–100.

Kallinka, E. 1943. *Agamemnon in der* Ilias. Vienna.

Kannicht, R. 2004. *Tragicorum Graecorum Fragmenta.* Vols. 5.1–5.2. Göttingen. Abbreviated TrGF.

Kaplan, N. 1991. "Ideology, Technology, and the Future of Writing Instruction." In Hawisher and Selfe 1991:11–42.

Karavites, P. 1992. *Promise-Giving and Treaty-Making: Homer and the Near East.* Leiden.

Katzung, P. G. 1960. *Die Diapeira in der Iliashandlung: Der Gesang von der Umstimmung des Griechenheeres.* PhD dissertation, University of Frankfurt.

Kawin, B. F. 1992. *How Movies Work.* Berkeley.

Kazazis, J. N., and A. Rengakos, eds. 1999. *Euphrosyne: Studies in Ancient Epic and its Legacy in Honor of Dimitris N. Maronitis.* Stuttgart.

Kearns, E. 2004. "The Gods in the Homeric Epics." In Fowler 2004:59–73.

Kelly, A. 2007. *A Referential Commentary and Lexicon to Iliad VIII.* Oxford.

———. 2010. "Hypertexting with Homer: Tlepolemus and Sarpedon on Heracles." In Tsagalis 2010c:259–276.

Kennedy, B. 2000. *M. Deleuze and Cinema: The Aesthetics of Sensation.* Edinburgh.

Kennedy, G. A. 1986. "Helen's Web Unraveled." *Arethusa* 19:5–14.

Kirk, G. S. 1962. *The Songs of Homer.* Cambridge.

———. 1978. "The Formal Duels in Books 3 and 7 of the *Iliad.*" In *Homer: Tradition and Invention,* ed. B. C. Fenik, 18–40. Leiden.

———. 1985. *The Iliad: A Commentary.* Vol. 1 (Books 1–4). Cambridge.

———. 1990. *The Iliad: A Commentary*. Vol. 2 (Books 5–8). Cambridge.

Kittay, J. 1981. "Descriptive Limits." *Yale French Studies* 61:225–243.

Kitts, M. 2005. *Sanctified Violence in Homeric Society: Oath-Making Rituals and Narratives in the* Iliad. Cambridge.

Knox, R., and J. Russo. 1989. "Agamemnon's Test: *Iliad* 2.73–75." *Classical Antiquity* 8:351–358.

Konstan, D. 2002. "Narrative Spaces." In *Ancient Narrative: Space in the Ancient Novel* (Supplement 1), ed. M. Paschalis and S. Frangoulidis, 1–11. Groningen.

Kopytoff, I. 1986. "The Cultural Biography of Things: Commodization as Process." In *The Social Life of Things: Commodities in Cultural Perspective*, ed. I. Kopytoff, 64–91. Cambridge.

Korre-Zografou, K. 1991. *Ο νεοελληνικός κεφαλόδεσμος*. Athens.

Korte, B. 1997. *Body Language in Literature*. Toronto.

Koselleck, R. 2000. *Zeitschriften: Studien zur Historik*. Frankfurt.

Kosslyn, S., and O. Koenig. 1992. *Wet Mind: The New Cognitive Neuroscience*. New York.

Krieger, M. 1992. *Ekphrasis: The Illusion of the Natural Sign*. Baltimore.

———. 2003 [1967]. "The Ekphrastic Principle and the Still Movement of Poetry; or Laocoon Revisited." In *Close Reading*, ed. F. Lentricchia and A. Dubois, 88–110. Durham, NC.

Krieter-Spiro, M. 2009. *Homers* Ilias: *Gesamtkomentar*. Vol. 3.2. Berlin.

Krischer, T. 1971. *Formale Konventionen der homerischen Epik*. Munich.

———. 1992. "Die Bogenprobe." *Hermes* 120:19–25.

Kristeva, J. 1974. *La révolution du langage poétique: L'avant-garde à la fin du XIXe siècle: Lautréamont et Mallarmé*. Paris.

Kullmann, T. 1995. *Vermenschlichte Natur: Zur Bedeutung von Landschaft und Wetter im englischen Roman von Ann Radcliffe bis Thomas Hardy*. Tübingen.

Kullmann, W. 1955. "Die Probe des Achaierheeres in der *Ilias*." *Museum Helveticum* 12:253–273.

———. 1956. *Das Wirken der Götter in der Ilias*. Berlin.

———. 1960. *Die Quellen der* Ilias (*Troischer Sagenkreis*). Wiesbaden.

———. 1984. "Oral Poetry Theory and Neoanalysis in Homeric Research." *Greek, Roman and Byzantine Studies* 25:307–324.

———. 1992. "Gods and Men in the *Iliad* and *Odyssey*." In W. Kullmann, *Homerische Motive: Beiträge zur Entstehung, Eigenart und Wirkung von* Ilias *und* Odyssee, ed. R. J. Müller, 243–263. Stuttgart (= *Harvard Studies in Classical Philology* 89:1–23).

———. 1993. "Festgehaltene Kenntnisse im Schiffskatalog und im Troerkatalog der *Ilias*." In *Vermittlung und Tradierung von Wissen in der griechischen Kultur*, ed. W. Kullmann and J. Althoff, 129–147. Tübingen.

————. 2002. *Realität, Imagination, und Theorie: Kleine Schriften zu Epos und Tragödie in der Antike.* Ed. A. Rengakos. Stuttgart.

————. 2009. "Poesie, Mythos und Realität im Schiffskatalog der *Ilias.*" *Hermes* 137:1–20.

————. 2012. "Neoanalysis between Orality and Literacy: Some Remarks Concerning the Development of Greek Myths Including the Legend of the Capture of Troy." In Montanari, Rengakos, and Tsagalis 2012:13–25.

Kveim, K. 1998. *The World Wide Web: An Instance of Walter Ong's Secondary Orality?* Master's thesis in Media and Communications, Goldsmiths College, University of London. http://www.angelfire.com/oh/kathrine/dissertation.html.

Labov, W. 1972. *Language in the Inner City: Studies in the Black English Vernacular.* Philadelphia.

Laird, A. 1996. "*Ut figura poesis*: Writing Art and the Art of Writing in Augustan Poetry." In *Art and Text in Roman Culture,* ed. J. Elsner, 75–102. Cambridge.

Lakoff, G., and M. Turner. 1989. *More than Cool Reason: A Field Guide to Poetic Metaphor.* Chicago.

Lämmli, F. 1948. "Meuterei oder Versuchung?" *Museum Helveticum* 5:83–95.

Landow, G. 1997. *Hypertext: The Convergence of Contemporary Critical Theory and Technology.* 2nd ed. Baltimore.

————. 2006. *Hypertext 3.0: Critical Theory and New Media in an Era of Globalization.* Baltimore.

Lang, A. 1906. *Homer and his Age.* London.

Lang, M. 1989. "Unreal Conditions in Homeric Narrative." *Greek, Roman and Byzantine Studies* 30:5–26.

Larsen, K. D. 2007. "Simile and Comparison in Homer: A Definition." *Classica et Mediaevalia* 58:5–63.

Latacz, J. 1977. *Kampfparänese, Kampfdarstellung und Kampfwirklichkeit in der* Ilias, *bei Kallinos und Tyrtaios.* Munich.

Latacz, J., et al. 2002. *Homers* Ilias: *Gesamtkommentar.* Vol. 1.2. Munich.

Lateiner, D. 1995. *Sardonic Smile: Nonverbal Behavior in Homeric Epic.* Ann Arbor.

Lattimore, R. 1951. *The* Iliad *of Homer.* Chicago.

Lausberg, H. 1990 [1960]. *Handbuch der literarischen Rhetorik: Eine Grundlegung der Wissenschaft.* 3rd ed. Stuttgart. Engl. trans. Leiden 1989.

Leaf, W. 1900–1902. *The Iliad.* London.

Lecomte, C. 1998. "L'Εὐρωπία d'Eumélos de Corinthe." In *D'Europe à Europe, I: Le mythe d'Europe dans l'art et la culture de l'antiquité au XVIIIe siècle; Actes du colloque tenu à l'ENS, Paris (24-26 Avril 1997),* ed. R. Poignault and O. Wattel-de Croizant, 71–79. Tours.

Lee, D. J. N. 1964. *The Similes of the* Iliad *and the* Odyssey *Compared.* Melbourne.

Lee, J. Y. 1996. "Charting the Codes of Cyberspace: A Rhetoric of Electronic Mail." In *Communication and Cyberspace*, ed. L. Strate, R. Jacobson, and S. Gibson, 275–296. Cresskill.

Le Fanu, M. 1997. "Metaphysics of the Long Take: Some Post-Bazinian Reflections." *P.O.V.: A Danish Journal of Film Studies* (4 Dec. 1997). http://pov. imv.au.dk/Issue_04/section_1/artclA.html.

Lefebvre, H. 1974. *La production de l'espace*. Paris.

Lehnert, G. 1896. *De scholiis ad Homerum rhetoricis*. Leipzig.

Lenk, B. 1937. "Oichalia 3(a)-(b)." *Real Encyclopädie* 17.2:2099–2101.

Lesky, A. 1947. *Thalatta: Der Weg der Griechen zum Meer*. Vienna.

———. 1966. "Bildwerk und Deutung bei Philostrat und Homer." In *Gesammelte Schriften: Aufsätze und Reden zu antiker und deutscher Dichtung und Kultur*, ed. W. Kraus, 11–25. Bern.

Lessing, G. E. 1893 [1766]. "Laokoon oder über die Grenzen der Malerei und Poesie." In *G. E. Lessings sämtliche Schriften*, ed. K. Lachmann, vol. 9. Stuttgart.

Lincoln, B. 1976. "The Indo-European Cattle-Raiding Myth." *History of Religions* 16:42–65.

———. 1981. *Priests, Warriors, and Cattle: A Study in the Ecology of Religions*. Berkeley.

Linde, C., and W. Labov. 1975. "Spatial Networks as a Site for the Study of Language and Thought." *Language* 51:924–939.

Lissarague, F. 1987. *The Aesthetics of the Greek Banquet: Images of Wine and Ritual*. Trans. A. Szegedy-Maszak. Princeton.

Llewellyn-Jones, L. 2003. *Aphrodite's Tortoise: The Veiled Woman of Ancient Greece*. Swansea.

———. 2011. "Dress." In Finkelberg 2011:1.221–223. London.

Löffler, I. 1963. *Die Melampodie: Versuch einer Rekonstruktion des Inhalts*. Meisenheim.

Lohmann, D. 1970. *Die Komposition der Reden in der* Ilias. Berlin.

———. 1992. "Homer als Erzähler: Die Athla im 23. Buch der *Ilias*." *Gymnasium* 99:289–319.

Lonsdale, S. H. 1990. *Creatures of Speech, Lion, Herding, and Hunting Similes in the* Iliad. Stuttgart.

Lord, A. B. 1960. *The Singer of Tales*. Ed. and with introduction by S. Mitchell and G. Nagy. Cambridge, MA. 2nd ed. 2000.

Lorimer, H. M. 1950. *Homer and the Monuments*. London.

Lotman, J. 1972. "Das Problem der künstlerischen Raumes," In *Die Struktur literarischer Texte*, ed. J. Lotman, 311–329. Munich.

Louden, B. 1993. "Pivotal Contrafactuals in Homeric Epic." *Classical Antiquity* 12:181–198.

———. 1999. *The Odyssey: Structure, Narration, and Meaning*. Baltimore.

———. 2006. *The* Iliad: *Structure, Myth, and Meaning*. Baltimore.

Lung, G. E. 1912. *Memnon: Archäologische Studien zur Aithiopis*. PhD dissertation, University of Bonn.

Lynch, K. 1960. *The Image of the City*. Boston.

Lyne, O. 1989. *Words and the Poet: Characteristic Techniques of Style in Vergil's* Aeneid. Oxford.

Lynn-George, M. 1988. *Epos: Word, Narrative and the* Iliad. London.

Mackay, E. A., ed. 2008. *Orality, Literacy, Memory in the Ancient Greek and Roman World*. Leiden.

Mackie, C. J. 2002. "Homeric Phthia." *Colby Quarterly* 38:1–11.

Mackie, H. 1996. *Talking Trojan: Speech and Community in the* Iliad. Lanham.

Macleod, C. W. 1982. *Homer: Iliad, Book XXIV*. Cambridge.

Maehler, H. 2004. *Bacchylides: A Selection*. Cambridge.

Maftei, M. 1976. *Antike Diskussionen über die Episode von Glaukos und Diomedes im VI. Buch der* Ilias. Meisenheim.

Malten, L. 1944. "Homer und die Lykischen Fürsten." *Hermes* 79:1–12.

Mamer, B. 2000. *Film Production Techniques: Creating the Accomplished Image*. Belmont, CA.

Mannsperger, B. 1998. "Die Mauer am Schiffslager der Achaier." *Studia Troica* 8:287–304.

———. 2001. "Das Stadtbild von Troia in der *Ilias*." In *Troia: Traum und Wirklichkeit*, ed. J. Latacz et al., 81–83. Darmstadt.

Mannsperger, P., and D. Mannsperger. 2002. "Die *Ilias* ist ein Heldenepos: Ilosgrab und Athena Ilias." In *Mauerschau: Festschrift für Manfred Korfmann*, ed. R. Aslan et al., 3.1075–1101. Remshalden-Grundbach.

Marcovich, M. 1962. "On the *Iliad*, XVI, 259–265." *American Journal of Philology* 83:288–291.

Marg, W. 1957. *Homer über die Dichtung*. Münster.

Margolin, U. 2003. "Cognitive Science, the Thinking Mind, and Literary Narrative." In Herman 2003:271–294.

Marin, T. 2008–2009. "Tradizione epiche sulla sosta di Achille a Sciro e la nascita di Neottolemo." *Incontri triestini di filologia classica* 8:211–238.

Marinatos, S. 1967. *Archaeologia Homerica: Kleidung, Haar- und Barttracht*. Vol. 1, chapter A–B. Göttingen.

Marks, J. 2002. "The Junction between the *Kypria* and the *Iliad*." *Phoenix* 56:1–24.

———. 2003. "Alternative *Odysseys*: The Case of Thoas and Odysseus." *Transactions of the American Philological Association* 133:209–226.

———. 2012. "ἀρχοὺς αὖ νηῶν ἐρέω: A Programmatic Function of the Iliadic Catalogue of Ships." In Montanari, Rengakos, and Tsagalis 2012:101–112.

Maronitis, D. N. 2004. *Homeric Megathemes: War, Homilia, Homecoming.* Trans. D. Connolly. Lanham.

Marschark, M. E. 1979. "The Syntax and Semantics of Comprehension." In *Perspectives in Experimental Linguistics,* ed. G. D. Prideaux, 52–72. Amsterdam.

Marschark, M. E., and R. R. Hunt. 1989. "A Reexamination of the Role of Imagery in Learning and Memory." *Journal of Experimental Psychology: Learning, Memory, and Cognition* 15:710–720.

Marschark, M. E., and A. Paivio. 1977. "Integrative Processing of Concrete and Abstract Sentences." *Journal of Verbal Learning and Verbal Behavior* 16:217–231.

Martin, R. P. 1989. *The Language of Heroes: Speech and Performance in the* Iliad. Ithaca, NY.

———. 1997. "Similes and Performance." In Bakker and Kahane 1997:138–166.

Massumi, B. 2002. *Parables for the Virtual: Movement, Affect, Sensation.* Durham, NC.

Matthews, V. J. 1974. *Panyassis of Halikarnassos, Text and Commentary.* Leiden.

Matz, D. 1995. *Ancient World Lists and Numbers: Numerical Phrases and Rosters in the Greco-Roman Civilizations.* Jefferson.

Mayer, R. E. 1983. "Can You Repeat That? Qualitative Effects of Repetition and Advance Organizers on Learning from Science Prose." *Journal of Educational Psychology* 75:40–49.

Mayo, C., and N. Henley. 1987. "Nonverbal Behavior: Barrier or Agent for Sex Role Change." In *Gender and Nonverbal Behavior,* ed. C. Mayo and N. Henley, 3–13. New York.

McCall, M. H., Jr. 1969. *Ancient Rhetorical Theories of Simile and Comparison.* Cambridge, MA.

McGlew, J. F. 1989. "Royal Power and the Achaean Assembly at *Iliad* 2.84–393." *Classical Antiquity* 8:283–295.

McHale, B. 1987. *Postmodernist Fiction.* London.

McHale, B., and M. Ron. 2008. "Tel Aviv School of Narrative Poetics." In Herman, Jahn, and Ryan 2005:582–584.

McInerney, J. 2010. *The Cattle of the Sun: Cows and Culture in the World of the Ancient Greeks.* Princeton.

Meijering, R. 1987. *Literary and Rhetorical Theories in Greek Scholia.* Groningen.

Meineke, A. 1843. *Analecta Alexandrina.* Berlin. Repr. 1964, Hildesheim.

Merkelbach, R., and M. L. West. 1967. *Fragmenta Hesiodea.* Oxford.

Merrifield, A. 1993. "Place and Space: A Lefebvrian Reconciliation." *Transactions of the Institute of British Geographers* 18:516–531.

Mette, H.-J. 1951. *Der Pfeilschuß des Pandaros: Neue Untersuchungen zur "homerischen"* Ilias. Halle.

———. 1961. "Schauen und Staunen." *Glotta* 39:49–71.

Meyer, H. 1975 [1963]. "Raumgestaltung und Raumsymbolik in der Erzählkunst." Reprinted in *Landschaft und Raum in der Erzählkunst*, ed. A. Ritter, 208–231. Darmstadt.

Mickelsen, D. 1981. "Types of Spatial Structure in Narrative." In *Spatial Form in Narrative*, ed. J. R. Smitten and A. Daghistany, 63–78. Ithaca, NY.

Miller, G. A. 1979. "Images and Models, Similes and Metaphors." In Ortony 1979c:202–250.

Minchin, E. 1996. "The Performance of Lists and Catalogues in the Homeric Epics." In *Voice into Text: Orality and Literacy in Ancient Greece*, ed. I. Worthington, 3–20. Leiden.

———. 2001. *Homer and the Resources of Memory: Some Applications of Cognitive Theory to the* Iliad *and the* Odyssey. Oxford.

———. 2008a. "Spatial Memory and the Composition of the *Iliad*." In Mackay 2008:9–34.

———. 2008b. "Communication without Words: Body Language, 'Pictureability,' and Memorability in the *Iliad*." *Ordia Prima* 7:17–38.

Mitry, J. 1997. *The Aesthetics and Psychology of the Cinema*. Trans. Christopher King. Bloomington.

Mitsi, E. 1991. *Writing Against Pictures: A Study of Ekphrasis in Epics by Homer, Virgil, Ariosto, Tasso and Spenser*. PhD dissertation, New York University.

———. 2007. "Violent Acts and Ovidian Artifacts in Marlowe's Hero and Leander." *Classical and Modern Literature* 27.2:1–16.

Mitsis, P. 2010. "Achilles *Polytropos* and Odysseus as Suitor: *Iliad* 9.307–429." In Mitsis and Tsagalis 2010:51–76.

Mitsis, P., and C. Tsagalis, eds. 2010. *Allusion, Authority, and Truth: Critical Perspectives on Greek Poetic and Rhetorical Praxis*. Berlin.

Mittell, J. 2007. "Film and Television Narrative." In Herman 2007:156–171.

Monsacré, H. 1984. *Les larmes d'Achille: Le héros, la femme et la souffrance dans la poésie d'Homère*. Paris.

Montanari, F., A. Rengakos, and C. Tsagalis, eds. 2009. *Brill's Companion to Hesiod*. Leiden.

———. 2012. *Homeric Contexts: Neoanalysis and the Interpretation of Oral Poetry*. Berlin.

Montiglio, S. 2000. *Silence in the Land of Logos*. Princeton.

Morris, I., and B. Powell, eds. 1997. *A New Companion to Homer*. Leiden.

Morrison, J. V. 1992a. *Homeric Misdirection: False Predictions in the* Iliad. Ann Arbor.

————. 1992b. "Alternatives to the Epic Tradition: Homer's Challenges in the *Iliad*." *Transactions of the American Philological Association* 122:61–71.

Mosher, H. F. Jr. 1991. "Toward a Poetics of 'Descriptized' Narration." *Poetics Today* 12:425–445.

Most, G. W. 2006. *Hesiod: Theogony, Works and Days, Testimonia.* Cambridge, MA.

————. 2007. *Hesiod: The Shield, Catalogue of Women, Other Fragments.* Cambridge, MA.

Moulton, C. 1974. "Similes in the *Iliad*." *Hermes* 102:381–397.

————. 1977. *Similes in the Homeric Poems.* Göttingen.

Muellner, L. 1990. "The Simile of the Cranes and Pygmies: A Study of Homeric Metaphor." *Harvard Studies in Classical Philology* 93:59–101.

————. 1996. *The Anger of Achilles:* Mênis *in Greek Epic.* Ithaca, NY.

Mühlestein, H. 1987. *Homerische Namenstudien.* Frankfurt.

Müller, F. 1968. *Darstellung und poetische Funktion der Gegenstände in der Odyssee.* Doctoral dissertation, University of Marburg.

Murray, G. 1907. *The Rise of the Greek Epic.* Oxford.

Murray, O., ed. 1990. *Sympotica: A Symposium on the Symposion.* Oxford.

Nagler, M. 1974. *Spontaneity and Tradition: A Study in the Oral Art of Homer.* Berkeley.

Nagy, G. 1974. *Comparative Studies in Greek and Indic Meter.* Cambridge, MA.

————. 1979. *The Best of the Achaeans: Concepts of the Hero in Archaic Greek Poetry.* Baltimore.

————. 1990a. *Greek Mythology and Poetics.* Ithaca, NY.

————. 1990b. *Pindar's Homer: The Lyric Possession of an Epic Past.* Baltimore.

————. 2001. "Reading Bakhtin Reading the Classics: An Epic Fate for Conveyors of the Heroic Past." In *Bakhtin and the Classics*, ed. R. B. Branham, 71–96. Evanston.

————. 2003. *Homeric Responses.* Austin.

————. 2004. "Transmission of Archaic Greek Sympotic Songs: From Lesbos to Alexandria." *Critical Inquiry* 31.1:26–48.

————. 2009a. "Hesiod and the Ancient Biographical Traditions." In Montanari, Rengakos, and Tsagalis 2009:271–311.

————. 2009b. *Homer The Classic.* Online edition: http://chs.harvard.edu/wa/pageR?tn=ArticleWrapper&bdc=12&mn=3247.

————. 2009c. *Homer The Preclassic.* Online edition: http://chs.harvard.edu/wa/pageR?tn=ArticleWrapper&bdc=12&mn=3285.

————. 2009d. "The Fragmentary Muse and the Poetics of Refraction in Sappho, Sophocles, Offenbach." In *Theater des Fragments: Performative Strategien im Theater zwischen Antike und Postmoderne*, ed. A. Bierl et al., 69–102. Bielefeld.

Neal, T. 2006. *The Wounded Hero: Non-Fatal Injury in Homer's* Iliad. Bern.

Neer, R. 2010. *The Emergence of the Classical Style in Greek Sculpture.* Chicago.

Neisser, U. 1983. "Toward a Skillful Psychology." In *The Acquisition of Symbolic Skills,* ed. D. Rogers and J. A. Sloboda, 1–17. New York.

Nelles, W. 1997. *Frameworks: Narrative Levels and Embedded Narrative.* New York.

Nesselrath, H.-G. 1992. *Ungeschehenes Geschehen: "Beinahe Episoden" im griechischen und römischen Epos.* Stuttgart.

Nestle, W. 1968. "Odysseelandschaften." In *Griechische Studien: Untersuchungen zur Religion, Dichtung und Philosophie der Griechen,* 32–50. Repr. ed. Aalen. 1st ed. 1948, Stuttgart.

Niemeyer, H. G. 1996. *Sēmata: Über den Sinn griechischer Standbilder.* Hamburg.

Niese, B. 1882. *Die Entwickelung der homerischen Poesie.* Berlin.

Nimis, S. 1987. *Narrative Semiotics in the Epic Tradition: The Simile.* Bloomington.

Nora, P. 1996. *Realms of Memory: Rethinking the French Past.* Vol. 1. Ed. L. D. Kritzman. Trans. A. Goldhammer. New York.

Nöth, W. 1996. "The (Meta-)Textual Space." In *The Construal of Space in Language and Thought,* ed. M. Pütz and R. Dirven, 599–612. Berlin.

Nünlist, R. 1998. "Der homerische Erzähler und das sogenannte Sukzessionsgesetz." *Museum Helveticum* 55:2–8.

———. 2009. *The Ancient Critic at Work: Terms and Concepts of Literary Criticism in Greek Scholia.* Cambridge.

Nünning, A. 2009. "Formen und Funktionen literarischer Raumdarstellung: Grundlagen, Ansätze, narratologische Kategorien und neue Perspektiven." In *Raum und Bewegung in der Literatur: die Literaturwissenschaften und der Spatial Turn,* ed. W. Hallet and B. Neumann, 33–52. Bielefeld.

Oesterreicher, W. 1997. "Types of Orality in Text." In Bakker and Kahane 1997:190–214.

Olrik, A. 1992. *Principles for Oral Narrative Research.* Trans. K. Wolf and J. Jensen. Bloomington.

Onians, R. B. 1951. *The Origins of European Thought.* Cambridge.

Ong, W. J. 1982. *Orality and Literacy: The Technologizing of the Word.* London.

Ortony, A. 1979a. "The Role of Similarity in Similes and Metaphors." In Ortony 1979c:186–201.

———. 1979b. "Beyond Literal Similarity." *Psychological Review* 86:161–180.

Ortony, A., ed. 1979c. *Metaphor and Thought.* Cambridge.

O'Toole, L. M. 1980. "Dimensions of Semiotic Space in Narrative." *Poetics Today* 1:135–149.

Owen, E. T. 1946. *The Story of the* Iliad *as Told in the* Iliad. London.

Paivio, A. 1971. *Imagery and Verbal Processes.* New York.

———. 1975. "Perceptual Comparisons through the Mind's Eye." *Memory and Cognition* 3:635–647.

———. 1979. "Psychological Processes in the Comprehension of Metaphor." In Ortony 1979c:150–171.

———. 1986. *Mental Representations: A Dual Coding Approach.* New York.

Palm, J. 1965–1966. "Bemerkungen zur Ekphrase in der griechischen Literatur." *Kungliga Humanistiska Vetenskapssamfundet i Uppsala, Årsbok* 109–211.

Paoletti, O., and G. Neumann. 2003. "Una coppa-skyphos attica a figure nere con raffigurazioni erotiche." *Rivista dell'istituto nazionale d'archeologia e storia dell'arte* 58:79–106.

Parisinou, E. 2000. *The Light of the Gods: The Role of Light in Archaic and Classical Greek Art.* London.

Parks, W. 1990. *Verbal Dueling in Heroic Narrative: The Homeric and the Old English Traditions.* Princeton.

Parry, A. 1956. "The Language of Achilles." *Transactions of the American Philological Association* 87:1–7.

———. 1957. "Landscape in Greek Poetry." *Yale Classical Studies* 15:3–29.

Pavese, C. O. 1974. *Studi sulla tradizione epica rapsodica.* Rome.

Pedrick, V. 1994. "Reading in the Middle Voice: The Homeric Intertextuality of Pietro Pucci and John Peradotto." *Helios* 21:75–93.

Pelliccia, H. 1995. *Mind, Body, and Speech in Homer and Pindar.* Göttingen.

Peppermüller, R. 1962. "Die Glaukos-Diomedes Szene der *Ilias*: Spuren vorhomerischen Dichtung." *Wiener Studien* 75:5–21.

Perrone-Moisès, L. 1980. "Balzac et les fleurs de l'écritoire." *Poétique* 11:305–323.

Perutelli, A. 1978. "L'inversione speculare." *Materiali e discussioni* 1:87–98.

Pestalozzi, H. 1945. *Die* Achilleis *als Quelle der* Ilias. Erlenbach.

Petegorsky, D. 1982. *Context and Evocation: Studies in Early Greek and Sanskrit Poetry.* PhD dissertation, University of California at Berkeley.

Pfister, F. 1909. *Der Reliquienkult im Altertum.* Giessen.

Pfister, M. 1977. *Das Drama: Theorie und Analyse.* Munich.

Pier, J. 1999. "Three Dimensions of Space in the Narrative Text." *GRAAT: Publication des Groupes de Recherches Anglo-Américaines de l'Université François Rabelais de Tours* 21:191–205.

———. 2005a. "Chronotope." In Herman, Jahn, and Ryan 2005:64–65.

———. 2005b. "Metalepsis." In Herman, Jahn, and Ryan 2005:303–304.

———. 2009. "Metalepsis." In Hühn et al. 2009:190–203.

Pier, J., and J.-M. Schaeffer, eds. 2005. *Métalepses: Entorses au pacte de la représentation.* Paris.

Piérart, M. 1991. "Aspects de la transition en Argolide." In *La transizione del miceneo all'alto arcaismo: Dal palazzo alla città,* ed. D. Musti et al., 133–144. Rome.

———. 1992a. "Argos assoifée" and "Argos riche en cavales." In Piérart 1992b:119–148.

Piérart, M., ed. 1992b. *Polydipsion Argos: Argos de la fin des palais mycéniens à la constitution de l'état classique*. Athens.

Plescia, J. 1970. *The Oath and Perjury in Ancient Greece*. Tallahassee.

Postl, G. 2010. "Körperlicher Raum: Geschlecht und Performativität." In Günzel 2010:162–176.

Poulantzas, N. 1978. *State, Power, Socialism*. London.

Powell, B. 1978. "Word Patterns in the Catalogue of Ships (B 494–709): A Structural Analysis of Homeric Language." *Hermes* 106:255–264.

Prag, A. J. N. W. 1985. *The Oresteia: Iconographic and Narrative Tradition*. Chicago.

Prier, R. 1989. *Thauma Idesthai: The Phenomenology of Sight and Appearance in Archaic Greek*. Tallahassee.

Privitera, G. A. 1970. *Dionisio in Omero e nella poesia greca arcaica*. Rome.

Pucci, P. 1987. *Odysseus Polutropos: Interetextual Readings in the Odyssey and the Iliad*. Ithaca, NY.

———. 1996. "Between Narrative and Catalogue: Life and Death of the Poem." *Mètis* 11:5–24.

———. 1998. *The Song of the Sirens: Essays on Homer*. Lanham.

Purves, A. 2002. *Telling Space: Topography, Time, and Narrative from Homer to Xenophon*. PhD dissertation, University of Pennsylvania.

———. 2006a. "Unmarked Space: Odysseus and the Inland Journey." *Arethusa* 39:1–20.

———. 2006b. "Falling into Time in Homer's *Iliad*." *Classical Antiquity* 25:179–209.

———. 2010a. *Space and Time in Ancient Greek Narrative*. Cambridge.

———. 2010b. "Wind and Time in Homeric Epic." *Transactions of the American Philological Association* 140:323–325.

Putnam, M. J. 1998. *Vergil's Epic Designs*. New Haven.

Pylyshyn, Z. W. 2007. *Things and Places: How the Mind Connects with the World*. Cambridge, MA.

Raaflaub, K. A. 1991. "Homer und die Geschichte des 8. Jh.s v. Chr." In *Zweihundert Jahre Homer-Forschung: Rückblick und Ausblick*, ed. J. Latacz, 205–256. Stuttgart.

Rabel, R. J. 1993. "Cebriones the Diver: *Iliad* 16.733–76." *American Journal of Philology* 114:339–341.

Race, W. H. 1982. *The Classical Priamel from Homer to Boethius*. Leiden.

Rank, L. P. 1951. *Etymologiseering en verwante verschijnselen bij Homerus*. Assen.

Rawlinson, G. 1996. *Herodotus: Histories*. Ware, Hertfordshire.

Read, H. 1932. "Toward a Film Aesthetic." *Cinema Quarterly* 1.1:8–9.

Ready, J. L. 2011. *Character, Narrator, and Simile in the* Iliad. New York.

Reece, S. 1993. *The Stranger's Welcome: Oral Theory and the Aesthetics of the Homeric Hospitality Scene*. Ann Arbor.

————. 2009. *Homer's Winged Words: The Evolution of Early Greek Epic Diction in the Light of Oral Theory.* Leiden.

Reichel, M. 1994. *Fernbeziehungen in der* Ilias. Tübingen.

Reichel, W. 1901. *Über homerische Waffen.* 2nd ed. Vienna.

Reinhardt, K. 1961. *Die Ilias und ihr Dichter.* Göttingen.

Rengakos, A. 1995. "Zeit und Gleichzeitigkeit in den homerischen Epen." *Antike und Abendland* 41:1–33.

————. 1999. "Spannungsstrategien in den homerischen Epen." In Kazazis and Rengakos 1999:308–338.

————. 2002. "Zur narrativen Funktion der Telemachie." In *La mythologie de l'Odyssée: Hommage à Gabriel Germain,* ed. A. Hurst and F. Létoublon, 87–98. Geneva.

————. 2004. "Die *Argonautika* und das 'kyklische Gedicht.'" In Bierl, Schmitt, and Willi 2004:277–304.

————. 2006a. *Το χαμόγελο του Αχιλλέα: Θέματα αφήγησης και ποιητικής στα ομηρικά έπη.* Athens.

————. 2006b. "Du würdest Dich in Deinem Sinn täuschen lassen: Zur Ekphrasis in der hellenistischen Poesie." In *Die poetische Ekphrasis von Kunstwerken: Eine literarische Tradition der Grossdichtung in Antike, Mittelalter und früher Neuzeit,* ed. C. Ratkowitsch, 7–16. Vienna.

————. 2007. "The Smile of Achilles." In *Prizes and Contests in the Homeric Epics,* ed. M. Paizi-Apostolopoulou, A. Rengakos, and C. Tsagalis, 101–110. Athens.

Rescorla, R. A., and C. L. Cunningham. 1979. "Spatial Contiguity Facilitates Pavlovian Second-Order Conditioning." *Journal of Experimental Psychology: Animal Behavior Processes* 5:152–161.

Richardson, A. 2006. "Cognitive Literary Criticism." In *Literary Theory and Criticism,* ed. P. Waugh, 544–556. Oxford.

Richardson, N. J. 1993. *The Iliad: A Commentary.* Vol. 6 (Books 21–24). Cambridge.

————. 2006. "Homeric Professors in the Age of the Sophists." In *Oxford Readings in Ancient Literary Criticism,* ed. A. Laird, 62–86. Oxford.

Richardson, S. 1990. *The Homeric Narrator.* Nashville.

Rieu, E. V. 2003. *Homer: The* Odyssey. Rev. ed. by D. C. H. Rieu, with introduction by P. Jones. London.

Riffaterre, M. 1981. "Descriptive Imagery." *Yale French Studies* 61:107–125.

————. 1996. "Chronotopes in Diegesis." In *Fiction Updated: Theories of Fictionality, Narratology, and Poetics,* ed. C.-A. Mihailescu and W. Hamarneh, 244–266. Toronto.

Risch, E. 1974. *Wortbildung der homerischen Sprache.* 2nd ed. Berlin.

Rispoli, G. M. 1984. "φαντασία ed ἐνάργεια negli scoli all'*Iliade.*" *Vichiana* 13:311–339.

Ritter, A., ed. 1975. *Gestaltung von Landschaft und Raum in der Erzählkunst.* Darmstadt.

Rivers, W. H. R. 1910. "The Genealogical Method of Anthropological Inquiry." *Sociological Review* 3:1–12.

Roberts, W. R. 1924. *Rhetorica.* Vol. 11 of *The Works of Aristotle Translated.* Ed. W. D. Ross. Oxford.

Robertson, N. 2001. "Athena as Weather Goddess: The Aigis in Myth and Ritual." In *Athena in the Classical World,* ed. S. Deacey and A. Villing, 29–55. Leiden.

Rofel, L. 1997. "Rethinking Modernity: Space and Factory Discipline in China." In *Culture, Power, Place: Explorations in Critical Anthropology,* ed. A. Gupta and J. Ferguson, 155–178. Durham, N.C.

Römer, A. 1879. *Die exegetischen Scholien der* Ilias *im Codex Venetus B.* Munich.

Ronen, R. 1986. "Space in Fiction." *Poetics Today* 7:421–438.

Rosen, M. R., and I. Sluiter, eds. 2006. *City, Countryside, and the Spatial Organization of Value in Classical Antiquity.* Leiden.

Rossi, L. E. 1983. "Il simposio Greco arcaico e classico come spettacolo a se stesso." In *Spettacoli conviviali dall'antichità classica alle corti italiane del '400: Atti del VII Convegno di Studio, Viterbo, Maggio 1983,* ed. F. Doglio, 41–50. Viterbo.

Rubin, D. C. 1995. *Memory in Oral Traditions: The Cognitive Psychology of Epic, Ballads, and Counting-Out Rhymes.* Oxford.

Rusten, J. S. 1996. "Ekphrasis." *Oxford Classical Dictionary.* 3rd ed. Ed. S. Hornblower and A. Spawforth. Oxford.

Ryan, M.-L. 1990. "Stacks, Frames and Boundaries, or Narrative as Computer Language." *Poetics Today* 11:873–899.

———. 1991. *Possible Worlds, Artificial Intelligence and Narrative Theory.* Bloomington.

———. 2001. *Narrative as Virtual Reality: Immersion and Interactivity in Literature and Electronic Media.* Baltimore.

———. 2003. "Cognitive Maps and the Construction of Narrative Space." In Herman 2003:214–242.

———. 2009. "Space." In Hühn et al. 2009:420–433.

Said, E. 1995 [1978]. *Orientalism.* London.

Sale, W. M. 1987. "The Formularity of the Place Phrases of the *Iliad.*" *Transactions of the American Philological Association* 117:21–50.

Sammons, B. 2010. *The Art and Rhetoric of the Homeric Catalogue.* Oxford.

Sasse, S. 2010. "Poetischer Raum: Chronotopos und Geopoetik." In Günzel 2010:294–308.

Sauer, C. O. 1925. "The Morphology of Landscape." *University of California Publications in Geography* 2:19–54.

Schadewaldt, W. 1965. *Von Homers Welt und Werk: Aufsätze und Auslegungen zur homerischen Frage*. 4th ed. Stuttgart.

———. 1966. *Iliasstudien*. 3rd ed. Darmstadt.

———. 1975. *Die Aufbau der* Ilias: *Strukturen und Konzeptionen*. Frankfurt.

Scheid-Tissinier, E. 1994. *Les usages du don chez Homère*. Nancy.

Schein, S. 1984. *The Mortal Hero: An Introduction to Homer's Iliad*. Berkeley.

Schischwani, S. 1994. *Mündliche Quellen der* Odyssee. Doctoral dissertation, Freiburg University.

Schlögel, K. 2003. *Im Raume lesen wir die Zeit: Über Zivilisationsgeschichte und Geopolitik*. Munich.

Shklovsky, V. 1965. *Russian Formalist Criticism: Four Essays*. Trans. L. T. Lemon and M. J. Reis. Lincoln.

Schmitt, A. 1990. *Selbständigkeit und Abhängigkeit menschlichen Handelns bei Homer. Hermeneutische Untersuchungen zur Psychologie Homers*. Mainz.

Schmitt Pantel, P. 1992. *La cité au banquet: Histoire des répas publics dans les cités grecques*. Rome.

Schmitz, T. 1994. "Ist die *Odyssee* 'spannend'? Anmerkungen zur Erzähltechnik des homerischen Epos." *Philologus* 138:3–23.

Schoeck, G. 1961. Ilias *und* Aithiopis. Zurich.

Schroer, M. 2006. *Räume, Orte, Grenzen: Auf dem Weg zu einer Soziologie des Raums*. Frankfurt.

Schuchhardt, C. 1928. "Die Befestigung des achäischen Schiffslagers vor Troja." In *Festschrift zur Vierhundertjahrfeier des altes Gymnasiums zu Bremen 1528–1928*:422–433. Bremen.

Schwab, M. 2000. "Escape from the Image: Deleuze's Image-Ontology." In *The Brain is the Screen: Deleuze and the Philosophy of Cinema*, ed. G. Flaxman, 109–139. Minneapolis.

Scodel, R. 1992. "The Wits of Glaucus." *Transactions of the American Philological Association* 122:73–84.

———. 1999. *Credible Impossibilities: Conventions and Strategies of Verisimilitude in Homer and Greek Tragedy*. Stuttgart.

———. 2002. "Homeric Signs and Flashbulb Memory." In *Epea and Grammata: Oral and Written Communication in Ancient Greece*, ed. I. Worthington and J. M. Foley, 99–116. Leiden.

———. 2008. "Zielinski's Law Reconsidered." *Transactions and Proceedings of the American Philological Association* 138:107–125.

———. 2012. "Hesiod and the Epic Cycle." In Montanari, Rengakos, and Tsagalis 2012:501–515.

Scott, W. 1974. *The Oral Nature of the Homeric Simile*. Leiden.

———. 2009. *The Artistry of the Homeric Simile*. Hanover, NH.

Scully, S. 1990. *Homer and the Sacred City.* Ithaca, NY.

Severyns, A. 1938–1963. *Recherches sur la chrestomathie de Proclos*, I–IV. Paris.

Sharff, S. 1982. *The Elements of Cinema: Toward a Theory of Cinesthetic Impact.* New York.

Shay, J. 1995. *Achilles in Vietnam: Combat Trauma and the Undoing of Character.* New York.

Shepard, R. N. 1978. "The Mental Image." *American Psychologist* 33:125–137.

Sheppard, J. T. 1922. *The Pattern of the* Iliad. London.

Shipp, G. P. 1972. *Studies in the Language of Homer.* Cambridge.

Silk, M. S. 1974. *Interaction in Poetic Imagery.* Cambridge.

Simmel, G. 1995. "Über räumliche Projektionen sozialer Formen." In *Aufsätze und Abhandlungen 1901-1908*, ed. R. Kramme, A. Rammstedt, and O. Rammstedt, 1:201–220. Frankfurt.

Singor, H. W. 1995. "*Eni prôtoisi machesthai*: Some Remarks on the Iliadic Image of the Battlefield." In *Homeric Questions: Essays in Philology, Ancient History and Archaeology (Including the Papers of a Conference Organized by the Netherlands Institute at Athens, 15 May 1993)*, ed. J. P. Crielaard, 183–200. Amsterdam.

Skafte Jensen, M. 1999. *Dividing Homer: When and How Were the* Iliad *and the* Odyssey *Divided into Songs?* Special issue of *Symbolae Osloenses* 74:5–91.

Slatkin, L. M. 2011. *The Power of Thetis and Selected Essays.* Hellenic Studies 16. Washington, DC.

Slater, W., ed. 1991. *Dining in a Classical Context.* Ann Arbor.

Small, J. P. 1997. *Wax Tablets of the Mind: Cognitive Studies of Memory and Literacy in Antiquity.* London.

Snipes, K. 1988. "Literary Interpretation of the Scholia: The Similes of the *Iliad*." *American Journal of Philology* 109:196–222.

Snodgrass, A. 1999. *Arms and Armour of the Greeks.* 2nd ed. Baltimore.

Snyder, J. M. 1981. "The Web of Song: Weaving Imagery in Homer and the Lyric Poets." *Classical Journal* 76:193–196.

Soja, E. W. 1989. *Postmodern Geographies: The Reassertion of Space in Critical Social Theory.* London.

Sommerstein, A. H., and J. Fletscher. 2007. *Horkos: The Oath in Greek Society.* Exeter.

Sontag, S. 1966. *Against Interpretation and Other Essays.* New York.

———. 1982. *A Susan Sontag Reader.* New York.

Sorabji, R. 1972. *Aristotle on Memory.* London.

Sourvinou-Inwood, C. 1995. *"Reading" Greek Death: To the End of the Classical Period.* Oxford.

Spence, C., and J. Driver, eds. 2004. *Crossmodal Space and Crossmodal Attention.* New York.

Squire, M. 2011. *The* Iliad *in a Nutshell: Visualizing Epic on the Tabulae Iliacae.* Oxford.

Stanley, K. 1993. *The Shield of Homer*. Princeton.

Starke, F., and R. Nünlist. 2007. "Pandarus." *Brill's New Pauly*. Vol. 10:432–434.

Steiner, D. 2001. *Images in Mind: Statues in Archaic and Classical Greek Literature and Thought*. Princeton.

Steiner, G. 1955. "τὸ Ἄργος." *Lexikon des frühgriechischen Epos* (LfgrE) 1:1208–1210.

Sternberg, M. 1981. "Ordering the Unordered: Time, Space, and Descriptive Coherence." *Yale French Studies* 61:60–88.

Storch, H. 1957. *Die Erzählfunktion der homerischen Gleichnisse in der* Ilias. Doctoral dissertation, Tübingen.

Strasburger, G. 1954. *Die kleinen Kämpfer der* Ilias. Doctoral dissertation, Frankfurt.

Strate, L. 2000. "Hypermedia, Space, and Dimensionality." In Gibson and Oviedo 2000:267–286.

Strömberg, R. 1961. "Die Bellerophon-Erzählung in der *Ilias*." *Classica et Mediaevalia* 22:1–15.

Studniczka, F. 1909. "Zur Ara Pacis." *Abhandlungen sächsischen Gesellschaft* 27:901–944.

Suzuki, M. 1989. *Metamorphoses of Helen: Authority, Difference, and the Epic*. Ithaca, NY.

Tannen, D. 1989. *Talking Voices: Repetition, Dialogue, and Imagery in Conversational Discourse*. Cambridge.

Taplin, O. 1980. "The Shield of Achilles within the *Iliad*." *Greece and Rome* 27:1–21.

———. 1990. "Agamemnon's Role in the *Iliad*." In *Characterization and Individuality in Greek Literature*, ed. C. Pelling, 60–82. Oxford.

———. 1992. *Homeric Soundings: The Shaping of the* Iliad. Oxford.

Teng, N. Y., and S. Sun. 2002. "Grouping, Simile, and Oxymoron in Pictures: A Design-Based Cognitive Approach." *Metaphor and Symbol* 17:295–316.

Thalmann, W. G. 1984. *Conventions of Form and Thought in Early Greek Epic Poetry*. Baltimore.

———. 1988. *The Swineherd and the Bow: Representations of Class in the* Odyssey. Ithaca, NY.

Thomas, R. 1992. *Literacy and Orality in Ancient Greece*. Cambridge.

Thornton, A. 1984. *Homer's* Iliad: *Its Composition and the Motif of Supplication*. Göttingen.

Toepffer, J. 1894. "Aiakos." *Real Encyclopädie* 1:923–926.

Torres-Guerra, J. B. 1995. *La Tebaida homérica como fuente de Ilíada y Odisea*. Madrid.

Trachsel, A. 2007. *La Troade: Un paysage et son héritage littéraire; Les commentaires antiques sur la Troade, leur genèse et leur influence*. Basel.

Traill, D. 1989. "Gold Armor for Bronze and Homer's Use of Compensatory τιμή." *Classical Philology* 84:301–305.

Treu, M. 1968. *Von Homer zur Lyrik*. Munich.

Trypanis, C. A. 1963. "Brothers Fighting Together in the *Iliad*." *Rheinisches Museum*, n.s.,16:289–297.

Tsagalis, C. 2004. *Epic Grief: Personal Laments in Homer's* Iliad. Berlin.

———. 2008a. *Inscribing Sorrow: Fourth-Century Attic Funerary Epitaphs*. Berlin.

———. 2008b. *The Oral Palimpsest: Exploring Intertextuality in the Homeric Epics*. Hellenic Studies 29. Washington, DC.

———. 2009. "Poetry and Poetics in the Hesiodic Corpus." In Montanari, Rengakos, and Tsagalis 2009:131–177.

———. 2010a. "The Dynamic Hypertext: Lists and Catalogues in the Homeric Epics." In Tsagalis 2010c:323–347.

———. 2010b. "Epic Space Revisited: Narrative and Intertext in the Episode between Diomedes and Glaucus (*Il.* 6.119–236)." In Mitsis and Tsagalis 2010:87–113.

Tsagalis, C., ed. 2010c. *Homeric Hypertextuality*. Special issue of *Trends in Classics* 2.2.

———. 2011. "Intertextuality." In Finkelberg 2011:2.413–414. London.

———. Forthcoming. "*Cypria* fr. 19 (Bernabé, West): Further Considerations." *RFIC*.

Tsagarakis, O. 1977. *Nature and Background of Major Conceptions of Divine Power in Homer*. Amsterdam.

Tuan, Y.-F. 1977. *Space and Place*. London.

———. 1978. "Space, Time, and Place: A Humanistic Frame." In *Timing Space and Spacing Time*, ed. T. Carlstein, D. Parkes, and N. Thrift, 7–16. London.

Tulving, E. 1962. "Subjective Organization in Free Recall of 'Unrelated' Words." *Psychological Review* 9:344–354.

Turkeltaub, D. 2010. "Reading the Epic Past: The *Iliad* on Heroic Epic." In Mitsis and Tsagalis 2010:129–152.

Turner, M. 1992. "Language Is a Virus." *Poetics Today* 13.4:725–736.

Underwood, B. J. 1969. "Attributes of Memory." *Psychological Review* 76:559–573.

Untersteiner, M. 1971. "Eumelo di Corinto." *Scritti minori: Studi di letteratura e filosofia greca* 165–179. Brescia (= *Antiquitas* 1951–1952, 6–7:3–13).

Valeton, M. C. 1915. *De Iliadis fontibus et compositione*. Leiden.

Van Baak, J. J. 1983. *The Place of Space in Narration: A Semiotic Approach to the Problem of Literary Space*. Amsterdam.

Van Noppen, J.-P. 1996. "Language, Space and Theography: The Case of *Height* vs. *Depth*." In *The Construal of Space in Language and Thought*, ed. M. Pütz and R. Durven, 679–690. Berlin.

Van Rossum-Steenbeek, M. 1998. *Greek Readers' Digests? Studies on a Selection of Subliterary Papyri*. Leiden.

Van Wees, H. 1997. "Homeric Warfare." In Morris and Powell 1997:668–693.

———. 2005. "Clothes, Class and Gender in Homer." In *Body Language in the Greek and Roman Worlds*, ed. D. Cairns, 1–36. Swansea.

Vester, H. 1956. *Nestor: Funktion und Gestalt in der* Ilias. Doctoral dissertation, University of Tübingen.

Vernant, J.-P. 1996. *L'individu, la mort, l'amour*. Paris.

Vetta, M., ed. 1983. *Poesia e simposio nella Grecia antica*. Rome.

———. 2003. "L'epos di Pilo e Omero: Breve storia di una saga regionale." In *ΡΥΣΜΟΣ: Studi di poesia, metrica e musica greca offerti dagli allievi a Luigi Enrico Rossi per i suoi settant'anni*, ed. R. Nicolai, 13–33. Rome.

Vidal-Naquet, P. 1996. "Land and Sacrifice in the *Odyssey*: A Study of Religious and Mythical Meanings." In *Reading the* Odyssey: *Selected Interpretive Essays*, ed. S. L. Schein, 33–53. Princeton.

Visser, E. 1997. *Homers Katalog der Schiffe*. Stuttgart.

Vivante, P. 1970. *The Homeric Imagination: A Study of Homer's Poetic Perception of Reality*. Bloomington.

Vodoklys, E. J. 1992. *Blame Expression in the Epic Tradition*. London.

Von der Mühll, P. 1946. "Die Diapeira im B der *Ilias*." *Museum Helveticum* 3:197–209.

———. 1952. *Kritisches Hypomnema zur* Ilias. Basel.

Wagner, C. 2010. "Kognitiver Raum: Orientierung—Mental Maps—Datenverwaltung." In Günzel 2010:234–249.

Wagner, F. 2002. "Glissements et déphasages: Note sur la métalepse narrative." *Poétique* 130:235–253.

Wagner. P., ed. 1996. *Icons-Texts-Iconotexts: Essays on Ekphrasis and Intermediality*. Berlin.

Walcot, P. 1969. "ΧΡΥΣΕΙΑ ΧΑΛΚΕΙΩΝ: A Further Comment." *Classical Review*, n.s., 19:12–13.

Walz, C. 1832–1836. *Rhetores Graeci*. Vol. 1. Osnabrück.

Wathelet, P. 1992. "Argos et l'Argolide dans l'épopée." In Piérart 1992b:99–116.

Webb, R. 2009. *Ekphrasis, Imagination and Persuasion in Ancient Rhetorical Theory and Practice*. Surrey.

Webster, T. B. L. 1958. *From Mycenae to Homer*. London.

Wenz, K. 1997. *Raum, Raumsprache, Sprachräume: Zur Textsemiotik der Raumbeschreibung*. Tübingen.

West, M. L. 1973. "Greek Epic Poetry 200–700 B.C." *Classical Quarterly* 23:179–192.

———. 1982. *Greek Metre*. Oxford.

———. 1997. *The East Face of Helicon: West Asiatic Elements in Greek Poetry and Myth*. Oxford.

———. 1999. "Frühe Interpolationen in der *Ilias*." *Nachrichten der Akademie der Wissenschaften in Göttingen* 4:183–191.

———. 2001. *Studies in the Text and Transmission of the* Iliad. Munich.

———. 2002a. "'Eumelos': A Corinthian Epic Cycle?" *Journal of Hellenic Studies* 122:109–133.

———. 2002b. "The View from Lesbos." In *Epea Pteroenta: Beiträge zur Homerforschung: Festschrift für Wolfgang Kullmann zum 75. Geburtstag*, ed. M. Reichel and A. Rengakos, 207–219. Stuttgart.

———. 2003a. "*Iliad* and *Aethiopis*." *Classical Quarterly*, n.s., 53:1–14.

———. 2003b. *Homeric Hymns, Homeric Apocrypha, Lives of Homer*. Cambridge, MA.

———. 2007. *Indo-European Poetry and Myth*. Oxford.

———. 2011. *The Making of the* Iliad: *Discquisition and Analytical Commentary*. Oxford.

West, M. L., ed. 1998–2000. *Homerus: Ilias*. Vols. 1–2. Stuttgart.

West, M. L., and S. West. 1999. "Comment." In *Dividing Homer*, ed. M. S. Jensen, *Symbolae Osloenses* 74:68–73.

West-Pavlov, R. 2009. *Space in Theory: Kristeva, Foucault, Deleuze*. Amsterdam.

White, J. A. 1982. "Bellerophon in the 'Land of Nod': Some Notes on *Iliad* 6.153–211." *American Journal of Philology* 103:119–127.

Whitehead, A. 2009. *Memory*. London.

Whitman, C. E. 1958. *Homer and the Heroic Tradition*. Cambridge, MA.

Wigley, M. 1992. "Untitled: The Housing of Gender." In *Sexuality and Space*, ed. B. Colomina, 356–389. New York.

Wilamowitz-Moellendorff, U. von. 1920. *Die* Ilias *und Homer*. 2nd ed. Berlin.

Will, E. 1955. *Korinthiaka: Recherches sur l'histoire et la civilisation de Corinthe des origines aux guerres médiques*. Paris.

Willcock, M. M. 1970. "Aspects of the Gods of the *Iliad*." *Bulletin of the Institute of Classical Studies* 17:1–10.

———. 1984. *A Commentary on Homer's* Iliad: *Books XIII–XXIV*. London.

Wilson, J. R. 1979. "Καί κέ τις ὧδ' ἐρέει: An Homeric Device in Greek Literature." *Illinois Classical Studies* 4:1–15.

Wilson, P. C. 1951–1952. "Battle Scenes in the *Iliad*." *Classical Journal* 47:269–274, 299–300.

Wilson, P. 2009. "Thamyris the Thracian: The Archetypal Wandering Poet?" In *Wandering Poets in Ancient Greek Culture: Travel, Locality and Pan-Hellenism*, ed. R. Hunter and I. Rutherford, 46–79. Cambridge.

Winkler, M. M. 2007. "The *Iliad* and the Cinema." In *Troy: From Homer's* Iliad *to Hollywood Epic*, ed. M. M. Winkler, 43–67. Oxford.

Winograd, E., and V. E. Church. 1988. "Role of Spatial Location in Learning Face-Name Associations." *Memory and Cognition* 16:1–7.

Winter, I. 1994. "Light and Radiance as Aesthetic Values in the Art of Ancient Mesopotamia (and some Indian Parallels)." In *Art: The Integral Vision:*

Essays in Felicitation of Kapila Vatsyayan, ed. B. N. Saraswati et al., 123–132. New Delhi.

———. 1999. "The Aesthetic Value of Lapis Lazuli in Mesopotamia." In *Cornaline et pierres précieuses: La Méditerranée de l'Antiquité à l'Islam*, ed. A. Caubet, 43–58. Paris.

Worman, N. 2001. "The Voice which is Not One: Helen's Verbal Guises in Homeric Epic." In *Making Silence Speak: Women's Voices in Greek Literature and Society*, ed. A. Lardinois and L. McClure, 19–37. Princeton.

———. 2002. *The Cast of Character: Style in Greek Literature*. Austin.

Woronoff, M. 1983. "Rançon d'Hector et richesse des Troyens." *L'information littéraire* 35:33–36.

Yamagata, N. 1994. *Homeric Morality*. Leiden.

Yates, F. A. 1966. *The Art of Memory*. Chicago.

Zanker, G. 1981. "Enargeia in the Ancient Criticism of Poetry." *Rheinisches Museum* 124:297–311.

Zerubavel, E. 2003. *Time Maps: Collective Memory and the Social Shape of the Past*. Chicago.

Zielinski, T. 1901. "Die Behandlung gleichzeitiger Ereignisse im antiken Epos." *Philologus Supplement* 8.3:407–449.

Zimmermann, M. 2005. "Lycii, Lycia." *Brill's New Pauly* 7:916–920.

Zografou-Lyra, G. 1987. *Ο μύθος του Παλαμήδη στην αρχαία ελληνική γραμματεία*. Doctoral dissertation, University of Ioannina.

Zoran, G. 1984. "Towards a Theory of Space in Narrative." *Poetics Today* 5:309–335.

Index Locorum

Homer, *Iliad*, cont.

Book XXII 6, 136; XXII 25–32,
371; XXII 38–40, 25; XXII 39,
49n67; XXII 71–73, 50n70;
XXII 84–85, 25; XXII 99–130,
47; XXII 122, 34n33; XXII 145,
82; XXII 145–148, 82; XXII
153–156, 86n188; XXII 154–156,
8; XXII 156, 86n188, 157n12;
XXII 167–187, 143n123; XXII
194–198, 136; XXII 226–247, 43;
XXII 248, 70n125; XXII 308–311,
370; XXII 321–327, 33; XXII
331–366, 49; XXII 359–360, 59;
XXII 361–363, 49; XXII 370–371,
49 and n68; XXII 373–374,
51n72; XXII 405–411, 402, 403;
XXII 406, 403n76; XXII 410–411,
402; XXII 439, 139; XXII 440,
139; XXII 440–448, 139; XXII
442, 139; XXII 445, 139; XXII
459, 61; XXII 460, 77n149, 401;
XXII 468, 403n77; XXII 468–472,
378, 401, 402, 403; XXII
484–506, 234; XXII 507, 49n67

Book XXIII 59–61, 101n21; XXIII
80–81, 60n91; XXIII 71–74,
140n118; XXIII 83–84, 57n88;
XXIII 125–126, 108n38; XXIII
143, 101n21; XXIII 144, 100n15;
XXIII 205–211, 147; XXIII
257–897, 113n51; XXIII 258,
108n38; XXIII 258–259, 108;
XXIII 274–278, 114n56; XXIII
274–286, 114n56; XXIII 287–538,
109, 112; XXIII 288–351, 114n55;
XXIII 305–350, 113n52; XXIII
331, 110n44; XXIII 332, 110n44;
XXIII 333, 110n44; XXIII
358, 114, 121; XXIII 361, 114;
XXIII 362–372, 115n57; XXIII
375–381, 121; XXIII 378–381,
115; XXIII 382–400, 115; XXIII

391–396, 121; XXIII 419–421,
116; XXIII 448, 113n50; XXIII
448–498, 117; XXIII 450, 113n53;
XXIII 451, 116; XXIII 456–489,
113n52; XXIII 476, 113n51;
XXIII 516–527, 117; XXIII 555,
393; XXIII 555–557, 116n60;
XXIII 560–562, 378, 393; XXIII
621–623, 113n51; XXIII 638–642,
111; XXIII 677–680, 220, 222;
XXIII 679–680, 220n170;
XXIII 685, 118, 119n64; XXIII
686–688, 118; XXIII 688–690,
118; XXIII 690–691, 118; XXIII
694–695, 118; XXIII 695–698,
118; XXIII 707–709, 120; XXIII
708–709, 120n65; XXIII 710,
119; XXIII 711, 119; XXIII 714,
119; XXIII 716, 119; XXIII 725,
119; XXIII 725–726, 119; XXIII
727, 119; XXIII 727–728, 119;
XXIII 728, 119; XXIII 729, 119;
XXIII 730, 119; XXIII 731, 119;
XXIII 731–732, 119; XXIII 732,
119; XXIII 734–737, 120; XXIII
738–739, 120; XXIII 740–749,
406, 407 and n91; XXIII
741–749, 378; XXIII 757, 121;
XXIII 757–797, 121n67; XXIII
758–766, 121; XXIII 760–763,
121; XXIII 770–771, 121;
XXIII 798–799, 129; XXIII 799,
129n83; XXIII 807–808, 393,
394; XXIII 811–814, 69, 70n120;
XXIII 813–814, 122; XXIII 814,
68; XXIII 816, 70n120 and
125; XXIII 816–817, 122; XXIII
824–825, 394n50; XXIII 826–849,
124; XXIII 836–838, 125n75;
XXIII 843, 124; XXIII 845–847,
125; XXIII 852–854, 126;

Subject Index

abbreviated style, 70n122

Abydos, 36

Achaean camp, 6, 10, 16, 17, 23, 24 and n4, 27, 54, 60n93, 66, 75, 78, 85, 95–129, 130, 136, 146, 147, 148, 150, 178, 193, 201, 280, 331, 345, 407, 449, 452, 453, 454

Achaean wall, 54, 74, 95, 102–105, 102n25, 236, 333, 334, 452

Aenienis, 166

aesthetics of light, 445

Aetolia, 166, 167, 248, 251

agony, 54 and n79, 206

Aegina, 80, 175

Aisuetes, 78n150

Aithiopisstoff, 253

Aleion, 251 and n73

Alybe, 167

amplificatio, 382

anachrony, 32, 123n73, 170

anatopies, 32

androktasiai, 28–39, 37n40, 43, 52, 294n57, 450, 451

apostrophe, 34n33, 441n86

Arcadia, 166

Argolid, 166, 191, 456

Argos, 191–201, 456; Agamemnon's city, 194n74, 196n80, 197n87, 199n94, 417, 456; Agamemnon's and Diomedes' city, 161; as distant place, 161, 171, 248, 249, 250,
257, 455; Greece, 197n87, 199n95, 200 and nn96–98, n101, 201 and nn103–105, 249n65; in Theban myth, 196n81; Pelasgian, 166, 249n65, 456; Peloponnese; 250n68; Peloponnese/Greece, 200, 456

Arisbe, 161n20, 229n1, 407

aristeiai, 28, 46n59, 48, 52–61, 73n137, 223 and n177, 291, 304, 305, 307, 309 and n87, 313, 417, 418, 450, 451, 461

arthrology, 436; general, 429 and n44, 435n60; restrained, 429, 431, 432

Artucca, 239

Asia Minor, 7, 160, 161, 163, 165, 169n43, 214, 227, 229, 255, 458

Asine, 175

associative composition, 309, 310n92

Assuwa Confederacy, 239

asymmetrical, 354, 357, 450, 451

asymmetry, 351, 353, 359

Athens, 166, 226nn190 and 192

augmentative particularization, 389

Aulis, 165, 168

aural hypertextuality, 364–365

au-words, 77

balanced opposition, 30

base domain, 19, 268, 348, 349, 350, 351, 352, 353, 354, 355, 356, 357, 358, 362, 366, 369, 370, 459

CPSIA information can be obtained at www.ICGtesting.com
Printed in the USA
BVOW05s0554100314

347078BV00006B/14/P